DEMOCRACY IN THE MAKING
American Government and Politics

Second Edition

DEMOCRACY IN THE MAKING
American Government and Politics

Walter Dean Burnham
Massachusetts Institute of Technology

Prentice-Hall, Englewood Cliffs, New Jersey 07632

Library of Congress Cataloging-in-Publication Data
Burnham, Walter Dean.
    Democracy in the making.

    Includes bibliographies and indexes.
      1. United States—Politics and government.
I. Title.
JK274.B8523 1986   320.973   85-25782
ISBN 0-13-198508-6

To My Family, Friends, and Colleagues

Production Supervisor: Lisa Halttunen
Book Designer: Maureen Eide
Cover Designer: Lundgren Graphics
Cover Photo: Eddie Hironaka, The Image Bank
Photo Research: Joelle Burrows and Anita Duncan
Manufacturing Buyer: Barbara Kelly Kittle

Printed in the United States of America

10 9 8 7 6 5 4 3 2 1

Photo Credits: Frontispiece by Marc Anderson; *Chapter 1* by Jan Lukas, Photo Researchers; *Chapter 2* by the National Geographic Society, Courtesy U.S. Capitol Historical Society; *Chapter 3* by the Alabama Bureau of Publicity and Information; *Chapter 4* by Ed Lettau, Photo Researchers; *Chapter 5* by Chester Higgins, Jr., Photo Researchers; *Chapter 6* by Bettye Lane, Photo Researchers; *Chapter 7* by Ray Ellis, Photo Researchers; *Chapter 8* by Jan Lukas, Photo Researchers; *Chapter 9* by Sam C. Pierson, Jr., Photo Researchers; *Chapter 10* by UPI/Bettman Newsphotos; campaign buttons in Chapter 10 by Ben Blank; *Chapter 11* by Pete Souza, The White House; *Chapter 12* by the U.S. Postal Service; *Chapter 13* by Marc Anderson; *Chapter 14* by Stan Wakefield; *Chapter 15* Courtesy of the Bureau of Reclamation, Dept. of the Interior; *Chapter 16* by AP/Wide World Photos; *Chapter 17* by UPI/Bettman Newsphotos

ISBN 0-13-198508-6   01

Prentice-Hall International (UK) Limited, *London*
Prentice-Hall of Australia Pty. Limited, *Sydney*
Prentice-Hall of Canada Inc., *Toronto*
Prentice-Hall Hispanoamericana, S.A., *Mexico*
Prentice-Hall of India Private Limited, *New Delhi*
Prentice-Hall of Japan, Inc., *Tokyo*
Prentice-Hall of Southeast Asia Pte. Ltd., *Singapore*
Editora Prentice-Hall do Brasil, Ltda., *Rio de Janeiro*
Whitehall Books Limited, *Wellington, New Zealand*

OUTLINE

CONTENTS

chapter six

INTEREST GROUPS   153

chapter ten

CAMPAIGNS AND ELECTIONS 279

chapter eleven

THE PRESIDENCY 321

chapter twelve

BUREAUCRACY 353

─────────────── *chapter thirteen* ───────────────

CONGRESS 389

─────────────── *chapter fourteen* ───────────────

THE COURTS 427

chapter fifteen

PUBLIC POLICY AND THE FREE MARKET   465

PREFACE

President Ronald Reagan took office in January 1981 with a mission to change the course of American history. In order to do this, he had first to defeat an elected incumbent—Jimmy Carter—who was seeking reelection in 1980. This does not happen very often. The last time was in 1932, when incumbent Herbert Hoover (R) was defeated by New York Governor Franklin D. Roosevelt (D), and a whole political era came to an end. And lest anyone think that Reagan's election in 1980 was a fluke, he resoundingly proved the contrary by his landslide reelection in 1984 over Democrat Walter F. Mondale. In the process, Reagan carried 49 of the country's 50 states.

As Ronald Reagan took office, policies that had not been questioned for two generations were suddenly debatable, doubtable, and changeable. Policies that had been abandoned for the same two generations were dusted off, proposed, and carried out through legislation or executive action. How did our political system, supposedly so very resistant to change, produce the "Reagan Revolution?" How did it happen that he was able to oust Carter in the first place? "Let's look at the record."[1]

Reagan's political success has been significantly based on his appeal—much more effective than Carter's or Mondale's appeals—to certain enduring traditions and attitudes: our political culture. But a context of crisis was also necessary. Our political system, normally resistant to major change, is often strikingly responsive to such stress. And, in truth, the country in 1980 was in

---

[1] A phrase made famous by Alfred E. Smith, governor of New York (D, 1919–1921; 1923–1929) during his 1928 campaign for the presidency. Smith, the first Roman Catholic major-party nominee in American history, was trounced by Herbert Hoover (R, 1929–1933).

the midst of the most painful and comprehensive crisis in America's postwar history. For a few months the inflation rate was pushing 20 percent; interest rates were at an all-time high; American hostages were held by Iranian "students" for months on end; and everywhere there were signs of a serious "confidence gap," what Jimmy Carter diagnosed (but could not dispel) as a malaise in the national spirit. Ronald Reagan promised to attack that crisis on all fronts—to "take the government off the backs of the people," to unshackle the powers of American industry, to restore prosperity, to rebuild American power and prestige in the world, and—for that matter—to support a constitutional amendment banning abortion.

It has well been said that although Richard Nixon (and many other Presidents) sought the country's highest office in order to *be* something, Ronald Reagan bid for the presidency in order to *do* something.[2] His list of accomplishments has been impressive by any standard; this book discusses and analyzes many of them. By 1984 the atmosphere of crisis and gloom had lifted almost by magic, replaced by low inflation, economic boom, some American foreign-policy successes, and a rapid decline in the "confidence gap" of earlier years. Mr. Reagan's appeal to the fundamentals of our political culture—democracy, limited government, free enterprise, the hope of personal betterment, in short The American Dream—fit this vastly improved climate like a glove. His landslide reelection had become virtually a foregone conclusion.

But as President, Ronald Reagan too has found more than once that our problems seem to overwhelm our means of solving them. For the same political culture that Mr. Reagan invokes with such remarkable skill and success has also sustained a government that is remarkably complex and fragmented. This government includes a system of divided powers in which he must deal with a House of Representatives controlled by the opposition party, and a Constitution which made him a "lame duck" on the day of his second inaugural. Our political culture encourages us to expect a great deal from this government, but it also encourages us to be hostile and resentful whenever the government flexes its power muscles. This is the supreme and enduring dilemma of American politics.

When we become dissatisfied with the way our government works, we dig into our political culture and try to reform the present by imposing on it the idea of an enduring past. Is our economy growing little or not at all? Cut federal spending! Fire bureaucrats! Cut taxes! Deregulate! Are our political parties controlled by bosses? Reform the parties—and cure the ills of democracy with more democracy! Meanwhile, one set of major problems subsides (inflation, interest rates, the image of American impotence in the world) only to be replaced by another set (federal deficits of a scale never before seen in peacetime, huge trade deficits, the rapid decay of the country's core manufacturing industry). We can hardly be surprised that Mr. Reagan has come out in favor of a constitutional amendment requiring that the federal budget be balanced, and also in favor of a line-item veto to strike down particulars in that budget. And so far as political parties are concerned, they are so feeble that Congress often seems to be little more than an assemblage of 535 individuals united only by common and conflicting fears and ambitions. No wonder that many people have thought that we suffer from

---

[2] The phrase is by Boston Globe journalist Martin Nolan. Cited in Lou Cannon, *Reagan* (New York: G. P. Putnam's Sons, 1982), p. 410.

a "crisis of governability," that the American political system is in a state of permanent "receivership."[3]

If we would understand how American government works today, we also need to understand how it fails to work. Whether or not Ronald Reagan's presidency represents a true or a false dawn after the gloomy murk of the late 1970s, the United States really does confront entrenched political and economic stresses. The two are intimately related, and as anyone observing the 1985 budget struggle can see, they are of no mean size even in the relatively tranquil 1980s. In every chapter of this book, I have tried to show how our politics and institutions have made their contributions to these crises, and how they have responded to (and have sometimes been weakened by) them. From beginning to end, then, this is a problem-centered book. But rather than organize it around any possibly doctrinaire views, I have called upon the study of behavior, institutions, public policy, and history, whenever any of them seemed useful.

Writing an American government textbook is an awesome task, and revising it is scarcely less so. When I had at last reached the end, I thought of the medieval monk who wrote, "The end of the book: Thanks be to God."[4] Even scholars who have spent their entire professional lives unraveling particular mysteries of American politics must be overwhelmed by the effort of coping with the whole field. Yet in the end, the excitement of writing such a book quite overshadows the difficulties that appear en route. For no task of political science can be more important than making the subject live for our fellow citizens. And the professor-writer learns throughout the project—to see things, and particularly the connections among things, that would never have become clear in any other way. If any part of that excitement has been communicated to this book's readers, the author will be well content. American politics and government may be at times baffling, frustrating, irritating, even alarming; but they are never dull.

The Plan of the Book

Organization. The general plan of this book is not unusual. Starting with the social, cultural, economic, geographical, and religious bases of American political life, the text moves on to the Constitution and the rights that we enjoy (and sometimes fail to enjoy) under it. Our attention then turns to the forces that actively participate in and shape American political life today. These include interest groups, public opinion, and political parties. In response to a number of suggestions, this second edition also contains an entirely new chapter on the mass media and American politics.

We then go on to discuss the basic institutions of our national government and the policies carried on in its name. The text concludes with an epilogue that, like the rest of the book, was designed to be assigned to students. Each chapter has a number of boxes, marginal quotes, and marginal notes, and each ends with a summary and an annotated list of selected readings. Each of

[3] See, among other books, Samuel P. Huntington, *American Politics: The Promise of Disharmony* (Cambridge: Harvard Univ., 1982); Theodore Lowi, *The End of Liberalism* (New York: Norton, 1969, 1979); and Samuel P. Huntington, Michel Crozier, and Joji Watanuki, *The Crisis of Democracy* (New York: New York Univ., 1975). The notion of "permanent receivership" is Lowi's.
[4] Bruce M. Metzger, *The Text of the New Testament*, 2nd ed. (New York: Oxford University Press, 1973), p. 18.

them, of course, has also been thoroughly revised and updated to bring the story down to the mid-1980s. The appendices include the Declaration of Independence, the U.S. Constitution, *The Federalist*, Paper 10, by James Madison, and a list of the Presidents, Vice-Presidents, and Congresses of the United States. We have also provided a glossary and an index.

Distinctive Features. Although the format of *Democracy in the Making* may not be startling or experimental, the text itself is distinctive in several ways.

First, I believe that the policy changes begun by the Reagan administration in 1981 were the most sweeping and comprehensive in fifty years. There continues considerable debate among specialists as to whether 1980/1984 were segments of an *electoral* "critical realignment." There can be little debate that we have had a major *policy* realignment. All authors of introductory American government textbooks try to keep them as up to date as publishing schedules allow. I have done so here, of course, but I have also tried to explain the characteristics, the extent, and the aims of these policy changes and the philosophy behind them. Because so many of Mr. Reagan's policy programs and proposals have dealt with economics, much attention has been paid to economic ideas and policies.

Second, because I believe that President Reagan's election and achievements arose from a serious crisis in American government and politics, I have tried to explain the origins and consequences of that crisis.

Third, our society and our political culture did not appear overnight, and neither have our problems. Thus, I have tried to show how the past has made us what we are today. As a people, Americans may be ahistorical by comparison, say, with Europeans, who may have rather too much history. But like them, we have inherited a great and noble past, and this past continues to exert a weighty influence over our ideas and actions in the present. The discussion of history in this book presumes little or no knowledge of history and focuses on attitudes and expectations, not on names and dates.

Supplements. A *Study Guide and Workbook*, an *Instructor's Manual*, and a *Test Item File* have been prepared to accompany this book. Students should use the *Study Guide and Workbook* to review each chapter and master the common themes that run through the book. The *Instructor's Manual* provides an outline of the text, lecture suggestions, discussion topics, research projects, and essay questions for each chapter. The *Test Item File* is available in both book and computerized formats.

ACKNOWLEDGMENTS

No one can write a basic textbook without accumulating many intellectual debts. Nor can anyone come to know the scholarship of American polical science and doubt its high level of excellence or the achievements of recent generations. Like any introductory text on American government, this one rests squarely upon these achievements and those of the past. Of course, errors of interpretation are my responsibility alone.

I would also like to acknowledge and thank Prentice-Hall's editorial staff for helping to make this book a physical reality—sometimes by putting the author's feet to the fire so that deadlines would not be missed. My particular thanks go to my editor, Roger Samuel Draper, who sometimes had to put up with a temperamental author but remained helpful, courteous, and unflappable throughout. Thanks are due as well to Stan Wakefield, executive editor for social sciences and political-science editor, and Marjorie Turko, his assistant; to Jeannine Ciliotta, who edited portions of this edition; to Joelle Burrows, who did the photo research; and to Lisa Halttunen, production editor, whose diligence, expertise, and perseverance made it possible to produce the book on such a short schedule.

For technical and conceptual assistance on the first-edition manuscript I wish to thank Graeme Auton, Maurice Carroll, John DeMott, William Golightly, Michael Hoyt, Ronald Hrebenar, Dennis Ippolito, Susan Joseph, Marc Lilla, Frank Lynn, Steve Marcus, Tom Morganthau, Robert Rackleff, Hope Shannon, Rita Stollman, and Thomas Walker. And I should also give thanks to my personal assistants on this book, John Coleman, Katie Hope, and Steven Minicucci, all of whom gave sterling support and aid along the way.

For those who helped out with critiques and other assistance on the second edition I owe special thanks: D. Grier Stephenson, Jr. (Chapters 4, 5, and 13), Harry Holloway (Chapter 7), David Rosenblum (Chapter 12), and Graeme Auton (Chapter 17).

Various chapters of the manuscript were reviewed and often improved in both editions by the following fellow-teachers and scholars:

— Karl Andresen
  University of Wisconsin
— Paul R. Benson
  The Citadel
— Bruce A. Campbell
  University of Georgia
— Richard Chackerian
  Florida State University
— David Cingranelli
  State University of New York
  at Binghamton
— Guy C. Clifford
  Bridgewater State College
— Frank T. Colon
  Lehigh University
— Rita Cooley
  New York University
— Robert E. Craig
  University of New Hampshire
— Robert DiClerico
  West Virginia University
— John C. Donovan
  Bowdoin College
— George C. Edwards III
  Texas A & M University
— Louis R. Eltscher
  Rochester Institute of
  Technology
— Stephen Frantzich
  United States Naval Academy

— John Gauger
  Lehigh County Community
  College
— John Geczik
  Community College of
  Allegheny County
— Walter I. Giles
  Georgetown University
— Stefan Haag
  Austin Community College
— Gale Harrison
  Floyd Junior College
— J. C. Horton
  San Antonio College
— Richard Joslyn
  Temple University
— William Thomas Keating
  Arizona State University
— Charles W. Kegley
  University of South Carolina
— Ken Kiser
  Highland Community
  College
— William W. Lammers
  University of Southern
  California
— Richard J. Maiman
  University of Southern Maine
— David W. Moore
  University of New Hampshire

— Bruce Allen Murphy
  Pennsylvania State University
— Lawrence C. Pierce
  University of Oregon
— Donald R. Ranish
  Antelope Valley College
— Walter Rosenbaum
  University of Florida
— Robert C. Sahr
  Purdue University
— Roger Schaefer
  Texas Tech University
— L. Earl Shaw Jr.
  University of Minnesota

— Edward I. Sidlow
  Miami University of Ohio
— Henry Steck
  State University of New York
  at Cortland
— Robert Thompson
  University of South Carolina
— Henry A. Turner
  University of California at
  Santa Barbara
— Lawson Veasey
  University of Central Arkansas
— Francis Wilhoit
  Drake University

I am also grateful to the following reviewers for reading and commenting on the book in preparation for the second edition:

— John Gauger, Lehigh County Community College
— Stefan Haag, Austin Community College
— Gale Harrison, Floyd Junior College
— Ken Kiser, Highland Community College
— Henry Steck, State University of New York at Cortland

I thank all of them for their troubles, which (in one case) included retrieving a manuscript from the Poultry Science Department, where it had been sent by a mail-room clerk who could not make out the words Political Science Department.

Finally, I owe a very special debt of thanks to my children, John and Anne, and, above all, to my wife Patricia, for giving me the patience and support so essential to an author caught up in the toils of production deadlines. Such acknowledgments always occur in prefaces of this sort, and for very good reason. Anyone who has carried out a task of this size also knows how utterly inadequate—though necessary and proper—these acknowledgments are.

Walter Dean Burnham
Cambridge, Massachusetts

DEMOCRACY IN THE MAKING
American Government and Politics

chapter one

AMERICAN SOCIETY AND POLITICAL CULTURE

Our American form of government is constitutional, democratic, and representative. Many other countries boast constitutional, democratic, and representative forms of government, yet none of them is quite like ours. In most of these other countries, the powers of government are concentrated in a single institution, the legislature, which by itself can resolve any political dispute. Except at the ballot box, there can be no appeal.

Our democracy is one of the few that do not concentrate political power solely within a single branch of the central government. It is also one of the few that make each member state fairly independent of it. In most countries, those who control the central government try, to a greater or lesser extent (and with greater or lesser success), to control society. In our country, control over government itself is the great prize in the never-ending competitive struggle for power and influence.

The collective political character of the American people is remarkable, too. Our government may well be the world's most democratic, yet no other people distrusts government and its power so much. Like Huck Finn's father, we Americans find it natural to be "agin the guv'ment." Foreigners find it hard to understand that what to them is the main shortcoming of the American form of government—the fact that it hampers all authorities in doing whatever they want to do—has been to us its chief virtue. Almost all Americans, whatever their political attitudes, view government as a necessary evil, not as a thing good in itself.

This distinctly American view of how government should work, and not work, helps explain why our political system is not easily transplanted to other countries. When American-style democracies were established in much of Latin America and the Philippines, they flopped—and in the end were replaced by dictatorships.

"If there be any among us
who would wish to dissolve
this Union or to change its
republican form, let them
stand undisturbed as
monuments of the safety
with which error of opinion
may be tolerated where
reason is left free to
combat it."

Thomas Jefferson,
March 4, 1801

Indeed, our system of government creates problems even for us, the nation that invented it. Individual liberty is one of the most cherished of American values, but in politics and government, we can get nothing without paying for it in some way. We pay for our liberty by having to deal with a political system that is cumbersome and ponderous, wide open to organized pressures and influences of all kinds, and marked by major inefficiencies and occasional injustices. Is it worth the price? A large majority of Americans have always thought so. Can we afford to continue to pay this price as we move toward the twenty-first century? Quite a few people who understand and accept the basic principles of American government doubt that the answer will continue to be, "Yes, of course," as it has always been in the past.[1]

Whatever the answer may be, the question raises an absolutely essential point: Like the United States itself, the American political system is always under construction and always under challenge. Individual liberties, we sometimes discover, cannot always be reconciled with effective government. The rights of individuals, for example, often clash with the rights of larger groups. The balance between one goal and another cannot be fixed for all time; it moves as life moves. The American experiment in free government is no more finished today than it has ever been.

If we persevere, we shall find our way to a new balance, one that most of us can accept. But the road is neither straight nor narrow, and the end is not in sight. It never will be.

FOUNDATIONS

"Americans are the western
pilgrims, who are carrying
along with them that great
mass of arts, sciences,
vigour, and industry, which
began long since in the
east; they will finish the
great circle"

**Michel-Guillaume-Jean de
Crèvecoeur,**
1782

Our political system differs from most other democratic systems because we, as a people, differ from the other peoples who govern themselves democratically. For the most part, our ancestors came here because they were not satisfied with something about their native lands. Once here, they found a country very unlike the places they had left.

A Free Choice

We do not have any one set of biological ancestors: People have come here from the four corners of the globe. But with the single exception of the blacks, almost all the immigrants came by choice, to find a better life. Some of the immigrants came to escape religious or political persecution, others to escape famines, overpopulation, or poverty. But all *decided* to come. America is a nation of people who chose to be Americans, for themselves and their descendants. So Americans are perhaps more likely than other peoples to believe that individuals can change their lot by personal activity.

A New World

The land that these fortune hunters, religious sectarians, tinkerers, and farmers arrived in was called the New World, and indeed it was planted on the farthest fringe of the known earth. The people we call Indians were living

---

[1] See, for example, Lloyd Cutler, "To Form a Government," *Foreign Affairs*, 59 (1980), 126–43.

USDA, photo by R. B. Branstead

Most of the United States has enough water for farming, and some parts are as fertile as any place on earth.

here, but there were not enough of them to prevent the newcomers from imposing their own cultures, derived from Europe but becoming increasingly independent of it. In a world ruled mainly by kings and nobles, the political and social values of the early settlers were amazingly democratic. At a time when the land and the church were the bases of society, many settlers became traders and artisans, and many more dissented from the local church or from all churches.

A Continent-Nation

What a land the newcomers found! Even the early United States had far more territory than any European country except Russia. Now it is one of the largest countries in the world; only the Soviet Union, Canada, and China are bigger. Almost all of our country lies in the earth's temperate zone, where the climate is suited both for industry and farming. Most of the United States has enough water for farming, and some parts are about as fertile as any place on earth. Of those areas that are not suitable for agriculture, quite a few have large deposits of natural resources like coal, oil, and lumber.

At first, several empires competed over these great riches. France established itself in Canada and in much of what is now the American Midwest. Spain occupied most of the West and Southwest and the peninsula of Florida. The Netherlands and Sweden held small territories in New York and Delaware, respectively. Britain was a latecomer to these colonial enterprises, which in this case were not even carried out by the British government. Profit-making enterprises and private individuals simply staked claims—sometimes without informing the British government—and then proceeded to settle most of what is now our eastern seaboard.

After the French were ejected from their territories in the Midwest and Canada, in the French and Indian War of 1754–1763, the British colonists had less fear of foreign enemies. However, foreign empires continued to surround even the independent United States until 1815. From that year until December 7, 1941 thousands of miles of water separated us from any credible enemy. Our remoteness powerfully influenced the American national mentality and still does, although we are no longer as remote (see Chapter 17).

The Scarcity of Labor

Long after colonization began, our continent remained almost empty. Not until the late nineteenth century were there enough Americans to till our fields and staff our workshops, mines, forests, or mills. As our economy grew, its demand for new workers became voracious. The persistent shortage of labor was among the greatest themes of our history.

No Feudalism. The labor shortage made feudalism out of the question here. Feudalism binds people to the land. In America, there were too few men and women to populate more than a sliver of territory along the eastern seaboard. The frontier was always close at hand, and its lure frustrated all efforts to create a class of permanent white serfs or peasants.

Indenture, Slavery, and Machinery. Many landowners—especially in the South—were "land poor." They owned huge estates but had too few workers to cultivate their holdings, so they turned to other sources of supply. For example, they enticed men and women from Britain to the colonies by paying the costs of the voyage to the New World. These "indentured" servants, who had contracted to spend several years working off their debts, were not ideal employees. Often they came down with malaria and other diseases, and many ran off to the frontier before their terms of service ended.

A more practical but not complete solution to the labor shortage was found—black slavery. Blacks were more immune to tropical diseases than whites were; moreover, they could not bolt and lose themselves at the frontier.

Another answer was to cut the amount of human labor needed for any task, by mechanizing it. Thus began our national obsession with labor-saving devices.

The Practical Mind. The newness and vastness of this country, produced a society that valued practicality more than almost anything else. Enterpreneurship—the ability to organize resources and make them produce wealth—was and still is a quality that Americans admire. Those who possessed this quality in the highest degree—explorers like Daniel Boone, businessmen like Henry Ford, inventors like Thomas Edison—are the central figures of our national legend.

The Standard of Living. For those Americans who were not slaves, the shortage of labor was a blessing: It made wages and living standards higher in this country than anywhere else in the world. Although not, indeed, very high,

Intellectuals?

In France, the leading intellectuals are celebrities, as famous as the leading politicans, movie stars, and rock singers. In Germany and the German-speaking parts of Switzerland, reporters for serious newspapers often hold doctorates. In Britain, well-known writers and journalists commonly become members of Parliament. Indeed, it is much easier for intellectuals to earn a living in Western Europe than in the United States.

"Let the public throw bouquets to the inventors and in time we will all be happy."

Thomas Alva Edison,
1914

Thomas Alva Edison was a genius in the practical application of scientific principles.

AP/Wide World Photos

Chester Carlson is shown here with his prototype invention of the Xerox machine.

Xerox Corporation

Henry Ford is shown in his 1900 Model T.

UPI/Bettmann Newsphotos

they were high enough to have important historical consequences. In Europe, industrialization promoted the growth of a powerful socialist movement. In America, "socialism foundered on the shoals of roast beef and apple pie."[2]

THE MOVEMENT OF POPULATION

The foundations of our national consciousness have remained remarkably stable over the generations; the makeup and distribution of our people have not. Quite the contrary: Ours is a nation of immigrants and internal migrants. The mix of its races, ethnic groups, and religions seems to change constantly, and so does the relative population mix of the different regions.

The Immigrants

In the 1930s, President Franklin Roosevelt spoke before the Daughters of the American Revolution, whose members—almost all of them white, Protestant, and conservative—claim descent from men and women who fought on the American side during the War of Independence. The President's speech began with the greeting, "Fellow Immigrants"; it went on to describe the audience as the offspring of "immigrants and revolutionists." Mr. Roosevelt was right. His own ancestor Isaac Roosevelt had been the leader of the anti-British party in New York during the Revolution. Most Americans, however, descend from relatively recent immigrants—people who came here fewer than 400 years ago.

The Protestant Foundations. The European settlers who arrived from 1607 to 1880 came mostly from Great Britain, with sizable minorities from the Netherlands, Germany, and Scandinavia. They were mainly white, mainly British, and mainly Protestant.

From Ireland came the first really large immigration of Roman Catholics. Their arrival *en masse*, in the 1850s, provoked riots in our cities and created the antiforeign "Know-Nothing" movement. Until the 1880s, however, most immigrants resembled the existing population in culture, outlook, and religion. The "old immigration" was absorbed without much trouble.

The "New Immigration," 1880–1923. After 1880 or so, the pattern of immigration changed. The men, women, and children of the "new immigration" came from societies very unlike the United States. Large numbers of them were Eastern Orthodox and Roman Catholic peasants from southern and eastern Europe, or they were Jews mainly from eastern Europe. They came from countries—like Italy, and the Austrian and Russian Empires—that had few traditions of self-government. These new immigrants created more resentment here than earlier waves of immigration had, in part because they were quite different, in part because they were quite numerous.

The tide of the new immigration rose steadily from 1900 until 1914, when the outbreak of World War I ended it. During six of those years, over a million

---

[2] Werner Sombart,"American Capitalism's Economic Rewards," in John H. M. Laslett and Seymour M. Lipset, eds., *Failure of a Dream? Essays in the History of American Socialism* (New York: Doubleday, 1974), pp. 593–608. For a very similar argument, see also David M. Potter, *People of Plenty: Economic Abundance and the American Character* (Chicago: Univ. of Chicago, 1954).

The S.S. Patricia crossed
the Atlantic in December
1906, jammed with some of
our ancestors and bound for
our shores

. . . but they did not always
meet with open arms.

immigrants entered this country—about five-sixths of them from areas
outside northwest Europe. The 1910 census showed that more than one-third
of our population consisted of Americans born abroad and their children.

Many "native-stock" (that is, British) Americans feared that the country
had been swamped by "lesser breeds without the law," people who could not
be assimilated. So-called scientific racism, unhappily, was quite a respectable
philosophy before the Nazis, under Adolf Hitler, demonstrated its genocidal
results. Outright racism, however, was not the only source of hostility to the
new immigration. Organized labor, whose membership included many
immigrants, old and new, had long been against the unrestricted flow of
"greenhorns," mainly because so many were lured here by corporations
wanting to take advantage of cheaper and more docile pools of labor. The

Some Who Made It in a New Land

For many who come to its shores, America is true to its reputation as a land where hard work, luck and determination can be the key to a better life.

One such is James Kong, 39, a Korean who arrived in Chicago with his wife in 1976. Each worked two jobs at first, scrimping and saving until they could buy the small tailor shop where Mrs. Kong was a seamstress.

Kong now owns five dry-cleaning stores and a wholesale plant—enterprises that could do a million dollars' worth of business this year. How did it happen? "We have to work harder and longer hours or we wouldn't make the opportunities," says Kong.

Success on a grander scale came to Joe Nakash, an Israeli who came to New York in 1962 at the age of 19 with barely $25 in his pocket. He spent his first nights in the U.S. sleeping in subway stations. In the daytime, he looked for menial work—all he expected to find.

Nakash ended up creating Jordache Enterprises, maker of designer jeans and status-label clothing. His salary: About 1 million dollars per year. "In Israel, it was a big thing for me to think maybe I could be a driver for a rich man," says Nakash, 38. "But when I came to America, I saw it was possible for me to be a rich man."

When lawyer Luis Gomez-Dominguez, 59, came from Cuba in 1979, his first job was cutting grass in Miami parks. Today he is a city marketing manager and a prominent member of Miami's large Cuban-exile community. "My family and friends helped me," he reports. "But the real thing was that I began to work hard immediately."

Dung Anh Do, a Vietnamese who arrived in Denver in 1977, is another whose struggle may soon pay big dividends. After working as a janitor, a truck-driver and at a succession of other low-paying jobs, the immigrant recently was able to turn a spare time printing and copying business into Lion Press. His first month's income was $12,000.

For another Vietnamese, Mai Tran, 31, of San Francisco, a restaurant is seen as the springboard to a better life. She sold most of her belongings, pooled resources with a relative and borrowed $11,000 from friends to open a tiny cafe. The break-even point is in sight. "So far we are contributing our time and dollars for nothing, but it is worthwhile," she says. "We are building something here."

William L. Chaze, Reprinted from *U.S. News & World Report*, April 12, 1982. Copyright 1982, U.S. News and World Report, Inc.

result of these very diverse fears was the 1924 Immigration Act, which drastically cut the legal flow of immigrants and succeded, until 1945, in preserving the racial and ethnic balance of 1920.

The Newest Immigrants. The 1924 formula favored would-be immigrants from northwest Europe. In the 1960s, the federal government adopted new rules that favored people, of whatever origin, with skills needed in the United States. Besides these legal immigrants, however, illegal immigrants came in—as many as 10 million, mainly from Latin America.

Like the immigrants of the past, our newest immigrants come here to escape persecution and poverty. But they are not coming from Europe. Indeed the age of the European immigrant seems to be about over. From 1820 through 1950, a bit more than 90 percent of all immigrants to this country came from Europe and Canada. By 1974 to 1979, only a bit fewer than 20 percent did. The six new leading places of origin for *legal* immigrants—a minority of the total number—were, in descending order, Mexico, the Philippines, Cuba, Korea, the West Indies (besides Cuba), and Vietnam. If illegal immigration was included, the list would probably include nothing but Latin American countries, still headed by Mexico.

Now, social tensions erupt when large numbers of newcomers, with their "strange" languages, cultures, and appearance, suddenly arrive in an old American community. Some of these newcomers, especially those from

. . . And Some Who Didn't

The sanctuary movement is made up of possibly 2,200 United States church organizations who help Salvadorans and Guatemalans enter this country across the U.S.-Mexican border. Members of the sanctuary movement, many of them nuns and clergy, are breaking the law. Many of the illegal aliens will be deported and returned to their own countries when and if they are discovered. Some American sanctuary workers will face the possibility of prosecution for their part in bringing the Central Americans into the U.S. But movement members believe that Central Americans who are returned to their own countries face more severe punishments, including political persecution, imprisonment, and even death.

The State Department's position is that Salvadorans come here hoping to escape the poverty and civil war that plague their own country. That is not reason enough to be allowed to stay. In 1984, 13,373 Salvadorans requested refugee status. Only 378 received it. Only those who were able to demonstrate that they personally would be targets of persecution were granted refugee status. The others must return.

In its effort to locate illegal aliens from Central America, the Immigration Service has undercover agents working within the sanctuary movement. In Texas in February 1985, Jack Elder, a Catholic lay worker, was found guilty of helping Salvadorans to enter the country illegally. Stacey Merkt, a Methodist church worker, was found guilty of conspiring to transport the Salvadorans to a bus station. In Arizona in January 1985, sixteen others were indicted for transporting and sheltering illegal aliens. The group included two priests, three nuns, a minister, and several church workers. Members . . . believe their religious convictions justify their actions.

Americans in the late twentieth century come—literally—from "every race under heaven." Except for blacks and native Americans, they or their forebears *chose* to come—some to escape religious or political persecution, some to escape poverty and destitution, and some to escape both. Which is which? This is at the core of the debate between the Reagan administration and the members of the sanctuary movement. With 250 million people, the United States has long closed its borders to completely unrestricted immigration. But our culture gives strong support to accepting newcomers who seek freedom from political and religious oppression. In any case, the influx of newcomers in this generation will reshape the very foundations of the republic—the identity of the people itself. It has been so from the beginning; it is so now.

From Tom Morganthau, "No Hiding Place Here," *Newsweek*, March 4, 1985, pp. 14-15.

Mexico and other parts of Latin America, are not eager to learn English and assimilate into "our" society. And the numbers involved are vast: California may well have a Third World population majority by the end of this century. There, as elsewhere, the American experiment is sure to be tested.

That testing is an opportunity to consider what the experiment is all about: People rejected the fears, superstitions, and murderous lunacies of the past and attempted to create a society where individuals could be free to use their talents and skills. Many people in foreign lands are still prepared to suffer dreadful ordeals to come to America, with all its faults. Perhaps their ordeals will be worth it. Let us hope so.

The Blacks. Most of the immigrants, from the seventeenth century to the present, have been similar in many basic ways. One group, however, was different. Its members did not arrive here voluntarily; they came as slaves, in chains, against their will.

Black slavery and the organized racism that survived its formal end, in 1865, were and are a dreadful reproach to American society and politics. From the start, they undermined and mocked our national ideals. We can draw only one consolation from this terrible reality: We have struggled to overcome slavery and racism, and this struggle has become one of the great themes of our history. (See Chapter 5, "Civil Rights," for a more complete discussion.)

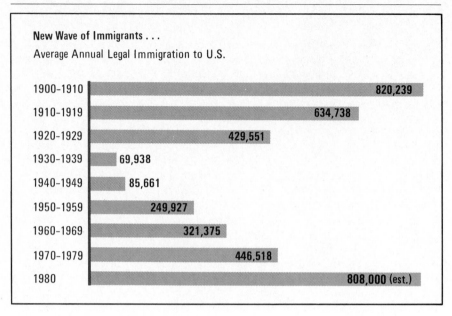

Figure 1-1   Immigration

New Wave of Immigrants . . .
Average Annual Legal Immigration to U.S.

1900–1910	820,239
1910–1919	634,738
1920–1929	429,551
1930–1939	69,938
1940–1949	85,661
1950–1959	249,927
1960–1969	321,375
1970–1979	446,518
1980	808,000 (est.)

And New Origins
Immigrants to U.S. by Region

1959		1979
60.9%	Europe	13.4%
8.9%	Asia	41.4%
1.1%	Africa	2.6%
0.5%	Oceania	1.0%
19.8%	Latin America	38.6%
8.9%	Canada	3.0%

Note: An additional 500,000 to 1 million persons are believed to enter the U.S. illegally each year.

Source: U.S. Immigration and Naturalization Service; 1980 estimate by Select Commission on Immigration and Refugee Policy.

"Island Communities"

Why have groups that in Europe felt compelled to exploit, persecute, and murder one another somehow managed to live in peace here?

One reason is that Americans of different backgrounds tend to keep to themselves. Cities like New York, for example, are an amazing agglomerate of races and nations. But if you look more closely, you find that Greek-Americans, for example, live in one neighborhood, Lebanese-Americans in another. Certain neighborhoods contain people of many ethnic backgrounds, but these people have something else in common: social background. By and

Americans like to settle beside other Americans of similar backgrounds and opinions. This tends to create "island communities," such as this Italian-American neighborhood in New York City.

large, Americans (in suburbs and rural areas, as well as in cities) like to settle beside other Americans of similar backgrounds and opinions. Each community of this sort is an island, so to speak, anchored in the sea of American culture and society, yet separate from all other "island communities."[3] The members of different groups do not collide because, to a great extent, they do not make contact.

Sometimes one community tries to dominate another; but more often, each simply insists on the freedom to run its own affairs. All dislike government control, especially control by the federal government. Independent communities of this kind are the social basis of federalism—the sharing of power between the federal government, on the one side, and states and localities, on the other (see Chapter 3).

"Island communities" cannot isolate themselves completely. In economic life, they can hardly isolate themselves at all. Most are involved in politics, too, if only to protect their independence and their interests. Sometimes, however, the members of a community have such strong views about some religious or moral issue that they attempt to impose their own point of view on everyone, everywhere. In 1981, for example, Arkansas adopted a statute requiring the biblical account of creation to receive "balanced" treatment in classrooms, along with the theory of evolution. However, many people in Arkansas come from a different kind of "island community" and do not share the fundamen-

---

[3] The term was coined by Robert Wiebe, a historian. See R. H. Wiebe, *The Search for Order, 1877–1920* (New York: Hill & Wang, 1969).

talist Christianity that inspired this law. Civil liberties groups denounced it as an "establishment of religion" and filed suit against it in state court.

In January 1982, a federal district judge overturned the Arkansas statute, arguing that creation science was not in fact a science but a religion, and that the sole purpose of the statute was to advance a specific religious belief. Similarly, in Texas, the state Board of Education in 1984 repealed the ten-year-old rule requiring that evolution be taught as only one among several theories of the origin of mankind, after a determination by the state Attorney General that the rule was unconstitutional. Both Louisiana and Mississippi have statutes regarding creation science that have yet to be overturned as of 1985, but both laws seem likely to be challenged. The Louisiana case is especially interesting because the Louisiana supreme court determined only that the state legislature did not exceed its authority in the area of educational policy by passing the bill—the law was not judged on its first amendment constitutionality. This case seems the most likely to end up in the U.S. Supreme Court.

In few other countries, if any, do courts decide what may be taught in classrooms. In the United States they are often called on to make such decisions. Sometimes, in fact, a case of this sort will move through a state system, be appealed to the federal courts, and ultimately be decided by the U.S. Supreme Court (see Chapter 14). A century and a half ago, that most astute observer, Alexis de Tocqueville, a French stateman and political writer, pointed out that "scarcely any question arises in the United States which does not become, sooner or later, a subject of judicial debate."[4] That is about as true now as it was in Tocqueville's day because our sociological federalism created a *political* federalism full of undefined boundaries. Only the courts can settle the claims of competing levels of government and "island communities." (See Chapter 3 for a longer discussion of the role of the courts in setting those boundaries.)

Negotiation and Compromise. If the "island communities" constantly collided and appealed to the courts, the American experiment would not have been possible. In fact, the relations of these communities are often quite friendly, since almost all of them share certain American values and ways of living. Local independence, of course, is one of these values. Within each community, local affairs are settled mainly by self-regulation, which requires the willingness and ability to negotiate and compromise. Most "island communities" are thus prepared to make external negotiations and compromises—those with other communities.

People who know how to encourage compromise, by stressing the values that different groups hold in common, have been and still are a major force in our politics. This was the secret of the political Bosses and machines that used to rule many of our cities. The Machine asked the groups it negotiated with, "How many votes do you have to offer?" They replied by asking, "What will you give in return?" The Machine appealed to voters' material interests, which most Americans accept and understand, not to the perennial battlegrounds of religion or class.[5]

---

[4] Alexis de Tocqueville, *Democracy in America*, Bradley Phillips, ed. (New York: Random House, 1944), I, 279.

[5] Seymour Mandelbaum, *Boss Tweed's New York* (New York: Wiley, 1965), pp. 182–85.

Internal Migration

The people who came to our country did not, for the most part, settle down and stay put. Neither, for the most part, do we, their descendants. Ours is a nation not only of immigrants but also of internal migrants.

The Frontier. Our birthrate was much higher in the eighteenth and nineteenth centuries than it is at present. Lack of opportunity, in some cases, lured men and women out of the settled parts of the country, toward the western frontier. Land was free or almost free in the West. Enormous deposits of minerals, including gold, were there, but no social elites, and in many places, almost no government.

The West was won mainly by sod-busting family farmers and their wives, not by adventurers and cowboys. Yet those men who first cleared a path through the wilderness, the frontiersmen, quickly became figures of national legend, our equivalents of Homeric and biblical heroes. That legend, although misleading, speaks to an important part of our culture: the individual's search for freedom and happiness (interpreted as an escape from the burdens, duties, and institutions of civilized society). That legend, implanted within each of us, has helped to shape our national character.

Closing the Frontier. Around 1800, when the frontier line stood just beyond the Allegheny Mountains, in western Pennsylvania, President Thomas Jefferson expressed a hope that it would take the American people a thousand years to reach the Pacific Ocean. Mr. Jefferson was in no hurry because he regarded the frontier as the backbone of the family farm, and the family farm as the backbone of American democracy. The American people were in a hurry, however. By midcentury, we had reached the Pacific, though the frontier (in the sense of large unsettled regions) lingered on for another forty or so years.

Today's Frontier: The Sunbelt. Although the frontier came to a close by the century's end, the westward movement of people continued. For the mental frontier—the search for independence and wealth—persisted long after the West had been peopled and built over. It persists to this day. Throughout the present century, men and women moved westward from the East and the Midwest, but the pace slowed until the early 1970s. Between 1970 and 1980, it picked up so much that the Sunbelt, the states of the South and Southwest, got seventeen more seats in the House of Representatives, at the expense of the Snowbelt, the states of the North and Midwest.

This dramatic population shift was not altogether voluntary. In part, it was caused by the loss of jobs in the Snowbelt, especially those in the industrial areas of the Midwest. In December 1984, Michigan's unemployment rate stood at 10.5 percent or higher, while in Texas, the rate was 6.2 percent. Although these differentials flattened out during the post-1982 recovery, census data reveals that in the mid-1980s, the population shift toward the Sunbelt states has continued without a pause. Low labor costs and good land values had long attracted industry to the South. Now there was a new attraction: low energy costs. Heating a house in Houston costs about 80 percent less than heating a house in Detroit. Even allowing for the greater need for air conditioning in Texas, energy costs are lower in the Sunbelt.

The Cities and the Suburbs. Since the beginnings of American history, the frontier of settlement has been moving steadily westward, and to that extent,

Jobs and low energy costs have drawn people from all over the country to the Sunbelt states. Cities like Dallas, shown here, have experienced an enormous population increase in the last decade.

the story of westward movement has been a single, continuous story. The movement from the countryside to the city, and from the city to the suburbs, has been far more complex—several stories, in fact, not just one.

Urbanization. When the U.S. Constitution was ratified, in 1788, about nine-tenths of all Americans then lived in the countryside. Philadelphia was our largest city, with about 54,000 people. The next largest was New York, with about 49,000. No other city in the United States had even as many as 20,000 people.

Immigration and the growth of industry fed people into the cities and caused them to expand into the surrounding countryside. By 1879, the number of Americans employed in agriculture amounted to less than half of the country's labor force. Not until 1920, however, did a majority of our people live in cities and towns with at least 2,500 inhabitants. This was just the beginning. By 1970, almost three-fourths of Americans lived in such cities and towns, and three-fifths lived in large metropolitan areas.

Suburbanization. Large metropolitan areas are more than just cities. The central cities are old, often crumbling, crowded, dirty, and poor. People who can afford to move out of them usually do so as soon as they can.

But recently a counter-movement has developed: "gentrification," or the return to and upgrading of certain central-city neighborhoods by "Yuppies." These "young upscale professionals" are frequently affluent, since both husband and wife work and are often childless. Many of them have preferred to move closer to work and to the centers of culture, entertainment, and the arts, which are concentrated in center cities. The rise of the Yuppie sector reminds us that the American social structure is not static but dynamically changing. Nevertheless, although their cultural and marketing influence is great, Yuppies still constitute a small minority of the entire labor force. And "gentrification" is both limited in scope and highly selective as to what parts of the central city it affects. Thus, although the old generalization about the decay of central cities needs to be somewhat modified today, it still has considerable validity.

By World War I (1914), the development of train and trolley networks had permitted middle- and upper-class people to work in the cities and live in the new suburbs built around them. After World War II, many lower-middle- and working-class whites escaped to the now older suburbs and to some newer ones. So metropolitan areas grew in population, even as the cities within them shrank.

What lured so many people out to the suburbs? For one thing, the urge to settle in "island communities" was still strong. Middle- and upper-class whites wanted to get away from poorer whites, and poorer whites wanted to get away from blacks (mostly from the South) and the Puerto Ricans who poured into the cities during the 1940s and 1950s. Rather than stay in the cities and work out the tensions produced by these migrations, many whites preferred to move.

Remember, too, that the countryside and the frontier have always been a part of our mental lives. Americans tolerate cities but do not appear to like them. We treat our cities as an urban frontier; means permitting, we move from the slums to the city's better neighborhoods and then on to the suburbs.[6]

Back to the Land? The process continues. The 1980 census shows that for the first time in more than a century, there were major population increases beyond urban areas, beyond the reach of any suburb, however sprawled out. As in the past, technical and economic developments prepared the way. Instant electronic communications, interstate highways, and other forms of quick transportation, have allowed many people to live out a rural ideal—not just mentally, but in the countryside itself.

The massive population shift to the Sunbelt and to the countryside will probably change the basis of American politics, like all major population shifts. The New Deal, which in the 1930s made the Democrats the majority party of the United States (see Chapter 10), was solidly anchored in the manual laborers and recent immigrants of our big cities. By the 1950s, this political anchoring had already been eroded by the move to the suburbs. The great southwestern and rural shift of the 1970s surely brought something new into our politics. Among its consequences, no doubt, were Ronald Reagan's victories in 1980 and 1984 and the Republican capture of the Senate in 1980, 1982, and 1984.

POLITICAL CULTURE

The word *culture* has many meanings. The rural ideal that lured many Americans out to the suburbs is an aspect of culture. So, too, are the symphonies of Beethoven, the plays of Shakespeare, Western movies, Bing Crosby, the Rolling Stones, and comic books. Culture embraces the tools we make, the thoughts we think, and everything else that we consciously create for our own, human, purposes.

---

[6] Samuel Lubell, *The Future of American Politics* (New York: Harper, 1952), especially Chapter 4, "The Frontier Reappears," and pp. 62–67, "The Old Tenement Trail."

Political culture is one part of culture as a whole. Its special field is power and the institutions that channel power: Congress, the presidency, the dogcatcher—not to mention the army, the navy, and the police. Political culture is a kind of transmission belt between the world of individuals and the world of political institutions, processes, and forms of behavior. It is also the way we learn to understand and accept those institutions, processes, and forms.

Consensus

Political culture varies from country to country. Within some countries, moreover, hostile political cultures may compete against one another. The Italian parliament, for example, contains members of parties that support fascism and monarchism, and several varieties each of liberalism, conservatism, socialism, and communism.

In fact, most European societies have been and still are divided by conflicts over economic and political systems, power, and religion—conflicts that date back to the French Revolution in the late eighteenth century, to the Protestant Reformation in the early sixteenth, and to even earlier struggles. *Class consciousness*—personal awareness of membership in a social class and the belief that class membership should influence political action—pervades European politics. Debates about the nature of "the good life," "the good economy," and "the good society" rage throughout European intellectual life.

In yet another class of countries—Britain springs to mind—most people accept certain basics, like parliamentary government, but disagree about many other social, cultural, political, and economic values.

The United States belongs—perhaps uniquely—to a third class of countries. Americans agree on a very wide front of issues. Some people dissent from this *consensus*, or general agreement, but they are relatively few, even among racial minorities and the poor.

Basic to the American consensus are the following: The United States, as most of us see it, is a society made by, and for, individuals who seek to improve their lot in life and think they can do so. Just as we value individualism, we value free cooperation among like-minded individuals. An exceptional diversity coexists with a broad commitment to a set of unifying ideas, The American Way of Life. This set of ideas has four major components: property, liberty, democracy, and religion.

Property. We have already mentioned that the United States is among the few industrial countries without an important socialist movement. The idea of equal property for all seems to have, and to have had, little support here. Private property and the right to acquire it have always struck most of us as basic human rights.

The weakness of socialism in the United States both fascinates and confuses Europeans. Some of the reasons have just been mentioned: our relatively high standard of living, along with the promise of the frontier, which led so many of us to think that we could solve our problems alone, as individuals.

Today, of course, we cannot hitch up our covered wagon and follow the sun. Yet socialism still has little support here. Most American workers do not consider themselves part of a "working class" whose interests are opposed to those of other classes. Americans as a whole seem to fear total economic

Mimi Forsyth, Monkmeyer

YOU CAN OWN THIS LAND

equality. Rightly or wrongly, most Americans think that people get out of life whatever rewards they have earned, and that the rich deserve their riches. Indeed, most of us admire wealth, identify with the wealthy, and hope to be wealthy ourselves, even if at times we are resentful.[7]

What Americans seem to want is not equality of wealth but equality of opportunity. The difference? If a medical school, let us say, decides to admit a certain number of poor applicants every year, regardless of their grades or the grades of other applicants, that policy promotes equality of *result*. Equality of *opportunity* means that all the applicants compete according to the same standard, usually grades. In an unequal world, however, a world where each of us faces different experiences with a different background, some people question just how "equal" equality of opportunity can really be. (We shall discuss that issue in Chapter 5, "Civil Rights.") In any case, most Americans oppose quotas and other policies that promote equality of result.

Liberty. The word *liberty* means "freedom." Freedom from what, however, and for what? To most Americans, liberty means freedom from restraints, the freedom of each one of us to do as we please. Of course, we know that we cannot enjoy absolute freedom, but it can always be our mental starting point. Anything short of absolute liberty is a compromise, however necessary such compromises have proven to be.

First and foremost, our conception of liberty, liberty as the absence of restraint, is the operational theory of our economic system. Of course, our economy has never been completely unregulated. But even now, after two generations of more or less steadily increasing regulation, it is still much less subject to government control than the economies of most other industrial nations—capitalist, socialist, or communist. (See Chapters 15 and 16 for a fuller discussion of our economy and government regulation of it.)

Our conception of liberty also manifests itself in other, sometimes conflicting ways. When President Reagan tried to reduce the size and impact of the federal government, he was acting in the name of liberty as many Americans understand it. But when other Americans, Reagan's bitter opponents, pub-

> *"But while property is considered as the basis of the freedom of the American yeomanry, there are other auxiliary supports; among which is the information of the people."*
>
> **Noah Webster,**
> 1787

---

[7] Robert E. Lane. *Political Ideology: Why the American Common Man Believes What He Does* (New York: Free Press, 1962), especially, pp. 57–81 and 413–35.

lished the names of alleged CIA agents abroad, they too were acting in the name of liberty, American-style. Complete freedom from restraint is always our ideal, and although we do not quite achieve it, we do come remarkably close.

Democracy. The Declaration of Independence proclaims that "All men are created equal." There has been a lot of dispute about the intended meaning of that phrase. When the future United States was first settled, in the seventeenth century, equality among men (to say nothing of women) hardly existed, even as an ideal. In England, for example, sumptuary laws kept certain clothing materials, such as ermine and silk, for "gentlemen" and "ladies." Only "gentlemen" and "ladies" could be addressed as "Mr." and "Mrs."—that is, if their ranks did not require them to be addressed as "My Lord" or "Your Grace." The son of a large landowner would have thought himself disgraced to work for a living, even as a doctor or a lawyer.

Many of the people who came to the colonies in the early period came here because, among other reasons, they hated such privilege and snobbery; they thought themselves as good as the gentry and wanted the world to recognize that claim. Every generation of immigrants to the United States has come in conscious rebellion against the customs, the ideas, and, especially, the privileged elites of the Old World. As a people, we have no need for aristocratic fripperies.

At first, these ideas of social equality did not have the field all to themselves. The earliest colonial constitution of South Carolina created a colonial aristocracy, complete with titles and heraldry. Even during the first generation of American independence, our political institutions were far from democratic—only white male property owners could vote, for example, in many states. But our institutions were far more democratic than those of Europe, and they became steadily more democratic as more men could own property. By the 1830s, most white men could vote in local, state, and national elections. By amendment to the Constitution in 1870, blacks were given the right to vote, although in many parts of the country they could not really do so until the 1960s. Women have been voting in national elections since an amendment to the Constitution in 1920.

Whatever our past imperfections, no serious doubt exists that the United States is by now a truly representative democracy. But our democracy remains limited in many ways. For one thing, it is a political but not a social democracy; in other words, it allows for gross inequalities of income and living conditions. These inequalities have political consequences, since they permit some people to make much more effective use of their political rights than others can—although in theory, they have no more rights than anyone else.

Indeed, our form of government is not absolutely democratic, even in the political sense. Every state, for example, elects two senators, so voters in states with small populations are, in effect, overrepresented in the Senate. The President is not elected by direct popular vote, and in certain circumstances, the candidate with fewer popular votes can win, *something that has already happened in the past.* As for the federal judiciary, it is not chosen by popular vote, although it is the most powerful court system in the world.

In fact, these *un*democratic elements of our political system probably do less to thwart the majority's will than some of the democratic elements do. It sounds like a contradiction, but it is not.

Our Constitution, you see, created a form of government that often prevents the federal government from acting with unity and vigor, because it is separated into three independent branches—executive, legislative, and judicial. In the beginning, the real focus of the federal government was the House of Representatives, which was also the most democratic part of the government. For a time, in fact, the House caucus of the majority party, the ancestors of today's Democrats (see Chapter 9), chose its presidential candidate and, thereby, the President (see Chapter 11). During those years, in other words, the party that controlled the House also controlled the executive branch of government.

Had this state of affairs continued, the United States might now have a parliamentary form of government (see Chapter 2)—which is to say, a government capable of acting more decisively. Instead, in the true American manner, the ills of democracy were cured with more democracy. By the 1830s, the Democratic candidate was chosen not by the House Democratic caucus but by broadly based conventions. The election itself became more democratic than it had been. The President, therefore, became more independent of Congress and much more important and powerful than before. But the power of the majority party was, in the long run, weakened because it now had to win control both of the House and of an independent presidency. Consequently, its capacity for representing the popular will declined.

Another case in point is the Seventeenth Amendment (1913), which provided for the direct popular election of senators, until then elected by state legislatures. Before 1913, many people viewed the Senate as a millionaires' club. But for the Seventeenth Amendment, the Senate might have lost democratic legitimacy and been abolished or made less powerful. A political party would then have been able to control the legislature by controlling only the House. It would then have been much easier for a political majority in the nation at large to become a political majority in the legislature—something that now requires control over the two houses of Congress, not just one.

In short, the progress of democracy created more and more islands of independent democratic power within our national government. The will of the majority was steadily diminished because each branch could check the other two. We have yet to find our way out of this.

Religion. In the seventeenth century, when the foundations of American society were laid, "established" churches claimed religious monopolies throughout Europe (see Chapter 4). Dissenters from these churches were often persecuted, hunted, tortured, and sometimes put to death.

The Protestant Church of England was among those claiming such a religious monopoly; however, it failed to suppress newer, dissenting varieties of Protestantism. Even the old faith, Roman Catholicism, kept some of its followers. Many Protestant Dissenters went to settle in North America. These men and women brought along a characteristic mentality. As Tocqueville put it:

> Having shaken off the authority of the Pope, [they] acknowledged no other religious supremacy. They brought with them into the New World a form of Christianity, which I cannot better describe than by styling it a democratic and republican religion. This sect contributed powerfully to the establishment of a democracy and a republic; and from the earliest settlement of the emigrants, politics and religion contracted an alliance which has never been dissolved.[8]

---

[8] Tocqueville, Democracy in America, I, 299.

The free exercise of religion.

This alliance, however important, was informal; it did not rest upon legal coercion. Quite the contrary, the First Amendment to the U.S. Constitution prevents Congress either from establishing a state church or from interfering with the free exercise of any religion. These prohibitions did not, as some people feared, promote atheism. In fact, the United States now has the highest levels of church attendance in the industrialized world. In contrast, countries like Britain, still encumbered with established churches, have the lowest levels. The religions of our country do not rely on the state's power, because they do not have to. Their enduring strength comes from the fact that many "island communities" define themselves through religion and thus take care to transmit their respective beliefs from generation to generation.

The 300 Religions. About 88 million Americans—a bit less than 40 percent of our people in the mid-1980s—seem not to belong to any organized religious group, but most of these millions are probably, in a cultural sense, Protestants. If so, about 62 percent of Americans are Protestant, 25 percent Roman Catholic and Eastern Orthodox, 3 percent Jewish, and 1 percent members of other religions. About 10 percent are conscious atheists or agnostics.

This reckoning does not exhaust the religious variety of the United States and, in fact, does not begin to reveal it. Protestant denominations differ from each other and are very numerous; their number changes constantly through mergers and splits. New religious groups form and disappear all the time. At any one moment, about 300 religious groups form and disappear all the time. At any one moment, about 300 religious denominations are active in the United States. They range in size from 55 members of the Primitive Advent Christian Church to the 49 million members of the Roman Catholic Church.

A Textbook Case: The Mormons. Some churches that proliferate in the United States were founded here. One of them, the Church of Jesus Christ of

AP/Wide World Photos

Hated for their creed or envied for their prosperity, the Mormons were driven westward until they finally found a haven in Salt Lake City, where they built the Mormon Tabernacle, shown here.

Latter-Day Saints—better known as the Mormon Church—was founded in the 1820s by Joseph Smith, a young man from upstate New York. Smith gave the Mormons their own sacred writings—the Book of Mormon, given to him, he said, by an angel—and their own doctrines and practices, among them polygamy.

The marriage of one man to several women infuriated public opinion in the 1820s and 1830s. Persecution forced the church and its members westward, first to Ohio and then to Illinois. But again the Mormons met with hostility from their neighbors, and it erupted into violence. Smith and his brother, Hyrum, were arrested on charges of treason and then murdered in jail by a mob.

Brigham Young, who succeeded Joseph Smith as head of the church, led the Mormons on a trek to a remote spot in what is now the state of Utah, far beyond the western frontier. The Mormons arrived in the Salt Lake Valley in 1847 and started to build their settlement. Pressure from the federal government forced them to give up polygamy, and Utah was soon after admitted to the Union (1896). Mormons have always formed a large majority of Utah's population and substantial minorities in neighboring states. To this day, they are a cohesive, separate community, and their church—one of the most rapidly growing religious bodies in America—is an important political force.

This is an American success story, and a classic one. It begins with a new and, to many, strange vision. Adversity and persecution strengthen the community's will to survive. After many trials and false turns, the community escapes to the farthest reaches of the frontier and creates an "island community" of like-minded men and women. There, they conquer the wilderness, survive, and triumph.

There is a postscript to the story, and it, too, is typical. More than a century ago the Mormons were persecuted by outsiders who viewed them as libertines and subversives. Today, no group of Americans is more conservative about many social issues.

Religion and Stability. Political parties and outlooks that openly oppose religion have little attraction for people in this country. Many of us are content to seek happiness in another life; many others seek happiness on earth by following God's law as they understand it. Even aspects of secular life—wordly success, for example—are regarded by many as proof of God's blessing: "God helps those who help themselves." Religion, in short, is a stumbling block to socialism. It makes many Americans content, as they see it, to leave well enough alone.

The "Civil Religion." Religion in a watered-down form helps to create our sense of what it means to be an American. Why watered-down? Because it is what religions share, not what divides them, that contributes to our national identity. These common elements, the American "civil religion,"[9] include belief in God; in what many Americans view as our country's divinely inspired destiny; and in the divine origin of property, liberty, and democracy.

The chief priest of the civil religion is the President, for the presidency, as Teddy Roosevelt said, is a "bully pulpit." Much of any President's power comes from the ability to understand and manipulate effectively the symbolic aspects of the office. Let us consider President Reagan's first inaugural address in January 1981. The address identified several deep, but not hopeless, crises facing the country. Then it pointed out why Americans—"this special breed"—could and would overcome them. Property, liberty, democracy, and God's benevolence toward the United States were invoked, as were heroes of the past—our political equivalent of saints and martyrs. Through heroism, self-sacrifice, and voluntary cooperation, Mr. Reagan assured us, we should fulfill this country's divine mission.

Political Subcultures: The Importance of Regionalism

The fundamentals of our political culture—property, liberty, democracy, and religion—are pretty much the same throughout the United States. Virtually all Americans believe that they should be free to strike it rich, take democracy for granted, respect religion, and wish to keep the government at arm's length. Such attitudes unite Americans of very different backgrounds.

We should remember that in our huge country, Americans are very different, too. On a given day, it might be 0°F in one part of the United States and 75°F a mere 2,500 miles away. The political cultures of the various regions do not differ quite as much, but they differ. These variations go back centuries, born not in this country but in Great Britain. They show how a common political culture, liberalism, can be interpreted in various ways under the influence of varying historical conditions.

In a sense, every state, town, and street has its own way of looking at the world, including the political world. But it is most useful for us to look at larger patterns of variation. One of the most useful was proposed some years ago by Daniel J. Elazar, who suggested that three political subcultures—"moralist," "individualist," and "traditionalist"—both coexist and compete within the American political universe.[10]

---

[9] Robert N. Bellah, "Civil Religion in America," in J. F. Childress and D. B. Harned, eds., *Secularization and the Protestant Prospect* (Philadelphia: Westminister, 1970), pp. 95–117. See also Will Herberg, *Protestant, Catholic, Jew* (New York: Doubleday, 1955).

[10] Daniel J. Elazar, *American Federalism: A View from the States* (New York: Crowell, 1966), pp. 79-140.

"Politics in America is the binding secular religion."

Theodore H. White,
Breach of Faith, 1975

The Moralist Subculture. The Puritans who founded New England were the spiritual fathers and mothers of our moralist political subculture. They, and those who drew inspiration from them, regarded politics not just as a way of getting what we want, but as a way of creating a good society and improving ourselves as human beings. The moralist subculture spread west to Minnesota and the Dakotas, peopled largely by northern European immigrants steeped in Dissenting Protestantism. Voters who live in states that are under strong moralist influence believe that government can act effectively. They do not tolerate incompetence, and still less do they tolerate governmental corruption. They are prone to support reform movements within and against the major political parties.

The Individualist Subculture. The political subculture of individualism assumes that the point of politics is to help individuals get what they want. Politics, in this view, is just another business. This tradition's political leaders tolerate corruption but not ideology, that is, consistent political principles (see Chapter 7). Here is the promised land of political machines, bosses, and patronage. The states most influenced by the individualist political subculture span a belt running from the Middle Atlantic states westward to the lower Midwest, an area with a large number of immigrants from Ireland and from southern and eastern Europe.

The Traditionalist Subculture. Like the moralist political subculture, traditionalism holds that individuals, with their noisy and sometimes harmful desires, are not the sole end of politics. The values embraced by the traditionalist subculture are family, community, and tradition. Its ideal of perfection lies not in the future but in the past, and that ideal would best be achieved by accepting the inevitable, not by struggling against it. The states, mostly in the South, that are dominated by this subculture lack strong political parties. These states have resisted the efforts of "outside agitators" who want to change their local institutions. Here is the true home of federalism (see Chapter 3).

The traditionalist subculture has its roots in the agricultural past of the South, and it has grown somewhat weaker as the South has become more industrial and more urban. Yet even in the South's industrial and urban centers, it remains fairly strong.

What's the Difference? If you go to the Mississippi River, where it divides Iowa from Illinois, you see two states that look almost the same. On each side, farms produce mainly pigs and corn. As a Marxist would say, the "productive forces" are identical. But the politics are totally different. Illinois has a history rich in political chicanery and corruption, not only in its cities but also in its rural areas. On the opposite bank of the Mississippi, in Iowa, the voters do not even tolerate gerrymandering (see Chapter 13). Iowa embraces the moralist ideals of the New Englanders and Scandinavians who first peopled it; Illinois reflects the developed political practices of people whose forebears came from the upper South, the Mid-Atlantic states, and eastern and southern Europe.

Electoral Implications. The traditions embodied by these three great political subcultures affect the general conduct of state and local politics—for example, the extent of public tolerance for Boss rule and corruption. These traditions also influence the fortunes of our national political parties and the coalitions formed inside and outside them. Just to take a few examples, the Democratic presidential candidate in 1972, George McGovern, and an independent candidate in 1980, John Anderson, both came out of the moralist subculture; both did best where that subculture was most powerful. George Wallace, who ran as an independent in 1968, came out of the Southern, traditionalist political culture; and in the South, he got a higher proportion of votes than he did elsewhere.

The flourishing of three separate political subcultures is an important aspect of the sociological federalism that lies at the heart of political federalism. It makes building and maintaining political coalitions very difficult.

SUMMARY

Our American political system is constitutional, representative, and democratic. It is a remarkable system, despite some obvious flaws. No other democratic form of government is quite like it. Only the American political system separates political power among the legislative, executive, and judicial branches, thus ensuring a never-ending competitive struggle for power and influence within the federal government itself.

The collective political character of the American people is remarkable, too. Probably no other nation is so cantankerously libertarian, so distrustful of government authority. The American system is democratic, for it has popular support. But the system often paralyzes the majority, making it ineffective. This paradox could not have endured over so many generations but for special, if not unique, conditions, which lie deep within American society.

First, the United States is a nation founded by immigrants. Some of them came to escape religious and political persecution, others, to escape famine and poverty. But all viewed America as a promised land, where they would have a chance for a better life. These immigrants formed a society with a culture whose values were not simply an extension of the Old World but, rather, something new. Feudalism and aristocracy, for example, never took hold here.

Second, the early settlers of America had the good fortune to emigrate to one of the largest countries in the world—a country rich in natural resources and safe, for over a century, from attack by foreign powers. A scarcity of laborers and a wealth of natural resources meant that Americans could be better off than Europeans. That is the main reason why a sizable socialist movement never developed here, as it did in the industrialized countries of Europe.

The newness, spaciousness, and vast natural resources of America helped create a society that emphasized the values of individualism, acquisitiveness, and practicality. The migration westward to the frontier fulfilled those values. The frontiersman, who rapidly became a romanticized part of America's folklore and history, was self-reliant and bold. The frontier tradition and rural life still influence our thoughts and acts—one reason for the population shift, after World War II, from the cities to the suburbs and rural areas.

Despite the enormous number of religious, cultural, racial, and economic groups that coexist and compete within American society, we have avoided—

with a few exceptions—violent conflict over public matters. Indeed the history of American politics has fulfilled the Founding Fathers' hope of maintaining "domestic tranquility." One reason is that Americans have tended to settle "island communities" of like-minded people and families. Another is the strength here of organized religion. But we Americans pay a price for this "domestic tranquility." We—and, more disturbing, our leaders—have great difficulty understanding societies different from our own. As a people, we have sometimes persecuted dissenters and nonconformists. And the cost of our national attachment to individual freedom has often been much higher than we like to think. Why else, after all, do we have 11,000 or so deaths from handguns every year, while Britain has only 30 or so and Japan even fewer?

Finally, we often have trouble recognizing the problems within our own political system. For it has been so enveloped in consensus that it is often regarded as unchangeable—as part of the "natural order of things"—and thus beyond analysis or evaluation. An eminent political theorist once asked, "Can a people 'born equal' ever understand peoples elsewhere that have to become so? Can it ever understand itself?"[11] We cannot answer either question here. But we can try to understand why they are important.

SUGGESTED READINGS

DANIEL BELL, *The Cultural Contradictions of Capitalism*. New York: Basic Books, 1976. A penetrating analysis of the enduring tensions between morality and pleasure, hedonism and self-denial, and collective social needs and individual self-will in modern America.

LOUIS HARTZ, *The Liberal Tradition in America*. New York: Harcourt, 1955. The classic analysis of the causes, characteristics, and consequences of the American consensus. Do not let Hartz's constant namedropping deter you.

———ed., *The Founding of New Societies*. New York: Harcourt, 1964. Hartz's introductory essay and chapter on the United States are well worth reading. Both are more accessible to readers than the tougher parts of his *Liberal Tradition*, while covering—and expanding—much of the same ground.

SAMUEL P. HUNTINGTON, *American Politics: The Promise of Disharmony*. Cambridge: Harvard Univ., 1982. The shrewder observers of American politics know that our wide agreement on the basics does not mean we have no conflict at all. Rather, our conflicts are diffused among many groups. The disharmony produced by our form of government makes our political system "drift," so deadlocks prevent decisive action by the government and the people who control it. Huntington is very concerned about this.

ROBERT E. LANE, *Political Ideology: Why the American Common Man Believes What He Does*. New York: Free Press, 1962. A classic, although perhaps somewhat outdated, analysis of the beliefs of Americans.

DAVID M. POTTER, *People of Plenty: Economic Affluence and the American Character*. Chicago: Univ. of Chicago, 1954. An elegant and powerful, but simple, discussion of the role of affluence in shaping American political culture.

ALEXIS DE TOCQUEVILLE, *Democracy in America*. Any edition; first published in English in New York in 1839. The French statesman and writer Alexis de Tocqueville visited and dissected America and its democracy a century and a half ago, yet it is amazing how many of Tocqueville's insights are still fresh, vital, and pertinent. There may be no other country whose politics and culture can still be described by a work of the 1830s. *Democracy in America* is a masterpiece that every person concerned with understanding American politics should read.

---

[11] Louis Hartz, *The Liberal Tradition in America* (New York: Harcourt, 1955), p. 309.

chapter two

THE CONSTITUTION

The text of the treaty that ended the American Revolution arrived in the United States in March 1783. Our army, which had not been paid for months, was verging upon mutiny.

In those days, Congress had no regular meeting place. At this moment, it had assembled in Pennsylvania's State House (today's Independence Hall), then also used by Pennsylvania's Executive Council. Like Congress, the council did not pay its soldiers promptly, and they too were mutinous. In June 1783, they attacked the State House and sent Congress packing off to Nassau Hall, at what is now Princeton University, in New Jersey.

Poor Congress! Although responsible for these debts, it lacked the ability to pay them. Under the constitution then in force, the **Articles of Confederation,** Congress could declare that a state owed a certain sum to the federal treasury, but it could not levy a tax on any citizen or business. Only the state legislatures could do that, and often they would not.

Congress wanted a more independent taxing power, and to that end it proposed a 5 percent import duty to pay off the Revolutionary War debt of $42 million. Under the Articles, the states had to give their consent—their unanimous consent. But only twelve of the thirteen states agreed to the new tax. Rhode Island, then as now the smallest state, held out against it. After nearly two years, Congress sent delegates to Rhode Island, but en route, they found out that Virginia, then the largest and most important state, had revoked its resolution supporting the import duty. Sadly, they returned home.

When the army did at last disband, the United States lacked even the pretense of military power. The country was surrounded by foreign, potentially hostile forces.

Britain held on to Canada and, despite the peace treaty with the United States, to army garrisons and frontier posts in our Northwest Territory, today's Midwest. Spain occupied much of what is now our West and Deep South, controlled the Mississippi River, and lusted after Tennessee and Kentucky. Without fear of reprisal, pirates on the high seas insolently preyed upon our merchant ships.

The leading men of the United States feared these threats from abroad, but most Americans largely ignored them. In fact, the foreign menace failed not only to produce a strong sense of internal unity but also to prevent very serious internal class conflicts. In the 1780s, hard times drove small farmers to demand legislation postponing or canceling debts. The same people wanted "cheap money": paper currency issued without adequate amounts of precious metals to back it up. Small farmers are usually debtors, or borrowers, and cheap money, in effect, lets them pay back less than they had borrowed. Of course, the urban and trading classes—those who loaned money—wanted state governments to uphold the sanctity of contracts and the "soundness" (or constant value) of money.

Each state had to deal alone with these conflicts because the Articles did not provide for an effective federal government to mitigate or resolve them. What the Articles had created was less a nation of thirteen states than a confederation among thirteen more or less-independent states. Georgia, for example, officially called itself The State of Georgia, by the Grace of God Free, Sovereign and Independent. As for Congress, John Adams, our second President (1797-1801), described it as a diplomatic assembly where representatives acted as if they were ambassadors in a foreign country. It was so powerless and unimportant that when John Hancock (the first signer of the Declaration of Independence and the governor of Massachusetts) was elected "president" of Congress, in 1785, he did not even bother to take up office.

The American experiment appeared to be failing. But there was one great difference between our political mentality then and now. In the early 1780s, we had a constitution—the Articles—but it had been ratified only recently, in 1777, and when it failed, many people assumed that it should be replaced. In fact, it was—by our present Constitution. That Constitution has now endured so long that most of us think of it as eternal and unchangeable. In this, we differ quite profoundly from the men and women of the revolutionary generation, who were committed to a set of political principles but not to particular forms of government.

ENGLAND AND AMERICA

The Founders of the United States—the men and women who rebelled against Britain and created our system of government—were Americans, like us. Their political culture was the starting point of our political culture. The nation they created and shaped was the starting point of the nation we live in today, but it was a different nation. Two centuries ago the United States was little more than a string of settlements up and down the Atlantic coast, few of them more than 100 miles inland. Philadelphia, then the country's largest city, had only 54,000 people. More than 90 percent of employed adults were farmers or farm laborers.

The Founders' political culture was different from ours, too. The first permanent English settlement in what is now the United States was planted in 1607 at Jamestown, Virginia. Until 1776—for 169 years—most of the land along the eastern seaboard of North America was a colony of England. During

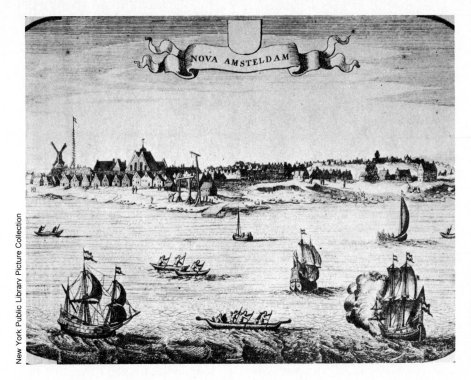

Two centuries ago, the United States was little more than a string of settlements up and down the Atlantic Coast. This illustration shows New Amsterdam (now New York City) in the 1700s.

those years, the men and women who lived in those colonies were Englishmen and Englishwomen, not Americans. When George Washington, Thomas Jefferson, and John Adams went to school, they learned English, not American, history. They read Shakespeare and Milton, not American writers. The political liberties they learned to value were "the liberties of Englishmen."

Until the 1760s, the colonies' dependence on Britain seemed normal and natural, for until then the English colonies had to share the North American continent with two rival empires: those of France and Spain.[1] In 1763, after a war of seven years, the French colonial empire in Canada was ceded to Britain, so the British colonists no longer had to worry about the threat of "French slavery" next door. British rule in the thirteen colonies then became more and more irksome. Somehow, suddenly, the whole colonial connection had become a problem. A decade of controversy between colonial malcontents and the British government then followed. At last, on July 2, 1776, the Second Continental Congress resolved "that these United Colonies are, and of Right ought to be, Free and Independent States."[2]

But as other countries have discovered more recently, political independence comes much more easily than cultural and economic independence. In 1776 we had neither. Indeed, we had not yet evolved an independent form of government.

---

[1] The French and Spanish were living in their respective American empires, but (except in Quebec and Louisiana) there were relatively few. Although the United States took over much of the land controlled by the French and Spanish empires in North America, these cultures contributed little to our political development. This country was created in the former English colonies; and as it expanded, it imposed its own institutions and political culture on the rest of the country.

[2] U.S. Declaration of Independence. See Appendix.

The Conservative Revolutionists

The men who declared American independence were not rebels against a social order. For the most part, they were people of means: merchants and large landowners. They had many grievances, large and small, but no wish to change the foundations of society. As they saw it, they were merely seeking to protect the purity of tradition from the malignant innovations of the British government.

The Liberties of Englishmen. The most bitterly controversial of these innovations had to do with taxation. Until 1763, colonial taxes were voted by colonial legislatures. Then, the British Parliament for the first time imposed a direct tax on the colonies. From their colonists' point of view, this tax was indeed an innovation. As John Adams said, the colonists "desire nothing new; they wish only to keep their own privileges. They were for 150 years allowed to tax themselves," and all they asked was to go on doing so.

From Britain's point of view, however, Parliament was not a local legislature, but the legislature of the empire as a whole, and it had as much right to impose taxes in Boston, Massachusetts, as in Boston, England. Remember that most of the people of Boston, England, could not vote and thus were not personally represented in Parliament. Yet they had to pay taxes. Why then should the people of Boston, Massachusetts, not pay taxes merely because they were not personally represented in Parliament? In short, the British were coming to view Parliament as a sovereign body; we did not.

Many of the colonists were convinced that their traditional liberties as Englishmen also included the right to trade freely with the rest of the world. Here, too, the liberties of Englishmen looked different in England. After all,

Americans protest against a direct tax imposed by the British Parliament, the stamp tax, by hanging a stamp distributor in effigy.

The Metropolitan Museum of Art, bequest of Charles Allen Munn

the English government had always claimed the right to regulate foreign trade. From mid-seventeenth century onward, it had interfered quite actively with colonial trade, specifying which products could be exported, in whose boats, and in what quantities. Had the colonists submitted to these laws—which, for example, required that all colonial goods be carried in ships owned by British subjects resident in Britain—ours would still be an agricultural country exporting most of its products to the Mother Country. That is what Britain hoped to make us. We did not accept their plan, but it is very doubtful that colonial claim to free trade had any traditional basis. Of course, the claim was made in all sincerity.

Some of the colonists' ideas about the liberties of Englishmen had more substance: for example, the idea that government ought to be subject to controls. The oldest and probably the most important of these controls is known by its Latin name, **habeas corpus** ("You should have the body"). Since 1678 this had required that within a few days of a person's arrest, English legal authorities must specify the violation with which the person is charged. This in effect prevented arbitrary arrest, the arrest of people simply because they had displeased the government. To the present day, *habeas corpus* is a bedrock of our civil liberties. In the late seventeenth century, the English government was also prevented by law from requiring that civilians quarter (or house) military troops. But this prohibition did not apply to the colonies, an irritant that contributed to the drive for American independence.

A Social Contract

Another English idea the colonists brought across the Atlantic was the principle that governments should in some sense represent the governed. Although the colonists did not take this idea at all literally, as we do today, they did believe that governments should derive their just powers, to quote the Declaration of Independence (1776), "from the Consent of the Governed." Why? Because in the long run, people will obey a government only if they think that it serves their interests. Government, as the colonists saw it, had its origins in a compact, or contract, among the people. Each individual contracts to accept authority, but only for reasons of personal advantage. When governments do not serve the interests of individuals, the result is tyranny, discontent, and rebellion.

This **contract theory** was elaborated in quite different forms by a number of philosophers. Probably its most influential source—especially here—was John Locke's (1632–1704) *Second Treatise of Civil Government* (1690). Locke argued that governments have no automatic right to obedience; they earn that right by following natural law, the law of human nature, which is the same in all human hearts and in all times and places. By nature, Locke thought, all human beings seek to protect their lives, their liberty, and their property. Some people seek, as well, other people's lives, liberty, and property. Were there no government, these wicked people would dominate those who merely minded their own business. Therefore the latter, among themselves, made a contract to maintain by force a common set of rules: the law. Thus, said Locke, government came into the world.

Locke believed that he could see the record of these events in what he knew about primitive peoples. But if we knew that our ancestors had agreed to join in a **social contract,** have we ourselves done so? No matter, according to Locke. In the first place, most of us join the contract implicitly, simply by obeying the law. Besides, it would be *rational* to join it, and that is the important thing. However, it is rational only if the government protects your life, your liberty, and your property, since you submit to the social contract only to protect them. Life, liberty, and property are **natural rights,** so to speak, rights that were created by God, not by government. Governments are legitimate only if they respect the natural rights that brought them into existence. When they violate these natural rights, they break the social contract and are no longer legitimate. The people now have a natural right of rebellion.

Locke did not invent the idea of government as a contract among the people; he refined it and applied it to a particular historic event, Britain's Glorious Revolution (1688-1689). By 1688, the idea itself had a long history. In 1620, twelve years before Locke was born, the Pilgrims founded the second colony of English-speaking men and women on the Atlantic seacoast, at Plymouth, Massachusetts. On November 11, the passengers on the *Mayflower* signed an agreement in which they "solemnly and mutually . . . covenant and combine ourselves into a civil Body Politic." They agreed to frame laws and regulations "as shall be thought most meet [suitable] for the general Good of the Colony," and in return they promised "all due Submission and Obedience." In short, they signed a social contract.

THE DECLARATION OF INDEPENDENCE

By 1776, many Americans wanted to end the contract between the people of Britain and the people of the thirteen colonies. Perhaps, as those Americans thought, the British had broken that contract; perhaps, again, it had merely outlived its usefulness. In any case, the idea of government as a contract was then still very much alive.

Another View of the Revolution

In 1827 Judge Mellen Chamberlain, then twenty-one, interviewed Captain Levi Preston of Danvers, then ninety-one and a veteran of the assault on the British retreating from Concord on April 19, 1775. The following dialogue ensued:

M.C.: Captain Preston, why did you go to the Concord Fight, the 19th of April, 1775?

L.P.: Why did I go?

M.C.: Yes, my histories tell me that you men of the Revolution took up arms against "intolerable oppressions."

L.P.: What were they? Oppressions? I didn't feel them.

M.C.: What, were you not oppressed by the Stamp Act?

L.P.: I never saw one of those stamps, and always understood that Governor Bernard put them all in Castle William. I am certain I never paid a penny for one of them.

M.C.: Well, what then about the tea-tax?

L.P.: Tea-tax! I never drank a drop of the stuff; the boys threw it all overboard.

M.C.: Then I suppose you had been reading Harrington or Sidney and Locke about the eternal principles of liberty.

L.P.: Never heard of 'em. We read only the Bible, the Catechism, Watt's Psalms and Hymns, and the Almanack.

M.C.: Well, then, what was the matter? and what did you mean in going to the fight?

L.P.: Young man, what we meant in going for those red-coats was this: we always had governed ourselves, and we always meant to. They didn't mean we should.

From Mellen Chamberlain, *John Adams: The Statesman of the American Revolution, with other Essays and Addresses, Historical and Literary.*

Consider, for example, the second paragraph of the Declaration of Independence (see Appendix). After announcing the fact of American independence, the signers assert that all men "are endowed by their Creator with certain unalienable [that is, natural] Rights, [and] that among these are Life, Liberty, and the Pursuit of Happiness"—by which they probably meant property. Governments, they next declare, "are instituted among Men, deriving their just Powers from the Consent of the Governed." And "whenever any Form of Government becomes destructive of these Ends"—life, liberty, and the pursuit of happiness "it is the Right of the People to alter or to abolish it."

Next, consider the long shopping list of complaints that follows this wonderful statement of principle. The king of England, we are told, has quartered "large Bodies of Armed Troops" among civilians in peacetime. He has imposed taxes "without our Consent." He has cut off "our Trade with all Parts of the World." He has taken away "our Charters, abolishing our most valuable Laws." As for "our British Brethren," they have been warned by us against attempts to create "an unwarrantable Jurisdiction over us." Alas, they "have been deaf to the Voice of Justice." The course was clear: "all political Connection between" the people of the colonies and the people of Great Britain "is and ought to be totally dissolved."

The United States of America had been born.

Nothing of importance happened today.

Entry in the diary of King George III,
July 4, 1776

EARLY "WRITTEN" CONSTITUTIONS

Eleven years passed between the signing of the Declaration of Independence, on July 4, 1776, and the framing of the U.S. Constitution, in 1787. These were years of political uncertainty and experiment. Constitutions came and went.

The importance we attach to constitutions and constitutionalism is a part of our British heritage. Britain has a constitution and takes it very seriously indeed, but it is "unwritten"—a misleading term, in a way. Parts of the British constitution are written down, but they consist of ordinary laws, which Parliament can repeal at any time. (By contrast, the U.S. Congress cannot by itself repeal any part of our Constitution.) Other parts of the British constitution are not written down in any legal document and simply exist in the public mind; for instance, the principle that Parliament, rather than the king, chooses the government.

Since the coming of independence, our constitutions have been "written" ones. All their provisions are set down in words, and they are somehow distinguished from the ordinary body of laws. One of the earliest of these constitutions was adopted in 1780 by the state of Massachusetts. "The body politic," its Preamble declares, "is formed by a voluntary association of individuals: It is a social compact, by which the whole people covenants [agrees] with each citizen, and each citizen with the whole people, that all shall be governed by certain laws for the common good." The citizens enter into this compact "to provide for an equitable mode of making laws, as well as for an impartial interpretation, and a faithful execution of them."[3] Note that the framers of this constitution explicitly distinguish between the *making*, the *execution*, and the *interpretation* of laws.

---

[3] Quoted in Ronald M. Peters, Jr., *The Massachusetts Constitution of 1780: A Social Compact* (Amherst: Univ. of Massachusetts, 1978), Appendix pp. 195-201.

Separation of Powers. The framers of the Massachusetts constitution thought they had found a way to ensure that good laws would be carried out and interpreted well, and it was a new way. Under the British constitution, Parliament is more than just a legislative body: It directly controls both the executive and the judiciary. Massachusetts rejected this system. Instead it provided that

> the legislative department shall never exercise the executive and judicial powers, or either of them: The executive shall never exercise the legislative and judicial powers, or either of them: The judicial shall never exercise the legislative and executive powers, or either of them: to the end it may be a government of laws and not of men.[4]

This separation of powers among the legislative, executive, and judicial branches was surely an obstacle to despotic government. But it also separated the components of political power without putting them back together again, so it was also an obstacle to effective government. We shall be discussing this problem time and again.

Growing Pains. The Articles of Confederation

Our first national constitution was a written one: the Articles of Confederation. It was a failure. Article I set up the United States of America, but Article II kept for each state any power not actually granted to Congress, and very few powers were granted to Congress.

Because Congress was the only branch of the national government, the system created by the Articles was more or less parliamentary. Congress elected a "president" who had no clear functions. There was no judicial system. Each state legislature sent three to seven representatives to Congress, but each state had only one vote. Nine out of the thirteen votes were needed to pass any law. Congress could not levy taxes or regulate commerce among the states. Its powers to wage war and make foreign policy were limited. Indeed, it had no way of enforcing any of its laws.

The Failure of the Articles. The system established under the Articles, despite its failure, was a natural one for the United States. In colonial times, no American central government existed, only a number of colonial governments that reported directly to Britain. These colonies, now states, were very different from one another, but they were very much alike in their hostility to centralization. The truth is that in 1787 and 1788, this country was far from united in resolving to throw out the Articles. We threw them out mainly because the most politically conscious part of our population wanted to do so.

The Threat at Home: Shays's Rebellion. In the 1780s and for a long time thereafter, the United States was a nation mainly of small farmers, most of them constantly in debt. In the early 1780s many of them could not repay the money they had borrowed. The farmers demanded laws to suspend debt, and they seemed likely to get them because farmers were almost everywhere a majority of the voters.

---

[4] Peters, *The Massachusetts Constitution*, p. 201.

In some states, local judges let indebted farmers off the hook, but not in Massachusetts, where farmers who failed to pay their bills were thrown into jail. In the fall of 1786, farmers protested by blocking the entrances to a number of county courthouses. The governor of Massachusetts called out the militia, and the farmers were chased home. But they feared that their leaders, including a man named Daniel Shays, might be accused of treason, so they headed for Springfield to prevent the state courts from trying the rebels. When they got there, they were again opposed by the militia and again defeated.

The next spring, Massachusetts elected a new legislature, which managed to defuse some of the farmers' anger. But the conditions that had produced the rebellion were general throughout the United States. Under the Articles, Congress had not been able to help the Massachusetts state government, and it would not be able to help other states with similar problems.

The Annapolis Convention

Shays's rebellion and the controversies that produced it frightened many people, especially the well-to-do people who stood to lose by suspension of debt payments. The two men most responsible for the replacement of the Articles, Alexander Hamilton (1757–1804) and James Madison (1751–1836)—neither of whom was at all rich—first engineered a commercial conference at Annapolis, Maryland, in 1786. In form, the conference met to discuss matters such as trade and internal transport. All thirteen states were invited, but only five sent delegates, not enough for a valid conference. It was held anyway, and Hamilton and Madison got what they really wanted: a resolution calling on the states to hold a convention to revise the Articles. The two men then asked Congress to sponsor such a convention, but Congress dragged its heels. The states however, proceeded to elect delegates—74 in all, although only 55 attended. Finally, Congress, too, approved the project, but only to *revise* the Articles, not to replace them.

THE CONSTITUTIONAL CONVENTION: A GROUP PORTRAIT

The Constitutional Convention met in Philadelphia in the spring and summer of 1787. By and large, the "nationalist" faction—those who wanted a stronger national government—were in control. George Washington, who had commanded the American Armed Forces during the Revolution, attended as a delegate from Virginia. A nationalist, he was elected chairman of the Constitutional Convention. Hamilton and Madison had managed to be chosen delegates from New York and Virginia, respectively. But some of the delegates, like Elbridge Gerry of Massachusetts and George Mason of Virginia, strongly opposed any important change in the Articles.

The Unrepresentative Representatives

The convention's 55 delegates belonged to perhaps the most remarkable generation this country has ever produced, a generation that first rebelled against a king anointed by God and then created and tried one political experiment after another. They were remarkably full of self-confidence.

To begin with, the delegates were men; not a single woman was invited to be among them. They were not quite representative of the people in other ways, too: They were more likely to live in the cities of the Atlantic seaboard than in back-country farms, and they were mostly lawyers, plantation owners, or merchants. Many held or had held state office. At a time when large numbers of people were completely uneducated, half the delegates had college degrees. Quite a few of them were wealthy.

At least two of the central figures—Benjamin Franklin and George Washington—were men of international renown. Others, like Alexander Hamilton and Edmund Randolph, were prominent in state and national politics. About three-quarters of the delegates had served in Congress, and a third or so had fought in the Revolution.

Of the 55 delegates who actually attended the convention, only about 30 played important roles. The convention's inner elite, the four men who most influenced its decisions, were George Washington, James Madison, Gouverneur Morris, and James Wilson. (Hamilton is not included because his proposals for centralization were too extreme.)

Although he rarely spoke, George Washington stood first among the delegates, for he was not only the commander of the victorious army that had won our independence but the patriot who had refused to seize power at the war's end. Washington's willingness to serve as president of the convention reassured the public, united the nationalists, and disarmed opposition.

A Meeting of Minds

The delegates' point of view was not radically different from that of other Americans. Like most of their fellow countrymen, they viewed government as a contract among individuals who voluntarily and rationally agree to form and obey government. They were not, in theory, democrats, but they accepted a degree of popular participation in government. Although their object was the creation of a stronger central government, they feared despotism as much as

James Madison (top), "the Father of the Constitution," and Alexander Hamilton (below), Madison's collaborator and later his political opponent.

National Geographic Society Photographer, Courtesy U.S. Capitol Historical Society

The Constitutional Convention, Philadelphia, 1787. George Washington, the convention's president, is standing at the center of the podium.

other Americans did. For them, governments existed to protect the natural rights—life, liberty, and property. Protecting those rights was more important to them than creating an effective government machine. Above all, the delegates were thoroughly practical, or to use today's word, *pragmatic*. They wanted practical solutions to practical problems—results, not talk.

In one way, the delegates were *not* typical of Americans in 1787. Unlike most of our people, they were very much aware of the world beyond the seas—of Britain, still an enemy; of France, a sometime ally and doubtful friend; of our trading partners in Europe, Africa, and Asia. They knew that foreigners laughed at American independence, American interests, and American ideas, and they meant to change that.

Behind Closed Doors

The delegates agreed to hold all their meetings in secret and to reveal nothing until they had finished—a wise idea, since the convention ignored its mandate to revise the Articles and instead produced a wholly new constitution. Philadelphia's lively newspapers respected the rule of secrecy; not until the 1830s were the journals of James Madison and others who participated in the convention made public. From these accounts, we have learned most of what we know about the framing of the Constitution.

Because the convention was held in total secrecy, none of its members did any grandstanding—none of them took extreme, self-serving, or false positions to please the public. No delegate had to worry that his statements or views might be misinterpreted by the press. All the delegates had to worry about was creating a system of government for a new nation of continental size.

The delegates in Philadelphia might have chosen between two obvious courses of action. They could have done what Congress told them to do—revise the Article—by giving Congress the power to tax. But the nationalists wanted a government capable of promoting economic growth, protecting the interests of landlords and the business community, and defending the country against foreigners; and they were convinced that the Articles, however revised, could not provide this stronger government. The Articles were largely ignored.

The second obvious course, the one favored by Alexander Hamilton, was to create a strong national government and to turn the states into mere local agencies of its power. If Hamilton had won out, the President and Congress would now appoint state and local officials. Such proposals never had the slightest chance of adoption.

The delegates chose a third course of action—one they themselves invented at the convention—a compromise between Hamilton's ideas and the complete decentralization that actually existed in 1787. They did indeed create a strong national government with supremacy over the states in its sphere of action, but they also took care to limit that sphere and to give the states a supremacy of their own. The states, in other words, were each given an independent basis of power, not reduced to the condition of mere agents of the national government. This system is called *federalism* (see Chapter 3).

No clear cut decision was ever made to throw out the Articles and frame a wholly new constitution, but that happened anyway, because the advocates of a wholly new constitution took the initative.

The convention was supposed to convene in early May, but delegates trickled in so slowly that not until May 25 did it have a quorum of seven states. The Virginia delegation used this time to work out the so-called **Virginia Plan**, drawn up mostly by James Madison and presented to the convention on May 25. It differed in many ways from the constitution finally adopted, but it too called for a strong national government. Since the delegates found themselves debating the Virginia Plan, the real question before them was *what kind* of strong national government should be created, not *whether* a strong national government should be created at all.

The National Legislature

The Virginia Plan. Like the Articles of Confederation, the Virginia Plan was to some extent parliamentary, since under it, Congress would have chosen the president. Once chosen, however, the president was to be independent. Congress was to have great power: Its laws were to be enforced in all states, and it was even to be given the power of striking down any state law that stood in the way of the "national purpose." The states were to be represented in Congress according to population, so that the larger states would be much stronger than they had been under the Articles.

Under the Articles, moreover, Congress consisted of one house only. The Virginia Plan proposed a Congress of two houses, one to be elected by the people, the other by the lower house, from nominations submitted by the state legislatures. The plan would also have set up a "council of revision," empowered to veto acts of Congress. By putting the veto power on the convention's agenda, the Virginia Plan, in effect, prevented the emergence of a true parliamentary system in the United States, since a modern parliament (see below) must have freedom from outside control.

The New Jersey Plan. Details of the Virginia plan reflect Virginia's large population. But if population were to be the basis of each state's representation in Congress, the bigger states might control or even devour the smaller ones. New Jersey, one of the smaller states, therefore proposed its own plan. The **New Jersey Plan** would have increased the power of the national government, mainly by making acts of Congress the supreme law of the land, enforceable in state courts. (This provision reappeared in the Constitution as finally adopted.) But it would have given Congress only one representative from each state, each representative chosen by a state legislature. The plan was a mere patchwork put together by many people who could agree on only one point: fear of a national government controlled by the big states.

When the Virginia Plan was put to the convention, it passed, seven votes to three.

The Connecticut Plan, or The Great Compromise. Although the Virginia Plan had carried the convention, many of the smaller states could not accept it. The 3 that voted against it—New Jersey, New York, and Delaware—occupied the center of the Atlantic seaboard. If they refused to join the United States, it would be divided into 2 completely separated parts.

At this point, July 1787, debate raged mainly over the composition of Congress, not over the plan's other features. Connecticut's delegates, especially Roger Sherman, saw that the Virginia Plan itself offered a way of reconciling the interests of the large states with those of the small ones, for it proposed a Congress of two houses. The **Connecticut Plan,** or **Great Compromise,** allocated the members of each house among the states in a different way. In the upper house, each state, regardless of population, would have two members, each elected by the state legislatures. Here, the small states were to have equal representation. But in the lower house, each state would be represented according to population. In this house, therefore, the big states would have a greater voice. On July 16, the convention accepted the Great Compromise, five votes to four. The United States got its legislature—one representing not only people but also states, which were now incorporated into the Constitution's foundation.

The Importance of Slavery

The Great Compromise did not, as it happens, make population the sole basis for representation in the lower house. Some of our people were not legally human; they were slaves. The southern states, where slaves were most numerous, wanted to count them for the purpose of representation; the northern states did not. The Great Compromise proposed to count three-fifths of them, and three-fifths it was.

Bear in mind that slaves were property and that slaveowners, like other owners of property, wanted a stronger national government to protect their interests. At that time, the economies of half the states depended on slave labor. Not until the early nineteenth century, as slavery became intolerable to many people, did slaveowners change their strategy and try to protect the "peculiar institution" by promoting "states' rights" (see Chapter 3). Indeed,

Negroes for Sale.

A Cargo of very fine stout Men and Women, in good order and fit for immediate service, just imported from the Windward Coast of Africa, in the Ship Two Brothers.—— Conditions are one half Cash or Produce, the other half payable the first of January next, giving Bond and Security if required.

The Sale to be opened at 10 o'Clock each Day, in Mr. Bourdeaux's Yard, at No. 48, on the Bay.
May 19, 1784.   JOHN MITCHELL.

not until the 1830s, when militant abolitionism first became a mass movement, was it clear that the North and the South were moving in opposite directions.

In 1787, slaves were owned in the North, where attitudes toward slavery were not very different from those in the South. A sort of genial philosophic opposition to slavery was quite common among southern slaveowners. In fact, had the invention of the cotton gin in 1793 not made cotton growing very profitable, Virginia might well have abolished slavery on its own.

"Other Persons." The delegates at the convention, embarrassed by the words *slave* and *slavery*, never used them. Instead, they referred to "other persons," a category that included slaves and American Indians. Despite the delegates' reticence, two additional provisions do in fact deal with slavery. One prohibited Congress from passing any law against the African slave trade until 1808, implicitly permitting it to ban importation thereafter. (It did.) The second provision gave Congress the right to pass fugitive slave acts, requiring federal assistance for masters whose slaves fled to free soil within the United States. Congress passed its first such act in 1793.

Trade and Manufactures

Slavery was only one difference between the North and the South, and not necessarily the most important. For one thing, their respective economies were quite different, and they remained so after slavery had been abolished. The South was mainly agricultural: It exported tobacco, rice, cotton, indigo, and other crops to the North and to Europe. The North had more trade and more manufacturing than the South, but its manufactured goods were costlier than similar items made in Britain.

The South wanted to send its crops abroad and import these cheaper manufactured goods. The North wanted to place a tax, called a **tariff,** on foreign manufactures, so they would not be cheaper than those of the North. The South, in other words, wanted **free trade** and the North wanted **protection.**

The delegates to the Constitutional Convention tried to resolve these controversies by prohibiting Congress from taxing goods exported from any state, but not from taxing imported goods. The South got a provision requiring treaties between the United States and foreign powers to be approved by a two-thirds vote of the Senate, so a Northern-dominated Congress would not be able to ratify treaties that interfered directly with southern trade. But tariffs on imports would require no more than a majority vote of both houses. These tariffs were a great cause of sectional hostility in the years leading up to the Civil War and, in fact, right up to the 1930s.

The National Executive

Most people expected George Washington to be the first man to fill whatever kind of executive office the Constitutional Convention resolved to create. General Washington had already had a chance to be a dictator, and he had refused. The trust he rightly inspired made the delegates willing to create a powerful presidency.

In fact, they did. They placed the executive branch wholly in the President's hands. (In a parliamentary government, the policy of the executive is set by the cabinet as a whole, not by the prime minister.) They permitted the President to appoint ambassadors, judges, and other "officers of the United States," including the cabinet, and gave him the power to make treaties—all subject to a two-thirds vote of the Senate.

They also resolved to make the President wholly independent of Congress, which participates in presidential elections only in unusual circumstances (see Chapter 11). In fact, they gave the President a veto, though not an absolute one, over acts of Congress.

These were enormous powers, but one thing was and is lacking among them: institutional control over Congress. Precisely because the President and

John Marshall, third Chief Justice of the U.S. Supreme Court and the creator of the doctrine of judicial review.

Congress are elected independently, the President cannot be sure of congressional support. This omission was quite deliberate. The delegates wanted the President to be independent of Congress, but they also wanted Congress to be independent of the presidency.

The National Judiciary

The Articles of Confederation had not provided for a national judiciary. Although the delegates to the Convention paid less attention to the judicial branch than to the executive and legislative, they did create a national judiciary—also an independent one. Its independence was secured in several ways. Because the President could appoint judges only with the consent of the Senate, neither had complete control over judicial selection. Judges, once chosen, were to serve during "good behavior"—for life, in effect. Except for the unusual and difficult process of impeachment and removal from office, the whole of the "judicial power of the United States" was placed in the hands of the judicial branch. In Britain, on the contrary, the House of Lords (a part of the legislature) was also the highest court.

The delegates provided for what they called a "Supreme Court" and also for "lesser courts" but did not delineate the latter, permitting Congress to set them up as it pleased. (At present, there are two levels of lower courts: district courts and U.S. courts of appeals; see Chapter 14.) Nowhere among the powers of the U.S. Supreme Court did the delegates include what has come to be its chief power—**judicial review,** the right to judge the actions of the other branches and levels of government and to declare them unconstitutional. But as we shall see, the delegates created a system that, as a whole, made judicial review a necessity.

The Rising Sun

The Constitution was signed by the delegates on September 17, 1787. Only 39 of the 55 delegates actually signed it; others left early; still others, like Elbridge Gerry, refused to sign. The whole future of the project was not all clear, because it still had to be approved by at least nine states.

On the day of signing, Benjamin Franklin spoke last. Often, he said, he had looked at the sun shining behind the president's chair, "without being able to tell whether it was rising or setting. But now, at length, I have the happiness to know it is a rising, and not a setting sun."

A MATTER OF INTERPRETATION

Those who framed the Constitution did not pretend to be democrats. Quite the contrary, they wanted to protect the rights and interests of the well-to-do. In fact, certain historians have argued that the Constitution was in essence a tactic in a class struggle.

Charles Beard

The first and foremost of these historians was Charles Beard (1874–1948), who published *An Economic Interpretation of the Constitution* in 1913. As a group, Beard noted, the delegates were very different from the ordinary Americans of

1787—much more likely to have a financial interest in bank trade, and manufacturing, and to live or own property in cities. Delegates who derived their incomes chiefly from farming were large planters rather than small farmers (who were not represented at the Convention at all). The delegates, then, were the kinds of people who were threatened by Shays's Rebellion and by the efforts of state governments to aid debtors. Beard argued that they were a class-conscious, wordly, urban elite that wanted a strong national government to protect its economic interests from the "excesses of democracy."

Beard's Critics

Beard's work has its critics, of course. In *We the People* (1958), Forrest McDonald argued that by 1787, our economy was too complicated to support a simple struggle of rich against poor. The rich themselves were very much divided over the Constitution: Elbridge Gerry of Massachusetts, one of the richest men in the country, refused to sign, and he worked against ratification. No doubt the rich wanted to protect the rights of property, but not all rich people thought those rights would be best served by the new Constitution; many, however, had other reasons for supporting it. Nor were all the Constitution's supporters rich. Madison and Hamilton were men of limited means and heavy debts. McDonald therefore concluded that the Constitution was not a weapon of the rich against the poor but the outcome of a political consensus that included members of all classes.

History, Politics, and the Constitution

Historians, as one of them once said, tend to interpret the past as though it were the present going on at some other time.[5] They impose the political controversies and attitudes of their own day upon the events and people of the past. Beard wrote during the Progressive Era (ca. 1905–1915), a time when class struggle was especially prominent in our politics. McDonald wrote in the 1950s, a time of relatively quiet prosperity. These very different political climates colored their respective outlooks on the past.

In a sense, it is not really necessary to choose between Beard's interpretation and McDonald's. For the Constitution combines, and was meant to combine, elements of elitism with elements of democracy. The electorates of the thirteen states were not democratic, but they were enormous by eighteenth-century standards. In most places, only property owners could vote, but land was cheap and easy to get. The exclusion of blacks and women offends against present-day ideas of democracy but not against those of 1787. Our country was far from perfectly democratic in 1787, but it was much more democratic in its own terms than in ours. The delegates knew and accepted this: They made no effort to diminish the size of the electorate.

These large and diverse electorates, however, exposed the United States to what the delegates regarded as fearful dangers. As Madison put it, the "unequal distribution of property" is "the most common and durable source of factions." Factions are "adverse to the rights of other citizens," or worse yet, to the "interests of the community as a whole." Suppose, says Madison,

---

[5] Herbert Butterfield.

How Thomas Jefferson Wrote the Declaration of Independence: In His Own Words

Dear Sir,

The committee of five met; no such thing as a sub-Committee was proposed, but they unanimously pressed on myself alone to undertake the draught. I consented; I drew it; but before I reported it to the committee, I communicated it separately to Dr. Franklin and Mr. Adams, requesting their corrections, because they were two members of whose judgment and amendments I wished most to have the benefit before presenting it to the committee . . . Their alterations were two or three only, and merely verbal. I then wrote a fair copy, reported it to the committee, and from them, unaltered, to Congress . . .

Pickering's observations, and Mr. Adams' in addition, "that it contained no new ideas, that it is a common-place compilation, its sentiments hachnied in Congress for two years before, and its essence contained in Otis's pamphlet" may all be true. Of that I am not to be the judge. Richard Henry Lee charged it as copied from Locke's treatis on government. Otis' pamphlet I never saw and whether I had gathered my ideas from reading or reflection I do not know. I only know that I turned to neither book nor pamphlet while writing it. I did not consider it as any part of my charge to invent new ideas altogether, and to offer no sentiment which had ever been expressed before. Had Mr. Adams been so restrained, Congress would have lost the benefit of his bold and impressive advocations of the rights of Revolution. For no man's confident and fervid addresses, more than Mr. Adams', encouraged and supported us through the difficulties surrounding us, which, like the ceaseless action of gravity weighed on us by night and day. Yet on the same ground, we may ask what of these elevated thoughts was new, or can be affirmed never before to have entered the conceptions of man?

Whether, also, the sentiments of Independence, and the reasons for declaring it, which make so great a portion of the instrument, had been hackneyed in Congress for two years before the 4th of July '76, or this dictum also of Mr. Adams be another slip of memory, let history say. This, however, I will say for Mr. Adams, that he supported the Declaration with zeal and ability, fighting fearlessly for every word of it. As to myself, I thought it a duty to be, on that occasion, a passive auditor of the opinions of others, more impartial judges than I could be, of its merits or demerits. During the debate I was sitting by Doctor Franklin, and he observed that I was writhing a little under the acrimonious criticisms of some of its parts; and it was on that occasion, that by way of comfort, he told me the story of John Thompson, the hatter, and his new sign . . .

Thomas Jefferson to James Madison. Letter of August 30, 1823

---

that a bill is put forward to regulate debts. "It is a question to which the creditors [lenders] are parties on the one side and the debtors [borrowers] on the other. Justice ought to hold the balance between them." In fact, "the most powerful faction must be expected to prevail"—in a democracy, the majority, which includes more debtors than creditors. "Hence it is that such democracies . . . have ever [always] been found incompatible with personal security or the rights of property."[6]

No doubt, fear for "the rights of property" inspired much of what the delegates did. But they did not attempt to protect property by suppressing the political rights of the people. Instead, they tried to balance the effects. They hoped to control democracy, not to eliminate it. They included in the Constitution specific prohibitions against some of the things they feared, such as the annulment of contracts (see Chapter 3). And they created a form of government meant to be strong enough to prevent the states—which at first were more democratic than the federal government—from threatening natural rights, but not so strong as to threaten the states themselves.

---

[6] *The Federalist*, Paper 10. See Appendix.

This engraving shows Congress voting independence in 1776.

Their way of making the federal government simultaneously both strong and weak was ingenious. On the one hand, they gave the federal government very substantial powers (see Chapter 3). On the other, the delegates separated those powers among the three branches of the federal government and made it very difficult for any one of them to act without cooperation from the others. Should the popular faction control Congress, for example, the President could veto any bill that threatened life, liberty, or property. The President could enforce the law but not enact it, could spend money but not appropriate it. Neither the President nor the Congress could alone appoint judges.

These **checks and balances** among the three branches of the federal government would stymie the power of any "mobocracy" that controlled only one of them. And because congressmen, senators, and Presidents would be elected by somewhat different electorates at different times, they would each represent different "factions." Besides, even if the mobocracy did take over the federal government as a whole, it would still have to share power with thirteen separate state governments, some of which were less democratic, some more so. The **separation of powers** among the three branches of the federal government and the **division of powers** between it and the states have worked much as the delegates expected them to. No faction, no mobocracy, has ever controlled the government of the United States, because it is not one government but 80,000 governments.

Finally, we ought to bear in mind that the delegates were an elite, but an *American* elite. Their political values were not so very different from the values of the small farmers. Almost all Americans accepted a certain amount of popular government, and almost all wanted a government that would respect and protect life, liberty, and property—despite differences of interpretation. The proof is the fact that we, in our vastly more democratic society, manage to live under the same Constitution the delegates worked out in Philadelphia 200 years ago. That Constitution is by far the oldest such document in the world.

"[The Constitution] was framed upon the theory that the peoples of the several states must sink or swim together, and that in the long run prosperity and salvation are in union and not division."

Benjamin N. Cardozo,
Justice of the U.S. Supreme Court,
1935

Ratifications of the Constitution

DELAWARE. The Convention, consisting of thirty members, met December 3, 1787, and ratified the Constitution unanimously, December 7, 1787.

PENNSYLVANIA. The Convention (called by the Act of November 6, 1787), consisting of sixty-nine members, met at Philadelphia on November 21, 1787, with Frederick Augustus Muhlenberg as President. The Constitution was ratified December 12, 1787, by a vote of forty-six to twenty-three.

NEW JERSEY. Under the Act of Oct. 29, 1787, thirty-nine delegates (three chosen from each county) met in Convention at Trenton, Dec. 11, 1787, with John Stevens as President. The Constitution was unanimously ratified December 18, 1787.

GEORGIA. The Convention, consisting of twenty-six members, with John Wheat as President, met at Augusta, December 25, 1787. The Constitution was unanimously ratified, January 2, 1788.

CONNECTICUT. Under the Act of Oct. 16, 1787, the Convention, consisting of one hundred seventy-three members, with Nathan Griswold as President, met at Hartford, on January 1, 1788. The Constitution was ratified by a vote of one hundred twenty-eight to forty on January 9, 1788.

MASSACHUSETTS. Under the Act of October 25, 1787, the Convention, consisting of three hundred sixty-four members, with Governor John Hancock as President, met at Boston, January 9, 1788. The Constitution was ratified by a vote of one hundred eighty-seven to one hundred sixty-eight, February 16, 1788.

MARYLAND. The Convention, consisting of seventy-six delegates (of whom seventy-four attended), with George Plater as President, met at Annapolis, April 21, 1788. The Constitution was ratified, April 26, 1788, by a vote of sixty-three to eleven.

SOUTH CAROLINA. Under the act of January 18, 1788, the Convention, to which two hundred thirty-six delegates were chosen, met at Charleston, May 12, 1788, with Governor Thomas Pinckney as President. The Constitution was ratified, May 23, 1788, by a vote of one hundred forty-nine to seventy-three.

NEW HAMPSHIRE. The Convention, consisting of one hundred thirteen delegates, met at Exeter, February 13, 1788, with Governor John Sullivan as President. The Constitution was ratified, June 21, 1788, at Concord, by a vote of fifty-seven to forty-seven.

VIRGINIA. Under Act of October 25, 1787, the Convention met at Richmond on June 2, 1788, consisting of one hundred seventy delegates, with Edmund Pendleton as President. The Constitution was ratified June 25, 1788, by a vote of eighty-nine to seventy-nine.

NEW YORK. The Convention, consisting of sixty-five members, met at Poughkeepsie, June 17, 1788, with Governor George Clinton as President. The Constitution was ratified July 26, 1788, by a vote of thirty to twenty-seven.

NORTH CAROLINA. The Convention, consisting of two hundred twenty-eight members, met at Hillsboro, July 21, 1788. Ratification of the Constitution was rejected, August 4, 1788, by a vote of one hundred ninety-three to seventy-five. It was finally ratified November 21, 1789, by a Convention which met Nov. 16, 1789.

RHODE ISLAND. The Convention, consisting of seventy members, met at South Kingston, March 8, 1790. The Constitution was ratified May 29, 1790, by a vote of thirty-four to thirty-two.

Close votes (less than 55% in favor):

VIRGINIA	MASSACHUSETTS
NEW YORK	NEW HAMPSHIRE

Originally rejected, then approved after beginning of new government.:

NORTH CAROLINA	RHODE ISLAND

From Charles Warren, *The Making of the Constitution,* (Boston: Little, Brown, 1928), pp. 819-20.

THE STRUGGLE TO RATIFY

A majority of delegates from each state voted to accept the Constitution, though some delegates refused to sign it. Framing it was only half the job, however. The Constitution still had to be ratified in the states, one by one.

The Process of Ratification

Each state's voters elected delegates to a state convention. Not until nine such conventions had voted to ratify would the Constitution become the law of the land.

Delaware, Pennsylvania, New Jersey, Georgia, and Connecticut were the first states to ratify the Constitution, by January 1788. All but Pennsylvania had small populations, and Georgia had a common border with the Spanish Empire, along the Florida border.

Public opinion in three large states—Massachusetts, Virginia, and New York[7]—was more evenly divided between supporters of the new Constitution, (the Federalists) and their opponents, (the Anti-Federalists). Massachusetts fell in line in February. Maryland, South Carolina, and New Hampshire followed in April, May, and June, respectively. When Virginia fell in line, on June 25, the federal government went into business.

Postscript. Even after New York had joined the roster of states voting to ratify the Constitution, on July 26, 1788, two states still held out: North Carolina and Rhode Island. Until they voted to ratify, they remained outside the United States.

North Carolina first voted against the Constitution by a margin of two to one but ratified it, reluctantly, in November 1789. As for Rhode Island, its politics were controlled by small farmers, the sort of people the new Constitution had been created to bridle. In most states, these small farmers were hostile to it. At first Rhode Island would not even consider the Constitution and did not ratify it until 1790, under duress and by only a slim margin.

THE ENDURING CONSTITUTION

The struggle for ratification was bitter, but the bitterness persisted for only a few years. By the time of Thomas Jefferson's election as President, in 1800, it had disappeared, and the Constitution became part of our "civil religion" (see Chapter 1), above and beyond political dispute.

Why? Because the Constitution turned out to be a victory both for the Federalists and the Anti-Federalists. Under President George Washington (1789–1797), the Federalists were able to create the stronger national government they wanted. That government, however, could not prevent their more democratic opponents, the Jeffersonian Republicans, from growing stronger. In 1800, the Jeffersonian Republicans elected Thomas Jefferson (1801–1809) as President; and the Federalists, as an organized party, withered away. But Jefferson accepted the government and many policies he had inherited from them. The Jeffersonian Republicans (see Chapter 9), dominated the *politics* of the country, but the *government* was in essence a Federalist government.

Today the United States is a far more democratic country than it was in 1788 or in 1800. In fact, we are now so democratic that if the people the delegates called "the mobocracy"—those with little or no property—wanted the government to seize the property of the rich, the institutions created in

---

[7] To influence the hard-fought and sometimes bitter contest in New York, Hamilton, Madison, and John Jay wrote a series of essays published as *The Federalist*. These essays—which treated of the new constitution, political theory in general, and conditions in the United States—not only helped ratify the Constitution in New York but also became political classics.

Figure 2-1 Ratification of the Constitution

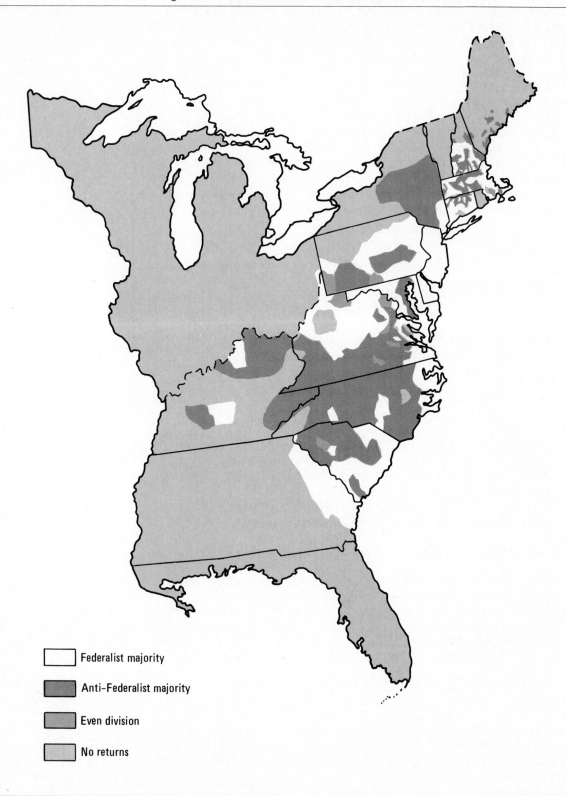

Federalist majority

Anti-Federalist majority

Even division

No returns

1787 could not prevent it from doing so. The Constitution's clever clockwork mechanisms—the divisions and separations of power, the checks and balances—could not prevent it, for to work, these mechanisms assumed a society that was not completely democratic. Yet, in the two centuries since Rhode Island was dragged unwillingly into the Union, there has never been any thoroughgoing attempt here to challenge the principle of private property. If there had been, the Constitution might not have survived for a generation, let alone for two centuries.

We have already seen why Americans accept inequalities of wealth, but the reasons are worth recounting. Our country is big, and it is rich in resources. Americans tend to think that more wealth can always be created, so we are less apt to covet the wealth of those who already have it. Almost all Americans regard life, liberty, and property as their birthright. We have rich and poor, but the rich and the poor rarely think of themselves as hereditary armies, separate and warring nations.

The Constitution did not create these American political ideas; it rests upon them. If they change, we may find that the Constitution is not immortal.

THE ADAPTABLE CONSTITUTION

Edmund Burke (1729–1797), one of the greatest of conservative political thinkers, once said that a political order that cannot change is a political order that cannot save itself. By endowing the Constitution with a means of changing it, the delegates ensured that ours would not be such a political order. Yet, although our Constitution has changed a good deal in the last two centuries, the political philosophy that inspired it, and its practical effects on our government and politics, have changed very little.

Changing the Constitution: The Amendment Route

The most obvious—but not the only—way of changing the Constitution is the one specified in the text itself: the amendment route. The Constitution began to be amended before it was ratified. During the ratification controversy, the Anti-Federalists complained that it lacked a "Bill of Rights" protecting specific political liberties. The Federalists promised to add one if the original text was ratified, and in 1789–1791 they kept their promise (see Chapter 4).

Methods of Amendment. Amendments can be proposed in two ways and ratified in two ways. Proposals can be made by two-thirds of both houses of Congress voting separately or by a national convention called by Congress at the request of two-thirds of the state legislatures (now 34 of 50). Once proposed, amendments can be ratified by vote of three-quarters of the state legislatures (38 out of 50) or by state conventions in three-quarters of the states.

With one exception—the Twenty-first Amendment (1933)—all amendments to the U.S. Constitution have been proposed by a two-thirds vote in both houses of Congress and then ratified by the state legislatures of three-quarters of the states. No constitutional amendment has ever been proposed by a national convention called by Congress at the request of two-thirds of the state legislatures, and it is not clear what would happen if Congress ever called such a convention.

The question is not at all theoretical, because for years advocates of

"The basis of our political system is the right of the people to make and to alter their constitutions of government."

George Washington,
Farewell Address,
September 17, 1796

The Amendments: A Brief Tour

Many amendments have been proposed, but only 26 have so far been ratified.

The first 10 amendments, also called the U.S. Bill of Rights, restricted the federal government's power to threaten life, liberty, and property (see Chapter 4). Other amendments, too, have expanded our civil liberties and civil rights. The Civil War amendments—the 13th (1865), 14th (1868), and 15th (1870)—were meant to give the former black slaves the status and rights of citizenship (see Chapter 5). They were used, as well, to extend the U.S. Bill of Rights to the states (see Chapter 4), but first they were used by the courts to prohibit most of the federal government's efforts to regulate business (see Chapter 4).

A number of amendments have expanded the electorate:

15th (1870) gave blacks the vote

17th (1913) provided for the election of senators by direct popular vote

19th (1920) gave women the vote

23rd (1961) allowed residents of Washington, D.C. to vote in national elections

24th (1964) in effect, banned poll taxes

26th (1971) gave 18-year-olds the right to vote

A few amendments changed the way the federal government works:

12th (1804) altered rules for electing Presidents and Vice-Presidents (see Chapter 10)

16th (1913) gave Congress power to impose an income tax

20th (1933) changed the day on which the President and Vice-President take office

22nd (1951) limited any President to 2 consecutive terms in office

25th (1967) revised the order of succession when a President dies or becomes too sick to carry out the duties of office

One amendment canceled out an earlier one:

21st (1933) abolished Prohibition, the 18th (1919)

Except for the 14th, 15th, and 16th, the amendments have had little effect on the actual workings of government. They *have* enlarged the electorate and, therefore, changed our political system—the climate in which government operates. That is their real importance.

---

balanced budgets (see Chapter 16) have been attempting to get state legislatures to request such a convention. By October 1982, they had 31 of the needed 34, almost the required two-thirds. Should a national convention be called to consider an amendment requiring a balanced federal budget, it is not clear whether the convention could take up other proposed amendments, too.

Changing the Constitution: Other Routes

Amendment is the only way of changing the text of the Constitution, but not the only way of changing the way it actually works. Unlike Britain, we have a written constitution, but our living Constitution, the Constitution as it really works, is not just a single written document.

Judicial Review. By dividing and separating the powers of government, the delegates to the Constitutional Convention tried to ensure that no single person or institution would control the United States. The relative independence of all branches and levels of government ensured conflict among them, but the delegates did not create a mechanism for resolving these conflicts. In time, the U.S. Supreme Court transformed itself into such a mechanism, by taking for itself the power of judicial review: in essence, the rights of interpreting the Constitution and deciding whether any act of government conforms to it. This power has enormous impact on the way the Constitution actually works (see Chapters 4, 5, and 14).

Presidential Prerogative. Article I, section 8 gives Congress, and only Congress, the power to declare war. But in the last 35 years, the United States has been involved in two major wars, Korea and Vietnam (see Chapter 17), and neither was declared by Congress. Presidents Harry Truman and Lyndon Johnson claimed the right, as commanders in chief of the armed forces, to send American troops into combat in aid of treaty allies. **Presidential prerogatives,** like this one, are powers claimed without specific grants by the Constitution or Congress (see Chapters 11 and 17).

President Reagan also exercised this prerogative twice during his first term. In the first of these exercises of power, he sent Marines ashore in Lebanon in 1982, and subsequently sent the battleship New Jersey and other parts of the navy against Moslem rebels in the hills overlooking Beirut. In the second, in 1983, he sent troops to invade and occupy Grenada in order to remove a Marxist government that had just taken power in a coup. It is important to stress, however, that the War Powers Resolution of 1973 required the President to return to Congress for approval of his Lebanese intervention. The whole Grenada operation was completed within the 60-day limit on presidential military interventions specified by the resolution, so there was no need to go to Congress for continuing authorization.

Congressional Initiative. The Constitution specifically permits the President to veto acts passed by Congress. In the years since 1932, however, Congress has increasingly resorted to a limited veto over the President, the so-called legislative veto. This device makes it possible for Congress—sometimes by resolution of disapproval passed in one house, sometimes requiring the disapproval of both houses—to void actions of executive agencies. The reason for the growth of the legislative veto over fifty years is that Congress these days must delegate large amounts of its powers to the executive when it passes laws. For instance, during World War II it was necessary to have wage and price controls covering the whole economy. Congress passed a general act to that effect, but it had to leave it up to an executive agency, the Office of Price Administration, to implement its intent by issuing detailed regulations. In the end, the OPA regulations filled a five-foot shelf of books. Today, the Internal Revenue Service issues an even greater volume of rulings and decisions. Congress simply cannot go into this kind of detail when it passes laws, so it has to delegate much of its authority to executive agencies and independent regulatory commissions.

But a question arises: How can Congress effectively check on or monitor the actions taken by these agencies? The most practical device that seemed to be the legislative veto, by which one house or both (depending on the statute) could disallow an agency regulation or decision within a fixed period of time (often 60 days) after it was issued. By 1983, nearly 200 federal laws contained such a provision. But was it constitutional? All Presidents of both parties, from Hoover to Reagan, had objected to the legislative veto as infringing on the President's constitutional authority, since the Constitution requires that anything with statutory force must be presented to the President for his signature or veto.

Finally the matter was brought to the Supreme Court, and in 1983 the Court ruled that the legislative veto was indeed unconstitutional for exactly that reason.[8] Chief Justice Burger, writing for the majority, underscored that the

---

[8] *Immigration & Naturalization Service* v. *Chadha,* 51 U.S. Law Week 4907 (1983).

In 1942, Price Administrator Leon Henderson asked for farm price and wage controls from Congress. Congress passed a general law to that effect, and by the end of the war the Office of Price Administration regulations filled a five-foot shelf of books.

legislative veto was an unacceptable breach in the Constitution's scheme for separating legislative and executive power. The problem of Congress's capacity to effectively monitor the powers it has to delegate to executive agencies remains both real and acute. But the Court told the legislators that they "cannot get there from here" by using the legislative veto. It is arguable that by its action in the *Chadha* case the Supreme Court struck down more acts of Congress (or at least parts of more acts) in one day than in all of its preceding history—according to Justice White's dissenting opinion, nearly 200 of them. Without doubt, this is one of the most important constitutional decisions ever rendered by the High Court. Separation of powers—in a quite rigorous interpretation—remains one of the centerpieces of American constitutional doctrine and, thus, of American political practice.

Political Realities. The U.S. Constitution makes no mention of political parties. Our first parties started to evolve almost immediately after the convention, however (see Chapter 9). Among other things, the parties soon undermined the original method of electing the President and Vice-President. Under Article II—and even today—the President is really chosen not by the voting public but by an electoral college. When you vote for a President, you are really voting for presidential electors. Originally, the electoral college chose the President and Vice-President in a single ballot. Each elector had two votes, and the candidate who received a majority became President, the next-strongest contender, Vice-President.

By 1800, the Republican party (not today's Republican party but the ancestor of today's Democrats) had become so highly organized that all the Republican members of the electoral college voted both for Thomas Jefferson, the party's presidential candidate, and Aaron Burr, its vice-presidential candidate. This forced the election into the House of Representatives. It was obvious that as long as parties existed, this would continue to happen. The

Twelfth Amendment (1804) solved the problem by electing the President and the Vice–President on separate ballots. (See Chapter 10 for a longer account of the procedures for electing a President.)

Political realities have changed not only the text of the Constitution but also the way it works. From the end of the Civil War to the mid-1930s, for instance, many of the federal government's few efforts to regulate business were declared unconstitutional by the U.S. Supreme Court. By and large, the public did not demand such regulation until the Great Depression, in the 1930s. When it did so, the politicians responded but not, at first, the justices: One after another, the Court struck down the Roosevelt Administration's programs to stimulate and control the economy.

In 1936, President Roosevelt was reelected by a landslide. Next year, the Supreme Court started to find that Mr. Roosevelt's programs were not unconstitutional after all. Eventually, Mr. Roosevelt managed to appoint several justices, and by 1941, the Court had become a nine-man "Roosevelt Court." As the celebrated humorist Finley Peter Dunne put it, "The supreme Coort follows th' iliction returns."

THE PARLIAMENTARY SYSTEM

The fact that the living Constitution, the Constitution as it really works, is more than just a "written" document calls to mind the British Constitution, which is said to be "unwritten." Despite this similarity, and despite the historic ties between Britain and the United States, the two constitutions are very different, above all because Britain's form of government is parliamentary. Before we see what that means, let us identify the essential features of our own system.

First, the U.S. Constitution is not a law like other laws; it stands above them and differs in form. Federal laws need only to be approved by majorities in each house of Congress and signed by the President. But the original Constitution had to be ratified by the states, and so do amendments to it. The President plays no part in amending the Constitution; neither does the judiciary. No one individual, no one branch or level of American government alone can amend the fundamental law of the land.

Second, no one branch of the federal government fully controls the others. No one branch can exercise the full range of governmental powers. The President runs the executive branch but cannot appropriate the funds needed to run it. Congress can appropriate them but cannot directly control the way they are spent. The President appoints high-level officials; the Senate confirms them. Congress passes laws; the President can veto them. The federal courts have the final say about the laws' constitutionality, but federal judges are nominated by the President and confirmed by the Senate.

Third, the federal government as a whole is supreme over the state governments, *but only within its sphere*. We shall see in Chapter 3 that, in fact, the limits of federal power over the states are not very clear. They change all the time. Still, it is clear that the federal government cannot abolish the states and that, in practice, the states have much independence. By no means are state officials mere local representatives of the federal government.

The separation of powers among the branches of the federal government and the division of powers between it and the states make our government quite unlike that of any other country. But our government lacks something

Franklin on the Turkey versus the Eagle

Others object to the "Bald Eagle" as looking too much like a "Dindon", or Turkey. For my own part, I wish the Bald Eagle had not been chosen as the Representative of our Country: he is a Bird of bad moral Character; he does not get his living honestly; you may have seen him perch'd on some dead Tree, near the River where, too lazy to fish for himself, he watches the Labour of the Fishing-Hawk; and, when that diligent Bird has at length taken a Fish, and is bearing it to his Nest for the support of his Mate and young ones, the Bald Eagle pursues him, and takes it from him. With all this Injustice he is never in good Case; but, like those among Men who live by Sharping and Robbing, he is generally poor, and often very lousy. Besides, he is a rank Coward; the little "King-Bird", not bigger than a Sparrow, attacks him boldly and drives him out of the District. He is therefore by no means a proper emblem for the brave and honest Cincinnati of America, who have driven all the "King-birds" from our Country; though exactly fit for that Order of Knights, which the French call Chevaliers d'Industrie.

I am, on this account, not displeas'd that the Figure is not known as a Bald Eagle, but looks more like A Turk'y. For in Truth, the Turk'y is in comparison a much more respectable Bird, and withal a true original Native of America. Eagles have been found in all Countries, but the Turk'y was peculiar to ours; the first of the Species seen in Europe being brought to France by the Jesuits from Canada, and serv'd up at the Wedding Table of Charles the Ninth. He is, though a little vain and silly, it is true, but not the worse emblem for that, a Bird of Courage, and would not hesitate to attack a Grenadier of the British Guards, who should presume to invade his Farm Yard with a "red" Coat on . . .

Benjamin Franklin

that most other governments have, something called sovereignty. Sovereignty is simply the answer to the most basic question in politics: "Who's in charge here?" A sovereign state is a state where you can point to a single person or institution and say: "This person" or "this institution is in charge." The power that this person or institution, the sovereign, enjoys must in theory be unlimited. In the government of the United States, no one person or institution has unlimited power—either in theory or in practice. In this sense, our government is not sovereign.

Parliaments

Most governments *are* sovereign. The sovereign may be a person, a queen, let us say. It may also be an institution. The **parliamentary system** is a system of legislative sovereignty; parliament is the sovereign. Its powers are unlimited. It chooses the executive, whose members almost always sit in parliament. If they lose the confidence of parliament, they must resign, and parliament chooses a new executive. If it cannot do so, a new parliament must be elected by the voters. There is no written constitution, but this means that constitutional laws are merely laws; they can be repealed by any parliament at any time. (Congress, you will remember, cannot amend the Constitution by itself.) A parliament cannot recognize "natural rights"; in parliamentary states, the citizens have only those rights that the legislature, (parliament) thinks they ought to have. Local governments and the court system exist at the pleasure of parliament, which can create, divide, and abolish them at pleasure. The legislature is the only source of law and political power.

Parliamentary Theory and Practice. When the parliamentary system first emerged in its mature form in Britain during the early 1840s, there were no strong parties. Governments changed continually because few of them had dependable majorities in Parliament, and every time any government lost an important vote, it had to resign. British politicians came to see that the parliamentary system can work only if strong parties create dependable majorities; by the late 1860s, strong parties had emerged.

From then onward, the leaders of the governing party, who are also the leaders of the British government, have usually been able to compel the members of their own party in Parliament to support them. Only in moments of grave political crisis can this power fail them. Indeed, some political scientists would say that, most of the time, it is really the cabinet (made up of the most important leaders) that is sovereign. At any rate, the cabinet (and therefore the executive) clearly has more independence of Parliament than mere definitions might suggest.

Another parliamentary fact of life is the fundamental similarity between our civil liberties and the civil liberties enjoyed by people in Britain and other democratic parliamentary states. In theory, no parliament could accept the idea of "natural rights," rights that would limit its sovereignty. In practice, no parliament passes laws compelling people to believe that two and two make five simply because it could do so. The political cultures of the United States and Britain, for example, have much in common, and this tends to make our political systems less different than they seem to be.[9]

Why Not Here?

The parliamentary system is good enough for Britain and most of the other democracies. Why isn't it good enough for us? Why didn't the delegates to the Constitutional Convention set up a parliamentary system here?

First, even in Britain, the parliamentary system did not really exist in 1787. Then and for some time afterward, the British monarch was the real head of the executive and chose its members. The executive needed a majority in Parliament to function effectively but not to stay in office.

Second, our system was not, at first, so different from a parliamentary system as it now seems to be. True, the President and Congress were elected separately. But the real center of government was the House of Representatives. From 1808 to 1820, the majority caucus in the House, the ancestors of today's Democrats, actually chose the party's presidential candidate and, perforce, the President (see Chapter 9). Not until the Age of Jackson (1829-1837) did presidential elections and the presidential office become truly independent.

Nonetheless, the parliamentary system was evolving in 1787, but the delegates—perhaps without quite realizing it—set the United States on a different path. They might have made the government sovereign, for instance, but instead, they did their best to ensure that it would not be. They so divided and separated the powers of government that it can hardly ever act as it pleases and often cannot act at all. People who are used to parliamentary

---

[9] Britain, of course, is only one of many countries governed under the parliamentary system, but it was the first country to be so governed and the country where that system took and kept its classic form.

regimes think that this is the chief disadvantage of our system. They find it hard to understand that, to us, it is the system's chief *virtue*.

Some critics, even American critics, say that our system makes this country ungovernable. Others say that it tends to prevent the majority from overcoming the power of important interest groups (see Chapter 6), even when they represent only a minority. In any case, it is clear that we fear tyranny more than we love efficiency, much as the delegates did and much as our descendants are likely to do.

―――――――――――――――― SUMMARY ――――――――――――――――

The Declaration of Independence and the Constitution of 1787 launched the United States of America. Both were rooted in the theory of social contract: the idea that the people, to protect their "natural rights"—life, liberty, and property—contract among themselves to form governments, which are legitimate if and only if they protect those rights.

The Constitution of 1787 was not the first written constitution in our country's history. Several state constitutions came first, and so did our first national constitution, the Articles of Confederation (1777). The United States, as created by the Articles, was nothing more than a confederation of thirteen quite separate states. Threats from abroad and the fear that small farmers might use their political power to demand laws annulling debts led many people to think a stronger government was needed. By 1787, Alexander Hamilton and James Madison had engineered the meeting of a Constitutional Convention in Philadelphia.

Delegates to the convention were a self-conscious elite—wealthier, better educated, better informed about the outside world than most Americans were. They decided to ignore their mandate from Congress—to revise the Articles—and instead framed a wholly new constitution. They tried to balance off a number of competing interests: small states and large ones; the North and the South; slave states and free states; agricultural states and states where manufacturing and trade were important. Finally, they had to balance the interests of the well-to-do and the poor.

The delegates tried to create a government strong enough to protect what they viewed as the national interest, but not so strong as to threaten life, liberty, and property. They attempted to do this by separating the powers of the federal government among three branches—legislative, executive, and judicial—and by dividing the powers of the federal government from those of the states. These separations and divisions of power mean that in our country the national government is not sovereign, for no one person or institution has ultimate control over the United States. All officeholders and all institutions must share powers with one another, and this sharing of powers by independent institutions distinguishes our form of government from the parliamentary system, in which the legislature is sovereign.

Once the Constitution had been signed by the delegates, in September 1787, it had to be ratified by nine of the thirteen states. Despite the limits it placed on the power of the federal government, the Anti-Federalists thought it made the government too powerful, and they opposed it bitterly. Nonetheless, by July 1788, the supporters of the new Constitution had persuaded nine states to ratify it, and the federal government was in business. In short order, the Constitution ceased to be controversial.

The Constitution has proved to be highly adaptable. Its text has so far been amended 26 times. The living Constitution, the Constitution as it really functions, has also changed in response to judicial review, presidential prerogative, congressional initiatives, and political reality.

We have now lived under the Constitution of 1787 for two centuries. Yet many people wonder if our system of government still works. Precisely because it sets such great store by life, liberty, and property, it may provide less well for other good things—effective government, for example. No constitution has ever been immortal, nor is our own Constitution the stronger if we ignore our problems. In the past, debate over the Constitution made our constitutional system more vigorous, not weaker.

Few if any countries have maintained the same form of government with such persistence and devotion as the United States has. But it is not the Constitution that has made us so stable. Our political stability, and thus our acceptance of the Constitution, rests upon certain shared political and social attitudes. Those attitudes—now as in 1787—favor life, liberty, and property. Should they be undermined, the Constitution may be undermined as well.

SUGGESTED READINGS

CHARLES A. BEARD, *An Economic Interpretation of the Constitution*. New York: Macmillan, 1913. Classic formulation of the argument that the Founding Fathers were not demigods but prosperous men who had made investments and required a stronger central government to protect them.

CONGRESSIONAL RESEARCH SERVICE (Library of Congress), *The Constitution of the United States of America: Analysis and Interpretation*. Washington, D.C.: GPO, 1972, with 1978 supplement. The last (and official) word as to the meaning of the document in a book so large that it will soon have to be divided into two volumes. A most valuable source reference.

EDWARD S. CORWIN, *The Constitution and What It Means Today*, 14th ed., rev. by Harold W. Chase and Craig R. Ducat. Princeton: Princeton Univ., 1978. This classic, whose first edition appeared in 1920, gives a detailed clause-by-clause analysis of the Constitution's current meaning, primarily as interpreted by the Supreme Court since it first staked out the power of judicial review in 1803. Again, indispensable as a reference.

ALEXANDER HAMILTON, JAMES MADISON, and JOHN JAY, *The Federalist*. Originally appeared in the *New York Packet*, 1787–1788. Convenient edition: Clinton Rossiter, New York: New American Library, 1961. Best edition: Benjamin F. Wright, Cambridge: Harvard Univ., 1961. The classic and indispensable source for studying the manifest objectives of three members of the convention's "inner elite" who drafted the Constitution.

FORREST MCDONALD, *We the People*. Chicago: Univ. of Chicago, 1958. Systematic refutation of Beard's thesis, demonstrating that there was no clear-cut relationship between the wealth of the men at the Constitutional Convention and their support for the document either then or in the ratification struggle.

ALEXIS DE TOCQUEVILLE, *Democracy in America* (2 vols.). Originally published in 1835, available in many current editions. The classic analysis of American politics and society by an impressively perceptive French observer. A generally useful work. Much of it deals directly and more tangentially with the sociological-cultural background of the American Constitution and constitutionalism.

chapter three

FEDERALISM

The clock, not an oath, transforms a President-elect into a President. At exactly 12 noon, January 20, 1981, Ronald Wilson Reagan became the 39th man to hold the office of the presidency.

Mr. Reagan was the most conservative President to be elected in two generations, and he had managed to get the highest proportion of the popular vote any President had won since 1972. Some people hoped, and others feared, that January 20, 1981, was the beginning of the end for the welfare state.

After solemnly swearing to defend the Constitution to the best of his ability, "so help me God," Ronald Reagan stepped up to the lectern and gave his inaugural address. Like most of his speeches, it had a conservative slant but used themes and ideas that appealed to all Americans, not just to conservatives.

"It is my intention," he said, to restore "the distinction between the powers granted to the federal government and those reserved to the states and to the people." A few weeks later, Mr. Reagan tried to do just that: He proposed what he called "the New Federalism."

As usual in matters of government, the chief questions were money and power. When Ronald Reagan took office, the federal government had about 500 spending programs earmarked for specific purposes: "categorical grants." Mr. Reagan wanted to combine 85 of them into 6 "block grants," grants for general purposes.

For example, 34 programs, including one to educate handicapped children and another, for juvenile delinquents, would be merged into a block grant for education. The new grant would be distributed among the states, which would be free to spend it for any educational purpose; it would not be limited to handicapped and delinquent children. States would therefore be able to drop programs they disliked. They would not have to follow elaborate federal guidelines. They would assume more responsibility for the services they provided, and the federal government would assume less.

As always, there was a catch.

It is easier to cut funding for general block grants than for specific spending programs. Mr. Reagan meant to fund his 6 block grants with 25 percent less money than the 85 categorical grants were receiving.

The New Federalism was authentic Americana. As one journalist put it, its basic features—"self-reliance, decentralized government, voter accountability—are just what 9 out of 10 governors would endorse." But they would endorse it only "so long as it didn't apply to them." Let's see what happened to the New Federalism.

First, certain specific programs that Mr. Reagan wanted to merge into his block grants were very popular. Some quite literally assisted widows and orphans. In 1980, for instance, Congress had made the federal government responsible for funding and regulating the care and placement of foster children. Politicians, however conservative, find it very hard to vote against foster children, which is a lot like voting against Christmas. Indeed, the fight to keep the program out of the block grants was led by a Republican congressman from California named John Rousselot, who is about as conservative as you can get in serious politics.

"I'm a great believer in block grants," Rousselot insisted. "But I honestly don't think that foster care should be lost in it. The basic point is to try to get these kids into a good family and not get lost in the system as we once did. Many states just weren't keeping track."[1]

The most liberal member of Congress would not have put it differently.

Of course, not all these programs help widows and orphans. Some are downright controversial. For example, one program gave poor people money to hire lawyers. Conservatives are especially hostile to this program, and all the conservatives in Congress would no doubt like to abolish it indirectly, by including it in a block grant. Not all of them voted to do so, however. One of those who did not, Representative M. Caldwell Butler (R–Va.), admitted that he had voted to save the program because it was popular in his district.

Remember: All congressmen—liberal and conservative, Republican and Democratic—must run for reelection every two years.

And when people actually got to thinking about "the distinction between the powers granted to the federal government and those reserved to the states and to the people," even conservatives could not define the boundary between these powers. Two fairly conservative governors proposed a swap in which Washington would pay for Medicaid, while each state would pick up all the costs of educating its own children. Education, they argued, lay within the states' historic field of responsibility; Medicaid, however, was a form of income maintenance, a federal responsibility.

Another fairly conservative governor claimed that education, though "basically" a state responsibility, was not altogether so. He wanted the federal government to pay for the most expensive programs.

Governors of all parties and all points of view do not want the states to pay for budget-busting programs.

---

[1] *The New York Times,* July 2, 1981.

Local self-government is an American tradition. Liberals or conservatives, we believe in it and practice it. But when we try to draw exact boundaries between the responsibilities of the federal government and the states, we get into trouble. People who embrace the general idea of states' rights often find it hard to live with the details.

To find out what happened to the New Federalism, read on.

_____THE MEANING OF FEDERALISM_____

Few countries besides our own debate the nature and extent of the national government's control over regional governments. Most national governments can do anything they want to do, for most countries are **unitary states.**[2] Regional governments in these countries—Britain and France, for example— are mere agents of the national government, which can regulate them, overrule them, and abolish them. In the early 1970s, for instance, Britain's counties, which had endured for hundreds of years, were legislated out of existence and replaced by a set of new counties made up by bureaucrats and politicians in London.

At the other extreme, a **confederation,** such as the United States under the Articles of Confederation (see Chapter 2) or Switzerland today, is a mere league of regional governments. The national government has only those powers delegated to it by the regional governments.

As for our **federal system,** it was unique when first created at the Constitutional Convention in 1787, and still is. Like a confederation's regional governments, the American states exist by right, not just by the whim of the **federal government.** But the federal, or national, government is equally independent of the states, for it, too, derives its title from the Constitution. Within its own sphere of authority, it is supreme, but all powers not specifically granted to it are "reserved to the states respectively, or to the people."[3]

Federalism and Liberty

In 1787, the states were the great reality of American politics, and the federal government was little more than a complicated theoretical improvisation. The federal government was expected to frustrate the states' democratic tendencies—above all, by preventing state governments from suspending the obligation to repay private debts (see Chapter 2). Debts are a form of property, and property, as the Founding Fathers saw it, is essential to liberty. The states' very existence, however, prevented the federal government from itself threatening liberty.

Do federal systems promote liberty, in the Founders' sense or in any other? Consider some specific cases. The Soviet Union is organized along federal

---

[2] States meaning "national entities," not "the fifty states" of our country.

[3] Note that the term *federal* is applied both to the *federal,* or national, government and to the *federal* system, in which power is shared by the federal government, on the one hand, and state governments, on the other.

Institut Pedagogique National

In France, a unitary state, the ministry of education in Paris controls the schools—this means that the central government in Paris decides what will be taught in this classroom and all others throughout the country.

"We are inclined to confuse freedom and democracy, which we regard as moral principles, with the way in which these are practiced in America—with capitalism, federalism and the two-party system, which are not moral principles, but simply the accepted practices of the American people."

James William Fulbright,
U.S. Senator, March 27, 1964

lines, yet it is a dictatorship. The unitary states of Britain and France are democratic; the unitary states of Chile and Cuba are not.

The reality of a nation's political life hangs on more than just its written documents. Quite as important—perhaps more so—are its political culture, social values, and historical memories. These unwritten features of a nation's political system can utterly nullify the written ones. The Soviet Union, for example, is not only a dictatorship but also a highly centralized country, despite its ostensibly federal structure. Our federal system, by contrast, is very real—not because it is sanctified by the Constitution, but because it reflects important elements in our political culture, notably our perennial distrust of concentrated power.

Yet, even if federal systems are not inherently democratic, they do differ from unitary systems. Take education. In France, a unitary state, the ministry of education in Paris controls the schools throughout the country, as well as in all overseas territories. One education minister boasted that at any time of day, he knew just what the pupils at every school in France were learning. No doubt he exaggerated, but the central government in Paris certainly prescribes the curriculum in every one of these schools.

At first, our federal government had almost nothing to do with education. At no time has it paid more than 8 percent of the total cost of American education, and it has never tried to do much more than set general standards. Most of the real work of deciding what goes on in our classrooms, and paying for it, is done by the 50 states and their 15,000 local school districts.

Who Gains? Who Loses?

Since the states are a vital part of our political culture and practice, their precise powers generate much controversy, and they always have. When the Constitution was framed, the demand for states' rights came chiefly from the small farmers and the men who led them, like Thomas Jefferson and Patrick

62   **FEDERALISM**

Henry. The "nationalists"—Alexander Hamilton, for instance—spoke mainly for the better-off people, who in 1787 wanted a strong government to conduct foreign relations, provide for the common defense, develop the national economy, and protect private property. These people tended to be "nationalists" because their aims were national in character. Besides, federal elections were less undemocratic than were some state elections (see Chapter 10); also

"Socialism" in California?

In 1934, a novelist named Upton Sinclair ran for governor of California on the Democratic ticket. He offered a program that he called "End Poverty in California," EPIC for short. A few associates of President Franklin D. Roosevelt feared that Sinclair might actually become governor.

"Well," Roosevelt replied, "Perhaps they'll get EPIC in California. What difference, I ask you, would that make in Dutchess County, New York, or Lincoln County, Maine? If it has fatal consequences in one place, it has little effect on the rest of the country. If a new and apparently fanatical program works well, it will be copied. If it doesn't, you won't hear of it again."

Paul F. Boller, Jr., *Presidential Anecdotes* (New York: Oxford University Press, 1981, p. 260). Upton Sinclair did not win California's governorship in 1934, although the tide of the New Deal flowed very strongly indeed. Sinclair took about 38 percent of the vote.

Upton Sinclair ran for governor of California in 1934. He was regarded by many as a dangerous left-winger and was defeated in a landslide.

the federal bureaucracy (see Chapter 12), so far as it existed, was more genteel than those of the states.

The Democratic Revolution of the 1820s (see Chapter 10) gave small farmers and other people of limited means some influence in federal elections, so these people and their leaders feared the federal government less. For that very reason, powerful economic interests began to entrench themselves in state governments, some of which were more or less "for sale." States' rights acquired a different political meaning and became, in effect, a barrier against political and social change. Its chief supporters were southern slaveowners before the Civil War, southern segregationists after it, and big business. Business liked states' rights because state regulation of its activities usually meant little or no regulation.

Meanwhile, reformers discovered that the fastest way to undo the status quo was to convert the federal government to their side. First, the opponents of slavery prodded the federal government to abolish it. Later on, organized labor, blacks and other minorities, aiders of the poor, and liberals in general sought to use the federal government's powers to promote their own causes.

Federalism usually benefits the "haves," not the "have nots," because it fragments political power into many local units. This in itself inhibits the sort of large-scale national programs that liberals tend to favor. Besides, these small local units are more easily manipulated by money than is country as a whole, and the "haves," by definition, have money. Even in localities that manage to resist manipulation, elections are mostly dominated by conventional local issues, if only because basic social and political change is hard to bring about on a purely local basis. So local politics is mostly the politics of the status quo. Change, when it comes, is usually imposed by the federal government.

The Federal "Laboratory." Not all supporters of states' rights are businessmen and segregationists. There are and always have been liberals who want to experiment on the state or local level, who do not wish to be bossed around by bureaucrats in Washington. Federalism, in fact, makes the United States into a sort of laboratory, with many experiments going on at the same time.

"Cultural Federalism." Remember that even if federalism does benefit the "haves," it survives because it is rooted in the political culture of this country (see Chapter 1). Local self-government is an American tradition, and so is fear of centralization. Americans are much more diverse than just about any other people, and this mental and cultural federalism is the bedrock of our political federalism (see Chapter 1). While the one endures, so too will the other.

The Politics of Federalism

Representative Thomas P. O'Neill (D–Mass.), the 55th Speaker of the House of Representatives, has a favorite saying: "All politics is local politics." This saying is itself a product of federalism. In a unitary state, all serious politics is national politics. Parties are often strong enough to free elected officials from the need to coddle particular groups of local voters (see Chapter 9). In our country, however, every officeholder but the President must appeal to the prejudices of local voters concerned mainly with local issues.

All the members of both houses of Congress are local politicians who win local primaries, not national figures chosen by the national parties. So both houses are both local and national institutions. Many members of the House

Speaker of the House Tip O'Neill's favorite saying is: "All politics is local politics." The Speaker is shown here on the campaign trail in his district in Massachusetts, practicing local politics.

represent districts no larger than city neighborhoods. As for the Senate, each state, no matter how small, elects two senators, so the interests of tiny groups of people can loom very large in that house of only 100 members. (William Fulbright, for example, chairman of the Senate Foreign Relations Committee from 1961 to 1974, devoted a great deal of his time and power to protecting the interests of the chicken farmers of his home state, Arkansas.)

Bargaining and Rivalry

Our congressmen, senators, and all other politicians must speak for their own constituents and leave the country as a whole to its own devices. By its nature, the federal system pits towns and cities against one another and against states, and it pits states against one another and against the federal government. Rivalry is its essence.

The states, however, cannot abolish one another or the federal government and the federal government cannot abolish any of the states. Rarely does one side utterly defeat the other. More often than not, when either side wants something, it must bargain. Bargaining, like rivalry, lies at the heart of federalism.

When rivals bargain, both must give up something to get something—the *quid pro quo*, or in plain English, "the what for the which." What does the federal government have that the states want? In a word, money; in fact, the federal government receives about two-thirds of all U.S. tax revenues. What can states and localities give in return? They can comply with federal policies and implement and support them. The states get money for programs that may help reelect their politicians. The federal government makes its policies more legitimate and popular than they would be if it tried to impose them on the states directly. Besides, well-led, well-organized state agencies (many, alas, are neither) can carry out federal programs effectively and cheaply.

Both sides pay a price for their bargain. The states lose much practical autonomy and sometimes become administrative arms of the federal government. They become financially dependent on Washington, and any President can intimidate them by threatening to cut back popular programs. As for the

A Failure: The Oakland Project

Back in the 1960s, federal officials agreed to give Oakland, California, $23 million to build a ship terminal and airport hangar. Their idea was to promote economic development and create new jobs, especially for the city's unemployed black population.

Work started in 1966. Four years on, little had been built and few jobs created. The whole project was going nowhere.

Why? One problem was that every decision had to be fought out among seven federal agencies, three state and local government bodies, and a multitude of private businesses and civic groups. Each had its own game to play, and each held up the project. Bargaining became an end in itself. Besides, Oakland's local politicians and officials only understood traditional city functions: the police department, garbage collection, sewers, and the like. The hangar project was out of their range.

There was a political problem, too. Many decades ago, California got rid of political parties and labels in local elections. Oakland's public officials had no body of organized supporters to mobilize on behalf of the program. Then too, apart from the traditional city services, they expected private individuals and groups to provide for themselves. Their attitudes toward government and its functions were so voluntaristic (one definition of voluntarism: "If you don't like what I'm doing, I quit.") that they had no use for organized political support. The poor people and minority groups who were supposed to benefit from the project were not even organized effectively. Public opinion was so nebulous that it hardly existed.

Oakland's political void was responsible for problems much like those that bedevil American foreign-aid programs in many Third World countries: incompetence and indifference among the local officials who received the aid, and a public that could not be organized to support it. This void, together with the endless rounds of negotiations and consultations among official and private groups, stymied the program.

Such stories give bureaucracy a bad name and convey the impression that we "can't get from there to here" when we rely on government. That impression is by no means invariably correct, but it is a living part of our political tradition.

This story is extracted from Jeffrey Pressman's brilliant *Federal Programs and City Politics: The Dynamics of Federal Aid in Oakland* (Berkeley: Univ. of California, 1975).

federal government, it must see its policies transformed into fifty separate policies because the levels of wealth, economies, political cultures, and resources of the fifty states are quite different. So too is the competence of the fifty state bureaucracies.

THE FRAMERS' SCHEME

To borrow a phrase, the Framers of the Constitution knew that they could not write the cookbooks of the future; they made no attempt to settle beforehand every conflict that might arise among the states or between the states and the federal government. Instead they designed a comprehensible scheme and let us fill in the details to suit ourselves.

The starting point of the Framers' scheme was their aim in creating the federal government: to promote economic development and freedom balanced by stability, and to carry on defense and foreign relations. They kept these aims in mind when they allocated powers between the federal government and the states, denied certain powers to the states, imposed certain obligations on the federal government, and required the states to cooperate with one another.

Enumerated, Implied, and Inherent Powers

Enumerated Powers. Most of the federal government's **enumerated powers** those specifically granted to it by the Constitution—deal with the areas of policy it was created to handle: economic development, internal stability, foreign policy, and defense. Certain powers, such as taxing goods exported from states, are explicitly denied to the federal government. Others—for example, the power to pass **ex post facto laws,** which make actions illegal only after they have been committed—were denied to all levels of government.

Implied Powers. The Framers knew perfectly well that no such collection of explicit powers could possibly be sufficient. So they wrote into the Constitution the so-called **elastic clause** (Article I, sec. 8), which gives Congress the power "To make all Laws which shall be necessary and proper for carrying into Execution" the enumerated powers. When Congress does so, it is said to exercise its **implied powers.**

Twice in this country's early history, for example, Congress created a central bank, the Bank of the United States, to carry out its enumerated power of regulating the currency. Both the first and second Banks of the United States generated much opposition. Indeed, the State of Maryland attempted to tax the second one to death. (See the section on *McCulloch* v. *Maryland.*) The legal controversies provoked by the elastic clause feed the unique powers of the federal court system, especially those of the U.S. Supreme Court. (See the section on "Boundaries.")

Inherent Powers. A third category of federal powers was neither granted explicitly nor implied by the elastic clause. These **inherent powers,** mainly connected with foreign relations, are thought to belong to the federal government by definition, simply because it is a national government, which must have certain powers to be worthy of the name. In 1936, for example, the U.S. Supreme Court ruled on these grounds that under the Neutrality Act, the president can forbid the export of American weapons.[4]

Concurrent Powers

The Framers created another happy hunting ground of litigation in the **concurrent powers**—those granted both to the federal government and to the states. Taxation is the most important of the concurrent powers and, therefore, the most important source of the legal problems.

In 1819 (in *McCulloch* v. *Maryland*) the U.S. Supreme Court ruled that states could not tax the federal government, a ruling that still stands. Until 1939, in fact, each level of government was not allowed to tax the employees of the other levels.[5] Those days are over. As of 1985, almost 85 percent of our people lived in the 41 states that levy personal income taxes, and they feel the impact of the concurrent powers in a very practical and sometimes, annoying way.

---

[4] *U.S.* v. *Curtiss-Wright Export Corp.,* 299 U.S. 304 (1936).
[5] *Graves* v. *New York ex. Rel. O'Keefe,* 306 U.S. 466 (1939), overruling *Collector* v. *Day,* 11 Wall. 113 (1871).

Restrictions on State Governments

To repeat: the federal government was created mainly for the sake of economic development, certain individual rights, internal stability, defense, and foreign policy. The powers specifically granted to the federal government deal mostly with these functions, and so do the powers specifically denied to the states.

The states cannot conduct an independent foreign policy. Unless they are actually invaded, they cannot carry out military and naval operations. They cannot coin money, debase it, or pass laws that impair the obligation of contracts, including debt. They cannot tax imports or exports, except to pay for state inspections.

Finally, they cannot grant titles of nobility—a reminder that in 1787, monarchy and aristocracy had not altogether ceased to be practical politics in this neck of the woods.

These might appear to be straightforward limits, yet they, too, generate controversy and litigation.

Severance Taxes. Some states, for example, levy "severance taxes" on natural resources exported to other states. Usually, these taxes are low enough for the courts to ignore. In recent years, however, certain energy-rich states have taken to levying very high severance taxes on oil, natural gas, and coal—so high that they appear to resemble export duties, which the U.S. Constitution forbids.

The U.S. Supreme Court could clear up the mess if it wanted to, but its ways are enigmatic. In 1981 the Court struck down a Louisiana severance tax on the grounds that it was too high. Yet in 1982, it approved a Montana severance tax of 30 percent because that state levied it on all consumers, not just on out-of-state consumers.

Congress, too, could resolve these problems. But the economic interests involved are huge and the politics troublesome, so no one expects Congress to act in the near future.

Federal Obligations to the States

The restrictions on state governments are inexact because the states constantly think of new ways to elude them. For quite the opposite reason, one of the federal government's obligations to the states—its responsibility to ensure "a republican form of government"—is equally obscure: No state has ever tried to establish a monarchy. For want of such an effort, this provision has not been much interpreted in the courts.

Another such obligation requires the federal government to act as the ultimate guarantor of stability, by protecting the states from domestic violence and invasion. The President, however, has not always waited for a request from state officials before sending in troops to put down civil disorders, although the Constitution seems to require a request.

Interstate Relations: Comity

Federalism involves more than just the relations between the federal government, on the one hand, and the states, on the other. The Framers aimed to transform a league of states into a nation, and they did so not only by creating

In recent years, oil-rich states such as Louisiana have taken to levying very high severance taxes on their greatest national resource.

Shell Offshore, Inc.

the federal government but also by requiring the states to practice comity among one another. In other words, the states must recognize one another's laws and treat one another's citizens as they do their own, instead of behaving as if they were sovereign empires, as they did under the Articles of Confederation (see Chapter 2).

"Full Faith and Credit." First, the Constitution commands the states to give what it calls "full faith and credit" to one another's laws and court decisions. "Full faith and credit" now means that people with civil judgments (see Chapter 14) pending in one state cannot evade them by moving to another state, because the legal machinery would have to enforce the first state's decision.

This seems clear and simple, but it is not. Take divorce, for example. Nevada grants divorces, sometimes for quite imaginative reasons, to residents of only six weeks' standing. Must other states respect the validity of a Nevada divorce? Apparently not, so this may be the only country in the world where it is, or ever has been, possible to be married and single at the same time.

"Privileges and Immunities." "The citizens of each state shall be entitled to all the privileges and immunities of the citizens of the several States" (Article IV, sec. 2). Again, the meaning does seem clear: States may not discriminate against one another's citizens but they do so all the time. Out-of-state students at public universities, for example, pay higher tuition fees than state residents do. Sometimes even residency is not enough. In Maine, you can fish for lobsters only if you have a fishing license, and you can apply for such a license only if you were *born* in Maine.

Extradition. Another dark area of constitutional law is **extradition.** When a person accused of a crime flees from one state to another, the second state must extradite (remove) that person to the accusing state. Originally, Article

Only those who were born in Maine can fish for lobsters—an example of one state's discrimination against residents of the other 49 states.

Maine Division of Tourism

IV also required states to extradite fugitive slaves to their masters. The section on fugitive slaves and the laws passed to enforce it were ignored in many places, however—a typical problem of federalism, which rests upon an amazing diversity of attitudes.

Such problems by no means vanished with the passing of slavery. Until quite recently, for instance, northern states occasionally refused to extradite blacks to the South, especially when they appeared to be present or future victims of racial injustice. The question of how much "faith and credit" states must grant one another is and always has been a delicate one.

Interstate Compacts. One clause (Article I, sec. 10) that promotes comity among states is phrased negatively: "No State shall, without the Consent of Congress . . . enter into any Agreement or Compact with another State, or with a Foreign Power, . . . " The wording implies that if Congress does consent, states *can* enter into such compacts. In fact, they do enter into them—more and more often. Consider the classic case, the Port Authority of New York. By World War I, the New York metropolitan area had spread into nearby parts of New Jersey and Connecticut. The three states decided (in 1921) to create a common authority to deal with regional problems of transportation—problems that the federal government did not want to solve and that individual state governments could not solve alone.

Foreign Compacts. The wording of Article I, section 10 implies that states can enter into compacts not only with other states but also with foreign powers, and they do that too, more and more often. For example, fifteen western states and the Canadian provinces of British Columbia and Alberta have signed a compact limiting the weight of the trucks on their roads. A compact between the Canadian province of Quebec and the energy-poor states of New England will provide New England with Quebec's abundant hydroelectric power.

These foreign compacts remind us that federalism is still in a real sense an experiment, just as it was in 1787. It has evolved in ways that the Framers could not have imagined and might not have liked, and in the future it will evolve in ways that we cannot imagine and might not like.

__ BOUNDARIES: THE FEDERAL SYSTEM EVOLVES __

Our Constitution separates and divides all the powers of government so thoroughly that each branch of government in the United States, at every level, must prove its right to act before acting. Competition and conflict arise at the boundary points, where the branches and levels meet or collide, for the Framers of the Constitution did not attempt to settle every dispute before it arose. In fact, they did not provide any mechanism for resolving disputes about who has the power to do what. Such disputes must be resolved. In the fullness of time, a way was found.

The U.S. Supreme Court as Boundary Setter

Although the Constitution provided no mechanism for ending the disputes generated by federalism, it did create the federal court system to resolve legal disputes, in general. Eventually, the U.S. Supreme Court simply took for itself the role of boundary setter by calling into existence what lawyers term **judicial review:** the power to judge the constitutionality of any act by any government authority federal, state, and local (see Chapter 14). We accept this amazing claim, which is made so fully by no other court system in the world, because we must: We need a way of deciding who has the power to do what, and only the Court has given us one.

McCulloch v. Maryland

The Court first claimed the power of judicial review in 1803, in the case of *Marbury* v. *Madison* (see Chapter 14). Not until 1819, however, did it make any general claim to regulate federal-state relations.

Three years before it did so, in 1816, Congress chartered the Second Bank of the United States, a central bank created to issue a noninflationary currency and to regulate the country's financial system. Such a currency benefits those who lend money, as opposed to those who borrow it; inflation permits debtors to repay less, in real terms, than they borrowed. Besides, it always has been much easier for big rather than small businesses to borrow money from the bank. By and large, the bank favored the well-to-do.

Many state governments, the banks they chartered, and small farmers and businessmen claimed that Congress did not have the right to charter a bank. The state of Maryland actually tried to drive the bank out of business by levying a tax on it. James McCulloch, an official at the bank's Baltimore office, refused to pay the tax.

Of course, the Constitution did not specifically grant Congress the right to charter a bank. It did give Congress a great many specific powers over the economy, however, including the power to coin and regulate money. It also permitted Congress to pass any law "necessary and proper" to achieve those ends.

Chief Justice John Marshall (see Chapter 14) was a strong nationalist, and the Court was very much under his influence. When *McCulloch* v. *Maryland* came up to the Court for review, in 1819, it ruled that Congress could indeed charter a central bank and that the states had no power to tax it out of existence—or even to tax it at all.[6]

States could levy taxes, of course, but only for legitimate purposes. "The power to tax involves the power to destroy," Marshall observed, and the destruction of the federal government is not a legitimate end of state taxation. The Constitution was ordained by the people, not by the states, and the federal government is supreme within its sphere. States therefore cannot meddle with its lawful actions.

McCulloch v. *Maryland* established the doctrine of **intergovernmental immunities,** which prohibits the federal government and the state governments from taxing each other's "instrumentalities." You can observe one result of this doctrine in the financial pages of a newspaper. Note that the bonds issued by state and local governments pay lower interest rates ("yield") than corporate bonds. The reason? Interest on municipal bonds is exempt from the "big bite," federal income taxes; the interest on privately issued bonds is not.

> *"Let the end be legitimate, let it be within the scope of the Constitution, and all means which are appropriate, which are plainly adapted to that end, which are not prohibited, but consistent with the letter and spirit of the Constitution, are constitutional."*
>
> **Chief Justice John Marshall,**
> McCulloch v. Maryland (1819)

---

[6] *McCulloch* v. *Maryland,* 4 Wheat. 316 (1819).

Dual Federalism

McCulloch v. *Maryland* was both a political conflict between the states and the federal government and an economic and social conflict between the forces entrenched on each side—small farmers and businessmen on one side, large landowners and big business on the other. By the late 1820s, though, the Democratic Revolution had transformed the political earth and heavens: The federal government, under President Andrew Jackson (1829-1837), became much less "aristocratic," while the powerful economic interests that had supported a nationalist policy sought refuge in state governments.

The conflict between the states and the federal government was still partly a socioeconomic one, but the forces aligned on each side had changed dramatically. Above all, big business was no longer keen on getting federal help and protection; it now wanted cheap government and little or no regulation. If it had to submit to regulation, it preferred state regulation, which often meant no regulation at all. Who should regulate business: the federal government or the states? After the Civil War, this became the great problem of federal—state relations.

Plainly enough, the federal government (Article I, sec. 8) had the power "To regulate Commerce with foreign Nations, and among the several States." Could it also regulate **intrastate commerce,** commerce within a state? Did the elastic ("necessary and proper") clause of the same article and section allow it to regulate intrastate commerce, not as an end but as a means of regulating **interstate commerce,** commerce among states? Just what *is* interstate commerce, anyway? Such questions agitated politicians, judges, and lawyers.

From about 1900 to 1937, the federal courts, especially the U.S. Supreme Court, seemed less intent on defining the respective powers of the federal government and the states and more intent on conjuring up a very large gray area where neither could act. As far as the courts tolerated economic regulation, they distinguished between federal and state spheres of authority by creating a legal doctrine called **dual federalism.** Goods and services stayed within the sphere of intrastate commerce and, therefore, under state regulation, until they crossed state lines. At this point, they entered interstate commerce, the federal sphere.

Under this definition, manufacturing was an intrastate activity. Indeed, in the sugar trust case (1895), the U.S. Supreme Court ruled that although one company refined over 90 percent of American sugar, it could not be prosecuted as a monopoly under the Sherman Antitrust Act because the act applied only to interstate commerce, and refining was "manufacturing," not commerce.[7]

When the distinction between intrastate and interstate commerce did not do the job, the Supreme Court rediscovered the Tenth Amendment: "The powers not delegated to the United States by the Constitution, nor prohibited by it to the States, are reserved to the States respectively, or to the people." By this means, in 1918, the Court struck down a 1916 act of Congress prohibiting child labor.[8]

---

[7] *U.S.* v. *E. C. Knight & Co.,* 156 U.S. 1 (1895), implicitly overruled in *N.L.R.B.* v. *Jones & Laughlin Steel Corp.,* 301 U.S. 1 (1937).

[8] *Hammer* v. *Dagenhart,* 247 U.S. 251 (1918), explicitly overruled in *U.S.* v. *Darby,* 312 U.S. 100 (1940).

The New York Stock Exchange. The crash of October 29, 1929, eventually changed the balance of political forces in the United States and the workings of all of our institutions, including federalism.

Cooperative Federalism

On "Black Tuesday," October 29, 1929, the stock market collapsed. That day's calamitous fall in stock prices opened the longest and most severe depression in American history. Most people expected the federal government to do something about the economy, but dual federalism and other legal doctrines stood in the way.

The electorate and the executive branch abandoned the ideal of an unregulated economy long before the courts did. President Herbert Hoover (1929—1933), who believed that the Depression would "burn itself out, naturally," was defeated in the 1932 presidential election by Franklin Delano Roosevelt (1933—1945). Mr. Roosevelt did not bring into office any particular outlook on economics, but he was willing to experiment with economic regulation. (See Chapters 10 and 11 for details.) His New Deal did not in itself end the Depression, but it was popular—popular with the electorate, at any rate. The "nine old men" of the U.S. Supreme Court continued to reject government, especially federal, regulation of business. One by one, the Court threw out many of Mr. Roosevelt's programs.

The President was, however, triumphantly reelected in 1936. In the next year, he tried to "pack" the Court by expanding its size, but this strategy failed (see Chapter 14). Still, it is said that the Court follows the election returns, and it apparently did so: In the "switch in time that saved nine," it discovered that Mr. Roosevelt's programs were constitutional after all. In 1937, it ruled that manufacturing was not an inherently local activity and could therefore be regulated, as interstate commerce, by the federal government,[9] and four years later, the Court permitted the federal government to ban child labor.[10]

President Roosevelt had by 1941 appointed seven justices. The "Roosevelt Court" actually upheld a fine against a farmer who—solely for his own family's use—had grown wheat on eleven more acres than the federal government allowed him to cultivate.[11] If that is not local production, what is? Dual federalism was dead.

Yet even now we see occasional faint stirrings of dual federalism. In 1976, the U.S. Supreme Court struck down an act that extended federal minimum-wage-and-hour laws to employees of state and local governments. The grounds? By a 5 to 4 majority the Court declared that the Tenth Amendment protects states from federal encroachment in such matters as employment.[12] The boundary debate goes on.

_____ THE PRICE OF FEDERALISM: FEDERAL AID _____

By now, the federal government has pretty well established its right to act in most fields of policy. Boundary struggles still abound, of course; state and local governments still resent getting orders from Washington. One thing, however, they are always happy to get from the federal government: money—without "strings," if you please.

Grants-in-Aid

Question: "What has 500 parts, costs $83 billion and is condemned by almost everybody?" Answer: "The chaotic system of 500 federal grant programs."

National Journal,
January 3, 1981

For 200 years now, the federal government has in fact given the states **grants-in-aid** of money and other resources. Most early grants were used to finance "internal improvements," like roads and schools. President Franklin Roosevelt put the federal government into the business of funding social programs. By 1950, federal grants-in-aid to states and localities amounted to $2 billion a year.

After John Kennedy became President in 1961, the number and size of federal grants exploded. The economy was then growing. Tax revenues went up, although tax rates were cut. Social spending seemed both painless and right. In a mere 10 years, from 1960 to 1970, the proportion of state and local spending paid for by the federal treasury doubled, from 10 percent to 20 percent.

Table 3–1 Historical Trend of Federal Grant-in-Aid Outlays

1950	$2,253
1955	3,207
1960	7,020
1965	10,904
1970	24,014
1975	49,834
1980	91,451
1985 estimate	107,016

Special Analyses, Special Analysis H Federal Aid to State and Local Governments (Washington, D.C.: GPO, 1985), p. H-19.

The "Big Three" and the "Medium Four"

In the early 1980s, the number of grant-in-aid programs stood at almost 500. But only 25 of them accounted for 81 percent of all the federal money that flowed into state and local coffers. The "big three" programs—accounting for almost two-thirds (in 1981) of all federal grant money—were education, health, and income maintenance. Just below them were the "medium four": transportation, revenue sharing (see below), community and regional develop-

[9] N.L.R.B. v. Jones & Laughlin Steel Corp., 301 U.S. 1 (1937).
[11] Wickard v. Filburn, 317 U.S. 111 (1942).
[12] The National League of Cities v. Usery, 49 L.Ed. 2nd 245 (1976).

ment, and natural resources and the environment. These 7 made up $94.2 billion, or 97.7 percent, of the federal government's total grant-in-aid bill, $96.3 billion (1981).

Getting It

The State and Local Lobby. As the grant-in-aid bill grew larger, so too did the state-and-local lobby. Each level of government tried to get its share of the loot by setting up its own offices, complete with lawyers, publicists, accountants, financial wizards, and social scientists. Cities formed the National League of Cities and the Conference of Mayors; counties, the National Association of Counties; and states, the National Governor's Association and National Association of State Legislatures.

In addition, associations were formed to protect the interests of state judges, attorneys-general, and secretaries of agriculture; for members of school boards; for state-and-local employees—and this is just the beginning because the list of such national associations takes up almost a page of small type in the Washington, D.C., telephone book. Of course, all states and most large cities have their own offices in Washington, too.

The Lure. Each of these formidable organizations seeks to get as much money as possible from the federal government but to minimize the strings attached to that money. Most often, however, they will take it even if they have no control at all over how to spend it.

Why? Politics and finance. For funds, most state and local governments rely on property taxes, sales and excise (luxury) taxes, license fees, and income taxes. State constitutions often limit tax levels in detail. Higher taxes may require not just routine bills but constitutional amendments, which in turn may require the voters' approval. On top of this, state constitutions often limit a state's power to borrow money. Federal taxes are not hemmed in by such limits and neither is the federal government's borrowing power. Finally, the federal government can, if it chooses, finance itself by just printing money (see Chapter 16).

In any case, the federal government's ability to pay its own way, and to survive if it does not, clearly goes beyond that of state governments. States must therefore seek in Washington the money they cannot raise themselves. (See Chapter 15 for a description of public finances.)

There is another reason, too, why states and localities often humble themselves before the federal moneybags. In a sense, money from Washington is free money. Each of us pays for it through taxes, but so do all other federal taxpayers. State taxes are raised within one state only. Some states are poor and cannot finance expensive programs. Especially in these states, politicians need federal money to promote their own interests and those of the people they represent.

The Paperwork Jungle. Once state and local governments began to receive vastly larger and more numerous federal grants, in the 1960s, they succeeded in cutting many of the strings. Until the 1960s, most federal money came in the form of **categorical grants,** for specific purposes, with uniform rules. These rules grew more numerous and burdensome each year.

Besides, Congress did little to coordinate or review grants after they had been made, so they proliferated. One culprit was the committee system (see

"A national debt, if it is not excessive, will be to us a national blessing."

Alexander Hamilton,
April 30, 1791

Chapter 13). Each committee has many subcommittees, and each subcommittee has a chairperson and a staff eager to claim credit for solving a major national problem through a major new program. Subcommittees often try to solve the same problems by offering their own programs, and the result of their conjoint egoism is overlap, conflict, and duplication.

THE STRUGGLE OVER FEDERALISM, 1963–

Lyndon Johnson used to tell a story about his college days. A political science professor once gave him a test with only a single question: "Discuss fully what the federal Constitution has to say about education."

"So I did," said Johnson, "and, Hell, it must have gone on for ten pages or so. Well, I got that paper back with a big red F across it." The U.S. Constitution says nothing about education.

"I decided right then and there that if there wasn't anything in the Constitution on the subject of education, there ought to have been. And I decided I was going to do something about it, and if you look at the bills that were passed during my administration, I think you might say that I have."[13]

In fact, during Lyndon Johnson's time as President, 1963-1969, the nature of federal spending and the boundaries between state and federal authority changed fundamentally. These changes created many of the issues fought out in the political wars of the 1970s, issues that helped make Ronald Reagan our President in 1981.

Lyndon Johnson: "Creative Federalism"

President Lyndon Johnson maneuvered through Congress the spending bills that vastly increased the number and amount of federal grants. As states and localities became more dependent on federal funds, the strings attached to them grew more irksome. Mr. Johnson tried to cut some of the strings by making greater use of **block** (or **broad-based**) **grants,** which could be spent, at the discretion of states and localities, on any program within certain very broad limits. Mr. Johnson created two such grants: one for public health and one for law enforcement. More were created in the 1970s, to fund (among other things) employment training and community development.

Richard Nixon: The First "New Federalism"

The idea of cutting the strings that came with federal grants appealed even more to President Richard Nixon (1969–1973), a Republican, than it had to President Johnson, a Democrat. Mr. Nixon's **revenue-sharing program** allowed state and local officials to use federal grants for almost anything. Washington, in effect, simply passed along its tax dollars to state and local governments and made no effort to direct or control the money's use. Mr. Nixon called this policy "The New Federalism."

Now that state and local governments had been partly liberated from the toils of federal red tape, they did not always spend their grants wisely. Some

---

[13] Paul F. Boller, *Presidential Anecdotes* (New York: Oxford Univ. Press, 1982), pp. 322–23.

Fighting Fire With Fire

Here, in case you ever wondered, is a list of federal agencies that in 1979 were involved in fire prevention and control:

Agriculture Department
- Farmers Home Administration
- Forest Service
- Rural Development Service
- Science and Education Administration
- Soil Conservation Service

Commerce Department
- Economic Development Administration
- Maritime Administration
- National Bureau of Standards
- National Oceanic and Atmospheric Administration

Energy Department
- Energy Research Centers

Health, Education and Welfare Department*
- Office of Education
- Public Health Service
- Social Security Administration

Housing and Urban Development Department
- Federal Housing Commissioner
- Community Planning and Development Office
- Policy Development and Research Office
- Consumer Affairs Office

Interior Department
- Bureau of Indian Affairs
- Bureau of Land Management
- Bureau of Mines

Justice Department
- Federal Bureau of Investigation
- Law Enforcement Assistance Administration

* Now the Health and Human Services Department

Labor Department
- Employment and Training Administration
- Mine Safety and Health Administration
- Occupational Safety and Health Administration

Transportation Department
- Federal Aviation Administration
- Federal Railroad Administration
- Materials Transportation Bureau
- National Highway Traffic Safety Administration
- Urban Mass Transportation Administration
- U.S. Coast Guard

Treasury Department
- Bureau of Alcohol, Tobacco and Firearms
- Bureau of Governmental Financial Operations
- Office of Revenue Sharing

Office of Personnel Management

Consumer Product Safety Commission

Federal Communications Commission

Federal Emergency Management Agency
- Defense Civil Preparedness Agency
- Federal Disaster Assistance Administration
- Federal Preparedness Agency
- U.S. Fire Administration

General Service Administration
- Federal Supply Service
- Public Buildings Service

National Aeronautics and Space Administration

National Transportation Safety Board

Nuclear Regulatory Commission

National Academy of Sciences

National Science Foundation

Transportation Safety Institute

places used revenue-sharing money to build tennis courts. Funds from the law-enforcement block grant were used to buy helicopters and riot-control tanks. Employment-training funds often found their way into the salaries of career officials—whom New York's Mayor Edward I. Koch later called "poverty pimps"—instead of helping state and local governments to hire the hard-core unemployed, the grant's original aim.

In fact, the controls and red tape of the bad old days had not been entirely pointless. The new order had produced follies, abuses, and plain frauds.

The Carter Administration

From 1972 to 1978, categorical grants—federal grant money with strings—fell from 90 percent to 73 percent. President Jimmy Carter (1977-1981) believed that the abuses were related to this decline, so he shifted the gears of policy and raised the number of categorical grants. Meanwhile, revenue sharing held steady, and block grants were cut. By 1981, categorical grants went back up to about 80 percent of all federal grant money.

Perhaps Mr. Carter's policies held down abuses, but they also increased the number and complexity of federal grant programs. As of 1981, there were about 500 such programs, but no one knew the exact number or the exact amount spent on them. The duplication was quite remarkable. For instance, no fewer than 49 agencies sponsored programs to control and prevent fires. Each of these programs had its own application forms, its own financing procedures, its own bureaucracy, its own interests, and its own constituency. (See the section "Iron Triangles," Chapter 12.)

The Reagan Administration

President Ronald Reagan, like President Nixon, described his grant-in-aid policy as the New Federalism. But Mr. Reagan's New Federalism really was new. Mr. Nixon and Mr. Johnson before him had given states and localities more and more money and made them more and more dependent on federal aid. Mr. Reagan's New Federalism was meant to undo that dependence.

Mr. Reagan sent to Congress a plan (described at the start of this chapter) to combine 85 categorical grants into 6 block grants. These 6 grants would receive 25 percent less funding than the programs they were to replace. Yet Mr. Reagan promised that the level of services to the "truly needy" would not be cut, just the duplication and the red tape.

The President got his 25 percent cut in funding. But he failed to persuade Congress to eliminate 56 of the 85 programs; their supporters in and outside Congress were simply too strong. He could not quiet all the doubts about the fairness of what he was doing. The average cost of administering these 85 programs came to about 4 percent of total expenses. Even abolishing adminstration would not have made up for a 25 percent cut. Besides, despite Mr. Reagan's claim that there would be no "winners or losers" in the New Federalism, he chose mainly to cut programs that aided the poor.

Congress, however, did cut federal aid to state and local governments—and drastically. In 1970, federal aid accounted for about 23 percent of their budgets. By 1975 the proportion had grown to 29 percent, and by 1980, to about 32 percent. But in 1982, the first full fiscal year under Mr. Reagan, it fell to 21 percent—a drop of more than one—third. By 1984, federal aid accounted for less than 20 percent of state and local budgets. States and localities could not make up these cuts by better administration. Many could not try to raise their own taxes to make up for lost federal funding, because if they did so, their people and businesses might move to states with lower taxes.

Mr. Reagan was aware of this problem. During the 1980 presidential campaign, he had promised to give the states a way to finance the programs he proposed to cut from the federal budget. In 1982, as President, he suggested giving them the revenues from certain federal excise (luxury) taxes.

By the time of the fiscal 1986 budget debates, however, very little was heard about this New Federalism. Instead, President Reagan urged the nation's governors and mayors to accept his reductions and eliminations of many federal aid programs, such as general revenue sharing, urban development action grants, community development block grants, sewage plant construction grants, and subsidies to urban mass transit. According to the president, there was "no justification" for the federal government to provide aid to states and localities that enjoyed budget surpluses of $52 billion in 1984, and the time had come to make some "tough calls."

Transfer Payments. Even without Mr. Reagan's version of the New Federalism, federal aid to state and local governments had been going down, not only in its absolute amount but also as a proportion of all federal aid to all recipients. In the 1978 fiscal year, 66 percent of federal aid went to governments; by 1981 that figure had dropped to 58 percent, and it was expected to be only about 50 percent by 1984.[14] A higher proportion of the federal government's money was now going directly to individuals, in the form of **transfer payments,** such as Social Security (see Chapter 15).

[14] *Congressional Quarterly Weekly Report,* 1982 p. 2050.

Figure 3-1   Federal Aid Trends since 1976

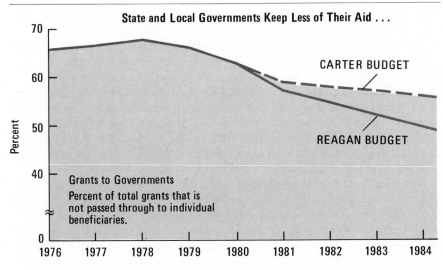

State and Local Governments Keep Less of Their Aid . . .

Grants to Governments
Percent of total grants that is not passed through to individual beneficiaries.

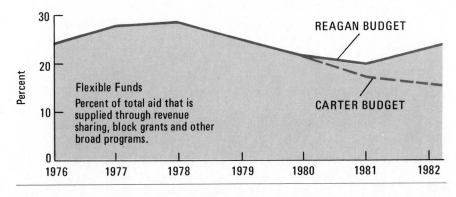

But Grants Now Have Fewer Strings Attached.

Flexible Funds
Percent of total aid that is supplied through revenue sharing, block grants and other broad programs.

Discretionary and Nondiscretionary Spending. Transfer payments are paid out mostly through **entitlement programs,** which define eligibility—who is covered and for how much—and permit any eligible person to claim the money. Control over this kind of spending has been difficult to achieve—a major reason for the mushrooming fiscal troubles of Social Security (see Chapter 15), the biggest of all entitlement programs. Officially described (in budget documents) as "relatively uncontrollable," this kind of spending is in effect **nondiscretionary.** The struggle to bring it under control was important to the politics of Ronald Reagan. Aid to governments is far easier to limit. If Congress appropriates, let us say, $5 million to support local sewer building, $5 million is all there is to be spent. Congress can directly limit the federal government's commitment, so these programs are called **discretionary spending.**

Because nondiscretionary spending is so hard to cut, direct aid to individuals (which is nondiscretionary) will tend to become a higher proportion of federal aid, even if aid to governments is not being cut. And when the federal government tries to cut its budget (see Chapters 11 and 15), it tends to cut discretionary rather than nondiscretionary spending.

The Politics of Control

In principle, block grants do have their advantages: They can increase the independence and administrative competence of state governments, lower the cost of federal programs, and make those programs more flexible. Yet even after a decade of much ballyhooed experiment with block grants, almost nine-tenths of the dollar amount of federal aid to the states was paid out in the form of categorical grants. Despite all the dark mumblings about centralization, the federal bureaucracy, and so on, Congress has relied chiefly on categorical grants because it fears that without them, many states would sabotage many programs—by willful noncompliance, administrative ineptitude, or, in some cases, outright corruption.

Why? Remember that the federal government often gets involved in social programs because their intended beneficiaries, the working class and the poor, lack strong political and social organization, especially as compared with similar groups in other democratic countries. In the United States, these groups often have no labor unions or sympathetic local political parties to pressure state governments. At the federal level, they are more strongly represented. Therefore they rely on the federal government both to fund programs that benefit them and to ensure that those programs are actually carried out.

SOME CONCLUSIONS

Ours is a large country, full of people who have diverse ideas about what is good, true, and beautiful. For the most part we fear and resent the idea of centralized government, much as the Framers of the Constitution did. This fear, handed down over generations, helps us to live under our noble but antique Constitution. Centralized government may be good enough for the British, French, or Swedes—to name only three peoples who govern themselves democratically—and most of the other peoples of the world, but it is not good enough for us.

Still, we pay a price for all good things. The price of federalism is the gross inequality among our fifty states. Each state provides its citizens with a different level of services. Civil liberties and civil rights are better protected in some states than in others, and some states' economies are much healthier than others.

Perhaps we shall remove these inequalities, perhaps not. In either case, some sort of federalism will survive, for it is a part of our culture as well as our politics.

SUMMARY

The federal system gives the federal government, on the one hand, and the states, on the other, an independent basis for existence. It was unique in 1787, when first created, and it still is. Most nations are ruled as unitary states; their regional governments carry out the orders of the central government and can be abolished by it. Certain other countries, the Soviet Union, for example, are federal in form but highly centralized in practice.

Federalism has deep roots in our political culture—in our fear of centralization and our cultural diversity. By and large, states' rights are supported by, and benefit, conservatives, but some liberals, too, are chiefly concerned to carry out their ideas on the local level. Most of them, however, look to nationwide schemes of improvement, and federalism frustrates such schemes.

The Framers of the Constitution did not attempt to settle in advance every conflict that might arise between the states and the federal government. Instead, they put together a comprehensible scheme and let us fill in the details. The Framers created the federal government mainly for the sake of economic development, liberty, foreign policy, stability, and defense. Most of the enumerated powers—those specifically granted to the federal government by the Constitution—deal with these functions. The Framers knew that these powers would not be sufficient, so they wrote into the Constitution the "elastic clause," giving Congress the right to pass laws "necessary and proper" to carry out its enumerated powers. Certain powers are denied to the states, again mainly to ensure the federal government's supremacy in the sphere of economics, defense, and foreign policy. The states were barred as well from threatening the rights of property by suspending the obligation to repay debts. Finally, the Constitution requires that the states cooperate among themselves.

Because our Constitution does not exhaustively separate the federal government's powers from those of the states, competition and conflict arise at the boundary points. Before any government can act, it must show that it has the right to do so. The U.S. Supreme Court took for itself the power of deciding who has the right to do what. We have accepted its claim because such decisions had to be made, and we had no other means of making them.

In *McCulloch* v. *Maryland* (1819), the Court (under Chief Justice John Marshall) ruled that the federal government does indeed have broad powers under the elastic clause. But later in the century, under the doctrine of dual federalism, the Court refused to let the federal government regulate intrastate commerce, which it defined quite broadly, to include all manufacturing. Not until the late 1930s did it permit the federal government to assume large powers of economic regulation.

States often resist the authority of the federal government but rarely its money. Federal grants-in-aid are of three kinds: categorical grants, made for specific programs; block grants, for broad categories of spending; and revenue-sharing, which can be spent as states and localities see fit. From the mid-1960s to the mid-1970s, states and localities became more dependent on federal grants but got more freedom in spending them. President Carter then shifted the emphasis back to federal controls.

President Reagan took office intending to restore "those powers granted to the states and to the people." During his first year in office, he proposed the creation of 6 new block grants, largely free of strings, to replace 85 categorical grants, largely controlled by the federal government. Mr. Reagan was denied the centerpiece of his New Federalism—the 6 block grants—but he did persuade Congress to accept a 25 percent cut in spending.

After two centuries, federalism is still an experiment. It is still in the forefront of political debate, still "in the news." It has evolved in ways that the Constitution's framers could not have anticipated and might well have disliked, but this means only that the country itself has evolved in ways they could not have anticipated and might not have liked.

The Civil War killed off the states'-rights theory of federalism. The Great Depression and the New Deal killed off dual federalism. The federal government now enjoys a supremacy that would surely have dismayed Thomas Jefferson and many other Founding Fathers. That supremacy is not at all likely to go away or even to be reduced very much in the foreseeable future.

On the other hand, as Chief Justice Salmon P. Chase (1864–1873) put it, "The Constitution, in all its provisions, looks to an indestructible Union, composed of indestructible states."[15] He wrote those words in 1869. They still ring true.

SUGGESTED READINGS

MICHAEL BARONE and GRANT UJIFUSA, *The Almanac of American Politics 1984.* Washington: Barone, 1983. A concrete, vivid monument to "sociological federalism."

DANIEL J. ELAZAR, *American Federalism: A View from the States,* 2nd ed. New York: Crowell, 1972. Stresses the sociological underpinnings of American federalism, particularly our political subcultures. See also DANIEL J. ELAZAR and JOSEPH ZIKMUND II, eds., *The Ecology of American Political Culture: Readings.* New York: Crowell, 1975.

ROBER A. GOLDWIN, ed., *A Nation of States,* 2nd ed. Chicago: Rand, 1974. A useful collection of articles by leading contemporary specialists.

MORTON GRODZINS, *The American System.* Chicago: Rand, 1966. An exceptionally illuminating study of American federalism.

ALEXANDER HAMILTON, JAMES MADISON, and JOHN JAY, *The Federalist.* Any edition, e.g., Cambridge: Harvard Univ., 1961. Written in 1788, these essays are a permanent contribution to the literature of political science and, in fact, to literature in general. Nos. 1–9, 21–23, and 25 discuss the reasons for changing over from a "league" to a federal republic. No. 39 gives a more general view of "republicanism, nationalism, federalism." The balance between federal and state powers is treated in Nos. 32, 41–46, and 82. You may read the immortal No. 10 in the Appendix to this book.

---

[15] *Texas* v. *White*, 7 Wall. 700 (1869).

JEFFREY L. PRESSMAN, *Federal Programs and City Politics: The Dynamics of the Aid Process in Oakland.* Berkeley: Univ. of California, 1975. Pressman's brillant case study shows how and why governments at different levels often fail to work together.

MICHAEL D. REAGAN, *The New Federalism.* New York: Oxford Univ. Press, 1972. Michael Reagan—no relation of Ronald Reagan—focuses upon the development of federal grants-in-aid, the states' dependence on them, and the federal government's growing dominance within the American political system.

chapter four

CIVIL LIBERTIES

A woman was brutally murdered in Boston—one more crime among all too many. The police came to suspect one of her boyfriends, Osborne Sheppard. But there was something a little special about this case. The detective who was investigating wanted to search Sheppard's house for incriminating evidence. Having failed to locate the warrant which was proper for murder investigations, he tried to alter a warrant form that was usually used in drug cases, and got a local judge to go along with the altered warrant. The detective had no trouble at all finding the incriminating evidence he was looking for, including bloodstained clothing, in Sheppard's house. He also got his conviction.

But the Supreme Judicial Court of Massachusetts overturned Sheppard's conviction because of the exclusionary rule: The search warrant was technically imperfect. The Fourth Amendment to the Constitution prescribes a ban against "unreasonable searches and seizures" by law enforcement officers. Like the rest of the Bill of Rights, the Fourth Amendment was adopted for very good reasons—here, to prevent the kind of official arbitrariness that had been very recent experience in colonial times. The police must have a judge approve a search warrant before they search. In 1914, the Supreme Court decided that the only sure way to keep federal law enforcement officers from getting too enthusiastic in their pursuit of criminal suspects was to set the suspects free if they had been convicted on illegally obtained evidence.[1] In 1961, the Court further came to the conclusion that this "exclusionary rule" applied to state criminal trials as well.[2] If the police search and seize without warrants, or with defective or "cooked-up" warrants, who is safe from the midnight knock at the

---

[1] *Weeks* v. *United States,* 232 U.S. 383 (1914).
[2] *Mapp.* v. *Ohio,* 367 U.S. 643 (1961).

door? On the other hand, if police and prosecutors can't get convictions from evidence they have illegally obtained, their motivation to take shortcuts like these will presumably disappear.

But Sheppard's case in Boston—like many other famous or near-famous cases—is a hard one. And it went to the U.S. Supreme Court for a final decision. As one Supreme Court Justice put the matter in an earlier case, "Is the criminal to go free because the constable has blundered?" The Supreme Court, we should remember, only gets the hard cases; the easy ones are decided further further down the judicial system. Where is the line to be drawn between protecting even the least upright of citizens against official lawlessness, and freeing the guilty on procedural technicalities? What does the Fourth Amendment really command in cases like this, considering earlier decisions about its meaning by the Supreme Court?

In the end, the Court's majority in the Sheppard case held that the warrant really was defective but that the police had acted in good faith, believing that their search of Sheppard's home had been lawful.[3] The ultimate blunder had been made by the magistrate in approving the defective warrant. And how could that fact contribute to the fundamental purpose of the exclusionary rule, to discourage illegality by the police? So the Supreme Court reversed the Massachusetts court's decision and upheld Sheppard's conviction.

Major civil liberties issues often turn on very fine points of interpretation that laymen find hard to understand. They almost always involve making difficult judgments on intrinsically hard cases, striking a balance between two competing and equally valid claims. In Osborne Sheppard's case, one claim is the right of society to deal effectively with a serious crime and punish the guilty. The other is the rule laid down by the Fourth Amendment, that "The right of the people to be secure in their persons, houses, papers, and effects, against unreasonable searches and seizures, shall not be violated."

LIBERTY

If there were only one human being in all the world, that person would enjoy absolute liberty. The reality is that many people pursue liberty, each of them as he or she sees it. If any large number of people claimed absolute liberty, human life would be so "nasty, brutish, and short"[4] that it would appeal only to the strong or the insane. For although we want liberty, we also want and need order.

Besides, even in an orderly society, the liberty of one person often conflicts with the liberty of another. You are free to open a business, but someone else is quite as free to set up shop across the street, compete with you, and drive you bankrupt. Liberty means risk. Not, however, unlimited risk. You are not free to hire criminals to destroy your competitor's business, for example. "Your freedom to move your arm ends where my nose begins," said John Stuart Mill (1806–1873), a celebrated British economic and political philosopher, more than a hundred years ago.

When governments help to reconcile the conflicting liberties of individuals, they are promoting liberty. But to maintain public order, governments must

---

[3] *Massachusetts* v. *Sheppard*, 52 L.W. 5177 (1984).
[4] Thomas Hobbes, *Leviathan* (1651).

also restrain the liberties of all individuals. Sometimes, too, governments restrain liberty because their own interests are distinct from the interests of the people they govern.

These two threats to liberty are inherent in any kind of government. Democratic governments, in addition, pose a special kind of threat. Democratic government is government by the majority. Often that majority is tolerant of minorities or, at any rate, indifferent to them. But when the majority loses its tolerance, it can oppress dissenters with a moral force that greatly exceeds anything an undemocratic government could draw upon. Wars and national emergencies tend to stimulate this kind of intolerance.

Even in theory, our American freedoms are neither complete nor absolute; nor, in practice, have we always managed to reconcile freedom and order, the rights of majorities and minorities, and the rights of different and differing individuals. But most of the time we have tried, and much of the time we have succeeded. That is a noble achievement.

"By a faction, I understand a number of citizens, whether amounting to a majority or minority of the whole, who are united and actuated by some common impulse of passion, or of interest, adverse to the rights of other citizens, or to the permanent and aggregate interests of the community."

James Madison,
The Federalist, Paper 10
1787

A Lesson from the Past

Few Americans deny that **civil liberties**—the right to speak, meet, read, and worship freely, and the right to a fair trial—are important. Yet many of us think we can give a little here and a little there, especially when it is other people's civil liberties that must be given up. Much of the time, we do indeed have to settle for something less than perfect liberty. But sometimes the price of order is too high. No mathematical formula can tell us when order is or is not worth the price.

To make up your own mind, study the past. Consider the case of one country that thought it could dispense with a few civil liberties. The country was Germany. Germany's political culture was without doubt different from ours, but during the 1920s, Germany was a democratic state with many civil liberties. In 1933, the National Socialists (Nazis) took power. They did not attack free institutions in a single blow; they undermined them one by one, bit by bit. As Protestant clergyman Martin Niemoeller has been reputed to say, they

came first for the Communists, and I didn't speak up because I wasn't a Communist. Then they came for the Jews, and I didn't speak up because I wasn't a Jew. Then they came for the trade unionists, and I didn't speak up because I wasn't a trade unionist. Then they came for the Catholics, and I didn't speak up because I was a Protestant.

Finally, they came for Martin Niemoeller. "By that time, no one was left to speak up."

"What About the Communists?"

It is easy to say that Democrats, Republicans, and political independents ought to enjoy freedom of speech. But should Communists? Or Nazis? Does it matter that neither Communists nor Nazis would protect the free speech of others? If we tried to deny free speech only to them and to people like them, would we threaten everyone's free speech in the long run?

These and many related questions have given the U.S. Supreme Court a great deal of work, especially during the past fifty or so years. One important reason is the fluid boundary between "speech" and "incitement to violence." When public passions run high and "radical agitators" seem to be dangerous, almost *any* speech they make will be viewed by many officials, and much of the public, as "incitement." Civil libertarians argue that except in extreme circumstances, we should "keep speech unfettered and . . . allow the processes of law to be invoked only when the provocateurs among us move from speech to action."[5]

Even those who adopt this as the ideal must still answer very hard practical questions, for in matters of speech (as with liberty in general), you often come very close to someone else's nose when you move your own arm.

THE U.S. BILL OF RIGHTS

The U.S. Constitution, as proposed in 1787, had few guarantees of personal and political rights, but only because the Framers thought that our system of government, with its divided and separated powers, would by nature protect those rights. Lack of specific guarantees was used as an argument against ratification, however, so the Federalists promised to add them. (See Chapter 2.)

The Federalists honored their commitment. After the first national elections, in 1788, Congress proposed a group of amendments, ten of which were ratified by the end of 1791. These ten, later called the U.S. Bill of Rights, laid the basis for our civil liberties.

The First Amendment is the "crown jewel" of the U.S. Bill of Rights. It explicitly bars Congress from passing any law to "establish" a church (see

[5] *Dennis* v. *U.S.*, 341 U.S. 494 (1951) (dissenting opinion).

The Fourth Amendment to the Constitution prohibits "unreasonable" searches and seizures. There have been a number of cases before the Supreme Court in the past 10 years on the issue of what constitutes "reasonable" search and seizure procedures.

Dennis Lake, Photo Researchers, Inc.

section following, on "Separation of Church and State"), and from abridging freedom of worship, petition, assembly, speech, or the press. Lawyers and officials mostly accept the "firstness" of the First Amendment; they view the rights created by it as "preferred" rights.

The Second and Third Amendments give the people of the United States the right to form militias, "to keep and bear Arms," and to curb the common eighteenth-century malpractice of forcibly boarding troops in the houses of private civilians. The Fourth through the Eighth Amendments were designed to protect the legal rights of individuals and to ensure that they got "due process of law." These amendments prohibit "unreasonable" searches and seizures, double jeopardy, compulsory self-incrimination in trials, cruel and unusual punishments, and excessive bails; ensure that trials must be open, public, and speedy; give defendants a right to counsel; and guarantee just compensation to people whose property has been seized by government **(eminent domain)**. The final two Amendments, Nine and Ten, make it clear that the states and the people have powers and liberties not enumerated in the U.S. Constitution.

Note that the U.S. Bill of Rights protects the people from the government and aims only to prevent the government and the political majority it represents from depriving individuals of their liberty. It was not meant to protect individuals from the purely private actions of other individuals. Parents, corporations, and churches can place all the mean and silly restraints they deem necessary on their children, employees, and members—even if those restraints undermine the spirit of the U.S. Bill of Rights.

Stan Wakefield

The Role of the Courts

Who shall protect our civil liberties—from ourselves, if need be? The President, who is elected by the majority and usually reflects its prejudices—or pretends to—cannot be relied upon to do so. Neither, for the same reason, can Congress. So it is up to the courts to protect our civil liberties. In particular, it is to federal judges, who are appointed rather than elected, and who serve as judges for life (see Chapter 14). Protecting civil liberties is the job of the least democratic branch of the government, precisely because it is the least democratic, since the will of the majority is among the greatest threats to individual liberty.

The courts give reality and meaning to our constitutional rights by interpreting them, deciding when they have been violated, and applying broad principles to particular cases. They adapt our eighteenth-century Constitution to the problems, needs, and follies of the present. Despite all the talk about **strict construction**—taking the text of the Constitution literally—judges have no choice but to adapt it.

For example, in 1791, when the Fourth Amendment, which prohibits "unreasonable searches and seizures," was ratified, there were no telephones and therefore no telephone wiretaps. Are wiretaps "reasonable"? The answer is not in the U.S. Constitution—not in so many words, at any rate. Besides, "unreasonable" is not a very clear word even when applied to the kinds of searches and seizures that people did know about 200 years ago. And what is meant by a "speedy" trial, "due process of law," and "excessive" bail? The courts must take these undefined and open-ended words and phrases from the heaven of the Constitution and bring them down to earth.

"We are under a Constitution, but the Constitution is what the judges say it is, and the judiciary is the safeguard of our liberty and of our property under the Constitution."

Charles Evans Hughes,
Chief Justice of the
U.S. Supreme Court, 1930–1941.
From a speech made in 1907

"Incorporation": The Bill of Rights and the States

When the federal government was born, in 1789, several of the thirteen original states were over 150 years old. All thirteen of them had their own political traditions and systems of government. By 1842, however, all of them had adopted constitutions similar in form to the U.S. Constitution, including more or less extensive bills of rights. Indeed, two of the earliest bills of rights—those of Virginia (1776) and Massachusetts (1780)—had helped to shape the U.S. Bill of Rights.

These state bills of rights were broadly similar to the federal one, but each was different and each was interpreted by a separate state court system. The citizens of different states, therefore, had different civil liberties, since the U.S. Bill of Rights restrained only the federal government.

Barron v. *Baltimore.* Between 1815 and 1822, the City of Baltimore decided to improve a few roads and streets. While making these improvements, the city diverted several streams, which deposited silt in Mr. John Barron's wharf. As a result, the wharf could no longer be used by large ships.

John Barron sued in federal court, claiming that the city had violated the Fifth Amendment, which (among other things) prohibits private property from being seized for public use "without just compensation." But when the case worked its way up to the U.S. Supreme Court, in 1833, the Court ruled that the U.S. Bill of Rights (including the Fifth Amendment) restricted only the federal government, not states and localities. Note that this opinion[6] was written by that archnationalist, Chief Justice John Marshall (see Chapter 3).

Barron v. *Baltimore* recognized what was truly a dual system of rights. The federal government had to respect the basic personal and political freedoms protected by the federal Bill of Rights. State governments, however, were restricted only by their own bills of rights, as interpreted by their own state courts. Until 1818, for example, The Congregational Church was established in Connecticut—and until 1830 in Massachusetts. The ministers of the church performed a number of state-related functions, among them delivering special election sermons before political elections. This practice was counter to the First Amendment of the U.S. Bill of Rights, but it was allowed by the respective states.

The Fourteenth Amendment. The dual system of rights persisted without serious legal challenge until 1868, when the Fourteenth Amendment was ratified. One clause of that amendment reads, "nor shall any *State* [my italics] deprive any person of life, liberty or property without due process of law." The **due-process clause,** as it has come to be known, invokes certain rights and, for the first time, prohibited the states from violating them. Certain legal scholars argued that the clause, in effect, "incorporated" the U.S. Bill of Rights into the Fourteenth Amendment, or that the amendment had extended the U.S. Bill of Rights, wholly or in part, to the states. They claimed, so to speak, that the due-process clause should be interpreted to read, "nor shall any State deprive any person of life, liberty, or property unless it observes the U.S. Bill of Rights." This reading of the clause was called the **incorporation theory.**

---

[6] *Barron* v. *Baltimore,* 7 Pet. 243 (1833).

Selective Incorporation. The U.S. Supreme Court has never fully accepted the incorporation theory. Only "fundamental" rights—those essential to liberty and justice—have been incorporated and must therefore be respected by the states.[7]

Which rights are indeed "fundamental"? It has been a long road, and by no means a straight one, but by now the Court has moved close to the view that all the major guarantees of the U.S. Bill of Rights are binding on the fifty states. At least four rights have not so far been incorporated: The Court has yet to rule on the right to keep and bear arms and the right to refuse to quarter soldiers (see Chapter 2). It *has* expressly ruled that the right to a grand jury hearing and the right to trial by jury in civil suits are not fundamental. Any of these four provisions might still be incorporated, but there has been little pressure on the Court to do so. The Eighth Amendment's ban on excessive bail and fines remains "unincorporated," but the Court would today regard such excesses as at least a violation of the basic standard of fairness the due process clause enshrines.

With these exceptions, the federal government and the states must now respect the same civil liberties. Incorporation, although selective, has created a uniform set of guarantees against abuses by all levels of government. The conservative Burger Court however, has begun to move the other way, notably in the very thorny field of Fourth Amendment search-and-seizure standards as applied to the states (see below). Most of the judicial incorporation of the past twenty years has probably come to stay, but the pendulum has by no means stopped moving. What seems to be happening is that some state courts, interpreting their own state constitutions, have become more protective of individual liberty than the U.S. Supreme Court has been in its interpretation of the Bill of Rights.

Rights in Conflict

Again and again, surveys and public opinion polls show that most of our people support the U.S. Bill of Rights. But this support is largely symbolic. When we get down to tough and concrete cases, opinion is often much more divided.[8] After all, the acid test of freedom of speech is "freedom for the thought that you hate," not for politically neutral or popular views. The rights of people caught up in the toils of the law present very similar problems. Pillars of society, and even ordinary people, rarely go on trial for serious crimes. When they do, they are well supplied with counsel and other legal defenses. Most of the leading criminal-procedure cases have involved rather unpleasant people who were in very big trouble—people like Danny Escobedo or Ernesto Miranda, for example (see below). When rights conflict, the boundaries between them must usually be drawn by the U.S. Supreme Court.

An Example: Public Speech versus Public Safety. On a day in 1946, a defrocked Catholic priest named Arthur Terminiello gave a speech in a Chicago auditorium. He attacked the Roosevelt Administration, blacks, Jews, and the "scum" who ran the government, but he did not suggest that any violent action be taken against them. Outside, a large crowd broke windows,

---

[7] *Palko* v. *Connecticut*, 302 U.S. 319 (1937).

[8] For a somewhat earlier but illuminating study on this point, see Samuel Stouffer, *Communism, Conformity and Civil Liberties* (New York: Doubleday, 1955).

"If there is any principle of the Constitution that more imperatively calls for attachment than any other it is the principle of free thought—not free thought for those who agree with us but freedom for the thought that we hate."

Oliver Wendell Holmes, Jr.,

Justice of the U.S. Supreme Court, 1902–1932. From *U.S.* v. *Schwimmer*, 279 U.S. 644, 653 (1928)

One conflict of rights is the right to freedom of speech versus the right of public safety or public order. Recently the Supreme Court has weighed heavily on the claims to free speech, even if they do conflict with public order.

threw stink bombs, battered down the doors, and fought with the police. It was Terminiello—however—not any member of the crowd—who was convicted by a local court for creating a breach of the peace.

Terminiello could pretty accurately be described as a fascist rabblerouser, but he was simply speaking his mind, such as it was. Do American citizens have a right to free speech only when their opinions are respectable, responsible, and intelligent? Who is to decide if someone's opinions *are* respectable, responsible, and intelligent? And don't the opinions have to be made known before anyone can tell?

Terminiello appealed his conviction right up to the U.S. Supreme Court. The City of Chicago argued that his remarks presented a "clear and present danger" to the peace and thus were not protected by the First Amendment. The Court did not agree: Speaking for the majority, Justice William O. Douglas (1939–1975) found that freedom of speech is meant "to invite dispute," even if it "induces a condition of unrest, creates dissatisfaction with things as they are, or even stirs the people to anger."[9] Terminiello's conviction was therefore thrown out, but the majority was a narrow one. A dissenting justice, Robert Jackson (1941–1954), suggested:

> The choice is not between order and liberty. It is between liberty with order and anarchy without either. There is danger that if the Court does not temper its doctrinaire logic with a little practical wisdom, it will convert the constitutional Bill of Rights into a suicide pact.

In fact, two years later the Court ruled the other way in a case similar to Terminiello's. A man named Feiner, a sidewalk orator in New York City, used derogatory and "inflammatory" language against the President, other public officials, and the American Legion. The small crowd around him got restive. A police officer ordered the speaker to stop and arrested him for breach of peace when he refused. Feiner's First Amendment claim was rejected by the

---

[9] *Terminiello* v. *Chicago*, 337 U.S. 1 (1949).

U.S. Supreme Court, however, since the Court felt that in this case, there had indeed been a "clear and present danger" of imminent riot.[10] More recently, the Court has gone much further in supporting claims to free speech, even if they conflict with public order.

In 1969, with no dissents, the Court declared that the Constitution does not "permit a state to forbid or prosecute advocacy of the use of force or of law violation except where such advocacy is directed to inciting or producing imminent lawless action and is likely to incite or produce such action."[11] That is coming very close to saying "almost anything goes."

---

[10] *Feiner* v. *New York,* 340 U.S. 315 (1951).
[11] *Brandenburg* v. *Ohio,* 395 U.S. 444 (1969).

A Right to Privacy?

Most civil liberties are mentioned in the text of the U.S. Constitution or its amendments. Some freedoms come into existence by judicial interpretation, however. One, the "right to privacy," was officially granted constitutional status by the U.S. Supreme Court in 1965, with its decision in the case of *Griswold* v. *Connecticut,* in which it struck down Connecticut's ban on the sale and use of birth-control devices.

A majority of the Court accepted the idea of a right to privacy, but there was much disagreement about the source of that right. Justice William O. Douglas argued that the explicit prohibitions of unreasonable searches and seizures, compulsory self-incrimination, or quartering of soldiers, together with all the

freedoms of expression and religious belief, combined to form a right to privacy. Chief Justice Earl Warren and Justices Arthur Goldberg and William Brennan thought that the right of privacy was also protected by the Ninth Amendment. Justice John Harlan regarded privacy as a part of the Fourteenth Amendment's guarantee of due process of law. Justices Hugo Black and Potter Stewart dissented, expressing reluctance to create rights that are not specifically set forth in the U.S. Constitution.

Whatever may legitimate the right to privacy, the Court has protected it since *Griswold.* Some of the Court's later decisions that deal with the right to privacy are briefly summarized below:

Stanley v. *Georgia* (1969)	The Court upheld the right to read and view obscene material in the privacy of the home.
Eisenstadt v. *Baird* (1972)	A Massachusetts law prohibiting the distribution of birth-control devices to unmarried people was here ruled unconstitutional.
Roe v. *Wade* (1973)	A woman's decision whether or not to terminate a pregnancy is protected (with some qualifications) against state encroachment by the right to privacy.
Planned Parenthood of Central Missouri v. *Danforth* (1976)	A pregnant woman's right to decide whether to terminate a pregnancy cannot be legally contingent upon consent of her husband (if married) or her parents (if a minor).
Carey v. *Population Services* (1977)	A New York law prohibiting the distribution of birth-control devices to persons under sixteen years of age is unconstitutional.
Akron v. *Akron Center for Reproductive Health* (1983)	The abortion right prevents government from requiring that all abortions after the first trimester be performed in a hospital.

An Example: Freedom of Religion versus Freedom from Religion. Not long ago, many teachers began the school day by reading the Lord's Prayer. In fact, the state of Pennsylvania required the reading of no fewer than ten verses from the Bible. When the law was challenged, in the early 1960s, the state argued that it merely aimed to help the students exercise their constitutional right to pray. The plaintiffs (those who were challenging the law) argued that the Bible readings were an establishment of religious beliefs contrary to their own. The U.S. Supreme Court not only struck down the law but implied that governments could not even encourage voluntary prayer in public schools.[12] In effect, it ruled that state sponsorship of religion amounted to establishment of religion, and it decided that prohibiting such an establishment was more important than the right to pray in public schools. Of course, the ruling in no way affected the right of purely private prayer in public schools.

An Example: Press Freedom versus Privacy. In 1971, six men brutally raped and murdered an eleven-year-old girl in Atlanta. The state of Georgia had passed a law against reporting the name of any rape victims, but a local TV station violated this law. The station was then sued by the victim's father, who claimed that it had trampled on his family's right of privacy. The U.S. Supreme Court's decision: The public's right to know and the stations freedom of speech outweighed the family's right to privacy.[13]

The Inescapable Need for Choice. Only hard cases reach the U.S. Supreme Court. The choices the Court must make are sometimes agonizing, and its decisions often provoke bitter dispute—even among Americans who support the Bill of Rights.

People like Terminiello, who deliberately inflame racist passions, are contemptible, but how easy it would be for public officials to suppress dissent by using their police powers! School prayer may be harmless in itself and acceptable to most people. Even so, what about the rights of that minority of Americans who pay for the public schools but do not believe in the Judeo-Christian Supreme Being or the divine origin of the Bible? And if states can require the reading of verses from the Bible, can they require readings from only the New Testament—that is, only Christian verses? As for the parents of that poor girl in Atlanta, it is easy to understand why they wanted to grieve in private. Yet the freedom of the press is so close to the core of our political liberty that any infringement diminishes the liberty of all Americans.

None of these decisions was conclusively "right," and none, perhaps, could have been; there are reasonable things to be said on both sides. Yet, the nine justices of the U.S. Supreme Court—who are also nine fallible human beings, despite their eminence—must somehow resolve such problems. As Justice Robert Jackson put it, "We [the Justices] are not final because we are infallible, but we are infallible only because we are final."[14]

FREEDOM OF SPEECH

In 1948, the Soviet Union's leading jurist, Andrei Vishinsky, observed that "in our Soviet state, naturally there can be no place for freedom of speech, press

---

[12] *Abington School District* v. *Schempp*, 374 U.S. 203 (1963); *Engel* v. *Vitale*, 370 U.S. 421 (1962).
[13] *Cox Broadcasting* v. *Cohn*, 420 U.S. 469 (1975).
[14] *Brown* v. *Allen*, 344 U.S. 443 (1953).

and so on for the foes of socialism.[15] Much later, in December 1981, Poland's Communist government declared martial law and tried to destroy the Solidarity labor union to suppress freedom of speech and political organization. Throughout the ages, all dictatorships of whatever kind have done the same. Of all the rights in the U.S. Constitution, freedom of speech and its cousins, freedom of press and assembly, are of fundamental importance— something that should be as obvious to all free people as it was to those who reject freedom. For if you do not have these rights, you have no political or civil rights.

So the U.S. Supreme Court, in recent decades, has bestowed a preferred position on First Amendment rights in general, and freedom of speech in particular. A preferred position, but not an absolute one. True, the words of the First Amendment do seem absolute: "Congress shall make no law . . . abridging the freedom of speech, or of the press; or the right of the people peaceably to assemble, and to petition the Government for a redress of grievances." Still, certain state and federal laws—those dealing with obscenity, false advertisements, libel, shouting in courtrooms, transferring military secrets to the enemy, and illegal picketing—do limit freedom of speech, and the courts have accepted the need for these limits. As Justice Oliver W. Holmes (1902–1932) put it, freedom of speech does not allow you falsely to yell "Fire!" in a crowded theater. The limits, in other words, balance the claims of free speech with those of public order and morals, and also with those of national security.

Even so, unpopular and cantankerous minorities have substantial protection. But these protections partly reflect the very accurate judgment that internal dissenters against our political, economic, and social order pose no serious threat to it. We have not always felt this secure against minorities. In fact, our level of protection is now this high because, among other reasons, the courts have reacted against the flagrant excesses committed in the past. The

---

[15] Quoted by Justice Douglas in *Dennis* v. *United States*, 341 U.S. 494 (1951) (dissenting opinion).

"Congress shall make no law . . . abridging the freedom of speech, or of the press; or the right of the people peaceably to assemble, and to petition the Government for a redress of grievances." The First Amendment.

record of these excesses is extensive and not at all pretty. Yet it should also remind us that judges, elected officials, and the American people have learned a good deal from their mistakes.

Free Expression and National Security

Nothing tests freedom like war, for nothing so threatens the majority's sense of security. Wars, too, often create a sense of national unity, but with a dark side: persecution of minorities outside that unity. Governments sometimes exploit this sense of national unity by creating internal enemies, usually minorities that the government finds troublesome.

The Sedition Act of 1798. The story of the first "mood crisis" that threatened our civil liberties began in France, in 1789, with the French Revolution. John Adams, our second President (1797–1801) and a Federalist, actively opposed the French revolutionists and waged a "half war" against them. The Federalists' Jeffersonian rivals (see Chapter 9) sympathized with a revolution they regarded as democratic in its aims. Strong attacks on Adams and his policy appeared in the Jeffersonian press and in Jeffersonian oratory.

Congress, dominated by the Federalists, passed a number of laws designed to quash these attacks. The Sedition Act of 1798, the most notorious, made it a crime to speak or print "any false, scandalous, and malicious" attack on the President, the Congress, or the government as a whole, or to publish anything that might bring them "into contempt or disrepute." In so many words, the act made it a crime to oppose the government either in speech or in print.

Twenty-five people, mostly Jeffersonians, were arrested under the Sedition Act and ten were convicted. Then the tables were turned; the Jeffersonians won the presidential election of 1800. The Sedition Act expired soon after, in March 1801; our country was well rid of it.

Back to Normal. The Sedition Act was hardly typical of our early history. The role of the federal government was then very limited. There was no FBI, no CIA (see Chapter 12), no other agency that could investigate or repress sedition, real or imagined. Military intelligence agencies did not exist until the late nineteenth century, and for a very long time thereafter they had only small staffs, which merely kept track of foreign military developments. Even if the national government had the will to attack civil liberties—and it rarely did—it usually did not have the means. Whatever censoring of opinion occurred was largely the work of state and local governments. This should not be surprising because, until recently, most government policies in this country were made and carried out by state and local governments.

Free Speech and the Civil War. The next major crisis—in many respects the worst in American history—erupted with the War between the States, the Civil War (1861–1865). In 1860 and 1861, eleven southern states seceded from the Union. Faced with a supreme crisis, President Abraham Lincoln (1861–1865) committed a number of outright violations of the U.S. Constitution. For example, he suspended the writ of *habeas corpus* (see Chapter 2) without authorization from Congress; he had leading southern sympathizers arrested and confined to Fort McHenry, Fort Warren, and other "American bastilles" without trial or any kind of due process. There were many Confederate sympathizers in the North. In September 1861, to prevent the Maryland legislature from passing an ordinance of secession, he sent the army to disperse it. In 1864, conditions in Kentucky had so deteriorated that Mr. Lincoln proclaimed martial law for the entire state. In Indiana, whose southern half was a hotbed of "Copperhead" (pro-Confederate) opposition to the Union war effort, military courts tried and convicted many people suspected of sedition.

This was all very serious business, and Mr. Lincoln was strongly criticized at the time as a "dictator." Yet there is another side to the coin. The President defended his actions as necessary to preserve the Union and thus the Constitution itself. Neither he nor the Republican party in Congress attempted to use the suppression of rebellion and sedition as a means of suppressing political opposition, nor did they seek any equivalent of the Sedition Act of 1798 (or the later Sedition Act of 1918 or the Smith Act of 1940). Considering the circumstances, speech and the press remained very free, and free elections continued to be held throughout the war, while the Democrats came out (in the 1864 election) for peace on Confederate terms.

The repression of rebels and seditious persons ended very soon after the crisis that had occasioned drastic measures. Subsequently, there were indeed occasional gross abuses against the freedoms of speech, press, and assembly—directed, for example, against blacks and Republicans in the South, after 1877, and against labor "agitators." But these abuses took place at the state and local level, and almost all of them were beyond the reach of the federal courts as the U.S. Supreme Court then defined the situation.

World War I. When the United States entered World War I, in 1917, a sudden and extraordinary outburst of public and official panic was directed against two groups: Americans with obvious personal links to Germany and Austria-Hungary, on the one hand—the "Great Hun Scare"—and socialists and other left-wing radicals opposed to the "imperialist war," on the other—the "Great Red Scare."

The Espionage and Sedition Acts of 1917 and 1918 made it illegal to say or do anything that might impair the American war effort, however remotely, or give aid or comfort to the enemy. Section 5, for instance, forbade anyone from "uttering, printing, writing, or publishing any disloyal, profane, scurrilous, or abusive language, or language intended to cause contempt, scorn, contumely or disrepute as regards the form of government of the United States." Anyone violating any provision of the act was liable to a fine of $10,000 or twenty years' imprisonment, or both.

Prosecutions under this and related statutes were, to say the least, frequent, vigorous, and sweeping. Some were rather whimsical. One case involved the suppression through censorship of a standard Hollywood historical movie about the American Revolution.[16] Why? Because such a film would tend to bring our British allies into public disrepute and thus impair the war effort. With this case as the standard, anything could and did go.

Many crimes prosecuted under these and similar acts were thought-crimes, pure and simple: One man, for example, was convicted for writing newspaper articles praising the German people and denouncing American entry into the war,[17] another for distributing leaflets urging draftees to resist the war.[18] A

---

[16] *U.S.* v. *The Spirit of '76*, 252 Fed. 946 D.C.S.D. Cal. (1917).

[17] *Frohwerk* v. *U.S.*, 249 U.S. 204 (1919).

[18] *Schenck* v. *U.S.*, 249 U.S. 47 (1919).

> *"We must learn to welcome and not to fear the voices of dissent. We must dare to think about 'unthinkable things' because when things become unthinkable, thinking stops and action becomes mindless."*
>
> **J. William Fulbright,**
> U.S. Senator, Speech in the Senate, 1964

Socialism

One case under the Sedition Act involved a man named Abrams who was accused and convicted of throwing out of a window some leaflets calling for the workers of the world to unite and praising the Russian Revolution. Abrams was sentenced—to 20 years in prison—by Judge Henry D. Clayton, who as a congressman had been one of the sponsors of the Clayton Antitrust Act (1914). Just before pronouncing sentence, Clayton said:

These defendants took the stand. They talked about capitalism and producers, and I tried to figure out what a capitalist and what a producer is as contemplated by them. After listening carefully to all they had to say, I came to the conclusion that a capitalist is a man with a decent suit of clothes, a minimum of $1.25 in his pocket, and a good character.

And when I tried to find out what the prisoners had produced, I was unable to find out anything at all. So far as I can learn, not one of them ever produced so much as a single potato. The only thing they know how to raise is hell, and to direct it against the government of the United States.

Zechariah Chafee Jr., *Free Speech in the United States* (Cambridge: Harvard Univ., 1941), p. 76.

third—who threw out of a window some leaflets that praised the Russian Revolution of November 1917 and urged the workers of the world to unite—was sentenced to 20 years in prison.[19] A woman named Anita Whitney was convicted (under a similar California statute) of belonging to an organization that advocated the violent overthrow of the government.[20] Eugene V. Debs, the Socialist candidate for president in 1912, was given a ten-year sentence for giving an antiwar speech.[21] (In 1920, while in federal prison, Debs again ran for President and got almost 1 million votes.) Each of these convictions was upheld by the U.S. Supreme Court.

Another federal statute, the Alien Act of 1918, granted the U.S. Attorney General sweeping powers to identify and deport "undesirable" aliens, chiefly radicals. However, only a warrant signed by the U.S. secretary of labor could lead to an effective arrest—a "safeguard" that had important consequences. In January 1920, President Woodrow Wilson's (1913–1921) Attorney General, A. Mitchell Palmer, organized a nationwide sweep of aliens suspected of belonging to the Communist Labor party. Many people were seized and searched without warrants, and a number of suspects eventually wound up in detention camps. One-third of the detainees were finally released for want of evidence, and very few were actually deported largely because of a very sharp conflict between Attorney General Palmer and Secretary of Labor William A. Wilson. The so-called Palmer Raids were the high-water mark of the Red Scare.

World War II and Its Aftermath. By 1920, the Sedition Act (and others like it) had been repealed, and the Red Scare had come to an end. World War II produced relatively few threats to civil liberties, although it did cause the federal government to place some 100,000 Japanese-Americans in detention

---

[19] *Abrams* v. *U.S.*, 250 U.S. 616 (1919).

[20] *Whitney* v. *California*, 274 U.S. 357 (1927).

[21] *Debs* v. *U.S.*, 249 U.S. 211 (1919).

Are You Now or Have You Ever Been a Communist?

From 1947 to 1956, tens of thousands of federal employees had to go before loyalty boards to keep their jobs by proving that they were not subversives. U.S. Civil Service Commission files record some of the questions put to them:

A geographer was asked:

"Have you provided any sort of religious training for your children?"

"Have you indicated that you favor redistribution of wealth?"

"Do you have any favorite newspaper columnists of the day?"

"Do you have any favorite radio or TV news commentators or news analysts?"

"Were you a regular purchaser of *The New York Times?*"

This question was put to an employee of the State Department:

"Have you ever discussed the subject of the dance in Russia with [deleted]?"

Another State Department employee was asked:

"What were your feelings at the time concerning racial equality? How about civil rights?"

An Interior Department employee was asked:

"At one time, or two, were you a strong advocate of the United Nations? Are you still?"

Other employees heard these questions:

"Have you ever had Negroes in your home?"

"There is a suspicion in the record that you are in sympathy with the underprivileged. Is this true?"

"When you were in [deleted's] home, did [deleted's] wife dress conventionally when she received her guests?"

"What do you think of female chastity?"

"When did you become engaged to your wife? You were married, I think, in May—when did you reach some sort of understanding?"

Perhaps 40,000 federal civilian employees were subjected to full-scale investigations during those 10 years. About 2,700 were dismissed for subversive activities or entanglements, and about 12,000 resigned.

From David Caute, *The Great Fear* (New York: Simon & Schuster, 1978), pp. 267–93; Robert Justin Goldstein, *Political Repression in Modern America* (New York: Schenkman Publishing Co., Inc., 1978), p. 303.

camps. For reasons described in Chapter 5, that action was a violation of civil rights, not of civil liberties.

At the war's end, communism seemed to be on the march everywhere. The U.S. Communist party had no real importance, but it was the most visible and nearest form of communism. The Republican party accused the Democrats of being "soft on communism," but it was the Democrats—the Justice Department of the Truman administration (1945–1953)—who first began to prosecute members of "the party" and its sympathizers, mostly under the Smith Act (1940) and the Internal Security Act (1950). (The Smith Act had first been used against Trotskyists—dissident Communists—much to the orthodox Communists' delight. It should be noted here that those who most need civil liberties often do not believe in them.) These two acts had made it illegal to teach, advocate, or belong to a group advocating the violent overthrow of the government, and they required Communist organizations to register with the government.

McCarthyism. From 1939 on, conservatives dominated Congress. Republicans and southern Democrats were hostile to the New Deal (see Chapter 10) and to the leftist ideas within it. The House "Dies Committee," named after Martin Dies, the Texas Democrat who chaired it, was set up in 1939 to investigate radicals. Later it was made permanent, as the House Un-American Activities Committee (HUAC). In early 1950, Senator Joseph McCarthy (R-Wis.) entered the lists by claiming that Communist subversion and

Senator Joseph R. McCarthy at the Army-McCarthy hearings. The senator started his attack on actors, retired dentists, writers, and the like. In 1954, he took on the army, and it destroyed him.

"The master myth of the cold war is that the Communist bloc is a monolith, composed of governments which are not really governments at all, but organized conspiracies . . . all equally resolute and implacable in their determination to destroy the free world."

J. William Fulbright,

U.S. Senator, Speech in the Senate, 1964

infiltration flourished throughout the federal government. McCarthy was an important actor in the Red Scare of 1950–1954, but politicians of both parties gave him much company.

At first, the U.S. Supreme Court shared the public's fear of communism and its desire to take strong measures against it. In 1951, the Court went along with the federal government's prosecution of eleven Communist leaders accused of violating the Smith Act by forming a group to overthrow the government by force. The Court admitted that the eleven Communists had never actually used violence but argued that the government did not dare wait for them to act, since waiting would mean "that the Communist plotting is protected during its period of incubation." If the government could "move only after imminent action" had been taken, it "would, of course, be too late."[22]

Was this really so obvious? The advocates of civil liberties for Communists did not and do not claim that communism is a good thing; they hold only that there is a clear distinction between "thought" and "action," and that however earnestly the Communists may yearn to overthrow the government, their yearnings alone are ineffectual. Nonetheless, the Court had given a green light to further prosecutions. From 1951 to 1956, the government (controlled by the Republicans after 1952) tried and convicted 121 additional Communists. The Court allowed all 121 convictions to stand.

As the American public began to get used to the reality of Soviet power, Congress turned to other issues. Many anti-Communist laws were struck down by the U.S. Supreme Court, which made others, like the Smith Act, unenforceable; still others were repealed by Congress or they expired.

Vietnam. Unlike our other wars, the war in Vietnam (see Chapter 17) produced little sense of national unity or patriotism—in fact, it was downright unpopular. Opposition was so widespread that it could not be blamed on "enemies," not, at any rate, without attacking millions of people. So there were relatively few threats to civil liberties during the war, and the U.S.

---

[22] *Dennis* v. *U.S.*, 341 U.S. 494 (1951).

Supreme Court did not always support the government when it did threaten them. In 1968, it is true, the Court upheld the conviction of a young man who burned his draft card as an antiwar protest, refusing to view the act as "symbolic speech," protected by the First Amendment.[23] A year later, however, it decided that officials could not suspend students who had protested against the war by wearing black armbands to school.[24] In 1974, it struck down the conviction of a student who had flown an American flag with a peace symbol on it.[25]

Freedom of Speech versus Public Order

The officials who prevented their students from wearing black armbands in school said that they aimed only to keep order, not to suppress unpopular opinions. The Court replied that free speech is more important than order.

Suppose, however, that the Ku Klux Klan (KKK), with its long history of racist hostility against blacks, were to hold a rally in a black neighborhood. There would surely be violence, perhaps deaths. Should the police stop such a rally? Do they have the right to? Is that right consistent with civil liberties?

These are hard questions to answer, and even if you answer all of them in the affirmative, there are more questions to answer. When do the police stop the rally, for example? Before it even starts? After it starts but before anyone makes a racist speech? After the speeches but before the audience reacts violently? Or only after the actual violence begins?

A Clear and Present Danger. No formula or test for deciding when the government may limit free speech has ever been supported by a majority of the Court for any length of time. The most famous of all its efforts to devise such a formula is the **clear-and-present-danger test,** first devised by Mr. Justice Holmes. Holmes wanted courts to consider not only the content of a speech but also the circumstances in which it was given. The important question is whether or not "the words are used in such circumstances and are of such a nature as to create a clear and present danger that they will bring about a substantive evil," such as violence, "which government has the right to prevent."[26]

The clear-and-present-danger standard is anything but precise, and different Court majorities at different times have interpreted it in many ways. This lack of consistency itself generated much criticism from civil libertarians. Justice Hugo L. Black (1937–1971) insisted that the First Amendment's ban against congressional action restricting free expression was absolute, or nearly so. Otherwise, he argued, it could be set aside whenever Congress and the Court wanted to do so. In fact, over the years, the Court's decisions have come closer to Black's absolute view than ever before.

"Fighting Words." One day in 1942, a man named Chaplinsky, who belonged to the Jehovah's Witnesses, gave a speech in Rochester, New Hampshire. He attacked other Christian churches and, in particular, called Roman Catholicism a "racket." Chaplinsky's audience jeered and threatened him. Instead of

---

[23] *U.S.* v. *O'Brien,* 391 U.S. 905 (1969).

[24] *Tinker* v. *Des Moines School District,* 393 U.S. 503 (1969).

[25] *Spence* v. *Washington,* 418 U.S. 405 (1974).

[26] *Schenck* v. *United States,* 249 U.S. 47 (1919).

Bringing the war home, students at the University of California (Berkeley) demonstrate in 1966 against the Vietnam War.

waiting for the fun to start, the police decided to move him away from the crowd, but when they seized him, he resisted and shouted at the city marshal, "You are a goddamned racketeer" and "the whole city government of Rochester are fascists or agents of fascists." He was then arrested, charged with violating a law against calling another person "offensive and derisive names" in public, and convicted.

Chaplinsky appealed all the way up to the U.S. Supreme Court, and there he lost. The Court ruled that his personal attacks on the city marshal were not protected speech, and that profane, libelous, or insulting words "are of such slight social value, that any benefit to be derived from them is clearly outweighed by the social interest in order and morality." However, it denied First Amendment protections only to "fighting words," not to the substance of Chaplinsky's attacks on other Christian churches.[27]

Demonstrations. Suppose a group of people go to Washington, D.C., march down Pennsylvania Avenue, gather on the steps of the Capitol, make speeches for this or against that, and deliver a petition to Congress. These rights—the freedoms of speech, assembly, and petition—are all protected by the First Amendment. Among the complaints of the American colonists against George III were his government's efforts to interfere with just these freedoms.

But here too there are limits. Demonstrations can disturb the public convenience, which local officials—if they do not discriminate in any way—can protect by requiring demonstrators to apply for licenses. Of course, demonstrations with the avowed object of disrupting the government can be, and have been, suppressed by the police; like "fighting words," they have not been granted First Amendment protection by the courts.

The Court seems increasingly willing to allow government regulation of the *way* or manner in which a demonstration is carried out, so long as the regulation is not based on content (that is, so long as the restriction is not

---

[27] *Chaplinsky* v. *New Hampshire*, 315 U.S. 568 (1942).

aimed at the idea or message the demonstration is supposed to convey). For instance, to protest budget cutbacks that some thought harmed the poor, the Community for Creative Non-Violence, a Washington organization, set up a tent city in Lafayette Park, just across Pennsylvania Avenue from the White House. The goal was to dramatize the plight of homeless people. Lafayette Park is under the supervision of the National Park Service of the Department of the Interior. Park Service regulations permitted a 24-hour vigil in Lafayette Park but banned sleeping and camping. Members of CCNV contended that sleeping and camping were constitutionally protected forms of speech essential to conveying their message. Not so, said seven justices of the Supreme Court. As long as the regulations (1) were applied equally to everyone, (2) were not designed to squelch particular points of view, and (3) were intended to serve a significant government interest (such as protecting the beauty of the park), they were valid under the First Amendment. Besides, the majority reasoned, sleeping and camping were not the only means to convey criticism of the President's budget policies.[28]

Freedom of the Press

Thomas Jefferson once wrote that if forced to choose between "a government without newspapers or newspapers without a government" he would "not hesitate for a moment to prefer the latter." Think of anything that is important to you: the rate of inflation, the rate of unemployment, books, movies, and records. We know about these things only because the press tells us about them.

We often complain about the irresponsibility of the press, and sometimes these complaints are valid. But the press of Jefferson's day was far more irresponsible than that of our own, and Jefferson was its frequent victim. As with other freedoms, the case for freedom of the press does not rest on the virtues of individual newspapers and reporters but on the role that the mass media and reporters play in our society—despite the faults they share with the rest of us.

"Prior Restraint." Some newspapers have very few virtues indeed. In 1931, one of these worthless papers provoked the most important of the U.S. Supreme Court's rulings on freedom of the press.

A certain Mr. Near owned an anti-Semitic scandal sheet, *The Saturday Press*, in Minnesota. (An example of its tone: "Practically every vendor of vile hooch, every owner of a moonshine still, every snake-faced gangster and embryonic yegg in the Twin Cities is a JEW.")[29] The state of Minnesota had on its books a gag law permitting it to ban any "malicious, scandalous and defamatory" newspaper or magazine. *The Saturday Press* was surely malicious, scandalous, and defamatory, but when Near's case reached the U.S. Supreme Court, it ruled in his favor. Why? Because the state had suppressed his paper to head off future maliciousness, scandal, and defamation; it had not attempted to punish Near for anything he had already published. To use the legal term, Minnesota had attempted to place a **prior restraint** on *The*

This tent city was set up across the street from the White House to dramatize the plight of homeless people. Its backers were forced to move, and the Supreme Court later upheld the regulations that banned sleeping and camping in the park.

UPI/Bettmann Newsphotos

---

[28] *Clark* v. *CCNV*, 52 U.S.L.W. 4986 (1984).

[29] Zechariah Chafee, Jr., *Free Speech in the United States* (Cambridge: Harvard Univ., 1941), p. 377.

Saturday Press instead of waiting for it to publish an objectionable article and *then* taking it to court and seeking to punish it for publishing that particular piece.[30]

National Security. There is almost no room in American constitutional law for prior restraint, which is the essence of censorship. However, the U.S. Supreme Court, has never absolutely barred the way to prior restraint, especially in cases involving national security.

In 1971, for example, *The New York Times* obtained and started to publish a classified Defense Department study that later became famous as "The Pentagon Papers." President Richard Nixon's Attorney General, John Mitchell—later convicted and sentenced for his part in the Watergate Affair—asked the federal courts to prohibit further publication of the papers. A U.S. District Court granted Mitchell an injunction against *The Times*, but the U.S. Supreme Court refused to uphold it (see Chapter 14). Nonetheless, the Court raised a number of red flags. First, the majority, six to three, was relatively narrow. Moreover, the Court based its refusal on what it called the government's failure to meet the burden of "showing justification for the enforcement of such a restraint." Finally, a majority was not persuaded that Congress had even authorized courts to issue such an injunction. This left open the possibility that if the government ever made its case, prior restraint might be granted.[31]

In fact, in one instance, it has been granted. As a condition of employment, all agents of the Central Intelligence Agency (CIA) must sign an agreement not to publish anything about their duties unless they get prior clearance from the agency (see Chapter 17). In 1980, the Court ruled that such agreements are indeed legally enforceable.

Another case might have made law but did not. In 1979, *The Progressive* magazine announced plans to publish an article that would show anyone how to build an atomic bomb. The article had been written from unclassified materials placed on the open stacks of a U.S. government library. Nonetheless, the federal government sought a prior-restraint injunction, and a district court granted it under the terms of the Atomic Energy Act of 1954, which prohibits the publication of information that might be useful in the manufacture of nuclear weapons.[32]

At this point, however, the federal government abandoned the case, for it became clear that the information in the article was already available in other publications. So this is one of many cases that never became a Supreme Court landmark.

The virtual impossibility of preventing anything from being published does not, by the way, permit the press to do exactly as it pleases, whatever damage it may inflict on others. The press can be punished *after the fact* for publishing certain kinds of information. The line is thus very sharply drawn between *prior restraint* and *subsequent punishment*, a line first marked out in the *Near* case, about fifty years ago.

Radio and Television: A More Limited Freedom. Unlike the print media, the electronic (or broadcast) media have been regulated by government from the first, since the public "owns" the airwaves. To broadcast over the airwaves,

---

[30] *Near* v. *Minnesota,* 283 U.S. 697 (1931).

[31] *New York Times Co.* v. *U.S.,* 403 U.S. 713 (1971).

[32] *United States* v. *Progressive, Inc.,* 467 F. Supp. 990 (S.D. Wis.), *appeal dismissed,* 610 F. 2d 819 7th Cir. (1979).

the owners of radio and TV stations must get licenses from the Federal Communications Commissions (FCC). One aspect of licensing is the requirement that television (but not radio) stations provide a certain minimum of public affairs programming each week; and sometimes (as in Boston in 1982), licenses are not renewed.

This unusual degree of regulation is justified chiefly by the argument that only a limited number of radio frequencies and television channels can be created, so regulators must allocate them among competing bidders. Print, the argument goes, is available to anyone, and in quantity. But, in fact, there are fewer newspaper than TV stations.

The licensing process does not permit the FCC to censor anything that broadcasters transmit or to interfere with the right of free speech. But two FCC regulations do directly affect the flow of politically related speech on the air. One of these, the **fairness doctrine,** requires a variety of viewpoints to be presented on issues of public importance. If licensees make editorial statements or endorse political candidates, the opposition has the right to respond on the same medium.[33] The second is the **equal-time rule,** designed to ensure that all candidates for public office have an equal opportunity to present their cases. In recent years, this rule has been waived to permit "major" candidates to participate in presidential debates without "minor" candidates.

Since broadcast programs reach a general audience in ways that print messages do not, the U.S. Supreme Court has ruled that obscenity or profanity can be eliminated from TV and radio programming by government regulation—at least when children are likely to be listening.[34] In fact, there are many gray areas here, especially with the advent of cable TV, which often broadcasts extensive displays of concupiscence, to say nothing of dirty words. But they play after 8 P.M., when, broadcasters claim, few children are watching. No doubt, more court cases will test the amount of flesh and profanity that can be put on TV screens.

Unprotected Speech: Obscenity and Libel

At last we arrive at two forms of expression that are not protected by the First Amendment: **obscenity** and **libel.**

Obscenity. To start with the obvious, obscenity has something to do with sex. But not all sex is obscene. What is obscene in one place, moreover, is not necessarily obscene in another.

Under the liberal regime of Chief Justice Earl Warren (1953–1969), the U.S. Supreme Court limited obscenity to "hard-core" pornography, whatever that may be. His successor, Chief Justice Warren Burger (1969–   ), tried to provide an exact definition. The Burger Court described as obscene those works that "appeal to the prurient"—lewd—"interest in sex," that portray "sexual conduct in a patently offensive way," and that "do not have serious literary, artistic, political, or scientific value." As examples of obscenity, it cited photographs of masturbation and sexual intercourse "and lewd exhibition of the genitals."[35] Photographs of this sort are, in fact, sold in many stores. No

---

[33] *Red Lion Broadcasting Company* v. *Federal Communications Commisson,* 395 U.S. 367 (1969).

[34] *F.C.C.* v. *Pacific Foundation,* 438 U.S. 726 (1978).

[35] *Miller* v. *California,* 413 U.S. 15 (1973).

Eugene Gordon

one can stop obscenity everywhere, because it is still hard to define and, therefore, to prove, and because the Burger Court permitted localities to define obscenity by their own "community standards."

All this gives the Court a lot of work to do, since it is sometimes called on to decide if a publication devoted to sex has any "redeeming social importance or value."[36] This means that in recent years the justices have screened a great many "dirty" films. Justice Hugo L. Black complained about this some years ago, but to no avail. Actually, although the Court upholds a larger percentage of obscenity prosecutions, the cases are fewer now. This is because social standards are more permissive. Some movies and prime-time television programs that barely cause a stir today would easily have been judged obscene thirty years ago.

Whatever else one may say about the Court's failure to develop a clearcut test for obscenity and pornography, some progress has been made. Not until 1933 did bureaucratic decision making allow James Joyce's classic novel, *Ulysses* (1922) to be legally imported into the United States. And not until the 1960s was Henry Miller's notable novel trilogy *The Rosy Crucifixion* (1949, 1953, 1960) published in the United States. Books are no longer "banned in Boston" by the Watch and Ward Society as they were until recent decades, and everyone who chooses to do so can now read D. H. Lawrence's "naughty" but great novel, *Lady Chatterley's Lover* (1928).

Libel. The other form of unprotected expression is libel, publishing untruthful statements that attack the character or reputation of a person or group. Spoken defamation of character is called **slander.**

People accused of libel can defend themselves by proving that their attacks were truthful. You are free, for instance, to write that someone convicted of murder is a murderer. Write that of someone who has not been convicted, and you can be sued for libel. That is one reason why newspapers refer to "alleged" murderers.

Much of the law of libel appears to hang on whether or not the Court views the injured party as a "public figure" or a "private person." Public officials cannot recover damages (restitution) for libel unless they show that an attack was not only false but also "malicious."[37] Apparently the U.S. Supreme Court thinks that the overall benefits of public debate about officials and their doings pretty much outweigh any damage that might be done to their reputations by false but not malicious charges.

The category of "public officials" includes retired army generals, too, as CBS learned when it telecast a "60 Minutes" story on Vietnam commander General William Westmoreland. Asking for a judgment greater than $120 million, Westmoreland sued CBS for claiming (falsely, he argued) that he had deliberately understated enemy troop strength and misled his superiors (including President Lyndon Johnson) in that tragic war two decades ago. The case was finally settled early in 1985 before it went to the jury, with neither CBS nor Westmoreland paying any money as part of the settlement. (This case is covered in detail in Chapter 8, "The Media.") Just the serious possibility of an award of that magnitude, however, is enough to make even the largest communication companies think twice before they print or broadcast statements about present and past officials. Some say such a

[36] *Roth* v. *United States*, 354 U.S. 476 (1957).
[37] *The New York Times* v. *Sullivan*, 376 U.S. 254 (1964).

possibility will prevent journalists from fulfilling their "watchdog" function under the First Amendment.

The position of *public figures* is much less clear than that of *public officials*. As far as the category of "public figures" can be defined—and the definition has varied—its members have few of the classical protections that libel laws give to completely private persons. Moreover, juries can and do demand evidence of "actual malice" before convicting of libel anyone accused of attacking a public figure. Even so, in mid-1982 the president of Mobil Oil Company, a "public figure," won a $2 million judgment against *The Washington Post*, which had printed articles alleging that he had used Mobil's money to "set up his son" in the shipping business and enrich himself with millions of dollars in Mobil contracts.

FREEDOM OF RELIGION

"Congress," begins the First Amendment, "shall make no law respecting an establishment of religion, or prohibiting the free exercise thereof." The desire to enjoy this freedom was among the chief reasons our country was settled, and it still brings men and women to our shores.

Separation of Church and State

In 1607, when the English planted their first permanent settlement in North America, the term *established church* had a specific legal meaning. The established Church of England had a religious monopoly; all other forms of worship were illegal. All priests of the church were government officials. After the "Glorious Revolution," of 1688–1689, the state stopped "poking windows into men's souls." But all government officials still had to belong to the established church, which still had great powers of taxation.

The First Amendment plainly bans an established church in this sense—a state church. Does it also ban any government involvement in religion, or does it merely prevent the government from favoring one religion as opposed to any of the others?

Direct Aid. Religious groups have both secular and religious aims. At times the line is quite easy to draw. For example, in 1899 the U.S. Supreme Court permitted the federal government to give funds to a Roman Catholic hospital that was open to all poor people.[38] Religious schools are a harder problem. The Court has permitted states to fund new buildings at church-related colleges and universities, but only if those buildings were to be used for teaching secular subjects.[39] States have also been allowed to provide secular textbooks to students in sectarian schools and to subsidize the costs of busing children to them (as part of a policy of providing such services to children in *all* schools, public and private).[40] But the Court drew the line when the states of

---

[38] *Bradfield* v. *Roberts*, 175 U.S. 291 (1899).

[39] *Tilton* v. *Richardson*, 403 U.S. 602 (1971).

[40] *Everson* v. *Board of Education*, 330 U.S. 1 (1947); *Board of Education* v. *Allen*, 392 U.S. 236 (1968).

Rhode Island and Pennsylvania attempted to eke out the pay of teachers at Roman Catholic parochial schools.

The Court's most general statement, in 1971, requires government aid to religious schools to be secular in aim and effect and to avoid "an excessive entanglement with religion."[41]

School Prayers. Suppose states attempt merely to promote religion in general, without involving themselves in the affairs of specific denominations. Until quite recently they tried to do so by requiring prayers and providing religious instruction in public schools.

The U.S. Supreme Court began to chip away at religious instruction in our schools in 1948, striking down an Illinois law that set aside "released time" for it during school hours.[42] Not until 1962 did the Court ban prayers in school itself.[43] Right now, the Court requires that the government observe strict neutrality toward religion in general, not just toward specific denominations. Many southerners and conservatives, however, support a constitutional amendment that would overturn this ruling. Nearly two dozen states, including Alabama, tried to get around the school prayer ban by calling for a "moment of silence" at the beginning of each school day. In 1985, the Supreme Court struck down the Alabama law under the First Amendment's Establishment Clause.[44]

What happens when the state-backed religious expression takes place outside the schoolhouse? Here the justices tend to be more lenient, stressing the need to accommodate the commands of the Constitution with the religious heritages of the nation. The Court narrowly approved a nativity scene in a public park in Pawtucket, Rhode Island, as well as public funds for a chaplain in the Nebraska legislature.[45] To do otherwise, some thought, would call into question the inscription "In God We Trust" on coins, Thanksgiving Day proclamations, and other manifestations of religion in public life.

Evolution. In 1925, the state of Tennessee attempted to prosecute a young teacher for instructing his pupils in the theory of evolution. Although the state won the so-called Monkey Trial, the law was dead: The teaching of evolution soon became not only legal but almost universal, and public schools ignored the biblical account of God's creating the world in six days.

In the mid-1970s, traditionalists started a compaign to include "scientific creationism"—a "scientific" justification of the biblical account—in school programs. They succeeded in Arkansas, but in 1982 a federal district court struck down, as an establishment of religion, an Arkansas law requiring that scientific creationism be taught alongside evolution. The state declined to appeal, so the case never reached the U.S. Supreme Court.

The Free Exercise of Religion

By and large, we Americans practice our own religions and let other people practice theirs. Certain religions, however, call for animal sacrifice. Others permit polygamy. Besides, what is to prevent anyone from calling anything a

[41] *Lemon* v. *Kurtzman*, 304 U.S. 602 (1971).

[42] *Illinois ex rel. McCollum* v. *Board of Education*, 333 U.S. 203 (1948); but the Court upheld a New York released-time program in *Zorach* v. *Clauson*, 343 U.S. 306 (1952).

[43] *Engel* v. *Vitale*, 370 U.S. 421 (1962).

[44] *Wallace* v. *Jaffree*, (1985).

[45] *Lynch* v. *Donnelly*, 52 U.S.L.W. 4317; *Marsh* v. *Chambers*, 51 U.S.L.W. 5162 (1983).

"religion"? Constitutionally, nothing whatever. The U.S. Supreme Court has refused to determine whether any group claiming to be a religious group is or is not.[46] This refusal has some very concrete consequences, notably the extensive federal tax exemptions that religious groups enjoy.

We are not, however, at liberty to *practice* anything we please in the name of religion. The distinction between belief and practice is in many ways analogous to the distinction between speech and action in free-speech cases. A religion cannot make legal what would otherwise be illegal. "Crime is not the less odious" as one U.S. Supreme Court justice put it, "because sanctioned by what any particular sect may designate as religion."[47]

In 1878, for example, the Supreme Court upheld the bigamy conviction of a man who, in keeping with then-prevailing tenets of Mormonism, had taken several wives. Governments, too, can act against religious practices that endanger public safety. The authorities, for instance, can insist that anyone be vaccinated against communicable diseases, including people whose religions prohibit vaccination. Courts have even upheld bans on rattlesnake-handling ceremonies.

Religious leaders themselves must obey the secular law of the state. In 1982 the Reverend Sun Myung Moon, founder and leader of the Unification

This nativity scene in Pawtucket, Rhode Island, caused a case to be brought before the Supreme Court because it was placed in a public park. The Supreme Court eventually ruled that it could appear in the park.

[46] *United States* v. *Ballard*, 322 U.S. 78 (1944).
[47] *Davis* v. *Beason*, 133 U.S. 333 (1890).

A Dissent

Only one justice dissented from the U.S. Supreme Court's decision in the Flag Salute cases of 1940, when the Court upheld Pennsylvania school officials who had suspended two children for refusing to salute the flag. The lone dissenter was Justice, later Chief Justice, Harlan Fiske Stone (1925-1946), who wrote:

The guarantees of civil liberty are but guarantees of freedom of the human mind and spirit and of reasonable freedom and opportunity to express them. . . . The very essence of the liberty which they guarantee is the freedom of the individual from compulsion as to what he shall think and what he shall say, at least where the compulsion is to bear false witness to his religion. If these guarantees are to have any meaning they must, I think, be deemed to withhold from the state any authority to compel belief or the expression of it where that expression violates religious convictions.

The Constitution expresses more than the conviction of the people that democratic processes must be preserved at all costs. It is also an expression of faith and a command that freedom of mind and spirit must be preserved, which government must obey, if it is to adhere to that justice and moderation without which no free government can exist.

Stone's view became the law of the land within 3 years.

From *Minersville School District* v. *Gobitis*, 310 U.S. 586 (1940) (dissenting opinion).

Church, was convicted of federal income-tax evasion. (He was charged with diverting some of the church's tax-exempt money to his own personal use without declaring the income on IRS Form 1040.) Churches as organizations are tax-exempt, but priests, ministers, rabbis, and the like must pay personal income taxes, along with everyone else who owes them.

Apart from these limits, the U.S. Supreme Court has generally insisted on the widest possible scope for free exercise of religion. Besides refusing to define religion, the Court has also struck down restraints on religious meetings, censorship of religious messages, taxes on religious evangelism, the denial of government benefits on grounds of religion, and application of compulsory school attendance laws that run counter to religious teachings.[48]

The Flag Salute Cases. Most of the time, the government has protected the "free exercise of religion." But on one occasion it did not. The year was 1940. Nazi Germany was conquering almost all of Europe. Japan was occupying much of Asia. Many people in the United States thought we would soon be at war. They were right.

Some school districts decided to encourage their pupils' love of country by staging flag-salute ceremonies. In one of these districts in Pennsylvania, two children who belonged to Jehovah's Witnesses refused to salute the flag. Now, the Witnesses believe, among other things, that their members should not swear loyalty to mere earthly governments, like that of the United States, and they regard the flag salute as worship of "graven images." Moreover, the Witnesses are unpopular with other religions, which their literature condemns as "rackets." The two pupils were suspended by school officials, whom the U.S. Supreme Court upheld because, at the time, it regarded national unity as more important than religious freedom.[49]

---

[48] See, for example, *Cantwell* v. *Connecticut*, 310 U.S. 296 (1940); *Murdock* v. *Pennsylvania*, 319 U.S. 105 (1943); *Sherbert* v. *Verner*, 374 U.S. 398 (1963); *Wisconsin* v. *Yoder*, 406 U.S. 205 (1972).

[49] *Minersville School District* v. *Gobitis*, 310 U.S. 586 (1940).

State-directed persecutions of Jehovah's Witnesses became epidemic. Children who refused to salute the flag were suspended, but if their parents then refused to end the suspension by having their children salute the flag, state law officers prosecuted them for violating state compulsory school-attendance laws.

Three years passed. By 1943 it was clear that the denial of religious liberty to Jehovah's Witnesses was not helping to defeat Germany and Japan. When another of these cases came before the Court in 1943, the 1940 decision was overruled. Justice Robert H. Jackson (1941–1954), writing for the majority, gave the interpretation that has ever since been the law of the land:

> If there is any fixed star in our constitutional constellation, it is that no official, high or petty, can prescribe what shall be orthodox in politics, nationalism, religion, or other matters of opinion, or force citizens to confess by word or act their faith therein. If there are any circumstances which permit an exception, they do not now occur to us.[50]

THE RIGHTS OF CRIMINAL DEFENDANTS

In January 1960, Manuel Valtierra was shot and killed in Chicago. The police arrested Valtierra's brother-in-law, Danny Escobedo, but released him after questioning. A few days later, they rearrested Escobedo and questioned him again. This time he asked to see a lawyer, but his request was denied. Hour followed hour, and still the police kept asking questions. At last, Danny Escobedo told them that he himself had killed Manuel Valtierra. He was tried for murder and convicted.

Escobedo appealed. His lawyers argued that the Sixth Amendment, which protects the right to counsel, gave him the right to be represented by counsel not only at the trial but also at the police interrogation. In 1964, by a vote of five justices to four, the U.S. Supreme Court supported them. Escobedo's conviction was overturned on the grounds that his confession had been obtained improperly.[51] He was now a free man.

No one ever proved that Danny Escobedo did *not* kill Manuel Valtierra. Under our system, that has never been necessary, for it has always been up to the prosecution to prove that a defendant is guilty (see Chapter 14). In addition, however, no one proved that Danny Escobedo's confession was less true because it had been gotten improperly. Its truth or falsity was not the issue; the issue was whether the police had respected Danny Escobedo's civil liberties.

The Escobedo decision put the Court on a collision course with public opinion, which undoubtedly wants to see criminals punished, with no "nonsense" about their "rights." Nothing, in fact, poses the problem of civil liberties so directly and painfully as the rights of defendants. The public's sense of justice is deeply offended when someone who is almost certainly guilty of a serious crime gets off on what appears to be a technicality. This sense of justice must be taken into account, with the idea that communities—not to mention the victims of crimes—have rights that cannot be ignored. What the public chooses to ignore is that at any moment, any one of us may be accused of a crime and so become a defendant. Cases like *Escobedo* are

---

[50] *West Virginia State Board of Education* v. *Barnette,* 319 U.S. 624 (1943).
[51] *Escobedo* v. *Illinois,* 378 U.S. 478 (1964).

The rights of defendants are essential to freedom. If the police do not respect these rights, the case against the defendant may be overturned.

very hard indeed, because the balance is so nearly even; and that helps to explain why it was decided by a 5 to 4 vote.

Nonetheless, the rights of defendants are essential to freedom. No single group is more at the mercy of the government's power—and of any abuse of that power—than are criminal defendants, and the conflict between their rights and the rights of others is characteristic of civil liberties in general. Yet the Court cannot indefinitely maintain standards that lie far beyond the limits of what public opinion will tolerate. The balance between defendants' rights and the rights of others reflects this fact in the longer run. No one is likely to be wholly satisfied with that balance, but that is only to be expected in any field of American politics.

Evidence and Testimony

One part of the balance between defendants' rights and the rights of society is our need to make it possible for the police to gather evidence and for prosecutors to extract testimony. The U.S. Constitution prohibits "unreasonable searches and seizures" and the issuing of search warrants unless there is "probable cause" to believe that a search might produce some evidence of particular crimes. It also permits defendants to refuse to incriminate themselves at their trials. How then do we protect these guarantees and also permit the police to do their job?

Searches and Seizures. For one thing, the police must observe certain procedures while conducting any search: They must have the consent of the person who controls the premises, "probable cause" to fear for their own safety or to think that evidence may be destroyed, or a search warrant issued by a court. While making any arrest, the police may search suspects and the areas the suspects control.

The Exclusionary Rule. In 1914, the U.S. Supreme Court dealt with the case of a man whose house had been searched by federal agents without a warrant and without probable cause. It ruled that the evidence so seized could not be introduced against him—the so-called **exclusionary rule.**[52] The aim of that rule was very clear: If police and prosecutors cannot prosecute defendants by using the fruits of an illegal search or seizure, they have no incentive to engage in illegal searches and seizures. For many decades, the exclusionary rule applied only to federal law-enforcement officers, but in 1961 the U.S. Supreme Court extended it to the states.[53]

The whole matter of searches, seizures, and arrest warrants is one of formidable complexity. The facts of particular cases are often very individual, so that generalization is difficult. In 1981, for example, the Court ruled on two search cases. In one of them, a speeding car had been stopped by a New York patrolman. Smelling marijuana in the car, he advised the driver and his friends of their rights[54] and then proceeded to search the whole car without a warrant, finding cocaine. Was this illegally seized evidence following an illegal search? In 1981 the Court decided that it was not.[55] But on the same day it ruled against an apparently quite similar search in California.[56] This is one more set of cases demonstrating the confusion that can arise from a chronic lack of agreement.

Impatient with the "social costs" of the exclusionary rule, the Court cut back its application in a 1984 case. Relying on a warrant that reviewing courts later decided was defective, police in Burbank, California, conducted searches that led to drug-related arrests. The lower courts said that the Constitution required that the evidence be declared inadmissible. Six justices concluded, however, that the evidence should *not* be kept out of the trial if the police act "in the objectively reasonable belief" that their conduct does not violate the Fourth Amendment. In such cases, the exclusionary rule could have no deterrent effect, so there was no gain in throwing out evidence that otherwise was perfectly valid.[57]

Taking the Fifth. "I refuse to answer that question on the grounds that my answer may tend to incriminate me." Hardly a glorious reply, but an essential protection of civil liberties, nonetheless. And it's in the Constitution: "No person . . . shall be compelled in any criminal case to be a witness against himself." This part of the Fifth Amendment, along with due process, protects all of us from the torturer's rack.

The Miranda Case. Early in 1963, an 18-year-old woman was kidnapped and raped near Phoenix, Arizona. The police soon arrested a poor, mentally

---

[52] *Weeks* v. *United States*, 232 U.S. 383 (1914).

[53] *Mapp* v. *Ohio*, 367 U.S. 643 (1961), in part overruling *Wolf* v. *Colorado*, 338 U.S. 25 (1949).

[54] Required since *Miranda* v. *Arizona*, 384 U.S. 436 (1966).

[55] *New York* v. *Belton*, 453 U.S. 454. (1981)

[56] *Robbins* v. *California*, 453 U.S. 420 (1981).

[57] *United States* v. *Leon*, 52 U.S.L.W. 5155 (1984).

disturbed man named Ernesto Miranda, 23 years old. He confessed after 2 hours of questioning and was convicted.

On appeal, however, Miranda's lawyers pointed out that the police had never told him that he had a right to be represented by a lawyer and, if he chose, to remain silent. In 1966, the U.S. Supreme Court decided that the police have to make these points clear to any suspect before questioning. By only a five to four majority, the Court ruled in Miranda's favor, even though no one presented any evidence that Miranda's confession had been coerced.[58] Later on, the Burger Court not only failed to expand the Miranda ruling but indeed chipped away at it. Many thought that the Warren Court had tilted the balance too much in favor of persons accused of crimes, making the job of the police too difficult. In two decisions[59] the Court decided that statements made by a defendant, inadmissible in direct trial testimony because of the police's failure to inform the suspect of his or her *Miranda* rights, could nonetheless be used to attack the credibility of a defendant's assertions on the witness stand. Moreover, a suspect under *Miranda* may voluntarily waive the right to silence and counsel, but such waivers can be challenged later. Now, rather than deciding whether confessions are voluntary (as in the pre-*Miranda* days), courts have to decide whether the waivers were voluntary when the suspects decided to talk to the police anyway. And because *Miranda* applies only to interrogations, statements made by a suspect outside of an interrogation may still be used, regardless of whether police gave the required warnings. Then in 1984, the justices added a "public safety exception" to *Miranda*, which allows police to ask suspects about the location of weapons before advising them of their *Miranda* rights.[60]

Fair Trial

Clarence Earl Gideon was a drifter; his life was a succession of disasters. In 1961, Gideon was charged with stealing some beer, wine, and change from a poolroom in Panama City, Florida. He was convicted and sent to jail for five years. In prison, Gideon became a "jailhouse lawyer," obsessed with the notion that he had been denied a fair trial because he had been too poor to hire a lawyer.

Now, the Sixth Amendment declares, "In all criminal prosecutions, the accused shall enjoy the right . . . to have the Assistance of Counsel for his defense." Originally this provision applied only to federal trials. Not until 1938 did the U.S. Supreme Court rule that all indigent criminal defendants, even in federal cases, have a right to court-appointed counsel.[61] In 1942, it refused to extend that right to noncapital state trials,[62] and it clung to that refusal until Clarence Earl Gideon brought before it his strange, sad life. But in 1963 the Court ruled that anyone "who is too poor to hire a lawyer cannot be assured of a fair trial unless counsel is provided for him"—in state trials and for any felony, not just capital crimes.[63]

---

[58] *Miranda* v. *Arizona*, 384 U.S. 436 (1966).

[59] *Harris* v. *New York*, 401 U.S. 22 (1971); *Oregon* v. *Hass*, 420 U.S. 714 (1975).

[60] *New York* v. *Quarles*, 52 U.S.L.W. 4790 (1984).

[61] *Johnson* v. *Zerbst*, 304 U.S. 458 (1938).

[62] *Betts* v. *Brady*, 316 U.S. 455 (1942).

[63] *Gideon* v. *Wainwright*, 372 U.S. 455 (1963).

Clarence Earl Gideon was granted a new trial. This time he got a court-appointed lawyer and was acquitted. More recently, the Burger Court has extended the right to counsel to misdemeanor or minor offenses for which a jail sentence of any length is imposed.[64]

Trials in the States. The year was 1923. Five black men were tried in Phillips County, Arkansas, for murdering a white man. At the trial, the court and the area around it were invaded by a crowd "that threatened the most dangerous consequences to anyone" who voted for acquittal. The defense counsel did not dare to ask for a delay or request that the trial be moved to some other place. He had no consultations with his clients, did not challenge any proposed juryman, call any witnesses, or put the defendants on the stand. The whole trial was over in less than an hour, and it took the jury less than five minutes to convict the defendants of first-degree murder.

The U.S. Supreme Court later concluded that "no juryman could have voted for an acquittal and continued to live in Phillips County, and if any prisoner, by any chance, had been acquitted by a jury, he could not have escaped the mob." It ruled that the five defendants had indeed been denied "due process."[65]

Most trials, like this one, are held in the states—though most are vastly more fair!—so ensuring fair trials is largely a matter of extending the Fifth and Sixth Amendments to state courts. Those amendments protect the rights to "due process of law," to "a speedy and public trial by an impartial jury," "to be informed of the nature and cause of the accusation," "to be confronted with the witnesses" of an alleged crime, and "to have the Assistance of Counsel."

As matters stand now, states must give defendants "fair notice," which includes a formal statement of charges, and must tell them when and where their trials will be held. During the trial itself, criminal defendants have a right to have their cases heard by juries that are representative of the communities or general areas from which the jurors are drawn. Trials must be open to the public and take place reasonably soon after the charges have been made. Witnesses against defendants must be subject to cross-examination by defense lawyers. Defendants must be given **compulsory process,** letting them compel witnesses to testify. All procedures before and during the trial must meet standards of due process and fundamental fairness. And if defendants are acquitted, they may never be retried for the very same offenses, since this would constitute **double jeopardy.**

Cruel and Unusual Punishment

Back at the turn of the century, a man was sentenced to fifteen years at hard labor for falsifying a public document.[66] The U.S. Supreme Court, however, found the penalty so out of proportion to the offense as to be "cruel and unusual punishment," banned by the Eighth Amendment.

[64] *Scott* v. *Illinois*, 440 U.S. 367 (1979).

[65] *Moore* v. *Dempsey*, 261 U.S. 86 (1923).

[66] *Weems* v. *U.S.*, 217 U.S. 349 (1910).

"I believe there are more instances of the abridgment of the freedom of the people by gradual and silent encroachments of those in power than by violent and sudden usurpations."

James Madison,
Speech in the Virginia Convention, 1788

Capital Punishment. Yet never has it ruled that the death penalty, **capital punishment,** is cruel and unusual in itself. It may be cruel, but in the past it was not at all unusual. Until 1972, many states imposed capital punishment for quite a few crimes, including rape, and many let juries decide whether or not to condemn convicts to death.

Over the years, the inequality of this practice among the states created what the U.S. Supreme Court called a "wanton and freakish" pattern, one that amounted to cruel and unusual punishment. In 1972, the Court in effect threw out all state laws providing for capital punishment and halted all pending executions, but it also invited the states to draw up more precise laws that would impose the penalty more consistently.[67] By the end of 1979, thirty-five states had done so. Capital punishment can now be imposed only for the most heinous crimes, mostly murder—not for lesser crimes, even rape (assuming that no life is taken in the act). Only a small number of executions have taken place since 1979, although hundreds of prisoners await execution on "death row."

Today the death penalty is among the most hotly contested of all so-called social issues. Many who oppose it believe it to be a "cruel and unusual punishment" in today's constitutional world and, therefore, prohibited by the Eighth Amendment. Its supporters often claim that it not only deters people who would otherwise commit heinous crimes but also gives society as a whole the power to protect itself, to avenge victims of crime, and to hold down prison costs. Every public-opinion survey reveals overwhelming public support for the death penalty. This in part reflects the fact that our levels of violent crime are extraordinarily high as compared with those of other industrialized countries.

SUMMARY

Civil liberties are the freedoms of speech, assembly, and religion, and the right to a fair trial. They protect individual citizens from the power of the government, and, in the larger sense, from the intolerance of the majority. These liberties are deeply embedded in our political culture.

Nonetheless, our civil liberties have occasionally been threatened, mainly in wartime, for they can flourish only among a self-confident people, and wars make us fearful. Unpopular minorities often become the objects of that fear, especially when governments use fear to promote a sense of national unity.

The United States has passed through several periods of national intolerance, most recently in the 1950s. Despite those aberrations, our civil liberties have become stronger and more numerous. The U.S. Supreme Court has gradually forced the states to respect the U.S. Bill of Rights—the first ten amendments to the Constitution. Of course, the federal government has always had to abide by them. Thanks to our state and federal constitutions and to the U.S. Supreme Court, we are now, for the most part, free to say or write whatever we please and to worship as we please or not at all. And when individuals are accused of committing crimes, they do not stand utterly alone

---

[67] *Furman* v. *Georgia; Jackson* v. *Georgia; Branch* v. *Texas,* 408 U.S. 238 (1972). *Gregg* v. *Georgia,* 428 U.S. 153 (1976), approved some new laws.

against the power of the state. Our system of civil liberties is now fairly uniform from state to state.

The struggle for civil liberties is continual. There will always be conflicts among the interests of freedom and order, tensions between the majority and the minority, and friction about the legitimate rights of different people. We have often been a cantankerous and sometimes an intolerant people, and we accept far too much violence and disregard for the rights of others. Still, our record for protecting the civil liberties of the American people has been an impressive one. As Americans, many of us believe that the Bill of Rights gives us by far the highest level of individual freedoms in the world. Yet a number of advanced democratic countries, with very different legal systems, enjoy freedoms pretty much equal to our own. Our record, at any rate, can stand comparison with those of other free societies, to say nothing of unfree societies. That is a noble accomplishment.

SUGGESTED READINGS

ZECHARIAH CHAFEE, JR., *Free Speech in the United States.* Cambridge: Harvard Univ., 1941. Illuminating discussion, particularly valuable for its detailed analyses of the major cases of the World War I era.

NORMAN DORSEN, PAUL BENDER, and BURT NUEBORNE, *Political and Civil Rights in the United States,* 4th ed. Boston: Little, Brown, 1976, with updated biennial supplements. One of many casebooks on the market—a very good one that concentrates on Bill of Rights cases.

FRED W. FRIENDLY, *Minnesota Rag.* New York: Random House, 1981. The story of the Supreme Court's landmark free press decision in *Near* v. *Minnesota.*

NAT HENTOFF, *The First Freedom: The Tumultuous History of Free Speech in America.* New York: Delacorte, 1980. A lively and popular account of how the long, long trail of American civil liberties has led to the present levels of protection for free speech.

J. DAVID HERSCHEL, *Fourth Amendment Rights.* Lexington, Mass.: Lexington Books, 1979. A useful account of searches and seizures and related issues.

YALE KAMISAR, WAYNE R. LaFAVE, and JEROLD H. ISRAEL, *Basic Criminal Procedure,* 5th ed. St. Paul, Minn.: West, 1980, with annual supplements. Useful resource on the rapidly changing rules of criminal procedure.

ANTHONY LEWIS, *Gideon's Trumpet.* New York: Random House, 1964. The well-written story of Clarence Gideon and how the right to counsel came to the Supreme Court.

J. W. PELTASON, *Corwin and Peltason's Understanding the Constitution,* 10th ed. New York: Holt, 1985. A valuable reference to the meaning of each clause in the Constitution as developed in the leading Supreme Court decisions.

BERNARD SCHWARTZ, *The Great Rights of Mankind: A History of the American Bill of Rights.* New York: Oxford Univ. Press, 1977. One of the country's leading constitutional lawyers gives a succinct and useful account of the constitutional development of our civil liberties.

CHARLES E. SILBERMAN, *Criminal Violence and Criminal Justice.* New York: Random House, 1978. A competent guide to the basics of the American criminal-justice system.

FRANK J. SORAUF, *The Wall of Separation: The Constitutional Politics of Church and State.* Princeton: Princeton Univ., 1976. Presents broad coverage of the church-state cases that shape public policy today.

chapter five

CIVIL RIGHTS

On May 25, 1942, Fred Korematsu, an American citizen of Japanese ancestry, was arrested while leaving a post office in Oakland, California. About half a year earlier, the United States had declared war against Japan following the surprise attack on Pearl Harbor in Hawaii. Executive Order 9066, issued that May, ordered all Japanese on the West Coast—including American citizens and the American-born—into "relocation" camps. Fred Korematsu had refused to report to such a camp and was then charged with violating a curfew on persons of Japanese descent and failing to leave an area declared off-limits to them. He was convicted of these crimes and sent to jail. The 120,000 people—two-thirds of them American citizens—who did report spent the rest of World War II in detention, in remote areas of Nevada, Utah, Idaho, and California. By the time they returned to their homes, they had lost 90 percent of their property. Most of it was never returned.

American citizens? Relocation camps? Just forty years ago? In the United States of America? Can all this be true? It is true.[1]

---

[1] For an excellent and comprehensive review of this civil rights disaster, see Jacobus TenBroek, Edward N. Barnhart, and Floyd W. Matson, *Prejudice, War and the Constitution: Causes and Consequences of the Evacuation of the Japanese Americans in World War II* (Berkeley: Univ. of California, 1968).

In May 1942, Germany controlled most of Europe. Japan controlled most of Asia. Americans were scared.

Our fear produced the relocation camps. Fear was selective, however. German-Americans and Italian-Americans were not ordered into relocation camps—not, of course, that they should have been—only Japanese-Americans were. It cannot be a coincidence that German-Americans and Italian-Americans are whites and that Japanese-Americans are not.

That, in fact, was the reason for Executive Order 9066. General J. L. DeWitt, who actually issued it, was frank: "It makes no difference whether he is an American citizen," said the general. "He is still Japanese. You needn't worry about the Italians at all, except in certain cases. Also the same for the Germans, except in individual cases. But we must worry about the Japanese all of the time until he is wiped off the map." The issue very clearly was not what people did or were suspected of doing, but what they were—and what they were not. They were not whites. The Japanese-Americans were victims of American racism. Even Governor Earl Warren of California, who, a decade later, became Chief Justice of the United States, approved the order.

The Appeal. Fred Korematsu appealed his conviction right up to the U.S. Supreme Court. It was not among the Court's finer hours: By a vote of six to three, the justices upheld the constitutionality of the Executive Order 9066, for the majority feared to challenge the judgment of a local military commander at a time of acute emergency.

A young Japanese-American awaits evacuation in the spring of 1942.

National Archives

One of the dissenting justices pointed out that the decision was "like a loaded gun" that could be used against any minority by any government official at any time of "emergency." But the Court's decision still stands, the gun is still loaded.[2]

An American Dilemma. The case of Fred Korematsu was no exception to the rule: The rule is that whites and nonwhites have by law been treated very differently in the United States and still are. Our national ideal proclaims that "all men are created equal," but our national reality is the reality of "two nations, separate and unequal." The conflict between what we believe and what we do was always our greatest national weakness. It still is.

At one time or other, just about all the minority groups in this country have been victimized by social and legal discrimination. But discrimination does not even have the negative virtue of falling equally on all minorities. In the United States, one minority group has suffered uniquely: black people.

Not so many years ago, in many places black people were forced by law into segregated schools. In railway stations they often had to sit in special sections reserved for blacks. They could not stay at good hotels or eat at good restaurants or even at most bad ones. They could not stop at most gas stations to use the toilets. In many places they could not sit down in a bus if any white person was standing. Most public accommodations—movies, recreational facilities, swimming pools, and the like—were closed to blacks or rigidly segregated. The professions and most skilled trades were largely off-limits to them. They could not play on any major-league sports team. Many hospitals would not admit them as patients or as physicans. In the southern states, where, until recently, the majority of blacks lived, most could not vote. They were subjected to discrimination in every sphere of life.

This is not ancient history. It did not end in 1865 or even in 1945. It only *started* to end in the 1950s and 1960s, and it has not entirely ended yet.

——— SLAVERY AND ITS AFTERMATH ———

Before the Civil War, it was not quite clear that blacks were legally human. Of the 4.4 million blacks enumerated by the 1860 census, about 89 percent were slaves. The U.S. Supreme Court (in the 1857 Dred Scott case) had ruled that black people "had no rights which the white man was bound to respect."[3] However, this decision created an uproar in the North and helped elect President Abraham Lincoln (1861–1865), who opposed the spread of slavery. One by one, the southern states then left the union, and the United States plunged into a bloody civil war.

The South was finally defeated in 1865. Lincoln's Republican party, which had a strong "Radical" antislavery element, controlled both houses of Congress and most state legislatures. In the war's aftermath, the Republicans pushed through the three "Civil War" Amendments—the thirteenth, fourteenth, and fifteenth—meant to give blacks legal citizenship and to protect their status as citizens.

---

[2] *Korematsu* v. *U.S.*, 323 U.S. 214 (1944).
[3] *Dred Scott* v. *Sandford*, 19 How. 393 (1857).

The Thirteenth Amendment

Ratified in 1865, the Thirteenth Amendment simply banned slavery in the United States. In 1865 and 1866, however, southern state legislatures passed "black codes" that pretty much nullified the amendment. These codes angered public opinion in the North and led in turn to the Reconstruction Act (1867) and the Fourteenth (1868) and Fifteenth (1870) Amendments.

The Fourteenth Amendment

The first section of the Fourteenth Amendment was clearly meant to protect the civil rights of black people, especially in the South. "No State," it declares, "shall make or enforce any law which shall abridge the privileges or immunities of citizens of the United States; nor shall any State deprive any person of life, liberty, or property without due process of law; nor deny to any person within its jurisdiction the equal protection of the laws."

The language is clear, yet the amendment's "privileges and immunities" clause was largely gutted by the U.S. Supreme Court in 1873, when butchers from New Orleans tried to use the new amendment to block a local policy that created a slaughterhouse monopoly.[4] Still, it is important to recall Justice Miller's words from the majority opinion: "The existence of laws in the States where the newly emancipated negroes resided, which discriminated with gross injustice and hardship against them as a class, was the evil to be remedied by [the equal protection] clause and by it such laws are forbidden."

Due Process. Some legal theorists believed that the second clause of the first section of the amendment—the one that prohibits any state from depriving "any person of life, liberty, or property without due process of law"— extended the federal Bill of Rights to state governments. (Originally, it had applied only to the federal government; see Chapter 4). The U.S. Supreme Court came to accept that view quite slowly and, even today, not quite completely. From 1886 to 1937 the Court chiefly viewed the **due-process clause** as a brake on government regulation of business and industry, on the ground that a corporation was a "corporate person." In fact, in one standard work on the U.S. Constitution, 117 of 188 pages on the due-process clause are devoted to decisions protecting the due process of corporations; only 71 pages cover decisions protecting individuals.[5]

Equal Protection. The third clause of the first section provides that no state shall "deny to any person . . . the equal protection of the laws." Some of the amendment's authors apparently thought that the **equal-protection clause** would let black men vote on equal terms with white men. (When doubts on that point arose, the Republicans tried to clear them up with the Fifteenth Amendment; see the section on voting rights, following.) From the start, the equal-protection clause had a second aim: extension of federal civil rights protection to a group—black people—subject to discrimination as a group and not only as individuals.

---

[4] *Slaughter-House Cases,* 16 Wall. 36 (1873).

[5] Edward S. Corwin, ed., *The Constitution of the United States of America: Analysis and Interpretation* (Washington, D.C.: 1953), pp. 963ff.

Say, for example, that an unsuitably dressed white man is refused admission to a fancy restaurant. He cannot appear before a court and claim to be a victim of group discrimination, because white men *as a group* have not been subjected to it. An individual has no more right to enter a particular restaurant than to play center field for the New York Yankees. However, a black person denied admission to the same restaurant for the same reasons might be viewed as a victim of group, not individual, discrimination, because in this case group discrimination is a historical reality.

Apparently the authors of the Fourteenth Amendment intended to permit black people to challenge acts of group discrimination committed against them. Whatever they may or may not have meant, the U.S. Supreme Court at first rejected the idea: In 1883, it ruled that discrimination by private businesses was not state action within the meaning of the Fourteenth Amendment, so they could discriminate all they pleased.[6]

"Separate but Equal." For the time being, the 1883 civil rights cases made the world safe for private discrimination. What about discrimination practiced by state governments? Remember the words of the equal-protection clause: No state shall "deny to any person within its jurisdiction the equal protection of the laws."

The state of Louisiana had on its books a so-called **Jim Crow law** (one of many) that required blacks and whites to be seated separately on trains. This particular bit of injustice was perpetrated by the state, not by the railroads. A man named Herman Plessy, who was only one-eighth black, challenged the law. The U.S. Supreme Court upheld its constitutionality (in 1896) by entering a fantasy world: It argued (in *Plessy* v. *Ferguson*) that the separation of the races did not imply the superiority of one to the other. If indeed racial segregation seemed to imply such a superiority, it was "not by reason of

---

[6] *Civil Rights Cases*, 109 U.S. 3 (1883). Note the tone of Justice Bradley's opinion for the Court: "When a man has emerged from slavery and by the aid of benificent legislation has shaken off the inseparable concomitants of that state, there must be some stage in the progress of his elevation when he takes the rank of a mere citizen, and ceases to be the special favorite of the laws, and when his rights as a citizen, or a man, are to be protected in the ordinary modes by which other men's rights are protected."

Peonage

Peonage is a relationship between employer and worker, usually landlord and tenant farmer in the countryside, in which the worker is held in compulsory servitude to the master to work off indebtedness. For many decades, the U.S. Supreme Court has ruled that peonage, like outright slavery, is prohibited by the Thirteenth Amendment. After the Civil War, a number of Southern states made repeated and ingenious efforts to give legal backing to peonage. In case after case, extending from 1911 to 1944, the Court struck down these laws as violations of the Thirteenth Amendment. (See, e.g., *Pollock* v. *Williams* 322 U.S. 4 [1944].) Like many other such southern

practices in this period, peonage laws were in fact overwhelmingly aimed at landless black farm workers.

Amazingly enough, a trickle of peonage cases keeps flowing, right down to the present day, mostly involving farm workers who are illegal aliens and their employers. These employers have been convicted in federal courts for violations of civil-rights acts; they have no constitutional leg to stand on.

Such cases remind us, however, that involuntary servitude is still with us and is more persistent than one might think.

anything found in the act, but solely because the colored race chooses to put that construction upon it."[7] The equal-protection clause merely required that the black sections be similar to the white sections—"separate but equal."

Three years after *Plessy* v. *Ferguson*, the "separate but equal" doctrine was explicitly extended to school systems.[8] The equal-protection clause, although framed as a weapon against discrimination, had been distorted into a legal rationale for it.

Voting Rights: The Fifteenth Amendment

When the Radical Republicans, who dominated Congress after the Civil War's end, saw that the Fourteenth Amendment did not protect black voting rights, they pushed through the Fifteenth Amendment (1870): "The right of citizens of the United States to vote shall not be denied or abridged by the United States or by any State on account of race, color, or previous condition of servitude."

The language is certainly clear enough, and until 1877, when the federal government stopped supervising elections in the South, the amendment did its job. It was then effectively nullified. The reaction to the Black Codes had taught southern legislatures a lesson: the danger of formally expelling blacks from the electorate while northern Republicans still took an interest in the rights of their black political clients. At first, corruption, fraud, and occasional organized racist violence were enough to discourage most black voters. By the 1890s, the eleven state legislatures of the former Confederacy were sufficiently confident of northern indifference to pass a whole series of laws—remarkable for their ingenuity and effectiveness—that achieved the purge they had

---

[7] *Plessy* v. *Ferguson*, 163 U.S. 537 (1896). Overruled by *Brown* v. *Board of Education*, 347 U.S. 483 (1954).

[8] *Cumming* v. *County Board of Education*, 175 U.S. 528 (1899).

"The right of citizens of the United States, who are eighteen years of age or older, to vote shall not be denied or abridged by the United States or by any State on account of age." The Twenty-sixth Amendment was passed in 1971.

AP/Wide World Photos

worked for since 1877. From about 1900 through the 1960s, these laws excluded the vast majority of Southern blacks—especially rural blacks—from the fundamental American right to vote.

Some of these laws required the voters to demonstrate their literacy; others required that they pay a poll tax or demonstrate such personal attributes as "good character" before voting. Occasionally a state would go too far, and the U.S. Supreme Court drew the line. Oklahoma, for example, enacted a "grandfather clause" that allowed anyone who had voted before January 1, 1867, or any descendant of such a person, to vote without having to pass literacy or other tests.[9] The trick was the date, chosen to eliminate blacks, none of whose ancestors had voted before the passage of the Reconstruction Act, in March 1867.

Some black voters stayed on the rolls even in the South, but they had no political pull whatever. After Reconstruction, the South became almost solidly Democratic (see Chapters 9 and 10), and Democratic party primaries (Chapters 9 and 10) were restricted to whites through the legal fiction (accepted by the U.S. Supreme Court as late as 1935[10] that the party, like the Kiwanis, was a private society. The Court did not abolish the "white primary" until 1944,[11] when it finally noticed that the Texas Democratic party was indissolubly linked with the state and with the state action, so that a white primary was therefore the kind of state action prohibited by the Fifteenth Amendment.

"A Dream Deferred"

At the end of the Civil War, our country had apparently committed itself to equality for black people. The constitutional and legal foundations of full black citizenship had been created; blacks were the voting majority in several southern states. Thirty years later, everything had changed. A lily-white Democratic party controlled the South; the northern Democrats were conservative, the Republicans even more so. The U.S. Supreme Court had turned the Civil War amendments on their heads and had thrown out most of the civil rights laws passed after the war.

The End of Reconstruction Politics. One reason for the debacle was the instability of the radical political conditions and coalitions that emerged during the Civil War. Blacks were a minority even in most southern states. When Reconstruction came to an end after 1877, the Republicans lost interest in the black minority and its problems, and it was reduced to political impotence. Southern whites were overwhelmingly Democratic, and their leaders were an important part of the national Democratic coalition. In 1894, when (for the first time since 1860) the Democrats controlled the presidency and both houses of Congress, they repealed all the remaining Reconstruction acts, although some civil rights laws remained, unenforced, on the books.

The Spirit of the Age. The late nineteenth century was the age of "rugged individualism." The idea that people ought to be viewed as members of groups was hardly a new one, but it did not fit in with the spirit of the age, nor did government regulation of business to prevent discrimination.

---

[9] *Guinn* v. *U.S.* 238 U.S. 347 (1915).

[10] *Grovey* v. *Townsend* 295 U.S. 45 (1935).

[11] *Smith* v. *Allwright*, 321 U.S. 649 (1944).

Moreover, by the late nineteenth century, racism had been worked up into a pseudoscience, often linked with "Social Darwinism," the notion that superior individuals survive better and so rise to the top of society. Racism of this sort gave a veneer of scientific respectability to the systematic suppression of black rights and was another pervasive feature of the spirit of the age. In fact, not until after the fall of Hitler did "scientific racism" cease to be respectable among civilized people in this and in other countries.

Finally, the effort to achieve equality for blacks petered out because it required an effort of will that was beyond us. Slavery is an ancient institution throughout the world and had existed here almost from the beginnings of settlement. In 1860 the vast majority of blacks in the United States were slaves. Five years later they were all, in theory, free men and women. By historical standards, that is both basic and instant social change. Theoretical freedom could have become real freedom only with a vast national effort, but that effort could not have been sustained. In the first place, it is hard to sustain any political movement beyond the point of crisis. Besides, making blacks into full citizens would have required—and still does require—many compromises with strong traditions: our usual hostility to federal intervention in local matters (see Chapter 3), for example.

THE CIVIL RIGHTS REVOLUTION

In the last full year before the Civil War, 1860, the vast majority of American blacks lived in the rural South, and they continued to live there until the mechanization of southern agriculture in the twentieth century. Machines cost money, and most southern blacks had little money and little access to banks, so black farmers were forced to move to the cities of the North and the Midwest. (That, by the way, is the reason why blacks today own less land in the South than they did 100 years ago.)

Cities are often cold and indifferent places, but that was exactly why blacks were able to become organized in them. By World War I, urban black professionals had their own pressure group (see Chapter 6), the National Association for the Advancement of Colored People (the NAACP, formed in 1909), and a black press, including newspapers such as Chicago's *Defender* and New York's *Amsterdam News*.

The spirit of the age changed, too. It was less and less the fashion to view society as a heap of isolated individuals colliding with other isolated individuals. Social science—a new term—treated individuals as members of social groups, with group as well as individual interests. Particularly after 1933, the American people began to take federal intervention in domestic affairs for granted (see Chapter 3), and local control retreated before the federal government's power. The Democrats, although they remained the party of the South, also became the party of the northern and midwestern cities and of blacks, and they shed much of their former conservatism.

Finally, by 1940 the United States saw itself as a world power, and in that role we claimed to act on behalf of freedom and against tyranny (see Chapter 17). How then could we deny that same freedom to 10 percent of our own people? Moreover, the liberation of Black Africa and much of Asia from European colonial rule, after 1945, created a very strong foreign-policy incentive for federal action against racial discrimination at home. When African diplomats in Washington, D.C., or in the United Nations were denied

An Insult to Democracy

It started in June, 1938, when the Hurok office received a routine request from Howard University, asking for a Marian Anderson concert. Hurok named a date, April 9, 1939, and a reservation was requested at Constitution Hall, the only large auditorium in Washington.

Sorry, replied officers of the D.A.R. [Daughters of the American Revolution, whose members claim descent from U.S. soldiers in the American Revolution], owners of the hall, it was taken for that date. Hurok suggested others. *All* dates were taken, replied the D.A.R. Investigation showed that a clause in the rental contract prohibited Negroes from appearing there.

The world was shocked. Leading musicians whom Marian did not know canceled their concerts at Constitution Hall; journalists, government and religious leaders, public and private citizens alike, rose as one. This insult to American democracy was more than they could stand.

"I am ashamed to play at Constitution Hall," said Jascha Heifitz, one of the world's leading violinists.

"One of the most monstrous and stupid things that has happened in America in years," said Heywood Broun, journalist.

Walter Damrosch, composer-conductor; Deems Taylor, critic; Lawrence Tibbett, Metropolitan star and president of the American Guild of Musical Artists; Fiorello La Guardia, Mayor of New York City, and hundreds of others sent the D.A.R. wires of protest. Wired Deems Taylor:

> This action subverts the clear meaning of the U.S. Constitution, in particular the Bill of Rights, and places your organization in the camp of those who seek to destroy democracy, justice, and liberty.

Then came the climax: In her syndicated newspaper column, "My Day," Eleanor Roosevelt [wife of President Franklin Roosevelt] announced her resignation from the D.A.R. Newspapers all over the country headlined her resignation, and a wave of others followed. Mrs. Giuseppe Boghetti; Josephine Truslow Adams, of the Massachusetts Adamses; Dr. Elsie Mitchell, of California. Others set up their own D.A.R. with a policy of nondiscrimination. Furthermore, some local chapters of the D.A.R. objected to Washington's action. This, Marian said later, confirmed her opinion that a whole group must not be condemned for the actions of a new.

Not everyone sympathized with Marian. Columnist Westbrook Pegler called her a "hitherto obscure Negro singer," and hinted that the whole affair was a publicity stunt. "An obscure singer"—after Salzberg, L'Opera de Paris, the White House, Carnegie Hall, and winning the Grand Prix du Chant for the best recorded voice in Europe!

"Perhaps," said Mr. Hurok, "Mr. Pegler was trying to be funny." . . .

Meanwhile Howard University, more eager than ever for a Marian Anderson concert, asked the Washington, D.C., Board of Education of the use of the auditorium at Central High School. The request was denied. Over a thousand indignant citizens formed a protest committee, picketed the board's office, and sent them a petition with thousands of signatures. The request was still denied. The high school students themselves wrote an editorial for their school paper:

> Let us hope that it [the Board] does reconsider and do Central the honor of playing host to one of the musical world's greatest artists, as well as prove to the rest of the world that this country holds no grudges because of race or color.

The principal of Central High, unwilling to have the students criticize their Board of Education, suppressed the editorial before it was published.

On February 24, Mr. Hurok made an announcement. Marian Anderson would sing in Washington, D.C. She would sing out-of-doors within earshot of the D.A.R.'s Constitution Hall. At the invitation of the United States Department of the Interior, she would sing an Easter Sunday Concert at the Lincoln Memorial. . . .

Easter Sunday dawned cloudy, gray. Busy bellhops all over Washington murmured the same prayer: "Please don't let it rain."

Mr. Hurok met Marian and her mother at the station. While police sirens shrieked, he drove them to the home of the former governor of Pennsylvania, Gifford Pinchot, where they would remain until concert time. . . .

They drove to the Lincoln Memorial, again escorted by police. The past few days had been filled with rumors, even threats against Marian's personal safety. "But as Marian walked beside me along the roped-off aisle and up the steps to the platform, where great men and women of America stood to honor her," said Mr. Hurok, "the arm which I took to steady her was steadier than my own."

The bellhops' prayers had been answered. The sky

AP/Wide World Photos

was blue, and the sun shown down on blossoming cherry trees and soft spring grass. Congressmen, some born in the South, were there. Also present were Supreme Court Justices, Secretary of the Treasury Morgenthau, and dozens of other dignitaries. . . . Seventy-five thousand people, men, women, children,

Negro and white, stood side by side, faces upturned, eyes, ears, and hearts fixed on her.

Together they sang "The Star Spangled Banner."

Sherlee P. Newman, *Marian Anderson, Lady from Philadelphia*, The Westminster Press, Philadelphia, 1966.

service at restaurants, there were serious international complications. So our developing awareness of the general conflict between our ideals and our reality was much enlivened by the growing awareness that we had important interests to protect abroad. Racism—by seriously contaminating the image of the United States—was getting very much in the way of these interests.

Discrimination had been a fact of life for generations. Now it was to become something quite different: an officially recognized fact and, what is more, a Problem with a capital P.

Strategies: Moving into Court

Discrimination was a problem for black people long before it achieved official recognition. At first, the NAACP and other civil-rights groups tried to get the elected branches of the federal government to move against discrimination. In the 1930s, these groups tried and failed to persuade Congress to pass federal laws to outlaw poll taxes and lynching and to guarantee voting rights and fair employment. They also pressured Presidents Roosevelt (1933–1945) and

Truman (1945–1953) to adopt executive orders (see Chapter 11) banning specific kinds of racial discrimination—in the armed forces, for example. The order against discrimination in the armed forces did indeed come, but only in 1950. When the strategy of working through the elected branches paid off at all, it paid off slowly.

By the 1940s, blacks were relying on the courts to recognize and protect their civil rights, and for the same reason that we must rely on the courts to protect our civil liberties (see Chapter 4): Civil liberties and civil rights protect minorities from the majority, so they cannot be upheld by those branches of government that are responsible to the majority. Not until most blacks had moved to the North and had formed alliances with other groups would a political, as opposed to a legal, strategy be at all realistic.

First Breakthrough: Schools. The agenda of the civil-rights struggle was enormously broad: Nothing less than a fundamental change in the legal and political status of 16 million people (in 1950). The battle lines were drawn over issues such as voting rights, public accommodations, public education, employment, housing, and just about every other aspect of life. School desegregation was the first important constitutional breakthrough. Racially segregated schools had a long history in the North and in the South. The U.S. Supreme Court had blessed them in 1896 and had always viewed the public schools as a matter for states and localities, whose only constitutional obligation was to provide a "separate but equal" education.

Separate but Unequal. To begin with, the NAACP and its allies showed that segregated education did not *in fact* provide an equal education for blacks. They then showed that segregation *could not* do so—that the *Plessy* v. *Ferguson* formula, "separate but equal," was a contradiction.

Because justices of the U.S. Supreme Court were lawyers, they were familiar with law schools and with the requirements of a good legal education. The NAACP therefore decided to prove to the Court that a law student could not get adequate training in a racially segregated state law school, even if the dollar amounts spent on it equaled dollar amounts spent on white law schools. The assault on the "separate but equal" doctrine would then be extended to public education in general.

In 1938 the U.S. Supreme Court ruled in favor of a black student seeking admission to an all-white state law school in Missouri because there was no law school for blacks.[12] The larger principle, "separate but equal," was not tested until 1950, when a black student sued for admission to the all-white University of Texas Law School. The state claimed that the UT Law School and another, black, law school were separate but equal. The justices took a hard look at this so-called equality and concluded that it was fraudulent. The UT Law School was opened to blacks.[13]

By the early 1950s, the NAACP's legal offensive against the "separate but equal" doctrine was fully prepared. In 1951 a black clergyman in Topeka, Kansas, took his daughter, Linda Brown, to an all-white grade school and tried to have her enrolled. Kansas was among the few states outside the South with a school segregation law, and Brown was turned down. At the same time, exactly similar cases were under way in South Carolina, Virginia, Delaware, and the District of Columbia. (Congress still permitted racially segregated public schools to operate in the nation's capital!) In each of these cases, the

---

[12] *Missouri ex rel. Gaines* v. *Canada*, 305 U.S. 337 (1938).
[13] *Sweatt* v. *Painter*, 339 U.S. 629 (1950).

NAACP provided the legal and financial resources for the appeals to the U.S. Supreme Court.

The political implications of overturning the "separate but equal" doctrine were explosive, as the U.S. Supreme Court well knew. Brown's case first appeared before the Court in the fall of 1952, and it was argued in December. Rather unusually, the justices refused to decide these cases during the 1952 term and ordered that they be reargued in the fall of 1953. In the interval, Chief Justice Fred M. Vinson (1946–1953) died and was replaced by Earl Warren (Chief Justice, 1953–1969). Some have claimed that the decision to reargue, rather than hand down a decision in 1953, resulted from a sharp division within the Court over whether to strike down *Plessy*. Be that as it may, the Court was slow, deliberate, and politically conscious from beginning to end.

Within the Court, pressure for a unanimous decision written by the Chief Justice of the United States was overwhelming and eventually carried the day. (In fact, for many years, the Court was to decide just about all civil-rights cases unanimously.) *Brown* v. *Board of Education* overruled *Plessy* v. *Ferguson*, and established the principle that "in the field of public education the doctrine of 'separate but equal' has no place. Separate educational facilities are inherently unequal."[14] The next year Topeka's school board was ordered to begin desegregating its system, as were the other school boards involved in the companion cases.

Brown's impact went far beyond segregated education—indeed, beyond education itself—for the Court's reasoning set it on a new and important course. The justices made no effort to claim that the Framers of the Fourteenth Amendment had intended to ban racially segregated schools. Instead, they made their case by drawing upon the research of social scientists— among others, a Swedish sociologist named Gunnar Myrdal—who believed that discrimination promoted feelings of inferiority.[15] Social scientists had always played an important role in the civil-rights coalition; once the Supreme Court took notice of them, they began to play an important role in American government.

But Brown's impact took a while to be felt. Almost a decade went by before many segregated school districts began to comply with the Court's ruling. Some resistance was even violent. Finally, it took legislation by Congress in 1964 and 1965 to make significant compliance apparent.

Ever since, the Court has been vigorously attacked by opponents of the *Brown* decision for relying on social science findings and arguments rather than on legal ones. In truth, it could well have omitted social science altogether and based its decision on purely legal reasoning or on the plain fact that separate schools were not and could not be equal. However the justices chose to justify their decision to overturn the separate-but-equal doctrine, they would have been attacked for extending the Fourteenth Amendment's equal-protection clause far beyond its Framers' intentions.

Should they have done so? Remember, this happens all the time in constitutional cases. Recall Chief Justice John Marshall's words, in *McCulloch* v. *Maryland* (1819) (see Chapter 3): "This provision is made in a constitution, intended to endure for ages to come, and consequently, to be adapted to the various crises of human affairs."[16] Rulings on the Constitution are not babies

---

[14] *Brown* v. *Board of Education*, 347 U.S. 483 (1954).

[15] Gunnar Myrdal, *An American Dilemma* (New York: Harper, 1944).

[16] Wheat, 316 (1819).

In this decade, integrated classes are quite common—but the struggle for civil rights is not yet over for Americans.

brought by judicial storks; they are politics of the highest order. Racial discrimination cannot be reconciled with any present-day understanding of equal protection under the law. If social scientists have discovered that it also produces psychological and social injustices, their findings should be heeded, not ignored.

The Battle for Civil Rights

On Monday, February 1, 1960, a group of young blacks, mostly college students, went into a drugstore in Greensboro, North Carolina. They sat down at the lunch counter and asked for service, but the manager told them that blacks could not be served. They refused to leave, and eventually the police came and arrested them.

The young blacks came back on following days with more and more friends—and enemies. By the end of the week, the store was jammed with young blacks and whites. The former continued to sit at the counter while "the white boys waved Confederate flags, chanted and cursed."[17] The store's lunch counter was closed the following Monday, and the local demonstration came to an end. But the "sit-in" movement had begun. By mid-April it had spread throughout the South; within a year and a half, 70,000 blacks and their white sympathizers had been involved in these demonstrations. A major force within the larger civil-rights revolution was under way.

Night after night, the television news showed films of young blacks being dragged out of drugstores and restaurants. Day after day, newspaper editorials denounced segregation in the South—as though there were no segregation

[17] Donald R. Matthews and James W. Prothro, *Negroes and the New Southern Politics* (New York: Harcourt, 1966), pp. 407–8.

A black "sit-in" demonstrator is pulled from a Woolworth store lunch counter and beaten. This took place in Jackson, Mississippi, in 1963.

in the North. President John F. Kennedy (1961–1963) submitted to Congress a civil-rights bill to ban discrimination in public accommodations, but Congress refused to pass it.

On November 22, 1963, President Kennedy was assassinated. Kennedy's successor, Lyndon Johnson (1963–1969), himself a southerner, appealed to Congress to pass the civil-rights bill as a tribute to the dead President's memory. After months of debate, on July 2, 1964, the 1964 Civil Rights Act was signed into law. The protesters at Greensboro had triumphed.

"Black Power." Although still committed to nonviolence, the civil-rights movement could not control the flow of events. On February 1, 1965, Martin Luther King, Jr., a southern Baptist minister who was the chief civil-rights leader of the day, was arrested with 770 demonstrators in Selma, Alabama, protesting against the state's voter registration law. White violence in Selma pushed the civil-rights movement toward greater militancy. Angry demonstrations and speeches were the order of the day, and not only in the South: In midsummer, King slipped away from Selma and led 20,000 people in a march through Chicago to protest local segregation. Black anger and frustration in the Watts section of Los Angeles then boiled over into a riot that left 34 people dead and 200 businesses destroyed. Certain black leaders stopped talking about civil rights and desegregation and started talking about "black power."

Back in Selma, 200 Alabama state police officers had attacked demonstrators with tear gas, whips, and nightsticks; a white civil-rights worker had been killed by four members of the Ku Klux Klan; and President Johnson had sent in the national guard. But the summer ended with a civil-rights victory: the passage and signing of the Voting Rights Act of 1965.

"Easy" and "Hard" Areas of the Law

The earliest targets of the movement were state laws that enforced segregation (in public schools, for instance) or that established clearly separate standards for blacks and whites (such as voter registration laws). Segregation in these "easy" areas resulted from the direct action of states and localities and could be attacked by striking down specific laws or passing new ones.

Private discrimination is much more difficult to reach by any government agency, law, or decree. So too is "passive segregation," particularly in northern public schools, where no laws required segregation. School districts and individual schools simply have "catchment areas" from which they draw students. These areas are based on local patterns of residence and, therefore, on residential segregation. Some of this segregation comes about voluntarily, for Americans commonly wish to live among people similar to themselves (see Chapter 1). But a great deal of it has been created by systematic patterns of discrimination against racial "outsiders," patterns enforced by banks, insurance companies, and realtors, all of whom play an important role in maintaining the boundaries (and therefore the existence) of the nation's urban black ghettoes.[18]

---

[18] A first-rate exploration of these and other even more coercive elements in the history of the Chicago ghetto is Allan Spear, *Black Chicago: The Making of a Negro Ghetto, 1890–1920* (Chicago: Univ. of Chicago, 1967). See also an older classic, St. Clair Drake and Horace R. Cayton, *Black Metropolis* (New York: Harcourt, 1945), bringing the story of the Chicago ghetto and its people up to World War II; and Gilbert Osofsky's parallel study of Harlem, *Harlem: The Making of a Ghetto, 1890–1930* (New York: Harper, 1963).

Twenty Years On

GREENSBORO, N.C., Feb. 1—Four black men, for the most part heavier and more prosperous and certainly less grim, returned here today to a lunch counter at the F. W. Woolworth's store where they were refused service 20 years ago, an event that galvanized the civil rights movement of the 1960s.

While some officials of the city and Woolworth's helped celebrate the long-ago moment that breached the barriers of a segregated society, other city officials were bracing for an anti-Ku Klux Klan march and rally tomorrow that has evoked new fears of violence.

Tonight the Mayor proclaimed a limited state of emergency in the hope of heading off any armed confrontation between pro-Klan elements and the members of the Communist Workers Party who are among the demonstrators. Last Nov. 3, five members of the Communist Workers Party were slain while protesting Klan violence.

Today, in the re-enactment of the lunch counter sit-in, the four men were supposed to have eaten a breakfast served by Aubrey C. Lewis, a black vice president of Woolworth's. But in the flurry of celebration and the crush of newsmen, they never got to eat.

"Twenty years ago I could not get served here," said Franklin McCain. "I come back today and still can't get served."

The city has erected a marker to commemorate the sit-in, which added to the momentum of the Alabama boycott declared by the Rev. Martin Luther King, Jr., and carried the demand for equal treatment from lunch counter to cafeteria line to the streets.

Within two months after the four freshmen at the North Carolina A & T State University perched on stools and ordered coffee from a white waitress, the sit-in movement spread to 54 cities in nine Southern states. Within a year, more than 100 cities had experienced some attempt at desegregation of public facilities by college students. The four men are today working successfully in their careers.

What They Are Doing Today

Joseph McNeil is a stockbroker with E. F. Hutton Inc. in Fayetteville, N.C. Before moving to Fayetteville, he was a banker in New York City for eight years. Mr. McCain is a group leader in the marketing technical department of Celanese Corporation in Charlotte, N.C. David Richmond lives on a farm in Franklin, N.C., and Ezell Blair Jr., who has changed his name to Jibreel Khazan, is an evaluator for the CETA program in Bedford, Mass.

Their return today to what one called "the birthplace of a whirlwind" was the cornerstone of a day filled with anniversary activities and remarkable ironies.

Andrew Young, the former chief United States representative at the United Nations, was present for a news conference and made a speech to students at North Carolina A & T. The four honored men held another news conference and attended breakfasts and a luncheon. A memorial statue was unveiled honoring a man who was slain in a civil rights disturbance at the college in 1969.

Mr. Young, whom the Klan fought so bitterly in the 1960s, said that he saw no real threat from their members. He described them as coming mostly from a group of poor, undereducated white Americans who had been left out of the mainstream and were frustrated and fearful as they saw blacks gain upward mobility.

"We have to be as concerned for the poor whites being left out of the mainstream as blacks," he said and added: "I am much more concerned about some of the people who hold public office here who have a very sophisticated racist mentality. I think they may be a lot more dangerous than the Klan."

And the four men who led the sit-ins of two decades ago said that they would not join tomorrow's march.

The march and rally is being sponsored by a group that calls itself the Feb. 2 Mobilization Committee, under the auspices of the Inter-religious Foundation for Community Organizations, a national organization situated in New York City and supported mostly by churches and foundations.

One of the major organizations participating in the rally is the Southern Christian Leadership Conference, once led by Dr. King. Another is the Communist Workers Party, which has refused to promise that its members will be unarmed as they walk a four-mile route to the Greensboro Coliseum for the rally. The members maintain that to announce in advance that they are without weapons would be to invite physical attacks from Klansmen and Klan sympathizers.

Consequently, the party was expelled from the coalition until it made such a promise, but its members will march tomorrow nevertheless.

In other developments, Gov. James B. Hunt Jr. today activated the North Carolina National Guard to help local law-enforcement agencies handle the thousands of marchers expected to arrive here from Prince Georges County, Maryland; Cincinnati, and various points in North Carolina.

Mayor James Melvin and the Greensboro City

Except in the more flagrant cases—for example, racially discriminatory restrictive housing covenants—"state action" to maintain passive segregation is much more difficult to identify than it had been in the classic southern cases. Yet passive segregation is about as thorough in the North as formal discrimination used to be in the South, and it makes school desegregation nearly impossible in many cases. Constitutional law comes up against the hard reality that most white Americans do not want to live near large numbers of blacks. People who have enough money to make their own choices usually "vote with their feet" by moving out of reach when the prospect threatens, the so-called white flight (see Chapter 1).

Voting Rights

The 1964 Civil Rights Act, and other early attempts to secure black voting rights, failed because the opponents of discrimination had to move case by case. President Johnson was largely responsible for the 1965 Voting Rights Act, which simply abolished literacy tests everywhere and permitted the Attorney General to send examiners to specific areas (named in the act) to register voters. The 1965 act also barred states and localities mostly in the South from changing their election systems unless they got clearance from the Attorney General or the U.S. District Court for the District of Columbia (see Chapter 14).

Voting itself is clearly one of the "easy" areas of dispute, but the 1965 Voting Rights Act did touch on one of the harder areas, too. Under the act, any proposed *change* in any system of election can be rejected if it dilutes black voting power, even if it was not intended to do so. The act was therefore an attack on discrimination that seems to be "in the nature of things," not only on deliberate discrimination.

In 1982 the Voting Rights Act was extended, this time for twenty years, and this time with a major difference: *All existing* election systems are now covered. Before 1982, a person who thought that a particular electoral practice outside the South was racially discriminatory had to prove discriminatory *intent*. Now, with the 1982 extension, a violation of the act in *any* part of the United States occurs if the electoral practice in question has a discriminatory *effect*. Obviously it is easier to show the consequences of a policy than to show convincingly the motivations for it. This change may lead to a shift of political power in areas of the country where blacks or Hispanics amount to at least a sizable minority of the population.

Without doubt, the Voting Rights Act has been a success because it brought federal power to bear directly on local elections. As a result, it has created—for the first time in American history—a mass black electorate that has helped elect over 5,000 black officials, including the mayors of some of the largest cities in the United States. These voters provided a solid base for Jesse Jackson's unsuccessful bid for the Democratic presidential nomination in

Title VII of the 1964 Civil Rights Act prohibits discrimination on grounds of physical handicaps, among other things. Here, a blind woman is working as a telephone operator.

1984. The wishes and needs of black people are now a political fact of life, one that is here to stay. Black leaders can now appeal to the self-interest, not just to the idealism, of white politicians.

These are changes of truly fundamental importance—changes that could not have been accomplished without a change in law. They were made possible by changes in the attitudes of white Americans about the basic rights of U.S. citizens, and the law itself then reinforced the new attitudes.

The Civil Rights Acts of 1964 and 1968

There was much less change in attitudes about private discrimination than about public discrimination. As we have seen, back in 1883 the U.S. Supreme Court ruled that the Fourteenth Amendment's equal-protection clause applied only to governments, not to private individuals and enterprises. "Public accommodations"—privately owned enterprises open to the public—could therefore discriminate all they liked.

Although discrimination in public accommodations was harder to deal with than voting rights had been, it was much simpler than discrimination in housing and jobs. It is much easier to prove that a theater, let us say, will not admit blacks as customers than to prove that it will not hire them as employees; after all, it cannot hire everyone. Besides, many difficulties that blacks face in seeking employment stem not from deliberate discrimination but from "the nature of things"—from poverty, poor educational opportunities, and every kind of social problem. These problems are largely the heritage of past discrimination. We, in the present, are not directly responsible for all of them, nor could they be resolved right away even if we had the will to do so.

The 1964 Civil Rights Act. The first effort to attack discrimination in public accommodations, housing, and jobs was the Civil Rights Act of 1964. In addition, parts of the act dealt, not very successfully, with voting rights.

Public Accommodations. Title II of the 1964 act banned racial discrimination in public places of business whose products or customers move about in interstate commerce—just about everything and everybody. Title II has been rigorously enforced; these kinds of discrimination are largely behind us.

Title II was upheld by the U.S. Supreme Court in 1964. At first, the Court held on to the traditional view that some kinds of state action—in this case, the licensing and regulation of businesses by states—must be involved to justify a civil-rights law.[19] In 1973 it simply declared that "The Constitution places no value on discrimination." Americans have no constitutional right at all to discriminate.[20]

Employment. Title VII of the 1964 act forbids employers (in interstate commerce) from discriminating against would-be employees on grounds of race, religion, national origin, physical handicap, sex, or age. Certain exceptions are permitted: Religious schools, for instance, can take into account the religious views of prospective teachers, and a theatrical producer does not have to hire a woman to play Romeo or a man to play Juliet.

Because the whole problem of employment is a "hard" issue, this part of the act has been only a mixed success. Blatant discrimination has been discouraged; we shall never again see job advertisements that say, "No Irishmen need apply." But many of the difficulties that blacks face in finding jobs, particularly good ones, stem more from the heritage of past discrimination than from discrimination in the present. No issue generates such bitterness as the effort to undo that heritage.

Housing. On a blistering hot day in July 1919, a young black man named Eugene Williams decided to go for a swim at a whites-only beach on the South Side of Chicago. He was stoned by whites and drowned. Blacks then retaliated by attacking whites, and the Chicago Race Riot of 1919 was on. For five days of death and destruction, the riot swirled through the city.

The story behind the story of the riot began about 1914, when blacks started moving into Chicago from the rural South. Whites resented the newcomers and tried to keep them out of white neighborhoods. Sometimes the whites failed because certain realtors would settle blacks in one house on a white block, hoping to make the whites panic and sell their houses to these realtors—at bargain prices. "Blockbusting" was the name of this sleazy operation.

After the riot, many whites tried to fight the blockbusters by writing into real estate contracts **restrictive covenants,** that bound buyers not to sell their houses to blacks or to members of other groups such as Jews and Roman Catholics. Restrictive covenants solidified Chicago's black ghetto, whose boundaries—fixed by housing contracts in surrounding neighborhoods—changed little until the end of World War II.

In 1948 the U.S. Supreme Court prohibited federal, state, and local courts from enforcing restrictive covenants, on the ground that in doing so they were tolerating and even promoting residential discrimination—"state action."[21] But restrictive covenants were only one reason for the ghetto. Another was the continuing (though, in most areas, illegal) practice of blockbusting by realtors. Yet another was "redlining" by banks, which often refused to grant mortgages in areas that blacks were moving into, thus speeding up "white flight." The

---

[19] *Heart of Atlanta Motel* v. *U.S.,* 379 U.S. 421 (1964).
[20] *Norwood* v. *Harrison,* 413 U.S. 455 (1973).
[21] *Shelly* v. *Kraemer,* 334 U.S. 1 (1948).

Figure 5-1 Areas of Black Residence in Chicago, 1920

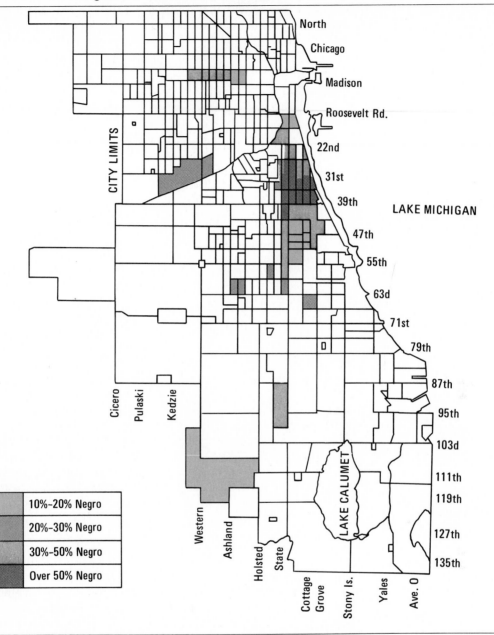

Source: Based on Ernest W. Burgess and Charles Newcomb, eds., *Census Data of the City of Chicago* (Chicago: Univ. of Chicago, 1931).

federal government itself contributed mightily to white flight by encouraging the growth of the suburbs (see Chapter 3).

The ultimate reason for the ghetto, to put it baldly, was racial prejudice— the root cause of white flight, restrictive covenants, blockbusting, and redlining. Banning restrictive covenants did not permit blacks to move out of the ghetto; the ghetto just grew bigger.

The Civil Rights Act of 1968. Congress attempted to root out the remaining causes of residential segregation in the 1968 Civil Rights Act, which bans

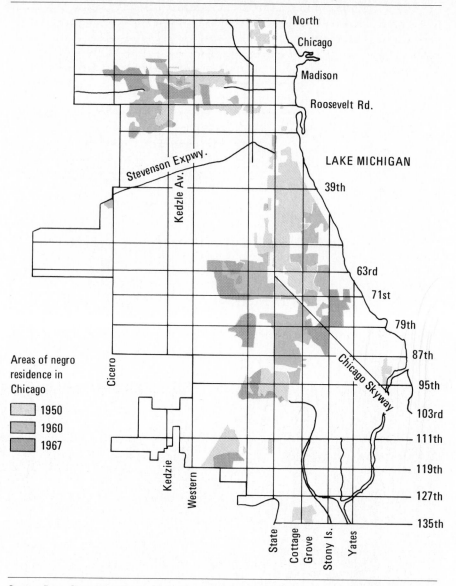

Figure 5-2   Areas of Black Residence in Chicago, 1967

Source: From *Chicago's Widening Color Gap*, Interuniversity Social Research Committee: Report No. 2 (Chicago, 1967).

racial, religious, and (since 1974) sex discrimination in the sale or rental of housing—more than 80 percent of it, in any case. The act also outlaws blockbusting and redlining.

But the ghetto persists. First, people who think they are victims of housing discrimination have to take their cases to federal court, and that is slow and expensive (see Chapter 14). Housing, besides, is a typical family's major investment—one that lies at the core of social life. And the issues involved in housing touch the heart of important industries in our economy, like banking and construction, that are well represented by lobbies in Washington (see Chapter 6).

Finally, access to housing is overwhelmingly determined by income, and in the early 1980s, the average income of black households was only 55 percent to 60 percent that of white households. Because our stock of public housing is very small by comparison with most Western countries, these black households have to compete for housing in the private realty market. With their often grossly inadequate financial resources, they live where they can.

Busing

De facto residential segregation was widespread in the North, and that made school integration harder to achieve in the North than in the segregated South. How do you create racial balance in Chicago's (or New York's or Boston's or Philadelphia's) school system if parts of the city are wholly white and parts wholly black?

The U.S. Supreme Court decided in the early 1970s that the only way was **busing:** The transportation of pupils from the areas where they lived to schools in other areas. Instead of attacking the laws that tolerated or encouraged segregation, the courts attacked the *fact* of segregation, whatever its cause. Busing was imposed first on Charlotte, North Carolina, in 1971,[22] and federal judges soon insisted on it, too, in several northern cities.

Some cities, like Denver, Colorado, accepted busing in peace. Others, especially Boston, exploded with anger and, from time to time, violence. No doubt about it: Busing was unpopular—among both blacks and whites—and

The first day of class in Boston in 1974. Black students arrive for the first time to integrate South Boston High School.

---
[22] *Swann* v. *Charlotte Mecklenburg Board of Education,* 401 U.S. 1 (1971).

UPI/Bettmann Newsphotos

made the country more conservative. Boston (which in the 1972 Democratic presidential primary had voted for the liberal George McGovern) voted for the conservative George Wallace in the 1976 Democratic presidential primary. Irish South Boston ("Southie") voted Republican in the 1976 presidential election—for the first time since the founding of the Republican party, 120 years earlier. It repeated this marvel in 1980.

Hostility to busing was due not only to racism pure and simple, but also to the belief that busing undermined our traditions of local government and majority rule. When Boston's School Board refused to organize the busing ordered by the U.S. District Court, the court itself became, in effect, a local school board. Without doubt, a strong majority of Boston's voters opposed the district court's policy. The school board was elected by the voters and was responsible to them, but its policies had produced a segregated school system. The right of the majority to control its own future confronted the minority's right to participate in a fundamental American institution, the public schools. That was the tragedy of Boston.

Boston's busing took place entirely within city limits. Some cities simply did not have enough whites to bus. Detroit was one of these cities: By 1970, black students were the large majority in the local school district, while in the three surrounding counties 87 percent of the students were white. In 1972, a federal judge did the obvious: He ordered busing across city and county lines, including a total of 54 separate school districts—even though most of the suburban districts involved in the plan had not transgressed the Constitution.

The local political furor was enormous: Candidate George Wallace carried white suburban Detroit by a large majority in the 1972 Democratic presidential primary. Busing was overwhelmingly opposed by white public opinion—so much so that many people concluded that busing could not in the long run produce the desired results in huge metropolitan areas. Of course, there was an important legal objection: The district court's decision overrode county and town boundaries.

The U.S. Supreme Court, at the vortex of this rapidly gathering storm, decided by a 5 to 4 vote that local governments could not be brushed aside if—as in this particular case—the boundaries of the original school districts had not been created with intent to maintain a racially segregated school system or if local governments were not the causes of the racial segregation between school districts.[23] Busing as a remedy for school segregation now usually stops at the city line, perhaps simply because five justices outvote four.

Affirmative Action

Perhaps nothing in the chronicles of civil-rights controversy generated more bitterness than **affirmative action**. Affirmative action is more than just an inconvenience: It affects us directly in our pocketbooks, and many people regard it as an assault on our basic values. There is even a good deal of disagreement about what it is. Let us get down to cases.

The Bakke Case. Allan Bakke, a white engineer, twice applied to the medical school of the University of California at Davis, and twice he was rejected. Bakke claimed that some of the students who had been admitted to the

---

[23] *Milliken* v. *Bradley*, 418 U.S. 717 (1974).

school—blacks let in under an affirmative action program—were less qualified than he was. This program, he argued, thus subjected him to racial discrimination. Bakke further argued that the medical school should have chosen its entering class by "meritocratic" criteria—grades—for grades measure precisely and establish a standard of fairness.

Do they? The medical school thought not. It argued that many things go into the making of a good doctor, not just grades. Beyond that, it challenged the idea that grades actually measure ability: Given the obstacles faced by blacks, a black applicant with a B average might be more able than a white applicant with an A average. In any case, the battle of life is far from equal; many of us enjoy advantages of birth, not of ability—so the medical school reasoned—and society should try to compensate for these underserved advantages. The Davis medical school tried to do so by reserving for black students sixteen places in its entering class. It called this affirmative action, promoting desegregation. Bakke called it a quota.

The whole case received much national attention, and passions ran high on both sides. Few values stand so high in the American pantheon as our commitment to individual achievement and reward for it. Yet in the present

One definition of meritocracy: "From him, according to his abilities; to him, according to his SAT scores."

Table 5-1 Employed Persons 16 Years and Over, by Race and Occupational Groups

RACE AND OCCUPATIONAL GROUP	1980	
	Number	*Percent Distribution*
White:		
White-collar workers	46,539,000	53.9%
Professional and technical workers	14,230,000	16.5
Managers and administrators, except farm	10,350,000	12.0
Sales workers	5,859,000	6.8
Clerical workers	16,101,000	18.6
Blue-collar workers	28,896,000	31.1
Craft and kindred workers	11,488,000	13.3
Operatives, except transport	8,765,000	10.1
Transport equipment operatives	2,938,000	3.4
Nonfarm laborers	3,704,000	4.3
Private household workers	694,000	0.8
Service workers, except private household	9,748,000	11.3
Farm workers	2,504,000	2.9
Total	86,380,000	100.0
Black and Other:		
White-collar workers	4,270,000	39.2
Professional and technical workers	1,383,000	12.7
Managers and administrators, except farm	569,000	5.2
Sales workers	313,000	2.9
Clerical workers	2,005,000	18.4
Blue-collar workers	3,904,000	35.8
Craft and kindred workers	1,041,000	9.6
Operatives, except transport	1,580,000	14.5
Transport equipment operatives	530,000	4.9
Nonfarm laborers	752,000	6.9
Private household workers	346,000	3.2
Service workers, except private household	2,169,000	19.9
Farm workers	200,000	1.8
Total	10,890,000	100.0

SOURCE: Department of Labor, Bureau of Labor Statistics.

generation, with its burdensome and still recent legacy of massive racial discrimination, a pure meritocratic standard would prevent almost all black applicants from getting into most graduate, medical, and law schools. Affirmative action came into being because of this reality.

Again, the U.S. Supreme Court was at the vortex. In 1978 its decision was utterly diffuse, for no opinion reflected the view of a majority of justices. By five justices to four, the Court ruled that Bakke should be admitted to the medical school.[24] But it could not agree on why. Justice Powell, in one opinion, argued that the medical school's admissions officers had stepped over the line separating "affirmative action" from an outright racial "quota." The University of California thus had the burden of showing that Bakke would not have been admitted had the special minority admissions program not existed. Of course, the whole point of Bakke's suit was the likelihood that he would have qualified for admission on a straight meritocratic basis.

Yet the Court did say that "affirmative action" was constitutional and even praised the affirmative action program of the Harvard Law School. Harvard's admissions committee does not specify beforehand how many black students will be admitted in any year. But in an effort to get a "balanced" class, it does consider the race of applicants. Because race is only one consideration among many, Justice Powell argued that Harvard was acting affirmatively to promote desegregation, not imposing a racial quota. This distinction struck many people as vague, if not false. Expect more litigation.[25]

The Weber Case. The Allan Bakke of employment was a 38-year-old white man named Brian Weber, who had been rejected by a skilled-crafts training program set up by his employer, Kaiser Aluminum, and his union, the United Steelworkers. More than half the openings in the program had been set aside for blacks, and a number of blacks with less seniority than Weber had been accepted. Weber sued the union on grounds similar to Bakke's.

This case had a curious ending, similar in a way to the outcome of the nineteenth-century civil-rights cases (see p. 123): In 1979 the Court ruled that the ban on racial discrimination in employment in the 1964 Civil Rights Act did not prohibit affirmative action in the private sector, even affirmative action that involved discrimination against whites.[26] In a second case, decided in 1980, the Court upheld a 1977 law that required at least 10 percent of federal works contracts to go to minority-owned businesses.[27]

But what happens when hard times require layoffs? In Memphis, Tennessee, several years ago, black residents sued the city fire department under the 1964 Civil Rights Act, claiming that there was racial discrimination in the department's hiring and promotion policies. In 1980, the city agreed to hire and promote more black firefighters. In 1981, a local budget deficit prompted the city to lay off some employees in the fire department. The city used the seniority rules that were part of the union contract the city had with the firefighters: last hired, first fired. This would mean that more blacks than whites would be laid off. In 1984, the Supreme Court ruled that the 1964 Act does not prevent an employer from applying an existing seniority rule even when there is an adverse impact on less senior members of a racial minority. The only exception would be a situation where less senior employees could

---

[24] *Regents of the University of California* v. *Bakke*, 438 U.S. 265 (1978).

[25] *Regents of the University of California* v. *Bakke*, 438 U.S. 265 (1978).

[26] *Steelworkers* v. *Weber*, 443 U.S. 193 (1979).

[27] *Fullilove* v. *Klutznick*, 652 Ed. 2nd 902 (1980).

show that they had been *actual* victims of the employer's past discrimination.[28]

There the matter now stands. Affirmative action, in some sense, is clearly constitutional. The U.S. Supreme Court has yet to define to everyone's satisfaction the permissible limits of affirmative action. And it may never do so. However defined, affirmative action is unpopular, so the Court may think it wiser not to present a clear target for attack.

Black people have won equality before the law, but they have not won social or, still more, economic equality. Some day, perhaps, we shall be able to say that all Americans truly are equal. But we have a long way to go, and there will be very large obstacles along the way.

THE WOMEN'S MOVEMENT AND WOMEN'S RIGHTS

Like the rights of blacks—but still more so—the problem of women's rights is only in part a legal problem. Women are now approaching equality in law: They have the vote, and the number of laws and regulations that apply solely to them is on the decline. But women are still not socially equal to men. When the man of the house comes home, he usually expects to find his dinner cooked by his wife, his house cleaned by his wife, and his children cared by for by his wife. His wife. His house. His children. On average, women earn 59¢ for each $1 men earn, even when they do the same work. By and large, they do *not* do the same work: For the most part, women are crowded into the lower rungs of the occupational hierarchy.

Votes for Women

In the United States, voting is the symbol of full citizenship, so the first goal of the organized women's movement was the vote. The U.S. Constitution itself did not deny the vote to women or to anyone else (see Chapter 2); qualifications for voting were left to the states, and the states limited the franchise to men. There was, however, a curious omission in the states' franchise codes: They prevented women from voting but not from running for office. As long ago as 1872, a woman, Victoria Claflin Woodhull, ran for President as the nominee of the National Woman's Suffrage Association.

The association's first victory came in 1869, when the newly formed Wyoming Territory gave women the right to vote and hold office. The next year, the Fifteenth Amendment was ratified, forbidding denial of the franchise "on account of race, color, or previous condition of servitude." But not on account of sex. Another fifty years would pass before women could vote in every state of the union.

The movement to grant votes to women—the "suffragette" movement—picked up steam after 1900, not only in the United States but also abroad. In this country, women could now vote in many western states, but each state had its own rules and its own standards. The women's movement wanted a constitutional amendment guaranteeing the right of women to vote everywhere in the United States. Neither major party was enthusiastic. The movement turned militant and sometimes violent. It still got nowhere.

Then came World War I. In 1917, after suffragettes had picketed the White House (which was touting the war as a war for democracy), President

---

[28] *Firefighters Union* v. *Stotts*, 52 U.S.L.W. 4767 (1984).

American Indians Became Citizens in 1924!

The long bloody struggle between the expanding United States of America and the many tribes and nations of the American Indian was brought to a close in the late 1800s. In 1887, the Dawes Act was passed by Congress, which provided for the granting of "individual" landholdings to Indians who would denounce their "tribal" holdings. In 1890, the Battle of Wounded Knee broke the back of Indian resistance. In 1893, the Dawes Commission was created under the Dawes Act; its aim was to secure the assent of the chiefs of the Five Civilized Nations in extinguishing tribal lands and allotting property to individuals. The bloodshed that had begun soon after the arrival of the Spanish in the sixteenth century and the British and the French in the seventeenth century was over, but the Indians' troubles were not.

For the most part, life for American Indians in the twentieth century has been marked by poverty, poor education, and unemployment. Throughout the 1970s, their unemployment rate was about 40 percent, roughly 10 times the national average (see table). The American Indian population today is some 800,000, living both off and on reservations.

Indians were made American citizens by congressional approval on June 15, 1924.

Federal Indian Reservations

STATE	NO. OF RESER.	TRIBALLY OWNED ACREAGE	ALLOTTED ACREAGE	NO. OF PERSONS	AVG. (%) UNEMP. RATE	MAJOR TRIBES AND/OR NATIVES
Alaska	1	86,741	299,400	72,664	51	Aleut, Eskimo, Athapascan, Haida, Tingit, Tsimpshian
Arizona	20	19,554,391	252,972	145,258	21	Navajo, Apache, Papago, Hopi, Yavapai, Pima
California	78	500,036	73,014	11,608	35	Hoopa, Paiute, Yurok, Karok, Mission Bands
Colorado	2	752,017	3,878	2,285	57	Ute
Florida	3	79,015	—	1,567	31	Seminole, Miccosukee
Idaho	4	459,756	334,475	5,847	30	Shoshone, Bannock, Nez Perce
Iowa	1	4,164	0	649	34	Sac and Fox
Kansas	4	5,504	22,522	2,225	17	Potawatomi, Kickapoo, Iowa
Louisiana	2	374	—	554	7	Chitimacha, Coushatta
Maine	3	71,568	—	1,247	20	Passamaquoddy, Penobscot, Maliseet
Michigan	5	12,039	9,247	3,354	50	Chippewa, Potawatomi, Ottawa
Minnesota	14	712,125	50,750	16,476	50	Chippewa, Sioux
Mississippi	1	17,478	18	4,490	18	Choctaw
Montana	7	2,170,265	3,051,321	16,483	27	Blackfeet, Crow, Sioux, Assiniboine, Cheyenne
Nebraska	3	22,275	42,531	3,318	42	Omaha, Winnebago, Santee Sioux
Nevada	23	1,067,674	78,388	6,281	30	Paiute, Shoshone, Washoe
New Mexico	24	6,462,826	677,845	104,153	20	Zuni, Apache, Navajo
New York	6	—	—	8,753	23	Seneca, Mohawk, Onondaga, Oneida
North Carolina	1	56,460	—	5,925	17	Cherokee
North Dakota	5	200,683	650,481	18,386	31	Sioux, Chippewa, Mandan, Arikara, Hidatsa
Oklahoma	—	85,566	1,145,871	126,213	15	Cherokee, Creek, Choctaw, Chickasaw, Osage, Cheyenne, Arapahoe, Kiowa, Comanche
Oregon	—	615,692	11,293	3,873	20	Warm Springs, Wasco, Paiute, Umatilla, Siletz
S. Dakota	9	2,572,817	2,516,505	42,439	34	Sioux
Utah	6	2,249,068	34,525	8,755	20	Ute, Goshute, Southern Paiute
Washington	26	1,996,018	497,219	34,940	35	Yakima, Lummi, Quinault
Wisconsin	15	328,437	80,886	16,544	34	Chippewa, Oneida, Winnebago
Wyoming	1	1,791,808	94,927	6,926	37	Shoshone, Arapahoe

Note: Data as of 1979. *Source:* Bureau of Indian Affairs, U.S. Department of the Interior.

Civil Rights and the American Indian

The American Indian Movement (AIM) is an organization of the American Indian civil-rights movement. In 1972, members of AIM briefly took over the headquarters of the Bureau of Indian Affairs, in Washington, D.C. They complained that the bureau had created the tribal councils on reservations in 1934 as a way of perpetuating paternalistic control over Indian development. In 1973, about 200 Sioux, led by members of AIM, seized the tiny village of Wounded Knee, South Dakota, site of the last great massacre of American Indians by the U.S. cavalry in 1890 (about 200 Indian men, women, and children were killed—and 29 sol-

diers). Among their demands was a review of the more than 300 treaties between the Indians and the federal government that AIM alleges have been broken. Wounded Knee was occupied for 70 days before the militants surrendered. The leaders were eventually brought to trial, but the case was dismissed on grounds of misconduct by the prosecution.

The return to Wounded Knee in 1981 by a small band of AIM Dakota Sioux, who occupied the Yellow Thunder Camp in the Black Hills.

UPI/Bettmann Newsphotos

Woodrow Wilson (1913–1921) endorsed the principle of equal suffrage. An amendment to that effect passed the House in 1918 but failed in the Senate. Finally, in 1919, the amendment passed both houses and was sent to the states for ratification. In 1920, when Tennessee ratified the Nineteenth Amendment, women got the vote throughout the United States.

The Latent Period: 1920s to 1960s

Fifty years of struggle had ended with an important but largely symbolic victory. One woman had been elected to the House in 1916, before the Nineteenth Amendment, but no woman was elected to the Senate until 1932, and in 1985 there were only two women senators. Not until 1933 was any woman appointed to the cabinet; even today, almost all cabinet officers are male. President Reagan did appoint the first woman justice of the U.S. Supreme Court, Sandra Day O'Connor, in 1981 (see Chapter 14).

In fact, the women's movement pretty much collapsed after the ratification of the Nineteenth Amendment, which removed one of the most important legal inequalities between men and women, if not the most important one. Further advances would have to be made in the sphere of private life—including the family—and in 1920, private life was pretty much outside of the government's domain. Moreover, the end of World War I was also the end of many changes in our national way of life. During the war, many women went to work in factories. After it, they went back to the kitchen. The Great Depression caused widespread unemployment, so women could not come out of the home in really massive numbers until they were needed in the war effort of the 1940s. After that, they again retreated to their kitchens.

In the late 1950s and early 1960s, however, the economy was expanding giddily. Businesses could not find enough workers, so they raised their wage rates in hope of enticing women out of their homes. They succeeded: Millions of women took jobs—mostly, as secretaries, waitresses, and the like—jobs

Table 5–2 Women in the Working Population

YEAR[1]	NUMBER (thousands)	PERCENT OF FEMALE POPULATION AGED 10 AND OVER[1]	PERCENT OF TOTAL WORKING POPULATION AGED 10 AND OVER[1]
1880	2,647	14.7%	15.2%
1890	4,006	17.4	17.2
1900	5,319	18.8	18.3
1910	7,445	21.5	19.9
1920	8,637	21.4	20.4
1930	10,752	22.0	22.0
1940	12,845	25.4	24.3
1950	18,412	33.9	17.3
1960[2]	23,272	37.8	19.4
1970	31,560	43.4	22.5
1979	43,531	51.1	26.6
1980	44,733	51.7	26.9

[1] For 1880–1930, data relate to population and gainful workers at ages 10 and over; for 1940, to ages 14 and over; for 1950–78, to population at ages 16 and over.

[2] Beginning in 1960, figures include Alaska and Hawaii.

SOURCES: Department of Commerce, Bureau of the Census, and Department of Labor, Bureau of Labor Statistics.

with flexible hours and little responsibility, so they could be home by the time the kids got out of school. But they were working —for income—and this gave them the beginnings of economic independence.

One thing did not change: the fact that women, because they were women, had a status in society quite different from the status of men, because they were men. A revived women's movement was upon us.

Women's Liberation

At a press conference in the early 1960s, President Kennedy was asked what the government was "doing for women." He paused for a long moment and said: "Not enough, I'm sure." He then promised to appoint a commission to study the matter. When the commission made its report, it turned out that Mr. Kennedy had been right: The government had not been doing enough for women. "Women's issues" were nonissues.

In 1963, Betty Freidan published what became the first manifesto of the revived women's movement, *The Feminine Mystique*. Friedan pointed out that women suffer as a class not only from discrimination but also from false values that encourage them to find fulfillment through their husbands and children, rather than through their own work. In 1963, there was no women's movement to challenge these social facts. Political activists were just becoming involved with the civil-rights movement. Later in the decade, they turned their attention to the Vietnam War (see Chapter 17). The women who joined these movements found themselves typing news sheets and manifestos, not writing them.

Even so, the movement of the mid- to late 1960s gave a large number of women political experience. Moreover, the "spirit of the age" was receptive to demands for liberation. When, in the early 1970s, the contemporary women's movement emerged, the country was ready to listen to it.

At first, the women's movement asserted itself less in politics and law than in attempts to change the private lives of men and women. Many women rejected the roles of sex object, servant, and Earth Mother. They sought equality with men in the kitchen and the bedroom. These changes were hard on both men and on women. Neither the innovators nor the inheritors have quite learned to live with them.

The Equal Rights Amendment

In 1972 Congress proposed a constitutional amendment (see Chapter 2) reading, "Equality of rights under the law shall not be denied or abridged by the United States or by any State on account of sex." This Equal Rights Amendment (ERA) seemed harmless enough. Yet a protracted struggle against it was eventually successful in 1982.

In part, the amendment was just a symbol, for it was not at all clear how sweeping its practical effects would have been. It was already illegal to discriminate against women in pay and hiring. Certain of the amendment's enemies claimed it would legalize coeducational toilets, but such toilets were already quite legal and existed in a number of colleges. Similarly, the barrier to the participation of women in armed combat was a mere law that could be repealed at any time.

Why then did the Equal Rights Amendment become so controversial? Perhaps the reason was that many people, including many women, disliked the things they thought it symbolized. Some regarded it as a symbolic challenge to traditional values: the home, the family, motherhood, what have you. Others believed that the subordination of women to men is ordained by God. Finally, many women probably opposed the ERA because they resented the movement standing behind it, a movement that in their view belittled the value of housework and motherhood—and thus of their own lives.

To a very large extent, moreover, the ERA got caught up in the undertow of growing and organized hostility to abortion on demand, legalized by the Supreme Court (see Chapter 14) and to female homosexuality. Some people seemed to equate the women's movement with approval of both. Certain leaders of the women's movement have also recently argued that big business worked against ratification, since the adoption of ERA might have provided a firmer constitutional basis for eliminating the time-honored practice of paying women lower salaries than men for the same work.

At first, however, the amendment had clear sailing; it easily made its way through many state legislatures. In the late 1970s, it ran into more resistance, and by 1979, the original deadline, it was still three states short of the 38 needed for ratification. With President Jimmy Carter's approval, Congress extended the deadline to July 1, 1982. But in 1982, the President was Ronald Reagan, who opposed the ERA. Despite a massive last-ditch lobbying effort by advocates of the ERA, it was still three states short when the second deadline ran out.

Public opinion strongly supported the amendment. Even so, the Republican party, at Mr. Reagan's behest, did not endorse the ERA in either 1980 or 1984 (breaking a forty-year tradition). In any case, there is very little doubt that the ERA—despite this defeat—will continue to haunt the American political agenda.

Women and the Law

One reason to doubt the real (as opposed to the symbolic) importance of the Equal Rights Amendment is the fact that much civil-rights law applies to sex as well as to race discrimination and so, as well, does the first section of the Fourteenth Amendment. In the 1970s the U.S. Supreme Court struck down many state laws that discriminated against women and recognized them as a group with common problems and a common need for legal protection, but it still permitted women to be excluded from certain jobs and duties of citizenship. For example, when Congress in 1980 required young men, but not young women, to register for a military draft (see Chapter 17), the Court refused to interfere.

AN OVERVIEW

In the late 1970s, women earned only about 60 percent as much as men who did comparable work. The median income of black families was only 59 percent of the corresponding figure for white families. Unemployment among black teenagers in the mid-1980s was close to three times that of white teenagers. Overall black unemployment was twice that of whites.

These differences do not all result from legal or constitutional inequality, but they make it harder for blacks to use their legal and constitutional rights. Black people have the right to go to college, for example, but not always the

Table 5-3 The Changing Work Force

		WHITE WOMEN (PERCENT)	MINORITIES* (PERCENT)
Total Work Force	1970	37.8%	15.9%
	1975	39.6	19.4
	1980	42.4	26.1
Managers	1970	10.7	3.6
	1975	10.7	4.5
	1980	11.2	5.2

* Includes blacks, Eskimos, American Indians, Orientals, and other racial groups of both sexes. Hispanics are classified as white.

SOURCE: Bureau of Labor Statistics.

income. And in some ways even blatant discrimination is very much alive—in housing, for instance—despite a multitude of laws and court decisions. The purely economic disparities between whites and blacks are so great that we still seem to be moving toward "two societies—separate and unequal."

Have we achieved nothing? Of course not.

Suppose that tomorrow morning, Japan were again to bomb Pearl Harbor—admittedly, an unlikely possibility. Would Japanese-Americans again be herded into relocation camps? Would their property again be seized without compensation? We cannot be absolutely sure, but the answer is probably no. It is worthwhile recalling that in 1979 and 1980, when the Iranian government held Americans hostage in Teheran (see Chapter 17), we did not retaliate in kind against the thousands of Iranians in this country, people who were *not* American citizens and who, in many cases, were openly hostile to us. We shall someday look back on this with pride.

White women and minorities now account for more than half the national work force, but in managerial positions, white males remain dominant.

SUMMARY

The case of Fred Korematsu and the story of the 120,000 Japanese-Americans placed in U.S. relocation camps during the World War II remind us that we have not always lived up to the ideal of equality before the law. Black people have been the main victims of American discrimination. Before the Civil War, black slaves were not legally human. The Civil War amendments—numbers 13, 14, and 15—were meant to bring legal and political equality to blacks. At first, however, the U.S. Supreme Court in effect nullified those amendments by permitting southern states to enact elaborate codes of legally mandated segregation and by permitting private individuals and businesses to discriminate all they pleased. Discrimination and segregation were common both in the North and in the South.

Early in the twentieth century, blacks started moving out of the rural South. Slowly and painfully, a black professional class emerged and formed organizations to protect the rights of blacks. The elected branches of the federal government did not offer much assistance, so the civil-rights movement took its case to the federal courts. This phase of the struggle came to a climax with *Brown* v. *Board of Education*, in 1954, the case that struck down racial segregation in public schools.

By the 1960s, civil rights had become a mass movement, with the muscle to enter the political arena. Congress passed a number of laws, including the Voting Rights Act of 1965, that created a black electorate. The Civil Rights Act of 1964 banned discrimination in public accommodations and in employment, and the Civil Rights Act of 1968 did the same for housing.

By then, the cutting edge of the movement had moved from the South to the North and was hitting the "hard" issues that more directly touch our economic and social lives. Black and white rights often collided. School busing was bitterly resisted in parts of the country, and affirmative action created even more bitterness.

When the struggle for black rights was already well under way, in the late 1960s, the struggle for women's rights started to revive. Of course, women had won the right to vote in 1920, with the Nineteenth Amendment. The women's movement then entered upon a long sleep, which ended in the early 1960s, when millions of American women went to work. This, together with the political ferment of the 1960s, caused more women to question their subordination to men. By the 1970s, the purely legal aspects of that subordination had been diminished, despite the defeat (in 1982) of the Equal Rights Amendment. But the social and economic relations between women and men are harder and more painful to change.

Blacks and women have made real legal and political gains in the past twenty years. That struggle is to some extent won. Battle lines are now drawn over social and economic issues that will be hard to resolve—issues that no society has ever resolved. It is to our credit that we keep trying; because important shortcomings continue, the struggle to eliminate them will continue to be an essential feature of our politics.

SUGGESTED READINGS

NORMAN DORSEN, *Discrimination and Civil Rights*. Boston: Little, Brown, 1969, and many subsequent editions. Standard and excellent book of constitutional cases in the civil-rights field.

JOHN HOPE FRANKLIN, *From Slavery to Freedom*, 4th ed. New York: Knopf, 1974. The best account of the history of blacks in America.

JUDITH HOLE and ELLEN LEVINE, *Rebirth of Feminism*. New York: Quadrangle, 1973. An account of the rise of the recent women's movement.

RICHARD KLUGER, *Simple Justice*. New York: Random House, 1977. An exhaustive—indeed definitive—account of the entire legal, political, and social setting of the Supreme Court's landmark desegregation case, *Brown* v. *Board of Education*.

J. W. PELTASON, *58 Lonely Men*. Urbana, Ill.: Univ. of Illinois, 1970. Dramatic story of the federal judges in the South who were faced with the task of enforcing the Supreme Court's 1954 school segregation decision.

JACOBUS tenBROEK, EDWARD N. BARNHART, and FLOYD W. MATSON, *Prejudice, War and the Constitution*. Berkeley: Univ. of California, 1968. Brilliant and comprehensive account of the West Coast Japanese-American detentions during World War II.

J. HARVIE WILKINSON III, *From Brown to Bakke: The Supreme Court and School Integration, 1954–1978*. New York: Oxford Univ. Press, 1979. A conservative account by a former Supreme Court law clerk and law professor who is now a judge on the United States Court of Appeals for the Fourth Circuit. The volume captures the growing stress over the integration issue as events have moved from the elimination of legally prescribed racial segregation to affirmative action.

C. VANN WOODWARD, *The Strange Career of Jim Crow.* New York: Oxford Univ. Press, 1957. Succinct and lucid account of the rise of Jim Crow segregation practices in the South, by the country's foremost historian of the South. The best recent discussion of the origins and effects of southern voting rights discriminations against blacks is J. Morgan Kousser, *The Shaping of Southern Politics: Suffrage Restriction and the Establishment of the One-Party South, 1880–1910.* New Haven: Yale Univ., 1974.

chapter six

INTEREST GROUPS

On October 9, 1983, James G. Watt resigned from his cabinet post as Secretary of the Interior. Watt's popularity during his tenure in this position had declined steadily until many interest groups were openly hostile toward him. Most observers agree that Watt's political downfall came as a direct result of a series of policies and statements that offended a large number of interest groups. Many of Watt's policies seemed to be in direct opposition to the positions of major interest groups affected by them. In addition, Watt seemed to display a remarkable knack for offending people with his public statements.

Soon after he became Secretary of the Interior, environmental groups began calling for his resignation. Watt believed that previous policies had overemphasized conservation. He favored, instead, the development of public resources for economic growth and security purposes. He wanted to use federally owned land for oil drilling, mining, logging, and other potentially profitable activities. President Reagan and other conservatives at first backed Watt's policies because he seemed to be supporting the free-market economy. On the other hand, environmentalists were outraged when Watt moved to open land that had been set aside as wilderness areas and ecological reserves to lease by oil and gas companies. These groups were further alienated by Watt's attempts to promote economic activity in wildlife refuges.

Not only did Watt present policies that were guaranteed to outrage environmentalists, but he also had a habit of making statements that displayed his contempt for them and many other groups. Watt infuriated liberals and conservatives alike with his unrestrained public comments and criticisms. For example, Watt compared environmentalists who criticized his policies to Communists and Nazis in their pursuit of "centralized planning and control of the society." Lining up Fourth of July activities on the Washington Mall, he banned rock music in general and the Beach

Boys in particular, saying that they attracted the "wrong element." Even the President and Mrs. Reagan came forward to say that they were Beach Boys fans. Secretary Watt also offended Native Americans by stating that their reservations were examples of the "failure of socialism" with the highest rates of unemployment, drug abuse, alcoholism, and venereal disease in the country. Then in one statement, Watt managed to offend four important voting groups. Referring jokingly to a newly formed coal advisory committee, Watt said, "I have a black, I have a woman, two Jews, and a cripple." Though he apologized for what he had said, Watt resigned one month later, admitting that this statement, especially, had hastened his departure from the cabinet.[1]

Policymakers in our society must continually interact with numerous organized interest groups. Watt's experience illustrates what can happen when the head of a major agency repeatedly alienates those groups.

DIVERSITY

Should you travel to a foreign country, go out into the countryside. In most rural districts—and even in some of the major cities—you will see that the great majority of faces are physically alike. Look at the way people walk, talk, and eat. In every aspect of life, you will see a distinct sameness.

Take the same kind of trip in most parts of the United States, and you will see a much greater diversity of people. Many other countries were founded as nation-states, a single nationality or closely related group of nationalities. The United States, too, once had a fairly homogeneous white population, but time and circumstance made our country a "house of all peoples." Even in the beginning, it was founded less on a specific nationality than on a set of liberating ideas—a fact essential to any understanding of our political culture and, indeed, of ourselves (see Chapter 1).

These ideas were superimposed on a country of continental vastness. Little more than a century ago, the North and South were so very different that they fought a war over their differences. As for religion, the country was a haven for religious groups of every conceivable kind. We have more than a hundred kinds of Protestants, three main denominations of Jews—Orthodox, Conservative, and Reform—and some smaller Jewish groups. The Roman Catholic Church, though monolithic in form, has in practice spawned a number of very distinct factions. There are also a great many splinter religions, sects, and cults, including people who believe in the divinity of a teenage boy and those who literally regard the dollar bill as reflecting the divine.

Our economy is as big and as varied as the country itself—all 3.6 million square miles of it, with its 240 million people. Ours is a major agricultural economy, a major manufacturing economy, a major commercial economy. Hardly anything is produced anywhere that is not produced here.

We sometimes forget that just as our system of government is almost unique, so too is our national diversity. Most other countries are much smaller

---

[1] Steven R. Weisman, "Watt Quits Post," *The New York Times*, October 10, 1983, pp. A1, D10; Joseph A. Davis, "Clark Named to Interior Post as Watt Resigns under Fire," *Congressional Quarterly*, October 15, 1983, pp. 2120-2123.

than ours, with many fewer people and much less diversity. Coping with our diversity is one of the central themes of American history and politics. How can a tax system satisfy a New York delicatessen owner, a Detroit auto worker, and a California tomato grower? How can a welfare policy meet the needs of the rural South and the urban North? How much should be spent on urban mass transit and how much on rural water supply? There are no "right" answers to any of these questions. We can only hope to reach some agreement that partly satisfies most of the groups competing for a piece of the pie, and that is why organizing people with common concerns, common interests, is such an important part of our politics.

Because Americans are so remarkably diverse, there are many common interests to organize. Material interests are probably the most important. All those who work for auto companies, for instance, or who own property, or who do not own it, have very strong reasons for organizing. So do people who share a common point of view—Roman Catholics or liberals, for example. Numbers of people who share common material concerns or points of view are called **interests,** and the groups that organize them are called **interest (or pressure) groups.**

Because our society is full of so many interests, it also has many interest groups, and this has always given our politics a "pluralist" flavor. Alexis de Tocqueville, who traveled through our country in the 1830s, noticed that

Associations

The number of formal associations in the United States is huge. The 1982 edition of the *Encyclopedia of Associations* identified 15,361 organizations. In the year after the publication of the 1982 edition, 1,460 new associations and projects were created. Some of these seem trivial or amusing from a public policy point of view—for example, the American Association of Aardvark Aficionados (600 members). A very great many do not engage in lobbying at all, and relatively few of those that do are really important in politics.

Broad Type or Function of Association	Number (1981)
Trade, business, and commercial	3,174
Chambers of Commerce (separate category)	108
Agricultural organizations and commodity exchanges	696
Labor unions, associations, and federations	239
Legal, governmental, public administration, and military organizations	571
Scientific, technical, and engineering associations	1,080
Educational organizations	1,008
Cultural organizations	1,436
Social welfare organizations	1,061
Health and medical organizations	1,474
Public affairs organizations	1,264
Veterans, hereditary, and patriotic organizations	206
Religious organizations	813
Fraternal, foreign-interest, nationality, and ethnic organizations	428
Hobby and avocational organizations	956
Sports organizations	519
Greek and non-Greek-letter Societies, associations, federations	319

"Whenever at the head of some undertaking you see government in France, or a man of rank in England, in the United States you will be sure to find an association."[2]

Our politics is still the politics of interest groups seeking to mold their objectives into public policy: Washington, D.C.; our 50 state capitals; and our 80,000 units of local government often seem to be overwhelmed by these groups. One publisher has compiled a listing of over 15,000 of them,[3] and it is very incomplete. In one field alone, business trade associations, there seem to be more than 20,000 international and national groups, as well as 25,000 on the regional and state levels, and perhaps 400,000 in localities.

GETTING ORGANIZED

In fact, there are more interest groups in this country than in any other. Americans are more likely to belong to interest groups than are the citizens of other Western democracies, more likely to belong to more than one, and more likely to make use of interest groups to influence the government.[4]

No doubt, as Tocqueville thought, our national character has much to do with this penchant for organization, but so too does the structure of our political institutions.

Federalism and the Interest Groups

A political scientist once described our federal system (see Chapter 3) as a "marble cake," for in it, all levels of government—federal, state, and local—share responsibility for most of the things they do.[5] He said, as well, that our political institutions created a "system of multiple cracks," meaning that "cracks" divide the layers (national, state, and local) of the federal structure from one another, and also that anyone seeking to influence a government decision has "multiple cracks" (opportunities) to get a favorable decision. A program, for example, might be passed by Congress, signed by the President, partly funded by the states, and implemented by local officials. In reality, most programs are vastly more complicated.

Fragmentation of power creates thousands upon teeming thousands of power centers throughout the United States. An interest group that loses a battle, say, in Congress can take up the cause in another branch of the federal government—or in the states, the counties, the cities, the townships, or the sewer districts. There is no one place where any interest group can win or lose all its battles, as there is in a parliamentary system, where the national legislature is supreme (see Chapter 2). American interest groups are highly localized, the better to influence the power centers at the grass roots.

[2] Alexis de Tocqueville, *Democracy in America*, Bradley Phillips, ed. (New York: Random House, 1944).

[3] Denise S. Akey, ed., *Encyclopedia of Associations*, 16th ed. (Detroit: Gale Research Co., 1981) with supplements.

[4] Gabriel Almond and Sidney Verba, *The Civic Culture* (Princeton: Princeton Univ., 1963).

[5] Morton Grodzins and Daniel Elazar, "Centralization and Decentralization in the American Federal System," in Robert A. Goodwin, ed., *A Nation of States* (Chicago: Rand, 1963).

Table 6-1 Membership and Use of Organizations in Politics

	USA	GREAT BRITAIN	WEST GERMANY	ITALY	MEXICO
Population belonging to some organization	57%	47%	44%	30%	24%
Population belonging to more than one organization	32	16	12	6	2
Population that would enlist the aid of a group to change unjust local regulations	56	34	13	7	26
Population that would enlist the aid of a group to influence national government	32	22	19	10	20

SOURCE: Compiled from Gabriel Almond and Sidney Verba, *The Civic Culture* (Princeton: Princeton Univ., 1963), pp. 194, 304, 320.

Political Parties and Interest Groups

Political parties and interest groups tend to flourish at each other's expense. American political parties are unusually weak by comparison with other democratic countries (see Chapter 9), so our interest groups are unusually strong. Countries with stronger parties—especially countries governed under the parliamentary system (see Chapter 2)—have weaker and smaller and fewer interest groups. Parliamentary government does not eliminate their influence, but it does reduce and channel the "cracks" in the machinery of government. In Western Europe, interest groups usually operate within the party system; the British Labour party, for example, is often dominated by the Trades Union Congress (TUC), the British labor federation.

Why do interest groups proliferate at the expense of political parties? Perhaps it is because both represent more or less the same interests, though in different ways, so that when parties do their job there is simply less "room" for interest groups. The job of a political party is to bring together many different interests—a precondition of effective government, but one that prevents many individual interests from securing their individual goals. And the interests that come together in a party may eventually decide they have little in common, as did many of the interests that formerly made up the Democratic party in the late 1960s and 1970s (see Chapters 9 and 10). Labor, various racial and ethnic minorities, and other interests that had formerly united within the Democrats then tried to represent themselves independently, each against all. This was one reason for the party's failure to govern effectively when it took power in 1977 under President Jimmy Carter (1977–1981). In fact, the growing strength and independence of interest groups makes it harder for any government to govern.

The strength of our interest groups and the weakness of our parties also diminishes the political influence of working people and the poor. For in the past, our parties—especially the Democrats—have given those two groups whatever representation they now have. As the Democrats become weaker, the ability of poor people to influence our political system grows weaker, too.[6]

---

[6] See Walter Dean Burnham, *The Current Crisis in American Politics* (New York: Oxford Univ. Press, 1982), "Changing Patterns in Congressional-Election Voting Participation." See also Walter Dean Burnham, "The Appearance and Disappearance of the American Voter," in Richard Rose, ed., *Electoral Participation: A Comparative Analysis* (Beverly Hills: Sage, 1980), pp. 35–74.

Classes and Interest Groups

A proverb declares that "the squeaky wheel gets the grease." But in politics not everyone can squeak equally. All interests are legally free to organize and to defend themselves. No single interest totally dominates the United States. In these senses, ours is a **pluralist society** and political system. Yet as one scholar put it, there is a "flaw in the pluralist heaven" of the United States— "The heavenly chorus sings with a strong upper-class accent. . . . Probably 90 percent of the people cannot get into the pressure system."[7] He meant that although the system as a whole reflects many different interests, when examined more closely they have one thing in common: Their members belong to the middle and upper classes.

In fact, the people who join interest groups have higher incomes, higher levels of education, and higher social status than do our population at large. According to one survey, 69 percent of the poorest Americans did not belong to any organizations; about the same proportion of the highest income groups did. Only 14 percent of the lowest economic group held more than one membership, while 35 percent of the highest income groups did.[8]

Why? The well-to-do have more time and money to protect their very substantial and concrete interests; they have personal contacts, confidence, and a belief that they can force society to recognize their needs and desires. Finally, interest groups actively seek them out because it makes sense to "go hunting where the ducks are."[9]

In fact, few if any of this country's interest groups consist largely of poor people. Even the members and leaders of black interest groups such as the National Association for the Advancement of Colored People (NAACP, see Chapter 5) are chiefly middle class. In only one category of organizations do the poor outnumber the well-to-do: churches.

This state of affairs is only in part compensated for by groups that basically represent other interests but also attempt to represent the poor. Organized

---

[7] E. E. Schattschneider, *The Semisovereign People* (New York: Holt, 1975), p. 35.

[8] Herbert Hyman and Charles Wright, "Trends in Voluntary Association Memberships of American Adults, " *American Sociological Review*, 36 (April 1971), 191–206.

[9] James Q. Wilson, *Political Organizations* (New York: Basic Books, 1973), p. 59.

In general, the poor do not belong to interest groups and are not served by them. One reason for this is that they lack the belief that they can force society to recognize their needs and desires.

UPI/Bettmann Newsphotos

labor sometimes attempts to do so, but it also supports practices—seniority, for example—that make it harder for many poor people to get skilled jobs.

The Rise of Interest-Group Politics

A century ago, American political parties were much stronger than they are today (see Chapter 9). Only when they started to weaken, around the turn of the century, did interest groups become central to our politics. These groups tend to be formed "in waves,"[10] and there have been four such waves in our history: 1830–1860, the 1880s, 1895–1920, and the 1960s and 1970s.

The wave of 1895 to 1920 coincided with the emergence of radio, telephones, and national magazines—developments that made us, for the first time, a country with shared national ideas. Millions of "new immigrants" (see Chapter 1) arrived here and made our already complex society more complex. Business and technology became more specialized, and each specialty had its own interests to defend and needed its own group or groups to defend them.

Government, which now began to intervene in all aspects of domestic policy, became the sea in which interest groups had to swim. New laws, new programs, new agencies, and new bureaucracies always produce new interest groups. When the government initiated a new policy, a new interest group was usually formed to represent the people affected by it.

___THE ECONOMICS OF THE PRESSURE SYSTEM___

Among the many motives that cause people to join interest groups, one set of motives stands out: the economic ones. Perhaps they are the most important, perhaps not—but no one doubts that they are very important indeed.

Economic interpretations of behavior are often wrongly equated with Marxism. In fact, they are much more widespread. James Madison, our fourth President (1809–1817) and the "father of the Constitution" (see Chapter 2) argued that the chief cause of "faction"—the competition of groups with different interests—is the "unequal division of property."[11]

Another kind of economic conflict is regional conflict. In Madison's day, the industrial and commercial North competed with the agricultural South for control of the country. After 1840, that struggle tore the country apart. In the end, politics could not resolve it; only a long and bloody Civil War could. At the war's end, northern commercial and industrial interests were triumphant, and they dominated the country until 1932. Organized labor, and the racial and ethnic minorities of the urban North and Midwest, then united with such traditionally Democratic interests as southern farmers. Together they made the Democrats the majority party of the United States. Business was still important—it returned to the White House in 1952—but now it shared its power with other conflicting economic interests.

After World War II, hostility and even competition among these groups subsided. The American economy was supreme on earth, profits were high, and social peace seemed to be well worth its cost to business. By the mid-1970s, this state of affairs had come to an end; some people believed that a

---

[10] David B. Truman, *The Governmental Process* (New York: Knopf, 1951).
[11] Madison, *The Federalist*, Paper 10. See Appendix.

new class war was in the offing.[12] But even in the 1970s and early 1980s, interest conflicts were often very pluralized: It is not usual for the rich, as a single group, to oppose the poor, as a single group. Nor, usually, does business as a single group oppose labor.

Let us take one example. In 1982, President Reagan decided to support the largest peacetime tax increase in history—only a year after he had led the fight for the largest tax cut in American history. "Orthodox" conservatives supported the tax increase, but the "supply-side" conservatives opposed it (see Chapter 16). The Chamber of Commerce—an important business-interest group—officially opposed the tax increase, though not without a good deal of internal division. Many other business organizations—including those representing stockbrokers and bankers—were for it. Conflicts within interests are often at least as important, in the short run, as larger conflicts among classes or between business as a whole and labor as a whole.

Regional Interests. Many economic conflicts still pit region against region, as they did in the era before the Civil War. A farmer in Mississippi and a farmer in Illinois—who may share interests as farmers—may also have conflicting regional interests, and so may computer programmers in New York City and Houston. In particular, the Sunbelt—the South and West—competes with the Snowbelt—the North and Midwest—for people, business, and economic resources in general (see Chapter 3).

The Importance of Noneconomic Interests

Many important groups in the pressure system do not represent economic interests of any kind. Religious groups do not; neither do some groups of lobbyists, like the National Rifle Association (NRA). Some of these noneconomic groups, such as the Elks and the Kiwanis, are mainly social clubs and do not as a rule meddle in politics; political controversy might undermine

---

[12] See Frances F. Piven and Richard Cloward, *The New Class War* (New York: Pantheon, 1982).

Many important groups in the pressure system, such as Friends of the Earth, do not represent economic interests.

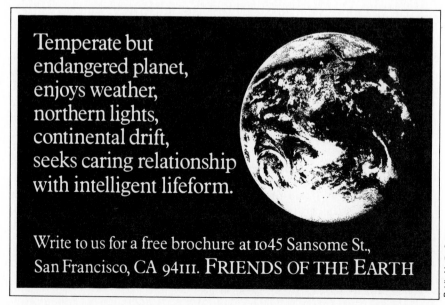

Temperate but endangered planet, enjoys weather, northern lights, continental drift, seeks caring relationship with intelligent lifeform.

Write to us for a free brochure at 1045 Sansome St., San Francisco, CA 94111. FRIENDS OF THE EARTH

Public Media Center

their internal harmony. Certain other noneconomic groups are up to their ears in politics. The NRA, which opposes gun control, is surely one of them. Another is the Moral Majority, which promotes its conception of Christian values through political pressure. The American Civil Liberties Union (ACLU), Common Cause, and Friends of the Earth stand very much on the other side of the political fence, but they too are noneconomic groups with political goals.

The Greater Importance of Economic Groups

The ACLU, the Moral Majority, and groups like them are important; from time to time, they change the way we live. But they are not the heavy hitters of pressure-group politics. The most numerous, persistent, and effective groups are those that represent economic interests—"selfish" groups that make demands on our political system and expect concrete economic benefits from new laws, regulations, and court rulings. At particular times and on particular issues, these groups can be beaten by others that have no economic basis. But day to day, year to year, and century to century, groups that represent major economic interests get their way because they can outspend their rivals.

THE HEAVY HITTERS

Money talks, but it needs a spokesman. Many groups in the United States speak for our society's major economic interests: business, labor, and agriculture—especially business. Of course, mere numbers of groups do not in themselves reveal any interest's political importance. Labor unions are much less numerous (at 174) than groups representing lobbyists (910), but these 174 labor unions have about 22 million members and are among the most powerful forces in the United States.

Business Groups

On every level of government—and in just about every state, city, county, and town—groups representing business make up the largest category of interest groups. Business is organized this thoroughly because it has money and many interests to defend at a time when governments at all levels are extensively involved in its activities (see Chapter 15). Decisions by government bodies can cost a business millions of dollars or save it millions. A few examples:

— For a very long time, the meat-packing industry has tried to get the Agriculture Department's permission to drop the strong warning label now required on processed meats that are made with meat scraps containing bone chips. An industry group estimated that the change would add an extra $513 million a year to sales.
— The long-suffering auto industry asked the Reagan Administration for relief from what it regarded as burdensome regulations that reduced its ability to compete with the lower-priced Japanese imports. The industry and the administration then agreed on a list of 34 such regulations, worth perhaps $1.5 billion annually in savings to the industry.

These are just two examples of the tens of thousands of such decisions that business lobbies seek in Washington each year.

On every level of government, groups representing business make up the largest single category of interest groups. Lee Iacocca, Chrysler Corporation chairman, is an active spokesman for the business community.

Business, for all its power, is not (as we have already seen) a single united bloc. There are many kinds of businesses, businessmen, and business groups.

The U.S. Chamber of Commerce. With its huge membership—4,000 local chambers of commerce and trade associations, 96,000 business firms,[13] and 215,000[14] individuals—the U.S. Chamber of Commerce has the numbers, the money, and the organization to influence decision making anywhere and everywhere. In the early 1980s, it collected dues to the tune of $57 million, had a total income of about $85 million, and spent more than $50 million "to advance," in the words of its credo, "human progress through an economic, political, and social system based on individual freedom, incentive, initiative, opportunity, and responsibility."[15]

Because the chamber is so large and so important, it deals with just about any kind of economic question: government regulation, spending, interest rates, taxes, and so on (see Chapter 16). Small companies make up 49 percent of the Chamber's membership,[16] but it is nonetheless dominated by big business.

Business Roundtable. Another very effective—but very different—business group, the Business Roundtable, is made up of about 190 chief executive officers of the largest companies in the United States. The Business Roundtable gets its clout not from money or numbers, but from the prestige and importance of its membership: When GM's chairman calls a Michigan senator, you can bet that he (or, when the day comes, she) will get past the senator's secretary.

Other Business Groups. The NAM. The oldest business pressure group (1895), the National Association of Manufacturers (NAM), has 13,000 member firms and represents fairly large corporations. Its budget comes to $7 million or so a year. Often, but on the whole wrongly, the NAM has been regarded as the chief organization representing the interests of our corporate fat cats. In fact, it has less political clout than some other business groups, particularly, in recent years, the Business Roundtable.

"What's good for the country is good for General Motors, and what is good for General Motors is good for the country."

Charles E. Wilson,
Secretary of Defense,
1953–1957

---

[13] *Encyclopedia of Associations*, (1982), 1.
[14] *Inc.* (Feb. 1982).
[15] Ibid.
[16] Ibid.

Small Business. The U.S. Chamber of Commerce includes many small businesses but is dominated by large ones. Two groups are devoted solely to small businesses: the National Federation of Independent Business (NFIB), with more than 500,000 members, and the National Small Business Association, with 50,000. Under President Jimmy Carter—who was himself the owner of a small business—these groups were able to get small businesses exempted from regulations that continued in force for larger firms.

Organized Labor

By definition, business is organized. Labor is not. Before labor unions came into being, each worker confronted each business as an individual, as many nonunion workers still do today. Unions organized individual workers and helped them, in most cases, to bargain collectively for better wages and working conditions.

Before the 1930s, the only major alliance for individual labor unions was the American Federation of Labor (AF of L), founded by Samuel Gompers in 1881 but not taking that name until 1886. At first, the AF of L embraced **voluntarism**—self-regulation and the least possible government interference—largely because the government before 1933, was hostile to labor. At first, too, the AF of L was politically neutral. Eventually, it started to play the game of politics for the same reason that business groups did: because the government was more and more involved with the economy and, therefore, with the interests of its members.

Organized labor's first political goal in the late nineteenth century was the ten-hour day—followed, when that was won, by the eight-hour day. Labor's money and manpower helped elect President Franklin D. Roosevelt (1933–1945) and his Democratic supporters in Congress (see Chapter 11).

The AFL-CIO. A bit fewer than two-thirds of this country's individual labor unions (108 out of 174) belong to the American Federation of Labor-Congress of Industrial Organizations. As its name suggests, the AFL-CIO is a fusion of two groups: the AF of L, which consisted mostly of craft unions, and the Congress of Industrial Organizations (CIO), which in 1935 split off from the AF of L and organized unskilled and semiskilled workers in large factories. The CIO was deeply involved in New Deal politics, the AF of L much less so.

After World War II, the labor movement as a whole lost much power as a result of bickering among unions and the growing strength of the Republicans. President Dwight Eisenhower (1953–1961) was the first Republican to occupy the White House in twenty years. In 1955, the AF of L and the CIO merged.

Resources. Big Labor's political clout—which at some times and in some places is very great—stems largely from its vast membership and financial resources. The AFL-CIO's 108 individual unions have about 17 million members, and union locals cover every nook and cranny of the United States. Labor's political arm, the Committee on Political Education (COPE), is the single most powerful political action committee (PAC, see below) in the United States. Individual labor unions usually have their own PACs, too.

Labor's Decline. Ordinarily, the political goals of business and labor conflict, so as one becomes more influential, the other must become less so. Apart from the ebb and flow of year-to-year politics, however, labor's political power has been declining.

Although the American labor force expanded by about 20 million workers in the 1970s, the number of union members stayed constant, at about 22 million; so the percentage of the labor force belonging to unions dropped from 25 percent in 1970 to 21 percent 10 years later. What happened? For one thing, many of the new jobs of the 1970s were created in the so-called Sunbelt (the South and West) where unions are weak, in part because of "right-to-work" laws, which prohibit labor contracts that require union membership as a condition of employment. In addition, many more new jobs have been created in service industries, where unions are weaker than in manufacturing, where unions are strong. In fact, during the last few years, our relatively well-paid manufacturing economy has been turning into a relatively poorly paid service economy. Moreover, many of the 20 million new workers have been women—very often women with low-paying white-collar jobs. Samuel Gompers once said, "Show me two white-collars on a picket line, and I'll organize the whole working class." It was not easy to organize white-collar workers in his day, and it is not much easier now.

Finally, organized labor's effectiveness and bargaining strength is weakened in periods of recession and high unemployment, and the recession that began in the summer of 1981 was the most serious since World War II. Around the turn of the century, a standard refrain among employers was, "The best cure for labor trouble is a long line of men outside the gate." During a boom, profits are high and labor is in short supply. Then labor's bargaining power goes up. When the bust comes, profits are low, and labor markets become glutted. Then labor's bargaining power declines.

Labor and Management. The recession that began in the summer of 1981 exposed many of organized labor's weaknesses. After the end of World War II, conflict between management and labor became more and more ritualized in most leading industries, mainly as a result of the great postwar economic boom. Major companies usually met labor's demands, since the additional costs could easily be passed on to consumers, who were not organized. At the commanding heights of our economy—roughly, the *Fortune* 500 leading corporations—labor and business established what amounted to a "ritually antagonistic partnership" during that boom. Small business, however, lacked these vast resources and market power and was therefore much more vigorously antilabor, both in negotiations and in politics.

When our economy grew weaker, in the 1970s and early 1980s, the increasingly poor shape of corporate balance sheets made even the biggest businesses ready to resist labor's demands. This resistance changed the power balance between labor and management. In the short run, at least, labor had to make substantial concessions, including "givebacks" of benefits negotiated in previous contracts. Despite the recovery which started in 1983, organized labor's position has remained weak, for many of the key industries where labor is strong (steel, for instance) have not really joined in the recovery.

THE FARM BLOC

People in most jobs get paid for what they do. Farmers, until recently, were different: They sometimes got paid for what they did not do, and the federal government forced them not to do it. Say that you owned a 900-acre soybean farm. The government would permit you to plant soybeans on only a part of your land, and it would pay you a subsidy for the soybeans you did not grow on the rest.

The Government on the Farm

Subsidies. That remarkable system ended in the 1970s, but the government stayed in the business of subsidizing farmers. It continued to set minimum prices for many crops and when actual market prices failed to reach those levels, government made up the difference. President Reagan's proposal, in 1981, to cut back on these **price supports** created a furor among farmers—and among their representatives in Congress, many of whom are Republicans. Luckily for farmers, the House Agricultural Committee—completely dominated by rural congressmen, not the President—is the most important maker of farm policy in Washington.

Price supports were not the only farm subsidy that survived into the 1980s. Another was the federal government's policy of buying surplus dairy products at fixed minimum prices considerably higher than market prices. (It accumulated a vast store of these surplus dairy products in its warehouses, and in 1981 began to give them away to the poor and the unemployed.) The U.S. Department of Agriculture's food-stamp program helps support farmers in a slightly different way. The stamps are used by their recipients—people who meet certain criteria, mainly low incomes—to buy food at local grocery stores. Food stamps are often viewed as a pure welfare program complete with welfare chiselers. But the people who use food stamps buy food at the going commercial rate, so the market for food products is much larger than it would otherwise be. Like some other programs, the food-stamp program is welfare for producers as well as for direct recipients.

Food stamps are often viewed as a pure welfare program—but the people who use them buy their food at the going retail rate, so the program is welfare for farm producers, as well.

The Grain Trade. Subsidies—direct and indirect—are only one of the government's ways of affecting farmers' income. The United States sells much of its grain crop abroad, and two of our largest customers have been mainland (Communist) China and the Soviet Union. Grain exports to those countries, which must be approved by the President, have been used as a way of bringing diplomatic pressure upon them.

When in 1980 President Carter cut grain exports to the Soviet Union, to punish it for invading Afghanistan (see Chapter 17), farmers lost money; they voted heavily against Mr. Carter in the November election. In North Dakota, for example—its wheat-based economy especially hurt by the embargo— President Carter's vote fell from 45.8 percent in 1976 to 26.3 percent in 1980, one of the biggest swings in the country. Farmers do not like hard times or the politicians whom they blame for them.

President Reagan ended the embargo and refused to reimpose it when in 1981, Poland's Communist government imposed martial law (see Chapter 17). In the summer of 1982 he even extended the existing grain agreement with the Soviets. This was good politics, but it was hard to explain to our European allies, angered by the administration's simultaneous attempts to ban the use of American technology—even in European products—to help build a natural–gas pipeline from the Soviet Union to Western Europe. Despite such efforts, the mid-1980s saw the worst economic crisis on the farm in fifty years. The crisis was fueled by high interest rates, a strong dollar, and sagging land and commodity prices—also the result of federal government policies.

Warehouses Bulge with Surplus Cheese, Butter, and Dried Milk

The other week, as in almost every other week of the year, more than 40 million pounds of surplus butter, cheese and dried milk, all of it bought by the nation's taxpayers, were hauled into spaces the Agriculture Department leases in 500 warehouses scattered across the country.

By the department's own calculations, if all of the dairy products that are already in those warehouses were loaded back into boxcars, the train would stretch from Washington, D.C., to New York City.

The surplus dairy products now in storage have a market value of $3 billion. In addition, the Federal Government will spend $40 million to $50 million this year to transport even more dairy products from privately owned processing plants to the warehouses and $40 million to $50 million more to store them.

In all, the Reagan Administration expects to pay $2 billion again this fiscal year, the same as last year, for a milk price support program that Agriculture Secretary John R. Block has said is "embarrassing, unacceptable and intolerable."

Stored in Huge Caves

A large part of the dairy surplus is brought each week into five gargantuan storage "caves" carved from the limestone that underlies the area around Kansas City. Most comes from private dairy cooperatives in Wisconsin and Minnesota, but some is shipped from as far away as California and Texas when the leased warehouse spaces there are full, as they sometimes are these days.

Every day, five days a week, trucks and trains bring more shipments of dried milk in 50-pound bags, cheddar cheese in 500-pound cardboard barrels, and butter packed in 65-pound cardboard boxes to the Commercial Distribution Center's 158 acres of caves here. The caves are actually man-made mines from which millions of tons of limestone were extracted for gravel.

One corridor, which twists among the supporting pillars for more than 200 yards, is now filled to its 17-foot ceiling with sacks of dried milk. In another, the four-foot-high cheese barrels are stacked four barrels high into the ceiling's gloom. And in one vast anteroom, kept at zero degrees Fahrenheit, are frozen boxes of butter, piled to the chamber's frigid top.

This mass of excess is in the warehouses today because the country's dairy farmers are still producing about 10 percent more milk than the public can consume.

No Limit on Production

More than half the milk that their cows yield is bottled and sold at contracted prices for distribution to consumers. The rest is sent to commercial manufacturing cooperatives, where it is processed into butter, cheese and dried milk.

What is not sold in supermarkets is bought, in bulk, by the Agriculture Department and stored in the warehouses until some of it can be parceled out for school lunches, to military installations or to countries receiving food purchase loans under the Food for Peace program. Recently, the Government has started giving a small portion of the surplus cheese and butter to low-income Americans.

Unlike all the other major price-supported farm commodities, there is no limit on how much a dairy farmer may produce and sell to the Government.

Currently, the Agriculture Department is buying the surplus milk for $13.10 a hundred pounds. Congress, which has received generous campaign contributions from the dairy industry, had been raising milk price supports twice each year until President Reagan put pressure on it to hold the supports at the $13.10 level last December.

Farm Groups

Most recent secretaries of agriculture have been chosen from the ranks of the largest farm groups: the American Farm Bureau Federation (AFBF), the National Farmers Union (NFU), and the Grange.[17] The AFBF, which mainly represents larger farmers, is strongest in the South, the Midwest, and New York State. It strongly opposes federal regulations of agriculture and is

---

[17] The Department of Agriculture was created by act of Congress in 1862. In 1889, its commissioner was named secretary of agriculture and became a member of the cabinet. Ezra Taft Benson (1953–1961), Earl Butz (1971–1976), and John R. Block (1981–) were all of the AFBF; and Orville Freeman (1961–1969) and Bob Bergland, (1977–1981) were of the NFU.

Surplus Is Increasing

Mr. Block hoped this would discourage excess production, but it has not, and each month since then the cows have produced more and the surplus has increased.

Virtually none of the mountains of butter, cheese and dried milk has spoiled, although some of the unprocessed cheese will soon have to be processed to preserve it.

"Despite all our efforts to move the dairy surplus into use, even by giving some of it away to charity, the outgoing isn't keeping up with the incoming," said James G. Schlick, the director of the Agriculture Department's Kansas City commodity office. "We're running as hard as we can, but the harder we run, the best we can do is barely stay in place."

Things have got so bad that Congress, with the acquiescence of the dairy industry, is now trying to fashion a new dairy price support program, probably one in which farmers would get the full $13.10 support rate on 90 percent of their milk and whatever the free market would bring for the rest.

Meanwhile, Mr. Schlick is looking for more storage space, especially for cheese, which is piling up faster than the butter or the dried milk.

Nor does the department expect any relief soon in the flow into the warehouses. Mr. Schlick is negotiating long-term contracts with warehouse owners, indicating that the Government will be needing their space for many years to come.

Seth S. King, *The New York Times*, July 6, 1982, p. A10.
By permission of *The New York Times* and the author.

conservative (hence, Republican) in its politics. The much more liberal NFU, strongest among the grain farmers of the upper Midwest, strongly backs government price supports and, usually, the Democrats. The Grange, once powerful in the Midwest, is now basically a social organization.

The 1970s produced a number of new and more militant farmers' groups. One of them, the National Farmers Organization (NFO), consisted of cattlemen who held boycotts and strikes and tried to raise prices by withholding products from the market. Another such group, the American Agricultural Movement, went in for modern publicity techniques: In 1977 it attempted to tie up traffic in Washington, D.C., by placing tractors in the street.

No other kind of group can match the power of the giants that represent business, labor, and agriculture. Yet issue by issue, all have been challenged and sometimes defeated.

Public-Interest Groups (PIGs)

One defect of the pressure system is the fact that special-interest groups are much better organized than is the public at large. **Public-interest groups** (PIGs) try to remedy that defect by representing what they view as the public interest, as opposed to the interests of specific groups.

PIGs are hardly new; abolitionist (antislavery) and prohibitionist societies were, in effect, groups of this type; so too is the American Civil Liberties Union (ACLU), which was formed in 1920. In the 1960s and 1970s, though, PIGs became more numerous, active, and effective—and better organized and financed. They were among the special features of the politics of that decade.

Consumer Protection. Manufacturers are among the best organized of all interests, but those who consume their products have no organization; we can buy or refuse to buy whatever products may be offered to us, but only as individuals.

Even that limited power can be used to good effect only if we are well informed about these products, and often we are not. Design flaws usually come to light only after they cause problems. One such flaw, in a car manufactured in the early 1960s, may well have caused many accidents and even a number of deaths. Ralph Nader uncovered this flaw, publicized it, and then went on to create one consumer group after another, among them the Center for Automobile Safety, the Center for Corporate Accountability, the Center for the Study of Responsive Law, and Public Citizen. Other consumer organizations include the Consumer Union, made up of many small consumer-protection groups, and the AFL-CIO's Consumer Protection Division.

Consumer lobbies have been around for quite a while, but they did not begin to influence policy making until the 1960s. Government action to protect essential consumer interests goes back much further—back at least to 1906 and the Pure Food and Drug Act, which reflected public awareness that the ancient rule of the market, "Let the buyer beware," would leave it unprotected against grave and imminent dangers to health and safety. The state, after all, is in the business of protecting public health and safety.

Single-Issue Groups

Long ago, a Democratic senator from Mississippi, one James K. Vardaman (1913–1919), would continually demand the repeal of the Fourteenth and Fifteenth Amendments, adopted at the end of the Civil War (see Chapters 4 and 5). Asked why he devoted so much time to a hopeless cause, he replied that a hopeless cause would get him reelected till the end of time.

Like Vardaman's election pitch, many of the controversies generated by **single-issue groups** could go on indefinitely without leading to any resolution that commands popular support. Those groups unite people around one and only one issue, often the only thing they have in common. But unlike the

"I would guess, sir, by the look on your face, that you are a single-issue person."

repeal of the Fourteenth and Fifteenth Amendments, these are serious issues, which produce quite serious struggles—struggles that cannot be settled, because their moral content makes compromise almost impossible. Abortion is, today, the most controversial of them.

Single-issue groups are not at all new; they have always been a characteristic feature of our politics, because our society is permeated by religion and, therefore, by religious values (see Chapter 1). Before the Civil War, the American Anti-Slavery Society was a single-issue group; so were the organizations that worked for the Eighteenth Amendment (1919), which banned the manufacture, sale, and use of alcoholic drinks.

Oddly enough, the Eighteenth Amendment was proposed and ratified even though the prohibitionists had not succeeded in electing their own candidates to office—a failure that foreshadowed the failure of prohibition itself. Adopted at a time of antiforeign, anticommunist zeal, the "noble experiment" was widely and openly flouted in almost all big cities, where public opinion respected the individual's sacred right to drink strong waters. It is quite possible that similar projects proposed by today's single-issue groups would come to grief for similar reasons.

Perhaps the most important of today's single-issue groups, the "right-to-life" (antiabortion) movement, rallied in opposition to the U.S. Supreme Court's 1973 decision striking down all state laws forbidding abortions (see Chapter 14).[18] Opinion polls consistently indicate that a majority of the public supports that decision, at least in principle. Nonetheless, it was and is utterly unacceptable to large portions of public opinion, including most Roman Catholics, quite a few fundamentalist Protestants, and some Orthodox Jews. For these opponents, the abortion issue was and is totally nonnegotiable; as a matter of religious principle, they regard abortion as murder. Those who

---

[18] *Roe* v. *Wade*, 410 U.S. 113 (1973).

Catholics for a Free Choice

Perhaps the most important of today's single-issue groups is the "right to life" (antiabortion) movement.

support *Roe* v. *Wade* are also organized and also view their cause as a stand for ultimate values—in their case, a woman's right to choose.

Alas, a political system—especially ours, which requires negotiation and compromise to function at all, let alone function effectively—cannot resolve such moral issues. Yet the conflict over abortion is not at all likely to go away. That is why the social issues (like abortion, admittedly an extreme case) tend to be much more disruptive and difficult to resolve than conflicts over economic or other "secular" questions. Deeply felt moral principles, and those who hold them, collide in a diverse society in which certain religious ideals are exceptionally important; and these issues cannot be settled (as economic issues can) with a new division of the pie of society's costs and benefits.

Such issues, unfortunately, have troubled us greatly in recent years, in part because the U.S. Supreme Court has repeatedly taken sides. Besides, many people fear what they view as a breakdown of law, order, and morality in a hedonistic age. There can be no doubt that social-issue battles, especially over abortion, contributed significantly to the 1982 defeat of the Equal Rights Amendment (see Chapter 5) and the post-1970 fracturing of the Democratic party (see Chapter 9).

Political Action Committees (PACs)

"You have the good guys, and you have the bad guys, and we're for the good guys," said William Holyater, the political director for the International Association of Machinists (IAM), a labor union. Like other interest groups, the IAM uses its money to reward its political friends and to defeat its political enemies.

When an interest group wants to elect or defeat candidates, but not to give its cash to a political party, it sets up a **political action committee, (PAC)**. PACs were specifically authorized by the 1971 Federal Election Campaign Act, but they had existed before then. By 1974, some 608 had been set up—mostly by businesses and labor unions—and they contributed $12.5 million to candidates for Congress. That was just the beginning. Six years later, in 1980, 2,779 PACs contributed more than $55.3 million. Many people—including

NCPAC Attacks, PROPAC Counters

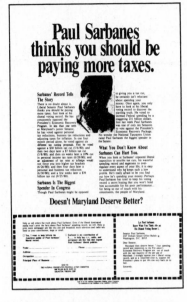

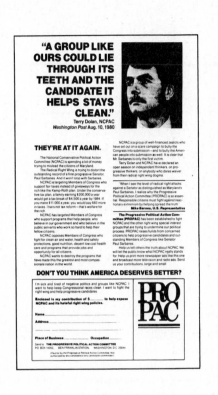

Before the 1980 election had cooled down, the National Conservative Political Action Committee (NCPAC) began targeting the liberal senators it hoped to unseat in 1982. NCPAC launched its attack early in 1981 with the above newspaper advertisement against Maryland Democrat Paul S. Sarbanes. A new liberal group, Progressive Political Action Committee (PROPAC), promptly responded with ads defending Sarbanes and criticizing what it called NCPAC's "scare campaign." A sample PROPAC ad is shown at the right.

some members of Congress itself—worry that we are well on our way to having "the best Congress that money can buy." Little wonder.

Incumbent congressmen got $37 million from PACs in 1980, challengers only $16 million. Incumbents took the lion's share because they tend to be reelected again and again (see Chapter 13), and when PACs can't beat them, they join them. Political principles and parties are all to the good, but the name of the interest-group game is "access"—access to decision makers. Contributions to incumbents of both parties are basic to getting it.

NCPAC. Most PACs have been set up by economic interest groups, especially business and labor. Some of them, however, represent people who share a common point of view—"ideological" interests (see Chapter 7). Of these PACs, by far the most important and well-known is the National Conservative Political Action Committee (NCPAC).

In 1978, NCPAC announced that it was "targeting" six liberal U.S. senators for defeat two years later. Came the 1980 election, and four of those six senators were duly defeated. The technique was brilliantly simple. Terry Dolan, NCPAC's founder, discovered that although federal law limited the amount that candidates and parties could spend themselves, there were no such limits on what others could spend on their behalf, provided that no

Table 6–2 Business PAC Contributions to Selected Congressional Leadership Campaigns in 1980 Elections

SENATE	LEADERSHIP POSITION	PAC CONTRIBUTION	TOTAL BUSINESS PAC CONTRIBUTION	TOTAL CONTRIBUTION
Jake Garn R–Utah	Banking-Chr.	$238,245	$191,534	$1,072,159
Bob Packwood R–Oregon	Commerce-Chr.	265,374	153,540	1,506,255
Robert Dole R–Kansas	Finance-Chr.	328,055	254,995	1,217,468
Barry Goldwater R–Arizona	Intelligence-Chr.	247,219	187,814	954,315

HOUSE	LEADERSHIP POSITION	PAC CONTRIBUTION	BUSINESS PAC CONTRIBUTION	TOTAL CONTRIBUTION
Thomas O'Neill D–Mass.	Speaker	$ 53,500	$ 29,400	$ 66,325
Jim Wright D–Texas	Maj. Leader	234,180	155,680	807,323
Jim Jones D–Okla.	Budget-Chr.	130,450	114,951	286,150
D. Rostenkowski D–Ill.	Ways & Means-Chr.	159,100	106,450	274,580
Jamie Whitten D–Miss	Appro.-Chr.	97,925	72,425	166,695
F. St. Germain D–RI	Banking-Chr.	63,700	46,900	133,170

SOURCE: From Federal Election Commission Data. Compiled by Common Cause, April 1981.

formal, organizational ties linked these groups to a candidate. NCPAC therefore collected money through direct-mail solicitation—form letters sent to conservatives throughout the United States—and then spent the money on independent advertising.

Some of these advertisements were television commercials directed solely *against* liberal incumbents—so-called negative propaganda—and not *for* anyone. For instance, one of these commercials, televised in Idaho, Indiana, and Iowa, showed slices of baloney, each with a price tag indicating the cost of the deficit spending each state's liberal senator had allegedly supported. "One very big piece of baloney," the announcer then claimed, "is [Frank Church, Birch Bayh, or John Culver] telling us he's fighting inflation." Each of these senators was defeated. These techniques were much less successful in 1982 and were hardly used in 1984. Times had changed.

Table 6–3 PAC Contributions to Federal Candidates:
1979–1980 Election Cycle (in millions)

PAC TYPE	TOTAL CONTRIBUTIONS	TO DEMOCRATS	TO REPUBLICANS
Corporation	$21.7	$ 7.8	$13.9
Labor union	14.2	13.2	0.9
Trade, health	17.2	7.6	9.6
Cooperatives	2.2	1.3	0.8
Unconnected	5.1	1.6	3.4
	$60.4	$31.6	$28.8

SOURCE: Federal Election Commission. Note: Columns may not add because of rounding.

No member of Congress likes to legislate in the dark. Congressmen constantly search for information because it tends to reduce risk and uncertainty. Information is therefore a basic political resource, even though everyone knows that interest groups mainly peddle information that helps them toot their own horns. No one, for example, knows more about an industry than the people who work for it. Besides, much information about the economy is hidden because it involves business secrets. Only once, during the New Deal era, has Congress ever subjected American business to a sweeping inquiry, complete with the power to compel disclosure of some of these secrets. Since then, Congress has to some extent lived off handouts from industry.

Congress does have a staff, but a relatively small one, so it must have other sources of data, news, and gossip. These sources provide such valuable commodities because they expect to make friends in Congress and influence people. Their attempts to influence politicians are called **lobbying.**

Direct Lobbying

"Bucks, booze, and broads": Our images of direct lobbying are mostly images from the past, rooted in historical fact but not typical of today's direct lobbyist, who is very likely to be more a technical expert than a con man.

Lobbyists. About 15,000 lobbyists ply their craft in Washington's many corridors. They include professionals who sell their talents to anyone who can afford them, and the staffs of particular interest groups. Some of these people are experts on public relations or on subjects that concern interest groups. Others know how to pull the right strings and open the right doors.

Former Congressmen. Among the people with some or all of these skills, one group stands out: former members of Congress—a small but important minority of the capital lobbying corps. Former U.S. senators are especially in demand among foreign governments and businesses.

"Superlawyers." During the mid- to late 1960s, Joseph Califano was a domestic affairs adviser to President Johnson (1963–1969). When Mr. Johnson left office in 1969, Califano returned to the practice of law. In the early 1970s, as a partner in his own firm, he helped persuade Congress to let a group of oil refiners, his clients, pay much less for its oil than competitors did. In 4 months, 56 companies made $164 million from this concession, which was then abolished. No doubt he was worth every penny of the $505,490 he got from his law firm in 1976.

Superlawyers like Califano, Paul Warnke, Thomas Austern, and Clark Clifford served in the highest offices of the executive branch and moved between them and private law firms. They know the game, and they know the players, just as former congressmen do.

Former Government Officials. Some industries—especially the defense industry—regularly hire retired government officials, who then lobby their former colleagues in government. So close is the relationship between such prime defense contractors as Lockheed, General Dynamics, and Rockwell International (aircraft), on the one hand, and the Defense Department, on the other, that some have called it "incestuous."

UPI/Bettmann Newsphotos

Attempts at influencing politicians are called lobbying because they often take place in building lobbies.

Other Lobbyists. The average lobbyist is usually a technical expert in public relations, law, politics, or one of the fields that concern interest groups. But public-interest and single-issue groups tend to rely on volunteer lobbyists—amateurs who sometimes beat the pros at their own game.

Governing for Bucks. A hundred or so years ago, in the days of what specialists call "the old lobby," when a lobbyist did not have enough votes to carry a state legislature, he often went out and bought extras. Whole legislatures were "owned" by the great economic powers of the day.

Direct bribery is now pretty rare, but we still see occasional glimpses of it, as in the so-called ABSCAM scandal (see Chapter 13). Influence can still be bought, but techniques have become more subtle, more indirect, and usually legal.

Honoraria. Let us say that a congressman gives a speech before a business group or labor union. The congressman then receives an honorarium, or fee, for making the speech. But suppose that instead of a normal fee, which might be from $2,000 to $5,000, the group pays $10,000. The extra money can be regarded as an indirect bribe.

Congress, in the mid-1970s, voluntarily limited its members to $25,000 a year in honoraria. But $25,000 was apparently too little of a good thing; in 1981, the House voted to double the yearly limit on outside earnings to $50,000. The Senate, always jealous of its rights as the upper house, then voted itself unlimited honoraria.

Indirect Lobbying

Influence is the stock in trade of lobbyists. Usually, they direct their talents at the people who make decisions. In a democracy, however, it is often possi-

Who Does What

By task and tactic these Washington representatives divide into three general categories:

First, there are the information gatherers. These representatives analyze and disseminate intelligence on national government affairs either confidentially for the private use of clients or more openly as a means of molding public opinion and the thinking of decision-makers. A number of Washington firms concentrate on gathering and interpreting information on national developments of particular interest to their subscribers. The intelligence function is also cited as an important responsibility of corporate, union and trade association representatives in [Washington] and their in-house legal staffs. Phyllis McGarth of the Conference Board, a New York-based research group, was recently quoted in the Wall Street Journal as saying that "The chief responsibility of the government affairs executive is monitoring, analyzing and communicating government related activity," and she rated the traditional lobbying function as of secondary importance. John Howland, Washington counsel for Westinghouse, commented to the Legal Times of Washington in January 1979 that corporate house counsel jobs in Washington "tend to get down to general information gathering". In the same general category of information collection and dissemination are the activities of certain Washington "think tanks" whose fellows often come from senior government positions and later return to them. Although the principle of scholarly objectivity is proclaimed, these institutions have not all shed their partisan colorations completely; and they provide prestigious Washington platforms from which the personal views (and biases) of their often transient scholars may influence government thinking.

Second, much Washington representation takes the form of legal counseling. Washington law firms specializing in communications, transportation or public utilities law help their client radio station, airline or gas company comply with the routine li-censing and reporting requirements of the regulatory agencies. They give legal counsel to corporate clients in regulatory commission hearings or in civil and criminal proceedings in a court of law. They provide legal expertise to clients commenting on proposed regulations or petitioning for special treatment under them. Increasingly, they are asked to undertake litigation against the government in their clients' behalf. In addition to enlisting the help of established Washington firms, more and more corporations are reportedly establishing or enlarging in-house legal staffs as part of their Washington representation. Some attorneys resist the label of "representative" and many disclaim any involvement in "lobbying." But as legal counsel to clients complying with or contesting some government regulation, they are surely representing the client's interest. And when they undertake a more activist role to prompt, revise or block some regulation or ruling, they are, in truth, lobbying, although not within the narrow definition of the existing statute.

By far the largest category of representational activity catalogued in this book is lobbying itself. Whether or not formally registered as lobbyists on Capitol Hill or as Foreign Agents with the Department of Justice, those Washington representatives whose principal objective is to stimulate government action favorable to (or block action unfavorable to) the interests of their employers, clients, or causes are lobbying. Their motives may be monetary or missionary or a mixture of both. They lobby in both the Legislative and Executive Branches of government. Appreciating the importance of public image to the cause they represent and the power of popular support from the "grass roots", some specialize in lobbying techniques which arouse public interest and which, like mass phone-in and mailing campaigns, draw the public into the persuasion process.

From *Washington Representatives 1981* (Washington, D.C.: Columbia Books, 1982).

ble—even necessary—to reach the few through the many. Influencing the decision makers indirectly, through public opinion or the appearance of public opinion, is called **indirect lobbying.**

Grassroots Lobbying. Perhaps the most common and effective form of indirect lobbying is "grassroots" lobbying. The champion at this sort of thing is the National Rifle Association (NRA), which claims that in 72 hours its members can send half-a-million letters to Congress. The "grassroots" are the

Those on both sides of the gun control issue try to influence decision makers indirectly, through public opinion.

group's membership, not the public at large, but of course the group manages the campaign to make it look spontaneous.

Media Campaigns. More diffuse and expensive than grassroots lobbying are *media campaigns*, which attempt to influence or change public opinion. In the late 1970s, for example, many Americans blamed the oil companies for higher oil prices. So those companies placed ads in newspapers and magazines to promote their own corporate virtues (as opposed to the usual ads promoting their products). These new-style ads presented the oil companies as good neighbors, social innovators, and victims of communist-inspired propaganda.

Protests and Demonstrations. Should a group lack the money to advertise in newspapers or on radio or TV, it can appeal to the public directly through news stories. Say that the people who live on a certain street want a sewer and cannot get one from their city government. They might decide to picket the mayor's office. Suppose that the mayor is on vacation. Will they abandon their plan? Why should they? The picketing is not intended to influence the mayor but to embarrass the mayor by creating bad publicity. It is a media event, which takes place mainly in the sense that it gets reported. Demonstrations and boycotts generate free publicity, too. Groups that lack traditional sources of political power—for example, the civil-rights, gay, and women's movements (see Chapter 5)—often resort to these techniques.

——LOBBIES IN ACTION: THE AWACS SALE (1981) ——

The date was October 28, 1981. All 100 senators were present in the Senate chamber. Lobbyists, staff members, relatives, reporters, and high government officials packed the galleries. The agenda: Should the U.S. Senate veto the Reagan Administration's proposed sale of AWACS[19] spy planes to Saudi Arabia? That day's vote was the first major foreign-policy showdown of Ronald Reagan's first year as President.

---

[19] Airborne Warning and Control System. Their radar systems can detect the movement of planes at considerable distances.

Passage of Arms

Since Israel was founded in 1948, American policy in the Middle East has "squared a circle." On the one hand, we have strong ties to Israel. On the other, we also have strong ties to the conservative Arab states of the Persian Gulf, especially Saudi Arabia, countries that oppose Israel. Sometimes we tilt to the one side, sometimes to the other.

President Reagan hoped that Israel and the conservative Arab states would submerge their differences for the greater good of opposing Soviet designs on the Middle East oil fields. In April 1981, the President announced that the United States would sell $8.5 billion worth of military equipment to the Saudis, including five AWACS planes. Many Americans opposed the deal because they feared that the aircraft would be used against Israel, not against pro-Soviet states. Under a law passed in 1976, the House of Representatives and the Senate together could veto the deal by passing resolutions of disapproval within thirty days of October 1, 1981, the day when Congress was formally notified of the sale. The battle was joined.

Early Defeats. In mid-October, the Democratic-controlled House voted 301 to 111—the President's first foreign-policy defeat in Congress. This, however, did not end the sale, because both houses had to vote against it. The Senate took up the question in late October. Here, too, the President's chances looked bleak: Opposition was led by Oregon's Senator Robert Packwood, a Republican, and the White House admitted that some 61 senators seemed to be leaning against the sale, enough to reject it. On October 15, the Senate Foreign Relations Committee voted against the President, 9 votes to 8. Thus things were going against the sale.

What happened next?

The Contenders: Interests in Conflict

If a fight among interest groups can be likened to boxing, the AWACS struggle was a heavyweight bout, for among the contenders were some of the strongest forces in the pressure system: the White House, the petroleum industry, the defense industry, and the Isreali lobby.

"The Great Persuader." Through most of Ronald Reagan's first year as President, 1981, he seemed invincible. *Time* magazine, paying homage to his gifts as a lobbyist, called him "the Great Persuader." In late September, Mr. Reagan got to work drumming up support in the Senate for the AWACS sale. The White House congressional liaison team had produced "detailed intelligence reports" on each senator, including "the ways he could be threatened or seduced or suckered." One such report described Senator Roger Jepsen (R–Iowa), originally an opponent of the sale, as "someone who could be bullied."[20] As it happened, the day before the final Senate vote—after a meeting with the President—Jepsen changed his mind.

Mr. Reagan allegedly promised money for a hospital in one senator's home state and a coal-fired power plant in another's.[21] He eventually discussed the

---

[20] *The New York Times*, December 30, 1981.
[21] *The Wall Street Journal*, October 14, 1981.

Oil supplies have become a consuming issue for several interest groups.

Shell Oil Co.

sale in person with 22 Republican senators, 14 of whom eventually supported him, and 22 Democrats, 10 of whom did. During the final week before the vote, he made 26 phone calls dealing with the AWACS sale.

Mr. Reagan viewed the deal itself as important, but he raised another issue perhaps the more important one: the President's credibility as a world leader. As he said to one wavering senator, "How can I convince foreign leaders that I'm in command when I can't sell five airplanes?"[22]

The Business Lobby. The AWACS sale represented $8.5 billion worth of military hardware right up front, with the prospect of even bigger money later on. These known and unknown billions were only part of the business community's stake. In 1981, the United States got 23 percent of its imported oil from Saudi Arabia, which in return bought $35 billion in goods and services from us. Several high Reagan officials had come to the administration directly from companies that made large sales to Saudi Arabia. One ad placed by Mobil Oil pointed to the 700 companies, in 42 states, that did business with the Saudis and the possible threat to this business if the sale fell through.

The Foreign Lobby. The Saudis hired Fred Dutton, a former aide to President John F. Kennedy, to represent their interests during the fight. For $200,000 a year, Dutton put on an extensive campaign including a round of $500 and $1,000 honoraria to congressmen and journalists. His argument: A vote against the sale was a vote to let Israel control our foreign policy.

Israel relied mainly on American Jewish organizations to present its side. In the past, they had been quite successful, but this time they were opposed not only by the Arabs but also by big business and by the White House.

Mr. Reagan Triumphs: AWACS for Sale

There were many explanations, but the result was the same in any case: On October 28, 1981, the Senate voted 52 votes to 48 against a resolution condemning the sale. Back in September, 61 senators had been leaning toward such a resolution, yet in the months that followed, senator after senator had fallen behind the president. Rarely has the President of the United States lost such a vote.

That remarkable fact suggests some important lessons. First, if the President really wants to win an important foreign-policy fight on a specific issue, the White House has very large institutional powers of persuasion: above all, the general belief that the President is and ought to be in charge of foreign policy. Second, the combination of the White House and big business is hard to beat, especially in a Republican-controlled Senate.

———— "TO CURE THE MISCHIEFS OF FACTION" ————

A hundred years ago, lobbies could simply buy and sell entire state legislatures and city councils—not all the time, of course, and not in all places. Lobbying today is much less corrupt than it once was. But the very fact of lobbying—simply because it is so expensive—turns influence and access into commodities that are bought and sold. There is certainly potential for abuse; perhaps, too, the system lends itself to abuse.

[22] *Time,* November 9, 1981.

Why not simply ban lobbying or place severe limits on it? For one thing, the First Amendment guarantees the right "to petition the Government for redress of grievances" (see Chapter 4), and that, in effect, is what lobbying is.

The second reason is grounded in the "politics of power." Lobbyists give decision makers information that is not easily found elsewhere. They provide a service—a self-interested one, of course—that Congress and the executive branch need. The pressure system could never be banned or even regulated vigorously enough to comply with the utopian expectations encouraged by some civics books. No government can possibly live in splendid isolation from the demands of leading economic groups, nor could any government ignore organizations that represent the views of important sections of public opinion.

Federal Regulation of Lobbying

Although an outright prohibition of lobbying would be neither constitutional nor realistic, we do not have to put up with any excess that lobbyists may care to inflict upon us. After all, the present arrangements are not the only possible arrangements, not by a long shot. Various regulations have been enacted from time to time—some of them merely cosmetic, others with good intentions. In neither case have they been very effective.

The Foreign Agents Registration Act of 1938. Shortly before World War II, hoping to throw the "spotlight of pitiless publicity" on foreign propaganda, Congress passed the Foreign Agents Registration Act (1938), which requires agents of foreign interests to register with the Justice Department. The act has been amended in ways that made it less effective: In 1966, for example, Congress exempted lawyers who provide "routine" legal services for foreign clients. As a result of this and other changes, the law is largely toothless, enforced only when scandals become so notorious that the government finds it more embarrassing to ignore than to use.

The Federal Regulation of Lobbying Act of 1946. Only one act of Congress—the Federal Regulation of Lobbying Act of 1946—deals with the general issue of lobbying on the federal level. The act simply requires paid lobbyists to register and to report their lobbying expenditures. But it was so vague that a federal appeals court once ruled that it violated the First Amendment. The U.S. Supreme Court overturned that decision and attempted to issue an opinion (see Chapter 14) tightening the law, but only by interpreting it in the most restrictive possible way, creating many loopholes and making the law largely pointless.

Regulations in this area do cut very close to the First Amendment's guarantees and must be drawn quite carefully to withstand judicial scrutiny. Had the will existed, this could have been done, but it has not.

Refusal to Register. Both the 1938 and 1946 acts require people who represent interests—foreign and domestic—to register with the government. Most lobbyists simply refuse to do so on the grounds that their chief activity is not lobbying. Other lobbyists say that providing information is not lobbying. Additional numbers of lobbyists fail to register because they are not *paid* to lobby. Besides, since only direct lobbying is covered by the Regulation of Lobbying Act, indirect lobbyists need not register or report their expenses, even in theory. Because media campaigns are the most expensive kinds of lobbying, this omission saps the act. Moreover, the act covers direct contact with congressmen only, not with their staffs. And a final limitation: It applies only to the lobbying of Congress; efforts to influence the minds and hearts of officials in the executive branch and to sway the courts do not have to be reported.

Since violations of these narrow rules are neither investigated nor prosecuted, the lobbies themselves decide what to report. According to some estimates, no more than one-third of Washington lobbyists have registered, and only about 1 percent of lobbying expenses are reported.

The act's deficiencies suggest obvious reforms: (1) broadening coverage to include the executive branch and the courts, (2) requiring that indirect lobbying be reported, and (3) creating an agency to monitor a new and stiffer law. We might also require that contributions to lobbying organizations be made public and that lobbyists keep records of their meetings with government officials.

No such law, nor even a more moderate one, is likely to emerge from Congress at any time in the foreseeable future. The groups that pressure Congress to do and not do things are lobbying organizations, so there is little effective pressure for reform of lobbying. In almost every year during the late 1970s and in 1980, strenuous efforts were made to persuade Congress to enact changes in the ineffective 1946 law. They all failed, even though each proposed bill was weaker than the preceding one.

Conflict-of-Interest Laws

Besides these laws that regulate—or, rather, fail to regulate—lobbying in the strict sense, Congress has passed a number of laws that fail to regulate influence-peddling in general. President Carter signed the most recent, the Government Ethics Act, on October 26, 1978. Among other things, the act attempts to control the so-called revolving-door problem: the employment by private companies of former high government officials. The act attempts to prevent these officials from representing anyone, formally or informally, on any matter pending before their former agencies for one year after they leave government service. The act also requires officers of all three branches of the federal government to make extensive financial disclosures to set up the Office of Government Ethics and machinery for appointing special prosecutors to investigate accusations of wrongdoing. These were indeed new limitations on lobbying, but very narrow ones, covering only a few aspects of the problem. It is still true that every comprehensive effort to strengthen the 1946 act has been defeated.

SUMMARY

Interest groups are a special and characteristic feature of American-style politics. Compared with people in other democratic and industrialized societies, Americans are much more likely to join interest groups and to use them to achieve political goals—perhaps because the United States is so large and diverse. In addition, the federal system requires the government in Washington to share power with 50 states and about 80,000 local governments. Interest groups are just as decentralized and numerous.

Our political parties, moreover, are weak, and their weakness makes interest groups strong. The strength of interest groups may be an obstacle to effective government, for they usually represent people in only one industry or people with only one point of view, not the coalitions represented by parties.

Parties also tend to champion the interests of the poor to a greater extent than interest groups do. By and large, interest groups represent the middle and upper classes.

The heavy hitters of the interest-group system are the major economic interests: business, labor, and agriculture. Public-interest and single-interest groups also play an important part in American politics. During the twentieth century, interest groups of all kinds increased dramatically in numbers, chiefly as a result of the government's more active role in the economy.

Interest groups take their points of view to the government through lobbying. Direct lobbying—contact between lobbyists and government officials—works best for established groups; the disadvantaged often resort to attention-getting protest tactics. Indirect lobbying, through the mass media and through letter-writing campaigns, can be very effective but also very expensive.

None of the laws that regulate interest groups work very well, and it is hard to believe that any were intended to work very well. Part of the problem is the fact that the very people—politicians—who benefit from the machinations of the interest groups also have the sole power to pass laws to control them. Even if the politicians really did want to control interest groups, the courts might not let them, because lobbying is to some extent protected by the First Amendment. Right opposes right—a typical problem of civil liberties (see Chapter 4) and one not likely to be solved in the near future.

SUGGESTED READINGS

JEFFREY M. BERRY, *Lobbying for the People*. Princeton: Princeton Univ., 1977. The best single study thus far on the "new" public-interest lobbying groups.

THEODORE J. LOWI, *The End of Liberalism*, 2nd ed. New York: Norton, 1979. The best and most comprehensive recent critique of interest-group domination of American politics and "interest-group liberalism."

MICHAEL J. MALBIN, ed. *Parties, Interest Groups and Campaign Finance Laws*. Washington, D.C.: American Enterprise Institute, 1980. A collection of essays by leading specialists on these subjects, generally mainstream reformist in approach.

LESTER W. MILBRATH, *Washington Lobbyists*. Chicago: Rand, 1963. A technically well-done academic study, quite good for its quotations from lobbyists and other men of affairs in Washington.

MANCUR OLSON, *The Logic of Collective Action*. Cambridge, Mass: Harvard Univ., 1965. An extremely important analysis of the formation, activity, and vitality of interest groups in American politics.

NORMAN J. ORNSTEIN and SHIRLEY ELDER, *Interest Groups, Lobbying and Policymaking*. Washington, D.C.: Congressional Quarterly Press, 1978. A very competent and up-to-date review of the subject but, in the usual CQ style, a little dry.

E. E. SCHATTSCHNEIDER, *The Semi-Sovereign People*. New York: Holt, 1960. An extremely important statement about the different roles and activities of pressure groups and parties in the American political system—written in very simple, easy-to-understand language. This is one of those books that can be understood by all, but the more you know, the more powerful its impact becomes.

DAVID B. TRUMAN, *The Governmental Process*. New York: Knopf, 1951. A modern classic.

JAMES Q. WILSON, *Political Organizations*. New York: Basic Books, 1973. A very intelligent attempt to develop to develop a theory of interest groups and parties. It stresses the incentive that each uses to attract members.

chapter seven

PUBLIC OPINION

Suppose we compare our Congress with the Italian parliament, which has two houses somewhat like those of Congress. Further suppose that the lower house, the Chamber of Deputies, has 435 seats, like the House of Representatives. Those seats in the Chamber returned in 1983 would be occupied by 6 Maoists, 130 Communists, 51 Socialists, 18 Social Democrats, 22 left-wing liberals, 144 Christian Democrats, 13 right-wing liberals, 30 Neofascists, and 21 whose views were too odd to be included in any of these other categories.

The U.S. House of Representatives elected a year later, in 1984, was composed of 253 Democrats and 182 Republicans. A masterpiece of simplicity! Yet Socialists, Communists, and Fascists are about as free to campaign in the United States as they are in Italy. In fact, they do campaign here; they simply lose. Almost always, only the Republicans and Democrats send representatives to Congress, because only they have real support from the electorate.

Republicans and Democrats differ in some ways, but they agree much more than they disagree. Their differences—though important—largely concern matters of emphasis, not fundamentals. If they had European-style political names, Democrats would be called "left-wing liberals" and Republicans, "right-wing liberals." Neither group seeks basic change in our political, social, and economic institutions, because the American people they represent do not appear to want such changes.

It is odd that our major political parties have so much more in common with each other than do those of Italy (and most other countries), for our people seemingly have much less in common. Italians may disagree on the most fundamental questions of political life: republicanism and monarchy; capitalism and communism; democracy and dictatorship—to name only three. We Americans settled these political questions long ago, and few of us seek to reopen them. But almost all the people of Italy are native Italians with a common culture and society. People settled in the United States fairly recently, however, and they came from almost every country on earth. We have forged a common political outlook from people with diverse national origins and cultures.

One further oddity: Because we try to cram all the opinions, interests, and life styles of the United States into two political parties, we must put up with a great deal of political fighting within parties—more, perhaps, than between parties. Americans may agree about the most fundamental questions of political life, but our diversity nonetheless generates an enormous amount of political conflict over lesser questions. As James Madison pointed out two centuries ago, the larger the political unit, the more complex the interests within it become.[1] The national politics of the United States are very complex indeed—so complex that we have four or five separate parties lurking within the common label of "Democrat" and at least two and a half within the GOP.

THE SHAPE OF PUBLIC OPINION: LIBERALS AND CONSERVATIVES

In the United States, most politically minded people call themselves *liberals, moderates,* or *conservatives.* Each of these terms has a long and convoluted history in our country and has meant different things at different times. Our aim is simply to understand how these terms are used now. We will not attempt to define *liberal* in a way that embraces both John Locke (1632-1704) and Senator Edward M. Kennedy (b. 1932), nor will we attempt to link the conservatism of Sir Robert Filmer (d. 1653)[2] with that of President Ronald Reagan (b. 1911). Nor will we attempt to define "true" liberalism or "true" conservatism. Liberals do not always agree among themselves, and neither do all conservatives, but public opinion nonetheless labels certain views as liberal and others as conservative. Our aim is merely to understand these labels. The Italian multiparty system is likely to appear confusing to Americans, but Italians might find confusing a simple two-party system in which virtually all political differences are fought out within two amorphous, umbrella-like parties.

The Origins

Modern American liberalism and conservatism developed in response to industrialization. Until the late 1960s, they were chiefly attitudes toward economic questions. At that point, racial, social, and moral issues came to the fore of American politics, and on these issues, too, there were liberal and "conservative" attitudes. First, however, let us investigate the economic bedrock.

Before 1933, the political influence of industry was overwhelming. We had no national welfare policy, no social safety nets. In this respect, we were far

---

[1] *The Federalist,* Paper 10. See Appendix.

[2] The author of *Patriarcha,* which Locke set out to refute in his first and second *Treatises on Government.*

behind many European countries. For most farmers, life was typically hard and uncertain, and it became truly desperate after 1929. Industrial workers lived and worked amid conditions just as grim, sometimes grimmer. In many industries the work week lasted 60 hours—10 hours a day, 6 days a week. The physical demands of machine production, and the hot, dirty, dangerous work environments that were then the rule, often wore out workers by the age of 45. When they wore out they were commonly discarded, left to fend for themselves and their families as best they could, sometimes with the help of private charity, local government doles, or soup kitchens.

For many, the conditions of social life were bad enough in the 1920s. In 1928, they became catastrophically bad with the onset of the Great Depression, and so they remained for about a decade. President Franklin D. Roosevelt (1933–1945), in his second inaugural address (January 1937), saw a third of the nation ill-housed, ill-clothed, and ill-nourished. Some of Mr. Roosevelts advisers, well knowing the dismal facts, argued in private that he should have said two-thirds.

Issues

The split between liberals and conservatives over economic issues widened during the decade of the Great Depression. The photo here shows a soup kitchen for the unemployed in 1929.

UPI/Bettmann Newsphotos

Economics. The decade-long calamity of the Great Depression gave rise to the modern activist state, responsible for upholding our national standard of living and for the fortunes of the economy as a whole. The activist state was created mainly by liberals; conservatives rejected it, except in matters such as national defense, for which the state was traditionally responsible. Although most liberals had no wish to eliminate private property, they feared the power and claims of big business. Conservatives supported that power and those goals; they wanted the government to be the partner of business, not its rival, or to leave business alone altogether. Their fundamental economic beliefs were two: first, that private enterprise and the market can provide for the greatest good for the greatest number, and second, that the mainspring of our economic system is the willingness of free individuals to run risks for the possibility of great reward. The liberals replied that business, left to itself, would dominate our society and politics, to the detriment of both our standard of living and our democracy. Only the activist state could restrain business, they thought—not only for the good of ordinary Americans but also (many liberals would add) for its own good.

Counterweight. As we have seen, the first counterweight was the use of the government's power to prevent business from dominating our society and politics. To that end, the government regulated business as it never had before. It also encouraged counterweights to business in the private economy—most notably, the Congress of Industrial Organizations (CIO), a federation of industrial unions (formed in 1935) that organized the work force in big industries such as automobiles and steel (see Chapter 6). Conservatives resisted this important change. Instead they supported the right of management to manage and the right of individuals to seek and get work without having to join labor unions. But in spite of conservative attacks, government grew larger. Then in the 1970s and 1980s this counterweight role of government was subject to mounting criticism by conservatives who sought to reduce government regulation and who assailed the power of unions.

Safety Nets. The activist state also created safety nets to protect individuals and, later, the environment—not because the liberals feared villainy in high economic places but because the aims of private enterprise are truly private.

Applications are taken for the first Social Security benefits. Although the Social Security Act took effect in 1935, the first benefits were not paid out until 1940.

The chief such aim is profit, and spending money to protect the environment and to mitigate the hardships of the poor, the old, and the weak is to no one's private profit.

Conservatives viewed such safety nets as Social Security (1935) and the Fair Labor Standards Act (1938) as signposts on the road to serfdom. Over time, they said, such safety nets would undermine our self-reliance and turn Congress into an auction, with each member trying to outbid the others in providing popular but expensive domestic welfare programs.

By now, the core safety-net programs, like Social Security, have been accepted by many conservatives. President Ronald Reagan used to attack Social Security in days gone by, when he urged us to rely on voluntary pension programs operated by private insurance companies. But in the 1980 presidential campaign and again in 1984, he repeatedly pledged to safeguard Social Security, which has long had overwhelming support.[3]

But although conservatives by and large accepted a core of safety-net programs, albeit perhaps reluctantly, liberals found themselves pushed to the right. The mounting costs of social programs, from Social Security to school lunches, could not be forever ignored. Bulging federal deficits in the 1980s, deficits that experts projected would increase year after year, were widely recognized as a threat to the nation's future growth and prosperity. That the problem was real enough was dramatically apparent when old-fashioned liberal Walter Mondale cited federal deficit as a priority issue in his 1984 campaign for president. Virtually everyone agreed that there had to be a safety net, but the task of curbing federal deficits to maintain the health of the economy had been forced to the fore.[4]

---

[3] During the first Reagan administration when the President's powers were at their peak in 1981, a moderate Social Security proposal construed by the Senate as undermining benefits was turned down by a vote of 96 to 0. Then early in the second Reagan administration when the need to cut deficits—and the federal budget—assumed top priority, modest proposals to trim Social Security benefits were put forth with great caution and as a last resort.

[4] The Democratic platform of 1984 muffled, or avoided altogether, many of the themes long characteristic of the party's platforms. See *The New York Times*, July 22, 1984, p. 25.

Economic Management. In the 1930s, few liberals worried about the costs and results of government activity. In fact, the Depression convinced liberals that the government must direct the economy as a whole.

It was John Maynard Keynes (1883–1946), British economist, who provided the theory and technique of the new economic management. He believed that during the depression phases of the business cycle, governments should deliberately spend more money than they took in—"deficit spending"—to pump funds into the economy, promote consumption, and stimulate industrial production (see Chapter 16). Conservatives have always been critical of Keynesian economics, and the inflation, declining investment, and lower industrial growth of the early 1970s made them more critical yet. Keynes's formula called for the government to restrain demand during boom periods as well as to stimulate it during busts. That would mean running a budget surplus at a time of strong, sustained prosperity in the private economy, not just running a deficit at a time of recession or depression. Conservatives pointed out—correctly, as it happens—that Keynes's balanced model broke down in the face of political reality, since it is easy to vote for higher spending but much harder to vote for spending cuts. Harder still is voting for a major tax increase to damp down an economic boom.

Conservatives also say that Keynesianism works poorly when the private economy's problem is to encourage investment, not to stimulate demand and consumption. Keynesianism in practice often seemed to produce what conservative economist James M. Buchanan called "democracy in deficit."[5] Rightly or wrongly, conservatives blame these deficits for most of the country's economic difficulties, and many have supported a constitutional amendment requiring the government to run a balanced budget.

Conservatives themselves split with the "supply-siders," a group that was especially prominent in opposition to increasing taxes as a solution to the deficits of the 1980s. Their ideas were not really original: Their origins lay in nineteenth-century classical economics. But their ideas gained popularity in the late 1970s and 1980s. Essentially they argued that priority should be given not to consumer spending, as Keynes thought, but to producers who supplied economic goods and services. They therefore advocated that the best policies to manage the economy so that it would create jobs and growth were to reduce taxes and government regulation of business. Supply-siders then stood in opposition to the liberals who advocated tax increases as a basic part of the answer to the problem of deficits.[6] Liberal–conservative differences in economic matters persisted in the 1980s but took somewhat altered forms in response to the problems of the times.[7] Readers might note that these shifting alignments took place *within* the traditional two-party system of Republicans and Democrats.

---

[5] James M. Buchanan, *Democracy in Deficit* (New York: Academic Press, 1977).

[6] One statement of these ideas is Bruce R. Bartlett, *Reaganomics: Supply-Side Economics in Action* (Westport, Conn: Arlington House, 1981). Foreword by U.S. Representative Jack Kemp.

[7] The clash between liberals and conservatives in 1984 ranged broadly over the spectrum of issues, since Mondale included cuts in the defense spending (relative to the budget projected by the President) as necessary to reduce deficits. Domestic policy became intertwined with issues of foreign and defense policy. This tendency to merge domestic and international issues (including defense policy) added to the range and complexity of liberal–conservative differences.

Foreign and Defense Policy. Economic liberals long confronted economic conservatives in a fairly clear way. This is not true of foreign and defense policy, where the line of conflict is drawn less clearly between liberals and conservatives than between conservatives and Cold War liberals, on the one hand, and dovish liberals, on the other.

From the end of World War II, in 1945, to the late 1960s, Democrats and Republicans, liberals and conservatives all regarded the "containment" of communism (see Chapter 17) as a legitimate goal of foreign policy. Two liberal Presidents, John F. Kennedy (1961–1963) and Lyndon B. Johnson (1963–1969), committed the United States to a war in Vietnam, a disaster sufficient to convince many liberals that the United States should no longer "police the world." Conservatives then changed their attitudes about foreign policy, too: It was a conservative Republican President, Richard Nixon (1969–1974), who first opened up relations with Communist China.

Realpolitik, hard-nosed realism, led many conservatives to accept not only trade and diplomatic ties with communist states but also strategic [nuclear] arms limitation talks with the Soviet Union, the so-called SALT talks (Strategic Arms Limitations Talks). These happened to be liberal objectives, too, though for somewhat different reasons.

From the mid-1970s onward, the ground began to shift. Conservatives started to criticize SALT and to support, once again, aggressive anticommunism coupled with high military spending. The 1980 campaign probably confused more than it clarified the positions of the candidates. Reagan advocated increased military spending but also sought to moderate his image as a hawkish and militantly anticommunist leader. Meanwhile, President Carter also advocated increased defense spending but sought to divert attention from the leadership issue in general and from the Iranian hostage crisis in particular.

The 1984 election perhaps offered somewhat clearer contrasts than 1980. President Reagan continued as an advocate of substantial increases in defense spending, regardless of the deficits, as a prerequisite to negotiations with the Russians. But, as in 1980, during the 1984 campaign Reagan appeared to soften his position on the possibility of negotiations with the Russians and to move away from some of his militantly anticommunist statements. Challenger Mondale also advocated *some* increase in defense spending but made it clear that the task of reducing deficits required cuts in defense spending relative to the budgets advocated by the President. Significantly, Mondale frankly advocated protectionism in matters of auto imports, a position at odds with the free trade posture of liberal leaders in an earlier era (FDR to Lyndon Johnson). There were some pretty clear contrasts, but there were plenty of opportunities for confusion on these and other matters as well. Some conservatives worried about the impact of heavy defense spending on the horrendous federal deficits. And liberals, or some of them anyway, worried that the challenger seemed too reluctant to show the flag on the world scene, while at home he appeared willing to respond to special interest pressures. Those who sought clear, consistent contrasts on domestic and foreign policy were likely to be a bit frustrated.

Social Issues. As though all this were not complicated enough, a new set of divisions cut disastrously through the Democratic coalition of economic liberals (see Chapter 9). These so-called *social issues* include abortion, student protest, homosexuality, psychoactive drugs, and other topics of the 1960s,

Table 7–1   Public Opinion: Economic versus Cultural Issues

ECONOMIC ISSUES	CULTURAL ISSUES		TOTALS
	% Liberal	% Conservative	
% Liberal	10	30	40
% Conservative	25	35	60
Totals	35	65	100

SOURCE: Michael Barone and Grant Ujifusa, *The Almanac of American Politics 1982* (Washington, D.C.: Barone & Co., 1981), p. xiii. By permission.

1970s, and 1980s. A related set of controversies involving civil rights (see Chapter 5) and civil liberties (see Chapter 4) divides public opinion in roughly the way that social issues do.

Social issues, by the way, have divided us in the past: prohibition in the 1920s, for example (see Chapter 6). But prohibition divided both major political parties about evenly between Wets and Drys. With the repeal of the Eighteenth Amendment in 1933, the federal government got out of the prohibition business. From then until the 1960s, social issues receded into the background while economic and foreign policy problems occupied center stage.

Social issues reentered our political life during the series of cultural revolutions that began in the 1960s.

"Acid, amnesty, and abortion," among other matters, divided old Democrats—New Deal economic liberals, often ethnic Catholics—from new-class Democrats—well-educated, affluent, issue-oriented men and women who often came from old Republican families. Such issues contributed to the tumultuous 1968 Democratic National Convention in Chicago and the defeat of Democratic nominees Hubert Humphrey in 1968 and George McGovern in 1972. Watergate, helped defeat Republican President Ford in 1976. Indeed, in the 1970s and beyond, the range and variety of social issues that impinged upon the political arena appeared to intensify, not diminish (see Table 7–1). Included were issues such as the gender gap and feminism, gay rights, school prayers, busing, affirmative action, gun control, and abortion—just to cite some of the most prominent.[8] Feelings seemed to become more polarized and compromise more difficult to achieve. The contention between the pro and the antiabortion factions is a good example. These special-issue publics pulled at both major parties, but they probably hurt the Democrats more than the Republicans. Certainly, when the Democrats lost in 1980 and again in 1984, they were charged with being overly responsive to special interests, such as labor, feminists, and blacks.

Added to the confusion surrounding these social issues was the fact that the public over the decade from 1972 to 1982 became more liberal on some matters but more conservative on others. Thus, approval of interracial marriages and open housing rose, as did the percentage willing to vote for a woman for president. These reactions suggested a liberal trend, but conserva-

---

[8] Note also Asher's treatment of the growing complexity of the political spectrum. He refers to these "social issues" as "alternative lifestyles." In any event, they compounded the subject matter or issue dimensions on which people could take liberal or conservative positions. See Herbert B. Asher, *Presidential Elections and American Politics: Voters, Candidates, and Campaigns Since 1952*, 3rd ed. (Homewood, Ill.: Dorsey, 1984), pp. 18ff.

tive reactions were apparent too. The percentage of those who felt that their federal income taxes were too high went up, as did support for capital punishment. Similarly on the increase was the percentage of respondents who felt the courts were not harsh enough with criminals.[9] One could not say there was a clear liberal trend, but neither were people becoming uniformly more conservative on all such issues. These social issues and the diverse reactions to them added to the problems of interpreting public opinion.

Cross-Cutting

Despite the vigor of some of the ideological disputes between liberals and conservatives, most Americans care little for ideology. Even those of us who call ourselves liberals, moderates, or conservatives—and many do not—bear those labels about as loosely as the label of party. When asked general questions about attitudes toward government, most Americans reply that it is "too big"—surely a conservative response. But not so fast! For when Americans are asked about *specific programs* in fields such as health, education, and Social Security, large majorities support government action—a liberal response.[10] Public opinion appears to embrace two overlapping majorities: ideological (theoretical) conservatives and operational (real-world) liberals. Most Americans are *cross-cutters;* that is, they are not notably consistent and do not seem much concerned about the discrepancies that occur. Most people feel quite free to sound off about the evils of government in general, then turn around and vote for specific programs desired.

Only a rather small minority of us think consistently about politics. Jews and blacks, for example, tend to be ideologically and operationally liberal; well–educated white Anglo–Saxon Protestants in managerial and some professional occupations tend to be ideologically and operationally conservative. But most Americans seem to float between these two extremes. The concrete political choices they make (such as voting) are much more influenced by immediate and tangible needs than by ideological attitudes. In 1980, for example, only 11 percent of Ronald Reagan's supporters voted for him chiefly because he was a "true conservative"; 38 percent said it was "time for a change." In 1984, with relatively good economic conditions prevailing, Reagan's leadership qualities mattered far more than specific issue positions or ideology.

The Leaders and the Led

Political leaders are more consistent than the rank and file, the majority of whose political ideas tend to be cross-cutting or somewhat inconsistent. A poll taken in California (by the *Los Angeles Times*) asked members and leaders of both major parties about social issues, including school prayers, the death penalty, and the Equal Rights Amendment (ERA, see Chapter 6). The results were illuminating. On every issue except ERA, the Democratic leaders stood

[9] John P. Robinson and John A. Fleishman, "Ideological Trends in American Public Opinion," in L. John Martin, ed., "Polling and the Democratic Consensus," *Annals of the American Academy of Political and Social Science*, 472 (March 1984), 55.

[10] Lloyd A. Free and Hadley Cantril, *The Political Beliefs of Americans* (New Brunswick, N.J.: Rutgers Univ., 1967).

alone, far off in left field, on several issues—further away from the Democratic rank and file than the Republican leaders were.[11]

The leaders, activists, and elites among us are often dedicated conservatives or liberals who tend to have fairly consistent ideas—or worry about the inconsistencies. But much of the public does not take politics that seriously. It tends to be *apolitical*. The public at large gives politics a lower priority and therefore is not much bothered about consistency or the lack of it in political matters. Traditional social values are seen as fine. But this does not mean people have a consistent scheme of well-thought-out values. The average voter therefore tends to be rather pragmatic and is swayed more by what is happening at the time of the election rather than by long-term ideological commitments. This outlook helps explain why American voters can get by with only two large but ill-defined political parties, while splinter parties flourish in other countries.

The National Mood: Liberal or Conservative?

Many people who lived through the 1960s look back to them as years of experiment. Yet Richard Nixon won the 1968 presidential election at the high tide of liberalism. The public at large seemed tired of those experiments and their beneficiaries, especially blacks and young people. The 1970s, for the most part, were years of relative conservatism. At their end, Jimmy Carter, perhaps the most conservative Democratic President since Grover Cleveland, lost to Ronald Reagan, perhaps the most conservative Republican President since Calvin Coolidge.

The gross results seem to suggest a steady shift to the right. But opinion polls (see below) do not always sustain that impression. One poll suggests that from 1977 to 1981, the proportion of white voters who called themselves conservatives went up by 6 percentage points, the proportion of moderates went down by 4 points, and that of liberals held steady. Other polls point to greater conservative gains—but at the expense of moderates, not liberals. Ideological self-identification has to be treated with some caution. As we have just noted most people, as distinct from activists and elites, tend not to be ideological in their thinking. Robinson and Fleishman included this caution in their study of a number of polls that looked at people's ideological prefer-

---

[11] Those who study party convention delegates often find their opinions somewhat divergent from those of the party rank and file. See Barbara G. Farah, "Delegate Polls: 1944 to 1984," *Public Opinion* (Aug.-Sept. 1984), 13.

Table 7-2   Personal Political Views in California, 1981: Party Leaders and Followers

	DEMOCRATS		REPUBLICANS		
	Leaders	Registered Voters	Leaders	Registered Voters	TOTAL POPULATION
Very Liberal	24%	6%	1%	2%	5%
Somewhat Liberal	41	20	3	9	16
Middle of Road	24	40	14	27	37
Somewhat Conservative	8	21	52	41	28
Very Conservative	2	10	30	20	12

ences over time. They did find a general shift over the decade ending in 1982 "in the conservative direction" but reminded readers this was "among that minority with an ideological preference."[12] There is good evidence that the term *conservative* gained popularity over time, at least among those who used such terms.

When we turn from labels to specific issues, the picture is still murky. Take defense spending. On this, as on most matters, the disagreement between liberals and conservatives is not absolute. Some liberals support increased levels of defense spending for an aggressive policy of anticommunism. Most liberals do not, however, and most conservatives do.

Let us start with 1969, the first year of Richard Nixon's presidency.

1969–1975: Detente. Richard Nixon had a conservative Republican background, campaigned in 1968 as a conservative, and as President, pleased conservatives much of the time. Yet when he was President, from 1969 to 1974, defense spending fell from about 10 percent of the gross national product (GNP) to about 6 percent. Part of this decline, but not all of it, resulted from congressional budget cuts. It was Nixon, too, who opened up **detente** a lessening of tensions between the United States and the Soviet Union (see Chapter 17), began to normalize relations with mainland (Communist) China, and created an all-volunteer (undrafted) army. During these years, the boundaries between liberalism and conservatism, particularly on foreign-

---

[12] Robinson and Fleishman, "Ideological Trends in American Public Opinion."

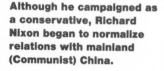

Although he campaigned as a conservative, Richard Nixon began to normalize relations with mainland (Communist) China.

UPI/Bettmann Newsphotos

policy issues, were blurred. Liberals hated Nixon and Nixon hated them, but many of his policies were in fact liberal policies.

The confusion between the liberal and conservative element of Mr. Nixon's presidency came to a head in Vietnam. In 1969 he apparently recognized that the United States would have to withdraw from that war-torn land. As President, however, he did not wish to lose the war, so he prolonged it while at the same time attempting to withdraw from it. We lost anyway (see Chapter 17).

Vietnam made the voters—liberal *and* conservative—skeptical of foreign military involvements, a skepticism that persisted even after the end of detente.

1976–1979: Ford and Carter. In 1975, leftist movements aided by the Soviet Union took over two of Portugal's African colonies, Angola and Mozambique. Conservatives who had opposed detente now opposed it even more strongly and carried a large part of public opinion. Those who supported higher military spending and those who supported lower military spending were now about equal in number. But President Gerald Ford (1974–1977) could not persuade Congress to approve aid to anticommunists in Angola. The wound of Vietnam was still open.

1979–1980: Carter. On November 4, 1979, a group of Iranian militants broke into the U.S. Embassy in Teheran and took its occupants hostage. President Carter could do nothing to get them released and they remained in captivity until January 30, 1981, the day of Ronald Reagan's inauguration as President (see Chapter 17). In December 1980, moreover, the Soviet Union had invaded neighboring Afghanistan to prop up a Communist government, and there, too we could do little or nothing (see Chapter 17). Many people, Mr. Carter among them, now demanded higher defense spending and a more aggressive anticommunist policy. But it was Mr. Reagan, not Mr. Carter, who benefited from the popularity of this demand.

1981–1984: Reagan. Reagan swept into office pledging to increase defense spending and to "stand up" for America abroad. He was strongly identified with a militant anticommunist posture. But as time passed, public support for the administration wavered. It was apparent that the public did not want American soldiers fighting and dying abroad, in Central America or in Beirut. And support for increased defense spending fell even in the early years of the first Reagan administration (see Figure 7–1). By 1984, mounting federal deficits intensified pressures to cut spending. Gallup polls showed that the

Table 7–3 "Philosophy" and Party, 1980

PARTY	"PHILOSOPHY"			
	Liberal	Moderate	Conservative	None
Democrats	9%	22%	8%	4%
Republicans	2	11	12	3
Independents	4	12	7	—
No Affiliation	—	—	—	6
Total	15	45	27	13

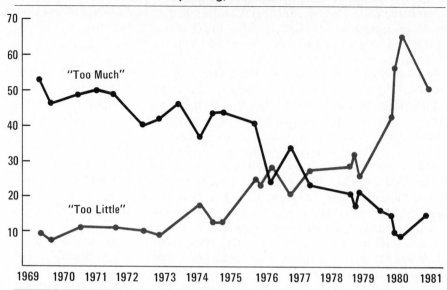

Figure 7-1   Public Preferences for Increased or Reduced U.S. Defense Spending, 1969-1981

Source: Bruce Rusett and Ronald de Luca, " 'Don't Tread on Me': Public Opinion and Foreign Policy in the Eighties," *Political Science Quarterly*, 96, no. 3 (Fall 1981), 381-99, at p. 384.

public preferred cuts in defense spending to tax increases or cuts in entitle-ment programs like Social Security.[13]

The national mood in the 1980s was probably a complex mixture, although a conservative drift was apparent in some respects. When traditional liberal Walter Mondale in 1984 felt obliged to deal with federal deficits as a priority issue, it was clear that even liberal elites felt constrained to acknowledge a relatively conservative agenda. The public at large appeared ambivalent. On the one hand, there was still considerable support for specific social programs and a willingness to cut defense spending. The welfare state still enjoyed much popular support and reflected priorities of a liberal nature. On the other hand, the public also reacted strongly against tax increase proposals, a stance that many observers and participants, including the vast majority of Demo-crats seeking House and Senate seats, felt the election of 1984 confirmed. This opposition to tax increases had profoundly conservative implications in limiting social welfare spending, especially if deficits were to be cut. The public seemed to want government programs but without added taxes. This ambivalence was well reflected in Everett Carll Ladd's analysis of the 1980 election and has application to 1984. Ladd argued that there was "broad support of Americans in all social strata for the 'service state' as revealed in surveys conducted annually since 1973. . . ." But Ladd also claimed that confidence in government and in leaders had fallen, that large majorities blamed government for inflation, and that the "sense is widespread across the United States that the state is clumsy, inefficient, and wasteful."[14] The

---

[13] See, for instance, a *Gallup Report* as early as February, 1983, pp. 16ff. More than a year later, in discussions of the budget for fiscal 1985 (to begin in the fall of 1984), similar public preferences were apparent. See *Gallup Report* (April 1984), 10ff.

[14] Everett Carll Ladd, *Where Have All the Voters Gone? The Fracturing of America's Political Parties*, 2nd ed. (New York: Norton, 1982), p. 104.

government that brought the benefits also brought problems. This mixture was hard to characterize clearly, but perhaps it titled more to the conservatives than to the liberals, at least while the unease and the opposition to tax increases persisted.

Volatility. The swings in defense spending attitudes remind us that public opinion at times is volatile and may be influenced by short-term forces. Certainly, opinion in 1980 was quite volatile. Prior to the election, President Carter and challenger Senator Ted Kennedy rose and fell in the polls. During the campaigns, signs of volatility appeared in the mixed attitudes toward both candidates, in the high percentage of late-deciders, and in the impact of events such as the last campaign debate and the Iranian hostage crisis.

In 1984, however, less volatility was apparent. All through the election year Ronald Reagan had an approval rating consistently close to 55 percent, and he finally won 59 percent of the vote. As for the surveys of public attitudes toward defense spending, one could argue that people did for a time want to increase defense spending; but once the increases were in place under Reagan, people did not want the further increases Reagan continued to advocate. They wanted more, but not as much as Reagan instituted. In this sense, one could say that their response was a rational reaction to changing circumstances.

In part, opinion volatility depends upon the issue. Recall that our analysis above suggests much of the public is fairly apolitical, pragmatic, and not notably concerned with consistency. Hence, on many issues there will be a certain "softness," due to relatively uninterested people who have no strong feelings about the matter—and may or may *not* tell the pollsters they have "no opinion." Nevertheless, there are some matters on which opinion—or a good deal of it—may solidify. By early 1984, Reagan had a solid majority of supporters who knew and liked him and stuck with him with considerable consistency. So it depends on circumstances, and we must be wary when we try to interpret the firmness and stability of opinions cited by pollsters and others.

THE MAKING OF PUBLIC OPINION

Gilbert and Sullivan apparently believed that political opinions emerge from the solitary depths of the personality or even from our animal nature:

> I often think it's comical
> How nature always does contrive
> That every boy and every gal,
> That's born into the world alive,
> Is either a little Liberal,
> Or else a little Conservative.[15]

---

[15] From *Iolanthe* (1882). *Liberal* and *Conservative* are used here in the sense of the parties that bear those names.

Table 7-4 Self-Identified Independent New Voters

YEAR	PERCENT
1952	26%
1960	34
1964	34
1968	48
1972	50
1976	47

SOURCE: Norman H. Nie, Sidney Verba, and John R. Petrocik, *The Changing American Voter*, 2nd ed. (Cambridge: Harvard Univ., 1979), p. 365.

Perhaps Gilbert and Sullivan were on to something, after all. Research on the psychological origins of fascism suggests that personality characteristics do predispose some people to support certain kinds of political movements.[16] But most of our opinions—including political opinions—take shape in our social environment. The process of acquiring political opinions—**political socialization**—it begins in the cradle and ends in the grave.

The Family

The earliest and chief agent of all kinds of **socialization**—learning to behave as a human being—is the family. Political socialization, too, begins—and sometimes pretty much ends—there: Children of Republicans tend to be Republicans, children of Democrats to be Democrats. Children who do not share their parents' partisan preferences are usually indifferent to politics, not sympathetic to the other party. Support for parties, like religions, has a kind of "hereditary" quality.

The hereditary transmission of party sympathies is now less common—one aspect of the parties' decline (see Chapter 9). In 1952, only 29 percent of first-time voters did not identify with a major party. In 1964, the proportion had increased to 34 percent; and in 1972, it reached 50 percent.[17]

At what age do children first learn about politics? A 1967 survey of a group of elementary school children showed that just over half the second graders could not define "Democratic" and "Republican" or say which party they "belonged to." Most sixth graders managed to answer these questions, although they were hazy about what each party stood for.

---

[16] See, for example, Harold D. Lasswell, *Psychopathology and Politics* (Chicago: Univ. of Chicago, 1977); and especially Theodor Adorno et al., *The Authoritarian Personality* (New York: Harper, 1950), a pathbreaking work in this field.

[17] One author writes "One of the most well-documented findings of political-attitude research is that young adults have weaker party identification than have their elders." See Paul R. Abramson, *Political Attitudes in America: Formation and Change* (San Francisco: Freeman, 1983), p. 106.

Table 7-5 Percentage of Whites Who Are Strong Party Identifiers by Years of Birth, 1952 and 1980

	1952			1980	
Year of Birth	Age at Time of Election	% Strong Identifiers	Year of Birth	Age at Time of Election	% Strong Identifiers
1924–1931	21–28	30	1956–1962	18–24	11
1916–1923	29–36	24	1948–1955	25–32	17
1908–1915	37–44	32	1940–1947	33–40	16
1900–1907	45–52	34	1932–1939	41–48	27
1892–1899	53–60	46	1924–1931	49–56	24
1884–1891	61–68	43	1916–1923	57–64	29
1876–1883	69–76	49	1908–1915	65–72	39
ALL WHITES		35	ALL WHITES		23

SOURCE: Paul R. Abramson, *Political Attitudes in America: Formation and Change* (San Francisco: W. H. Freeman, 1983), p. 108.

The Enduring Family. Although, it is often hard to define the separate contribution made by the family in shaping the political identity of the young, one thing does seem very clear: The American family's decay as a transmitter of traditional social values—including political values—has been exaggerated. In the 1970s, for example, two sociologists went to Muncie, Indiana, to examine the lives and attitudes of the people.[18] *Middletown*, the first modern study of an American community, had been made in Muncie fifty years earlier.[19] Fifty years is a longish time in the history of any modern society, and in the interval, Muncie's economy and society changed considerably. But more impressive was the *lack* of change in many traditional social and political attitudes.

The second study showed that in Muncie, at any rate, the family was still the basic unit of society, still the basic agent of socialization, and still a conservative social force. How conservative? In the late 1970s, fully 50 percent of high school students believed that the Book of Genesis, literally interpreted, described the origin of humankind more accurately than did the theory of evolution. In the mid-1920s, 72 percent had thought so. In large measure, such attitudes come from the family.

The family endured, but it was changing. Marriage remained the ideal, but couples tended to marry later and preferred to have smaller families rather than large ones. Another change was the large number of women—many married and with children—who left the home for jobs in the marketplace. Sex roles and stereotypes began to change as well, in the home and outside it. It became more acceptable for young couples to live together out of wedlock or for a young woman to raise her children alone. The family both endured and adapted as increasingly diverse life styles sprang up.

Gender

In the 1980 election, a marked difference between the votes of men and women led to much talk of the "gender gap." Reagan won 55 percent of the male vote; Carter won 36 percent. Women split their vote almost evenly: 47 percent for Reagan, 45 percent for Carter. Sex differences in voting were not entirely a novelty. Previous studies found that women, more pacific than men, opposed the use of force abroad and at home. Women also were generally found to be more religious and moralistic than men. But until 1980 the votes of men and women revealed little difference in relation to parties and presidential candidates. Because other differences relating to religion, region, and social class were of diminished importance in the 1980 returns, the gender gap stood out all the more. And the media made much of it.

Poole and Zeigler, in their extended study of womens politics through the early 1980s, were not much impressed by the gender gap. Instead they found differences *among* women, with employed women tending to be more liberal than housewives on social welfare issues. They then speculated that the growth of women in the work force might in time shift the nation's politics toward the left in support of social welfare policies.[20] But women were not uniformly liberal. On most civil rights policies they reacted much the way men

---

[18] Theodore Caplow et al., *Middletown Families* (Minneapolis: Univ. of Minnesota, 1982).
[19] Robert S. Lynd and Helen Merrell Lynd, *Middletown: A Study in American Culture* (New York: Harcourt, 1929).
[20] Keith T. Poole and L. Harmon Zeigler, *Women, Public Opinion, and Politics: The Changing Political Attitudes of American Women* (New York: Longman, 1985), p. 148.

Women did not turn out as a bloc in support of Geraldine Ferraro on the Democratic ticket in 1984. In general, in the voting in the 1984 election, it did not appear that men and women divided sharply along gender lines.

did, but they had a greater tendency to oppose busing and abortion. On foreign policy, women tended to be more liberal than men in favoring a nuclear freeze and better relations with Russia. There were some differences, but overall, Poole and Zeigler argued that women were *not* a cohesive bloc that could be contrasted with men.

The 1984 returns appeared to confirm this cautious view of the gender gap and the diversity of women's opinions. Certainly women did not turn out as a bloc in support of Geraldine Ferraro on the Democratic ticket. Her presence on the ticket may have hurt more than it helped, according to an NBC exit poll. Even among women, slightly higher percentages (24 percent), said her presence made them less likely to vote Democratic than the 19 percent who said it made them more likely to vote for the ticket.

After the election, talk of the gender gap died down. But the fact that women did not vote as a massive bloc did not mean all gender differences were somehow unreal. More realistic is the realization that women differ among themselves just as men do, and that on most matters men and women would not divide sharply along gender lines.

The Schools

Before World War I (1914–1918), the vast majority of Americans did not finish high school. Down to the end of the Great Depression of the 1930s, only about half of all Americans aged 18 to 35, and fewer still of their elders, had high school diplomas. For that other half, formal education was short and relatively unimportant.

Yet by the end of the 1970s, about five-sixths of the same group of Americans had high school diplomas, and 45 percent had been to college. Far

Table 7-6	Education of Americans by Age Group				
YEAR OF 18TH BIRTHDAY	AGE IN 1982	HIGH SCHOOL 1–3 YEARS	HIGH SCHOOL 4 YEARS	COLLEGE 1–3 YEARS	COLLEGE 4 YEARS OR MORE
1963–1972	37–46	15.3%	39.2%	21.8%	23.8%
1953–1962	47–56	22.9	42.0	15.5	19.6
1943–1952	57–66	32.5	40.1	12.4	15.0
1933–1942	67–76	40.1	37.3	11.6	11.0
before 1933	77 and older	59.9	23.3	8.3	8.5

more people were staying in school far longer than at any time in the past. Education had become one of the strongest shared experiences of the American people—a political experience, among other things.

Going to School. Pupils learn important lessons from real life, not just from textbooks. Perhaps the most important is respect for authority. Another is the expectation that punishment will follow the breaking of any major rule. These, in themselves, are the most important of all political messages. Most of us discover, too, that loyalty—to other students, to teachers, to a school, or to the United States—is often valued more highly than creativeness or integrity.

Of late, some pupils have seen their schools transformed into actual political battlegrounds: Efforts to ban certain books from school libraries have been made—and resisted; parents in some cities have demanded, and in part won, community control over curriculum and the hiring and firing of teachers; and busing has turned many schools into literal, not just figurative, battlegrounds. These controversies surely heighten the political awareness of the pupils swept up in them, but they do not necessarily promote any particular political point of view.

College. Elementary and high schools build discipline and conformity. Colleges, by contrast, tend to break them down. Professors, especially in the liberal arts, tend to be liberals, and they often they encourage "critical" attitudes among their students. In any event, colleges and universities force their students to ask questions and weigh evidence, and these experiences make college-educated Americans more politically aware and liberal than those whose education stopped at high school. Indeed, college seniors are more politically aware and more liberal than college sophomores.

Although today's college students are not as demonstrative as those of the 1960s and 1970s, college graduates tend to be more political and more liberal than our population at large.

During the 1984 election campaigns there was talk of campuses turning conservative, with growing numbers of students willing to describe themselves as Republican. As often happens in the media, reports of the death of college liberalism were probably exaggerated. The exit polls showed that Reagan did well in *all* age groups. We normally expect older voters to be more heavily Republican than younger ones, but Reagan countered the usual drop-off in Republican strength among the young. If Republican candidates can hold this increased support from the younger generation, Democrats could be in long-term trouble.

Religion

A century and a half ago, Alexis de Tocqueville noted that the influence of religion was more pervasive and intense in the United States than in Europe.

It still is. Tocqueville also marveled that religion was not nearly so divisive here as in Europe. He perceived that we had avoided European-style religious controversies because, at the very outset of our national existence, we had the wisdom to separate church and state (see Chapter 4). He was surely right about this, as about so many other aspects of American life.

This is not to say that religious differences do not enter our politics—not at all. In the nineteenth century, a political fault-line, or fracture, separated different kinds of Christians. One group, consisting of Evangelical Protestants, stressed "right behavior," salvation through personal grace and "rebirth"; the other, consisting of Roman Catholics and many members of Protestant denominations, such as Episcopalian and Lutheran, stressed "right belief," salvation through liturgical and sacramental life. Evangelical Protestants, in particular, have repeatedly tried to make essentially religious conceptions of morality binding on the American people as a whole. They had notable success in 1919 through the ratification of the Eighteenth Amendment, which banned the manufacture, possession, and sale of liquor. There was great opposition to effort of this sort, however—opposition in which Episcopalians and Roman Catholics were prominent. In 1933, the Eighteenth Amendment was repealed by the Twenty-first Amendment.

The persistence of religious values is a major reason why the two parties are more alike than different and, above all, why socialism never caught on in the United States. No party can expect to get a foothold in the affections of the American public if it does not give lip service, at any rate, to the Judeo-Christian fundamentals. Neither can any politician.

Some politicians repeat essentially religious formulas obsessively. Nelson Rockefeller, governor of New York (1959–1976) and Ford's Vice-President (1974–1977), used to invoke "the Brotherhood of Man under the Fatherhood of God" in almost every speech. The reporters who covered him dubbed this phrase "BOMFOG."

Historic Ties. Religion is politically important, too, because certain religious groups have historic ties with certain parties. Outside the South, members of most Protestant denominations have been largely Republican. The connection between Protestantism and Republicanism became weaker during the New Deal (see Chapter 10), when social class (see the next section) became an important point of political difference. But the connection is still there, to some extent. The historic exception, southern white Protestants, used to be overwhelmingly Democratic, but in the past two decades, large numbers of them have defected to the Republicans in presidential elections.

Roman Catholics were at one time overwhelmingly Democratic, as a result both of their relative poverty and the discrimination and hostility they encountered at the hands of native-stock (and largely Republican) white Protestants. By now, Roman Catholics are actually better off than Protestants and have defected in large numbers to the Republican party.

American Jews have been overwhelmingly Democratic and liberal—rich to poor, top to bottom. Strikingly well-educated and increasingly affluent, they play an important role in the internal politics of the Democratic party. International and domestic issues may have pushed some Jewish Americans toward the open arms of the Republican party, but the bulk of them have maintained their liberal and Democratic leanings.

In the 1984 election, religion became an issue, albeit a multifaceted one. Certainly there was much talk of abortion, school prayers, and the separation

UPI/Bettmann Newsphotos

of church and state. Conservative Christians weighed in with their pronounce-ments, as did Catholic bishops and others. Much dispute arose about the proper role of religious leaders in political campaigns, whether they dealt with so-called religious issues such as school prayers, or with secular issues such as poverty and the threat of nuclear warfare. While many of the candidates from the President on down sounded off on the need to reinforce religion, others sought to stress the importance of keeping church and state separate. In the actual voting, as revealed in exit polls, Reagan carried the Catholic vote, by a margin of about 55 percent, somewhat improving his 1980 record. White Protestants swung more heavily to Reagan, and the largest swing of all was among white born-again (or evangelical) Protestants: Their margin for the President was five to one over his Democratic challenger Walter Mondale. On the other hand, Jewish voters had been badly divided in 1980, in part because of their suspicions about Jimmy Carter's support for Israel. They swung 13 percentage points toward Mondale in 1984, giving him a nearly two-to-one lead over the President.[21] It seems very probable that this return to a normally heavy Democratic Jewish vote in 1984 was helped by a reaction against Reagan's obvious and close ties to the religious (mostly Protestant) right. Religious antagonisms have an old history in American politics. Sometimes they are bound up with the campaign itself, as in 1928, 1960 and—to a lesser but very visible extent—in 1984. Most of the time other issues come to the fore.

In the 1984 election, much dispute arose about the proper role of religious leaders in political campaigns. One such dispute involved Governor Mario Cuomo of New York and Archbishop John O'Connor; the issue was voting or not voting for a candidate according to his or her stand on the abortion issue.

[21] For an explanation of the persistence of Jewish liberalism, see the comment by a leading political sociologist who is himself Jewish, Seymour Martin Lipset, in his "Most Jews Are Still Both Democrats and Liberals," *Washington Post National Weekly Edition*, January 4, 1985, p. 22.

Social Class

Parties in Europe often describe themselves as "working class" or "middle class" in outlook and support, and they are so described by others. Before the 1930s, neither of our own major parties was regarded as the party of one class or another, nor did the members of any class consistently vote for any particular party. Consciousness of class no doubt influenced the way some people voted, but it was only one such influence and, in many cases, not the most important one. By and large, there is not much reason to suppose that different classes had markedly different points of view about the basic questions of politics and economics. Most people believed, as did Ralph Waldo Emerson (1803–1882), that "the government that governs best is the government that governs least" and that business itself ought to look after its own affairs.

The Great Depression, which began in 1929, made many people doubt these propositions. President Herbert Hoover (1929–1933) and most Republicans were convinced that the Depression could end only through the normal workings of the business cycle, without government intervention. Anyone who could not wait for the Depression to "burn itself out" was not, perforce, a Republican. After 1930 there were millions of these people, so the Democrats could and did make political hay by calling for greater federal intervention in the economy.

Of course, not all manual workers then voted Democratic, nor all middle- and upper-class people, Republican. After all, the Democratic President, Franklin D. Roosevelt (1933–1945), was himself a man of impeccably aristocratic descent. Nonetheless, middle- and upper-class voters had a clear tendency to polarize around the Republicans, and working-class voters around the Democrats. With millions of voters, such general tendencies counted then and still do. The elections of 1940 and 1948 were the most class-polarized in American history. The Democrats won both.

Hard times during the Depression, then World War II, polarized the electorate; but the prosperity of the 1950s and 1960s blurred class lines. During most of these years, unemployment and inflation were low, and wages climbed. Many working-class people earned enough money to lead middle-class lives; in some cases, this meant voting Republican.

By the mid-1970s, the steady rise in our national standard of living had come to an end, at least for the time being. But blame could not be fixed on one party or the other, and our economy, though less healthy than it had been ten or twenty years earlier, was not really a disaster. Fewer people, especially fewer poor people, were voting at all (see Chapter 9).

The Reagan administration in the early 1980s changed national policies in directions that critics saw as "initiating a new class war."[22] One critic in the mid-1980s even wrote of a new inequality arising from changes in the population, the parties, and national policies. Thomas Byrne Edsall argued that the Republicans had become the party of the affluent and the middle class, including much of the business world. A new majority, they favored conservative economic policies that benefited them, such as taxes and regulations. But, Edsall argued pointedly, these policies hurt those who were less well off and thereby fostered the "new inequality."[23] Whatever the truth of

---

[22] Frances F. Piven and Richard Cloward, *The New Class War* (New York: Pantheon, 1982).
[23] *The New Politics of Inequality* (New York: Norton, 1984).

these charges, Reagan did well among most income groups and occupations in 1980 and 1984. In the 1984 sweep, Reagan, in the CBS/*New York Times* exit poll, carried all income groups but the lowest, those with incomes under $12,500. Even the union vote gave Mondale a meager majority of 53 percent to Reagan's 45 percent. Reagan did pretty well across the board, and it appeared that social class differences were of diminishing importance.

Race

The experience of immigration from all parts of the world, and then the American experience, gave our earlier settlers (and us, their descendants) a common political point of view in spite of much cultural diversity. But one group of immigrants was different. Its members did not come here by choice, and when they got here they found slavery, not freedom. Among blacks these collective experiences created a collective point of view that is different—though not *very* different—from that of other Americans.

Until the 1930s, collective memories of the past made Republicans of most blacks who could vote—a small minority (see Chapter 5). It was the New Deal that made blacks into Democrats, and by the 1980s, blacks were about as lopsidedly Democratic as they had once been lopsidedly Republican. In the early 1980s they made up less than 2 percent of the Republican party's voting base, but nearly 20 percent of the Democratic party's.

Economic and social questions generate the biggest differences between blacks and whites; many more blacks, for instance, support affirmative action (see Chapter 5) and federal government spending for social programs (see Chapter 15). Blacks and whites share much more common ground on foreign policy and defense issues, however, which do not affect our lives quite so directly.

Analyzing the shift to the Democratic party, one could argue that the nation's racial attitudes have changed much since World War II, when segregation widely prevailed. In addition, one can argue that blacks and whites were not far apart on many matters. They differed sharply on some things that mattered a good deal to blacks, however, such as affirmative action. And the Reagan administration aroused strong antipathy from blacks. Blacks were strongly wedded to traditional New Deal liberal policies of social welfare and civil rights. Reagan's claims that his policies benefited all,

Table 7–7   Polled Black–White Opinions on Various Issues

YEAR OF POLL	ISSUE	WHITE	BLACK
1978	Favor death penalty	72%	46%
1978	Favor curbing sales of pornography to adults	44	24
1979	Government should take over oil companies	19	42
1980	Unemployment is more important than inflation	37	60
1980	Programs of the 1960s made things better	28	51
1981	Food-stamp spending should be cut	55	17
1981	Respondent personally hurt by Reagan budget cut	38	76
1981	Federal level of government most efficient	18	41
1981	Approve President Reagan's handling of his job	66	13
1981	Military spending should be increased	57	33
1981	Favor busing for school integration	13	41
1981	Believe laziness a major cause of black unemployment	43	7

including blacks, were roundly rejected by much of the black community. In 1980 about 85 percent of blacks backed Carter, and 55 percent of whites favored Reagan. Then in 1984, according to the CBS/*New York Times* exit poll, a whopping 90 percent of blacks voted for Mondale while 66 percent of whites nationally endorsed Reagan, a margin reinforced by the 72 percent of southern whites for Reagan. This tendency for the parties to split along racial lines was hardly welcome news. Even though blacks and whites could agree on many issues, there were certainly some pronounced differences, and the Reagan Administration seemed to bring them out.

Regional Differences

The United States of America, all 3.6 million square miles of it, includes bits of what were formerly parts of the British, French, Spanish, Dutch, Russian, and Swedish empires. The union of these gigantic and very different territories into a single country was not inevitable; they might have become many separate nations, and although they did not, they are still different, with somewhat different political cultures. In 1984 Reagan carried all regions, but he did his best in the South, Midwest, and West, while gaining just a bare majority in the East. (These regional variations were discussed in Chapter 1.)

POLLING AND SURVEYS

In the first decades of the present century, the *Literary Digest* magazine conducted a nationwide opinion poll before each presidential election. By the 1930s, this pool had literally millions of respondents. The *Digest* simply mailed off ballots to people whose names it took from telephone books and lists of magazine subscribers and automobile owners. Up through and including the 1932 election, it always picked the winner. But in 1936, the pool indicated that Governor Alfred Landon of Kansas, the Republican candidate, would get 62 percent of the vote to President Franklin Roosevelt's 38 percent. In fact, Mr. Roosevelt won by 25 percentage points. The *Digest* soon folded.

Where did it go wrong? Simple. Its poll sought to divine the intentions of the electorate as a whole, or at any rate the intentions of those people who actually voted. In 1936, most working-class people did not have telephones, cars, or magazine subscriptions, but they had very strong reasons for voting overwhelmingly for Franklin Roosevelt. Those who received the poll ballot were relatively well-off and therefore relatively more Republican than were the electorate as a whole. Moreover, not all the people who received ballots mailed them back to the magazine. Those who did were probably more political than those who did not. The *Digest* poll did not survey the electorate as a whole, only the part of it that was well-to-do and Republican.

Straw Polls and Scientific Polls

The earliest polls, like the *Digest*, were straw polls (or straw votes), which have a common weakness: The people who respond to them are self-selected. You might, for instance, take a straw poll by standing on a street corner and putting questions to anyone who passed. The problem is that pollsters cannot know if the people who agree to respond really who typify the group under

Ken Karp

For a poll to be scientific, the pollster must choose representative members of the population. These members make up what pollsters call a sample.

study. Scientific polls try to ensure that the respondents, as a group, are actually typical. The *Literary Digest* disaster showed[24] that if opinion polls were ever to be useful, they would have to be conducted scientifically.

Sampling. One way of predicting the outcome of an election would be to get in touch with all the voters individually. That method would hardly be practical.[25] Pollsters therefore make a scale model of the group they wish to investigate. A model of the adult population of the United States might consist of 1,500 to 2,500 people, each one representing 50,000 or more adult Americans. Those 1,500 or 2,500 people if correctly chosen would give answers similar to those that 80 million to 125 million adult Americans might give. In polling and statistics jargon, the larger group, whose opinions the pollster want assessed, is called the **population,** or **universe.** The people actually questioned, whose opinions represent those of the universe, make up the **sample.**

For a poll to be scientific, the sample must typify the universe. The members of the sample cannot be self-selected; the pollster must choose them to avoid biasing the sample. You could not divine the intentions of the national electorate with a sample chosen entirely in Manhattan or Peoria. The sample must be a mix that reflects our national mix; those chosen in this way are called **representative samples**.

Finally, the individuals in the sample must be chosen at random. A **random sample** of the national electorate, might include *some* people from Peoria, but

---

[24] Though not, perhaps, for all time. After the Reagan–Carter debates, ABC television invited its viewers to phone in their responses to the candidates' performances. The network did acknowledge that its sample was not representative.

[25] The Census Bureau comes close to conducting a door-to-door survey of all Americans, but even with its financial resources, it has been accused of undercounting a number of groups, especially blacks, Hispanics, and other minorities. The census of course, is not an investigation of public opinion but a collection of demographic information about the American people.

A Pollster's Day

Diane Bentley [not her real name] does interviewing for both Louis Harris and Pat Caddell. To follow her as she makes her rounds is to peer behind the wizard's curtain and see polling as it really is. The practice is a far cry from what the pollsters would have us believe.

Diane began working as a poll-taker several years ago. Originally, she did it principally to get out of the house, since her children were both well along in school. Now, however, with family money tight, the pay is an important incentive, so she takes on any polling assignment she can get. Most pollsters imply that they have their own special force of fieldworkers, but in fact many interviewers like Diane find it necessary to work for two or more polling firms.

On a Tuesday morning in June, Diane went to a working-class section of New Haven, Connecticut, where she had to complete ten interviews. Some firms tell their interviewers to start at a certain house and work in a particular direction, but this day she was simply given a map of the neighborhood and told to begin wherever she wanted.

"If I get to choose, I like to drive around the area a bit. I look for parked cars, toys in the yard. That means that it's more likely people are around and I don't have to waste time at empty houses."

Judged by Diane's standards, the neighborhood did not look very promising, but she managed to find a street where there were a few cars. The first house she tried was surrounded by a chain link fence. The door had two locks on it and a small decal which said the premises were protected by Lectronic Alarm Systems. One supposed it was a home of a middle-aged couple, with perhaps a son in the service and a married daughter living in Indiana. The occupants, one guessed, were conservative in their politics, but no one answered the door, so whatever their views, they went unrecorded.

Next door was a rather run-down two-family house.

No one was home on one side. An older man answered Diane's knock on the other side and she was pleased, as it is harder to find men at home during the day. Her pleasure was brief, however, because the man spoke so little English that an interview was impossible. Diane tried to explain what she had wanted, but her attempt left him confused and her embarrassed.

Diane crossed the street to talk with a woman who was hanging up her wash. Diane introduced herself, though with the oversized button she wore on her blouse that was hardly necessary. Diane's manner is naturally friendly, and three years of work as a poll-taker has polished her ability to put people at ease. Nevertheless, the woman refused to be interviewed; she said she had too much housework to do before her daughter came home from kindergarten. Diane persisted, saying that it was important to express one's opinion and that the whole thing was strictly confidential, but the woman still said no.

Diane looked down a side street, hoping for some sign that things would get better, but the houses looked just the same as those she had left. "This is a bad start. Sometimes the first three places I'll try, I'll get three interviews, one, two, three. Then there are days like today."

In theory, every person in the United States must have an equal chance of being selected in a sample if the survey is to be reasonably representative. In practice, however, certain types of people are much easier to find than others. Housewives, retired people, and the unemployed may be found at any hour, but young working people are hard to track down. On many issues homebodies tend to have different opinions from those who are on the move. . . .

When Diane Bentley interviews at night, her husband usually drives her around, though the arrangement is not completely satisfactory. "While I'm doing my interview, I sometimes worry about him out there in the car." Diane has interviewed all over Connecticut, in rich areas and very poor ones. Her one real phobia is dogs. She walked by one house without hesitating; a large German shepherd was sleeping on the porch.

Diane finally succeeded at the sixth house. A woman returning from the supermarket with two large bags of groceries said she would be willing to talk for a little while. Diane did not mention that the survey would take more than an hour. If she had, the woman would probably have declined, as would most people. . . .

Diane did not know who was the principal client for the survey she was conducting, but most of the questions dealt with energy problems which made her guess that the client was either an oil company or a public utility.

Diane followed the woman into the kitchen and sat down with her clipboard to conduct the interview while the woman put away her groceries. Diane said she just wanted "your reaction to these questions—it doesn't have to be something you would stand by." The first questions asked whether there was an energy shortage, either locally or nationally, and whether there would be one in the future. The woman hesitated. "Well, I think the gas crisis was manufactured by the companies." Diane checked the boxes that said there was no energy shortage.

Diane is essentially paid according to the number of interviews she does, so she moved crisply through the questionnaire, politely but firmly insisting on specific answers to the questions she put. As the interview went on, however, the woman got increasingly impatient. "Everything you're asking me is yes or no, black or white. I just don't think that way." She felt trapped by a question which asked her to agree or disagree with the statement, "Since Henry Kissinger failed to make peace between Egypt and Israel it looks as though he is losing his touch as a peacemaker."

She said she had never liked Kissinger. Were she to take the question literally, she must answer no, for she believed he never had had a touch as a peacemaker. But that answer, as she could plainly see, would be taken as an endorsement of Kissinger. On the other hand, she could not bring herself to say yes, as that implied that she has until recently supported him.

Diane was pleasant but persistent. "Just answer the question as best you can. Choose whichever is the lesser of two evils." The woman still could not subscribe to either of the two offered alternatives. Diane eventually put her down as "not sure" when in fact the woman had a clear and strong opinion about Kissinger. . . .

The woman interviewed by Diane Bentley was unemployed. The man with whom she lived (the poll had categories only for "married" or "single") was a truck driver. There were four posters taped to her kitchen walls. One of them said more about her attitude to the energy crisis than her answers to any of the questions which Diane asked her. It showed a half-dozen greedy and bloated figures, each one representing a major oil company. Underneath, there was a caption: "Don't blame the truckers, it's these motherfuckers."

There were also signs of her habits. In addition to a refrigerator and a gas stove, the kitchen was equipped with a toaster-oven, an iron, a blender, and an AM/FM radio. In the next room there was a stereo and a portable television. For all her hostility toward the power industry, she was still its dependent customer.

Michael Wheeler, *Lies, Damn Lies, and Statistics: The Manipulation of Public Opinion in America* (New York: Liveright, 1976), pp. 88-91.

if it does, *all* the adults in Peoria must have an equal chance of being selected. A pollster might, for instance, take a Peoria telephone book and call the tenth name in it. (These days, unlike in 1936, almost anyone likely to vote will have a telephone.) If that person is not in, the pollster will then call the twentieth listing in the phone book, and so on.

Table 7-8   The 1980 Presidential Election: A Survey of Six Polls

POLL	REAGAN (R)	CARTER (D)	OTHERS	TWO-PARTY MEAN ERROR
Final Result:	51%	41%	8%	—
Decision/Making/Information (Reagan); Nov. 3; N = 2,200	51	38	11	1.5%
NBC/Associated Press Oct. 22–24; N = 1,574	48	41	11	1.5
ABC/Louis Harris Oct. 22–Nov. 3; N = 16,000	47	42	10	2.5
Gallup/AIPO Oct. 30–Nov. 1; N = 1,950	47	44	8	3.5
CBS/New York *Times* Oct. 30–Nov. 1; N = 2,264	46	45	9	4.5
Washington *Post* Oct. 29–30; N = 1,100	44	47	9	6.5

Note that the Washington *Post*'s mean error was *above* the 4 percent mean error range and that their sample population (N) was *below* the 1,500 needed for representative sampling.

UPI/Bettmann Newsphoto

The pollsters who confidently looked forward to a Dewey Administration simply stopped sampling too soon—enough people switched their vote at the last minute to give Truman the election.

Sampling Error. However carefully pollsters use scientific sampling techniques, actual opinion—the opinion of the universe—may differ within certain limits from the views reported by the sample. These limits are called the sampling error. In most professional surveys, it is no greater than 4 percent either way.[26] The smaller the sample, the greater the chance for error. The margin of error for subgroups such as Protestants and Catholics goes up even more. Larger samples decrease the error margin somewhat but increase costs considerably. Samples of about 1,500 strike the right balance between accuracy and cost for most polling organizations.

The Election of 1948. Another problem with polls is the interval between the final poll and the election. It was apparently this problem that caused the debacle of 1948. The polls taken during that year's presidential campaign were scientific, but almost all of them were as disastrously wrong as the 1936 *Literary Digest* poll had been. In 1948, it seems, many voters may have

---

[26] In other words, if a poll reported that Tweedledee had the support of 48 percent of the voters and Tweedledum had 52 percent, their real levels of respective support might well be reversed, because 4 percent either way might mean 52-48. It might mean a greater spread, though, like 44 to 56.

switched from Governor Thomas Dewey (N.Y.), the Republican, to President Harry Truman, the Democrat, at the last moment, *after* the final polls had been taken. The pollsters who confidently looked forward to a Dewey Administration—almost all of them—simply put away their clipboards too soon.

Questions and Answers. If a pollster asked whether you would like an Olympic stadium built about two blocks from your house, you might say yes without even thinking about it. But suppose the pollster added that to pay for the stadium, your taxes would go up by 20 percent. You might then decide that you did not really need a world-class sports facility so close to home. Questions that do not tell us the price of one policy or the other may elicit questionable responses. The respondents may agree without having to weigh real-life alternatives.

Formats. Pollsters usually force their questions into one (or more) of three different formats. "Yes/no/maybe" questions give respondents only three choices, the third of which is really a nonanswer. If you think anything at all about any subject ("Do you like ice cream?" for example), it is often impossible to answer accurately with a simple categorical "yes" or "no."

Multiple-choice questions permit a wider range of choice:

Drawing by Dana Fradon; © 1981
The New Yorker Magazine, Inc.

> *Q:* How much do you think the government should spend for national defense in the years ahead?
> *Choose one:* A lot more than at present/ Somewhat more than at present/ The same as at present/ Somewhat less than at present/ A lot less than at present.

What should you say, however, if you think we should be spending more on conventional arms and less on nucler weapons, or the reverse? In other words, multiple-choice questions are still hard to answer if you have opinions with qualifications and different alternatives.

Open-ended questions ("What do you think about defense spending?") are meant to deal with just this possibility. People with well-thought-out opinions can explain them. But tabulating such reponses is much more costly than tabulating agree/disagree boxes. Again, there is a trade-off between accuracy and costs.

SUMMARY

The American people are remarkably diverse, but our political life is based on consensus—agreement—not on conflict over fundamentals. Our major political parties, Democratic and Republican, are more alike than different, and their similarities reflect common attitudes toward religion, property, liberty, and democracy. We acquire these attitudes from family, schools, and religious groups; from the social classes, races, and regions we are born into; and from the mass media—newspapers and television especially.

Consensus notwithstanding, Americans do disagree about politics, but the only ideologies (political principles) that have much support here are liberalism and conservatism. Many people, however, are cross-cutters: They have conservative attitudes but support liberal programs. Public opinion may have swung somewhat to the right from 1977 on, but the shift was probably not large—more a "creep" then a "swing," in all likelihood. Nor is there much reason to doubt that public opinion will continue to shift back and forth in future.

Politicians and businesses try to plumb our attitudes and views by taking public-opinion polls. In a modern, scientific poll, the pollsters decide in advance how many people to question. They try to make these people, the sample, representative of the larger group they are investigating, the universe. In an earlier kind of poll, called a straw poll, anyone who wished to participate could do so; there was no way of ensuring a representative sample, and the results were not reliable.

By and large, Americans tend not to be interested in political issues. We usually leave politics to the pros and to those who have a direct stake in the outcome of any issue. A few issues do generate strong public responses—sometimes, as in the Vietnam War, a highly polarized response, one that divides public opinion into opposed and hostile groups. When the public in a democracy cares about an issue and takes a united stand on it, politicans have good reason to defer to the majority.

SUGGESTED READINGS

PAUL R. ABRAMSON, *Political Attitudes in America: Formation and Change.* San Francisco: W. H. Freeman, 1983. Contains good analysis of basic political attitudes, such as party identification, political efficacy, political trust, and tolerance.

HERBERT B. ASHER, *Presidential Elections and American Politics: Voters, Candidates, and Campaigns Since 1952*, 3rd ed. Homewood, Ill.: Dorsey, 1984. Good coverage of the subject matter and literature, including sections on the media and financing of campaign.

EDWARD J. EPSTEIN, *News from Nowhere.* New York: Random House, 1973. Critical analysis of television network news programs.

ROBERT S. ERIKSON and NORMAN G. LUTTBEG, *American Public Opinion: Its Origins, Content and Impact*, 2nd ed. New York: Wiley, 1979. Up-to-date summary of the studies on American public opinion and politics.

MORRIS FIORINA, *Retrospective Voting in American National Elections.* New Haven: Yale Univ., 1981. Fiorina makes a compelling case for rationality among voters who are limited by the choices that politicians and campaigns give them.

HARRY HOLLOWAY with JOHN H. GEORGE, *Public Opinion: Coalitions, Elites, and Masses*, 2nd ed. New York: St. Martin's, 1985. A wide-ranging text that covers much ground from family to media and includes some analysis of elitist–pluralist alternatives.

V. O. KEY, JR., *Public Opinion and American Democracy.* New York: Knopf, 1961. A modern classic on major aspects of American public opinion, its structure, formation, and manipulation.

———, *The Responsible Electorate.* Cambridge: Harvard Univ., 1966. A wise and powerful little book, dedicated to the proposition that voters are not fools.

ROBERT E. LANE, *Political Ideology.* New York: Free Press, 1962. A classic modern statement of the belief systems of average Americans, bascd on in-depth interviews.

SEYMOUR MARTIN LIPSET and WILLIAM SCHNEIDER, *The Confidence Gap: Business, Labor, and Government in the Public Mind.* New York: Free Press, 1983. A massive survey and assessment of public attitudes towards government, business, and labor over time.

HAROLD MENDELSOHN and IRVING CRESPI, *Polls, Television and the New Politics.* Scranton, Penn.: Chandler, 1970. A useful study, giving a clear picture of how polls are constructed and used.

NORMAN H. NIE, SIDNEY VERBA, and JOHN R. PETROCIK, *The Changing American Voter*, 2nd ed. Cambridge: Harvard Univ., 1979. Comprehensive review of the major changes in American voter attitudes since 1960.

H. L. NIEBURG, *Public Opinion: Tracking and Targeting.* New York: Praeger, 1984. Reviews polling processes, techniques, and theories of public opinion.

chapter eight

THE MEDIA

After the Spanish-American War (1898), the United States occupied the Philippine Islands. Many Filipinos objected and fought a bloody guerrilla war that lasted for nearly four years, until 1902, when the "rebels" gave up. The war was far away in the jungles, and there was no television to bring it closer in 1902. It was an unknown war, and the American government did not need to worry very much about loss of support for the war effort among the American public. But over half a century later, during the years of active war in Vietnam (from 1965 to 1973)—again mostly in the jungles and against an enemy who relied mostly on guerrilla tactics—the American media had unlimited access to the battlefront. The result was that, through television, Americans could see the war's blood and gore in living color and in their own homes. The belief is widespread, especially in the Pentagon and among Vietnam "hawks," that media exposure subverted the American war effort by giving the public a dramatic view of the war that the government did not control.

In October 1983, the United States invaded Grenada to oust a Marxist regime. Media coverage did not hamper American military efforts on the island, for the American military, following White House directives, imposed a very effective news blackout. For the first two days this blackout was total. Some reporters made efforts to bypass it, but they were stymied. One group hired a boat on invasion day, but the Navy would not permit them to use its radio equipment to send out stories. Others who hired boats were chased away by naval and air units. Photographers who managed to take pictures of troops had their film confiscated.

After the first two days, the policy changed from outright blackout to careful management of a permitted media presence in Grenada. The press were admitted in small groups on condition that they stay with their official "tour guides," and for a very short time at that. The Pentagon's justification for this was concern for the

An evacuee from Grenada reacts after landing at Charleston Air Force Base. This photo was carried in newspapers and magazines all over the country and helped state the Reagan administration's view of the Grenada invasion.

physical safety of civilians in a war zone, which in itself would have come as real news to World War II and Vietnam War reporters. With the precedents of these wars in mind, the press was not charmed by this explanation.

News management continued. The first photographs of people on Grenada showed American medical students at St. George's University being evacuated. Of course they looked grateful and relieved. The troops were shown carrying out and completing a heroic rescue mission. The television image of the invasion was pretty much what the Reagan administration wanted it to be. Needless to say, the blood and gore were shielded from view.

Unlike our first two cases, the Grenada operation was brief, victoriously completed in less than a week. Maybe if other and more long-drawn-out wars involving American troops break out, it will not be so easy to control news as it was in Grenada. But these days, image is reality, or is on the way to becoming so. Nothing is more politically important than getting the image right. At least, this is what policy makers believe, and it is what they act upon.

When we think about the media, Mark Twain's famous comment about the weather frequently comes to mind: People often complain about it, but no one does anything about it. Unlike the weather, however, the media—particularly the electronic media—have become overwhelmingly influential only recently. Their greatest impact can be seen within the past twenty years, in fact. Newspapers, magazines, radio, and, above all, television now create the arena in which we understand the events of public life. They create our images of the nation and our society. Considering the media's pivotal position and the fact that those who hold it have not been elected to it it is not surprising that their performance often receives close scrutiny.

This chapter will examine the role of the media in political life today and the nature of the criticism that is leveled at these all-powerful opinion makers. First, however, let's take a look at the scope of the media in modern America and then see how—and when—they became so powerful.

THE SCOPE OF THE MEDIA

Television

The dominant mass medium in the United States today is television. Ninety-eight percent of all American households have at least one TV set, and the average set is on about 6½ hours a day, or over 40 hours a week. (By contrast, about three-quarters of the population reads newspapers, spending an average of 3½ hours per week on them. The average American also reads 2 magazines a week, spending about 1½ hours on them.) In 1980, there were 725 commercial television stations and 281 public television stations in the United States. The commercial stations are tied in with one of the three major national networks (ABC, CBS, or NBC), and they receive nearly 90 percent of all their programs from them. In addition, each of these networks owns the 5 stations allowed it by federal law, and—these are all in the largest media markets, of course—these 15 stations reach about 38 percent of the national viewer market. Over 98 percent of the revenue in the TV industry comes from advertisers.

Table 8–1   Advertising Expenditures: All Media, All Advertisers, 1867–1980

YEAR	TOTAL ADVERTISING EXPENDITURES IN $ MILLIONS (current)	PER CAPITA ADVERTISING EXPENDITURES, $ (current)	PER CAPITA ADVERTISING EXPENDITURES, $ (1980 or "constant")
1867	$ 50	$ 1.34	$ 10.31
1880	200	3.80	38.38
1890	360	5.71	61.40
1900	542	7.12	78.24
1909	1,142	12.62	119.06
1914	1,302	13.14	115.26
1922	2,607	23.69	127.37
1929	3,426	28.43	150.42
1933	1,302	10.36	70.96
1940	2,088	15.80	96.93
1950	5,710	37.64	125.89
1960	11,932	66.04	171.53
1970	19,600	95.67	170.84
1980	54,480	239.26	239.26

SOURCE: *Historical Statistics of the United States, Colonial Times to 1970* (Washington: GPO, 1975), II, 856; *Statistical Abstract of the United States 1982–83* (Washington: GPO, 1982), p. 566.

An increasingly important development in the television industry is the growth of cable (or "pay") television. In 1952 there were only 70 systems and 14,000 subscribers. By 1972 these figures had risen to 2,841 and 6 million, respectively. By 1982 there were 4,825 systems and 21 million subscribers, about one-quarter of all American households. In 1980, commercial TV's total net revenues were $8.8 billion; cable's total revenues were $2.24 billion.

Although cable may continue to expand in the decades ahead, its rate of expansion has recently leveled off sharply, and reports of the imminent demise of the major networks at cable's hands now appear vastly exaggerated. More likely, commercial, public, and cable offerings will continue to flourish together in the near future.

Radio

Virtually all Americans (99.9 percent, at the last estimate) have access to a radio in their homes or cars. The average American spends 18 hours a week listening to radio. There are many more radio stations than TV stations—about 4,500 AM stations and 2,800 FM stations—and more networks than in TV (8, compared with 3 in 1980). Radio stations are far cheaper to operate per unit than are television stations, and they offer considerable diversity of formats, with many programs designed for specialized audiences. In economic terms radio networks are far smaller than those in TV; but like TV stations commercial stations are overwhelmingly dependent on advertising for their revenues (99 percent of $3.6 billion gross revenue in 1980). No longer the dominant mass medium it was before the 1950s, radio is still used extensively to communicate messages with political content.

Newspapers

There were just over 1,700 English-language newspapers in the United States as of 1983, with a total circulation of about 62.5 million, or about 36,500 per paper, on average. Additionally, there were about 750 Sunday papers, with a circulation of about 56.3 million—73,000 per paper on average. Although newspapers do not have a truly national circulation in this country, as they do in Europe, papers such as *The New York Times* and the *Washington Post* do have a national orientation. *The Wall Street Journal* is at the top of daily circulation, with a readership of 2 million.

Magazines

Nearly 11,000 magazines and periodicals are marketed in the United States every year. Most of these are monthlies, designed for highly specialized markets—people interested in computers, electronics, fashion, stamps, or sports, for instance. The total annual revenues in this industry are about $12 billion. *Reader's Digest* (with a 1982 paid circulation of 17.9 million) and *TV Guide* (circulation of 17.0 million) have the largest circulations. The three top national weekly news magazines are *Time* (4.5 million), *Newsweek* (3.0 million) and *U.S. News & World Report* (3.0 million). *Time*, founded by Henry Luce in 1923, has occasionally played important roles in politics, particularly while Luce was alive, promoting causes of interest to himself (for instance, the Republican presidential candidacy of Wendell Willkie in 1940, or the so-called China Lobby in the early 1950s). *Newsweek*, owned by the Washington Post, is

The Media Monopoly

There are at least 10,830 magazines in the United States. They cover an extraordinary variety of subject matter and quality. Measuring ownership control of the total audience is more difficult in magazine than in newspaper publishing because some magazines are issued weekly, some biweekly, some monthly, some bimonthly, and some quarterly. The most reliable measure is the proportion of sales controlled by each owner. Among the 10,830 magazines, 20 corporations have just over 50 percent of the annual sales of total industry revenues of $12 billion. For 1981, these 20 corporations and their major magazines were, in order of their dominance:

1. Time, Inc.
    Time
    Life
    Sports Illustrated
    People
    Money
    Discover
2. Triangle Publications
    TV Guide
    Seventeen
3. Hearst Corp.
    Colonial Homes
    Cosmopolitan
    Country Living
    Electronic Products
    Good Housekeeping
    Harper's Bazaar
    House Beautiful
    Motor
    Motor Boating & Sailing
    Popular Mechanics
    Redbook
    Sports Afield
    Town & Country
4. CBS, Inc.
    American Photographer
    Audio
    Cycle World
    Family Weekly
    Field & Stream
    Mechanix Illustrated
    Road & Track
    Pickup, Van and 4WD
    Woman's Day
    World Tennis
5. McGraw-Hill
    American Machinist
    Architectural Record
    Aviation Week & Space Technology
    Business Week
    Byte

Chemical Engineering
Chemical Week
Coal Age
Electric World
Electrical Construction & Maintenance
Electronics
Engineering & Mining Journal
Engineering News Record
Fleet Owner
Modern Plastics
Postgraduate Medicine
Power
6. S.I. Newhouse & Sons (Condé Nast–Parade)
    Bride's Magazine
    Glamour
    GQ
    House & Garden
    Mademoiselle
    Self
    Vanity Fair
    Parade
    Vogue
7. Washington Post Co.
    Newsweek
    Washington Post Magazine
    Inside Sports
8. New York Times Co.
    Family Circle
    New York Times Magazine
    Golf Digest
    Tennis
9. Reader's Digest Association
    Reader's Digest
10. Playboy Enterprises
    Games
    Playboy
11. Meredith Corp.
    Better Homes & Gardens
    Metropolitan Home
    Sail
    Successful Farming
12. Penthouse International
    Forum
    Omni
    Penthouse
13. Ziff-Davis
    Boating
    Business & Commercial Aviation
    Car & Driver
    Cycle
    Flying
    Meetings & Conventions
    Modern Bride
    Pan Am Clipper
    Popular Electronics
    Psychology Today

            Skiing
            Stereo Review
            Yachting
        14. National Geographic Society
            National Geographic
            National Geographic World
        15. McCalls Publishing Co.
            McCall's
            Working Mother
        16. U.S. News & World Report
            U.S. News & World Report
        17. National Enquirer
            National Enquirer
        18. News America Publishing (Murdoch)
            New York Magazine
            Star
        19. Times Mirror Co.
            Cross Country Ski
            Golf
            Homeowners How-To
            Outdoor Life
            Popular Science
            Ski
            Ski Business
            Sporting News

        20. Petersen Publishing Co.
            Car Craft
            Guns & Ammo
            Hot Rod
            Ladies' Home Journal
            Lakeland Boating
            Motor Trend
            Motorcyclist
            Petersen's 4 Wheel & Off Road
            Petersen's Hunting
            Petersen's Photographic
            Pick Up
            Rudder
            Sea & Pacific Skipper
            Skin Diver
            Teen
            Van & 4WD

These twenty companies have 50.7 percent of all magazine revenues. Thus, 1 percent of magazine owners have more than half the revenues of all 10,830 magazines published regularly.

From Ben H. Bagdikian, *The Media Monopoly*. Boston: Beacon, 1983, pp. 10–14. Reprinted with permission.

somewhat more liberal than *Time* and has a wider diversity of signed comments and opinions. *U.S. News & World Report*, founded by conservative journalist David Lawrence and run by him for many years, has been acquired by Mortimer Zuckerman, real estate mogul and owner of *The Atlantic*. All three news magazines taken together had a 1982 paid circulation of 9.6 million, little more than half of *Reader's Digest*'s total.

Although a glance at the mass communications industry may suggest a wide variety of outlets, there is actually as much concentration at the top in this sphere as there is elsewhere in the business community. In the newspaper business, for example, the top 20 chain corporations (such as Hearst, Knight-Ridder, and Gannett) own an average of 21 papers per chain. These 20 corporations account for over half of all national newspaper circulation. Overall, 1 percent of newspaper owners own 34 percent of all daily newspapers sold in this country.[1] The situation is similar in the other media.

THE HISTORY OF MEDIA AND POLITICS IN AMERICA

The Early Years

"TV is the Great Legitimator," one media critic observed. "TV confers reality. Nothing happens in America, practically everyone seems to agree, until it

---

[1] Ben Bagdikian, *The Media Monopoly* (Boston: Beacon, 1983), p. 20.

happens on television."[2] And yet it was not always so. Consider the Constitutional Convention of 1787. As a media event, the convention was a total loss. The gathering of 55 men for several months in Philadelphia in the spring and summer of 1787 to perform the highest and most important of political acts— the drafting of a constitution—occurred under conditions of *total news blackout* from beginning to end, a favor asked of, and granted by, the local newspapers. Furthermore, the journals of the convention remained sealed under an information embargo until 1830, more than 40 years after the event.

If we were to have a Constitutional Convention today, a news blackout would be a total impossibility. The event would have to be wired for television, as party conventions are, complete with Dan Rather, Peter Jennings, or Tom Brokaw interviewing our latter-day Madisons and Hamiltons in the anchor booth overlooking the floor. Far from having a forty-year information embargo on the debates and preceedings, news leaks would be constant and plentiful. And all this would be transmitted instantaneously around the world.

Read Madison's *The Federalist*, Paper 10, as a piece of journalism, which it was, and compare it with a modern effort. *The Federalist*, Paper 10, is reprinted in the Appendix of this volume. In language and complexity of argument, *The Federalist* is far more substantial than anything likely to appear nowadays, even in a prestigious paper such as *The New York Times*. Although it was originally written for a newspaper, Madison's essay was not pitched to a mass audience as we understand it today.

In part, its level was appropriate because there *was* no mass audience in those days. News was scarce and hard to come by. Newsprint was expensive, based on rag-content paper rather than on pulp—one reason why newspapers of the 1790s still exist in archive libraries, but those of the 1890s have mostly disintegrated into dust. The presses were primitive hand-powered affairs with very low per-hour productivity. It could easily take two months for news to reach America from Europe by sailing ship, and it could take more than a month to spread from some major center like Philadelphia or New York into the American hinterland. This slow pace could and did have major consequences, the most famous of which was Andrew Jackson's 1815 defeat of the British at the Battle of New Orleans two weeks *after* the peace treaty had been signed in Belgium. Things are quite different today, needless to say. When President John F. Kennedy was assassinated on November 22, 1963, at least two-thirds of all Americans learned about it within *half an hour* after the event was first reported.

The emergence of a mass audience and a real national political market, complete with parties, conventions, organizers, bosses, and a fully mobilized electorate, could not occur until the late 1820s, during the "democratic revolution" associated with Andrew Jackson. The most democratizing elements of all were probably improvements in transportation and communication.

Construction of adequate roads, turnpikes, canals, and (after 1828) railroads powered by steam engines drastically curtailed the time needed for domestic news to reach its audiences. Establishment of regular transatlantic steamship lines in 1838 just as dramatically reduced the time needed for European news to reach this country. The invention of the telegraph in 1844 was another giant leap forward, though it took nearly another generation before the country was fully equipped to use this first electric device for

---

[2] William A. Henry III, "News as Entertainment: The Search for Dramatic Unity," in Elie Abel, ed., *What's News* (San Francisco: Institute for Contemporary Studies, 1981), p. 134.

THE

New-York Weekly JOURNAL.

Containing the freſheſt Advices, Foreign, and Domeſtick.

Numb. II.

MUNDAY November 12, 1733.

Mr. *Zenger*.

INcert the following in your next, and you'll oblige your Friend,
CATO.

Mira temporum felicitas ubi ſentiri quæ velis, & quæ ſentias dicere licit.
Tacit.

THE Liberty of the Preſs is a Subject of the greateſt Importance, and in which every Individual is as much concern'd as he is in any other Part of Liberty : Therefore it will not be improper to communicate to the Publick the Sentiments of a late excellent Writer upon this Point, ſuch is the Elegance and Perſpicuity of his Writings, ſuch the inimitable Force of his Reaſoning, that it will be difficult to ſay any Thing new that he has not ſaid, or not to ſay that much worſe which he has ſaid.

There are two Sorts of Monarchies, an abſolute and a limited one. In the firſt, the Liberty of the Preſs can never be maintained, it is inconſiſtent with it ; for what abſolute Monarch would ſuffer any Subject to animadvert on his Actions, when it is in his Power to declare the Crime, and to nominate the Puniſhment ? This would make it very dangerous to exerciſe ſuch a Liberty Beſides the Object againſt which thoſe Pens muſt be directed, is

their Sovereign, the ſole ſupream Magiſtrate ; for there being no Law in thoſe Monarchies, but the Will of the Prince, it makes it neceſſary for his Miniſters to conſult his Pleaſure, before any Thing can be undertaken : He is therefore properly chargeable with the Grievances of his Subjects, and what the Miniſter there acts being in Obedience to the Prince, he ought not to incur the Hatred of the People ; for it would be hard to impute that to him for a Crime, which is the Fruit of his Allegiance, and for refuſing which he might incur the Penalties of Treaſon. Beſides, in an abſolute Monarchy, the Will of the Prince being the Law, a Liberty of the Preſs to complain of Grievances would be complaining againſt the Law, and the Conſtitution, to which they have ſubmitted, or have been obliged to ſubmit ; and therefore, in one Senſe, may be ſaid to deſerve Puniſhment, So that under an abſolute Monarchy, I ſay, ſuch a Liberty is inconſiſtent with the Conſtitution, having no proper Subject in Politics, on which it might be exercis'd, and if exercis'd would incur a certain Penalty.

But in a limited Monarchy, as *England* is, our Laws are known, fixed, and eſtabliſhed. They are the ſtreight Rule and ſure Guide to direct the King, the Miniſters, and other his Subjects : And therefore an Offence againſt the Laws is ſuch an Offence againſt the Conſtitution as ought to receive a proper adequate Puniſhment ; the ſevera.
Conſti.

The front page of *The New-York Weekly Journal* for November 12, 1733.

transmitting information. During the 1830s, the so-called penny press dramatically reduced the costs of newspapers (by four-fifths in many cases) and substantially increased circulations. Much of the earlier press had been strongly partisan, but its reach was limited. With the penny-press revolution and the founding of mass-circulation political papers such as James Gordon Bennett's New York *Herald* (1835) and Horace Greeley's New York *Tribune*

GRAND CIVIC AND MILITARY PROCESSION

In Philadelphia, February 22d, 1832, being the 100th Anniversary of the Birth of

GEORGE WASHINGTON,

The Soldier and Statesman—the Brave and Good.

(columns of fine print describing the day's procession and celebration, including sections headed "Eighteen Pioneers", "BRICK MAKERS", "THE BRICKLAYERS", "THE PLASTERERS", "THE STONE CUTTERS", "Book-Binders and Sellers", "The Copper-Plate Printers", "The Tanners, Curriers,", "Tenth Marshal—JOHN WOELPPER. PHILADELPHIA ASSOCIATION OF YOUNG MEN", "Hunting Park Association", and "Twelfth Marshal—JAMES BAKER")

Albany Argus

Extra. Feb. 21.

An Honorable Treaty of Peace,

PROCURED BY

The valor of the

American Arms,

AND

THE

Patriotism, Persev

erance and Virtue

OF

THE

Supporters

of the War.

We received by express, at 12 o'clock this day, in connexion with the offices of the Evening Post, New-York Gazette, and Mercantile Advertiser, a copy of the Ratified Treaty, between this country and Great Britain, and hasten to lay it before the public. It was brought from Washington to Philadelphia in 14 hours, and from Philadelphia to New-York in 9, performing the whole distance from Washington to this city (240 miles) in 25 hours.—*Com. Adv.*

ARTICLE THE THIRD.

All prisoners of war taken on either side, as well by land as by sea, shall be restored as soon as practicable after the ratification of this treaty, and hereinafter mentioned, on their paying the debts which they may have contracted during their captivity.—The two contracting parties respectively engage to discharge in specie, the advances which may have been made by the other for the sustenance and maintenance of such prisoners.

shall have power to adjourn to such other place as they shall think fit. The said commissioners shall have power to ascertain and determine the points above mentioned, in conformity with the provisions of the said treaty of peace of one thousand seven hundred and eighty-three, and shall cause the boundary aforesaid, from the source of the river St. Croix to the river Iroquois or Cataraguy, to be surveyed and marked according to the said provisions. The said commissioners shall

pective reports, declarations, statements and decisions, and of their accounts, and of the journal of their proceedings, shall be delivered by them to the agents of his Britannic Majesty, and to the agents of the United States, who may be respectively appointed and authorised to manage the business on behalf of their respective governments. The commissioners shall be respectively paid in such manner as shall be agreed between the two contracting parties, such agreement being to be

Shown here are the front pages of newspapers published in 1815 and 1832.

(1841), mass communications media emerged, fully able to shape national opinion. The price/circulation revolution was consolidated by major reductions in newsprint, heavy reliance—for the time—on advertising, and the introduction of much more efficient, steam-powered presses.

The emergence of mass media is not, therefore, as modern a phenomenon as we commonly think. Greeley's Republican, antislavery New York *Tribune*, for example, reached 14.4 percent of presidential voters in New York State (who, by the way, constituted more than 90 percent of the state's adult white male citizens). Even in far-off Iowa, the *Tribune* reached 9.1 percent of all voters.[3] Abraham Lincoln, for one, had no doubt about the *Tribune*'s importance in spreading Republican gospel throughout the free states, and it was only one of several hundred papers that flourished in the 1850s.

The oral media were no less prominent in this era. When Lincoln ran for the Senate in 1858 against the Democratic incumbent, Stephen A. Douglas, their now-famous debates were the first event of their kind to receive national attention. Contemporary presidential debates—Kennedy–Nixon in 1960, Reagan–Carter in 1980 or Reagan–Mondale in 1984—are often unfavorably compared with these debates. If the criteria for judgment are the quality and coherence of ideas about serious political issues, the criticism seems well justified. Reading is believing.

Transition to the Modern Mass Media: 1880–1920

During the golden age of the party system, probably more than three-quarters of the press were partisan. Associated with press giants such as Joseph Pulitzer and William Randolph Hearst, new styles of news coverage and reporting developed at this time. For members of the new generation such as Pulitzer, journalistic standards of comprehensiveness, accuracy, and elimination of partisan slanting of the news were the strategy of the day. For Hearst and many imitators, a key to success was sensationalizing the news and, where possible, creating media events that could lend themselves to sensationalism. Perhaps the greatest coup for this *yellow journalism* was its work in paving the way for the Spanish-American War (1898) and the occupation of Cuba and the Philippines that followed. It should be stressed, however, that many of the founders of great newspaper chains in this period—including Pulitzer, Hearst, and Roy Howard—were crusaders whose papers frequently attacked and exposed not only corrupt political bosses but the buccaneering capitalism of the era. On the other hand, political conservatives, such as Adolph Ochs of *The New York Times*, could and did succeed as well. The key to success, ultimately, was the creation of a product that commanded strong loyalty among subscribers. In that day, that meant first and foremost an emphasis on news itself.

Underlying all these journalistic developments were fundamental shifts in the American economic and social system, specifically the rise of corporate capitalism and an increase in consumption as affluence and urbanization burgeoned. Producing a fat Sunday paper was an expensive business by 1900, and newspapers needed large volumes of advertising. Then, as now, advertising rates were tied to audience size, which newspapers attempted to increase

---

[3] Jeter A. Iseley, *Horace Greeley and the Republican Party, 1853–1861* (Princeton: Princeton Univ., 1947), Appendices A and B, pp. 337–38.

$50,000 REWARD.—WHO DESTROYED THE MAINE?—$50,000 REWAR

EDITION FOR GREATER NEW YORK

NEW YORK JOURNAL
AND ADVERTISER

NEW YORK, THURSDAY, FEBRUARY 17, 1898.—16 PAGES.   PRICE ONE CENT

DESTRUCTION OF THE WAR SHIP MAINE WAS THE WORK OF AN ENEI

$50,000!

$50,000 REWARD!
For the Detection of the
Perpetrator of
the Maine Outrage!

Assistant Secretary Roosevelt
Convinced the Explosion of

$50,000!

$50,000 REWAR

The World.   863,956

MAINE EXPLOSION CAUSED BY BOMB OR TORPEDO?

Capt. Sigsbee and Consul-General Lee Are in Doubt---The World Has Sent a
Special Tug, With Submarine Divers, to Havana to Find Out---Lee Asks for
an Immediate Court of Inquiry---Capt. Sigsbee's Suspicions.

CAPT. SIGSBEE, IN A SUPPRESSED DESPATCH TO THE STATE DEPARTMENT, SAYS THE ACCIDENT WAS MADE POSSIBLE BY AN ENEMY.

Dr. E. C. Pendleton, Just Arrived from Havana, Says He Overheard Talk There of a Plot to Blow Up the Ship---Capt
Zalinski, the Dynamite Expert, and Other Experts Report to The World that the Wreck Was Not
Accidental---Washington Officials Ready for Vigorous Action if Spanish Responsibility
Can Be Shown---Divers to Be Sent Down to Make Careful Examinations.

On February 15, 1898, the battleship Maine *exploded mysteriously in Havana harbor, killing 260 American sailors. She had been sent to Cuba to protect U.S. interests when Cuba revolted against Spain. The Spanish offered to submit the question of its responsibility to arbitration but the U.S. chose military intervention in April, after U.S. newspapers played national emotions into a fury*

U.S. newspapers' coverage of events leading up to the Spanish-American War roused national emotions and paved the way for the occupation of Cuba and the Philippines.

by curtailing their partisanship and adding a variety of features: sports, comics, homemaking, and rotogravure and magazine sections. Eventually, however, the news business became heavily concentrated. Horace Greeley, a poor farm boy from New Hampshire, had been able to start up the *Tribune* in 1841 with a few thousand dollars at most, but a similar effort required hundreds of thousands if not millions of dollars well before 1900.

The Modern Media: After 1920

In addition to newspapers, which have retained their fundamental importance, weekly news magazines began to appear early in the century, beginning with Henry Luce's *Time* in 1923. Until recently, weekly or biweekly magazines such as *The Saturday Evening Post, Collier's, Life,* and *Look* also played a

The cast and sound men get ready for an on-the-air broadcast of "Gang Busters," an early radio program.

major role in disseminating ideas, values, and information. Their sudden death in the 1960s and 1970s (some partially resurrected since then) is one of the dramatic media stories of recent times. For some magazines, the advent of color television seems to have supplied the *coup de grace*. But a vast population of magazines and periodicals continues to exist, nearly 11,000 at last count.

Another dramatic development within the print media over the past generation has been the disappearance of newspaper competition. According to a recent study by Ben H. Bagdikian, about 700 American cities had competing daily papers in 1920. By 1982, only 27 cities still enjoyed this competitive diversity.[4] Most of the disappearances have occurred since the end of World War II, caused largely by the tendency of advertisers to gravitate toward papers with the largest circulation and therefore the lowest rate for reaching each household.

The most obvious and important media development of the modern period has been the rise of the electronic media—first radio, then television. The first political use of radio was the broadcast of the 1920 election returns over the first commercial station, KDKA in Pittsburgh. By 1924, radio was broadcasting the divisions within the Democratic convention to a national audience, possibly with disastrous effects for the party. That audience heard, 102 times if they had the stamina, "Ala-a-a-bamuh casts twenty-four votes for Oscar W. Underwo-o-od." (John W. Davis was nominated on the 103rd ballot and went down to defeat with the lowest percentage of votes ever given a Democratic nominee.)

The golden age of radio as commercial entertainment occurred between

---

[4] *The Media Monopoly* pp. 105–12.

the mid–1920s and 1950. Situation comedies, adverture dramas, quiz shows, daytime soap operas, live coverage of professional sports events—all flourished. They were accompanied by advertising for diverse products, from automobiles to cigarettes to—soap. The many hundreds of stations were linked by major networks.

The media world of the 1930s looked strikingly similar to its counterpart in the 1980s, except for the television picture—but that was a colossal exception. Some politicians came to be virtuosos of radio: Franklin D. Roosevelt, Winston Churchill, and Adolf Hitler were the most famous examples of their time. Even much later, radio remained a very important medium for some politicians. Richard Nixon had serious trouble with a poor visual image during the debates with John F. Kennedy in the 1960 campaign. Gifted with a resonant voice, Nixon turned increasingly to radio in his subsequent campaigns. President Ronald Reagan, a virtuoso performer on all media channels, has regularly broadcast his message over radio every Saturday. This medium retains important political assets, including millions of listeners. In the days when radio had no competition from visual media, its impact was very great indeed, but it seems to have had shaping effects very different from those that television produces.

The communications specialist Marshall McLuhan has observed that radio is a "hot" medium and TV is "cool." This means that politicians can deliver messages on radio with an intensity and a sharpness that would be strange and off-putting on television. The implication is that a supremely dramatic, intense, "hot" figure such as Adolf Hitler might have had much more trouble projecting his confrontational, divisive rhetoric on TV than on radio. With FDR it's more difficult to say. His frequent "fireside chats" to the nation were artfully designed to be conversational in tone and were pitched as though he were a senior member of every hearer's family, a rather "cool" approach. Early in his administration, Jimmy Carter attempted something similar on TV but without marked success. One may doubt that the television medium made the crucial difference in that case.

Television was technologically well developed by 1926 and virtually ready for full commercial exploitation by the late 1930s. (In fact, FDR was the first

President Franklin D. Roosevelt was very successful in getting across his political message through "fireside chats" on the radio in the 1930s and 1940s. President Jimmy Carter, on the other hand, tried to use nationally televised "fireside chats," with disappointing results.

Richard Nixon appeared on national TV in 1952 to explain his financial backing from oil interests in an earlier Senate race. The speech was called the "Checkers speech" because in it he referred to the family dog, named Checkers. The speech was a great success with the public and saved his career; it might not have been possible without the use of television.

AP/Wide World Photos

President to appear on television, in 1939.) The outbreak of World War II delayed TV's progress, but by 1950 it was becoming a household appliance. In a sense, TV came into its own when the transcontinental coaxial cable was completed in 1951, just in time to permit nationwide broadcasting of the signing of the peace treaty with Japan, in San Francisco.

The last pre-television presidential campaign was therefore in 1948. By 1952, TV had already come to center stage, extensively covering both the conventions and the candidates' campaigns. It is worth noting that never since 1952 has a convention nomination gone beyond a single ballot. (Adlai Stevenson was nominated by the Democrats on the third ballot that year.) This is hardly accidental. Old-fashioned, deliberative, power-brokered conventions project a "hot" and very often disorderly image.

Another path-breaker in 1952 was Richard Nixon's "Checkers speech," which has acquired a certain camp-classic status among media aficionados. Nixon, a poor boy from California, had been given very substantial financial help by oil interests in his race for the Senate seat in 1950. When this matter came to light during the 1952 campaign, General Eisenhower distanced himself from his running mate and made it clear that he would have to leave the ticket if the matter were not resolved.

Nixon appeared on television and, in a classic performance, justified his uprightness in highly emotional terms. He had not profited; he had not become enriched; his wife, Pat, did not wear mink but only a "Republican cloth coat." And yes, someone had given the family their dog, Checkers; but he would never give the dog back, no matter what. The performance, which pundits dismissed as "tear-jerking," was a spectacular success with the public. Nixon's career was saved. Television made it all possible. Its impact, substantial in 1952, has become overwhelming in the 1980s.

IMPACT OF THE MEDIA

It is ironic that the media, who were responsible for salvaging Richard Nixon's career in 1952, were also responsible for exposing the abuses of power that led to his resignation from the presidency in 1974. The Watergate scandal is but one example of the vast influence of the media in America today. Nor is that influence limited to the political sphere. The impact of the media, particularly television, manifests itself often subtly but powerfully in all aspects of our lives.

Entertainment

People watch TV more to escape the strain of everyday existence than to come to terms with the world, but even as they escape, TV socializes them into the attitudes and behaviors suitable to members of a high consumption society. Watching J.R. and his friends and enemies, life and love on a cruise ship, a football game, or a police thriller takes viewers away from their own burdens and responsibilities as they watch others cope with theirs in exotic environments. Actors portray roles (tycoon, football player, private investigator, waitress) with which viewers can identify in ways that reinforce the structure of reality, though it has little to do with most viewers' lives.

The fundamental objective of TV entertainment is to deliver viewers to sponsors, whose commercials—scrupulously crafted at costs even higher than those of TV production in general—tirelessly stimulate wants and hawk the products that will satisfy them. Because the networks must ensure that their programs do not inadvertently trivialize or diminish the sponsor's message, they steer clear of thought-provoking subjects. The majority of people are most comfortable with familiar, unchallenging ideas; and so, to prevent their defecting to another channel, the networks, as a rule, avoid topics such as business, labor, politics, white-collar crime, students, the elderly, or mental illness. There is little room in the entertainment business for thought-provoking fare.

News

Although network news influences the thinking of more people than does any other social institution does,[5] it is shaped by the same commercial facts of life that govern all other commercial TV programs. Entertainment—that is, generating emotions such as pride, joy, anger, and fear—constitutes the primary objective of the news, with information provided as a kind of sideline. Obviously, a thirty-minute program frequently interrupted by commercials cannot go into anything in any depth. Stories that cannot be conveyed in a minute or so are generally omitted entirely. Furthermore, the need for good pictures, rather than merely talking heads, means that stories without lively dramatic action, no matter how important, will probably not be covered. The upshot is that stories on subjects such as corporate crime, price fixing, consumer fraud, Washington lobbyists, health care, or social security are broadcast much less often than their importance would warrant because they do not lend themselves to vivid pictures.

---

[5] Donna Woolfolk Cross, *Mediaspeak* (New York: Mentor, 1983), p. 81.

The need to be entertaining means that the news is affected by other constraints as well. News stories must be packaged; that is, they must have a clearly understandable theme that can be hung on a clear-cut dramatic peg and must fall nicely into a beginning, middle, and end. Stories that do not lend themselves to such a format frequently fail to make the TV news. The most important ingredient for a lively story, most newspeople believe, is "the presence of visually identifiable opponents clashing violently."[6]

Associated with the need to personalize the news is the tendency to give heavy coverage to leading political figures and celebrities of various kinds, as Herbert J. Gans and others have shown.[7] Roughly three of four people alluded to in the news are "Knowns," in Gans's terminology. "Unknowns" are usually shown either as protesters, rioters, and strikers or as victims, a kind of Greek chorus of figures in a general drama. In a segment on the farm crisis, for example, farmers about to go broke in Iowa will briefly be shown looking miserable, followed by shots of fields, tractors, and politicians disagreeing with each other.

Obviously, news of serious and complex issues can hardly win much entry into this stack of "packages." Once upon a time, the networks rather frequently ran half-hour documentaries, such as *"Harvest of Shame"* (about the plight of migrant farm workers) and *"The Selling of the Pentagon"* (title self-explanatory), which really did explore significant and controversial issues in a high-profile way. They don't do that as often any more, partly because of the immense corporate and conservative backlashes that such programs generated, but more because the day-to-day economics of the business and its incentives to blandness have tended to squeeze out such programs. Issues

---

[6] Edward Jay Epstein, *News From Nowhere* (New York: Vintage, 1973), p. 173.
[7] Herbert J. Gans, *Deciding What's News* (New York: Vintage, 1979), p. 8.

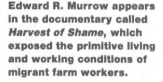

Edward R. Murrow appears in the documentary called *Harvest of Shame*, which exposed the primitive living and working conditions of migrant farm workers.

CBS Photography

surrounding complex problems such as inflation or the size of the federal deficit and its implications are only occasionally highlighted—by filming a supermarket and its customers, for example, and showing the increase in the average market basket's costs.

William A. Henry III has summarized the basic rules of news/entertainment as follows:

1. An event is always a better story than a trend or an idea, not only because it is easier to report an event in video and sound, but because it is more tangible, more unarguably "news."

2. A story must be essentially new. It must not repeat its main points no matter how tricky they are to grasp at first hearing. And it must strive to be "definitive"—so that assignment editors, always short of air time, can consider the topics "covered" for weeks or months to come.

3. Every story ought to have a dramatic unity, a clear line of conflict, with definable antagonists (reduced ideally to Homeric epithets) and a tangible prize at stake.

4. The longer a news story and . . . the more it resembles a traditional documentary or anything longer, the more it must resolve itself into neat, contained packages, allowing viewers to tune in late and commercials to fit naturally. Unless it exposes an undisputed national scandal—in which case it is probably insufficiently new—a documentary must not show the network taking sides.

5. A local television station should boost its community and succor community institutions. A national network should assert the interests of the nation—normally, as defined by its government—and should love the nation's friends and hate its enemies.

Obviously, then, there are many biases in television in general and in its news functions in particular. The news tends to "hype"—that is, to overdramatize and overpersonalize events—and it frames conflicts in terms of personal combat rather than the issues involved. It does little to encourage viewers to analyze issues, think independently, or learn from overall patterns. Yet TV news is the *prime* source of news for 67 percent of the American people,[8] and it profoundly influences political decision makers, who understand its impact on the public mind.

In addition to ongoing commercial and other pressure, there may be another factor discouraging controversial TV documentaries and other kinds of aggressive investigative reporting. Prominent figures have taken recently to suing the news media for libel. One such case was that of Israeli General Ariel Sharon, who sued *Time* magazine for a story that, in Sharon's view, accused him of direct responsibility for the 1982 massacres of Moslems by Christian militias in Lebanon. (It was the cover story, "Verdict on the Massacre," Feb. 21, 1983.) In early 1985, this suit resulted in the judgment that *Time* had committed important factual errors but had not acted with the deliberate malice required to prove libel under the Supreme Court's interpretation in *New York Times* v. *Sullivan*, 376 U.S. 254 (1964).

The other case involving a general was that of Vietnam commander William Westmoreland, who brought suit against CBS for its 1982 television documentary "The Uncounted Enemy: A Vietnam Deception." This program

---

[8] Doris A. Graber, *Mass Media and American Politics* (Washington, D.C.: Congressional Quarterly Press, 1980), p. x.

AP/Wide World Photos

General William Westmoreland (left) and Israeli General Ariel Sharon (right) both sued national news organizations for libel. Neither of the organizations that were sued, *Time* and CBS, had to pay out money in a libel judgment, but both had to spend much time and money to defend themselves.

charged that Westmoreland had tried to suppress higher estimates of enemy strength and that President Lyndon Johnson had thus been deceived about the real situation. The documentary's central argument was that there was a "conspiracy at the highest levels of American military intelligence" to pretend by deliberate undercounting that the war was going well, a fiction that the 1968 Tet offensive exploded.

As *Newsweek*'s review of the case points out (March 4, 1985, p. 59), Westmoreland's libel suit consumed 2½ years of litigation and hundreds of thousands of pages of documents. It cost Westmoreland and his conservative antimedia backers (notably the Capital Legal Foundation) some $3.3 million, and cost CBS that much or more. Quite unexpectedly, the trial suddenly ended a week before it was to go to the jury in early 1985, when Westmoreland agreed to settle out of court. The key reason for his doing so seems to have been that testimony by some of his former subordinates was so damaging that the jury might well have rendered a devastating verdict. It might have decided not just that CBS acted without malice (the final verdict in the Sharon–*Time* case), but that the charges were true.

Although neither *Time* nor CBS had to pay out money in a libel judgment, both media organizations and their key employees had the very time-consuming and expensive task of defending themselves in the courts. In both cases—seemingly much more in *Time*'s than CBS's—major inadequacies were revealed in the news-gathering and the news-presenting process. Cases like these will certainly prompt the major news organizations to clean up their acts. But they may have a chilling effect on future investigative reporting. They may also promote the antimedia attitudes among much of the public, especially among conservatives, by casting further doubt on the media's credibility. Issues involving freedom of the press can turn out to be very expensive matters these days!

It was largely in reaction to this malaise, and to Jimmy Carter as its symbol, that Ronald Reagan was elected in 1980. As his party's platform, his own statements, and his actions in office demonstrated, Reagan was pledged to major conservative change in our government's policies and priorities. But the television image that this matchless media virtuoso projected, in 1980 and still more in 1984, was that of cheerfulness, relentless optimism, and a whole-hearted belief that the traditional values and institutions of the society could and would be restored to their old vitality. If Reagan's election was largely based on reaction to the malaise that liberal media people, however inadvertently, contributed to creating, the irony bites deep. In any case, people who attempt to shape public opinion occasionally find that the impact they get is not the impact they sought.

IMPACT OF THE MEDIA ON POLITICS

There is considerable truth, then, to the idea that the media do not teach us what to *think* but rather define what we think *about*. They determine what information will be available and what won't. "By putting stories into perspective and interpreting them, media personnel assign meaning to the information and indicate the values by which it ought to be judged. . . . Because space is limited and because facts do not speak for themselves . . . the media have the power to control much of the raw material needed by political elites and the general public for thinking about the political world and planning political action. At times, newspeople even *generate* political action directly through their own investigations or indirectly through their capacity to stimulate pseudo-events."[9]

Electoral Politics and the Rise of Mass Media

The foundations of our electoral politics have been affected in the most profound ways by the rise of mass media, as well as by the urbanized, relatively affluent, and consumer-oriented society in which the media flourish. This has been the case for longer than is generally imagined. The first President who continuously worked on and with the media of his day was Theodore Roosevelt (R, 1901–1909), an immensely colorful and dramatic figure who made splendid copy for the Washington press corps. As William Randolph Hearst had created wholesale media events and emotions paving the way for the 1898 war with Spain, so did TR create media events of all sorts. An example was his decision in 1907 to send the navy (the "Great White Fleet") on a "good-will journey" around the world. He knew when the ships set off that there wasn't enough money appropriated to bring them back. He also knew that Congress would have to supply the money eventually (which it did, amidst some grumbling). He knew, further, that his image of activism, energy, and determination to show the flag against all possible enemies and rivals abroad would be enhanced by this event. Like much else in his administration, this was splendid theater. His masterly use of the media was a

[9] Graber, *Mass Media and American Politics*, p. 23.

major political asset, a great power resource. Subsequent Presidents were to learn permanent lessons from TR's example.

In 1916, President Woodrow Wilson (D, 1913–1921) ran for reelection. He had won his first term in 1912 only because the Republican party had been split down the middle when Theodore Roosevelt launched the Progressive party insurgency against incumbent William Howard Taft (R, 1909–1913). Republicans held the popular majority during this era, with an average national lead of about 8 percent over Democrats. Additionally, in 1916, World War I had been in progress in Europe for two years. A large part of the public wished to keep the United States neutral in that conflict, and Wilson's reelection strategy was shaped by that fact. His team organized the first advertising-oriented presidential campaign in American history. If Wilson's party affiliation was to be deemphasized, the obvious campaign strategy was to stress Wilson *the man*, and *in as bipartisan (or nonpartisan) a way as possible.* He could then hope to run far enough ahead of his ticket to win— which he did, barely. Throughout the campaign he kept his appeal simple— easy to send through the media and easy for the public to understand: "He kept us out of war." From this campaign, lessons for the future were also learned. The whole business has a very modern ring indeed.

As the dominant mass medium, television has made a huge difference to politics, but its impact must be understood in the context of other, mutually reinforcing changes in American life. Consumer society is much more developed than it was in 1916. Affluence levels are vastly higher. The American per-capita gross national product is at least three times larger now in real terms than it was in 1916, for example. With the rise of the consumer society have come entire groups of persuader professions that either didn't exist or were still in their infancy in 1916: advertising and public relations, motivational research, social and psychological techniques of discovering the structure of consumer preferences and the ways to mold and appeal to them, and of course, modern scientific survey research and polling, which grew directly out of commercial market-research efforts in the 1930s and 1940s.

The ascendancy of television as the context in which politics now occurs has also influenced the way in which public figures present themselves. Until the New Deal, politicians defined themselves as part of well-knit partisan teams. Now, however, the media have replaced the parties as the primary linkages between candidates and voters. As a result, a candidate's personality is more important than party affiliation or the issues in a campaign. Furthermore, as image grows in importance, the media become still more pivotal as the chief source of information about this essential quality.

The decay in the importance of the parties in the past generation has had differential effects, depending on the visibility of the office sought. Candidates for offices with low visibility—the House of Representatives, for example— frequently operate with budgets and in settings that preclude much television exposure. The result inevitably favors the incumbent. Such incumbent insulation was seen, for example, in 1980, when the Democrats were able to retain a 51-seat margin in the House, while losing the presidency and the Senate to the Republicans. In 1984, they did even better. In the wake of Ronald Reagan's landslide victory over Democratic challenger Walter Mondale (59 to 41 electoral votes), the Democrats made a net gain of 2 Senate seats and kept control of the house by a 71-seat margin. To do this, Democratic incumbents on the average ran nearly 20 percentage points ahead of Mondale in their congressional districts.

Marketing Candidates through the Media

As the current history of any modern presidential campaign shows, candidates for high-visibility offices essentially organize their campaigns as *media events*. When possible, the campaign schedules its activities to produce something newsworthy at a time when it will be picked up, free of charge, by the network evening news. Candidates who wish to succeed will also employ a wide diversity of media markets, not just television. As we have already seen, some candidates with appropriate voice qualities find radio a very attractive medium, not only because it is much less expensive than television commercials, but because it has a vast general reach; moreover, radio can be targeted to specialized audiences. But of course, television remains dominant. The higher and more visible the office, the more heavily the campaign must use it. National campaigns must spend most of their budgets for television advertising, and they must compete with each other in doing so. Even though political campaigns receive a preferred discount rate from the networks, the costs of TV advertising have increased tremendously in the past ten or fifteen years. Moreover, the spread of presidential primaries since 1971 has had a profound multiplier effect. The parties cannot and do not take sides, with cash or otherwise, in primary elections. Candidates must have their own packaged organizations and must be able to tap their own funds.

In fact, the techniques of campaigning are now indistinguishable from those used to market other commodities in America. As soap is sold, so candidates are sold, complete with appeals to fantasy and fear. And obviously, polling and pollsters are of absolutely central importance to today's political campaigns—for exactly the same reasons that they developed commercially in the first place. Market research is the name of the game. Polls are used to identify consumer preferences and to identify areas of strength and weakness in the candidate's image. Consumer preferences reveal targets, special groups in the electorate: for example, the so-called 480 different subgroups targeted by the "people machine" first used extensively in the 1960 Kennedy campaign. Areas of strengths and weaknesses are identified so that political operatives can reconfigure campaigns while they are going on. Later advertising can more adequately stress the positive and eliminate the negative image disclosed by the polling.

The Media as Kingmakers

Gatekeepers of the news, deciding who or what will be admitted, media people are also gatekeepers of the electoral process. "Overall," says Doris Graber, "the most important influence of the media on the voter . . . lies in shaping and reinforcing predispositions and influencing the initial selection of candidates. . . . Through focusing the voters' attention on selected individuals, their characteristics, and the issues for which they stand, the media also determine to a large extent what the crucial issues will be on which the competence of candidates will be judged. . . . All this occurs . . . often long before formal campaigning starts."[10]

One obvious way the media fulfill this gatekeeping function is by providing certain would-be candidates with the exposure they require to break the

---

[10] *Mass Media and American Politics*, p. 188.

anonymity barrier. *Name recognition* is the most vital of all assets in modern politics. Once, of course, this was hardly necessary. From the Democrats who chose James K. Polk as their standard bearer in 1844 to the Republicans who nominated Warren G. Harding on the tenth ballot in 1920, many political conventions chose "dark horses." (Polk and Harding won the elections.) These "dark horses" were completely unknown to the country at large until after they had been nominated, but they didn't *need* to be known. They could count on the party team and partisanship in the electorate to carry the day. Not today. Any candidate who cannot crack the anonymity barrier and secure personal name recognition is politically dead. This happened, for example, to Howard Baker's bid for the Republican nomination in 1980, and Reuben Askew's and Ernest F. Hollings's Democratic presidential campaigns in 1984.

Obviously, a candidate with expert media advisers and lots of money can go a long way to securing name recognition. But things are not that simple. The media is a huge amplifier, and amplification works hand in hand with damping down. It is not cost effective for network newspeople to spend a great deal of their limited time on candidates who have all the earmarks of also-rans. They tend to focus during campaigns on winners or possible winners, people who seem to have the capacity to create the dramatic horse races that are so preferred by the producers of news shows.

The kingmaking function of the media has several effects. First, people who cannot project an acceptable image are likely to be excluded from the pool of available political talent from the outset. We can only wonder whether either candidate in the 1860 presidential race—tall, gaunt Abraham Lincoln, with his lined, pock-marked face, confronting a short, potbellied Douglas—would have projected very well in today's media world. It could very well be that in a race between Abraham Lincoln and Robert Redford, Redford would win in a walk. And we can't be entirely sure that even Franklin D. Roosevelt could have

This photograph was taken at one of the Lincoln-Douglas debates. Neither of the candidates was what we today would consider photogenic—would that have eliminated them from the political process in a modern election?

The Bettmann Archive

survived TV exposure. The fact that he was paralyzed from the waist down could scarcely be hidden from public view as effectively on television as it was during the golden age of radio.

Another aspect of the media's kingmaking function is the tendency of newspeople, even before campaigns have gotten underway, to identify winners and losers, sometimes inaccurately. The labels can then take on a life and a reality of their own. Two classic cases occurred in the 1968 and 1972 New Hampshire Democratic primaries.

In 1968, television commentators and anchor persons claimed that challenger Eugene McCarthy was the winner over incumbent President Lyndon Johnson, despite the fact that Johnson led McCarthy by more than 4,000 votes and 7 percentage points. In 1972, Senator Edmund S. Muskie, Hubert Humphrey's 1968 running mate, had been billed by the media as the front-runner. But challenger George McGovern (who eventually won the nomination) gave Muskie an unexpectedly close race in New Hampshire. In the end, however, Muskie remained the front-runner, leading McGovern by more than 8,000 votes and over 9 percentage points. This did not stop the media from proclaiming that Muskie was the loser in New Hampshire. Such proclamations played a very powerful role in undermining the Muskie campaign thereafter. By announcing their version of reality during the critical early stages of the nominating process, the TV news media are strategically powerful in creating that reality.

Another effect of the rise in power of the media can be seen in the superficial way in which election campaigns are reported. A study found that print media and TV generally give about the same proportion of attention to the issues in a campaign. Both in print and on TV, over two-thirds of all coverage focuses on the campaign as a "race." Where the candidates stand on issues receives less than a third of the media's attention.[11]

It follows from our discussion, particularly of visibility and recognition, that the media perform a crucial agenda-setting function in modern American politics. What issues are important? What is to be decided? The answers to these questions center on what the media does, who has access to it, and on what terms. Some years ago, the political scientist Michael Lipsky called attention to the fact that protest was a political resource.[12] Powerless groups made up of faceless people need to gain access to national attention. They need to cross the anonymity barrier. And notably during the 1960s and early 1970s, demonstrations, riots, and other protests served admirably to achieve that purpose. Such events are dramatic, confrontational, and well adapted to visual coverage. They tend to be television news with a capital N. On the other side of the line, a key element in presidential power is that Presidents are always famous and influential. Compared with anyone else in the society, they have nearly unlimited access to the media sounding board any time they wish to use it. There are unwritten political rules about that too. For example, Presidents are not advised to "go to the well" too often or on too many different subjects of unequal importance and visibility. But the basic point holds true. And by the same token, issues, conditions or people who are ignored by the mass media will tend to be invisible to most of the public.

---

[11] Thomas E. Patterson, *The Mass Media Election* (New York: Praeger, 1980), p. 24.

[12] Michael Lipsky, "Protest as a Political Resource," *American Political Science Review*, 62 (1968), 1144–58.

We have been careful in this chapter to stress that media people are not Svengalis. They have no supernatural or hypnotic powers. Conservative analyst Kevin Phillips referred to the "Mediacracy," but there are important limits to its domination of the political process. The more that something is understood, felt, experienced, and lived in the average American's daily experience, the less he or she is swayed by the media's assessments of whether it is important or not. By its nature, the electoral market is not completely like a commercial sales market. Ideas, opinions, interests, and values remain of autonomous importance in shaping people's perceptions of politics and the choices they make. Parties have decayed—the Democratic party in particular—but they are still lively, and it is possible for them to make a comeback even in a media age. In fact, this may be occurring before our eyes. The Republican campaign of 1984, for example, surely stressed all the symbolism of which Ronald Reagan is an all-time master. But the party also issued a platform that was one of the sharpest, most keenly defined ideological statements of conservatism (or any other position) ever adopted by a major party. The 1984 choices on issues were indeed among the clearest partisan alternatives to be offered to voters in American history. And if this kind of polarization along party and ideological lines continues to develop in the years ahead, as it may well do, then the media will amplify that, too—as they amplify everything that comes within their purview.

And yet, concern about the impact of the media's consent-engineering technology on American democracy remains deep and pervasive among observers of the American scene. This concern is in large measure justified. One writer for *Newsweek* in the summer of 1984 wrote a splendid little essay on Ronald Reagan as the film hero Indiana Jones *(Raiders of the Lost Ark, Indiana Jones and the Temple of Doom)*. The author pointed out that many ordinary Americans appear willing and eager to respond to such upbeat heroic images.[13] After such a long sojourn in a malaise-filled wilderness, one could hardly blame them. Well and good, up to a point. American democratic politics has been splendid theater ever since the hullabaloo-filled "Tippecanoe and Tyler Too" campaign of 1840. But much can be lost through excessive use of the media in the political process. If symbol manipulation is substituted for serious discussion of our collective problems, the quality of public discourse is degraded. If we cannot distinguish between image and reality, the integrity of the relationship between rulers and ruled in a democratic society is seriously undermined. Reality is not primarily images. It is—well, reality: complex, difficult, laden with potential for real danger, and not readily packaged in two- or four-minute segments once a day. No founder of this nation, from Washington and Madison to Lincoln and beyond, ever believed that free government could be sustained without hard work on the part of all involved. Media imagery promotes the contrary view: Elections are horse races, the packages are all we need to understand reality, and we should live for, and think in, the short term only—preferably a short term that involves relaxing entertainment rather than serious work. Fortunately, reality has a habit of intruding on the imagery and spoiling the perfection of the show. It will continue to do so.

---

[13] Bruce Bawer, "Ronald Reagan as Indiana Jones," in *Newsweek*, August 27, 1984, p. 14.

SUMMARY

The mass media, especially television, now create the arena in which we understand the events of public life. Ninety-eight percent of all American households have at least one TV set, and the average set is on about 6 1/2 hours each day. Radio, newspapers, and magazines also supply the information with which we construct our view of the world. As an industry, the media are concentrated in a small number of hands, with fewer than fifty corporations commanding over half the combined national audience for all media.

The ascent of the media to the position of Great Legitimator, whereby nothing is seen to happen in the country until it happens on TV, is a relatively new phenomenon. No truly mass audience could coalesce until improvements in transportation and communication occurred between the late 1820s and the 1840s. During this period the "penny press" began to shape national opinion to a significant extent. Newspapers were extremely partisan during this era, although the rising costs of publishing eventually forced many to soften their positions in order to attract more readers. In the modern era, the appearance of news weekly magazines, the disappearance of competition among newspapers in many cities, and the advent of the electronic media have been milestones.

Between the mid-1920s and 1950, the "golden age of radio," some politicians used radio extensively and with great effect to reach and move a mass audience. Even after the widespread appearance of television in the 1950s, some continued to use radio to broadcast their message. The impact of TV, however, has increased phenomenally since the 1950s, and the medium now manifests itself in all aspects of our lives.

Because commercial television is dependent on advertising for its revenues, the need to be entertaining in order to keep viewers tuned in permeates all programming, including the news. In order to get into the news—and therefore enter the awareness of the American people—stories must satisfy several criteria for newsworthiness. They must be suitable for being conveyed quickly and dramatically, for instance, preferably with lively pictures. This characteristic creates a bias toward stories that can be described in terms of conflict or disagreement. It also creates a market for "photo opportunities" and other pseudo-events. Stories on subjects that are more abstract but more significant—social problems or economic news, for instance—are often ignored, as are other issues that are difficult to televise, such as corporate crime or the impact of specific policies and programs on the lives of ordinary people.

Television also has a great bias toward covering people who are already well known. The best example is the President, who has virtually unlimited access to prime coverage every day. On the other hand, many influential figures receive very little coverage in proportion to the importance of their positions in American life. These people include economic, labor, military, and business leaders, who are rarely in the news. In deciding who or what will get coverage, the media are strategically positioned as gatekeepers to the public consciousness.

Occasionally, media coverage can have an unpredictable effect, even on media people themselves. Instead of generating an impulse for reform, for example, exposing corruption in high places can inadvertently create instead an atmosphere of discouragement, apathy, and malaise. Voters are then more receptive to upbeat messages of optimism and faith in the very institutions that were under fire.

Electoral politics has been profoundly affected by the rise of the mass media, particularly television, as well as by the growth of the persuader professions, such as advertising and public relations, that mold public perceptions so effectively. Political parties have declined in importance as candidates present themselves directly to the electorate via the media. Of course, only those who look promising to the media get the kind of exposure that allows them to be candidates in the first place. In this sense, the media are now the kingmakers of the political process, deciding who will and will not be able to run effectively. Incumbents have the decided political advantage in such situations because they already have the name recognition that media people look for when deciding newsworthiness.

In order to maximize the coverage that they will receive, candidates now organize their campaigns as media events, and they spend most of their budgets for television advertising. After polls identify consumer preferences, advertising that is as vague and positive as possible is constructed to sell the candidate exactly as any other commodity is sold, complete with appeals to fantasy and fear. For their part, the media cover the campaign as if it were a horse race, with numerous projections about winners and losers eclipsing any real interest in the candidates' differences on the issues. It is no wonder that concern about the impact of the media on American democracy remains deep and pervasive among some observers.

―――――――――――― **SUGGESTED READINGS** ――――――――――

ELIE ABEL, ed., *What's News: The Media in American Society*. San Francisco: Institute for Contemporary Studies, 1981. Collection of useful essays on the subject by a group of communications scholars and newspeople.

BEN H. BAGDIKIAN, *The Media Monopoly*. Boston: Beacon 1983. Penetrating and crusading look at corporate concentration in the mass media, its consequences and implications.

W. LANCE BENNETT, *News: the Politics of Illusion*. New York: Longman, 1983. Stresses image creation and, particularly, the extent to which politicians manipulate the media and create news.

EDWARD JAY EPSTEIN, *News from Nowhere*. New York: Random House, 1973. This analysis that highlights particularly the commercial and production imperatives that help to determine shape and content of mass-media news.

DAVID HALBERSTAM, *The Powers That Be*. New York: Knopf, 1979. A skeptical review of the activities of the top media power structure and how these shape content, by a leading investigative reporter.

STEPHEN HESS, *The Washington Reporters*. Washington: Brookings, 1981. Comprehensive and illuminating review of the reporters, their work and political habitat. Based on surveys of reporters.

DAN NIMMO, *The Political Persuaders*. Englewood Cliffs, N.J.: Prentice-Hall, 1970. Slightly dated but still highly useful study of the persuasion industry as a whole.

THOMAS E. PATTERSON, *The Mass Media Election*. New York: Praeger, 1980. Makes all the important connections among media, persuasion industry, and political campaigning. Very useful as a guide to image production and processing in the 1980 and 1984 presidential elections.

ITHIEL DE SOLA POOL, *Technologies of Freedom*. Cambridge: Harvard Univ., 1983. Professor Pool's last work centers on the impact of new communication technologies on freedom of expression and information. Written with great authority and disturbing conclusions. Worth reading and pondering.

chapter nine

POLITICAL PARTIES

Our first federal election was held in 1788. Inevitably, George Washington was chosen as President. The leading light of his administration, Treasury Secretary Alexander Hamilton, acted more or less as Washington's "prime minister."[1]

Hamilton's mind percolated with schemes, projects, and ideas, some sounder than others. In 1790, Hamilton proposed the creation of a Bank of the United States,"[2] a government bank that would issue a stable currency and make large-scale loans. This was a most far-seeing idea; the only other country with a central bank was Great Britain. But if this plan was far-seeing, it was also controversial. To begin with, in 1790 the whole notion of banking—making money with money—struck many people as fundamentally wicked. Besides, certain groups of Americans—small farmers, for example, and small businessmen—had reason to fear that the bank would harm their interests, and there were a great many small farmers. According to the first census (1790), 94.9 percent of the American people lived in "rural territory," defined as farm country and small towns of fewer than 2,500. So as long as the Bank of the United States lasted, there was great political opposition to it. From beginning to end, agrarian interests were at the core of this opposition.

The leader of the congressmen opposing the Bank of the United States was the same James Madison who had earlier collaborated with Hamilton in the effort to frame and ratify the U.S. Constitution (see Chapter 2). These congressmen were a minority; most of their colleagues, calling themselves Federalists, backed Hamilton. Madison's

---

[1] The British prime minister's official title was and is "first lord of the treasury."
[2] The first Bank of the United States, not the second Bank, which provoked the celebrated case of *McCulloch* v. *Maryland* (see Chapter 3).

241

group, in opposition to what its leader darkly referred to as "doctrines and discourses circulated in favor of Monarchy and Aristocracy," adopted the sterner name of Republicans. [3]

Meanwhile, Washington's secretary of state, Thomas Jefferson, was himself troubled by Hamilton's "system" and the lack of effective opposition to it in Congress. "The only corrective of what is corrupt in our present form of government," he wrote a friend, "will be the augmentation of the numbers in the lower house [the House of Representatives], so as to get a more agricultural representation, which may put that interest above that of the stock-jobbers [stock brokers]." [4] *Jefferson and Madison then set up a newspaper to oppose Hamilton and his schemes, and in 1791 they traveled to New York, Hamilton's home state. There, they may or may not have met with his local political enemies, who were numerous. Hamilton, at any rate, thought he knew what was going on: In 1792 he declared, "Mr. Madison, cooperating with Mr. Jefferson, is at the head of a faction decidedly hostile to me and my administration."* [5] *He was right. Yet Jefferson actually complained to Madison about Hamilton's "daring to call the republican party a faction."* [6] *In 1794, Jefferson resigned from President Washington's cabinet.*

Hamilton's quarrel with Madison and Jefferson was the beginning of the American party system. In the fullness of time, it produced the Democratic party that we know today, the world's first modern political party. But Jefferson's complaint to Madison reminds us that political parties are intruders into our constitutional system. The Founding Fathers misunderstood, feared, and tried to thwart them. Certain of the Founders nonetheless created our first political parties—not because they wanted to, but because they discovered that parties are the indispensable engines of representative government.

As our government became more democratic—partly because parties made it so— they became even more indispensable. A present-day politician reasons, "We pay a price for all good things, and parties are the price we pay for democracy."

WHAT IS A POLITICAL PARTY?

Even in 1788, when the first federal elections were held, the American electorate included a higher proportion of adult males than did any other electorate. It was much larger (in absolute numbers) than even the electorate of Great Britain. Although voters here still had to meet certain property qualifications (copied from British models), many adult white men could in fact meet them. Some states never had such qualifications at all.[7] The early American republic was not fully democratic, of course, but not because property qualifications limited the right to vote. The real reason was a political culture that still required the lower ranks to defer to their social superiors.

---

[3] Noble E. Cunningham, Jr., "Beginnings of Party Organization" in Norman K. Rigjord, ed., *The Early American Party System* (New York: Harper, 1969), p. 39.

[4] Ibid., p. 33.

[5] Ibid., p. 41.

[6] Ibid.

[7] See details in J. R. Pole, *Political Representation in England and the Origins of the American Republic* (Berkeley: Univ. of California, 1966).

Candidates for office were often men of wealth, education, and high social standing. Campaigning in the modern sense was not very common, since most such men "stood" rather than "ran" for election (see Chapter 10). The parties of the day—Federalists and Republicans—were little more than caucuses of like-minded members of Congress, with little if any grassroots organization. Only after the War of 1812 did more fully democratic and egalitarian attitudes prevail. From 1818 to 1830, property qualifications were abolished in almost all states that still had them. Modern political parties were organized, and the proportion of adult white men who actually voted increased radically at all levels. In 1828, with the election of Andrew Jackson, the presidency itself was democratized.

These modern political parties were plebeian, not aristocratic, in nature. They brought new men to power—men who knew how to build mass party organizations, win the loyalty of active supporters, and get out the vote. Candidates now had to run for office in vigorous campaigns against tough competition. And if they would not condescend to play the new political game, or did not know how, they were swept aside by men who would and did.

"Politics is a business, that's what's the matter with it. That's what's the matter with everything."

Lincoln Steffens
(1866–1936), American journalist, editor, and reformer

What Parties Do

Parties Seek Votes. Unlike the old congressional caucuses and today's interest groups (see Chapter 6), political parties exist mainly to contest elections. Interest groups, by contrast, pursue their objectives by many means, of which elections are but one, and not necessarily the most important. Interest groups are mostly content to influence elections by aiding the candidates of major parties. Even groups that run their own candidates—the Prohibition and the Right-to-Life movements, for example—are not chiefly electoral organizations.

Parties Unite Interests. The groups that speak for particular interests commonly represent selfish, sometimes rather small groups of people. No party—especially in the United States—could hope to win elections if it did not attempt to build a coalition of many such groups. The Democrats and the Republicans each embrace literally dozens of them. Strong parties can unite interest groups for common purposes and force them to moderate their individual, often conflicting claims. Weak parties, like ours, find it hard to impose unity and order on the jungle of separate interests. As our parties have grown weaker, this problem has become more and more serious.

Parties Organize the Unorganized. The interest-group universe forms a very small—if extremely strategic—minority of our whole population: As E. E. Schattschneider once pointed out, "Probably 90 percent of the American people cannot get into the pressure system." When President Harry Truman (1945–1953) claimed to be the lobbyist of all the people who couldn't afford to hire their own, he was (in part) speaking as leader of a political party and making the point that in scope and purpose, his party differed from almost all interest groups, for the electoral system has a vastly broader base than the interest-group system. Many more poor people vote than join interest groups, so it is worthwhile for some politicians to organize the poor—men and women who lack individual sources of power and have strength only in numbers. Left-wing and liberal parties take these numbers and organize them, to use

One goal of Jesse Jackson's campaign for the Democratic nomination was to organize people who might not otherwise have voted.

their energies for political ends. Such parties have not made our society, or any other, a paradise for the poor, but they have given the poor whatever political strength they have.

Parties Form Governments. Political parties, however, also serve conservative interests—especially the foremost of all conservative interests: strong and stable government. Let us suppose that we had no parties in the United States. Each of the 435 members of Congress would then be completely independent of the others, of the 100 senators, and of the President. What would enable the various parts of our complicated national government to work together? Nothing. Even if the President, congressmen, and senators had only the national interest at heart, they would all have their own schemes, projects, and attitudes. Large-scale cooperation would be impossible. Parties and only parties can fuse a multitude of individuals into a political majority that embraces elected officials and those who elect them. Only parties can give them a common purpose and the moral authority to govern. Our parties, however, are weak, so they carry out these functions very imperfectly, sometimes not at all.

Parties Aid Government. When representative democracy first became practical politics, in the late eighteenth century, its opponents derided it as a kind of organized anarchy. In fact, democracies have been much more stable than other kinds of governments. One reason is that democracy, by its very nature, forces the political elite to discover what the people want and, as far as they can, to provide it. More than any other force in our society, these parties help the political chiefs stay in touch with the political Indians. Party organizations and activities (like primaries and conventions) link the voters and activists of any state with their elected officials and link the officials, voters, and activists of all fifty states. Through political parties, a democratic government receives more, and more accurate, information about the state of public feeling than any secret police could possibly collect. These links and the information they provide help the leaders of democratic governments, who are also party leaders, build support by paying the electorate in the coin of whatever public policies the electorate wants. Parties give legitimacy both to specific governments and to the idea of government.

Who Is a Party?

Compare these two sentences: "The Republicans are in power," and "The Republicans will choose their candidate in next Tuesday's primary." These two uses of the word *Republicans* are different, but they both refer to components of the same political party.

The Party-in-the-Electorate. How large is a party's base of support at elections? How solid is the base? In a democracy, of course, a political party's most important asset is its public support. Early in life, most of us acquire a general tendency to support one party or another, a **party identification** (see Chapter 7). The stronger the identification, the higher the probability that anyone will vote for his or her party's candidates; the weaker, the more likely that any person will not vote at all or will vote a **split ticket:** that is, support candidates of more than one party.

The Party-as-Organization. Many European parties have a group of enrolled supporters, usually one-fourth to one-tenth of their normal vote, who pay regular dues that support a wide range of activities: party newspapers, magazines, research institutions, and so on. Party supporters of this sort have no formal organization in the United States; our parties do not support extensive political activities of the government, which are common in Europe.

"Look, it doesn't mean I'm for him one hundred percent."

Drawing by Frank Modell © 1980 The New Yorker Magazine, Inc.

The hard core of American parties tends to be small, informal, and unpaid; its size and effectiveness varies from place to place. Chicago's Democratic machine, for example, is quite elaborately organized; but in California cities, party organization is amorphous and superficial. By and large, our major parties have little organization or ability to organize, and this seriously diminishes their ability to mobilize and educate the voters.

The Party-in-Government. Political parties control governments and give them a distinct political flavor. The President of the United States appoints some 1,500 high-level officials, who collectively make up "the administration." Most Presidents fill the overwhelming majority of these posts with members of their own parties.

At the outset of the modern party system, in the 1830s, winning control of the government was an end in itself. In the United States, only on occasion have we gone far beyond that stage. No doubt the Democrats and Republicans differ from each other, but the differences are considerably fewer than among Western Europe's political parties, many of which favor basic political and social transformations. In these countries, too, the parliamentary system makes it much easier for them to carry out their programs in office than it is for our political parties.

THE UNIQUENESS OF AMERICAN PARTIES

Most aspects of our culture developed quite recently, as such things are reckoned. But in one respect, the United States is a venerable greybeard among nations. Ours was the first country to enter the world of modern politics, with its written constitutions, popular elections, and mass political parties. Our written Constitution is the world's oldest. The Democratic party is not only the world's oldest existing modern political party, but it was also the very first. The Republican party is a full generation younger; but by European standards, it too is ancient as parties go. Our parties are still close to their original form and spirit. In many ways they are unique, as they were at the very beginning.

The Two-Party System

In Italy, 11 parties were represented in the legislature in 1982; in France, 4 parties; in West Germany, 3; in Britain, 7; and in Canada, 4. As for the United States, we have many **third** (or **minor) parties,** and from time to time, one or another of them does manage to sneak into Congress. But it is remarkable how rarely this happens. At almost every election, in almost every place in the United States, serious politics is confined to the Democrats and the Republicans.

Why? Political Culture. American authorities do not welcome third-party candidates joyously, especially those on the political fringe. Neither, many years ago, did the authorities in Italy and France, but hostility did not prevent strong Communist parties from emerging in those countries. Nor does the hostility of their American counterparts account for the failure of a strong Communist (or even Socialist) party to emerge here. What does? First and foremost, our political culture. In the United States, there is little debate about basic political questions and, as a result, little room for parties that oppose the existing order of things. We simply do not need a great many parties to ventilate the relatively narrow range of views that appeal to large numbers of our people.

Structural Reasons. In the United States, "all politics is local politics." Even the members of our national legislature are elected, one by one, each in a separate geographical district: senators from the fifty states, congressmen from the 435 congressional districts. No party can win electoral votes (for a presidential candidate) or elect a congressman or senator if it lacks concentrated local strength. Some countries, by contrast, elect some or all of their legislatures by **proportional representation,** a system that gives parties legislative seats in proportion to the total number of votes those parties win. Because their "electoral district" comprises the entire country or a large part of it, parties without local pockets of strength still manage to win seats. In the United States they cannot—to the detriment of third parties.

A second structural problem that third parties confront is the so-called **first-past-the-post system.** Presidential electors, congressmen, and senators need only a **plurality,** the largest number of votes, not a **majority,** 50 percent plus 1 vote. In a congressional race, if the Democrat got 35 percent of the vote; a Socialist, 33 percent; and a Republican, 32 percent, the Democrat would win.

We cannot, of course, require the electorate to give a majority to any candidate. But we could, like France, have a two-tiered electoral system: a second election in districts where no candidate got a majority. Such systems encourage bargaining among parties. For instance, to return to the example above, in other districts, the Socialists might have gotten more votes than either the Republicans or the Democrats. The Democrats and the Socialists might then agree to withdraw their candidates in districts where the other party was in the lead, advising their voters to support the remaining Socialist or Democratic candidates. In the first district, the Socialist would have a "straight race" against the Republican; in the second, the Democrat would contend against the Republican. The Socialists would then find it much easier to elect congressmen than they do at present.

Inertia. Finally, our politics have been dominated by two parties for so long that most Americans simply take the two-party system for granted and consider it a good thing. We sometimes make use of third parties to express our discontent with either the Democrats or the Republicans, but the major parties often get the message; and when they do, we go back to voting for them.

Two *Weak* Parties

Our parties are now the weakest in the democratic world. In many localities, they have hardly any organization; naturally, they inspire decreasing loyalty from the voters. It was not always so, yet the decline of our parties was not a sudden or an accidental event.

The Constitutional Structure. For one thing, the American form of government does not absolutely require strong parties, as parliamentary systems do. No parliamentary government can hold office without the support of a majority of the members of the legislature. This majority, whether of one party or of several, selects the prime minister from its ranks; and the prime

"Damn principles! Stick to your party."

Benjamin Disraeli,

prime minister of Britain during the reign of Queen Victoria

	Table 9–1 Split Control		
YEARS	PRESIDENT	SENATE	HOUSE
1919–1921	Wilson (D)	Republican	Republican
1931–1933	Hoover (R)	Republican	Democratic
1947–1949	Truman (D)	Republican	Republican
1955–1961	Eisenhower (R)	Democratic	Democratic
1969–1977	Nixon (R); Ford (R)	Democratic	Democratic
1981–1985	Reagan (R)	Republican	Democratic
1985–1987	Reagan (R)	Republican	Democratic

minister, in consultation with party leaders, selects the cabinet. If the government is defeated on any important proposal, it falls. The opposition party (or parties) then gets a chance to form a new parliamentary majority and, therefore, a new government. If it cannot do so, new elections are held. Since party discipline is the foundation of government, it is strong, and it is exercised vigilantly. Members of parliament who belong to the government party may be cast out from the party's ranks if they vote against the government. Gilbert and Sullivan, describe the process:

If they've a brain and cerebellum too,
They have to leave their brain outside,
And vote just as their leaders tell 'em to.[8]

Our constitutional system, by contrast, creates no such absolute need for party discipline. The executive and the legislature are separate, and the one cannot be voted out of office by the other. Offices are held for fixed terms, and elections are at fixed intervals. The President cannot sit in Congress, and members of Congress cannot serve in the executive branch.

Lack of Discipline. Because the institutional links between the President and Congress are so weak, Presidents have few weapons for bringing congressmen to heel. Congressmen are nominated locally, in their respective districts. As long as they stay in favor with local politicos or with a plurality of those who vote in the primaries, they can do as they please. Even the most popular Democratic President of this century, Franklin D. Roosevelt (1933–1945), failed in the 1938 Democratic primaries to purge uncooperative Democratic senators.

Like most of the problems our parties confront, this one is much more conspicuous among the Democrats than among the Republicans. In 1981, over strong objections of the Democratic House leadership, 48 Democrats in the House—the so-called boll weevils—supported the budget of Republican President Ronald Reagan. These 48 provided the margin of votes needed to pass the budget. Although the boll weevils generated much bitterness in the Democratic party, no serious effort was made in the Democratic caucus to impose sanctions against them, and all but a very few of them were reelected in 1982.

"Split Control." Under a parliamentary system, the party that controls the lower house of the legislature controls the government. In the United States, different parties can and do control different branches of the federal government, and even different (and coequal) houses of the legislative branch. For 24

[8] From *Iolanthe* (1882).

years of this century (as of 1985), the White House has been controlled by one party; either or both houses of Congress have been controlled by the other. During four of those years, control over Congress was itself divided. When President Reagan took office in 1981, for example, the Republicans took control of the Senate, but the Democrats kept control of the House, and each party kept control of its respective house in the 1982 and 1984 elections.

Split control is the complete antithesis of party responsibility, effective party control of the government. But it is only an extreme case of the more general point that our political system does not promote the creation or maintenance of strong or responsible parties, even when the same party has a majority in both houses.

Reform. Another problem for our parties is the tendency of Americans, especially upper-middle-class Americans, to view parties as a problem in need of reform. We have tried to reform our parties directly and to reform the government by putting it beyond the reach of conniving party leaders. These reforms have been only too successful.

In the old days, before the turn of the present century, there were no primaries. Party leaders had complete control over nominations to elective office. Not until the Pendleton Act of 1883 (see Chapter 12) did civil-service regulations interfere with the power of those leaders to appoint their own cronies and hangers-on to posts in the federal bureaucracy. Corruption was in many places a way of life. These were evils—no doubt about it—but they created a sense of party loyalty. They helped make parties strong and therefore made them effective instruments, both of good and evil. Primary systems, civil-service reform, and the public's growing intolerance for corruption have made parties weaker, but no substitutes have been created for them.

Coalitions. In the old days, too, party leaders were stronger because it was so much easier for them to "broker" political coalitions than it is for the would-be bosses of the present. Today, a plausible coalition must be forged from a great many groups. Until the twentieth century, few conflicts were national in extent. Interest groups could fight on the local level yet pool their efforts for a party's national candidates. Today's interest groups compete both locally and nationally. They consist, to a great extent, of issue-oriented activists who are ready to abandon any party that does not swallow their cause whole. To satisfy them, parties now take detailed stands on everything from highway speed limits to chemical warfare. The 1972 Democratic platform, for instance, ran to 60 pages. With parties forced to address so many issues, they spend much of their time in doctrinal arguments that split them into hostile factions.

Hostility to Politics. The 1972 election was one of the rare times in our recent history when the "reform" label was a burden to those who bore it—in this case, the Democrats. More commonly, all candidates call themselves reformers. We demand that our politicians rise above politics as usual, and we like to vote for the man, not the party. Often these are mere empty phrases, but they reflect a real national hostility to organized politics and parties, because political parties clash with important cultural ideals: individualism, free choice, and, at times, honesty.

The Remoteness of Politics. Perhaps nothing so weakens our political parties as the fact that many, if not most, Americans do not care a great deal about politics. We settled the basic questions about our society and government long

This Thomas Nast cartoon of 1871 caricatured Boss Tweed and became a symbol of the sometimes corrupt partnership between American businessmen and politicians.

Some organizations, such as the League of Women Voters, try to overcome Americans' indifference to politics.

League of Women Voters

ago, and we have one of the world's highest standards of living, relatively little class conflict, and a fair amount of social mobility.

Especially since the end of World War II in 1945, elections have not been life-and-death events for most of us. They mean more to the candidates and their families than to anyone else. Until quite recently, neither the Democrats nor the Republicans seemed to be proposing major changes in the way our government worked. As far as politics has any interest for us at all, we tend to see it chiefly as a kind of sport (see Chapter 7).

Some people argue that our indifference to politics is a good thing, since it reflects our social harmony. Perhaps that is true, but we pay a price for this indifference: the undermining of the strength of our political parties—perhaps to the point where we might not muster the will to act in a crisis.

Third Parties

Despite our general indifference to politics and our ingrained two-party system, the United States has been filled with minor parties. One list, compiled by the Inter-University Consortium for Political and Social Research, enumerates more than 1,100 separate party names that appeared from 1824 to the present. Of course, the overwhelming majority of these parties have been local and ephemeral. But 10 minor parties have won as much as 5 percent of the vote in national elections, and these 10 profoundly influenced the development of American politics. Two main kinds of "major" minor parties have crossed the 5 percent threshold.

"Bolts." One kind of party consisted of "bolts" from the major parties, factions that lost struggles within the Democratic or Republican parties and left to run their own candidates. Prime example: the Progressive Party of 1912. Bull Moose Republicans supported former President Theodore Roosevelt (1901–1909) against incumbent William H. Taft (1909–1913), divided the party, and unintentionally brought about the election of Woodrow Wilson, the Democrat. These "bolts" most often end quickly, though the previous state of things may never be quite restored.

Protest Movements. The second kind of "major" minor party consisted of protest movements, typically led by politicians who had little or no standing in the top leadership of the major parties. These protest movements represent important interests clamoring for national attention but unable to get it

Table 9–2 Significant Third Parties in American History

PARTY	YEAR OF MAXIMUM	PERCENTAGE OF VOTE	THEME
			Major Party Bolt (or Fragment) Type
American	1856	21.5%	Anti-Catholic; southern fragment of the Whig party
Constitutional Union	1860	12.6	Southern fragment of the (now dead) Whig party
Southern Democrat	1860	18.1	Bolters from nomination of Stephen A. Douglas; proto-Confederate
Progressive	1912	27.4	Bolters from nomination of William H. Taft (R); supporters of Theodore Roosevelt; in favor of various progressive reforms
			Protest Movement Type
Anti-Masonic	1832	7.8	Proto "Populist" movement against elitism and "privilege"
Free Soil	1848	10.1	Antislavery protest against both major parties
Greenback	1878	12.9	Farmer (and some labor) groups opposed to currency deflation and resumption of *de facto* gold standard
Populist	1894	11.5	Opposition to industrial capitalism and continuing currency deflation
Socialist	1912	6.0	High-water mark of socialist movement in opposition to industrial capitalism
Progressive	1924	16.6	Farmer–labor protest coalition against conservative business control of both parties
American Independent (Wallace)	1968	13.5	Protest against civil-rights revolution, cosmopolitan cultural and policital elites, etc.; very strong in South
Independent (Anderson)	1980	6.6	Liberal Republicans and some "New Class" Democrats opposed to both Reagan (R) and Carter (D); particularly strong in university towns, New England, and West Coast

through the major parties. We have had three such movements since World War I (which ended in 1918), and two of them were clearly associated with electoral realignments (see Chapter 10). The first, Robert LaFollette's 1924 Progressive party, was a farmer–labor coalition protesting the conservative nominees of both major parties. The second, George Wallace's 1968 American Independent movement, ventilated the grievances and resentments of middle America and helped dissolve the New Deal Democratic coalition. The third, John B. Anderson's independent 1980 presidential campaign, made substantial inroads among groups —especially on the East Coast and West Coast— that were unhappy with the major-party candidates, Ronald Reagan and Jimmy Carter.

The Lessons. Third parties, it is often said, raise issues that the major parties later take up and make their own. Up to a point, this is true. More precisely, many of these parties (especially the protest movements) reveal such acute and basic political tensions that one or both of the major parties must eventually accommodate the interests they represent. In any event, such movements were more common in the nineteenth century than they have been in the twentieth, and the last three—those of 1924, 1968, and 1980—were entirely limited to presidential candidates. Before World War I, however, third parties were often real movements, with candidates fielded at many levels, not just for the presidency. This important change appears to be linked to a general narrowing of political alternatives and a general decline of interest in politics.

THE RISE AND FALL OF THE AMERICAN POLITICAL PARTY

Few institutions were born amid more groaning and gnashing teeth than were political parties. The Founding Fathers feared them. In the early years of our Republic, the groups that called themselves parties were mere congressional factions, comprising men elected independently of one another, usually without real campaign organizations or, indeed, campaigns (see Chapter 10). Our political system was not strikingly democratic then, at least by later standards. So as late as 1824, only seventeen states chose their presidential electors by popular vote; in six other states, the state legislature chose the electors; and one state, Massachusetts, combined both methods. Even in states where electors were chosen by popular vote, only about a quarter of the white males voted. Women, of course, could not vote, and neither could almost all nonwhites.

Federalists and Jeffersonians

In 1787 and 1788, those who wanted to ratify the new Constitution were called Federalists (see Chapter 2). After the first federal elections, in 1788, that label was taken by the congressional majority that supported the policies of President Washington (1789–1797) and Alexander Hamilton, his treasury secretary. In Congress, James Madison led the opposition to Hamilton. Mr. Madison and Secretary Jefferson began to call themselves "republicans" and, by 1792, even referred to their supporters as the "republican party," the direct ancestor of today's Democratic party. But the two men did little organizing in the country at large.

President John Adams (1797–1801) was opposed with vigor by the now quite numerous republican newspapers. The Republican Party—now with a capital *R* and a capital *P*—organized local committees much more vigorously than the Federalists did. The Republican cause prospered. Jefferson negotiated an alliance with a leader of the New York Anti-Federalists, Aaron Burr, who in 1800 was Jefferson's vice-presidential running mate. The Republican alliance of 1800 was almost undone by its very strength. Each member of the electoral college had two votes, and the presidential candidate with the largest number of electoral votes was to become President; the runner-up, Vice President. All the Jeffersonian electors, a clear majority, voted the party ticket—Jefferson *and* Burr. Both therefore got the same number of votes. The election was then thrown into the House of Representatives, where Burr tried and failed to usurp the presidency himself. This fiasco produced the Twelfth Amendment, providing for separate electoral ballots for President and Vice-President—the first intrusion of parties into our constitutional system (see Chapter 11).

As President, Mr. Jefferson (1801–1809) was very much a party leader, but the idea of party made him uncomfortable. "Nothing shall be spared on my part," he wrote in a private letter, "to obliterate the traces of party and consolidate the nation, if it can be done without abandonment of principle."[9] However, the traces of party were obliterated only in the sense that the Federalist party disappeared as an organized opposition. From the end of the War of 1812 to the early 1820s—the "Era of Good Feeling"—the Republicans were the only organized party. During this time, the Republican party's presidential candidate—and, therefore, the President—was chosen by "King Caucus," the Republican members of the House of Representatives.

The Jacksonian Revolution

Internal divisions within the Republican party in time created two distinct factions, the National Republicans and the Democratic Republicans. In the 1824 presidential election, John Quincy Adams, a National Republican, was elected President by the House of Representatives, although he had fewer popular votes than the leader of the Democratic Republicans, Andrew Jackson. By 1828, almost all the states chose their electors by popular vote, and most property qualifications for voting had been abolished. General Jackson described the 1828 election, in which he again ran against Adams, as a contest between aristocracy and democracy. This time, he won. The Jacksonians began to call themselves Democrats, and the Democratic party was now launched into American politics.

Without doubt, the years from 1828 to 1840 were the most creative in the entire history of our political parties. President Jackson (1829–1837) was a master of men, determined not only to head the government but also to run it, and he used the Democratic party as the instrument of his rule. When Jackson took over, most federal officials were hostile to him and to his supporters—for the most part, westerners, small businessmen, farmers, and artisans. Jackson fired many of these officials and replaced them with good Democrats. This so-

Men by their constitutions are naturally divided into two parties: (1) Those who fear and distrust the people, and wish to draw all powers from them into the hands of the higher classes. (2) Those who identify themselves with the people, have confidence in them, cherish and consider them as the most honest and safe, although not the most wise depository of the public interests. In every country these two parties exist; and in every one where they are free to think, speak, and write, they will declare themselves.

Thomas Jefferson,
in a letter to Henry Lee,
August 10, 1824

---

[9] John M. Blum et al., *The National Experience* (New York: Harcourt, 1973), p. 158.

New York Public Library Picture Collection

called **spoils system** did not, of course, endear Andrew Jackson to the northeastern "aristocrats" of his own day or to the reformers of the future. But it democratized the federal government and made it responsive to the political majority of the day.

The Birth of Party Structures. In 1831, this country's first major third party, the Anti-Masons, had the bright idea of nominating its presidential candidate at a convention. The Democrats held their first convention in 1832. Delegates were chosen by state conventions made up of delegates selected in mass meetings at the grass roots. By the early 1840s, national conventions were drawing up party platforms; and by 1848, when the Democratic National Committee (DNC) was set up, the national Democratic party ceased to be a mere quadrennial eruption and became a continuous organization.

Party Democracy. The old Jeffersonian Republican party had chosen its presidential candidates at a caucus of Republican members of the House. The convention system, with its base at the grass roots and the state conventions, was far more democratic. Genteel politicians now lost out to a new and hungrier set of men, the party professionals. The spoils system made it possible for these political managers, often born in quite humble circumstances, to live "off" politics, not just "for" politics.

Getting out the Vote. The models of the new-style political businessmen were Martin Van Buren, of the Democrats, and Thurlow Weed, of the Whigs (the name taken in the 1830s by the National Republicans). These were the first "machine" politicians, party managers who built well-funded, centrally controlled, and phenomenally successful national campaign organizations. In 1824, before they existed, the voter turnout was a mere 25 percent of eligible adults (white men, in other words). In 1828, the first election preceded by a real campaign, the turnout more than doubled, to 56 percent, and it stayed at that level till 1840. By then, the Democrats were opposed by another fully developed political party, the Whigs. Between them, the Whigs and the Democrats pulled out 81 percent of the eligible vote. The two parties now vigorously competed in each of the 26 states, and the modern party system was a reality.

The (New) Republican Party

The Jacksonian party system was destroyed by the national debate over slavery. In 1854, the Democratic majority in Congress opened the way for slavery[10] in territories from which it had been excluded by the Missouri Compromise (1821). The resulting political explosion destroyed the Whig party in the North and heavily damaged the Democratic party, too. Out of the explosion came a new Republican party, which, over the next several years, came to dominate the "free states." All the free states were carried in 1860 by the Republican party's second presidential nominee and first President, Abraham Lincoln (1861–1865). The new party wished to contain slavery permanently within the states it then dominated. It also promised to give northeastern manufacturers protective tariffs (see Chapter 2) and an adequate banking system, and to give free lands to farmers.

The political realignment of 1854–1860 reorganized American electoral politics along sectional lines. Mr. Lincoln received only 125 popular votes in the eleven states that seceded from the Union after his election; but in the free states, he got a clear majority of the popular vote—over three other candidates. The Republican party captured hearts and minds in the Northeast and Midwest, especially those of Protestants in farms and small towns. The Democrats became the party of the South and had great support among Catholic immigrants in the North's cities. These lines of cleavage were to remain clearly visible a century later.

"The Republican party favors the privileged few and not the common everyday man. Ever since its inception, that party has been under the control of special privilege, and they concretely proved it in the Eightieth Congress."

President Harry S Truman
(1945–1953), in 1948

The Zenith of Party Politics. South of the Mason–Dixon line, voter turnouts were depressed by one-party politics. Elsewhere, however, they rose (in 1868 and 1888) to an all-time high of 87 percent. Parties were now better organized and more vigorous than ever before or since. Almost everyone identified with one major party or the other, and voters commonly voted straight party tickets. Party feeling was intense; the Republicans proverbially "waved the bloody shirt," equating the Democrats with disloyalty and rebellion. Rallies and parades commonly enlisted thousands and even hundreds of thousands of marchers. (For further details, see Chapter 10, "Campaigns and Elections.")

---

[10] Through the Kansas–Nebraska Act.

To Be or Not To be . . . A Republican

In the Ohio of those days it was natural to be a Republican; it was more than that; it was inevitable that one should be a Republican; it was not a matter of intellectual choice, it was a process of biological selection. The Republican party was not a faction, not a group, not a wing, it was an institution like those Emerson speaks of in his essay on Politics, rooted like oak-trees in the center around which men group themselves as best they can. It was a fundamental and self-evident thing, like life, and liberty, and the pursuit of happiness, or like the flag, or the federal judiciary. It was elemental, like gravity, the sun, the stars, the ocean. It was merely a synonym for patriotism, another name for the nation. One became in Urbana and in Ohio for many years, a Republican just as the Eskimo dons fur clothes. It was inconceivable that any self-respecting person should be a Democrat. There were, perhaps, Democrats in Lighttown; but then there were rebels in Alabama, and in the Ku-Klux-Klan, about which we read in the evening, in the Cincinnati Gazette.

Brand Whitlock, "Forty Years of It" in Stephen L. Hansen, *The Making of the Third Party System: Voters and Parties in Illinois, 1850–1876* (Ann Arbor, Mich.: UMI Research Press, 1980), pp. 203–4.

"The Democratic Party is the common sewer and loathesome receptacle of mankind. . . . It may not be true that every Democrat is a traitor, but it is true that every traitor is a Democrat."

Senator Oliver Hazard Perry Morton

(1823–1877), of Indiana; a prominent but unsuccessful candidate for the Republican presidential nomination in 1876

The "System of 1896." Party feeling was not only strong but also very localized. Especially after the election of 1896, one-party politics prevailed in much of the country. A very large part of the Northeast and Midwest, including a majority of working-class voters, was Republican; the "Solid South" had been solidly Democratic since the Civil War. As for the politically unstable West, it was the seedbed of antiparty revolts and reforms. Political sectionalism pitted the country's industrial heartland against the agricultural South and against the West, which depended on one-crop farming in some areas, on mining and lumber in others.

By the early years of the present century, one-party politics was so widespread that general elections were a sham. Political bosses in each party chose many candidates for office and, therefore, many elected officials.

The Age of Reform

One-party politics strengthened the parties or, at any rate, the party leaders. Powerful and vigorous parties and party leaders had never been much to the liking of our intellectuals. Admittedly, there was much to dislike, for the parties were deeply corrupt, and the leaders' control over nominations threatened to undermine our democratic legitimacy. The reformers attempted to weaken the bosses by attacking their control over nominations.

Primaries. The reformers' chosen instrument was the party **primary,** which allowed the voters themselves to choose each major party's candidates. Mississippi, in 1903, was the first state to adopt primaries for state offices; by 1917, about three-quarters of all states had done so. The first presidential primaries—to select delegates to the national conventions—appeared in 1912. But they did not become fundamentally important until 1972; as late as the 1940s, President Truman quite rightly referred to them as "eyewash."

Other Reforms. More important at the local level were reforms that barred the use of party labels in local elections; provided for the election of officials at large (from an entire city or town), to root out the evils of ward politics; and created many unelected public authorities controlled by experts.

The Cost of Reform. When Americans get into a reforming mood, our first thought is to "cure the ills of democracy with more democracy." Sometimes this creates additional ills. Direct primaries and the other reforms of this era were, and were meant to be, party-busting measures. They stripped party leaders of their most important power—control over nominations—and thereby undermined party discipline.

What was even worse, the primary system, especially in the South, tended to reinforce one-party politics, for the Democratic primary became a kind of substitute election. In all states, moreover, small numbers of voters, often belonging to certain well-organized local interests, usually dominate the primaries. In Boston, for example, the primary system puts local politics into the hands of the Irish, the largest element of the population but overall a minority. Politically committed minorities also have quite a disproportionate influence in primaries and sometimes give nominations to candidates who are not acceptable to the parties' usual supporters. In 1972, for instance, Senator George McGovern (D–S.D.), the Democratic presidential nominee chosen largely in primaries, got only 37.5 percent of the total vote in the general election.

Primaries tend to promote the power of big money, since as they become more numerous and important, they also become more expensive. This is a sad paradox, because they were intended, among other things, to weaken the power of wealthy interests connected with political bosses. What they really did was shift the focus of big money from the smoke-filled rooms of legend to the offices of political consultants, with their high-priced mass mailings and media campaigns.

The Great Depression and Its Aftermath

The election of 1896, which produced the Reform Era, also made the Republicans the normal majority party of the United States. From 1896 to 1932, the Democrats occupied the White House for only eight years, 1913 to 1921. They were a discredited party standing for little but the sectional interests and hatreds of the South. Not until the second-greatest shock in our national history, the Great Depression of the 1930s,[11] did the Republican party's grip on national politics finally end.

"People" vs. "Privilege." Before the 1930s, neither Democrats nor Republicans were regarded as the party of a particular social class, and class interests did not greatly influence the party preferences of most voters. In the Northeast, for example, most working-class people were Republicans, like their social superiors. Regional, not class, conflict was the heart of party rivalry and remained so until the Depression.

During the final years of the "system of 1896"—the 1920s—an unusually large number of working-class people simply did not vote at all. At the decade's end, in 1929, our boom economy went bust. The Republicans did not know how to revive it; the Democrats, meanwhile, were promising everything to everyone and, in any case, had not been in office when the economy crashed. Under Franklin D. Roosevelt, they won the election of 1932 by mobilizing the vote of millions of working-class nonvoters. In office, the

---

[11] The greatest shock, of course, was the Civil War.

Democrats experimented with programs intended to give work to the unemployed and to raise living standards. These programs did not end the Depression, but they did polarize the electorate along class lines. (See Chapter 10 for a further description of the realignment of 1932.)

The Revival of Parties. Despite the massive shift in party loyalties, the party organization of the Democrats and the Republicans changed relatively little during the 1930s and 1940s. Primaries became more common and, as we have seen, thwarted President Roosevelt's effort in 1938 to purge Democrats who opposed his policies. National conventions met as before; and between them, the Democratic and Republican national committees still gave continuous existence to the national Democratic and Republican parties.

Yet the Democratic party, at least, was now vastly better at doing its job, bringing out the vote, than it had been in the 1920s. Why? Not because of Mr. Roosevelt's popularity, although he was immensely popular. The real reason was that American parties can thrive only when a crisis forges a national understanding on some controversial issue—slavery, for example, or economic policy. Mr. Roosevelt's popularity was not rooted in a purely personal following but in public support for his policies and the party that made them possible, the Democrats.

We see this quite clearly in the election returns. In 1944, for example, President Roosevelt carried heavily Democratic Allegheny County (Pittsburgh and its environs) by a margin of 89,472 votes (out of 611,372)—quite a comfortable lead. Moreover, *all* other Democratic candidates did about as well as he did, with margins ranging from 75,626 to 81,887. In 1976, by contrast, Jimmy Carter won Allegheny County by 25,216 votes; the party's senatorial candidate lost by 211,755 votes; and two other statewide Democratic candidates won by 54,320 and 79,500 votes, respectively.

Mr. Carter was a loner who blazed across the political firmament and then disappeared. President Roosevelt was a party leader. Mr. Carter was elected President once and defeated once. President Roosevelt was elected once, then reelected three times.

The Age of Affluence

The Democrats were still strong enough in 1948 to pull off the miracle of President Harry Truman's victory over Thomas E. Dewey in an election that almost everyone thought the Republicans would win. Not until 1952 did the Republicans finally recapture the White House.

The Democrats. After World War II, affluence partly eliminated the economic issues that made the Democrats strong. One of the new issues, civil rights (see Chapter 5), deeply divided the Democratic coalition, pitting blacks and liberals on one side against southerners and many working-class whites on the other. These strains did not prevent the Democrats from retaking the White House in 1960 and keeping control of it—by a landslide—in 1964. If the Republicans are proverbially the "party of recession," however, the Democrats are proverbially the "party of war": Two World Wars and the Korean War (see Chapter 17) were all fought under Democratic Presidents. During the 1960s, under yet another Democratic President, John F. Kennedy, we slid into war in Vietnam (see Chapter 17). Then President Kennedy was assassinated, and his successor, Lyndon Johnson, escalated the war.

By 1968, opposition to the war in Vietnam was so intense that Senator Eugene McCarthy (D–Minn.), opposed President Johnson for the Democratic nomination. Mr. Johnson defeated McCarthy in the first primary, in New Hampshire, but by a very slender margin that revealed the extent of opposition to his policies. Mr. Johnson then left the Democratic race; Senator Robert F. Kennedy of New York (John Kennedy's brother) and Vice-President Hubert Humphrey entered it; then Senator Kennedy was assassinated, and the party went into disarray. The 1968 Democratic National Convention, in Chicago, was a shambles. Many liberals were openly hostile to Vice-President Humphrey, who had won the nomination, while riots outside the convention branded the Democrats as the party of civil disorder.

In an effort to win back the liberals, Vice-President Humphrey agreed to changes in the whole procedure for nominating presidential candidates. We shall examine these changes later in this chapter.

The Republicans. President Dwight D. Eisenhower's two victories, in 1952 and 1956, did not make the Republicans the majority party of the United States; they were victories for the man, not for the party. Mr. Eisenhower's Vice-President, Richard M. Nixon, lost the race for the presidency in 1960 by the narrowest of margins to John F. Kennedy.

Thereafter the party began to change, and change dramatically. Mr. Eisenhower and Mr. Nixon after him had been nominated with the support of the party's moderate Eastern Establishment. That Establishment was disestablished, in the early 1960s, by the growth of Republicanism in the South and the West. By 1964, these elements—which were very conservative indeed—compelled the party to nominate Senator Barry Goldwater of Arizona for President. Goldwater was then trounced by incumbent President Johnson.

In 1968, the party showed that it had learned its lesson by again nominating Richard M. Nixon for the presidency. Mr. Nixon's background was conservative, and he ran for the office as a conservative, although he was much *less* conservative than certain elements in the Republican party. For the country as a whole, Mr. Nixon's election appeared to signal the rise of a new and conservative majority. But in the Republican party itself, his nomination was a setback for the ultraconservatives, who accepted him only because they knew that they could not secure the election of a true believer.

Although Republican President Dwight D. Eisenhower won the 1952 and 1956 elections by substantial majorities, these victories did not help the Republican party as much as might have been expected. They were victories for the man, not for the party.

DECLINE AND FALL: CHANGE, REFORM, AND PARTY POLITICS

In the summer of 1974, Jimmy Carter, then the one-term ex-governor of Georgia, told his mother that he meant to run for President. "President of what?" she replied. It was a very proper question, for Jimmy Carter had no experience in national politics and was largely unknown outside Georgia. No major party had ever nominated anyone quite like him. He was a creation of the rules adopted by the Democratic party in 1968 and 1972, rules that changed the way delegates were sent to the convention and the workings of the convention itself. In fact, they produced a new kind of candidate.

The National Convention

Now, as in all the years since 1832, the supreme authority of both national parties is a national convention that meets once every four years. As always since 1840, it nominates the presidential and vice-presidential candidates, agrees on a party platform, makes its own rules, and judges the credentials of would-be delegates.

The Deliberative Convention. These apparent continuities hide quite real changes in the way that conventions go about their business. Not so long ago, before the proliferation of presidential primaries, national conventions were dominated by the leaders of state parties. As late as 1952, in fact, the power brokers denied the Democratic presidential nomination to the candidate who had won the most primaries, Senator Estes Kefauver (D–Tenn.), and gave it (on the third ballot) to Governor Adlai Stevenson (D–Ill.). This, by the way, was the most recent convention that took more than one ballot to choose a presidential candidate.

Before then, conventions usually involved much give-and-take among party leaders and the holding of at least several ballots, unless an incumbent was to be renominated. (The record: 103 ballots, in 1924, to nominate Democrat John W. Davis.) The Democrats were especially notorious for multiballot conventions because they had a rule requiring the nominee to get two-thirds of the delegate vote. The **two-thirds rule,** which in effect gave the South a veto over the convention, survived until 1936. Even presidential incumbents could not automatically expect renomination; from time to time, party leaders would make up their minds to throw one overboard, as they did with Democrat Franklin Pierce (1852) and Republican Chester Arthur (1884).

In short, the conventions of the past made their own decisions. No presidential candidate, not even an incumbent, could possibly have managed a convention by literally presenting it with a script, as President Nixon did in 1972. The conventions of the past were unruly, often riotous, and they sometimes arrived at very surprising decisions indeed.

Dark Horse Candidates. In the first place, past conventions did not always choose from among the front-runners, the best known contenders. In fact, they often nominated obscure even unimportant, men. These were the so-called **dark-horse candidates,** long shots who did not stand high on anyone's list of potential nominees but won because the front-runners were in deadlock. The first dark horse, James K. Polk, was so little known that a slogan of the 1844 campaign asked, "Who the hell is Polk?" (He had been Speaker of the House, from 1835 to 1839, and governor of Tennessee.) Polk won, of course. The last real dark horse elected President was Warren G. Harding, nominated on the tenth ballot at the Republican party's 1920 convention after the party's power brokers, meeting in the legendary smoke-filled room, decided that he was an acceptable figurehead. The last dark horse to get a major-party nomination, the hapless John W. Davis, a prominent Wall Street lawyer, went down to overwhelming defeat at the hands of President Calvin Coolidge (R).

Dark horses have disappeared from our political life and are not likely to reenter it. A Jimmy Carter can indeed come out of nowhere, but any candidate must be well known to the public by the time the convention meets. The realities of media campaigning now prevent would-be power brokers from choosing presidential nominees. It remains to be seen whether we shall again see multiballot conventions.

The Veep. In the past, too, presidential candidates often had running mates thrust upon them usually by party leaders. They looked for a man who would "balance the ticket" someone who did not live in the presidential candidate's part of the country or who belonged to a different faction of the party.

Stan Wakefield

Pleasing the presidential candidate was not a major consideration. Even in 1932, Franklin D. Roosevelt had to accept a southern conservative as his running mate—John Nance Garner, best known for his observation that the vice-presidency "ain't worth a bucket of warm spit." President Roosevelt never got along with Garner, personally or politically. In 1940, liberated from the two-thirds rule, FDR replaced him with an ardent liberal, Henry A. Wallace. But Wallace was so unpopular with party leaders that, over Roosevelt's objections, they forced him off the ticket at the next convention, in 1944.

As late as 1956, the Democratic presidential nominee, Adlai Stevenson, let the party's national convention choose between the two chief contenders for the vice-presidential slot. By then, the norms had changed: Stevenson was much criticized for indecisiveness, and the gesture has never been repeated. Conventions now accept whichever running mate the presidential nominee is pleased to select. In 1984, the Republican convention in Dallas renominated

The national convention meets once every four years to nominate the presidential and vice-presidential candidates, agree on the party platform, make its own rules, and judge the credentials of would-be delegates. Today the conventions are televised and covered extensively by the mass media.

Ronald Reagan and his running mate, George Bush, share their victorious moment at the 1984 Republican National Convention.

Ronald Reagan and George Bush together, on the same ballot—a first in American political history.

Favorite-Son Candidates. Now dead and departed, another feature of past conventions was the **favorite-son candidate.** At every convention, many state delegations refused to back any contender until late in the proceedings because they wanted to make bargains. Other delegations would be so hopelessly split among supporters of the various candidates that they were incapable of backing any of them. Such delegations would often attend the convention pledged to favorite sons, usually leading politicians in their own states, who were not serious contenders for the nomination. Under cover of the favorite son, they could conceal their own lack of unity or negotiate with the contenders.

The last favorite son who attempted to bargain with the front-runner was Governor Robert Meyner (D–N.J.), at the 1960 Democratic convention. John F. Kennedy was nominated on the first ballot, without making any concessions to Meyner. Since then, favorite-son candidates have been an irrelevant nuisance.

The Rubber-Stamp Convention. All these antique features of past conventions added up to one thing: Those conventions themselves chose their parties' presidential candidates. In 1980, however, Jimmy Carter and Ronald Reagan had their respective nominations in the bag weeks before the conventions met. In 1984, Reagan of course had no opposition at all for the Republican nomination. Walter Mondale, who had a very difficult nomination fight, nevertheless went over the top on the last primary day (June 5), and there was never any serious doubt what the outcome would be from then until his actual nomination on July 19. In both 1980 and 1984, well over two-thirds of the delegates were chosen in primaries, mostly pledged to candidates. The vice-presidential nomination was clearly to be the gift of the presidential candidate. Neither convention had much real work to do.

The Delegates Proliferate. Conventions have been stripped of their independence, in part, simply because delegates have become so much more numerous since the 1960s. The 1876 Democratic and Republican national conventions had a mere 738 and 756 delegates, respectively. By 1940, the number of delegates had climbed to 1,100 and 1,000, respectively; and by 1960, to 1,521 and 1,331—still far short of the 3,933 Democratic and 2,235 Republican convention delegates in 1984.

Large numbers frustrate the machinations of would-be leaders. In 1980, most of the 3,331 Democrats were committed to President Carter. But if Mr. Carter had lost on the first ballot, it would have been far more difficult to work out a deal than it had been among the 738 Democrats of 1876. Mr. Carter, quite rightly fearing that his support had waned in the last stages of delegate selection, insisted on nailing his delegates down. His forces demanded the adoption of the so-called faithful-delegate rule, which required all delegates to vote on the first ballot for the candidates to whom they were pledged. The rule was duly adopted. As his critics charged, this rule made the convention a rubber stamp, but it did logically flow from other recent developments, notably the increased importance of primaries. Although the rule was eliminated for 1984, the general point remains. Once, conventions were true deliberative bodies. They aren't today.

The Impact of Television. Had the 103 roll calls at the 1924 Democratic National Convention been televised, they would no doubt have made a hilarious, silly spectacle. (It was bad enough on the radio, already a significant force.) Controversy and disagreement are inevitable and necessary in politics, but they seem less impressive to the public than tranquility and agreement, however torpid. Now that the conventions' most intimate moments are witnessed on TV by millions of viewers, politicians are embarrassed by controversy, and do their best to suppress it. Perhaps they are wise to do so, for the conventions are filled with squads of eager reporters, whose professional self-interest often leads them to exaggerate the extent or importance of any disagreement they actually do find. (From a reporter's point of view, disagreement is news.) Network TV exposes the conventions to an audience of millions, and the larger the audience, the greater the tendency to treat the news as entertainment (see Chapter 8).

Reform

The 1968 Democratic Convention in Chicago was a media fiasco by anybody's standards. Inside the convention hall Democrats were describing each other as Fascists and communists. Outside, rioters clashed with police, to the chant of "The whole world is watching." It was.

The Democrats. In the true American manner, the Democrats decided to "cure the ills of democracy with more democracy": They adopted new rules, designed to make the party more genuinely democratic. One of them discouraged "midnight caucuses" of insiders, by requiring that state parties hold their meetings at fixed times and places. Another put an end to the *unit*

Walter Mondale and his running mate, Geraldine Ferraro, at the 1984 Democratic National Convention.

UPI/Bettmann Newsphotos

rule at national conventions, by which any state's entire delegate vote could be cast in a bloc, unanimously, if only a majority agreed. Later rules (adopted in 1972, for use in later conventions) banned *winner-take-all-primaries* that gave all of a state's delegate vote to whichever candidate got a mere plurality of the popular vote. All these rules were meant to help political minorities take part in state delegations, and they did. They also weakened the power of state political leaders.

With a second set of reforms, the Democrats made certain that more women, young people, and minorities would sit as delegates at future conventions. The party did not content itself with banning overt discrimination. Instead, it required state parties to ensure that women, young people, and minorities were *in fact* included in delegations, and included in certain specific proportions.

The new rules did not and do not require state parties to choose their delegates in presidential primaries. Even in 1984, some states still chose them through the old **caucus system,** in which local meetings of enrolled Democrats return delegates to state conventions, which in turn elect the delegates to the national convention. Nonetheless, the number of states holding presidential primaries rose inexorably—from 12 in 1960 to 35 in 1980. (This number did decline somewhat in 1984, to 28.)

The Midterm Conference. The 1972 convention, the first held under the new rules, decided to schedule a "charter conference," which met in 1974 and produced the first written party constitution. Above all, this document provided for the holding of a midterm national conference at the midpoint of each presidential term. (The first was held in 1978.) Midterm conferences were supposed to give the party a chance to thrash out and adopt ideas and policies, as opposed to candidates.

The Republicans Follow. The most dramatic rules changes came from the Democrats. The Republicans made changes, too, but not in response to strong internal pressure. Besides being better-behaved than the Democrats are, the

Republicans have more in common, both in politics and in social background, so they can more easily let their state parties go their separate ways. The Republicans tinkered with their rules simply to spruce up the party's image. Their most important innovation—the increased amount of money and technical aid the Republican National Committee gave to candidates—had nothing to do with rules.

The Price of Reform. The 1960 Democratic National Convention was a gathering of the party as a whole, attended in force by its great members: 85 percent of the Democratic governors, 68 percent of the party's U.S. senators, and 45 percent of its congressmen. In contrast, only 47 percent of the Democratic governors attended the party's 1976 convention, 18 percent of its U.S. senators, and 15 percent of its congressmen. Reforms aimed at reducing the bosses' role have succeeded so well that would-be Democratic candidates are no longer subjected to a peer review by other pros; instead, they are chosen by delegates who may have little knowledge of government and politics and may, in addition, come from the political fringes of the party.

Reforming the Reforms. At least this is what Democratic leaders believed when, following Carter's 1980 defeat, they tinkered with the rules yet again. For the 1984 convention, a special class of 568 superdelegates (about 14 percent of the total) was created. This was a category set aside for senators, representatives, and elected state and party officials. They did not have to compete in primaries, and they went to the convention technically unpledged, though in fact overwhelmingly for the eventual nominee, Walter F. Mondale.

But nothing seems to have worked very well. Under the initial reforms, the Democrats nominated two candidates between 1972 and 1980—George McGovern and Jimmy Carter. Following McGovern's 1972 nomination, he failed to win the support of many party officeholders and professionals, organized labor, and other major interest groups. Jimmy Carter patched up enough of this coalition in 1976 to win the presidency, but he could not work effectively with his own party's congressional leaders. It had perhaps been forgotten that factional candidates like McGovern could and occasionally did win party nominations under the old rules. Barry Goldwater's capture of the Republican nomination in 1964 is a modern case in point. It may also have been forgotten that the old system in itself did not prevent the emergence of weak candidates and weak Presidents throughout vast stretches of American history.

Table 9-3   Attendance at the Democratic Presidential Convention, 1956–1984

YEAR	SENATORS	REPRESENTATIVES	GOVERNORS
1956	90%	33%	100%
1960	68	45	85
1964	72	46	61
1968	68	39	83
1972*	36	15	80
1976	18	15	47
1980	14	15	76
1984	28	67	NA

* First postreform convention

AP/Wide World Photos

Democratic National Committee

(Left) Frank Fahrenkopf, Jr., chairman of the Republican National Committee. (Right) Paul Kirk, chairman of the Democratic National Committee.

In any case, the 1984 addition of the superdelegate contingent did not have the desired results. In the sharpest contrast to 1972, Walter F. Mondale was the candidate of choice among the core groups of party, labor, and other interest professionals. One preconvention survey of the congressional super-delegates, for example, revealed that Mondale—who had received only 38.5 percent of the primary vote over stiff opposition from Senator Gary Hart and the Rev. Jesse Jackson—was supported by 84 percent of these legislators. In retrospect, it would be difficult to claim that Mondale was a strong candidate with a clear set of appealing campaign themes.

Without power brokers, the critics of reform say, parties tend to fragment or to be taken over by demagogues. Perhaps so. But the problems that gave rise to the reforms in the first place were very real. And the addition of power brokers in 1984 did not seem to improve matters very much. Neither reform nor counter-reform has restored the Democratic party to political health. From 1972 through 1984, the Democrats suffered three electoral catastrophes—1972, 1980, and 1984—and from 1977 to 1981 they were notably ineffective as a party of government. Some people argue that the Democrats need a realignment, not reform. Later in this chapter, we shall see what they mean.

The National Organization

National conventions meet only once every four years. Between these conventions, the hopes and fears of our national parties are embodied in the Democratic and Republican national committees (the DNC and the RNC, respectively). Their fortunes have ebbed and flowed: During the late nineteenth century, they may have been more active than they are today; but in the 1920s, the Democratic National Committee did not even have a headquarters.

The National Committees. Even now, the Democratic and Republican national committees have relatively few functions, especially as compared with party organizations in Western Europe. There, parties run newspapers, social organizations, research and policy institutes, and propaganda campaigns. By contrast, the DNC and the RNC focus on national elections and on little else.

The National Chairperson. In form, each national committee elects its own chairperson. The reality is that the party's presidential candidate chooses the chairperson after winning the nomination. Should the candidate lose, the national committee announces that it is rebuilding the party, and the first step is to fire the chairperson and appoint a new one. After Jimmy Carter's 1980 defeat, for example, the DNC replaced Carter's handpicked chairman, John White, with Charles Manatt.

Campaign Committees in Congress. Alongside the DNC and the RNC, which concentrate on presidential campaigns, the Democrats and the Republicans have campaign committees in each house of Congress. They supply candidates with money, campaign materials, research, training, poll data, and speakers. By making such loaves and fishes available to candidates who vote with the party's majority, the campaign committees can reward party loyalists and punish deviations from the fold. But their ability to do so is limited, if only because they usually have so few resources at their disposal. In 1982, however, the Republican Congressional Campaign Committee had $30 million to spend.

Any candidate who relied chiefly on the resources of the national committees or the Congressional Campaign Committee would be naive. These days, presidential candidates always have their own committees, independent of the national committee and sometimes hostile to it. (The most notorious example, Richard Nixon's 1972 committee to Re-elect the President, was called CREEP, even by many Nixon supporters.) Congressional candidates, too, must have their own campaign organizations (see Chapter 10).

Fund Raising. The Democrats like to call themselves the "party of the people" and to call the Republicans the "party of privilege." Yet the Democrats get far more of their money from millionaires than the Republicans do, and Republicans get far more of theirs from small contributors. The reasons? For one thing, the Republicans started raising money through mass-mailing techniques much earlier than their rivals did; and mass mailings are clearly the most effective way of eliciting small contributions. Besides, the people who give money to political parties tend either to be strong liberals or strong conservatives. Conservatives are more numerous than liberals, and they give their money to the Republicans.

_____ "A DIME'S WORTH OF DIFFERENCE" _____

George Wallace, governor of Alabama and three-time presidential candidate, liked to say that "there isn't a dime's worth of difference" between the Democrats and the Republicans. He was wrong; there are many differences.

Style

For one thing, Democrats and Republicans are different kinds of people. There are a lot of jokes about these differences of style, and they tell a pretty clear story.

Republican or Democrat?

A favorite tale of one politician has to do with the advice of an older Senate page to the new pages. He said:

"It's sometimes difficult to tell the difference between a Republican senator and a Democratic senator. Nearly all senators—both Republicans and Democrats alike—look prosperous and distinguished and carry themselves with dignity. But if you really want to tell whether a particular senator is a Republican or a Democrat, observe how he comes into a room. A Republican senator struts into a room just as if he owns the place. On the other hand, a Democratic senator swaggers in as though he doesn't give a damn who owns it."

— Republicans, it is said, "usually wear hats and always clean their paintbrushes."

— Republicans hire exterminators; Democrats "step on the bugs."

— "Republican boys date Democratic girls. They plan to marry Republican girls, but feel they're entitled to a little fun first."

— "Republicans sleep in twin beds—some even in separate rooms. That is why there are more Democrats."

Republican conventions are usually efficient and well-behaved. The Democrats like to fight—especially among themselves. Inevitably, the record for the greatest number of ballots at any American convention—103, in 1924—is held by the Democrats. (The Republican record is a mere 36, in 1880.) The great humorist Will Rogers declared in the 1920s, "I belong to no organized political party. I am a Democrat."

Republicans differ from Democrats more today than ever, perhaps. The party realignment of the 1930s (see Chapter 10) made the Republicans a minority, and minorities tend to have more in common than majorities do. Republicans are more alike than Democrats are: in ethnicity (mostly northwest European), in religion (Protestant), in race (white), in politics (conservative), and in class (middle to upper). They vote more consistently for Republicans than Democrats vote for Democrats. Despite their minority standing, they won an average of 53 percent of the two-party vote in the six presidential elections from 1960 to 1980. The Democrats had an average of only 47 percent, although they have a clear if declining edge in registration and party identification.

The Issues

The Republicans, it is said, "are for virtue, the Democrats for Santa Claus."[12] In any case, they are different kinds of people, so they take different stands on public policy.

Party Platforms: 1984. It is often fashionable to sneer at party platforms as mere windowdressing. In fact, the two parties represent two very different parts of America. Scholars have shown that they really try to carry out their pledges when in office. This certainly happened following Ronald Reagan's first election in 1980, and with some spectacular policy results. The 1984 platform contrasts between the parties were very sharply defined. We mention but a few of the more important here.

Economic issues. Republicans came out in opposition to any attempt to increase taxes. Instead, they favored reducing deficits by cutting domestic government spending and providing more incentives for personal savings. The GOP also supported constitutional amendments requiring a balanced budget and giving the President a *line-item veto*, allowing him to strike down specific provisions in an appropriations bill without having to veto the entire package.

Democrats proposed reduction of the deficit by creating a tax system that is "both adequate and fair" (Walter Mondale, in his acceptance speech, was to come out flatly in favor of a tax increase), reassessing defense expenditures (i.e., slowing down their tremendous growth rate), and controlling health costs. Democrats also advocated capping the 1981-1984 Reagan tax cuts for

---

[12] Theodore H. White, *The Making of the President 1964* (New York: Mentor, 1965).

the wealthy and were flatly opposed to a budget-balancing constitutional amendment.

Republicans favored further limiting the federal role in education. Democrats, on the contrary, called for a restoration of Reagan's cuts in federal spending for education.

Republicans supported the right of the states (given them under the 1947 Taft-Hartley Act) to enact right-to-work laws that would outlaw mandatory union membership for workers. They also supported a subminimum wage standard for youth, to encourage employers to hire inexperienced workers. Democrats, as in every platform since 1948, would repeal the section of the Taft-Hartley Act (14-B) permitting states to pass right-to-work laws, and they were opposed to subminimum wage standards for young workers. On one issue after another, the two programs clashed irreconcilably, though the Democrats pulled in their horns on certain issues compared with their platforms of 1980 and earlier years.

Social Issues. As in 1980, the two parties divided most dramatically and emotionally over social issues. In 1980, the Republicans had abandoned support for an Equal Rights Amendment that they had consistently backed from 1940 through 1976 (see Chapter 5). In 1984, they made no mention of support or opposition as such, using vague phrases instead. They did oppose the concept of equal pay across gender lines for jobs of "comparable worth." Democrats, as in the past, endorsed the adoption of the Equal Rights Amendment and supported equal pay for work of comparable worth.

Republicans categorically supported a constitutional amendment banning abortion, opposed public financing for abortion, and supported appointment of federal judges who oppose abortion. Democrats equally firmly rejected a constitutional amendment banning abortion, taking a clear "pro-choice" stance on this explosive issue.

Opposing any gun controls, Republicans defended the "constitutional right to keep and bear arms," while the Democrats demanded "tough restraints on the manufacture, transportation, and sale of snub-nosed handguns which have no legitimate sporting use and are used in a high proportion of violent crimes."

One difference between the Democratic party and the Republican party in 1984 was support for the Equal Rights Amendment. Democrats supported passage of ERA, Republicans did not.

Republicanism in Action: President Reagan. Although the Democratic and Republican platforms were very different, Mr. Reagan carefully refrained from stressing these differences in his successful reelection campaign. Back in 1980, he had done somewhat the same, suggesting that things would somehow become very different if he became President. And in fact they did become different, along lines clearly spelled out in the 1980 GOP platform. For in 1981, as we recall, Mr. Reagan proposed, and Congress approved, major spending cuts in social programs, a huge increase in military spending, and a three-year tax cut. All these had been called for in the Republican platform.

The general setting of 1984, of course, was different. The President campaigned on a theme of success in office, of "America is back" (and standing tall) after a long crisis. The incumbent party was more interested in defending its major program accomplishments than proposing sweeping novelties. In 1985, in any case, the balance of political forces in Congress— especially in the House—was less favorable to carrying out Republican pledges than it had been in 1981.

Nevertheless, the platform gave some clear guidance as to what the President and his party wanted to do during the next four years. George Wallace was simply wrong when he said back in 1968 that there wasn't "a dime's worth of difference" between the Democrats and the Republicans. The difference now amounts to tens, if not hundreds, of billions of dollars.

The Divided Democrats

Why then have so many people agreed with Wallace that the two parties are alike? One reason is that some people, like Wallace himself, are so far from the center of American politics that from their point of view, the two parties really *are* alike. If you were a Prohibitionist, for example, you might be more impressed by the fact that both Ronald Reagan and Jimmy Carter drink alcohol than by their political differences.

Most people, however, think that the two parties are alike for another reason: what one political scientist calls the Democratic party's "internal two-party system."[13] Indeed the Democrats are even more divided than that; as House Speaker Thomas P. ("Tip") O'Neill points out, in any other democratic country they would be three, four, or even five separate parties. These parties within the Democratic party neutralize one another.

The Coalition Splits Up. The 1932 realignment, which made the Democrats the majority party of the United States, forged a coalition among five basic social groups—white southerners, labor unionists, northern ethnics, blacks, and middle-class liberals. These five united in the New Deal coalition but remained distinct and, in many ways, hostile to one another. They had joined together in economic crisis, but they drifted apart in the prosperity that followed World War II. Adlai Stevenson, the Democratic presidential candidate in 1952 and 1956, said, "If you want to live like a Republican, you have to vote like a Democrat." In fact, people who were living, or thought they were living, like Republicans voted like Republicans.

Prosperity was only one feature of the steady but silent social revolution that undermined the coalition. Many assimilated children of ethnic parents feel much less loyal to the Democrats than their ethnic parents did. Many white southerners find the Republicans more attuned to their conservative values than the Democrats are. The share of all workers belonging to labor unions has dropped relentlessly. Yet the Democrats have actually gained strength among blacks, who gave John F. Kennedy 68 percent of their votes in 1960 but voted 85 percent to 95 percent Democratic in all presidential elections thereafter. Finally, the Democrats have gained support among upper-income voters, who still mostly vote Republican, of course, but by smaller margins than they did in 1960.

The "New Class." These well-to-do Democrats may seem like an anomaly, what with the party's support for the welfare state. Oddity or not, they belong to what some have called a new class. In fact, it is a much-enlarged part of the upper-middle class, one that has a personal stake in social programs because many of its members are employed by them, with jobs in education, the professions, and government. Other people in this new class are newly prosperous men and women who, when they were children, heard about

---

[13] Everett C. Ladd, Jr. "The Democrats Have Their Own Two-Party System," *Fortune*, 96, no. 4 (October 1977), 212-26.

hardships of the Depression, and they are loyal to the beliefs of their parents. Still others were born into Republican families and were attracted to the Democrats, not by economic issues, but by matters such as foreign policy, women's rights, abortion, and the environment.

Democrats of the new class made George McGovern the party's presidential nominee in 1972. Large numbers of unionists, white ethnics, southerners, and other party regulars then went angrily into the waiting arms of the Republican party. Some of them are still there.

Will the Real Democratic Party Please Stand Up? The five social groups that united in the New Deal coalition still make up five parties within the Democratic party. There are other internal Democratic parties, too: ideologi-

Table 9-4   The War of the World Views in the Democratic Party

	NEW CLASS DEMOCRATS	OLD CLASS DEMOCRATS
Should divorce be easier or more difficult to obtain than it is now? 　Percentage answering "easier"	59%	21%
Should a pregnant woman be able to obtain a legal abortion if she is married and does not want any more children? 　Percentage answering "yes"	73	32
What is your opinion of someone having sexual relations with someone other than the marriage partner? 　Percentage thinking extramarital sex is always wrong	38	80
What is your opinion of sexual relations between two adults of the same sex? 　Percentage feeling homosexuality is always wrong	27	89
Do you think we are spending the right amount of money to protect the environment? 　Percentage thinking we are spending too little	85	49
Do you think there should be laws against marriages between blacks and whites? 　Percentage favoring laws against miscegenation	5	67
Which statement comes closest to your feelings about pornography laws? 　Percentage thinking "there should be laws against the distribution of pornography *whatever the age*"	13	55
In a community-wide vote on the housing issue, which law would you favor? 　Percentage choosing law allowing homeowner to decide, even if he prefers not to sell to blacks	33	78

SOURCE: Social Science Data Center, Univ. of Connecticut, in Ladd, ibid.

cal subparties. About 16 percent of all Democrats are liberal both on social and economic issues. A further 18 percent—more, you will note—are conservative on both. The "populists," who are economic liberals and social conservatives, make up 24 percent of the party's voters—the largest single group. An additional 13 percent are "libertarians," conservative on economic issues and liberal on social ones.[14]

Diversity is the party's strength—and its weakness. In some respects it has become a coalition of the outgroups of American society. The Democratic party remains, by decreasing margins, the country's normal majority party; but in many respects it is a strikingly ineffective political force. At the presidential level, the 1984 election ratified a fact that first became evident as long ago as 1952: When it comes to presidential voting, the United States is normally a Republican country these days.

The reformers who changed the party's rules in the 1960s and 1970s tried to make it more effective by making it more democratic. They appear to have failed. But there might be another way—a party realignment: a change in the makeup of the two parties and the balance of forces between them. Since 1854, a party called the Republican party has competed against a rival called the Democratic party. But the forces behind those parties, and their inner reality, have changed a good deal. They change at moments of **realignment,** when the political heaven and earth shift and a new majority comes into being (see Chapter 10). The last such moment was 1932, when the New Deal coalition was born, combining traditionally Democratic voters with traditional Republicans and with people who had not voted at all. What brought them together was the Depression and the threat it posed to their economic interests. These economic interests gave common ground to voters who were otherwise quite different.

The rise and success of Ronald Reagan squarely raises the question whether 1980 did not in fact inaugurate a new realignment. Opinion is divided on this point—not surprisingly when we consider that in the mid-1980s the Democrats had large majorities in the House of Representatives, among the governors of the states, and in many state legislatures. We can hardly answer that question now, but we should note that life is vastly more complicated than it was in any historical realignment. Government is vastly more active and intrusive in the lives of Americans, and far more cross-cutting issues arise from that activity than in the past. Thus, the social issues that now play such a large role in our politics have divided people whose economic views were similar, and united people whose economic views were different. The result of all these and other pressures has been a network of cross-cutting cleavages that have damaged Democratic coherence and effectiveness far more than Republican. The damage is a result of the Democratic coalition's heavy concentrations of people who are marginal to white upper-middle-class economic power and to its associated mainstream cultural values. They have little in common except this marginality; they fragment and break away easily under pressure. In retrospect, in fact, we could **argue** that the Mondale coalition of 1984 was in very large part the New Deal coalition of 1940. Partly with the help of the state the New Dealers created, the problem for the Democrats is that society as a whole is vastly better off, as well as much more complex, now than it was in 1940.

---

[14] Stuart Lilie and William S. Maddox, "An Alternative Analysis of Mass Belief Systems." A report of the Cato Institute Policy Analysis, San Francisco, 1980.

The More-or-Less United Republicans

Today's Democrats have very little in common with left-wing parties abroad. Indeed, it is hardly clear whether this motley collection of interests really deserves to be called a party. It is much easier to see the Republicans as a right-wing party. We have already seen that the people who call themselves Republicans have much more in common than Democrats have. That makes Republicans a much narrower slice of our population. Blacks, for example, are on the margins of the GOP. Catholics and Jews have much less influence in it than they have in the Democratic party. Of course, there are poor, black, Catholic, and Jewish Republicans, but they are far less numerous than poor, black, Catholic, and Jewish Democrats, or than white, Protestant Republicans. This demographic unity gives the Republicans a fair amount of political unity; they are much more buttoned down and disciplined than Democrats are.

Nonetheless, they are not a monolithic party by any means. Like the Democrats, they are a coalition of groups with different economic interests, ethnic backgrounds, and political outlooks. After the New Deal realignment, the Republican party fractured along two lines. Conservatives who did not wish to compromise with the New Deal separated from liberal-moderate Republicans who did. In foreign policy, there was a parallel but distinct cleavage between "internationalists" and "isolationists" (the latter especially concentrated, before World War II, in the Midwest).

A once-hallowed rule of thumb was that Republican conservatives and isolationists controlled the party's congressional delegations, while the liberals and moderates controlled the party's presidential nominations. Whatever truth there was in this old saw was eliminated by the "Goldwater revolution" of 1964, when the same Sunbelt-conservative forces took over the modern GOP. Moderate and liberal Republicans defected to the Democrats in droves. Lyndon Johnson became the first Democratic presidential candidate to carry Vermont—a 2-to-1 margin, no less—while Goldwater became the first Republican presidential candidate to carry once solid Mississippi, by more than 8 to 1. In 1964, the Sunbelt conservatives went down with Goldwater to defeat. Not until 1980, with Ronald Reagan as their standard-bearer, did they triumph.

Liberal-to-moderate Republicans have been strongest in the industrial northeast and in certain other northern and western states powerfully imbued with moralist subculture (see Chapter 1). They have long been a waning force within the party, if only because so many of their sons and daughters have defected to the new class Democrats. Ronald Reagan's election as President confirmed the new power balance and probably speeded it up.

The bottom line is simply this: The Republican leaders in Congress and in the executive branch are far more nearly united around a probusiness conservatism than the Democrats are united in opposition to it. And they rest on a far more cohesive base of support in the American public than do their Democratic counterparts.

HANDWRITING ON THE WALL: THE FUTURE OF PARTIES

It is entirely possible that in the year 2000, a minority Republican party will still confront, as it does today, a divided Democratic party. Interest groups, political action committees (PACs) and candidates' campaign committees may continue to flourish in the political terrain that the parties have been forced to abandon. But if so, will democracy have a future?

Parties and the Poor. One chief result of the continued decline of parties might well be a relative increase in the political power of the well-to-do, at the expense of the poor. Political parties, though they have not eliminated proverty, do give the poor whatever political power they have. Our political history shows that the well-to-do tend to benefit when and where parties have been eroded. What were those times and places? In the South from 1877, the end of Reconstruction (see Chapter 5), to the 1960s. In the country as a whole, from the mid-1890s to the turn of the century and during the 1920s. Political parties are simply "more necessary on the left than on the right. To suppress them would be an admirable way for the right to paralyze the left."[15]

Parties and Government. If, then, there were no parties, there would be little or no effective agitation for Social Security, minimum wages, civil rights, food stamps, and the like. Many conservatives would no doubt be overjoyed. Yet there would be a price to pay, and we would all have to pay it, including conservatives. In fact, we are paying some of it right now.

In the past, parties helped create popular support for our system of government and gave it legitimacy in the eyes of the people. Parties mobilized a political majority and placed its power and moral authority at the government's disposal. In short, they made the United States governable, and stable government is the foremost of all conservative interests. Now that we no longer have strong parties, we no longer have strong governments, and the two are directly related. They always have been.

When the federal government moved to Washington, D.C., from Philadelphia, in 1800, there were no parties in the modern sense. The government was planted "at a distance and out of sight."[16] Its headquarters had been tucked away in the swamps of then-remote Washington, and its bureaucracy was too small to make any real contact with the people. Indeed, there was nothing else that could do so. These weaknesses almost lost us the War of 1812. Not until 1828, when Andrew Jackson won the presidency, was there any means for creating a unity out of the innumerable fragments of our system of government, and between the government and the people.

The United States Army is far stronger now than it was in 1814, when the British burned down Washington. But armies are created and maintained by political will, and we are now back on the road to the political immobility that led to the disaster of 1814. No one knows where it is leading us now, but the signs are hardly encouraging.

SUMMARY

The Founding Fathers misunderstood, feared, and thwarted political parties, but created them nonetheless, since they are indispensable to representative government. Political parties help:

---

[15] Maurice Duverger, *Political Parties* (New York: Wiley, 1963), p. 426.
[16] James Sterling Young, *The Washington Community* (New York: Harcourt, 1966), p. 13.

- elect candidates, their primary aim
- unite pressure groups, whose individual and conflicting goals must otherwise dominate politics
- represent the interests of the poor, as far as those interests are represented at all
- give individual politicians common purposes
- form governments
- by mobilizing popular support, endow governments with the moral authority to govern

Our parties, the weakest in the democratic world, do not do any of these things very well. We suffer the consequences.

A party comprises three elements: (1) voters who regularly cast ballots for it; (2) the party organization, made up of activists who participate in campaigns and other party activities; and (3) the officials elected under the party's colors. In Western Europe, party organizations are very elaborate, and elected officials, especially in parliament, are subject to much party discipline. Our parties have little discipline and little organization. For better or for worse, our party system is unique. We have only two major parties, which substantially agree on the fundamentals of political and social life—democracy and private property—though not on all the details of what best guarantees them. Certain aspects of our electoral system—notably the election of all congressmen and senators in local constituencies, and the "first-past-the-post" system—also discourage third (or minor) parties. Besides, we are so used to the two-party system that we think it is good in itself. Despite this, we have had a great many third parties, some of which have served as harbingers of political dissatisfaction and critical realignment.

The weakness of our political parties is unique, too. The American constitutional system, which permits the executive to survive without support in Congress, does not promote strong parties, which we in any case tend to view as a problem in need of reform. Although in the late nineteenth century our parties were much stronger than they are today, these reforms (such as primaries) have succeeded all too well.

Our first political parties emerged during President Washington's administration (1789-1797), when the supporters of Treasury Secretary Alexander Hamilton called themselves "Federalists," and Hamilton's opponents—led by James Madison and Thomas Jefferson—took the name of "Republicans." Until the 1820s, candidates "stood" rather than "ran" for election, but by then the franchise had been granted so widely (though only to white males) that "new men," often of humble origin, swept aside the genteel type of candidate. In 1828, these new men made Andrew Jackson, himself a new man, President of the United States. President Jackson's supporters, a faction in the old Jeffersonian Republicans, now called themselves the "Democratic party." Another faction called itself the "Whigs." The modern party system had now been born and, with it, the apparatus of bosses, machines, activists, conventions, platforms, rallies, political patronage, and the rest.

The Whigs came to grief over the slavery question and were replaced (from 1854) by the Republican party, the present one of that name. From 1860 to 1932—especially after 1896—it was the normal majority party of the United States. Party politics were deeply regionalized, with the Republicans representing the Northeast and Midwest, and the Democrats the South. Not until the 1932 realignment did class conflict replace regional conflict as the mainspring of party competition. By uniting several quite disparate constituencies around support for an activist government, the Democrats became what they have been ever since: the normal majority party of the United States. At first, the Republicans opposed the government's efforts to smooth out the rough spots of the business cycle and to maintain living standards. Later—for a time, at any rate—they accepted those policies in principle, while differing with the Democrats over specifics.

Prosperity weakened the Democratic coalition by diminishing the importance of the economic issues that had created it. So, too, did new issues such as civil rights. By 1968 the Democrats, split as well over the Vietnam War, seemed ready to come apart. The 1968 convention attempted to smooth out these controversies by adopting new rules. They undercut the role of party leaders by making it possible for political unknowns like Jimmy Carter to appeal to the public directly through a vastly increased number of primaries. The convention became a mere rubber stamp. Still, as ever, a jumble of very disparate groups and outlooks, the Democratic party became less and less united.

By contrast, the Republican party, the minority, had far more common ground, both socially and politically. When conservatives from the South and West took the party away from the Eastern Establishment, the Republicans acquired even greater unity of purpose. The conservatives' first victory, in 1964, was the nomination of Senator Barry Goldwater of Arizona as the Republican presidential candidate, but that was followed by his catastrophic defeat in the general election. In 1980 and 1984 Ronald Reagan, another conservative, won not only the nomination but also the office.

Our parties, even the Republicans, are weak and appear to be growing weaker. Interest groups occupy the political terrain that the parties have abandoned. As a result, our political system is less able to contain the jungle of private and selfish interests, and our country is less governable. This road has led us to disaster in the past, and it may do so again.

—————— SUGGESTED READINGS ——————

WILFRED E. BINKLEY, *American Political Parties: Their Natural History*, 2nd ed. New York: Knopf, 1945. Quite old now, but still the best single-volume study of American parties and their historical development.

WILLIAM N. CHAMBERS and WALTER DEAN BURNHAM, eds. *The American Party Systems*, 2nd ed. New York: Oxford Univ. Press, 1975. A useful collection of essays by outstanding specialists on the major American parties and the "systems" they have dominated.

JOHN CHUBB and PAUL PETERSON, eds. *The New Direction in American Politics*. Washington: Brookings, 1985. A first-rate collection of essays on parties, elections, and policy in the Reagan years.

WILLIAM R. KEECH and DONALD R. MATTHEWS, *The Party's Choice*. Washington: Brookings, 1977. Analyzes the processes and nominations of American major-party conventions from 1940 through 1976.

V. O. KEY, JR., *Politics, Parties and Pressure Groups*. New York: Crowell, 1942 to 1963. Many of the details of this classic text, appearing in many editions over the years, are now outdated; but it remains a gold mine of information and insights by the greatest scholar on American electoral politics.

EVERETT C. LADD, JR., and CHARLES D. HADLEY, *Transformations of the American Party System*, 2nd ed. New York: Norton, 1978. Analysis of changes in American party organization and electoral behavior, with particular emphasis on changes since the coming of the New Deal to power in 1932–1933.

GERALD M. POMPER, ed. *Party Renewal in America*. New York: Praeger, 1980. Essays by leading specialists concerned with the problem of party decomposition and its implications.

AUSTIN RANNEY, *Curing the Mischiefs of Faction*. Berkeley: Univ. of California, 1975. Unsympathetic but penetrating analysis of the post-1968 reforms in national party structures and processes.

FRANK J. SORAUF, *Party Politics in America*, 3rd ed. Boston: Little, Brown, 1976. A fine contemporary text overview of the subject.

chapter ten

CAMPAIGNS AND ELECTIONS

American presidential campaigns officially begin on Labor Day, in September.[1] By tradition, the Democratic candidate goes to Cadillac Square, Detroit, where the Democrats quadrennially call to mind the Great Depression, Herbert Hoover, and the glorious memory of our four-term President, Franklin Delano Roosevelt. But on Labor Day 1980, President Carter, who liked to do things differently, started his campaign in Tuscumbia, Alabama.

Ronald Reagan, too, spent Labor Day 1980 in unlikely surroundings: Jersey City, New Jersey. Jersey City is not the sort of place where Republican Presidential candidates ordinarily campaign; as Mr. Reagan rightly said, "It's the home of Democrats." But as he also noted, "There are millions of Democrats as unhappy as we [Republicans] are with the way things are going."

Many of Jersey City's Democrats are first- and second-generation Americans. Mr. Reagan's campaign organizers saw to it that he was entertained at the rally by a group of Korean girls singing "God Bless America," an Irish bagpipe band in kilts, and a group of Polish dancers in peasant dress. The Korean girls, Irish musicians, and Polish dancers looked wonderful on television, and so did Mr. Reagan, in shirtsleeves, with a very visible Statue of Liberty in the background.

Later in the day, it was Ronald Reagan, the Republican, not President Carter, the Democrat, who went to Detroit—to attend a cookout in the suburban backyard of a steelworker named Emil Petri. Many of the twenty or so neighbors he invited were **unemployed steelworkers** *and auto workers.*

---

[1] The election campaign, of course; the campaign for the nomination begins much earlier.

Democrats, immigrants, the Statue of Liberty, unemployed workers—Mr. Reagan was bombarding his audience with symbols. In November, 26 percent of the people who identified themselves as Democrats, 43 percent of the members of labor union families, 46 percent of manual workers, and 47 percent of Catholic voters voted for Ronald Reagan. These inroads among traditional Democrats were exceptionally large for any Republican presidential candidate. Ronald Reagan defeated Jimmy Carter by a landslide.

A TALE OF THREE ELECTIONS

Ronald Reagan was a superb campaigner in many ways. Few American politicians of the 1970s or 1980s could deliver a speech as proficiently, and few better understood the symbols of American politics. But the basic elements of his performance on Labor Day 1980—the election rally, the systematic use of the mass media, the appeal to national symbols and special interests—are the "grammar" of campaigns, common to politicians in general for about 150 years.

In the beginning, our campaign system was very different. We can understand the present system only if we understand how it evolved so let us begin more or less at the beginning.

The Election of 1816. The eighth presidential election of the infant American Republic, in 1816, had little in common with twentieth-century elections.

There were two parties in 1816, but one of them, the Federalists, was on its last legs. The Republicans—not the present party of that name but an ancestor of today's Democrats (see Chapter 9)—had controlled the presidency and both houses of Congress since 1800. The party chose its presidential candidate at a *caucus*, or formal meeting, of the 159 Republicans in the House of Representatives. "King Caucus," as they called it then, chose James Monroe of Virginia, the last big name of the generation that had fought and won the Revolution. As Monroe's vice-presidential running mate, the caucus picked Daniel Tompkins of New York.

As for the Federalists, they were so much at death's door that it is not clear how they chose their candidate, Senator Rufus King, or even whether King knew he was a candidate for the presidency!

Table 10–1   Selecting Presidential Electors: 1816 Election

METHOD	NUMBER OF STATES	ELECTORAL VOTES			PERCENT
		James Monroe	*Rufus King*	*Total*	
Popular, at large	7	93	0	93	42.9%
Popular, districts	3	31	0	31	14.8
Legislature	9	59	34	93	42.9
Totals	19	183	34	217	100.0

Mr. Monroe won easily, with 183 electoral votes to King's 34. (See Chapter 11 for a description of the electoral college.) In only 10 states (of the 19 then forming the Republic) the electoral vote was based on the popular vote; in the other 9, state legislatures chose presidential electors. Even in the 10 states that elected them by popular votes, public interest in the election was low: In Pennsylvania, for example, only 18 percent of the eligible voters actually voted, as opposed to the 42 percent who voted for congressmen.

There was no national politics, only federal elections in 19 separate states. The government in Washington was "at a distance and out of sight," its activities largely invisible to the country at large. Political propriety still discouraged mass participation by the public and active power seeking by its elected representatives. Transportation and communications were too primitive to permit a national campaign. Until Mr. Monroe's nomination, on March 16, 1816, the 1816 campaign was wholly confined to the House of Representatives and to only one party, the Republicans. Whatever the Constitution's Framers had intended, the President was little more than a creature of the House Republican caucus.

The Election of 1880. Everything had changed by 1880. Presidential elections had been more or less democratic for at least fifty years. Two parties, the Democrats and the Republicans (the new party, not the old Jeffersonian Republicans), competed throughout the country—real mass parties, not just cliques in Congress—and in both, nominating conventions chose the candidates. The campaign was intense, and the country followed it eagerly. Almost all Americans called themselves Democrats or Republicans; the few independents were viewed as political idiots or as crooks for sale to the highest bidder.

There were no presidential primaries (see Chapter 9). From the local level to the national conventions, party leaders made the nominations. National conventions were small by today's standards—738 votes on the Democratic side, 756 on the Republican, as opposed to 1980's 3,331 and 1,994, respectively. At them, state party leaders and power brokers of various sorts wheeled and dealed, often in the smoke-filled rooms of political legend.

Hancock the Superb. The Democrats easily rallied around Winfield Scott Hancock (1824–1886), a Union general who, because of his large dimensions, was called "Hancock the Superb." The Republicans had much more trouble. Former President Ulysses S. Grant, despite the failures of his administration (1869–1877), was still popular among Republicans, particularly those who preferred the spoils system (see Chapter 9). Grant was opposed for the nomination by Senator James G. Blaine of Maine.

A full-fledged battle between the Grant ("Stalwart") and Blaine ("Half-Breed") forces produced a deadlock lasting through 35 ballots, a record. Finally, Blaine swung to a "dark horse," Representative James A. Garfield of Ohio. Chester A. Arthur, a notable "spoilsman" and Grant supporter, was nominated for Vice-President to give the ticket factional balance.

The Campaign. The two parties, having chosen their standard-bearers, then began a frenzy of campaigning: stump speeches, campaign flysheets in a dozen languages, constant rallies, and parades. Millions upon millions of pieces of campaign literature—about ten for each voter—were produced and distributed.

Canny politicians on both sides expected a close result, and they were right. The final vote: Garfield (R), 4,446,158; Hancock (D), 4,444,260; all others, 320,002. Garfield's national plurality—1,898 out of 9,210,420 votes cast—was less than 1 percent of the total. A bit under 80 percent of the whole potential electorate actually voted. This electorate was far more partisan than the electorate of 1816 or of 1980, for **party-line voting** was the rule; when a man voted for Garfield, he most often voted a straight Republican ticket.

The Limits of Democracy. Our electoral system was democratic in 1880, but only within limits. The voters elected all the members of the electoral college, which had long since been reduced to a rubber stamp. But women could not vote in any state;[2] black men, though enfranchised by the Fifteenth Amendment, were often effectively prevented from voting in some parts of the South (see Chapter 5).

Despite these and other failings, the 1880 election involved the general public much more than most elections before or since. The campaign was short—from September to November—but intense. As a result of party-line voting, the party that won the White House was more or less assured of controlling Congress—exactly what happened. Despite Mr. Garfield's almost nonexistent margin of victory, the Republicans took control of the House and kept control of the Senate. The party, not Mr. Garfield, won the election, and the party now ran the government.

The Election of 1980. Let us come down to very modern times—the 48th presidential election, held in 1980. How does the scene look now? Political parties are much weaker than they were in 1880 (see Chapter 9), and today's party leaders play a much smaller role in their undertakings. Delegates to the national conventions are now mostly chosen in direct primaries, and the convention is merely a rubber stamp, like the electoral college. In 1980, the Democrats eliminated even the possibility of an independent convention by adopting a rule that required the delegates to vote on the first—and now, in practice, *the only*—ballot for the candidates to whom they were pledged in the primaries.

Jimmy Carter, the sitting Democratic President, had clinched the nomination two months before the convention met in August. Since Mr. Carter had been chosen by the voters, he had the political clout to pick his running mate. Until World War II, party leaders made the choice. On the Democratic side, the campaign had begun a full year before the election; the Republicans began to contest their presidential nomination fully two years before the election. And as we shall see later in the chapter, in many respects 1984 was very similar to 1980.

Tactics. The candidates could not rely on strong party organizations or on politically committed newspapers. They still used the press and the rest of the mass media, but they had to work much harder to do so, and it cost them more money. Media events staged for TV took most of the candidates' time, and TV advertisements took most of their money.

Fewer Voters. Just days before the 1980 voting, almost all the opinion polls predicted a close election. But on Election Day, the national turnout was only 55 percent of the potential electorate. In New York, the turnout was lower than it had ever been in a presidential election. Remember that 79.4 percent of the potential electorate had voted in 1880; by 1980, the turnout was about 25 percent lower.

Voting for Candidates. Party-line voting was virtually dead by 1980. Jimmy Carter, for example, lost Ohio to Ronald Reagan by a margin of 454,131 votes, more than 10 percent of the total, and carried only 10 of the state's 88

---

[2] They could vote in the territory of Wyoming at that time, but territorial voters cast no vote for President.

countries. But U.S. Senator John Glenn, like Mr. Carter a Democrat, was reelected by a margin of more than 1.6 million votes, and he took all but one of the state's counties.

CAMPAIGNS: THE EVOLUTION

These three elections tell a single story: the story of the rise and fall of parties. The election of 1816 was held before the emergence of the party system and full manhood suffrage. The election of 1880 came at the high-water mark of the party system, which could then mobilize voters and produce a government subject to party control. The 1980 election embodied the politics of today's postparty era.

The Rise of Parties

Before Andrew Jackson's administration, there were no true mass parties (see Chapter 9) and no campaigns for the presidency or, until 1913, for the Senate. Seats in the House of Representatives were contested, but local notables decorously presented themselves to the public, "standing," as a rule, not "running" for office. Mostly, they presented themselves as individuals and not as representatives of a party.

During the golden age of the American party system—roughly from 1830 to 1900—campaigns were intense. Elections, like wars, were won by mobilizing every last party supporter, not by appealing to an independent "swing vote." With mass demonstrations and flamboyant, sometimes hysterical rhetoric, the parties promoted an apocalyptic state of mind among the faithful. If any additional votes were needed, they could be bought for ready money.

Campaigns of this sort required teamwork, unity, and the discipline of a machine. Parties had this teamwork, unity, and discipline because their organizations and leaders had complete control over nominations to office. Because there were no primaries, the popular voice spoke only on Election Day.

The New Style

The American way of campaigning—notably for President—began to change shortly after 1900; these changes were bound up with changes in American society itself.

Living standards in the United States had always been relatively high (see Chapter 1). At the turn of the century, the *nature* of those standards began to change. In 1816, or even in 1880, American families often made their own bars of soap or kegs of beer. The technical means for mass production of these goods were at hand, but mass production requires mass consumption; and for mass consumption, the people had to be talked into buying things they often made for themselves. This situation created a new industry: mass advertising, the study and creation of consumer preferences.

At about the same time, newspapers—which until late in the century were usually affiliated with political parties and partly subsidized by them—learned to increase their revenues by relying less on parties and more on advertisements. The popular press therefore cut its links with the parties and, in its new apolitical form, promoted an apolitical state of mind among its readers.

Drawing by Donald Reilly; © 1981 The New Yorker Magazine, Inc.

Playing the News. President Theodore Roosevelt (1901–1909) was the first virtuoso of the mass media, the first politician who knew how to provide the popular press with the sort of light news it required to fill its columns. In 1904, he won the first modern landslide election—the first election, that is, in which the candidate's personality played a larger role than his party's organizing ability. President Woodrow Wilson's (1913–1921) reelection campaign in 1916 was a model of the new style, an advertising campaign based on the slogan, "He kept us out of war," created by Ivy Lee, "the father of advertising." But Lee and his fellow experts worked solely for the President, not for the Democrats as a whole. Mr. Wilson kept his party at arm's length because it could not help him; after all, it had been in the minority since 1896. President Wilson was reelected by the narrowest of margins; as for the Democrats, they continued to be a minority party.

The new campaign style did not quickly replace the old one. Even the campaigns of the 1930s and 1940s were still organized by the parties and tended to benefit them. The Democrats, in particular, flourished from the top of the ticket to the bottom. Nonetheless, today's kind of campaign—in which essentially independent candidates use advertising techniques—has been with us for quite a long time. Indeed, this kind of campaign is actually as old as the mass-consumption society and economy that produced it.

Our parties today are weak and growing weaker (see Chapter 9), and more than anything else, the new style of campaigning caused their decline and its consequences. No longer are parties needed to mobilize and organize the vote, nor have they found any new role. They continue to exist partly because the law requires a mechanism for nominating candidates.

MONEY AND ELECTIONS

American elections cost. Like each election before it, the 1980 election set a record: more than a billion dollars for all national races. In one hotly contested congressional race in California, Representative Robert K. Dornan (R) and his challenger, Carey Peck (D), spent between them almost $2.5 million for a job that pays $60,663 a year and has a tenure of only two years. Theirs was by far the most expensive House election in American history so far, but records of this sort are surpassed quickly. Senate races are even more expensive. In 1984, Senator Jesse Helms (R–N.C.) spent $16.9 million in his successful reelection campaign, compared with $9.5 million spent by his Democratic rival, Governor James Hunt.

We should keep these admittedly large sums in perspective. In a single day, the Defense Department spends about as much as the cost of the 1980 national campaign. And a large corporation would expect to pay as much for a major ad campaign as all candidates for national office spend in a presidential year. In fact, our country is so big and so populous that we may be spending too little on elections, not too much.

The basic problem of campaign finances is the distribution of the expenditures, not their size. Some people can contribute very large amounts of money; others, nothing. Cynics say that money talks, and they have a point— a constitutional point, in fact. The U.S. Supreme Court ruled in 1976 that an attempt by Congress to limit the right of candidates to spend their own money was not constitutional because it denied them free speech. So when money talks, it has a right to constitutional protection.[3]

"Money is the mother's milk of politics."

Jesse Unruh,
Speaker of the California State Assembly (1961–1968)

Who Gives and Why?

Most contributors want something for their money. Many of them want to promote their worldly interests, others, a cause, often an ideological one. Many individuals contribute modest sums to political campaigns, but most campaign financing comes from special interest groups, especially business and labor unions. As a rule, conservative and Republican candidates have more money to spend than do liberals and Democrats. Liberals and Democrats, oddly enough, are more dependent on big contributors than are conservatives and Republicans, because the latter use direct mail more effectively to stimulate small contributions. (See Chapter 6 for a longer discussion of interest groups and their campaign contributions.)

"With the money I'm spending I could elect my chauffeur."

Attributed to Joseph P. Kennedy
by Fred Sparks, *National Star,* 9/28/74

---

[3] *Buckley* v. *Valeo,* 424 U.S. 1 (1976).

Figure 10-1   Rising Costs of Campaign Spending

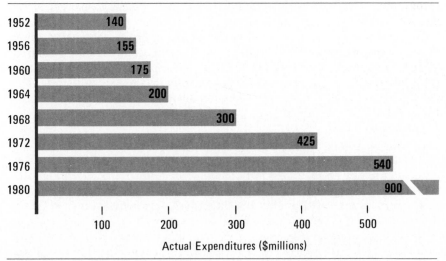

Year	Value
1952	140
1956	155
1960	175
1964	200
1968	300
1972	425
1976	540
1980	900

Actual Expenditures ($millions)

Source: Expenditures, Herbert E. Alexander; Consumer Price Index, U.S. Bureau of the Census.

Campaign-Finance Laws

Because members of Congress, especially powerful ones, benefit from the campaign contributions, they did not in the past regard them as a problem. In 1971, however, and then again in 1974, Congress was finally shamed into placing limits on the amount of money that candidates can receive and spend. It compelled them to disclose the sources and amounts of their money and the ways they spend it. It set up government subsidies for presidential campaigns. None of these reforms has worked very well; some had unexpected results.

The 1971 Reforms. The Federal Election Campaign Act of 1971 put limits on the candidates' spending and required all political committees to submit detailed financial statements if they received or spent at least $1,000 a year for candidates in federal campaigns. The glare of publicity cast by the 1971 law has greatly enriched political science scholarship on the subject of money and elections, but otherwise it has had little effect.

Campaign Subsidies. The most important of the campaign financing reforms that Congress enacted in 1971 provided for a partial public subsidy of presidential campaigns. When taxpayers check a special box on their tax forms, $1 of their tax payments goes into a fund later distributed among presidential candidates who meet certain conditions. As created in 1971, the subsidy covered only the general election. Candidates of major parties—those receiving 25 percent or more of the total vote cast in the previous election— receive sums amounting to 15 cents multiplied by the number of U.S. residents over the age of 18. Another formula determines the subsidy given to candidates of minor parties, those receiving at least 5 percent of the total vote in the previous election. New parties can be subsidized retroactively if their percentages of the total vote come up to the minimum level, 5 percent.

Major-party candidates who accept the subsidy cannot accept private campaign contributions[4] and cannot spend more money than they are entitled to under the subsidy formula.

The 1974 Campaign Financing Act. The Watergate Affair, and the astonishing variety of corrupt practices it revealed, forced Congress to pass the 1974 Campaign Financing Act, which extended the existing system of subsidies. Presidential candidates can now receive **matching funds,** to subsidize their primary campaigns. First, however, they must themselves raise a minimum of $100,000—including at least $5,000 in no fewer than 20 states—through contributions no greater than $250. Each candidate could receive as much as $5 million in matching funds, adjusted annually for any increase in the cost of living. Under the 1974 act, subsidies are now provided as well for the parties' national conventions.

Buckley v. *Valeo.* Besides extending the system of subsidies, the 1974 act attempted to limit the campaign spending of candidates for all federal offices, both in primaries and in general elections, and to limit the amount that contributors could donate to all federal candidates. These campaign spending limits were struck down by the U.S. Supreme Court in *Buckley* v. *Valeo,*[5] so

---

[4] Unless the tax checkoff fails to raise enough money to provide them with the full sum to which they are entitled.

[5] 424 U.S. 1 (1976).

that only presidential candidates who accept the federal subsidy must now accept spending limits. The Court did uphold limits on campaign contributions, with one curious exception: It permitted *candidates* to contribute as much money as they liked to *their own* campaigns.

In some respects the 1974 act is about the best we can expect. Huge unaccountable slush funds, laundered money, illegal contributions by corporations, and unlimited donations by individuals have been brought under about as much control as we can now expect. As for the federal subsidy, it has more or less equalized the campaign treasuries of the major parties and reduced, up to a point, the influence of big givers in presidential elections.

Some problems are still beyond solution. Wealthy candidates continue to have an advantage, especially in the primaries and primaries have become quite common (see Chapter 9). Congress, moreover, has refused to subsidize its own campaigns, to which the big money has now shifted. Finally, since third-party candidates get the subsidy only in proportion to their shares of the vote, they automatically get less than the Democrats and the Republicans do. This inequality may yet institutionalize the two-party system.

Walter Mondale and host Warren Beatty attend a fund-raising dinner dance during the 1984 campaign. Candidates necessarily spend a great deal of time attending such functions, but they are not in fact a major source of money in an election campaign.

Political Action Committees (PACs)

Perhaps the most telling criticism of the campaign-finance laws is the fact that they promoted the rise of political action committees (PACs)—without meaning to.

Businesses and labor unions are both barred by law from contributing directly to parties or candidates. Both skirted these laws by setting up and funding PACs, which then made the contributions their sponsoring businesses or unions could not. For years, organized labor pushed for a law that would explicitly legalize PACs, and in 1971 it got one. In 1972, the Supreme Court also blessed the PACs.

Like all other campaign contributors, PACs can give no more than $5,000 directly to any candidate for federal office. But when complex laws are written by ingenious men and women, equally ingenious men and women find ways around them. The National Conservative Political Action Committee (NCPAC, see Chapter 4) found one such way in 1978. The law limits only expenditures by *candidates* on their own behalf and contributions *directly* to candidates. It does nothing to limit what others, besides candidates, might choose to spend independently of them. Such limits might indeed violate our constitutional right to freedom of speech (see Chapter 4).

PACs, for example, can spend all the money they like on a candidate's behalf, as long as they spend it without the candidate's consent or knowledge. They can also spend freely on negative campaigns—against candidates, not for them. In 1980, NCPAC spent $1.2 million to defeat six liberal Democratic senators. Four of the six were in fact defeated.

Back in 1974, only 600 PACs had been set up; by 1980, there were 2,200. Labor had pressed for the legalization of PACs; yet between 1974 and 1980, its PACs increased from 303 to only 318. During the same 6 years, the number of business PACs went up from 450 to 1,226. The number of conservative PACs rose dramatically, too.

The Effect of PACs. The money spent by the various PACs is very great indeed, although it does not even approach the $10 million that Governor John D. Rockefeller III (D–W.Va.) spent to get reelected in 1980. But these sums can still overwhelm the small world of a congressional district or even, a state as NCPAC's 1980 successes may show. Conventional wisdom has it that money can win opportunities but not elections. Many candidates have indeed spent enormous amounts of their own and other people's money for the privilege of losing. Still, in 1980, the conservative PACs got the sort of President and Congress they wanted, and the major pieces of legislation to emerge from Congress in 1981—the 1981 Tax Act and the budget—plainly reflected those facts.

NATIONAL ELECTIONS: THE PRESIDENCY

Fifty senators and 435 members of the House are elected from separate electoral districts. All these elections are local elections, often dominated by local issues. The President, too, is elected in the 50 states, but in all of them, not in just one. Presidential elections therefore have a national dimension that is absent in all other elections. (See Chapter 13 for a description of elections to the Senate and the House.)

The President and the Party

President James Garfield, elected in 1880, was the creature of his party. He asked voters to support him as the Republican standard-bearer, not as an independent who just happened to have a party label, and his election was a party victory, not a personal one. Voters in 1880 tended to vote a straight party ticket, so candidates for the House and the Senate tried to wrap themselves in the flags of their parties. The political world was sharply divided between the light and the darkness: "The Republican Party is the ship, all else is the sea," proclaimed a late nineteenth-century slogan. Democrats were equally convinced of the great virtues of their own party and the wickedness of the Republicans.

A century later, the parties are in tatters. Jimmy Carter ran for the 1976 Democratic presidential nomination without any real support in the national Democratic party. As for Ronald Reagan—why, in 1976 he actually ran in the primaries against a President of his own party, Gerald Ford.

The Campaign Organization

Because candidates for the presidency wish to keep their parties at arm's length, they have their own campaign staffs, beholden solely to them.

The Pros. At the center is a core of paid professionals, including members of a new professional class who specialize in campaigning. One group of campaign consultants organizes the candidates' schedules and money-raising efforts. Another takes and analyzes public-opinion polls and helps the candidates to build images in the public mind.

The Inner Elite. More important even than the campaign professionals are the candidates' personal friends, the inner elite of unpaid outside advisers whom the candidates rely on to plot strategy. Most of these friends have known the candidates for years, and most are wealthy. Ronald Reagan was particularly well-endowed with such friends.

The Spear Carriers. The professionals and the inner elite are the backstairs of the campaign. The visible campaign consists of perhaps thousands who put the candidates in touch with the voters. These are the envelope stuffers, the door knockers, the leaflet distributors, and the telephone crew.

Richard Sobol, Stock, Boston

Vice-President George Bush and some members of his campaign staff on the road in the 1984 campaign.

Canvassing. Some candidates use their workers to conduct an old-fashioned **canvass.** This means that the candidate's supporters get a list of registered voters and then call each of them to elicit their political sympathies. If a voter supports the right candidate, the campaign worker notes this on a card. Late in the afternoon of Election Day, all of the people with cards get a second call, asking them if they have voted. If they have not, the candidate's supporters offer to deliver them by car to the polling place. Canvassing used to be a standard feature of every political campaign. It still works wonders, as it did, for example, in Mario Cuomo's (D) 1982 victory in the New York gubernatorial contest.

Not all candidates use the canvass. With the art of politics very much in decline, few political professionals know how to conduct a canvass, which takes a lot of campaign workers; usually there are too few. Most candidates rely on the mass media, not on their own campaign organizations, to reach the public.

Issues Experts. Another group of campaign workers comprises the issues experts, people who work up position papers. These usually have little impact unless they contain gaffes. Presidential candidates do produce such position papers—for decency's sake, perhaps, since we seem to expect them—but most candidates do not like to take clear-cut stands on issues. The plain fact is that politicians now have more to lose than to gain by saying what they really think. Two presidential candidates violated this precept in recent years: Senator Barry Goldwater (R–Ariz.) and former Senator George McGovern (D–S.D.). Goldwater lost with only 38.5 percent of the vote; McGovern went down with only 37.5 percent.

Strategies

The lessons of these defeats were learned by sensible politicians. McGovern lost so badly, even though he represented the majority party, because the Democrats were deeply divided. Many rank-and-file Democrats are closer to the Republicans than to liberal Democrats like McGovern (see Chapter 9). Republicans are more united, but they are the minority party and have been for half a century.

In an age when only two-thirds of the voters identify with either party and the remaining third call itself independent, the Democrats and the Republicans must bid for the free-floating center. Most of these independents neither know nor care much about politics; they respond to personalities, media images, and very broad appeals to national symbols and moods.

An Artful Campaign. Ronald Reagan had a reputation for strong conservative principles (or ideology) years before he won the 1980 election. In office, he launched what was in effect a conservative revolution in public policy. But what were his campaign themes in his 1984 bid for reelection? They were not ideological at all. Back in 1980, he had rhetorically asked, "Are you better off now than you were four years ago?" In 1984, his main themes were that "America is back" and standing tall, that his programs were working, that under his administration Americans had regained their pride and self-confidence. He invited Americans to compare how they felt in 1984 with how they felt when Jimmy Carter was still in office, in 1980. There wasn't a trace of ideology in all this. Instead, Reagan's campaign was a variant on one of the oldest themes in politics, whenever there is relative peace and relative prosperity: "You never had it so good." In 1900, William McKinley ran for reelection on the theme, "Four More Years of the Full Dinner Pail." In 1984, Ronald Reagan ran for reelection on the theme, "Four More Years of the Second American Revolution."

Focus. Most candidates, like Mr. Reagan, decide to campaign on their personalities, not their views. But they must have a strategy for dealing with the opposition. One strategy is to stress the candidate's positive side; the other is to run a negative campaign, one directed at the failings of the other party and its candidate. Most campaigns include both elements, so it is mainly a question of balance. Challengers of incumbents—especially incumbents whose popularity has slumped—will stress the negative. Incumbents, however, have records, so often they must run on them by stressing their own virtues.

Theme. Although presidential candidates have little reason to dwell on specific issues, they still need something to hang their hats on. This something must permit the candidates to win the largest possible share of the mainly indifferent and uninformed political center. The result is a perfect duplication of commercial advertising. Candidates who may differ little from their opponents are made to seem different with broad "themes," a substitute for the specific issues they would rather ignore. Ronald Reagan's theme in 1980 was "Can Do, America." Four years earlier, Carter, in his first bid for the presidency, had sounded the theme of "trust." John Kennedy's "Let's get America moving again," in 1960, was not much different from Mr. Reagan's "can do" slogan. Such themes are broad enough to avoid offending anyone, but they make the political products seem different. With luck, they will induce the electoral consumer to buy the candidate's "brand," rather than the competition's.

Television. After losing the 1960 campaign against John Kennedy, Richard Nixon decided that his TV manner left much to be desired, so in 1968 and 1972 he used more radio ads. But TV remains the chief mass medium of our times. Studies of public opinion show that most people do take the TV news more seriously than TV commercials. Candidates and their advisers therefore try to create media events (see Chapter 8) that will be covered—free of charge—on the nightly news. Indeed, the candidate's staff builds its schedule around news deadlines.

TV commercials, addressed to a mass public, must be vague and inoffensive. When the candidates want to reach specific groups—bankers, say, or union members, or conservatives or liberals—they use direct mail. Since a candidate knows in advance who will be getting these letters, they have more of the strong red meat of political controversy than anything that candidate might dare to say on TV.

Pressing the Flesh. If only to create media events for the benefit of television, the candidates must go out and mingle with the public—"press the flesh," as politicians call it. Although personal campaigning already seems rather old-fashioned, it is a fairly recent practice. Until 1896, presidential candidates did not go to the voters; the parties brought the voters to them—to their houses, in fact—sometimes, hundreds of thousands of voters were brought in

> *"A little vagueness goes a long way in this business."*
> **Governor Edmund G. Brown Jr.,**
> of California, as quoted in *The New York Times,* June 6, 1976

> *"If you can't dazzle 'em with brilliance, baffle 'em with bull."*
> **Slogan on the wall of Stuart Spencer,**
> Campaign Manager for Gerald Ford 1976

> *"Sometimes at the end of the day when I'm smiling and shaking hands, I want to kick them."*
> **Richard M. Nixon,**
> as quoted in Theodore H. White, *The Making of the President,* 1968

chartered trains. William Jennings Bryan in 1896 made the first "whistle-stop" campaign from a railroad car. William McKinley stayed at home and won.

The last great whistle-stop campaign was President Harry Truman's, in 1948. Presidential candidates still make personal appearances, but mainly in large metropolitan areas. Richard Nixon pledged in 1960 to visit all fifty states, and he did. Later, he and others concluded that he had wasted his time.

THE ELECTORAL COLLEGE

When we go to the polls in a presidential election, we feel that we are voting for one of the presidential candidates. But we aren't. We vote not for the candidates themselves but for presidential electors pledged to vote for them in the "real" election. This "real" election is held not in November, but in December. It is held not by the people at the polls but by 538 men and women assembled in all of the state capitals and, for 3 electors, in Washington, D.C. The only election that counts, constitutionally speaking, is the one associated with the electoral college. No candidate can be elected through this process unless he or she wins an absolute majority of the electoral vote (today, 270 votes). If more than two significant candidates are running and no one receives such an absolute majority of the electoral vote, then the election for President goes to the House of Representatives. There, each state delegation casts a single vote, and a majority of states (26) is necessary to elect.[6] If no vice-presidential candidate receives a majority of the electoral vote, the election is decided by the U.S. Senate, each senator casting one vote; an absolute majority of the Senate (51) is necessary to elect.[7]

The men of 1787 fashioned a powerful, single executive office on the model of the "patriot king" William III. But on what basis should he be chosen? Hereditary monarchy was out of the question. In fact, so great was the concern about the power potential of the presidency they were creating that the Constitutional Convention made serious and nearly successful attempts to give the President a single seven-year term with no possibility of reelection.[8] On the other hand, fears of legislative tyranny were an important reason for calling the 1787 Convention in the first place. And direct popular election of the President, though proposed at the Convention, was overwhelmingly

---

[6] The last time this happened was in 1825, following the inconclusive results of the four-candidate 1824 election. Despite Andrew Jackson's plurality of the electoral vote (99 out of 261), he was defeated by John Quincy Adams in the House election that followed. This result and Jackson's reaction to it have been a mighty incentive to the creation of the American party system. It should be noted, as a technical detail, that the Twelfth Amendment requires the House to vote for a maximum of three persons having the highest number of votes for President in the electoral college.

[7] The only occasion in which the Senate elected the Vice-President was in 1837. Although Martin Van Buren (D) won the 1836 election over a divided opposition, his vice-presidential running mate, Richard M. Johnson, was objectionable to the party in Virginia. Receiving exactly one-half of the electoral vote (147 of 294), Johnson was elected without difficulty by a Democratic Senate. In such Senate elections, the Twelfth Amendment limits the choice to the top two vote getters in the electoral college.

[8] As we know, the final draft of Article I gave the President a four-year term and left no provisions forbidding reelection. In 1947, Congress proposed, and in 1951 the states completed the ratification of, the Twenty–second (or "anti–FDR") Amendment, prohibiting more than one reelection (or a maximum of ten years in office for a President who, like Lyndon Johnson or Gerald Ford, had succeeded to the office from the vice-presidency). It is noteworthy that today considerable efforts are being made to fix the presidential term at six years with no reelection.

rejected. Of all the alternatives to what eventually happened, election of the President by Congress came closest to becoming reality. In the states, this was common practice and remained so until the middle of the nineteenth century. It normally meant that the governor was subordinated in practice, if not always in theory, to the dominant faction or party in the legislature. Had this path been taken at Philadelphia, it is conceivable that a parliamentary system with a figurehead chief of state would have emerged. But in the end, fears of just such a legislative ascendancy in the federal government prevailed.

The final choice at Philadelphia turned out to be the least successful of all the many compromises among contending interests that form our Constitution. The original provision was for an electoral college. Each state would appoint a number of electors equal to the total number of its senators and representatives. That has survived to this day, but nothing else has. Each elector was originally to vote for *two* candidates, with the presidency going to the one with the largest number of votes and the vice-presidency to his runner-up. If there were a tie between the two, the House of Representatives would then be called upon to decide the election. With the temporary rise of bitter partisan conflict between the Federalists and the Jeffersonians, the inevitable happened. In 1800, Thomas Jefferson and his running mate Aaron Burr each received 73 electoral votes (to 65 and 64, respectively, for Federalist incumbent John Adams and his running mate). So the lame-duck Federalist-controlled House of Representatives had the task of deciding which one of the Jeffersonians should be elected to the presidency. Results like this could be expected in every partisan election from then on. And so the first effort to fix the constitutional structure of presidential elections fell apart on the rock of party, considerably less than a generation after the new government was launched. In 1804, therefore, the Twelfth Amendment was adopted. Apart from the three electoral votes given to the District of Columbia by the Twenty–third Amendment (1961), the electoral college remains as defined in 1804.

How Many Electoral Votes Does Each State Have? From the beginning, the total electoral vote for any given state has been based on the total number of representatives to which it is entitled following the most recent census apportionment *plus* the number of senators to which it is entitled (always two, of course). The largest number of electoral votes in any state during the 1980s is in California (45 representatives plus 2 senators equals 47 electoral votes). The smallest number is 3, in states with only one representative (as of 1985 these were Alaska, Delaware, North Dakota, South Dakota, Vermont, and Wyoming). In 1961, the Twenty-third Amendment finally gave residents of the District of Columbia the right to vote in presidential elections—though of course the district has no senators and no voting representatives. The Twenty-third Amendment defines the district's total electoral vote as that to which it would be entitled if it were a state: 3 votes at present. When we add the entire national total, we find that there are 538 presidential electors, each casting a single vote (100 senators plus 435 representatives plus 3 for the District of Columbia).

Since the adoption of the Twelfth Amendment in 1804, each elector has cast a separate ballot for President and Vice-President. An absolute majority of electoral votes (today, 270) is necessary to elect either a President or a Vice-President. In the event that no candidate receives a majority for President, the House of Representatives must do the electing, choosing among the top three candidates receiving electoral votes. But the House on this one occasion votes

New York's presidential electors cast the state's 43 electoral votes after the 1968 election.

by state, whatever the size of its congressional delegation, and a majority of states (today, 26) is needed to elect. If no candidate for Vice-President receives an electoral-vote majority, the Senate is required to elect, with each senator casting one vote. A majority of the Senate (today, 51) is needed to elect.

How Does a Candidate Carry a State? By winning a simple plurality of a state's electoral votes, a candidate wins *all* the electoral votes of that state. The winner takes all. This means that not infrequently, the entire electoral vote of a state goes to a candidate who has won less than a majority of the total vote cast. For example, Ronald Reagan won conclusively over Jimmy Carter in 1980 and also secured an absolute majority (50.7 percent) of the total votes cast. But he carried 19 of his total of 44 states by less than a majority of the vote, winning 241 electors in his minority states and 248 in his majority states. Jimmy Carter fared even worse; only his native Georgia and the District of Columbia gave him absolute majorities (15 electoral votes in all), while the other 5 states he carried (34 electoral votes) were all won with less than a majority of their popular votes. But all this does not matter. Even if the winning plurality candidate should get only 35 percent of the vote in a state, he would win its whole electoral slate. In fact, this happened in Illinois in 1912, when Woodrow Wilson nevertheless won all 29 of the state's electoral votes. This leads to extremely "lumpy" results both statewide and often nationwide, as it shuts out the opposition entirely within each state. Thus, Reagan's 1980 victory over Carter of 9.7 percent in the total popular vote translated into a margin of 489 to 49 in the electoral vote. Needless to say, this system has produced major, long-standing objections and proposals for reform.

Problems and Controversies. Although we have lived with this system since 1804, we have not lived with it comfortably. Not a decade has gone by without extensive criticisms of the electoral college, both by politicians and outside observers. Criticisms focus on the lack of close fit between the popular and the electoral vote and on the lack of guarantee that the electors will vote for the candidate to whom they are pledged, the so-called faithless elector.

Lack of Close Fit between Results of Popular and Electoral Vote. We have seen that a simple plurality allowing the winner to take all produces distorted results in a presidential election. It also tends to squeeze out even massive third-party movements that are not strongly concentrated in some region of the country. (A case in point: Millard Fillmore, running as the Know-Nothing [American] candidate in 1856, won 21.5 percent of the popular vote but only 8 out of 296 electors, or 2.7 percent).

More disturbing still to some people is the always-present possibility that the front-runner in the popular vote could lose to the challenger in the electoral college. This is more than a possibility. It has happened on two occasions, in 1876 and 1888. It very nearly happened again in 1916, 1960, and 1976. In the 1976 election, a shift of 23,181 voters in Ohio and Wisconsin (.028 percent of the national vote) from Carter to Ford would have led to Ford's winning in the electoral college, through trailing Carter by 1.7 million in the national popular vote. Such an outcome would be unfair, and a President with that kind of negative mandate would have difficulty leading Congress and the country.

The "Faithless Elector" Problem. The founding fathers intended that presidential electors exercise personal and independent judgment in deciding for which candidate to cast their votes. Most analysts of American politics had assumed that the rise of party put an end to all that, reducing electors to the position of rubber stamps. Until very recent times, that assumption was well founded, but it rested on no basis of legal requirement or penalty at either the state or federal level. In the past generation, the practice of exercising personal, independent judgment has suddenly come into vogue, always on the far political right and mostly in or near the South. Although no such cases arose from 1820 through 1947, there have been six of them since 1948. The numbers are trivial; the principle and the potential for serious trouble are not. The universal norm for the past century and a half has been that popular vote, channeled through party, determines the winner of presidential elections. Legally unlimited elector discretion in the college may appeal to rugged individualists (or undemocrats), but it has the potential for working real mischief.

Proposals for Reform. How should we choose our President? Proposals range from totally scrapping the electoral college and choosing by direct popular vote, to requiring electoral districts or maintaining the electoral-vote structure but making the results in each state more nearly proportional to the popular vote. There is wide support for another reform proposal: the elimination of the *office* of elector, whether or not the states' electoral *votes* are retained. Such a reform, of course, would also eliminate the faithless-elector problem.

But there consensus probably ends. The present system may be unsatisfactory and capable of a spectacular misfire someday, but it has some assets in an enormous, continent-sized country with federalist political traditions and very large regional diversities. A candidate who receives less than an absolute majority of the vote but receives a majority in the electoral college is legitimately and constitutionally elected. This has happened in 14 out of the 39 presidential elections since 1828, or more than one-third of the time. Direct popular vote would have prevented the misfires of 1876 and 1888, as well as

A strict proportional distribution of the electoral vote in 1896 would have made William Jennings Bryan (shown here campaigning) the winner rather than William McKinley.

AP/Wide World Photos

the possibility of any such thing happening in the future. Regional appeals, still of vital importance to the calculations that go into presidential campaigns, would be eliminated.

Whether this seems a good or a bad thing depends on one's own views, but it should be stressed that there are real trade-offs involved. For one thing, if the entire country were a constituency, that might further accelerate programmed, packaged, and wired media candidacies. For another, the disappearance of the electoral college's usual majorities might be connected with a multicandidate scramble for the office. Were there enough of such people running, the plurality winner might be elected with less than 30 percent of the vote. Most proposals for a direct vote, recognizing this possibility, have some minimum—say, 40 percent of the popular vote—and a provision for a second or runoff election in the event that no candidate reaches it on the first round. But we recall that Jesse Jackson's 1984 campaign has explicitly challenged the legitimacy of the runoff system in southern primaries, since it works to the disadvantage of black candidates. That apart, one wonders about the possible consequences of applying it to the (admittedly very unusual) 1860 case, when Lincoln fell below such a threshold.

Proposals for requiring electoral-vote districts or for proportionalizing the existing electoral vote seek to give some form of recognition to minority representation within each state. They do not raise the tradeoff issues involved in eliminating federalism and regional campaign calculations from presidential elections. They have other problems, admittedly in relatively unusual cases. It can be readily shown that a strict proportional distribution of the electoral vote in 1896, carried let us say out to three decimal places, would have made William Jennings Bryan the winner rather than William McKinley, despite McKinley's absolute majority of the popular vote. (Work this out for yourself. The secret to the puzzle lies in the extra weight given to small states by the two senatorial electoral votes each state gets, and in the extreme

296   CAMPAIGNS AND ELECTIONS

lopsidedness of the results in various sections of the country.) Similarly, it can be demonstrated that Nixon rather than Kennedy would have been elected on a district system in 1960. In 1976 the result would have been a partisan *tie*, with 269 electoral votes for both Carter and Ford. And when no candidate gets an absolute majority of the electoral vote, the election is then thrown into the House of Representatives!

Many political interests are vitally involved in such proposals. Adoption of any of them would entail uncertain side effects and perplexing tradeoffs. It is thus hardly surprising that politicians and academic experts are deeply divided about proposals to revise the constitutional election mechanism. With all of its potential question marks, some form of direct election might well recommend itself as a means of selection better than the present system. And there seems little justification in any case for the continued existence of individual presidential electors. Every four years, it seems, the problem of the electoral college is raised amid much viewing with alarm. Some of the alarm may be justified. In any case, the problem then goes to sleep again as soon as another presidential election has come and gone without incident. Almost certainly, it will take a misfire as spectacular as the great Jefferson–Burr contest of 1801 to provide enough incentive to bring about any sort of change. In the meantime, the electoral college should not and will not be entirely forgotten. For example, when Bert Lance told Walter Mondale in 1984 that he should choose a southern vice-presidential nominee because a Democrat could not win without the South, he was talking about the traditional political realities of the electoral college. For better or for worse, all that would vanish if direct popular election were to replace it.

CRITICAL ELECTIONS

Most presidential elections simply give us a President. But some do more. They shape the majorities that will rule the political world for a generation or more.

Types of Elections. Elections are of three types. **Maintaining elections** do not change the balance of forces between the major parties. It's business as usual. Such were the elections of 1940, 1944, and 1948, which returned Franklin Roosevelt and Harry Truman. In **deviating elections,** public opinion appears to shift in one direction or the other, but without any permanent effect. The landslides of 1952 and 1956 (Dwight Eisenhower) and 1964 (Lyndon Johnson) were examples of this type. Finally, the **critical-realignment,** or **realigning elections,** are the rare moments of fundamental change in the political balance between parties and in the shape and thrust of public policy. The presidential elections of 1828 (Andrew Jackson), 1860 (Abraham Lincoln), 1896 (William McKinley), and 1932 (Franklin Roosevelt) were realigning elections.

The last of them, in 1932, made the Democrats the majority party, and they remain the majority party to this day. Conservatives and Republicans live in the hope of overturning the results of 1932 with a new realigning election that will create a conservative and Republican majority. There was much hope in 1968 that the time had come at last but those hopes were dashed by Watergate. The election of Ronald Reagan in 1980 also hailed as the start of a new era but it is too soon to tell.

Realigning elections have been our country's substitute for revolution. How and why do they come about? What are their symptoms and results? Let us take a look at the most recent realigning election, 1932—an election whose consequences are still very much with us.

1932: The New Deal

The realigning election of 1896 made the Republican party overwhelmingly dominant in most industrial areas of the Northeast and Midwest. The Democrats were then just a party of narrow sectional and parochial interests, especially the South's. The depression of the 1890s, when the Democrats were in office, proved to many people that they could not be trusted with the affairs of a modern industrial society. True, in 1912 the Republican party split between Teddy Roosevelt and William Howard Taft, and the Democrats took the White House under Woodrow Wilson. The Socialist party did very well too in 1912 but could not break the two-party system. After the United States entered World War I, in 1917, the Socialists faded. In 1920, the electorate returned to "normalcy"—to the Republicans, under Warren G. Harding.

A Signal. Four years later, in 1924, the Democrats nominated the probusiness conservative John W. Davis, and the Republicans nominated the probusiness conservative Calvin Coolidge. The dominance of conservative interests was disturbed only by the campaign of a third-party candidate, Robert M. LaFollette, a notable Republican senator from Wisconsin who ran on the Progressive party ticket. Backed by the American Federation of Labor (see Chapter 6), LaFollette actually beat Mr. Coolidge in Cleveland and almost did so in Pittsburgh and San Francisco. LaFollette lost, but he showed that the makings of a farmer-labor coalition lay in the streets.

In 1928 the Democrats got the message: They nominated the progressive governor of New York, Alfred E. Smith, the first Roman Catholic to win a major party's presidential nomination. Even his Republican opponent, Herbert Hoover, a famous humanitarian engineer, was cut from a new mold. But the election was dominated by the issues of Smith's Catholicism and Prohibition (of alcohol), adopted as national policy in 1920. These issues were mainly symbols of conflict between rural, small-town America and big-city America.

The previous realignment, that of 1896, had divided the country along different lines: the Republican side of the Northeast and the Midwest versus the Democratic side of the South. The new pattern produced a huge shift in voting patterns. Smith carried Massachusetts and Rhode Island and nearly took his home state, New York—all of which normally voted Republican in presidential elections. Mr. Hoover took half of the congenitally Democratic states of the former Confederacy. The vote in the heavily Catholic northern cities, where LaFollette had often done well in 1924, shifted decisively toward the Democrats. A realignment had started, but it was not yet complete.

The Depression. On October 29, 1929—"Black Tuesday"—prices on the New York Stock Exchange hit bottom. The Crash (as it came to be known) signaled economic collapse throughout the Western world; banks failed, and large cuts in production caused mass unemployment. By the winter of 1932, at the bottom of the Great Depression, our gross national product had plummeted to about two-thirds of its 1919 level. About 15 million Americans were unemployed, 25 percent of the work force. In 1931 and 1932 for the first and, so far, the only time, the American economy ran at a net loss, and in 1933, profits were pitifully small. Bread lines and "Hoovervilles"—encampments of the destitute—blighted every American city; local governments were almost bankrupt. "Safety nets" to protect the poor and the jobless did not exist.

To this day, economists disagree about the causes of the Depression, but there is no disagreement about its effects. It amounted to a complete breakdown of our economy and caused mass suffering and deprivations of a sort that most Americans today can hardly imagine.

Bottoming Out. President Hoover believed that the human costs of the Depression should be borne by private charity and local government. The job of the federal government was not to intervene directly in the economy or, still less, to pick up a huge welfare burden. Depressions would burn themselves out if left alone, as they had before. Mr. Hoover was not indifferent to the suffering of our people—far from it. But his commitment to laissez-faire economic theory (see Chapter 16) made it impossible for him to allow the federal government to help relieve such sufferings or to get the economy on the move. He, the Republican party, and most business people believed what a majority of Americans had always believed: that business should manage its own affairs.

This idea was shattered, at least for a time, by the Depression. The unemployed public needed a change. It could not wait for the bottoming out. Mr. Hoover's administration would not deliver the change they needed. The Democrats did not really know what kind of change to deliver, but they knew that one was needed. They were the alternative party at a time of crisis.

The Fateful Year. Meanwhile, Mr. Hoover hung on grimly at the White House. As the economy plunged toward bottom, in 1932, the country moved into an almost prerevolutionary state of unrest. Farmers were preventing court-ordered evictions of bankrupts and pouring milk into gutters rather than sell it at low prices. In the summer, the so-called Bonus Army of World War I veterans marched on Washington to demand early payment of their war bonus. The veterans were dispersed by the army.

Against this backdrop, the Democrats nominated Governor Franklin D. Roosevelt of New York. Mr. Roosevelt promised everything to everyone: a balanced budget but also a more active federal role in the economy. He won by a landslide vote of "no confidence" in the Hoover administration.

The Sea Change. During the lame-duck interval between the 1932 election and the change of government, on March 4, 1933, the nation's banking system collapsed. Franklin Delano Roosevelt took office at a moment of urgent crisis. In his first hundred days, he proposed one change after another for dealing with the economy. (Among other things, he persuaded Congress to create public-works agencies to employ the 25 percent of Americans who could not find work in the private sector.) The Roosevelt administration's New Deal did not end the Depression, but it did change the operational philosophy and constitutional role of the federal government. The strict laissez-faire policy was abandoned, not from socialist principle but for pure pragmatics. The government then became a permanent "senior partner" in the economy— regulating, encouraging, and threatening it.

President Roosevelt was personally popular, but his victories were not just personal victories. In 1934, for the first and, thus far, the only time in this century, the President's party gained seats in both houses of Congress in an off-year election. The realignment was continuing. Mr. Roosevelt's over- whelming 1936 reelection victory over Kansas Governor Alf Landon sealed the

Republicans' fate. Again, in 1940, 1944, and 1948, the New Deal's basic policies were ratified by the voting public. Dwight Eisenhower was the first Republican to break the spell, in 1952 and 1956. But—and this is a crucial point—Eisenhower did nothing to dismantle the New Deal; it was confirmed, not rejected, by his administration. The regulatory, interventionist state was now above politics, accepted by mainline Democrats and Republicans—or so it seemed.

Cause and Effect

What do these events tell us about our past, our present—and our future? Why do we have realigning elections, whereas other nations have revolutions?

Let's begin at the beginning. Our Constitution is now about 200 years old. Few countries have lived under the same form of government for this long. Although our governmental forms have changed little, our society is among the world's most dynamic. Our eighteenth-century institutions deal with a torrent of modern problems. In most countries, new problems lead to new institutions, but our country is not like most. Instead of changing our constitutional system, we change the political realities behind it.

What happens, roughly, is this: As new political issues and controversies come to the fore, politicians respond slowly—and our constitutional system even more so. Controversies build up, and the voters cast about for new choices, new solutions. New generations of men and women reject the parties of their parents. In the years just before the realigning election, third parties appear and point the way to the new order. In Congress, where it is less and less clear what each party stands for, party differences are blurred. The voters, disgusted with the candidates offered by the Democrats and the Republicans, stay away from the polls in large numbers.

The materials of realignment are now at hand. For an explosion, however, there must be a trigger of some sort, an event that sends the old system to "the trash heap of history." The Panic of the 1890s was one such trigger, and the Great Depression of the 1930s was another. But although serious economic troubles can no doubt shatter the political status quo, the trigger does not have to be economic. The realignment of 1860, for example, was set off by a

series of political decisions in Washington and points south, not by economic distress.

The triggering event changes the political landscape almost beyond recognition. Old and apparently secure elites are abruptly and forever ejected, replaced by new elites. The parties confront each other in bitterness and anger, divided by basic disagreement. After rising steeply, the temperature of politics peaks in the pivotal election itself.

People who have lived through a realignment period well remember the passion and intensity of those days. For example, a man who worked for Stephen A. Douglas, Abraham Lincoln's Democratic opponent in the 1858 Illinois senatorial election—two years before they competed for the presidency—wrote of the earlier election:

> It was no ordinary contest, in which political opponents skirmished for the amusement of an indifferent audience, but it was a great uprising of the people in which the masses were politically, and to a considerable extent socially divided, and arrayed against each other. In fact, it was a fierce and angry struggle, approximating the character of a revolution.[9]

Just so. To a greater or lesser extent, all realigning elections have "the character of a revolution." The contenders, who include a very large part of the adult population, see the stakes as nothing less than the future of the country.

When the new majority takes power, it does in fact change the direction of public policy and the relative importance of the various power blocs. But our realignments so far have never disturbed the basic liberal consensus: life, liberty, and property. They simply cause those principles to be interpreted in a new light. The realignment does not change the text of the Constitution, but it changes the way it works. Before the 1932 realignment, for example, the U.S. Supreme Court, on constitutional grounds, limited the federal government's powers over the economy. After 1937, it accepted the two basic elements of the New Deal: the federal welfare state and systematic government intervention to smooth out the business cycle.

---

[9] Quoted in Harry V. Jaffa, *Crisis of the House Divided: An Interpretation of the Lincoln—Douglas Debates* (New York: Doubleday, 1959), p. 23.

In the aftermath of critical realignment, the atmosphere of acute and general crisis cools off. The new balance of political forces and the new direction of public policy are ratified at subsequent elections, but in more placid circumstances. One of the two major parties—what Samuel Lubell called the "sun party"—takes a dominant position, the other (the "moon party") a subordinate one.[10] The Democrats dominated from 1828 to 1860, the Republicans from 1860 to the mid-1870s, neither party from about 1875 to 1896, the Republicans from 1896 to 1932, and the Democrats from 1932 on.

Cycles of Realignment

Until the 1930s, critical realignments occurred in cycles of about 38 years. But there has been no indisputable realignment, of the old style, at least, since the 1930s. President Reagan, no doubt, is attempting to bring one about, but there are important reasons for doubting whether he or anyone else can do so. In the past, realignments have been associated with our political parties and with voting for them, but the major parties have decayed so far that neither, perhaps, can serve as the driving force of a new political order.

The Realignment That Was Not. In 1968, many political scientists thought they were witnessing the first stage of the next realignment. Disorder and violence rocked college campuses and black slums. Public opinion, as measured in polls, turned sharply against the Johnson administration (1963–1969). The Democratic National Convention, in Chicago, was held under virtual siege by protesters against the war in Vietnam (see Chapter 17). Bitter divisions within the Democratic party weakened its presidential candidate, Hurbert H. Humphrey. With Governor George Wallace's (D–Ala.) independent bid for President, a third-party protest movement weighed in right on historical schedule. By appealing to the massive discontents of whites in the South and white workers in the North, Wallace carried five southern states and won a respectable 13.5 percent of the vote.

Some people thought that the United States was on the verge of a revolution in 1968. Conservatives were confident, however: They inferred from Richard Nixon's election as President that an "emerging Republican majority," as Kevin Phillips put it, was at hand. This supposed emerging majority was promptly submerged—in 1974 and in 1976.

Parties and Realignment

Jefferson County, in eastern Tennessee, has voted for the Republican nominee in each presidential election since 1868. Warren County, in western Tennessee, is almost as fixed on the Democratic side: It has failed to support the party of Jefferson, Jackson, and Roosevelt only twice, in 1968 and 1972. The two counties do not differ much economically or socially, but they do differ historically: In 1861, the small farmers of east Tennessee bitterly opposed the state's secession from the Union, but elsewhere in the South, similar kinds of people supported the Confederacy.

Most people ordinarily know little and care less about politics and government; but in times of realignment attitudes are different. Suddenly the public's loves and hates polarize around political issues which most people

[10] Samuel Lubell, *The Future of American Politics* (New York: Harper, 1952).

Table 10-2 Voting in Two Tennessee Counties: 1861 and 1980

COUNTY	VOTE ON SECESSION: 1861			PRESIDENTIAL VOTE: 1980		
Warren	Yes	1,419	99.2%	Carter (D)	6,021	61.1%
	No	12	0.8	Reagan (R)	3,680	37.4
				Anderson (I)	148	1.5
Jefferson	Yes	603	23.3	Carter (D)	3,180	30.8
	No	1,987	76.7	Reagan (R)	6,944	67.3
				Anderson (I)	201	1.9

believe to be of great importance. The parties suddenly embrace radically different positions on these issues. Voters side with one party or the other, and this party identification, once fixed, can be handed down from generation to generation, as it was in Tennessee.

Realignments aside, the parties usually do not embrace radically different policy positions. If the parties are weak and the important issues do not divide them sharply, it is much harder for a realignment to get under way. In the 1930s, the issues were economic, and the Democrats and the Republicans were divided on them. But the two parties had no historic attitudes about the major issues of the 1970s, such as abortion, the environment, and foreign policy. Party differences were much less clear-cut, so the Democrats and the Republicans were less suitable as vehicles for a realignment. They would have been so even if they had not been disintegrating—which they were.

Nonetheless, the parties still stand for different economic policies, and their differences came sharply into focus under President Reagan. In Congress, during Mr. Reagan's first year, the Democrats (except for a relatively small group of southern conservatives) and the Republicans divided sharply along party lines. If the issues of the 1980s continue to be economic, the parties may continue to be more and more different. That might not only ease the way to a new realignment but also make it easier for the electorate to influence public policy by voting for one party or the other.

THE RISE AND FALL OF THE AMERICAN VOTER

Voting for federal office is only one kind of political participation. Some people take an active part in local affairs and not only vote but also give money to candidates, parties, or PACs; some go to political meetings; some work for parties or candidates. The turnout on election day is therefore just one test of our political vitality, but it is a very important one.

Voting is important because, for most of us, it is the only way of having an impact on government. Society can be seen as a pyramid. Those at its very summit may have enough wealth, power, and status to have a permanent role in government. But the mass of citizens at the base of the pyramid, who have no individual power, who lack wealth, talent, or skill, can still influence the political system if only they vote.

Today's voting rates are as low as they have been since the beginnings of our democracy, in the late 1820s and the 1830s. They are lower than the voting rates in any other democratic country. Indeed, in many urban areas of the North and West, the voter turnout in the 1978 and 1980 congressional elections reached an all-time low. In 1978, the nationwide congressional turnout was a mere 37 percent of the potential electorate. In 1980, a presidential election year—when the rate of voting always goes up—only 55 percent of the potential electorate voted for president and only 50 percent for the congressional races. These miserable figures strikingly and sadly contrast with our own nineteenth-century turnouts—better than 80 percent outside the South in presidential years, and close to 70 percent in off-years.

The South. In the South, special in this as in so much else, devices meant to cut down the black vote (see Chapter 5) and the absence of party competition produced turnouts of less than 10 percent of the potential electotate in the 1926 and 1942 congressional elections. The 1965 Voting Rights Act and the emergence to two-party politics in much of the South pushed the 1978 congressional turnout up to about 28 percent, still lower than the rate—low though it was—in the rest of the country.

Turnout: 1900–1984. Because it was the South's peculiar history that produced these very low figures, we should separate its record of voter participation from the national record. In the rest of the country, diminished party competition and registration of voters and, in 1920, the beginning of votes for women all caused voting rates to fall steadily from 1900 to 1926, both in presidential and in off-year elections. (In Philadelphia, barely one-quarter of adult women registered in 1924, compared with more than three-fifths of the men.) As always, nonvoters tended to be poor. A vital ingredient in the New

By 1940, voter turnout had climbed to more than 70 percent of the estimated potential electorate. This crowd in Times Square has come out to read the latest bulletin on election night, 1940.

UPI/Bettmann Newsphotos

Deal realignment was its successful mobilization of the huge pool of nonvoters, mostly working-class, of both sexes.

By 1940, the turnout (outside the South) had climbed to more than 70 percent of the estimated potential electorate, a jump of 20 percent from the low point, the 1920 presidential election. It remained high until 1960 and then began to decline, a decline that continues to this day. Only about 55 percent of the eligible electorate (outside the South) voted in the 1984 presidential election, so we are back to the low levels of the early 1920s. The congressional turnout in 1984, at 52.5 for senators and 50.1 for representatives, equaled the low points of 1920 and 1924. This, by the way, is one reason for doubting that 1980 was a realigning election for in the past, such elections produced larger, not smaller, turnouts. That conclusion is reinforced by an important feature of the 1984 election. Despite Ronald Reagan's huge landslide, the Republicans picked up only 14 seats in the House of Representatives. Reagan carried 372 of the country's 435 congressional districts. But Republican congressional candidates won only 181 of them, the other 191 being won by Democrats, the first time that sort of thing has ever happened in American political history.

The Reasons. At present, all states but North Dakota require voters to register before Election Day. Although registration may indeed discourage voting, it and other procedural changes cannot account for the dramatic decline since 1960. By and large, these procedural changes have made it easier, not harder, to vote. The 1965 Voting Rights Act, for instance, cut to a uniform thirty days the residency requirement for voters in presidential elections, and many states have liberalized their personal registration laws. In North Dakota, the one state where registration has never been required, the turnout declined from 1960 to 1984 at a rate only somewhat lower than the rate of decline in the rest of the country.

Reducing the Voting Age. In 1984, some 60 years after women won the vote, they voted as often—or as rarely—as men did. In 1971, however, the voting base had been expanded yet again, by 7 percent, when the Twenty-sixth Amendment lowered the voting age from 21 to 18. Only about 35 percent of Americans aged 18 to 20 actually vote, as compared with about 61 percent of those 21 and over. Nothing like this gap has appeared in other democratic countries, and the greater geographic mobility of American young people cannot explain it; it is just too large.

Social Attitudes. The 1970s were a decade of resentment. Some people were alienated—"turned off," they said—by the social experiments of the previous two decades; others were alienated by the limited scope of those experiments. You might think such people would be less likely to vote, but in 1978 a researcher found relatively little difference between their voting habits and the voting habits of people who were satisfied with the performance of American government and politics. Nonvoters, he found, are passive, not alienated; they believe that their lives are controlled by chance and random events. Voters tend to think that they themselves control their own lives.[11] Of course those passive notions are more common among the poor than among other social classes.

Social Class. In fact, the poor make up about three-fourths of the "party of nonvoters." At the top of the social pyramid, three-quarters or so of the people who belong to the professional and managerial class voted for President in

---

[11] Arthur Hadley, *The Empty Polling Booth* (Englewood Cliffs, N.J.: Prentice-Hall, 1978).

Table 10–3 The 1984 Presidential Election: The Total Picture

CATEGORY	NUMBER	PERCENT OF POTENTIAL ELECTORATE
Potential electorate (citizens 18 and over)	168,336,000	100.0%
Estimated registered	127,000,000	75.4
Voted for President	92,645,261	55.0
Nonvoters	75,691,000	45.0
Reagan (R)	54,454,154	32.3
Mondale (D)	37,573,756	22.3
Other	617,351	0.4
Total vote for U.S. House	84,114,309	50.1
Nonvoters for House (excludes D.C.)	83,754,000	49.9
States with Senate elections:		
Potential electorate	87,962,000	100.0%
Voted for President	48,097,505	54.7
Voted for senator	46,221,898	52.5
Voted for U.S. House	42,794,972	48.7

1976. At the bottom, only about 45 percent of semiskilled and unskilled workers did. The pattern was much the same in 1980 and 1984. No such extreme differences occur in other democratic countries.

From 1960 onward, as voting rates have moved steadily down, they have fallen most among those groups whose members were least likely to vote in the first place: the poor and the uneducated. The gap in the voting habits of the different social classes widens all the time, so the well-to-do are a constantly growing proportion of the total active electorate.

Mostly Democrats. Fifty years ago, the New Deal realignment came about because the Democrats succeeded in mobilizing nonvoters, mostly working-class people. Today, too, the poor and the uneducated tend to vote for the Democrats if they vote at all, so the fall in electoral turnout and the decay of party organization hurt the Democrats far more than the Republicans.

It follows that if turnouts ever start to rise, the Democrats stand to gain. How might this be done? One thing is sure: The largely middle-class wars over cultural issues did not encourage Democratic nonvoters to turn out; it probably discouraged them. The massive increase in the ranks of nonvoters—about 75 million of them in 1984—is the most telling of all commentaries on the Democratic leaders' inability to raise issues that interest the people they claim to represent.

Does It Matter? Would it make a difference if the 75 million nonvoters came to the polls in the future? Perhaps not. Some people think that voters and nonvoters share a common set of social and political attitudes.[12] Perhaps,

---

[12] Raymond Wolfinger and Steven Rosenstone, "The Effect of Registration Laws on Voter Turnout," *American Political Science Review* (1978), 22–45. See also their book-length study, *Who Votes?* (New Haven: Yale Univ., 1980).

though, it would matter. In the first place, our very low rates of voting may undermine the legitimacy of our democratic system. Second, without doubt they affect the content of government policy. President Reagan, for example, had much more trouble persuading Congress to cut student loans—which mostly benefit people who vote—than persuading it to cut food stamps, which mostly benefit nonvoters.

Mr. Reagan won massive victories in 1980 and 1984, but they were based on some of the lowest and most class-skewed turnouts in American history. The low turnout does not diminish the importance of his victories and may, in fact, represent one aspect of their importance. Republicans still seem to represent a minority of all Americans, but Mr. Reagan's triumphs show that they are a well-to-do minority, much more unified and organized than their opponents.

THE 1984 ELECTION

We Americans are always in the happy position of knowing that our next presidential election will be held on the first Tuesday after the first Monday in November of the next leap year. In 1984 the appointed day was November 6. Everyone knew the date of the election and of every caucus, primary, and convention leading up to it. Candidates for the presidency therefore started campaigning very early—indeed, they have long been caught up in a virtual "permanent campaign."[13] The first event of the presidential season is now the Iowa caucus, held in the January before the voting, but most candidates take to the road long before then. The whole business literally takes years.

In fact, the quest for our highest office begins the day after the last election. It takes time to build organizations in all fifty states, to flatter reporters and party leaders, and to parade the candidate's name and face before an uncaring public. Many would-be Presidents start in earnest two years before Election Day, and that is none too early.

Choosing the Delegates

Most delegates to presidential nominating conventions are now chosen in primaries—not in every state, but each state that has a primary also has its own rules. In some states, delegates are distributed among candidates by **proportional representation;** the number of delegates that each gets reflects the candidate's share of the vote. Under the **winner-take-all** system, which only the Republicans now use, the person who wins the largest percentage takes all that state's convention delegates. In still other states, would-be delegates do not pledge to support particular candidates; a separate "beauty contest" gives the voters a chance to back one, although the preference vote is not always binding.

About a quarter of the delegates are chosen in statewide conventions. Delegates to those state conventions are elected by district caucuses that any registered party member may attend. The earliest caucuses, in Iowa and Maine, are now full-fledged media events; later ones are eclipsed by primaries.

---

[13] Sidney Blumenthal, *The Permanent Campaign*, rev. ed. (New York: Simon & Schuster, 1982).

The Road to San Francisco

President Reagan announced his candidacy for reelection in February 1984. He was assured of getting the Republican nomination and indeed had no opposition. As always, however, the Democrats were fighting among themselves. Walter Mondale, Jimmy Carter's Vice-President, entered the race and won the endorsement of the AFL-CIO, the national labor federation (see Chapter 6). Labor's support and the backing of many fellow politicians made Mondale the front-runner. Yet they also linked him with the special interests, with Washington, and with traditional liberalism. These were not sources of strength.

As expected, Mondale won in the Iowa caucuses; Colorado's Senator Gary Hart came in a strong second. Three candidates from the party's moderate wing—Senators John Glenn of Ohio and Ernest Hollings of South Carolina, and former Governor Reuben Askew of Florida—did not have much support. Neither did two candidates from the party's left, Senator Alan Cranston (Calif.) and former Senator George McGovern (S.D.), the disastrous candidate of 1972.

The New Hampshire primary, the first and most important of the lot, was held on February 23, 1984. Every four years that small, not especially virtuous or typical state is invaded by the candidates and by the wise men and women of the newspapers and TV. Indeed, the contest is now a major source of business, and state law actually requires New Hampshire's primary to precede all the others. The status of front-runner, usually conferred on the victor, tends to be self-fulfilling: Since 1952, no candidate of either party has become President without winning the first primary.

In February 1984 it was won by Hart. Yet even then the support of labor and the politicians gave Mondale more delegates overall. Mondale was tarnished as the front-runner, but Hart could never firmly establish himself in

Mondale addresses an AFL-CIO conference. Labor's support made him the front runner early on but also linked him with special interests and traditional liberalism—not sources of strength in the 1984 election.

UPI/Bettmann Newsphotos

the role. It was not for want of trying, however. The Colorado senator, McGovern's 1972 campaign manager, had revamped himself as a moderate; his theme, "new ideas," was meant to keep traditional liberalism at arm's length. Hart, moreover, put himself forward as the spokesman of a new class, the Yuppies (young urban professionals), many of whom are not ordinarily Democrats.

On February 24, the candidates and the mass media gratefully left New Hampshire and moved on to "Super Tuesday" (note the football metaphor) primaries in five states on March 13.[14] Hart did well, but Mondale survived and stayed ahead in the delegate count. Mondale had big victories in three primaries held in late March and early April: Illinois, New York, and Pennsylvania.[15] Then there was a lull, followed by the four-state[16] "Super Tuesday II" on May 8, which Hart swept. After Nebraska and Oregon voted (May 15), the survivors met in the June 5 "Super Bowl." Hart took California, but Mondale had never lost his lead in delegates, and his victory in New Jersey gave him enough support to clinch the nomination.[17]

Refusing to give up, Hart continued to maneuver in hopes of upsetting Mondale at the convention. The only other candidate still in the Democratic race was the Rev. Jesse Jackson, a black activist. Representing the extreme of militant liberalism, he took the black vote—the largest single bloc of Democrats—in primary after primary but generally failed to build a "rainbow coalition" of liberals, minorities, and the poor of all races. No doubt he was not helped in his efforts to do so by a remark he made describing Jews as "Hymies" and New York City as "Hymietown." Charges of anti-Semitism dogged his campaign and made it hard for Mondale and Hart to bid for his support without offending Jews, the only other ethnic group in the country that still supports the Democrats. Even so, Jesse Jackson showed that blacks do have a large number of votes and can use them in a disciplined way.

The Democrats held their convention in San Francisco, a symbol of cultural liberalism. Despite Hart's apparently greater popularity in polls against President Reagan, Mondale was nominated—not because he was the stronger candidate but because the party and the unions knew and trusted him. This may be a very good reason for electing a man President, yet it is clear that the American public did not think so.

The Republican convention met in Dallas, a symbol of the new conservatism. It duly nominated Mr. Reagan.

Fall Classic

We Americans have two kinds of elections. In one, people make up their minds early and don't budge. The speeches, the rallies, the motorcades, the debates, and the commercials do not seem to make the slightest bit of difference. In the other, both major-party candidates are weak, and the voters are indecisive. Obviously, 1984 was the kind of election that is over before it starts.

---

[14] Alabama, Florida, Georgia, Massachusetts, and Rhode Island.

[15] Connecticut, the District of Columbia, and Tennessee went to the polls at this time as well.

[16] Indiana, Maryland, North Carolina, and Ohio.

[17] The other states with primaries on this day were New Mexico, South Dakota, and West Virginia.

In what little we had of a campaign, Mr. Reagan congratulated himself on nearly eliminating inflation and on promoting the highest rise in income levels since 1951. Mondale was ignored when he suggested that future generations would resent our running up the highest deficit ever to finance a moment of false prosperity. His promise to reduce that deficit by raising taxes to pay it off was one of the most imprudent ever made by a politician. Besides, this was not the sort of issue that would bring out the millions of nonvoters, mostly low-income men and women of vague Democratic leanings.

Mondale did get a certain amount of play out of the "fairness" issue, the belief that Ronald Reagan had enriched the top fifth of American society at the expense of the bottom fifth. For better or worse, however, the poor are much less likely to vote than the rich, who do not view their own good fortune as unfair.

Ferraro. The one unpredictable influence in the campaign was Mondale's decision to make Rep. Geraldine Ferraro (N.Y.) his vice-presidential running mate, the first woman nominated by a major party for that office. Mondale's choice gave his ticket historic significance that may have been the only possible prize in a Republican year. Nonetheless, it seems to have made more people vote against the Democrats than for them. An intelligent, capable person, Ferraro did not have the credentials many voters expected of a Vice-President of the United States. Some Americans believed quite strongly that her presence on the ballot made a statement that was far more important than credentials, whose relevance is perhaps doubtful. A larger number of Americans objected to the idea of nominating a woman because she was a woman, and they carried the day.

Finally, Mr. Reagan won by using his inspired, though not infallible skills as a national cheerleader. Our political culture is an optimistic one, and there is also something in that old saw, "Laugh and the world laughs with you; cry and you cry alone." Mr. Reagan and the country laughed in a summer and fall of Olympic triumphs and relatively high employment; Mr. Mondale cried alone of deficits and difficulties. "Whine on, harvest moon," Vice-President George Bush commented.

The Day After

Never was the outcome of the 1984 presidential election in doubt—not in the primaries, not at the conventions, not during the campaign, and certainly not on voting day. As expected, Ronald Reagan won reelection by a landslide.

Table 10–4 The Presidential Vote, 1984

CANDIDATE	POPULAR VOTE	PERCENTAGE	ELECTORAL VOTE
Ronald W. Reagan (R)	54,454,154	58.8*	525
Walter F. Mondale (D)	37,573,756	40.6	13
All others	617,351	0.7	—
Total	92,645,261	100.0	

Reagan's percentage of 2-party vote: 59.17
Reagan's plurality: 16,880,398

* This figure is calculated on the basis of the total vote, not the 2-party vote.

Victorious in the whole country except Mondale's native Minnesota and the heavily black District of Columbia, Reagan carried the electoral college by a whopping 525-to-13 margin (Table 10-4). Since the birth of the American party system some 150 years ago, only one President had won a larger electoral vote: Franklin D. Roosevelt, in 1936.

Prevailing almost everywhere, the President had his greatest triumphs in the Mountain States, the Great Plains, and the South. Defeated almost everywhere, Mr. Mondale did best in the larger states of the Northeast and Midwest, and on the West Coast. Yet in the popular (as opposed to electoral) count, Mr. Reagan's 59.2 percent of the vote for the two major parties was by no means historic; it ranked only sixth among presidential landslides (Table 10-5).[18] Moreover it was a very lonely landslide, for Mr. Reagan had very short coattails; he carried relatively few Republicans into office with him.

These undoubted truths do not make Mr. Reagan's masterful performance on the stump a bit less impressive. Indeed, they do not even rule out sweeping claims that he won a mandate for his policies and his idea of the future. Instead, they point up a basic fact of politics: In years of relative peace and prosperity, incumbents almost always win. If they are very popular or their opponents are very unpopular, incumbents tend to win by a landslide. Mr. Reagan was a very popular incumbent running against a much less popular challenger in what most people saw as a time of peace and plenty. The results had always been predictable, and most observers had predicted them.

Rise and Fall. You can see how directly Mr. Reagan's popularity rose and fell with the economy by looking at the record of elections and public-opinion polls conducted from 1981 to 1984. Early in his first term, inflation dropped from its double-digit levels in 1980–1981 to less than 5 percent. At the same time, however, profit rates fell, stocks of goods piled up because consumers could not afford to buy them, and "real" interest rates (see Chapter 16) and unemployment stood at the highest levels since the Great Depression in the 1930s. Times were hard, and the Republican party paid the price for them in the congressional elections of 1982. Yet throughout the recession, polls showed that voters liked Ronald Reagan as a man and leader. Many people

---

[18] Calculated on a two-party basis. Calculated on the basis of the total vote, Mr. Reagan won the fifth-ranking landslide in our history.

Table 10–5 Twentieth-Century Presidential Landslides (Two-Party Vote)

YEAR	WINNER	PERCENTAGE	LOSER	PERCENTAGE
1920	Harding (R)	63.83	Cox (D)	36.17
1936	F. Roosevelt (D)	62.46	Landon (R)	37.54
1972	Nixon (R)	61.79	McGovern (D)	38.21
1964	L. Johnson (D)	61.34	Goldwater (R)	38.66
1904	T. Roosevelt (R)	60.01	Parker (D)	39.99
1984	Reagan (R)	59.17	Mondale (D)	40.83
1932	F. Roosevelt (D)	59.16	Hoover (R)	40.84
1928	Hoover (R)	58.80	Smith (D)	41.20
1956	Eisenhower (R)	57.76	Stevenson (D)	42.24
1952	Eisenhower (R)	55.40	Stevenson (D)	44.60
1980	Reagan (R)	55.30	Carter (D)	44.70

wanted to give him a chance, to see if his programs would work out or luck out in the end.

And they did, or at least so it seemed by Election Day. To a degree that surprised almost all forecasters,[19] the economy roared back from its troubles. Apparently, to be reelected, an incumbent chief executive must only "prime the pump" sufficiently to ensure vigorous economic growth.[20] Jimmy Carter failed to do this in 1980,[21] when the growth in per capital disposable income was actually negative (−0.6 percent) for the first time since 1932. Not by chance, that was the most recent time an incumbent President was not reelected.

Continental Drift. This model of the electorate's behavior may seem rather cynical. It is, but it is also hard to dispute. Much evidence seems to show that lacking detailed information about the economy or about any political subject, most Americans react mainly to short-term changes that directly affect their lives. In the 1982 election we were reacting mainly to the recession. In 1984 we were reacting mainly to its end.

There were other issues, however. When Ronald Reagan took charge in 1981, the country was in a state of confusion. Our humiliation at the hands of a few Iranian teenagers who had stormed the U.S. embassy in Teheran had lowered us in the eyes of the world. Taxes, bureaucracy, and the federal government were disliked by many Americans, especially in the West and the South. Cultural issues like abortion and school prayer had created deep divisions. The country seemed to be adrift.

Ronald Reagan had therefore promised to bring us much more than an economic recovery. Before he entered politics in the early 1960s, he had been prominent as a film actor in the 1930s and 1940s and as a television announcer in the 1950s. He was a man of another era, and that was exactly his attraction in a world where many people wanted to revive traditional values. By 1984 the White House had persuaded a sizable body of opinion that he had actually succeeded in reviving those values, at least to some extent. Mr. Reagan's campaign theme, "America is back," reflected this happy state of mind. For many Americans, the long national leadership crisis was finally at an end.

Not, of course, for all Americans. The profile of each candidate's voters suggests that ours is still a divided country, almost two countries. The Republicans claim the historical core of our population: relatively well-off, white, Protestant, and conservative. The Democrats get their support from a much more marginal America: the poor, blacks and other nonwhite minorities, women, single people, and the Jews. Pollsters found that the President's supporters stressed the issues of inflation, rising taxes, government spending, and leadership. Mr. Mondale's followers believed that "he cares about people like me," and pointed to unemployment, nuclear-arms control, environmental protection, and civil rights as the issues that concerned them.

---

[19] Since the recovery was in essence an old-fashioned deficit-induced revival similar to many in the past, this surprise was itself surprising. Without admitting it, Mr. Reagan took a few tips from John Maynard Keynes, the founding father of liberal economics (see Chapter 16).

[20] The classic study of the relationship between the economic cycle and the presidential election cycle is Edward R. Tufte's *Political Control of the Economy* (Princeton: Princeton Univ., 1978).

[21] Jack Germond and Jules Witcover, *Blue Smoke and Mirrors: How Reagan Won and Why Carter Lost the Election of 1980* (New York: Vintage, 1981).

Table 10-6 Vote for the House of Representatives, 1984

PARTY	VOTE	PERCENTAGE	SEATS Preelection	SEATS 1984	Swing
Republican	39,520,345	47.0	168	182	+14
Democratic	43,903,184	52.2	267	253	−14
All others	690,000	0.8	—	—	—
Total	84,114,309	100.0	435	435	. . .

Democratic percentage of 2-party vote: 52.63
Republican percentage of 2-party vote: 47.37
Democratic plurality: 4,382,839

The Lonely Landslide

The 1984 election broke a number of records. Here we will cite just two. First, in more than three-quarters of all contests for the House, the winners took over 60 percent of the vote. Closely connected to this remarkable statistic was another: Since the 1830s, no President has ever entered a term of office with less support in the House than Ronald Reagan had in 1985.

In fact, more than most landslides in our history, Mr. Reagan's reelection was largely a personal achievement and tribute. Republican strategists had dreamed that his coattails might restore to the party the 26 seats it had lost in the 1982 House elections, and produce a net gain of 1 or 2 seats in the Senate. It was not to be. In the end, the GOP picked up only 14 seats in the House, where the party balance now stood at 253 for the Democrats, 182 for the Republicans (Table 10-6). The party also lost 2 incumbent senators, in Illinois and Iowa, despite the President's victory in both states, and was beaten for the seat vacated by outgoing Senator Howard Baker of Tennessee. In exchange, the GOP added only 1 Senate seat, in Kentucky. It wound up with 53 senators, to the Democrats' 47—for the latter, a net increase of 2 (Table 10-7). These results were all the more disappointing to the Republicans because President Reagan, unlike Richard Nixon in 1972, had really tried to help his party's ticket.

Incumbents First. Why did a country that voted decisively for a conservative Republican President also elect a strongly Democratic House and weaken Republican control of the Senate? There was nothing really new about this; the voters have been sending mixed signals for quite a long time, mainly

Table 10-7 Vote for the U.S. Senate, 1984

PARTY	VOTE	PERCENTAGE	SEATS AT STAKE IN 1984 Held Preelection	SEATS AT STAKE IN 1984 Held after Election	Swing
Republican	22,857,480	49.5	19	17	−2
Democratic	22,994,745	49.7	14	16	+2
All others	369,673	0.8	—	—	—
Total	46,221,898	100.0			

Republicans (total): 53
Democrats (total): 47

Local Interests in a Local Race

The most expensive congressional election in the history of Connecticut was worth every penny for Democratic U.S. Rep. Bruce A. Morrison, who was re-elected to a second term in Congress Tuesday despite a Reagan landslide in the 3rd District.

"I didn't raise one dime too much and I didn't work one day too long or one hour too long," said Morrison, who spent $800,000 to withstand a challenge by former Republican Congressman Lawrence J. DeNardis.

Bruce Morrison, running in one of the most liberal districts in the nation, won re-election because he projected a basically conservative point of view.

Bruce Morrison took care of first things first.

"I'm a basically conservative voter," said a friend during Tuesday night's . . . vote tally. "But how can you vote against a guy whose main concern is local issues? Bruce Morrison's big concern is for the people of his district. Forget about national deficits or nuclear energy abuses. Bruce took care of the old and the poor. He was concerned about the things that the average person cared about. Ronald Reagan was popular but Bruce Morrison understood what politics meant at a local level."

"I just bought a restaurant," said one downtown New Haven bar owner. "My main deal voting for Morrison was that he was going to be worried about me as an individual. I have no problem with Larry DeNardis, but it seems to me that I can't wait for a lot of promises. I voted for Bruce Morrison because he already showed me that he was going to deliver on his promises."

"I voted for Morrison because he tended to local business," said a friend of mine who has moved on to the concrete pastures of New York, but who has maintained his Connecticut voting privileges. "He's always cared about my mother and my father and about the welfare of all the old folks in this district. I might have moved out of this district, but I think that Bruce Morrison has proved that he cares about the same things I care about."

Another friend of mine explained it differently.

"Reagan has his own deal," said my friend, "but he doesn't understand what makes people vote for him. I'd never vote for him because I'm a born Democrat and he's a Republican. But he stands for a lot of the things that I stand for. Bruce Morrison refuses to accept that there's a conservative tide sweeping the country, and so do I. There are problems that are both local and national, and I think that's why he was elected. People perceived that he wanted to fight for both local and national issues and that he was willing to sacrifice, but only if it was really necessary. That's the tradition of our area."

Another of my friends disagreed.

"Morrison won because of the Yalies," he said. "The Yalies gave him a plurality that he couldn't have had if it was up to local voters. Morrison is a liberal whose only concern is the well-being of the minorities."

And yet another viewpoint was espoused in a downtown ginmill, one of the more popular watering-holes in the city.

"The philosophies of the 60s and 70s are dead," a friend said. "The Democrats have got to start to stand for something positive, not something negative. Bruce Morrison understands that. That's why he won this year. He's not negative, he's positive. He wants things to happen, not stop."

"Bruce Morrison," said yet another friend, "stands for progress. The voters saw that."

George Wadley, "Around Town," *New Haven Register*, November 7, 1984, p. 2.

Some Data on This Race

MONEY RAISED (to Sept. 30, 1984)			VOTES CAST		
Candidate	Money	Percent of Money	Candidate	Vote	Percent
B. Morrison (D)	$1,143,047	67.3	B. Morrison (D) (incumbent, elected 1982)	129,230	52.6
L. DeNardis (R)	555,682	32.7	L. DeNardis (R) (ex-incumbent, lost 1982)	115,939	47.2
			Other	626	0.2
Total	$1,698,779*	100.0	Total	245,795	100.0

* This was the third most expensive out of 435 congressional contests in 1984.

because parties, party organizations, and party labels now count for very little (see Chapter 9). Incumbent senators and representatives run as individuals who can protect the interests of a state or a district and its people, not as members of a party seeking to promote a party program. Meanwhile, Presidents bypass their own parties and speak directly to the people by manipulating the newspapers and TV, in what political scientist Thomas Patterson calls the "mass media election."[22]

The divided outcome of 1984 was also a product of Mr. Reagan's utterly unideological message, "America is back." Here was the voice of incumbency, and it cast a glow over all other incumbents, most of whom were Democrats. On November 6, the electorate responded to such cues by voting in all sorts of officeholders, regardless of party.

To survive, all that congressional Democrats had to do was to run, on average, about 18 percentage points ahead of Walter Mondale in House races and 21 percent in the Senate. Large numbers of them did; some races had far greater spreads. In North Dakota, Walter Mondale took just 34.3 percent of the two-party vote; Byron Dorgan, a popular Democratic incumbent, won 78.7 percent, a spread of 44.4 percentage points! In New Jersey, Ronald Reagan had 60.5 percent of the two-party vote, taking all but 1 of the state's 21 counties. Yet incumbent Senator Bill Bradley (D) won no less than 64.7 percent of the vote and a majority in every single county. Among the 145 Democratic House incumbents, only 6 lost their seats (4.1 percent), and a mere 3 of the 114 Republican incumbents lost theirs, a high survival rate indeed!

The presidential result had much more impact on the fate of seats that were open, those without incumbents. Outside the South in 1984, the Democrats lost nearly half of the open positions last held by a member of the party; the Republicans held on to all of theirs. Unluckily for them, there were very few vacancies—only 17 out of 266 contested nonsouthern seats—6.4 percent, one of the lowest figures ever. Such small pickings did not threaten Democratic control of the House.

The Money Game

If 1984 was a year of incumbency, so in a sense is every year. As we have seen, the Republican party as a whole raises and spends far more money than the Democrats can. But this general truth does not explain the reality of 435 separate congressional districts and 50 different states. The true rule of thumb, which has few exceptions, is this: The safer a seat appears to be, the more lopsided are the resources available to the officeholder but not to the challenger. Most seats, moreover, are very safe. Incumbent Democrats usually have a clear financial advantage over their Republican opponents, and incumbent Republicans are similarly blessed.

You might think that big givers—wealthy people, for the most part—would support only Republicans in hopes of electing enough of them to the House and Senate to impose a consistently conservative program. In fact, few wealthy givers have ideological goals. What they want is access to decision makers, usually to have influence on specific questions—a tax exemption here, a subsidy there. If you know that an incumbent has a ten-to-one shot at

---

[22] Thomas F. Patterson, *The Mass Media Election* (New York: Praeger, 1980).

being reelected, you have good reason to bet on a sure thing, even a Democratic one, especially a committee chairman.

Room at the Top

Well-entrenched in Congress and well-funded by special interests, the Democrats are the experts in modern campaigning and district management. Congressional politics is unquestionably their strength; on this level and this level alone, they won the election of 1984. Yet the Republican party, which is even better funded by fairly similar special interests, has emerged as the normal presidential majority party.

Meanwhile, the old New Deal coalition (see Chapter 9) seems to have fallen apart, particularly in the South and the Mountain States. In principle, any Republican candidate should be able to defeat any Democratic candidate in 1988. Don't bet the farm on this probability, however.

Critical Realignment. Has Ronald Reagan brought to pass a critical realignment? In one sense, certainly. The President took office in 1981 with a coherent program for thorough change based squarely—and to a degree almost unique in our history—on a firm political ideology. To a truly remarkable extent, he reshaped the national agenda in a sweepingly conservative direction that will be hard to reverse, at least in the short run, no matter who succeeds him.

A few examples will show why. For one thing, the tax cuts of 1981-1983 shrunk the tax base and therefore the amount of money available to pay for social programs. So did the indexing of tax brackets to inflation, which started in 1985 (see Chapter 16). Mr. Reagan's huge budget deficit, by far the biggest ever, will have much the same effect. Our public policies have been realigned, whatever might have happened to our politics.

In any case, the Democrats have been behaving as if they were victims of a realignment, and they ought to know. Walter Mondale admitted after his defeat that he had not set forth a coherent theme and stuck with it. A good deal of mutual distaste continues to divide his followers, the core of the New Deal coalition, from Hart's and from conservative southern and western Democrats. What's more, the number of nonvoters was close to its historic high point in 1984, despite Mondale's unprecedented effort to register new Democrats.

Shopping for a Future. Party activists are now struggling among and within themselves to find themes that can match the power of Mr. Reagan's conservative optimism. New-generation, high-tech, or neoliberal Democrats say that to win a majority among the members of the white American middle class, the party must cut its historic ties to the interest groups that claim to represent labor, racial and ethnic minorities, women, and so forth. Others, like New York's Governor Mario Cuomo, fear that the proposed divorce might imply abandoning labor, racial and ethnic minorities, and women themselves.

One thing is not in doubt: The Democrats lack a common theme and rallying point. For the moment, at least, the ruling ideas of our time are on the other side—just the sort of thing that happened after every critical realignment in the past. But the Reagan administration will not be a true turning point in our history unless the "second American revolution" can make the economy perform reasonably well, with no major crises, over a fairly long period—a generation or more. In addition, the rest of the Reagan program will have to be a success, the corporate elite will have to keep its present unity, and the Democrats will have to remain in their present muddled state.

Such pleasant Republican dreams are by no means certain to come true. Plenty of doubts hang over our economy and our society. Very recent history seems to show that crisis and growth follow each other with great speed, and they are likely to go on doing so. In fact, we have good reason to think that worldwide economic change is taking place ever more rapidly, that it is disruptive and will remain so, and that no one has a model for understanding these upheavals, let alone controlling them. In such a world, will we have the luxury of the 30 or 35 stable years required for an era of realignment? As we said, don't bet the farm on it.

The odds do suggest that the Republicans will have the edge in 1988, all other things being equal. Yet rapid economic change, media-dominated campaigning, and widespread nonvoting have made things very unequal. If most voting Americans remain satisfied with their lives under conservative leadership, the Republicans may hang on to the White House, though not necessarily to the Senate. Will the conditions for general contentment endure? No one can tell. Should they collapse, we may find that the politics of the permanent campaign has changed the nature of critical alignment, if it has not eliminated the very chance of one.

_____ SUMMARY _____

Campaigns and elections change as our society and democracy change. In 1816, the winning presidential candidate, James Monroe, was nominated by a caucus of Democrats in the House of Representatives, and members of the electoral college that actually made him President were chosen mostly by state legislatures. In 1880, the candidates were nominated by party conventions. Parties were strong. Election was by popular vote. A century later, in 1980, candidates were nominated by rubber-stamp conventions, whose delegates were chosen mostly in primaries and caucuses. The parties were weak, and most candidates ran independent campaigns that advertised them as if they were breakfast cereal.

Such campaigns are expensive. Attempts to regulate campaign contributions and diminish the impact of big money have not been very successful. Congress limited the amount of campaign contributions, forced their disclosure, and attempted to replace them, in part, with federal subsidies for presidential elections. But the ingenuity of the lawmaker was frustrated by the ingenuity of the law skirter and by decision of the Supreme Court. Political action committees (PACs) were created by labor and business to pump money through independent campaigns.

Running for President has become a test of endurance, for the campaign now begins on the day after the last election. Candidates depend heavily on paid professionals and paid advertising, which concentrates on themes rather than issues.

Elections are of three types, and it is still not clear where the 1980 election fits in. Maintaining elections do not change the party balance; deviating elections do so, but only in the short run; and realigning elections reshape the political balance and, indeed, the Constitution itself.

The most recent of these realigning elections, in 1932, established the Democrats as the majority party of the United States. The federal government then assumed a responsibility to uphold living standards and to smooth out bumps in the business cycle. The coming of the new order was triggered by the Depression and anticipated by shifts in voting patterns in the 1928 presidential election.

The realignment was made possible, in part, by a high turnout among the poor, who tend to vote Democratic when they vote at all. Starting in 1960, the proportion of the potential electorate that votes began to fall, and it has fallen to the point at which only about half of all adult citizens voted in the 1984 presidential election. The decline is especially marked among the poor and the uneducated, who make up a majority of the party of nonvoters.

The social composition of the electorate is reflected in public policy. There was more resistance in Congress to cuts in student loans (a concern of the middle class) than to reductions in food stamps (a concern of the poor). The low voter turnout is now creating a political vacuum, "the dark underside of democracy," that is being filled largely by special interests.

SUGGESTED READINGS

HERBERT E. ALEXANDER, *Financing Politics: Money, Elections and Political Reform,* 2nd ed. Washington, D.C.: Congressional Quarterly, 1980. Up-to-date analysis by the leading expert in this field.

WALTER DEAN BURNHAM, *Critical Elections and the Mainsprings of American Politics.* New York: Norton, 1970. An account of realigning changes in American electoral politics, primarily from 1896 onward.

CONGRESSIONAL QUARTERLY, *Dollar Politics,* 3rd ed. Washington, D.C.: Congressional Quarterly, 1982. Very current and clearly presented discussion of the present state of law and practice in campaign finance, including an extensive review of the recent rise of political action committees (PACs).

PAUL W. DAVID, RALPH M. GOLDMAN, and RICHARD C. BAIN, *The Politics of National Party Conventions.* Washington, D.C.: Brookings, 1960. The definitive account of national nominating conventions in the prereform era, from the beginning through 1956.

JAMES W. DAVIS, *Presidential Primaries.* Westport: Greenwood Press, 1980. Good contemporary account of the rise and present impact of primaries on the presidential nomination process.

NORMAN H. NIE, SIDNEY VERBA, and JOHN R. PETROCIK, *The Changing American Voter,* 2nd ed. Cambridge: Harvard Univ., 1979. First-rate survey-based analysis of attitudinal changes and candidate choices in post-1960 American presidential elections.

BENJAMIN I. PAGE, *Choices and Echoes in Presidential Elections.* Chicago: Univ. of Chicago, 1978. Incisive and disturbing analysis of campaign tactics used by candidates in today's media-dominated elections; their implications for the health of democracy.

JAMES D. SUNDQUIST, *Dynamics of the Party System.* Washington, D.C.: Brookings, 1973. A valuable study of realignment dynamics and processes back to the disruption of the Jacksonian "system" in the 1850s; particularly useful both for its analytic style and its wealth of historical information.

STEPHEN J. WAYNE, *The Road to the White House.* New York: St. Martin's, 1980. A clear, well-written, and up-to-date review of the whole cycle of presidential election campaigning.

RAYMOND WOLFINGER and STEVEN J. ROSENSTONE, *Who Votes?* New Haven: Yale Univ., 1980. Short and well-crafted contemporary study of the problem of nonvoting in current American elections.

And on the 1984 election:

JACK GERMOND and JULES WITCOVER, *Wake Us When It's Over.* New York: Macmillan, 1985. Cynical but penetrating, and an immense reportorial performance.

ELLIS SANDOZ and C. V. CRABB, JR., eds. *Election 84: Landslide without a Mandate?* New York: New American Library, 1985. Collection of useful essays by election experts.

chapter eleven

THE PRESIDENCY

During World War II, Dr. Robert Oppenheimer directed the project that built the first atomic bomb. Yet he was quite distressed when the United States dropped it on Japan, in August 1945, a few months after Harry Truman became President. Oppenheimer and others soon devised a plan for sharing our atomic energy research with foreign countries. Hoping to persuade Mr. Truman to endorse this plan, Oppenheimer met one day with the President. At the end of the meeting, Mr. Truman wanted to know why Oppenheimer was so upset. Oppenheimer later remembered holding his hands out and saying, "Mr. President, I have blood on my hands."

Mr. Truman then gave him a handkerchief and replied, "I'm the President. I dropped the bomb. Take my handkerchief and wipe the blood off your hands."[1]

The American presidency has been described in many ways—among others, as an "elective monarchy." During the Civil War (1861–1865), Secretary of State William Seward observed that "we elect a king every four years and give him absolute power within certain limits, which after all he can interpret for himself."[2]

Indeed, Samuel Huntington, a well-known political scientist, once called our political arrangements a "Tudor polity": a state system that, in many

---

[1] Theodore H. White, *The Making of the President 1972*, (New York: Bantam, 1973), pp. 496–97.

[2] Edward S. Corwin, *The President, Office and Powers* (New York: New York Univ., 1957).

respects, is closer to the political system England had 400 years ago than to any other.[3] Within this "American-Tudor" political system, the President acts as "monarch," like Henry VIII and Elizabeth I, whose powers were, of course, much greater than those of present-day monarchs.

Of course, American Presidents usually do not make explicit claims to absolute power. (Sometimes, however, in extreme crises, Presidents come very close to acting as if they had such powers.) Huntington's analogy is not and cannot be exact. But consider the similarities between Presidents and Tudor monarchs and the differences between Presidents and prime ministers. Like Henry VIII, and unlike a prime minister, the President is a "single person"—a "monarch"[4] in the literal sense—who directs the executive as a whole. Like Henry VIII, the President chooses the chief officers of state—the members of his cabinet—and dismisses them at will. Like Henry VIII, the President holds office independently of the legislature and cannot be voted out of office by it (except for "high crimes and misdemeanors"). Yet the President, like Henry VIII, can veto acts of the legislature. And the President is the commander-in-chief of the armed forces, the supreme war chief who ultimately appoints and gives orders to all military officers—much as Henry VIII could.

Like the Tudor monarchs, too, our Presidents have repeatedly insisted that they have **prerogative powers,** powers inherent in the executive office itself, requiring neither constitutional nor legislative approval. In certain particularly notorious cases, the U.S. Supreme Court has refused, in principle, to accept such claims: once (in 1952) during the Korean War, when President Truman seized the steel mills in a labor dispute and once (in 1974) when President Nixon refused to release certain tape recordings related to the Watergate affair.[5]

The facts of political life suggest that a prerogative power really is inherent in the presidential office. Sometimes, it has been used vigorously, successfully, and without constitutional challenge. In 1861, for example, President Abraham Lincoln, on his own initiative, suspended the writ of *habeas corpus* (see Chapter 2); increased the size of the regular army and navy; paid out money from the Treasury, without congressional authorization or appropriation; arrested and imprisoned suspected Confederate sympathizers for long periods, without trial or any other legal process; and sent troops to break up the Maryland legislature and arrest some of its members.[6] None of these actions was ever successfully contested in the courts.[7] If the crisis is sufficiently grave, the President becomes, in effect, a kind of "Roman dictator"[8] and the Constitution's guarantees are put on the shelf for the duration of the

---

[3] Samuel P. Huntington, *Political Order in Changing Societies* (New Haven: Yale Univ., 1968), pp. 93–139.

[4] From the Greek *monos* ("alone") + *archein* ("to rule").

[5] *Youngstown Sheet & Tube Co.* v. *Sawyer*, 343 U.S. 579 (1952); *U.S.* v. *Nixon*, 418 U.S. 683 (1974). All the oral arguments and opinions in the *Nixon* case are contained in Leon Friedman, ed., *United States* v. *Nixon* (New York: Chelsea House, 1974), along with abundant background materials.

[6] See the discussion in Edward S. Corwin, *The President: Office and Powers* (New York: New York Univ., 1957), pp. 229–32, and notes.

[7] See Chief Justice Roger B. Taney's laments on this score in *Ex Parte Merryman*, 17 Fed. Cases. 145 (1861).

[8] That is, the President like a dictator in ancient Rome has effectively unlimited powers, but only for the duration of a crisis.

crisis.[9] Later on, after the crisis ends, the U.S. Supreme Court sometimes attempts to clean up the constitutional mess, but very often it does not. We do not yet know—especially in the present age of nuclear terror—what the ultimate limits of the President's "monarchical" power may really be.

Finally, our President, like a monarch but unlike a prime minister, serves as chief of state—the ceremonial leader of the people. In almost all modern political systems, that role is separated from the role of actually leading the government. But the two are fused in our presidency, just as they were in the Tudor monarchy, and their fusion reflects characteristically American attitudes about the nature and purposes of executive power. Presidents must represent "all the people," act for the common good, rise above partisan politics, and even provide "moral leadership." Yet we also expect them to be effective leaders—to bludgeon their policies through Congress and the countless agencies and departments of the executive branch. The presidency is the focal point for political leadership and for our sense of national identity—and these roles sometimes conflict.

Presidents and the presidency almost inevitably generate much controversy and confusion. Under Presidents Lyndon Johnson (1963–1969) and Richard Nixon (1969–1974), there was talk of an "imperial presidency"—of presidential excesses that had sapped the powers and rights of Congress.[10] But Mr. Johnson and Mr. Nixon were followed in office by Gerald Ford

---

[9] Clinton Rossiter, *Constitutional Dictatorship* (Princeton: Princeton Univ., 1948), pp. 207–314.

[10] This is the position taken by Arthur M. Schlesinger, Jr., in *The Imperial Presidency* (New York: Houghton, 1973).

Seal of our chief of state.

The White House

(1974–1977) and Jimmy Carter (1977–1981), whose weaknesses made many people wonder if the presidency had enough power, not too much. Can any one person fill the job? Would Ronald Reagan (1981–   ) and his successors be able to balance our yearning for effective presidential leadership, on the one hand, and for presidential virtue, on the other?

AN INDEPENDENT EXECUTIVE

The separation of powers among the executive, legislative, and judicial branches is the great fact of life in American government. Congress and the President are coequal—distinct, yet deeply involved in each other's activities.

The Sharing of Power

Article II of the Constitution sets forth the President's powers and responsibilities. It begins by declaring, "The executive power shall be vested in a President of the United States of America"—that is, in the President and the President alone. Article II then defines some of the major components of the executive power: The President shall "take Care that the Laws be faithfully executed. . . . " The President shall be commander-in-chief of the army and navy of the United States. With the advice and consent of the Senate, the President shall make treaties and nominate ambassadors, judges, and all other officers of the United States. And from time to time, the President shall give to the Congress information on the state of the union and recommend consideration of certain measures.

Each of these powers is limited. The President is the core of the executive branch, but Congress meddles, as it was meant to, with the execution of the laws and with the President's other powers, too. The Constitution gives Congress the most important of the weapons with which it checks the President: the power to legislate and to appropriate funds. It also confers on the Senate the duty to give its "advice and consent" to all treaties—by a two-thirds vote—and to many presidential appointments. The President can propose laws, appropriations of money, appointments of officials, and entanglements with foreign powers. But Congress decides whether these proposals will be accepted and in what form. Even the President's power to veto acts of Congress is qualified: Vetoes must be cast against an entire piece of legislation, not against specific provisions, and they can be overridden by a two-thirds vote of the House and Senate.

In Richard Neustadt's phrase, the Constitution creates a "government of separated institutions sharing powers."[11] The separation was intended to prevent "a gradual concentration of the several powers in the same department."[12] The sharing was designed to give the separate branches the incentive and the means to check one another. "Ambition," wrote James Madison, "must be made to counteract ambition."[13] The Constitution was designed to create—and does create—major institutional barriers to unified policy making.

[11] Richard E. Neustadt, *Presidential Power, The Politics of Leadership from FDR to Carter* (New York: Wiley, 1980), p. 26.
[12] James Madison, *The Federalist,* Paper 15 (New York: Mentor Books, 1961), p. 321.
[13] Ibid., p. 322.

Our President Is *Not* a Prime Minister

Under a parliamentary system, the head of government is the "prime minister" or "premier." Our President, too, is a head of government, but our President is not a prime minister. The basic differences are two: A prime minister is not the sole head of the executive, quite separate from the pretensions of the head of state (usually a hereditary monarch or a President elected by the legislature). A prime minister heads a team of political leaders, called the cabinet, and is only a "first among equals." The cabinet as a whole has collective responsibility for running the government. Second, a prime minister has the support of the legislature's majority.

The President

The President and the members of the U.S. Congress are elected by the voters, one by one. (More or less by the voters, in the President's case—as we shall soon see.) Congress cannot vote the President into office or out of it—unless they begin impeachment proceedings. The President has no assurance of support in Congress and, often, no expectation of it. The President, the members of the House, and those of the Senate have different and fixed terms, not concurrent ones.

As a result, different branches of the federal government can be controlled by different parties. During the eight years (1969–1977) of the Nixon and Ford Administrations, which were Republican, the Democrats managed to keep healthy majorities in the House and the Senate—even in 1972, when Richard Nixon won a landslide election over Senator George McGovern (D–S.D.). The very same thing had happened during 6 of the 8 years (1955–1961) of the Republican President before that, Dwight D. Eisenhower (1953–1961). In 1980, Ronald Reagan overwhelmed President Carter, the Democrats took a 51-seat majority in the House, and the Republicans, after 27 years, finally regained control of the Senate by 7 seats.

Divided party control of our executive and legislative branches reinforces their separation and further prevents unified policy making. Yet even when the same party controls both Congress and the White House, the two branches remain separate and independent. Despite heavy Democratic majorities in both Houses, President Carter and the Democratic Congress bickered continually.

The President's influence in Congress varies significantly from administration to administration and from issue to issue. The limits of presidential influence hang on the public's support for the various parts of the President's program, the party balance in Congress, and the President's personal skills. Most Presidents have at least some success with Congress during the early months of their administrations—the so-called honeymoon period—but with time, success becomes more and more elusive.

Prime Ministers. The rules of the parliamentary system require a prime minister to sit in the legislature and lead the party or the coalition that controls it. So the prime minister and the cabinet pretty much control the legislature and, thus, the keys to power. Of course, a Conservative party prime minister in Britain could not abolish private property, and a Labour party

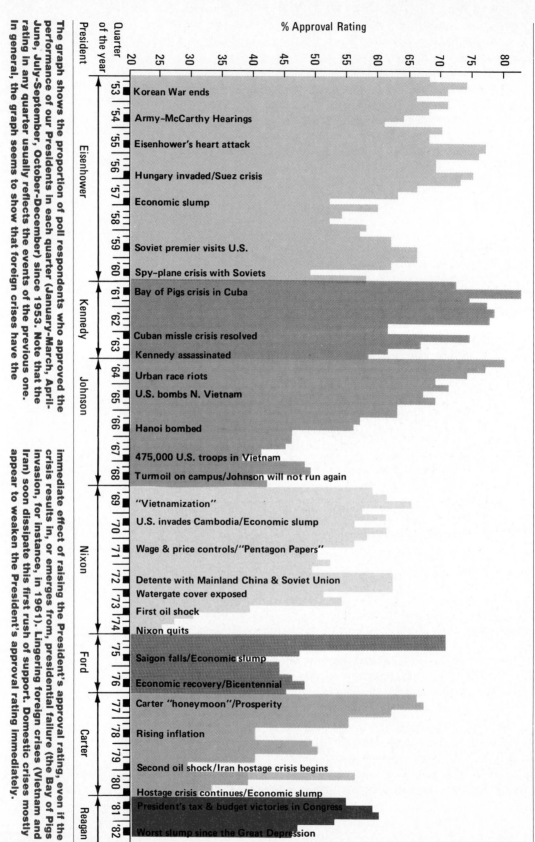

Figure 11-1 Trends in Presidential Approval Ratings by Years and Quarters, 1953–1982

% Approval Rating

President | Quarter of the year

Eisenhower
- '53 Korean War ends
- '54 Army-McCarthy Hearings
- '55 Eisenhower's heart attack
- '56 Hungary invaded/Suez crisis
- '57 Economic slump
- '58
- '59 Soviet premier visits U.S.
- '60 Spy-plane crisis with Soviets

Kennedy
- '61 Bay of Pigs crisis in Cuba
- '62
- '63 Cuban missle crisis resolved
       Kennedy assassinated

Johnson
- '64 Urban race riots
- '65 U.S. bombs N. Vietnam
- '66 Hanoi bombed
- '67 475,000 U.S. troops in Vietnam
- '68 Turmoil on campus/Johnson will not run again

Nixon
- '69 "Vietnamization"
- '70 U.S. invades Cambodia/Economic slump
- '71 Wage & price controls/"Pentagon Papers"
- '72 Detente with Mainland China & Soviet Union
- '73 Watergate cover exposed
       First oil shock
- '74 Nixon quits

Ford
- '75 Saigon falls/Economic slump
- '76 Economic recovery/Bicentennial

Carter
- '77 Carter "honeymoon"/Prosperity
- '78 Rising inflation
- '79
- '80 Second oil shock/Iran hostage crisis begins
       Hostage crisis continues/Economic slump

Reagan
- '81 President's tax & budget victories in Congress
- '82 Worst slump since the Great Depression

The graph shows the proportion of poll respondents who approved the performance of our Presidents in each quarter (January-March, April-June, July-September, October-December) since 1953. Note that the rating in any quarter usually reflects the events of the previous one. In general, the graph seems to show that foreign crises have the immediate effect of raising the President's approval rating, even if the crisis results in, or emerges from, presidential failure (the Bay of Pigs invasion, for instance, in 1961). Lingering foreign crises (Vietnam and Iran) soon dissipate this first rush of support. Domestic crises mostly appear to weaken the President's approval rating immediately.

prime minister could not abolish old-age pensions—their parties would revolt. But within the limits set by political conditions and the nature of their parties, prime ministers can do what they think right and wise. That is much more than any President can count on doing.

Presidential Timber

Because a prime minister leads a parliamentary party[14] and is elected by it, no outsider stands a chance. Most prime ministers have years of experience in parliament and in government office. Their colleagues have many opportunities to judge their abilities and their temperaments.

How different is the way we elect a President of the United States! Except in rare circumstances, Congress has no role whatever. The voters, who elect the President more or less directly through the rubber-stamp electoral college, do not always seem to care if the candidates have a suitable background in national politics or the skills that win influence on Capitol Hill. Perhaps the voters are not in a position to know. Many of our Presidents never served in Congress or, indeed, in any other branch of the federal government. Presidents Carter and Reagan had been governors. President Johnson, who was notably successful with Congress, had been a senator and a congressman, but so too had John F. Kennedy (1961–1963), who was not successful with legislators. During the nineteenth century, military service was among the well-traveled routes to the White House, but in the present century the only general to make it was Dwight D. Eisenhower.

---

[14] The members of a party who sit in parliament.

President Lyndon B. Johnson came to the presidency from a career as congressman and senator, and was very successful in his handling of Congress. President Dwight D. Eisenhower had been in the army all of his adult life; he found Congress harder to handle.

UPI/Bettmann Newsphotos

Presidents who were major military figures before becoming President:

George Washington (Revolutionary War)

Andrew Jackson (War of 1812)

Zachary Taylor (Mexican War)

Ulysses S. Grant (Civil War)

Dwight D. Eisenhower (World War II)

To this list might be added William Henry Harrison (1841), whose more modest contributions to Indian-fighting and the War of 1812 were his chief assets in the 1840 presidential campaign.

Of course, no one can be elected who cannot first be nominated, and recent changes in the way our parties nominate presidential candidates give obscure and inexperienced people even greater advantages than they used to have. When in 1975 Jimmy Carter announced his candidacy for the Democratic nomination, reporters asked, "Jimmy Who?" By devoting his full time to the campaign, he did well in the early primaries, moved ahead of better-known contenders, and soon emerged as the front-runner. Mr. Carter's "outsider campaign" quite deliberately stressed his *lack* of experience in Washington, politics, and the federal government, and his successor, Ronald Reagan, ran "against" Washington, too, even after he had been President for four years. The idea that ignorance of Washington is somehow a virtue obviously reflects public hostility to government, at least since the Watergate affair. But Presidents so chosen may not know how to run the government.

In fact, winning a presidential election has little to do with the ability to work with Congress, with the federal bureaucracy, and with the political parties. It has become an end in itself. Yet American parties have not always nominated presidential candidates with broad electoral appeal. In 1972, for example, the Democrats chose the very liberal Senator George McGovern, who was intensely disliked by moderates and conservatives, even in his own party. He was buried in the Nixon landslide. McGovern won the nomination because of his superior campaign organization, not because he was popular among Democratic voters, party leaders, or pressure groups. Elections, in other words—especially primary elections—do not always reflect political realities, let alone those of government. McGovern's case was not unique: The Republicans suffered a similar disaster in 1964, when Senator Barry Goldwater (R–Ariz.) ran as the party's nominee against incumbent Lyndon Johnson.

THE PRESIDENCY IN HISTORY

Some members of the Constitutional Convention feared that the President would be a monarch in disguise. Others at the convention worried that the President might be eclipsed by Congress. In a sense, both were right.

The First Presidents

The Framers expected George Washington to be our first President, and that expectation made them willing to experiment with a powerful presidency. Washington did not disappoint the confidence reposed in him: He retired after two terms in office, thereby ending all fears of monarchy (and, in addition, creating a precedent that stood until the 1940 election). This precedent was perhaps his most important contribution to the office.

George Washington was a strong and active President (1789–1797). Although he shaped the limits of the office by refusing to become a king, he shaped its opportunities as well. Instead of waiting passively for Congress to decide on the merits of this bill or that, he and his cabinet proposed policies and worked to build support for them in Congress. He started the practice of meeting regularly with his department heads as a cabinet, or collective group. He asserted the President's right—not explicitly mentioned in the Constitution—to remove officials unilaterally, without the Senate's approval or anyone else's. Some of Washington's innovations were negative ones—things that he did not do. Once, for example, he went to the Senate to discuss a matter and was treated, he thought, rudely. The Senate, it seems, wanted to "advise and consent" in private. President Washington left the Senate declaring, "I'll be damned if I ever go back to that place again." He never did. His later communications with the upper house were all in writing. And when the House of Representatives demanded certain papers and instructions dealing with a treaty, Washington, insisting that their disclosure would be a "dangerous precedent,"[15] refused to hand them over.

George Washington became President by force of his personal standing. He neither had nor needed a real party organization. Thomas Jefferson (1801–1809) was the first to use a political party—the Republicans (today's Democrats, see Chapter 9)—to win the election and then to organize support in Congress. Mr. Jefferson actually helped plan his party's congressional strategy. He showed that party politics could act as a bridge between the presidency and the Congress. His immediate successors were less adept at party leadership than he was. They were dominated by Congress, especially the (then) Republican Caucus in the House.[16]

---

[15] Quoted in Louis W. Koenig, *The Chief Executive*, 4th ed. (New York: Harcourt, 1981), p. 33.

[16] John Marshall, Jefferson's cousin and enemy, saw this point very early, at the time of the 1800 election. He commented that if Jefferson were elected, he would "embody himself in the House of Representatives, and by weakening the office of President," he would "increase his personal power." E. S. Corwin, *The President: Office and Powers* (New York: New York Univ., 1980), p. 18. The sad fate of Jefferson's successors revealed how shrewd and accurate Marshall's prophecy was.

The White House, the official name of the executive mansion, is the oldest public building in Washington. Its cornerstone was laid in 1792, and John Adams was its first resident.

American Airlines

Jacksonian Democracy

In Washington's day, and in Jefferson's, most members of the electoral college, which actually chooses the President, were appointed by state legislatures. Andrew Jackson (1829–1837) was the first President really elected by the people and the first to act, as he himself said, as their "direct representative."[17] In 1824, he made his first run for the office and won more popular votes than any of his opponents: John Quincy Adams, Henry Clay, and William Crawford. But none of the contenders had an electoral majority, so the President was chosen by the House of Representatives, where General Jackson's followers—mainly small farmers and people in the western states—were not well represented. Mr. Adams (1825–1829) became President.

By the 1828 presidential election, however, most of the states were choosing their electors by popular vote, and most states had eliminated property qualifications for voting. Andrew Jackson's coalition could not be stopped. He won the presidency in a landslide, and under his leadership the Democrats acquired the complete apparatus of modern party organization: a mass membership, party officials, a presidential nominating convention, and party platforms.

Andrew Jackson was a strong—in fact, a provocatively strong—leader. He was the first President to veto an act of Congress solely because he disagreed with it; his predecessors had vetoed only bills they thought unconstitutional. He purged from the executive branch officials he considered insufficiently sympathetic to him and his policies and replaced them with good Democrats—initiating the so-called **spoils system** (see Chapter 12). He challenged the states, and he challenged Congress. For the next century, strong Presidents took him as their model.

The Presidency, 1837–1932: Theory and Reality

Not all of Jackson's successors, by any means, were strong. Indeed, many of them were about as insignificant to their own contemporaries as they are to us.

The Limited Presidency. One group of Presidents and thinkers about the office believed that it should have only those powers specifically granted to it by the Constitution. Congress, they thought, was the rightful center of leadership. A President's job was merely to see that the laws were "faithfully executed," as the Constitution says, and no more.

This view of the presidency had its beginnings among Andrew Jackson's opponents in the Whig party (see Chapter 9), and it is sometimes called the "Whig theory" of presidential power. In the late nineteenth century, it was taken up by conservative Democrats; in the twentieth century, by conservative Republicans. Conservatives, regardless of party, have usually wanted to limit the President's power: They oppose big government, and the president is the spark plug of government. But liberals, too, find it convenient at times to demand limits on presidential power—especially when the President supports policies they oppose. It was liberals, not conservatives, who denounced the "imperial presidency" of Democrat Lyndon Johnson and Republican Richard Nixon.

---

[17] Clinton Rossiter, *The American Presidency*, 2nd ed. (New York: Harcourt, 1960), p. 92.

The rise of the modern interventionist state has not been kind to the Whig theory of presidential power. For in our system of government, the President is and must be the energetic force of government. No one, for example, doubted that President Reagan was a political conservative, but he hardly acted (and hardly could act) in the passive manner of a Grover Cleveland (1885–1889 and 1893–1897) or a William Howard Taft (1909–1913). President Eisenhower tried the Whig approach briefly, in 1953, but had to give it up almost immediately. The responsibilities of today's presidency are simply too vast for any Whig theory.

The Stewardship Theory. Liberals have more commonly argued that the President has the right and the duty to take any action in the national interest, as long as the action is not expressly barred by the Constitution. By the lights of this "stewardship theory," the President is the custodian of the national interest, as opposed to the special and limited interests that dominate Congress. Some conservatives, too, have taken up the stewardship theory because they think that domestic order and national security can be had only under a strong President who is also the commander-in-chief of our armed forces.

The Changing Presidency. Whatever the merits of these theories, real conditions, not theoretical ones, have changed the government, the presidency, and our expectations about them. Before the 1930s, the average citizen living in an average town might encounter only two kinds of federal officials: the letter carrier and the census taker. There was no standing draft, no federal income tax (before 1913), no Social Security, no food-stamp program, no Council of Economic Advisers, no Federal Reserve Board, and no National Labor Relations Board, to name just a few.

In a government of such limited scope, the presidency too was limited, and Congress was usually the dominant branch of government. Woodrow Wilson (1913–1921), who was a university president before he took to politics, quite accurately described this state of affairs in the title of his most famous book, *Congressional Government* (1885). Congressional government, in Professor Wilson's view, was hardly government at all. But most Americans expected little or no government.

Every so often, a great crisis brought forth a strong President. During the greatest of these crises, the Civil War, Abraham Lincoln (1861–1865) ignored legal limits on the size of the armed forces, used public funds and engineered loans without legislative authorization, closed the mails to "treasonable correspondence," and even partly suspended the writ of *habeas corpus* (see Chapters 2, 9, and 10). These and other actions were later submitted to Congress for formal ratification, but Lincoln made it clear that he was ready to act without congressional support.

At the war's end, the presidency was cut down to size. A series of weak and mostly obscure and undistinguished men—the so-called Bearded Presidents— held the office for the rest of the century and into the next. One strong President, Theodore Roosevelt (mustachioed, not bearded), interrupted the line of restrained presidencies. But there were no real crises during Teddy Roosevelt's administration (1901–1909), and, therefore, few opportunities for dramatic action.

Teddy Roosevelt hand-picked his successor, President Taft, one of the weakest of them all; but Mr. Taft was followed by Woodrow Wilson, who in many ways was the first modern President. Wilson came into office with a

The Laugh's on Taft

William Howard Taft (1909–1913), weighing somewhere between 300 and 350 pounds, was the heaviest President. While governor of the Philippines, he sent Elihu Root, Secretary of War (1899–1904), a telegram: "Took long horseback ride today; feeling fine." Root shot back a telegram of his own: "How is the horse?"

program to reorganize the banking system and tighten up the antitrust laws, among other domestic reforms, and he persuaded Congress to act on most of them. After the United States entered World War I, in 1917, he became in effect the dictator of the national economy—the first President who attempted to regulate business to any great extent. Railroads, for example, were nationalized (by statute) for the duration of the war. The remarkable thing about it all was that Mr. Wilson cajoled and used Congress for his own ends, instead of ignoring it, as President Lincoln had sometimes been forced to do.

Woodrow Wilson finally lost his magic touch. After World War I, he played a leading international role in negotiating the Treaty of Versailles, but he did not pay enough attention to the vanity of the still isolationist Senate, which refused to ratify the treaty. Nonetheless, he was among the first American Presidents to play a great role in international diplomacy, and he looked forward to the emergence of the United States as a world power.

The Modern Presidency

Andrew Jackson, Abraham Lincoln, Theodore Roosevelt, and Woodrow Wilson were strong Presidents, but mainly through the force of events and their own personalities. By and large, the public expected weak Presidents, not strong ones. It expected weak government or none at all.

Strong Presidents usually emerged in times of crisis. After 1929, our country was, by earlier standards, in a state of almost permanent crisis. That reconciled us to the much stronger presidency of modern times and to Big Government. First came the Great Depression of the 1930s, which forced the federal government to become responsible for much of the country's economy. Then our role in World War II made the United States a world power. By historical standards, these events occurred almost in the twinkling of an eye. But they so changed the federal government and our expectations of it that even President Reagan, who intended to cut the government's power, had to act as a strong President in order to do so.

The power that the Presidents won was taken from Congress, weakening it permanently. The public came to look on the President as the leader of the government and the country, not just of the executive branch. When a policy seemed to be needed for this problem or that crisis, the President was expected to propose such a policy. Congress found itself reacting to the President's actions, and sometimes it did not have enough information or unity for a serious challenge.

The modern presidency was in large part created by Franklin D. Roosevelt (1933–1945), who served during the great transformations that placed the President at the head of an enormous domestic bureaucracy and military machine. His New Deal may or may not have helped to end the Depression, but it (and the mobilization to fight World War II) did create the idea that the president should and would deal with national problems actively, with a program.

The Presidency Today. By the fall of 1973, the Watergate scandal had wrecked Richard Nixon's presidency. Indeed, Congress had begun to lumber along on the road to impeach him. Public-opinion polls showed that he was less popular than any President since the beginning of public-opinion polls. The President himself was a ruin of a man, hardly able to concentrate on affairs of state. At this point, the Arab-Israeli war of 1973 broke out. To pressure

The Drabbest President

The list of plausible candidates is very long. My favorite is Calvin Coolidge (1923–1929), often called "Silent Cal" because of his extreme taciturnity. Coolidge almost certainly slept more than any other President—up to twelve hours a day, as a rule. The poet and author Dorothy Parker, informed of his death in 1933, inquired, "Calvin Coolidge has died? How can you tell?"

Yet his colorless personality could itself become colorful. For example, at a dinner party President Coolidge was seated next to an attractive woman. The dinner passed in total silence. The lady became more and more uncomfortable. Finally, turning to the President, she said, "Mr. President, I have a bet with a friend that I can get you to say at least three words to me this evening." Giving her a wintry smile, Coolidge replied, "You lose."

Western countries friendly to Israel, Arab countries stopped selling them oil. Quite suddenly, the economies of the whole Western world were shaken.

How did Congress respond? So great was the expectation that the President could deal with a crisis of this sort that Congress delegated to President Nixon—*the very man it was preparing to impeach*—the power to impose rationing of gasoline.

Obviously, the powers of the presidency have proved very difficult to cut down. It would now be more difficult for a President to get us into a war, as President Truman did in Korea and Presidents Kennedy and Johnson did in Vietnam; but that is mainly because of the Vietnam War's effect on public opinion, not because of the War Powers Act of 1973 (see below and Chapter 16). Indeed, the old debate about the nature and scope of presidential power has largely disappeared. President Reagan, although a conservative, was an activist President, not only in foreign and defense policy, but—every bit as much—in domestic affairs. Any President must try to seem like a strong leader, because that is clearly what the public wants and expects.

ASPECTS OF PRESIDENTIAL LEADERSHIP

During the 1980 presidential campaign, Ronald Reagan asked the voters:

> Are you better off than you were four years ago? Is it easier for you to go and buy things in the stores . . . ? Is there more or less unemployment in the country . . . ? Is America as respected throughout the world as it was? Do you feel that our security is as safe, that we're as strong as we were four years ago?

These five questions, especially the first one—"Are you better off than you were four years ago?"—may have defeated President Carter. We not only think that the President is in charge of the economy and the world, but also that it is up to the President to make each of us happy.

We know that the President is not really in charge of the economy, and still less in charge of the world. But our expectations of what Presidents can do have grown very much more rapidly than their abilities to fulfill those expectations. Most foreign and domestic crises cannot be predicted. Most government policies are inherited from previous administrations. Much of

UPI/Bettmann Newsphotos

what we expect from a President—for example, a low rate of inflation and unemployment, and a high degree of happiness—may well be impossible (see Chapter 16).

What can Presidents do? Their job, perhaps, is less to formulate and execute policies than to impose some sort of coherence on a government that consists of millions and millions of separate individuals. The President sets the national agenda and makes the people feel that this agenda is somehow being met.

Chief Executive

A famous story about Abraham Lincoln illustrates the powers of the President as head of the executive branch. In 1862, Lincoln told his cabinet that he intended to issue a proclamation freeing the slaves in those states still under Confederate control. The cabinet voted unanimously against any immediate action. "Seven nays, one aye," said Mr. Lincoln. "The ayes have it."

Mr. Lincoln got his way because the President is the sole head of the executive branch—the cabinet-level departments, the agencies and bureaus, and the several million civil and military employees. These millions run the vast juggernaut of laws and programs and make the day-to-day decisions that collectively add up to federal policy. Unlike prime ministers, Presidents do not have to share control over policy with the cabinet or with anyone else. Not in theory, at any rate.

Appointments. Presidents, however, cannot themselves sit beside the desks of all bureaucrats and approve or reject all decisions that they make. Their

PRESIDENT LINCOLN AND HIS CABINET, WITH LIEUT GEN! SCOTT.
IN THE COUNCIL CHAMBER AT THE WHITE HOUSE

A President has final say over the cabinet even if all its members vote against him, as once happened to President Lincoln.

power rests upon the chain of command linking them with every private and secretary. The first level of this chain is composed of the heads of the executive departments, who make up the cabinet, and the heads of the administrative agencies. These people and their immediate subordinates—deputy secretaries, under secretaries, and deputy under secretaries—are "political" officials. They are nominated by the President and confirmed by a majority vote of the Senate, and their job is to represent to their departments the wishes of the President and the political majority behind the President. (Often, however, they do just the opposite.) The President appoints about 1,500 of these officials who, together, make up "the administration."

The appointment of the 1,500 is the first task of newly elected Presidents and usually occupies much of the 10 weeks that separate the election from the inauguration. Some of the people a President might wish to choose may not be willing to serve in government, because they would have to take too great a cut in pay. Others may be politically convenient—popular, let us say, with Congress or with interest groups—but incompetent. Building an administration requires compromises between the President's desires and sense of reality.

Limits of Power. Once men and women are appointed to posts in departments and agencies, they no longer represent the President and the President alone, if they ever did. Surrounded daily by the employees of their own departments and agencies, they come to represent those they work with to the president. They find, too, that Congress controls the organization, staffing, and funding of their departments or agencies. Therefore they have to take Congress into account when making a decision, not just the President. Finally, all but the top 1,500 employees of the government do not work for the President in any sense at all; they work for the *government*. Presidents come and go; they stay. Bureaucrats fall into the habit of viewing the President's policies as a mere interruption of their eternal routines. As President Truman said of Dwight Eisenhower, his successor, "He'll sit here in the White House, and he'll say, 'Do this! Do that!' *And nothing will happen.* Poor Ike—it won't be a bit like the Army. He'll find it very frustrating."[18]

Most presidents come into office thinking that the executive branch can be easily and crisply run. What they learn, eventually, is that there is more to running the executive than "Do this! Do that!" They find, too, that they themselves get little credit if their appointees do good jobs but are blamed if those appointees turn out to be incompetent. Managing the executive is neither glamorous nor politically rewarding.

Help. In theory and in fact, Presidents can dismiss any of their cabinet appointees whenever they want to do so. In practice, this power is not enough to impose the President's will on the federal bureaucracy. Cabinet officers very rapidly become advocates for their departmental interests, which often conflict with the President's. This bureaucratic fact of life has been a persistent theme of complaint from Presidents since Franklin Roosevelt.

President James Buchanan (1857–1861) worked over his own correspondence, with only a single secretary to help him. President Cleveland answered his own telephone! But how often did a telephone ring in those days? The modern presidency has needed—and, to some extent, has acquired—*a personal staff* adequate to develop a program and supervise the bureaucracy. Back in 1937, a commission on reforming the executive branch issued a report whose bottom line was, "The President needs help." Congress responded in 1939 by passing a Reorganization Act that, among other things, set up the **Executive Office of the President** and authorized Presidents to submit reorganization proposals to Congress whenever they wished (see Chapter 12).

In time, the Executive Office of the President acquired many operating units, each with its own separate staff. Most of the assistants who see the President daily work in the **White House Office.** Next to it, the three most important and deeply institutionalized branches of the Executive Office are the Office of Management and Budget (OMB), the National Security Council (NSC), and the Council of Economic Advisers. Each branch gathers information for the President and attempts to coordinate the policies of the various parts of the executive branch.

The Office of Management and Budget. Established as far back as 1921 (but then called the Bureau of the Budget), the OMB prepares the executive budget—the document in which the President sets forth the administration's spending priorities. OMB is the nerve center where the divergent demands and competing interests of the cabinet departments are brought into line with the President's policy objectives (see Chapter 12).

---

[18] Quoted in Richard E. Neustadt, *Presidential Power* (New York: Wiley, 1980), p. 9.

Figure 11-2 Executive Office of the President

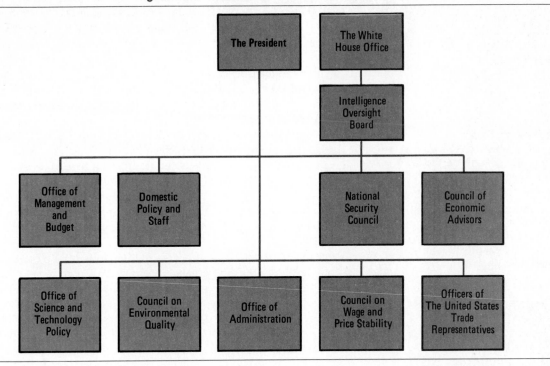

Source: *U.S. Government Manual, 1980/81* (Washington, D.C.: GPO, 1982).

The National Security Council. In 1947, when it had finally become clear that the United States, after decades of isolation, had taken on permanent worldwide responsibilities, Congress set up the NSC. Its statutory members include the President, the Vice-President, the Secretary of state, and the secretary of defense; and its statutory advisers include the chairman of the Joint Chiefs of Staff and the Director of Central Intelligence. It is run by a presidential assistant called the National Security Adviser (see Chapter 17).

The Council of Economic Advisers. By the end of World War II, it had also become clear that the federal government had taken on a permanent responsibility for managing the American economy. The Council of Economic Advisers, with three members, was set up by the Employment Act of 1946. It keeps abreast of developments in the economy, advises the President about them, and helps prepare the Economic Report of the President, which must now by law be submitted to Congress each year.

The Cabinet. The relative importance of the Executive Office staff, on the one hand, and the cabinet departments, on the other, varies from administration to administration. Some Presidents—John Kennedy, Lyndon Johnson, and Richard Nixon, for example—worked closely with a few cabinet members but never used the cabinet itself as a decision-making body. More generally, Presidents come into office intending to consult the cabinet as a whole on important questions of policy. What they always find out is that any reliance on the cabinet undercuts their own power.

Both Presidents Carter and Reagan started out by attempting to raise the status of the cabinet, and both came to rely on loyalists within the White

Robert McFarlane, National Security Adviser.

Beryl Sprinkle, head of the Council of Economic Advisers.

Larry Speakes, White House Press Secretary.

House. Recent experience seems to show that the cabinet simply cannot act as a decision-making body or even as an advisory one. The interests represented by the various departments are too diverse, and no common bond unites them.

Chief of Staff. Another of the pieties often proclaimed by new Presidents is the idea that all of the top members of their staff will have equal importance and equal access. Sooner or later, one of these people emerges as the favored adviser and "chief of staff" with clear authority over the others. Equality can be maintained only in the absence of conflict. Once conflicts break out—and they will—the President must come down on one side or the other and thereby give it and its members ascendancy. Internal bickering, in addition, usually embarrasses the President, who may appoint a chief of staff simply to impose order or the illusion of order. All Presidents come into office pledged to openness and debate; and they all leave office under a cloud, for openness and debate give administrations the appearance of indecision, weakness, and incompetence.

First, the President comes to rely on the White House staff. Then the staff sifts itself out, and the President comes to rely on an inner circle of loyalists. Does this increasing dependence on smaller and smaller groups of people really serve the President or, for that matter, the American people? Some argue that it restricts the flow of information to the top and isolates the President from criticism, even from reality. Perhaps so, but inner circles continue to emerge in the White House.

Chief Diplomat

More than anything else, foreign relations lets the presidency come into its own and shows it in the fullness of its potential powers. "The President alone," declared the U.S. Supreme Court (in 1936), "has the power to speak or listen as a representative of the nation. He *makes* treaties with the advice and consent of the Senate; but he alone negotiates. Into the field of negotiation the Senate cannot intrude."[19] It is the President, too, who appoints our ambassadors abroad, gives them their orders, and receives from them information, often secret, about foreign countries.

The people at large, who have less interest in foreign than in domestic policy, "expect the President to act in foreign affairs and reward him with their confidence."[20] Indeed, until the late 1960s, politicians generally agreed that "politics stops at the water's edge," so Presidents could usually expect bipartisan support in foreign policy. This tradition has been much weakened by the Vietnam War, which destroyed the Cold War consensus that was its basis, but the tradition is not dead.

Since Vietnam, Congress has forced the President to increase intelligence information to members of both houses. It has expanded its foreign policy staff and given itself the power to veto arms sales to foreign countries (see Chapter 6), and it has used the power of the purse strings to bar aid to certain countries and to set conditions for granting aid to others. But the President is

---

[19] *U.S.* v. *Curtiss-Wright Export Corporation*, 299 U.S. 304 (1936).
[20] Aaron Wildavsky, "The Two Presidencies" in *The Presidency*, A. Wildavsky, ed. (Boston: Little, Brown, 1969), p. 234.

still the moving force in our foreign policy; Congress only responds, with more or less vigor, to the President's policies.

Making Treaties. The Senate has always had the right to turn down treaties negotiated by the President; and it has used that right—most notably in 1920, when it declined to ratify the Treaty of Versailles, ending World War I. But it now makes a fuss over treaties almost as a matter of routine, although it does not turn them down routinely. In 1977, for example, President Carter signed treaties that required the United States to surrender control over the Panama Canal by the year 2000. Only after 38 emotional days of argument and uncertainty did the Senate ratify the treaties, by a single-vote margin. Because they had to be implemented through certain ordinary law that must be passed by *both* houses of Congress, they were later, in effect, considered anew—again with much controversy. This time, the House forced President Carter to make important concessions.

In fact, the Senate actually refused to act on another of Mr. Carter's treaties. In 1980, the United States and the Soviet Union signed the Strategic Arms Limitation (SALT) Agreement, which placed controls on certain kinds of nuclear weapons (see Chapter 17). SALT was so controversial that Mr. Carter, knowing the Senate would turn it down, finally withdrew it.

The Soviets do not fully understand our system of government and the culture that has shaped it. They may have assumed that the Senate's unwillingness to ratify the treaty reflected presidential insincerity in negotiating it. In fact, in most democratic countries, the executive has complete control over foreign policy, and the fact that our President's control is subject

AP/Wide World Photos

Chief of Staff Donald Regan.

Brown Brothers

President Woodrow Wilson attended the Versailles Peace Conference to sign the treaty of 1919. Here, he is shown with the other Allied heads of state (from left) Lloyd George of Britain, Orlando of Italy, and Clemenceau of France. President Wilson is on the right.

to definite limits is hard for foreigners to understand. This lack of understanding often complicates our foreign relations.

Commander-In-Chief

Beyond all doubt, the Constitution makes the President commander-in-chief of the U.S. armed forces. But the implications of this title are not beyond doubt. A commander, to say nothing of a commander-in-chief, clearly has the right and power to move units from place to place. But suppose that the President were to order a unit from Fort Bragg, North Carolina, to a trouble spot—Lebanon, let us say—where our soldiers were then drawn into combat. And suppose that the fighting then escalated into a major war. These are not mere suppositions: Just this sort of thing has happened twice, in Korea and in Vietnam (see Chapter 17).

Presidents have always claimed the right, as commander-in-chief, to commit troops to action without formal declarations of war by Congress. Many small-scale interventions have resulted from this claim, the earliest in 1805, when President Jefferson sent ships against the Barbary Pirates, in the Mediterranean. The first "police action" on the Yalu River, in Korea, did not occur in 1950, during the Korean War, but in 1871, when President Ulysses S. Grant (1869–1877) sent a detachment of Marines there.

The 1973 War Powers Resolution. Korea and Vietnam were major wars, not just "interventions." One result of Vietnam was the 1973 War Powers Resolution, which permits the President to commit troops abroad for no longer than sixty days. If, within that time, Congress does not agree to the commitment, or if it votes—in a resolution not subject to presidential veto—to withdraw the troops, then they must be withdrawn (see Chapter 17). No serious test of the resolution has yet occurred. In any case, it simply makes it much harder for the President to use force in circumstances that public opinion does not regard as a threat to national security. If such a threat were to materialize, Congress would surely approve any presidential action, as it retroactively approved President Lincoln's activities in the spring of 1861. Were the ultimate disaster—nuclear war—to erupt suddenly, no one can suppose that the War Powers Resolution would interfere with an American response. That response would be made by the President and, quite likely, the President alone.

The "Power of the Purse Strings." A more effective check on the President's powers as commander-in-chief—but only if Congress will use it—is the "power of the purse strings," the so-called appropriations check. In the early 1970s, Congress greatly cut the defense spending proposed by Presidents Nixon and Ford; but during the Carter Administration, it was much more willing to spend for defense. By 1985, in the face of federal deficits approaching $200 billion, its enthusiasm for such expenditures had greatly cooled, although President Reagan's had not. Congress looks at new weapons systems much less passively than it did in the 1950s and 1960s, and this in itself trims the President's sails.

The Voters Decide. Finally, the electorate itself has a certain amount of control over the President's power as commander-in-chief. Presidents Truman and Johnson, who committed American forces to Korea and Vietnam, became

Beyond all doubt, the Constitution makes the President commander-in-chief of the U.S. armed forces.

so unpopular that they did not run for reelection. Thereafter, the public became even more cautious about U.S. military operations abroad. President Reagan, for example, might have involved the United States more heavily in the violence in El Salvador and Nicaragua, but public opposition, clearly reflected in Congress, deterred him. In December 1982, Congress rejected Mr. Reagan's proposal to fund the MX missile system (see Chapter 17), the first rejection since World War II of any defense system proposed by a President. But that rejection was not the end of the story; the MX system seemed to be heading toward another showdown between the President and the Congress early in 1985.

In one respect—and it is a vital one—neither the public nor Congress has any control at all over the President's warmaking power, and it is hard to see how they could. Before responding to a nuclear attack, the President would not have enough time to ask Congress for a declaration of war; despite the terrible finality of these weapons, they must be used, if they be used at all, as soon as any threat looms on the radar screens. For this reason alone, a congressional power on which the Founding Fathers set great store—the power to declare war—no longer has much meaning, if any. In all likelihood, the last formal declaration of war in American history was made on December 11, 1941, against Germany and Italy.

Chief Legislator

The Constitution vests in Congress the exclusive power to make laws; and the President, of course, is not a member of Congress. But Presidents do participate in lawmaking. From the start, they had the power to veto acts of

Gerald Ford became President of the United States in late 1974. In his 1975 State-of-the-Union Address, he admitted, "The state of our Union is not good." In the 1976 State-of-the-Union Address, getting ready for reelection, he said, "The state of our Union is better." In 1977, bidding farewell, he declared, "The state of our Union is sound."

Congress, and from the start, the stronger Presidents have lobbied for some bills and against others. Not until the 1930s, however, did the White House take the liberty of actually sending bills up to Congress. That liberty is now routine; in fact, the congressional workload now comes mostly from the executive branch.

Presidents cannot always get what they want from Congress, but they can force it to spend most of its time dealing with their own proposals. In January, at the start of each new session of Congress, the President comes in person to Capitol Hill and delivers the **State-of-the-Union Address,** announcing to the assembled representatives and senators what the administration hopes they will do. The President's annual economic report makes proposals for managing the economy. The annual executive budget puts forward the President's ideas about taxes and government spending. These general statements are followed up by the texts of bills proposed by the President.

The White House Congressional Liaison Office then steps into action as it directs a day-to-day effort to sway Congress. Cabinet members and other top officials come up to Capitol Hill and testify, as needed, before congressional committees, and they lobby individual members of Congress. Often the President telephones members of Congress or invites them to the White House. (See Chapter 6 for an account of one such presidential effort.)

Presidents rarely get from Congress all, or even most, of what they want. Now and then a President will have a good year on Capitol Hill, but such years are conspicuous by their rarity: Woodrow Wilson had two of them (1913 and 1916); so did Franklin Roosevelt (1933 and 1934) and Lyndon Johnson (1965 and 1966); Ronald Reagan had one good year, 1981, but his proposals in the remaining three years of his first term encountered congressional resistance.

More often than not, Presidents are frustrated, limited, and defied by Congress. Between 1954 and 1975, Congress accepted their proposals less than half the time in every year except 1954, 1964, 1965, 1966, and 1968. As might be anticipated, Presidents have been more successful when their parties controlled Congress than during times of split control; but in either case, their failures were more numerous than their successes.[21] Despite the great resources of the presidency, one resource is altogether lacking: a consistent, committed party majority in Congress. Each piece of major legislation may require a new coalition to be forged in Congress, and that takes time. Unlike a prime minister, the President must develop not only a legislative program but also support for that program.

How difficult it is to build such coalitions could be illustrated by most bills that come before Congress, but let us take two cases: President Reagan's 3-year tax cut, in 1981, and his tax increases, in 1982. Both passed the House of Representatives by rather close votes. But in the first case, Republican conservatives lined up in the majority with more than 40 conservative Democrats. The vote on the tax increase was totally different, although it, too, passed. Carrying the measure by a 226 to 207 vote were 103 Republicans, 93 northern Democrats, and 49 southern Democrats. Such staunch House liberals as Paul Simon (D–Ill.) joined with Robert Michel (R–Ill.), the conservative House minority leader, in support of the increases; liberals like Barney Frank (D–Mass.) and conservatives like Jack Kemp (R–N.Y.) joined forces in opposition. The 1981 and 1982 coalitions had little in common, even though President Reagan won both times.

---

[21] George C. Edwards III, *Presidential Influence in Congress* (San Francisco: Freeman, 1980), pp. 13–15.

Party Leader

Presidents did not always have to build a different coalition for each measure they wanted; once, they could count on the support of most members of Congress who belonged to their own parties. Party ties are now very much weaker than they used to be. But they are still much stronger in Congress than they are in the country as a whole (see Chapter 13), so the President's position as party leader does have some importance.

Presidents are *unofficial* party leaders; they occupy no formal party post, and their fellow Democrats or Republicans in Congress are quite at liberty to defy them. But many congressmen are bound to link their own political fortunes to those of a President of their own party. An incumbent President, besides, can impose a party chairman on the party's national committee and thereby control the national party's activities—whatever that may be worth. (Not a great deal; see Chapter 9.) However, the President's power to appoint "officers of the United States" (Article II, section II of the Constitution) is a very real one, and it often helps congressmen to see the wisdom of the President's point of view.

These powers of control and persuasion sometimes amount to more and sometimes to less; it depends on the President. Throughout his term, President Carter had heavy Democratic majorities in both houses of Congress, but he could not organize those majorities behind his program. His energy and conservation bills—two of the most important proposals that he submitted to Congress—emerged from it in radically altered form, and it never even dealt with his welfare-reform proposals.

Mr. Carter's experience was unusual only in degree. President Kennedy was opposed by many Democrats in Congress and was not able to get much of his program enacted, although he seemed to like the role of party leader more than Mr. Carter did. Even Franklin Roosevelt, probably the most effective and enthusiastic party leader of this century, had difficulties in Congress in 1937 and 1938. He then tried and failed to purge certain incumbents in the Democratic primaries of 1938. But taken as a whole, Mr. Roosevelt's record shows that effective party leadership does make a difference.

Ronald Reagan's presidency showed both the importance and limits of party leadership. In 1981, Senate and House Republicans voted together on important issues, and President Reagan got most of what he wanted from Congress, particularly his tax and budget proposals. Those proposals failed to generate immediately the major economic recovery he had promised. So in the 1982 session, when elections loomed in November, the Republicans in Congress were far less united.

Leader of the People and Chief Preacher

We have seen that the President is literally a "monarch," a "single person" vested with the whole power of the executive. The office is redolent with "the divinity that doth hedge a king," for the President and the President alone is elected by the whole people, and alone embodies their will. The people quite naturally look to the President as our national leader. If the President speaks out, the people and the world will listen. Not all Presidents have known how to use this awesome power. Used wisely and well, it is the power to change the world.

Best

The five "best" Presidents, from a 1982 *Chicago Tribune* survey (ranked from very "best" *down*):

Abraham Lincoln
Franklin D. Roosevelt
George Washington
Theodore Roosevelt
Thomas Jefferson

President Theodore Roosevelt said that the White House was "a bully pulpit." It still is. When a President says, as Ronald Reagan said, that we should cut domestic spending and taxes and raise defense spending, that is what we will be debating for the next four years. When the President decides, as Jimmy Carter decided, that "human rights" will be an issue in our foreign relations, it is an issue. Presidents do not always get their way, but they can always shape the substance and tone of public debate. They can set the government in a certain direction, even if they cannot always get it to move very far. They can make the country feel that it has a government not just millions of independent bureaucrats. They can set goals and make the people believe that we are making progress—however slow, unsteady, or painful— toward them. They can educate and exhort and inspire. These indeed are a President's major powers, for they are the keys to all the rest.

VICE-PRESIDENTS AND THE PRESIDENTIAL SUCCESSION

An old joke tells the story of a woman with two sons. "One ran away to sea and the other became Vice-President, and neither was heard of again." And in truth, how many of us remember the lives and deeds of the worthy William R. King (1853—died in office during that year), Levi P. Morton (1889–1893), William A. Wheeler (1877–1881), or James S. Sherman (1909–1912)?

Under the Constitution, the formal powers of our Vice-Presidents are hardly impressive: They can preside over the Senate and cast their vote in case of a tie. Since tie votes are rare, and presiding over the Senate is usually dull, Vice-Presidents visit the Senate rarely, if at all. John Nance Garner (1933–1941), Franklin Roosevelt's first Vice-President, said (inelegantly but truly) that the office was not worth "a pitcher of warm spit." John Adams, Washington's Vice-President, described the position as the "most insignificant office that ever the invention of man contrived or his imagination conceived." Its importance lies not in what the Vice-President *is* but in what the Vice-President might *become*.

Choosing the Vice-President

The original text of the Constitution (as ratified in 1789) did not provide for a separate ballot to elect the President and the Vice-President. Each state chose members of an electoral college, and each member cast a ballot for two persons. The candidate, if any, with a majority of the whole number of electors became President; the second-ranking candidate became Vice-President.

The Twelfth Amendment. The presidential election of 1800 was the first full-fledged party contest. All the Republican electors cast votes both for Thomas Jefferson and Aaron Burr. Since each man received the same number of electoral votes, the contest was thrown into the House of Representatives, which, after a long struggle, chose Mr. Jefferson. The emergence of political parties made it quite possible that a similar difficulty might present itself at each and every presidential election. So the Twelfth Amendment, ratified in 1804, kept the electoral college but required it to cast separate ballots for President and Vice-President. A majority of electoral votes is still needed for election to either post. If no candidate receives a majority, the President is chosen by the House of Representatives from among the top three candidates, with the representatives from each state voting as a unit and a majority of all states being necessary for election. The Vice-President, should no candidate get a majority in the electoral college, is chosen by the Senate, which decides between the two candidates having the greatest number of electoral votes. A majority of votes in the entire Senate is needed for election.

The Twenty-fifth Amendment. Not all the problems relating to the Vice-Presidency and the succession to the presidency were removed by the Twelfth Amendment. Until 1967, for example, there was no way of filling a vacancy in the vice-presidency if it occurred between elections. This gap in our institutions bothered people a great deal after President Kennedy was assassinated in 1963, for when Lyndon Johnson became President, the office of Vice-President fell vacant. The Twenty-fifth Amendment, ratified in 1967, directs the President to nominate a Vice-President, who must then be confirmed both by the House and the Senate. This procedure has been used twice. When Spiro Agnew resigned the vice-presidency, in 1973, President Nixon nominated Gerald Ford to replace him. When Mr. Nixon resigned the presidency, in 1974, Mr. Ford succeeded to the office and nominated Nelson Rockefeller to fill the vice-presidential vacancy.

The Role of the Vice-President

Because the formal powers of the vice-presidency are limited, the real authority of the office depends on any President's willingness to delegate important work to the Vice-President. By statute, Vice-Presidents sit on the National Security Council, and they are usually included in the cabinet, but their influence, if any, is wholly up to the President.

One important political change has made our Vice-Presidents more visible and useful than they used to be. Until some point after the end of World War II, in 1945, vice-presidential candidates were chosen not by the presidential nominee but by the party elite. As a result, Presidents often completely ignored their Vice-Presidents. Franklin Roosevelt, for example, rarely met with his third and last Vice-President, Harry Truman, and he never gave Mr. Truman the slightest information on the course of the war. The reason? Harry Truman, who became President on Mr. Roosevelt's death in April 1945, had been forced on him by a 1944 Democratic convention in revolt against the liberalism of Vice-President Henry Wallace.

In recent years, presidential candidates have chosen their running mates by themselves—the first major appointments they make. Therefore, the Vice-President is not only personally acceptable to the President but also, in a sense, the "President's man." Walter F. Mondale (1977–1981) was an active and visible Vice-President because President Carter, who had chosen him, liked and trusted him too.

Most recent Presidents have started out fully intending to give their Vice-Presidents real power and authority. These intentions have failed to end the

Success

Presidents who succeeded to the office from the vice-presidency:

John Tyler (1841)
Andrew Johnson (1865)
Chester A. Arthur (1881)
Theodore Roosevelt (1901)
Calvin Coolidge (1923)
Harry S Truman (1945)
Lyndon B. Johnson (1963)
Gerald R. Ford (1974)

This, by the way, is exactly one-fifth of all our Presidents, suggesting the potential importance of the vice-presidential selection process.

Until 1945, vice-presidential candidates were chosen by the party elite at the national convention. Since then, the choice has usually been left to the presidential nominee. In 1984, Walter Mondale interviewed several candidates before choosing Geraldine Ferraro as his running mate.

Art Stein, Photo Researchers, Inc.

Vice-President's complete dependence on the President, however, for Presidents do not want to diminish their own power by sharing it with anyone else. Nor do they have to: The Vice-President can be used effectively as an adviser without in any way threatening the President's prerogatives.

At the very least, Presidents ought to ensure that Vice-Presidents know and understand the policies and responsibilities they might one day inherit. During World War II, President Roosevelt did not even tell Vice-President Truman that the United States was developing an atomic bomb, which Mr. Truman learned about little more than three months before he decided to drop it on Japan. By making the Vice-President a statutory member of the National Security Council, the National Security Act of 1947 probably guarantees that no future Vice-President will ever be so deeply ignorant of high policy as Harry Truman was when he took office.

The Twenty-fifth Amendment also tried to wrestle with the agonizing and by no means merely academic problem of presidential illnesses. The most celebrated and dramatic of such an illness occurred in the last years of Woodrow Wilson's presidency. On August 25, 1919, while campaigning across the country to build support for the ratification of the Treaty of Versailles, Mr. Wilson had a nervous collapse; on the following October 2, he suffered a stroke that fully incapacitated him for many months. His wife, Edith Bolling Galt Wilson served in effect as acting President from the fall of 1919 to the end of Wilson's term, on March 4, 1921. At any rate, she was in charge during those eighteen months. When President James A. Garfield was shot by a disappointed office seeker on July 2, 1881, he lingered on until September 19. During the interval, neither he nor anyone else was truly President. Perhaps this gap in our institutions had little impact on the conduct of government then; that would hardly be so now.

Succession

Nine Presidents have died in office—four of them in this century. All of them were succeeded by their Vice-Presidents. The tenth death almost occurred in March 1981, when President Reagan was shot by a deranged young man. Before the Twenty-fifth Amendment was ratified, in 1967, there was always a chance that the President might die at a time when the vice-presidency was vacant. Had Lyndon Jonhson died in 1964, for example, there would have been no Vice-President to succeed him, and the Speaker of the House, John McCormack, would have become President. The Twenty-fifth Amendment permits the President to nominate a Vice-President (in the event of a vacancy), who must then be confirmed by a majority vote of both houses of Congress.

What if a President becomes insane or mentally incompetent? The Twenty-fifth Amendment attempts to make provision for such contingencies by setting forth procedures that allow the Vice-President to become acting President and for the President to resume the duties of office upon recovery. But no one supposes that the amendment can or does resolve all of the terribly difficult and embarrassing problems that could arise in such circumstances; it is merely the only way we now have of trying to deal with them. Perhaps we should choose our Presidents in a way that minimizes the more obvious mental-health risks. Only the most optimistic among us could think that we are doing so now.

THE PERSONAL PRESIDENCY

The American presidency is more than an institution; it is a set of possibilities that some Presidents have used effectively and others have not. The individual holder of the office makes a great deal of difference, not only because different people might promote different policies, but also because a President's power hangs largely on personality—on the ability to define and clarify issues, build public support, explain solutions, and negotiate deals.

So much hangs on the President's personality that it makes sense to study the way different kinds of personalities handle the responsibilities of the office. Such a study has been made by James David Barber, who claims that each of our Presidents had one of four basic personality patterns and that these patterns, together with events in the real world, "set in motion" the course of each administration.[22]

Two aspects of presidential behavior are especially important, according to Barber. The first is the level of activity that Presidents bring to the job—what Barber calls their "active" or "passive" attitude toward its demands. The second is the kind of satisfactions they derive from it, satisfactions that Barber classifies as "positive" and "negative." The "active-positive" Presidents are flexible men of high self-esteem, who set store mainly by results. The included, in Barber's view, Franklin Roosevelt, Harry Truman, and John Kennedy. The "active-negative" Presidents are compulsive and aggressive. They emphasize getting and keeping power. Among these Presidents were Woodrow, Wilson, Lyndon Johnson, and Richard Nixon. By contrast the "passive-positive," including William Howard Taft and Warren G. Harding, were compliant and mainly wanted the affection of others. Finally, the "passive-negative" Presidents, among them Calvin Coolidge and Dwight Eisenhower, were dutiful but vague and bent on avoiding conflict.

Barber, of course, admires the active-positive Presidents—those he calls progressive, dynamic, and practical. Passive Presidents of either type, as Barber sees it, do not confront political reality; under them, the government tends to drift. But the really dangerous Presidents, he thinks, are the active-negatives, who are drawn into disasters because they lack flexibility and regard all criticism as personal and destructive. Woodrow Wilson's presidency thus came to grief because he could not compromise with the Senate over the Treaty of Versailles; Johnson's was destroyed by his personal commitment to his Vietnam policy; and Nixon's went aground on the treacherous rocks of Watergate.

Barber's parceling out of Presidents into particular categories is not beyond challenge. For example, he calls Dwight Eisenhower a passive-negative President, but some recent studies claim that Mr. Eisenhower was far more active, influential, and able than Barber allowed. In 1977, Barber classified Jimmy Carter as an active-positive President, but by 1980 most voters did not regard Mr. Carter's presidency as a success.

The present openness of our presidential nominating system to "outsiders" makes it harder than ever to judge a candidate's personality traits. The politicians that other politicians and the people are likely to know most about are those in Washington, especially those in Congress. The fact that these

---

[22] James David Barber, *The Presidential Character*, 3rd ed. (Englewood Cliffs, N.J.: Prentice-Hall, 1985).

Assassination

Assassinated Presidents:

Abraham Lincoln (1865)
James A. Garfield (1881)
William McKinley (1901)
John F. Kennedy (1963)

Presidents who were targets of unsuccessful assassination attempts:

Andrew Jackson (1835)
Franklin D. Roosevelt (1933) (as President-elect)
Harry S Truman (1951)
Gerald Ford (1976) (twice)
Ronald Reagan (1981)

Of this list, one was actually wounded—Ronald Reagan, in 1981.

politicians are now less likely to be nominated, and also less likely to serve as delegates at presidential nominating conventions (see Chapters 9 and 10), makes it more likely that each new President will be something of an enigma, both personally and politically. There are very real dangers in all this.

THE LIMITS OF POWER

Although the Framers of the Constitution meant to create a strong presidency—a "single person" vested with all the powers of the executive branch—the limits of presidential authority are often more obvious. All the President's powers and responsibilities must be shared with the other branches of

A President's power hangs largely on personality. Each President projects an image, especially during casual moments and vacation trips.

Jack Kightlinger, The White House

government and with millions of bureaucrats. We expect the President to run the government and the country, and more often than not, the reality falls far short of that expectation.

At times, however, the office and its holder seem to shake free of these limits. Many people remember the late 1960s and the early 1970s—the days of the "imperial presidency," of Lyndon Johnson followed by Richard Nixon. These two Presidents escalated the Vietnam War and kept us in it, without ever bothering to ask Congress for a declaration of war. Why do the powers of the office seem to expand and contract like an accordion?

The Imperial Presidency

For the most part, our Presidents have power over the executive branch and only over the executive branch. They have vastly less power in dealing with Congress than prime ministers have dealing with parliaments. In 1914, Walter Lippmann (1899–1974), a famous political writer, argued that the Constitution gives Presidents so little authority that, in times of crisis, they must rely on their **prerogative powers**[23]—powers that, according to Presidents, are "inherent" in their office. Presidents are especially prone to use these powers in wartime, and they have twice been used to take this country into war.

Lippman was getting at a fundamental point about the American Constitution, a point that is often ignored. In the ordinary course of things, our system is so full of opportunities for stalemate that normal politics under the Constitution is the politics of drift. Frequently this very drift produces a crisis so acute that decisive action becomes absolutely necessary. The halls of Congress, the editorials of newspapers, the living rooms of millions of families suddenly resound with the cry, "Do something!" At that point, the Constitution itself may in effect be set aside and a kind of Roman dictatorship established by the President. The presidency feeds on crisis; and it is at just such times that the President most resembles a Tudor monarch.

Our own time is a time of permanent crisis, so the powers of the President have been permanently enlarged. Thoughtful men and women worry about this enlargement and its implications, for in an acute crisis, we must depend far too much on the judgment of a single, fallible, perhaps simply mistaken human being. Perhaps, too, the Roman dictatorship might be made permanent. One of our recent Presidents probably wanted to make it so, and we might have another such President in the future.

The President as "Pitiful, Helpless Giant"

How do we square these legitimate fears of an "imperial presidency" with the equally legitimate complaints that our President is too weak? From Richard Nixon's descent in the storm of Watergate, in 1973, until (at the very least) the inauguration of Ronald Reagan, in 1981, the presidency looked anything but imperial. Drift, not mastery, was very much in the air, and it made Americans extremely uncomfortable.

The point of this complaint hangs on two observations about the modern presidency. First, the range of the President's responsibilities has far outstripped the means available to tackle them. Liberal activist Presidents are likely to be swamped by these responsibilities and to ignore many of them for

---

[23] Walter Lippman, *Drift and Mastery* (New York: Macmillan, 1914).

Presidential Character

Active-Positive Presidents (high self-esteem, flexibility, emphasis on results):

   Franklin Roosevelt
   Harry Truman
   John Kennedy

Active-Negative Presidents (compulsive, aggressive, emphasis on gaining and keeping power):

   Woodrow Wilson
   Lyndon Johnson
   Richard Nixon

Passive-Positive Presidents (compliant, other-directed, emphasis on gaining affection):

   William H. Taft
   Warren Harding

Passive-Negative Presidents (dutiful, vague, emphasis on avoiding conflict):

   Calvin Coolidge
   Dwight Eisenhower

Adapted from James D. Barber, *The Presidential Character: Predicting Performance in the White House* © 1972. Reprinted by permission of Prentice-Hall.

sheer want of time. More conservative Presidents, too, are harried by constant crises abroad and, often enough, at home too. The second observation is that the President lacks any institutional means of securing sufficient and reliable support in Congress. In its first year, the Reagan administration seemed to have such support, but so strong are the presures of fragmentation that by 1982 its hold over Congress was noticeably weakening, and it grew even weaker as Reagan began his second term in 1985.

Many proposals have been made for righting these wrongs. To name only two: a "collegiate presidency" composed of a President supported by as many as twelve executive Vice-Presidents, or the adoption here of a parliamentary system. None of the many proposals will get anywhere in the near future. But they should remind us that the realities of the twentieth century have strained the fabric of divided government bequeathed to us by the Founding Fathers. In any event, it is perfectly possible to have a presidency that is somehow both too strong and too weak at the same time.

SUMMARY

The President of the United States is a kind of "elective monarch," literally a "single person" who directs the executive as a whole. Our Presidents are elected independently of Congress, but without its consent, they can exercise few constitutional powers; and because they have no assurance of support in either house, the "sharing of powers" often leads to deadlock. And the election of our Presidents more or less directly by the voters (rather than by the legislature, as a prime minister is elected) sometimes gives us Presidents who lack the temperament, skills, or experience needed to curry favor in Congress.

George Washington defined the limits of the presidency by retiring after two terms, and he defined its opportunities by vigorously asserting its powers. Thomas Jefferson was the first President to use a political party to forge links with Congress. Andrew Jackson used the Democratic party to democratize the presidency and the federal bureaucracy, and to provide himself with a base of support for his sometimes provocative assertions of presidential power. Many Americans, however, wanted a President who would exercise only those powers specifically granted to the office in the Constitution. Others felt that the President must take any action in the national interest not actually prohibited by the Constitution. Indeed, during the Civil War, the supreme crisis of our history, Abraham Lincoln violated the Constitution repeatedly to preserve the Union.

Woodrow Wilson was in many ways the first modern President. He came into office with a program of domestic reforms and, later on, played a great part on the stage of world diplomacy. But toward the end of his term and in the 1920s, that kind of activist leadership was rejected. Not until the presidency of Franklin D. Roosevelt did the activist state and the activist presidency become permanent realities.

By now, the expectation that the President will *lead* the country is so strong that even a conservative President like Ronald Reagan had to satisfy that expectation by acting as a "strong" President.

Yet the constitutional powers of the office are still, in many ways, inadequate, notably because the President has no assurance of support in

Congress. Sometimes the President appears to be a "pitiful, helpless giant," beset and dominated by enemies. Sometimes—at moments of crisis, like the Civil War—the President becomes almost a temporary dictator, setting the Constitution aside. Since World War II, the United States has been almost permanently embroiled in one sort of crisis or other, and this is why we often hear complaints about an "imperial presidency."

The President's responsibilities have grown over the past two centuries, but the President does not have the power to meet those responsibilities. Our expectations of what Presidents can and should do are beyond fulfillment. Presidents must be accountable to Congress, but they should also be able to govern. If we are to judge them by results, we must give them a reasonable chance to shape those results. Otherwise, we shall have to scale down our expectations of what the President—and the federal government as a whole—can do.

SUGGESTED READINGS

JAMES DAVID BARBER, *The Presidential Character*, 3rd ed. Englewood Cliffs, N.J.: Prentice-Hall, 1985. When everything is centered on one man, research naturally turns to that one man's personal characteristics. Barber's is the most ambitious effort to deal with presidential personalities.

EDWARD S. CORWIN, *The President: Office and Powers*, rev. ed. New York: New York Univ., 1980. A classic study by a leading constitutional analyst who cared greatly about the rules of the game and was worried by what he saw.

THOMAS E. CRONIN, *The State of the Presidency*, 2nd ed. Boston: Little, Brown, 1980. Stresses the political side of the presidency, with particular attention to the constraints on the chief executive.

THOMAS E. CRONIN and REXFORD G. TUGWELL, eds., *The Presidency Reappraised*. New York: Praeger, 1977. A good contemporary collection of essays, reflecting concerns arising in the immediate aftermath of Vietnam and Watergate.

RICHARD E. NEUSTADT, *Presidential Power*, rev. ed. New York: Wiley, 1980. A rich example of modern "mirror of princes" literature, informing Presidents and others about the ways in which they could increase their power resources, and the pitfalls en route.

RICHARD M. PIOUS, *The American Presidency*. New York: Basic Books, 1979. The best and most complete up-to-date text on the presidency and the issues surrounding it.

CLINTON ROSSITER, *The American Presidency*, 2nd ed. New York: Harcourt, 1960. A classic by one of the leading specialists on the subject; seems a bit too cheerful and meliorist nowadays, in the wake of Vietnam and Watergate.

——— *Constitutional Dictatorship*. Princeton: Princeton Univ., 1948. A first-rate comparative study of "exceptional government" in Western democracies with a great deal of material on the activities of American Presidents in crisis; gives a good sense of what Corwin is worried about.

AARON WILDAVSKY, ed., *The Presidency*. Boston: Little, Brown, 1969. Old now, but a superlative collection of important essays on every aspect of the subject by leading scholars.

chapter twelve

BUREAUCRACY

In July 1981, the majority of the Professional Air Traffic Controllers Organization's (PATCO's) members voted to strike. Their demands included higher wages (members had rejected an offer of $38,000 a year); annual salary increases that would stay ahead of inflation; a four-day work week; and after twenty years' employment, a retirement pension equal to 75 percent of the base salary. By staying off their jobs, the air traffic controllers intended to ground virtually all flights in this country until their demands were met. What was unusual about this strike was that the federal government, in a series of actions headed by President Reagan. responded by doing everything in its power to render the strike ineffective.

First, the government reduced flight schedules and called air traffic control supervisors and retired controllers back into service. Next, the government ordered military air traffic controllers from their bases into service at civilian airports. While some union leaders accused the government of union busting, this protest was not a strong one. Why? The reason is that, in this case, the strike was illegal, and the federal government had every right to try to stop it. Although air traffic controllers may not fit our image of bureaucrats, they are part of the federal bureaucracy, and they had signed an oath stating they would never strike. By his actions, President Reagan aimed to see to it that those oaths were honored or that the controllers lost their jobs.

To gain public support for these moves, President Reagan appeared on national television, explaining the strike from the government's viewpoint. He told the American people that the PATCO members who had walked off their jobs were breaking the law. He said further that if the air traffic controllers were not back at work in two days, they would permanently lose their jobs.

Most PATCO members believed in their union, and they thought that the government would have no choice but to meet their demands. Without them, PATCO members maintained, there were not enough trained air traffic controllers to keep the country flying safely. They believed further that the safety risk was too critical for mere substitutes to handle. They counted on the President's fear of a serious accident to force him into backing down and giving PATCO members what they wanted. Only about 1,000 of the striking air traffic controllers returned to work following the President's speech.

Unfortunately for the air traffic controllers, PATCO's reasoning was dead wrong. The government's flight reduction and temporary fill-in system worked, and no accidents occurred. To PATCO's surprise, members who did not return to work within the President's deadline were fired, just as Mr. Reagan had promised. PATCO's officials were arrested.

Even some labor leaders spoke out against the strike, despite the fact that the government was acting against a union. United Auto Workers' president, Donald Fraser, admonished PATCO for its actions, saying the union's actions had hurt the labor movement. By not consulting the AFL-CIO before the strike, PATCO had eliminated the possibility of industry-wide support from other airline unions. In addition to being illegal, without this support, PATCO's absence from service was manageable.

PATCO members, fired in 1981, did not regain their jobs. In October of that year, the Federal Labor Relations Authority decertified the union. PATCO filed for bankruptcy in December 1981, just five months after it had tried to halt U.S. air traffic and force the government into meeting its demands.[1]

——————— WHAT IS A BUREAUCRACY? ———————

The very people who create and fund federal bureaucracies—the members of Congress—routinely make political hay by denouncing them; and so too do the very presidential candidates who would lead them. With so many Davids aiming slingshots at the bureaucratic Goliath, how does it survive? Because we cannot do without it.

All societies but the most primitive must have institutions to provide goods and services. These institutions must be run by staffs although not all such staffs are bureaucracies. In a traditional society, the chief and the assistants often inherit their positions. *Administration*, if that is the word for it, is traditional, highly personalized, and informal. At times, however, special individuals claiming special powers come to the fore and provide a new kind of leadership, one that is called charismatic. Moses, Jesus, Mohammed, and the Buddha were leaders of this sort; and so, at a very different level, were Alexander the Great, Napoleon, and (unfortunately) Adolf Hitler. Charismatic leaders often appear in revolutions or at times of crisis. In our own history, two exceptionally charismatic leaders—Presidents Abraham Lincoln and Franklin D. Roosevelt—have emerged out of such crises.

---

[1] This account is derived from David H. Rosenbloom and Jay M. Shafritz, *Essentials of Labor Relations* (Reston, Va.: Reston, 1983).

Until quite recently, traditional and charismatic authority prevailed almost everywhere. Why not everywhere? Why not now? One reason is the sheer difficulty of running a coherent administration on either basis. Traditional authority, dependent on the whims of a single chief, may lack order, system, continuity and predictability. Lines of authority may not be clearly specified. Few written rules—or none—grant, limit, or define power. Administrative procedures are rudimentary. In medieval England, "the Treasury," for example, was literally a treasure, a chest full of coins and precious gems. It was kept in the king's immediate possession, and when the king moved, it moved with him.

To an even greater extent than traditional authority, charismatic authority hangs on the influence of a single individual, the charismatic chief. When that individual dies, the movement must adapt itself to the ordinary routine of the world; the revolution institutionalizes itself. Thus, for example, Jesus and his band of apostles give way to the Christian Church—eventually, to many Christian churches.

Some of these churches resembled the original charismatic band of Jesus and his disciples. Others eventually became large organizations with millions of members, with staffs organized in an elaborate hierarchy, each level having its own specialized function or functions. Max Weber (1864–1920), the famous sociologist who developed a theory of bureaucracy, argued that any large organization must be, or become, bureaucratic in form, function, and outlook. Jesus and his disciples had no worldly interests to administer; the government of medieval England had few responsibilities that could not be financed from a chest small enough to be carried about. But as society became larger and more complex, it demanded a larger, more complex, and more sophisticated government. Private organizations, too, had to adjust to the new scale of society. Bureaucracies were by no means new, but they became more numerous. Eventually they became the way to run most kinds of organizations, public and private.

Max Weber argued that any large organization must be, or become, bureaucratic in form, function, and outlook.

Fred Gatlin, U.S. Census Bureau

The basic features of bureaucracy are two: specialization and hierarchy. Specialization, or the division of labor, is the separation of tasks so as to promote efficiency and expertise. Each official has a specialized function and is appointed and promoted by demonstrating a mastery of it, often through competitive exams—and in any case, not through personal connections with the chief or underlings. Hierarchy, or the ordering of authority by levels, is used to coordinate the activities of all those engaged in different specializations. Authority is clearly defined and placed in relation to the levels above and below it, so it is always clear who can give orders to whom. In addition, in order to delineate precisely what the specialists are supposed to be doing and the scope of hierarchical authority, bureaucracies describe each position in a written statement and are based on formal rules and procedures. Consequently, since they are based on *positions*, not individuals, bureaucracies are impersonal and do not depend on the whims, prejudices, or inspirations of the chief.

This is an idealized description, of course. In the real world, we find elements of all three types of rule; it is entirely possible for bureaucracies to be both "traditional" and "charismatic" in some respects. Many bureaucracies have autocratic and whimsical bosses, and many are staffed by people who owe their jobs to connections, chance, or corruption—although today, this is rare in the federal bureaucracy. Nonetheless, modern bureaucratic government, in the United States and elsewhere, has most of the characteristics that Max Weber spelled out many years ago. Authority is exercised in a rational, legal, precise way. Detailed, often numbered regulations specify and limit the tasks of each employee. Such organizations are basically different from those founded mainly on tradition or charisma.

THE MAKING OF A BUREAUCRACY

Bureaucracies in this real, in-between sense existed as many as 4,000 years ago, especially in large and populous early civilizations such as Babylonia, Egypt, and China. When the U.S. Constitution was adopted in 1789, most of Europe's bigger countries were giving birth to such bureaucracies. But Britain, from which we derive most of our political traditions, was in this respect the most backward of these countries. As for the United States, the apparatus of government was so tiny it is rather hard to speak of bureaucracy at all.

Just how small was our new government? When Congress passed the 1798 Appropriations Act, it allocated $8,850 for the salaries of the secretary of state and the seven clerks who assisted him and $500 for stationery, printing, and other such incidentals. For the United States Army, the total pay allocated in that year was $264,824; and the grand total of all appropriations for the War Department (an ancestor of today's Defense Department) was $1,411,798. In his 1982 budget, President Reagan proposed to spend $18.5 billion on our foreign relations and $219 billion on defense.

Although the federal establishment has grown vastly since 1789, one thing has not changed: Neither in 1789 nor today, after 26 amendments, does our Constitution refer to a bureaucracy, in name or in fact. It does give the president power to appoint "Ambassadors, other public Ministers and Consuls, Judges of the [U.S.] supreme Court, and all other Officers of the United States whose Appointments are not herein provided for, and which shall be established by law." The last category—"all other officers"—includes what is now called "the bureaucracy," and the provisions dealing with this category are vague in the extreme. Congress could bestow the power of making these appointments to the President alone, to the department heads (appointed by the President), or to the law courts. Congress itself, of course, received the power to create all executive department, to control them by appropriating or refusing funds, and to establish their missions.

In 1789, when the federal government was set up, the federal administration consisted very largely of genteel amateurs, almost all of them Federalists. When Thomas Jefferson became President, in 1801, he found only six Republicans[2] holding federal office, and "these were chiefly half-breeds." President Jefferson thereupon fired more than 100 high officials and replaced them with members of what he called the "natural aristocracy"—his own Republicans.

The Spoils System. Despite President Jefferson's efforts, what we had by way of a bureaucracy continued to be small, politically conservative, genteel, and long-lived. When Andrew Jackson entered the White House, in 1829, he confronted a government whose appointed officials were overwhelmingly hostile to him and to his Democratic party, which therefore faced obstacles in carrying out its policies. President Jackson proceeded to fire more federal officials than all of his predecessors combined and replaced them with members of his own party a procedure known as **spoils system.** By liberating the bureaucracy from a coterie of Northeastern "aristocrats," he transformed it into the servant of the political majority and made it possible for small-time politicians to live off, as well as for, politics. The Democratic party dominated the bureaucracy and was also partly subsidized by it.

Civil-Service Reform. The spoils system survived Andrew Jackson, but his successors were less able to use it as a means of controlling the bureaucracy. After the end of the Civil War, in 1865, we had many more bureaucrats to control—100,000 in 1880, as compared with only 37,000 in 1861. In Europe, especially in the German Empire, full-fledged and prestigious professional bureaucracies had long since emerged. Many educated Americans admired the German bureaucracy and longed for the United States to imitate it. They wanted most government offices to be thought of as positions requiring technical or professional skills, not political connections and skills. They wanted these officials to be appointed and promoted under a **merit system,** in other words, through competitive exams. And they wanted most officials, once appointed, to have tenure, or security in office.

The struggle for civil-service reform was fought out mostly within the Republican party. In 1880, the party's dominant "Stalwart" faction, which bitterly opposed reform, could not prevent the nomination of James A. Garfield, a tepid reformer. He was duly elected, but in July 1881, a disappointed officeseeker named Charles J. Guiteau fatally shot him, shouting, "I am a Stalwart, and Arthur is President now!" The attack simply made the cause of reform irresistible. Even President Chester A. Arthur, though a Stalwart, supported it.

Congress finally had to give the reform movement a part of what it wanted. The Pendleton Act (1883) set up the Civil Service Commission, charged with

---

[2] Not Republicans in the modern sense, for there were none until 1854, but Jeffersonian Republicans, opponents of the Federalists (see Chapter 9).

Job Hunting

A Congressman whose heart was set on a foreign mission had tried for some time without success to get the appointment. At length he decided to use more indirect tactics. One day he called on the President [Andrew Jackson], who, as usual, was smoking his pipe. "General Jackson," he said, "I am about to ask you a favor—a favor, sir, that will cost you nothing, and the government nothing, but will gratify me exceedingly." "It's granted, sir," said Jackson. "What is it?" "Well, General," said the Congressman, "I have an old father at home who has as great an esteem for your character as one man can have for another. Before I left home, he charged me to get for him, if possible, one of General Jackson's pipes, and that is the favor I now ask of you." "Oh, certainly," said Jackson, laughing and ringing the bell. When the servant came, he told him to bring two or three clean pipes. "Excuse me," said the Congressman, "but may I ask you for that very pipe you have just been smoking?" "This one?" said Jackson. "By all means, if you prefer it." He began to empty it of ashes, but the Congressman interrupted him again. "No, General," he said, "don't empty out the tobacco. I want that pipe, just as it is, just as it left your lips." When Jackson obligingly handed it to him, he put it carefully in a piece of paper, thanked Jackson for the precious gift, and left the room with the air of a man who had just achieved his highest ambition. Three weeks later he got his appointment and departed on a mission to one of the South American countries.

From *Presidential Anecdotes* by Paul F. Boller, Jr. Copyright 1981 by Paul F. Boller, Jr. Reprinted by permission of Oxford Univ. Press, Inc.

running the government's personnel system—including the competitive exams that the act required for filling certain positions—and prohibited the dismissal of government employees for refusing to make campaign contributions. At the outset, only about 10 percent of all federal positions were filled by competitive exams, but the proportion was gradually expanded. It now amounts to about 90 percent of the total.

The Interstate Commerce Commission. The United States now had the beginnings of a really professional bureaucracy, although its size and scope were still quite small. Most members of the federal bureaucracy, ran and staffed the Post Office, the Customs Office, or the Immigration Service; administered Civil War pensions; or dealt with the Indian nations. Whatever little regulation of business was tolerated occurred chiefly at the state level; the federal government interfered in such matters only when they were plainly beyond the capacity of individual states. In 1887, for example, Congress created the Interstate Commerce Commission (ICC) to regulate interstate railroads. The ICC, however, was not and is not an executive agency, under the President's direct control, but an independent commission, insulated from political interference. This was to be an important bureaucratic model of the future.

The New Deal. As long as the federal bureaucracy was mainly concerned with delivering the mail, paying war pensions, and dealing with the Indians, its roles and powers were not considered highly controversial by most members of the political community. Ordinary laws defined these roles and powers, for the most part; aside from some serious misgivings concerning the federal government's dealings with Indian tribes, there was little debate as to what the bureaucracy should do or how things should be done. Economy and efficiency were considered the self-evident and uncontroversial objects of public management.

A railroad yard. The
Interstate Commerce
Commission (ICC) was set
up to regulate interstate
railroads in 1887.

The bureaucracy entered a period of very rapid growth during the Great Depression of the 1930s. President Herbert Hoover (1929–1933) insisted that the government could only stand back and let the Depression "burn itself out." By 1932, however, one-quarter of our work force was unemployed, and industrial production had fallen by almost one-half since 1929. The end was not in sight. At first, very hesitantly and inconsistently, the Democrats argued that the federal government had the right and the duty to help end the Depression and prevent future ones. That issue was to dominate politics for another generation.

When the Democrats, under Franklin D. Roosevelt, took control of both Congress and the White House, in 1933, they set up independent agencies to regulate banks, stock exchanges, the communications industry, transportation, and labor relations; emergency relief agencies, like the Works Projects Administration (WPA); and executive agencies to administer agricultural price supports, unemployment compensation, and the new Social Security system. The number of federal employees shot up from about 600,000 in 1932 to more than 1.4 million in 1941; the federal budget, from $3.6 billion to $13.6 billion.

Discretionary Powers. During the Depression, as Congress brought industry after industry under federal regulation, it found that it could not legislate all or even most aspects of the new regulations. More and more, it had to content itself with defining general standards and objectives and letting the agencies fill in the details. At first, the U.S. Supreme Court interfered with the new approach by ruling that it delegated legislative powers to the executive branch, without establishing adequate guidance, and therefore, in effect, violated the Constitution's separation of powers.[3] But after President Roosevelt's triumphant reelection in 1936, the Court judiciously concluded that Congress could indeed grant **discretionary powers** to federal agencies, as long as it set forth adequate standards and guidelines in the law. Today Congress quite routinely grants the executive branch some very broad discretionary powers: In 1970, for example, it permitted the President to impose wage-and-price controls throughout the American economy.[4]

Much of the time, the legal guidelines and standards are so vague that bureaucracies make their own policies. Take the granting of tax exemptions by the Internal Revenue Service (IRS). Under its interpretation of the federal tax code, in 1970, the IRS issued a regulation that denied tax exemption to segregated private schools. Five years later, it watered down this absolute decree by issuing a set of guidelines. In 1978, it proposed a new and more stringent set of regulations, but congressional criticism killed them. In 1982, the Reagan administration first tried to grant these schools tax exemption; but after several changes in direction, it was at last beaten back to the old policy. All these bureaucratic zigs and zags were authorized by the very same law.

The Permanent Debate. The bureaucracy's vastly increased size and powers have been bought at a price. Until the 1930s, most Americans took for granted the bureaucracy and its functions. Not so after 1933. The New Deal reforms were controversial, yet so, too, was the old policy of economic noninvolvement. The bureaucracy was mired into a permanent swamp of controversy and doubt. It is still there.

The Limits of Neutrality. Debate over the role and powers of the government raged fiercely in the 1930s, when the New Deal agencies were first set up. Since the people who worked for those agencies owed their jobs to the Democratic party, many of them campaigned for the party's candidates. The liberal Democrats who controlled Congress in the mid-1930s benefited from this campaigning and therefore had no wish to stop it. In the elections of 1938, however, the liberal Democrats lost control of Congress to a coalition of conservative Democrats and Republicans. Even though the Democrats remained the majority party, the **conservative coalition** soon forced through Congress the Hatch Act (1939), which prohibits civil-service employees from "taking active part in political management or campaigns."

Between them, the Pendleton Act of 1883 and the Hatch Act may have seemed to have neutralized the bureaucracy as a political force. Not so. Individual civil servants may perhaps be politically neutral, but not the civil service as a whole or the departments and agencies it comprises. Each of these departments and agencies is involved in a sort of bureaucratic "war of all against all"; each department and agency must seek to defend its interests within the maze of our constitutional system. Each must secure the good will of the President and the executive branch, to which it belongs; each must seek to cultivate good will in Congress, which funds and creates—and sometimes

---

[3] See, for example, *Schechter Poultry Corp.* v. *U.S.*, 295 U.S. 495 (1935).
[4] In the Economic Stabilization Act.

shuts down—agencies; each must try to cultivate the mass media, interest groups, the major political parties, and the public at large. With power so very fragmented and no one quite in control, departments and agencies must play politics or go under.

THE FEDERAL BUREAUCRACY TODAY

Richard Nixon, elected President in 1968, had a long record of attacking the federal bureaucracy for its alleged unresponsiveness, inefficiency, and even disloyalty to the nation. In 1976, Jimmy Carter also attacked the federal bureaucracy during his presidential campaign and vowed to make it more efficient through massive reorganization, if given the opportunity. In 1980, Ronald Reagan pledged to reduce drastically the bureaucracy's size and power. Even though the themes of these three successful presidential candidates were different, their common tactic of attacking the bureaucracy is striking. Denunciations of the federal bureaucracy have become an essential part of our political stock in trade, the negative equivalent of motherhood, apple pie, and the flag.

One would think that the federal bureaucracy had grown madly in recent years, considering the hostility our politicians direct at it. It has not. The simple truth is that its numbers have not grown consistently at all. What has grown is the scope of its impact on Americans' daily lives. It is not bigger; it is more intrusive.

Who They Are

Let's look at the facts:

— The federal government had about 2.8 million civilian employees in 1984, not so very much more than the 2.4 million it had in 1952, no more than the 2.8 million it had in 1969. The level of federal employment has not gone steadily up or steadily down.

— Moreover, federal employment has drastically *declined* as a proportion of total government employment (federal, state, and local)—from about 40 percent in 1952 to 17 percent in 1984. Bureaucracy is growing all right, but only the bureaucracies of state and local governments, which employed 4.2 million people in 1952 but had 16.3 million employees in 1984.

— The "pointy headed" and "distant" federal bureaucrats of political lore do not, for the most part, live and work in Washington, D.C. Seven-eighths of them work in regional, local, and foreign offices, among the people they serve. If there is a problem, physical distance is not it.

— About 80 percent of federal bureaucrats hold white-collar jobs. Men outnumber women by about 2 to 1; the average age is about 40; and members of racial minorities make up somewhat more than 20 percent of the total. Thirteen years is the average length of service.[5]

---

[5] Gerard S. Gryski, *Bureaucratic Policy Making in a Technological Society* (Cambridge: Schenckman, 1981), p. 36.

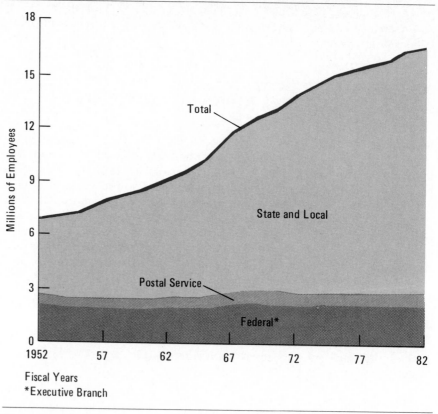

Figure 12-1   Government Civilian Employment

Fiscal Years
*Executive Branch

Source: *Special Analyses, Budget of the United States Government, Fiscal Year 1986* (Washington, D.C.: 1985), p. I–11.

Merit Systems

In 1905, a celebrated politician of New York's Tammany Hall observed that "the civil-service law [the Pendleton Act] is the curse of the nation. I know more than one young man . . . who worked for the ticket and was overflowing with patriotism, but when he was knocked out by the civil-service humbug [by competitive exams] he got to hate his country and became an Anarchist . . . And just think! He might be a patriot except for that cussed civil service."[6]

Anarchism should now be raging among us because about 90 percent of all federal employees—far more than in Plunkitt's day—are now covered by one of several merit systems.

The Civil-Service System. The largest and oldest is the original civil-service system, run since the federal civil-service reform of 1978 by the Office of Personnel Management (OPM). This agency oversees the use of competitive exams for filling positions in about 60 percent of the federal government's

---

[6] William L. Riordan, *Plunkitt of Tammany Hall* (New York: Dutton, 1969; orig. ed. 1905), pp. 11–12.

Table 12-1 Government Employment and Population, 1952–1984

FISCAL YEAR	GOVERNMENT EMPLOYMENT				POPULATION
	Federal Executive Branch (thousands)	State and Local Governments (thousands)	All Governmental Units (thousands)	Federal as Percent of All Governmental Units	Federal Employment per 1,000 Population
1952	2,574	4,134	6,708	38.4	16.3
1953	2,532	4,282	6,814	37.2	15.8
1954	2,382	4,552	6,934	34.4	14.6
1955	2,371	4,728	7,099	33.4	14.3
1956	2,372	5,064	7,436	31.9	14.0
1957	2,391	5,380	7,771	30.8	13.9
1958	2,355	5,630	7,985	29.5	13.5
1959	2,355	5,806	8,161	28.8	13.2
1960	2,371	6,073	8,444	28.1	13.1
1961	2,407	6,295	8,702	27.7	13.1
1962	2,485	6,533	9,018	27.6	13.3
1963	2,490	6,834	9,324	26.7	13.2
1964	2,469	7,236	9,705	25.4	12.9
1965	2,496	7,683	10,179	24.5	12.8
1966	2,664	8,259	10,923	24.4	13.6
1967	2,877	8,730	11,607	24.8	14.5
1968	2,951	9,141	12,092	24.4	14.7
1969	2,980	9,496	12,476	23.9	14.7
1970	2,944	9,869	12,813	23.0	14.4
1971	2,883	10,372	13,255	21.8	13.9
1972	2,823	10,896	13,719	20.6	13.5
1973	2,775	11,286	14,061	19.7	13.2
1974	2,847	11,713	14,560	19.6	13.4
1975	2,848	12,114	14,962	19.0	13.3
1976	2,832	12,282	15,114	18.7	13.2
1977	2,789	12,704	15,493	18.0	12.8
1978	2,820	13,050	15,870	17.8	12.9
1979	2,823	13,308	16,131	17.5	12.8
1980	2,821	13,445	16,266	17.3	12.7
1981	2,806	13,274	16,080	17.5	12.2
1982	2,768	13,207	15,975	17.3	11.9
1983	2,819	13,226	16,045	17.6	12.0
1984	2,854	13,440	16,294	17.5	12.0

SOURCE: *Special Analyses, Budget of the United States Government, Fiscal Year 1986* (Washington, D.C.: GPO, 1985), p. I-11.

civilian jobs. All of these clerical, professional, administrative, technical, managerial, and supervisory posts are classified under a General Schedule (GS) ranging from grade 1 to 18. Clerical and subprofessional positions are in the lowest grades. Middle-management and professional positions are graded GS–12 to GS–15. For the most part, grades GS–16 to GS–18, which used to be called the "supergrades," have been converted to a Senior Executive Service. This was one of President Carter's most ambitious administrative reforms. Members of the SES can be transferred from agency to agency, region to region, and position to position (within the SES) with little formal procedure. Thus, they can be moved around to where they are most needed and assigned the work they can do best without regard to the rigidities of promotion procedure, demotion, or position classification that characterize such movement in the rest of the General Schedule. College graduates start off at GS–5 to GS–7, depending on their qualifications. People with a master's degree or higher begin at GS–7, GS–9, or GS–11.[7]

Special Merit Systems. A further 30 percent of all the federal government's civilian employees work for agencies—including the public health service, the Federal Bureau of Investigation (FBI), the Central Intelligence Agency (CIA), the foreign service, and the postal system—that are thought to be too specialized for the civil-service program and thus have their own personnel systems, also based on merit.

The Unprotected. About 10 percent of the federal government's civilian employees, including some members of the SES, are not covered by merit systems at all. Only about 2,000 of them occupy posts of great importance—cabinet secretaries, assistant secretaries, under secretaries, agency heads, some bureau chiefs, and other sundry policy makers. Appointed by the President or with his approval, these are the people whom newspaper and TV reporters speak of as "the Administration." To prevent them from political encroachment upon merit system employees, the 1978 civil-service reform created the Merit Systems Protection Board (MSPB).

The Executive Departments

Until 1967, we got along with a Constitution that did not mention the executive departments. The Twenty-fifth Amendment, ratified in that year, did at last refer to "the principal officers of the executive departments." Yet the earliest departments date from George Washington's time.

The thirteen cabinet-level departments of the early 1980s came into being gradually, over 200 years. Proposals to add new departments are commonplace; so are proposals to abolish existing ones. President Reagan came into office intending to abolish no fewer than two—Energy and Education—but Congress, not the President, creates departments and abolishes them.

The Core Departments. Under the Articles of Confederation (see Chapter 2), there were no federal departments at all, merely Congress and a few clerks. The Constitution of 1789 was written precisely to create a true federal government, but government was then thought to have only a few legitimate functions: foreign relations, government finance, defense, mail delivery, and law and order. In the beginning, Congress provided for these few, and for little else, by setting up four departments: State (1789), Treasury (1789), War (1789), and the Navy (1798). (The Department of War, which ran the army, was in 1947 fused with the Navy Department and the new Department of the Air Force to form the Department of Defense.) The federal government inherited the Post Office from the old Confederation (see Chapter 2). President Washington appointed the first Attorney-General, the government's chief legal officer, in 1789, but the Justice Department was created only in 1870.

---

[7] The uniformed military bureaucracy has a parallel structure, but is divided into three basic classifications not readily crossed. At the bottom are enlisted personnel, grades E-1 through E-9 (private and seaman recruit through sergeant major and master chief petty officer, in the army and the navy, respectively). In the middle are four warrant officer grades, W-1 through W-4; at the top are commissioned officers, from grades O-1 through O-10 (second lieutenant and ensign through four-star (full) general and admiral, in the army and the navy, respectively).

The Clientele Departments. Except for the Treasury, none of the core departments really dealt with internal affairs. Of government in the internal sense, we had very little, and that little was mostly taken care of by the states. There was but one important exception: the Post Office Department, one of the original departments and ever afterward the largest civilian employer in the federal government. The need for an effective, nationally supported postal service was recognized from the first because letters were then the only form of remote communication. From Andrew Jackson's time (1829–1837) on, the postmaster general was often an important figure, for throughout the nineteenth century and well into the twentieth, local postmasterships were key party patronage plums. But by 1970, letters (and the mail in general) were only one among many forms of remote communication, and in that year Congress replaced the department with the U.S. Postal Service, an independent federal agency. It is headed by a postmaster general, but one who is neither a member of the cabinet nor a leader in party politics.

Apart from the Postal Service, we felt no need for an elaborate federal machinery of internal government until the mid-nineteenth century. A number of departments were set up then, primarily to service—rather than to regulate—the private economy. Three departments fit this pattern and sought to promote the general interests of very specific constituencies: Agriculture[8] (1889); Commerce, and Labor both in 1913. The Department of the Interior was established earlier, in 1849, largely to deal with Indian affairs. It is important to bear in mind, though, that even departments in the service of a clientele group, such as farmers, may sometimes be engaged in regulation of their activities. For instance, nowadays, although Agriculture is still a clientele department, it has responsibility for administering a number of programs that place restrictions on the planting and marketing of crops.

The Modern Departments. For a time, these departments kept up with our expectations of what an American government ought to do. These expectations changed by the mid-1930s, but none of the agencies created by the New Deal was given cabinet rank. In 1953, however, a number of agencies were brought together in a new department—Health, Education and Welfare (HEW). Then in 1979, HEW was split in two—Health and Human Services, and Education. Lyndon Johnson's "Great Society" produced two cabinet-level departments: Housing and Urban Development (HUD) in 1965, and Transportation, in 1967. President Carter created the two departments, Energy (1977) and Education (1979), that Ronald Reagan wished to dismantle.

Hardly anyone wants to do away with the State or Defense Departments, although many people want to change their policies. The mere existence of all the modern departments, not just Energy and Education, is controversial, for all must function in areas of policy that are not illuminated by a clear consensus about the limits or very legitimacy of federal action. Indeed, Mr. Reagan's desire to abolish the Energy and Education Departments was just as controversial as the departments themselves. He met with great resistance in Congress, and the two departments continued to exist.

U.S. Postal Service

The Postal Service started out as a cabinet-level department but is now a public corporation. Here a Postal Service employee is shown operating an optical character reader, which reads zip codes and sorts mail.

---

[8] Agriculture was set up under the Morrill (Land-Grant) Act in 1862, but under a commissioner. The first secretary of agriculture, with a place in the cabinet, was established by act of Congress in 1889.

In the mid-nineteenth century, a number of departments were set up to service—but not regulate—the private economy. Agriculture was made a cabinet-level department in 1889, and it promotes the interest of a special constituency.

Independent Executive Agencies

Some executive agencies (those agencies controlled by the President) are not important enough to be made cabinet-level departments but are too important—or too well-connected politically—to be brought into a cabinet-level department. These agencies have therefore remained independent—directly under the President and, in some cases, independent of the President. They include the Veterans Administration (VA), the Environmental Protection Agency (EPA), the National Aeronautics and Space Administration (NASA), the Agency for International Development (AID), and the Small Business Administration (SBA).

Independent Regulatory Commissions

Independent regulatory commissions are another type of federal bureaucratic agency. Among them are the Interstate Commerce Commission, the Securities and Exchange Commission, the Federal Communications Commission, the Federal Trade Commission, and a number of others. These agencies are frequently concerned with establishing rates, entry, and rules for fair practices in the industries or aspects of the economy under their jurisdiction. For example, before being phased out as part of the broad effort to deregulate the economy, the Civil Aeronautics Board set rates, approved routes, and controlled entry into the commercial airline industry. The Federal Trade Commission is concerned with fair marketing practices and antitrust measures; the National Labor Relations Board seeks to develop provisions for assuring that collective bargaining practices are fair.

The President not only appoints the top personnel of most other agencies but he also dismisses them at will. In theory, the President is their boss; in practice, the executive departments and agencies have their own interests to promote, and they promote them vigorously, usually with the help of the President's appointees. Even in theory, however, independent regulatory

NASA (the National Aeronautics and Space Administration) is an executive agency. Here, the mission operations control room of the Johnson Space Center is shown during a Space Shuttle Columbia TV transmission from Earth orbit.

agencies are much more removed from the President's control than are other agencies. The President nominates members of independent commissions but subject to certain legal guidelines that prescribe their professional qualifications and partisan ties. Moreover, the terms of these members do not run concurrently (begin and end simultaneously). They are staggered; so at any one time, independent commissions usually include members appointed by more than one President. And the President cannot dismiss them at will.

The Federal Reserve Board—"the Fed"—regulates commercial banks, controls the money supply, and sets interest rates (see Chapter 16). It is the most important of the independent regulatory commission. (In one sense, the Fed is also an executive agency: At the direction of the Treasury Department, it buys and sells foreign currencies to raise or lower the dollar's price in relation to them.)

Independent regulatory commissions are sometimes called "the headless fourth branch of government." Congress created them to ensure "expert" regulation, largely of the private economy, "free of politics." Making their

A Rite of Spring

One of the most notorious results of the fear of budget cuts is the end-of-the-fiscal-year spending spree . . . It was a traditional rite of spring in Washington until a few years ago, when the end of the fiscal year was changed from June 30 to September 30. Now the season—harvest time—couldn't be more perfect, and the ritual remains the same. As the midnight hour approaches, each agency desperately tries to use up all its appropriated funds for that year so it won't appear to have been overbudgeted.

Several years ago Senator William Proxmire got hold of a memo sent by Admiral Elmo Zumwalt, then chief of naval operations, to his key subordinates, urging them to spend $400 million quickly before the fiscal year ended. When Proxmire held hearings on the memo and on the navy's efforts to get rid of the money by paying high claims to shipping contractors,

Admiral Isaac Kidd, chief of the naval materiel command, explained: "We must . . . commit those funds within the prescribed period in order not to be put in a position of disadvantage later on by someone being able to say, "Well, you asked for money, but you did not spend it, so we are going to take it away or cut your budget next year."

How did Admiral Kidd meet this crisis? "We have gone with teams of competent contract people from Washington to outlying field activities to look over their books with them . . . to see in what areas there is susceptibility to improved capability to commit funds." As every taxpayer knows, there is never a shortage of that susceptibility.

Charles Peters, *How Washington Really Works* (Reading, Mass.: Addison, 1980), p. 39.

policies subject to presidential control was considered too dangerous. This flight from politics—especially in dealing with important areas of the private economy—is a strong and persistent characteristic of American government. Europeans have great difficulty understanding how a central bank like the Federal Reserve Board can possibly be independent of the rest of the government; in Europe, the policies of central banks fit into integrated budget and fiscal policies, adopted by cabinets. But this is not the American way, for better or worse.

Numbers: Money and Manpower

Budgets are very important to departments and agencies, both administratively and as indicators of their relative importance in the politics of the federal bureaucracy. If you want to know how important a program, objective, or department really is, find out how much money is spent on it and how many workers that money will buy. In fact, you could write a history of recent times simply by examining year-to-year and decade-to-decade changes of this sort. However, one should never conclude that budgets and the number of personnel are the only indicators of administrative power in the federal government. For instance, the State Department is relatively small in funds and staff, but its influence is felt worldwide on a daily basis.

By Department. The federal government includes about 35 separate departments and independent agencies, but a small number of them accounts for a high proportion of its 2.9 million civilian employees: Defense (with a staff of 893,000); Health and Human Services (136,000); and the Treasury (110,000). About 527,000 men and women work for the U.S. Postal Service.

Health and Human Services has the largest budget: $228 billion in fiscal 1981, which is 35 percent of all federal spending. Defense comes next, with

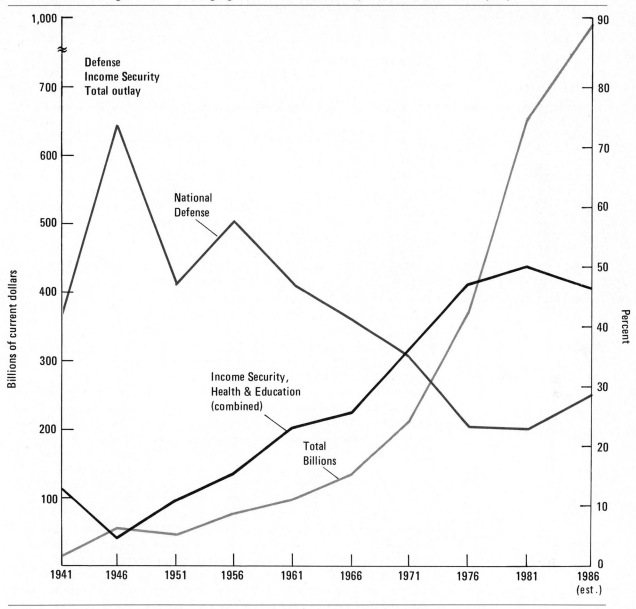

Figure 12–2 Changing Patterns of Federal Expenditures, 1941–1986 (est.)

$156 billion, 24 percent of the 1981 total. Until about 1970—except during the Depression—national defense accounted for a much higher proportion of total spending because the overall federal budget, in absolute dollars, was very much smaller. As a proportion of the gross national product (GNP), defense spending was small, only 1 percent of GNP until 1941, except during World War I. From the outbreak of the Korean War in 1950, until the Vietnam War wound down after 1970, defense and space claimed almost 10 percent of a vastly larger GNP. By 1981, that share had been cut to a bit more than 5 percent.

Since the early 1960s, the real change has been the growth of domestic spending for Social Security, health, education, and welfare. In 1950, federal expenditures for "income security," health, and education accounted for only 1.9 percent of our GNP. By 1965, this share had gone up to 4.3 percent, and by fiscal year 1981, to 11.1 percent. In 1972, for only the second time in American history,[9] spending for these items exceeded total expenditures on defense, international relations, and space. The new balance persisted, which explains much of recent American history. Despite cost overruns and sniping from liberals, national defense is not in itself politically or socially controversial. Social Security is another political sacred cow. Almost all the vastly expanded programs in the Departments of Education and Health and Human Services (HSS) are controversial.

By Areas of Responsibility. Not all the federal government's social-welfare spending falls under the budget of Health and Human Services, and the Defense Department does not spend every dollar appropriated to protect the United States from foreign enemies. Departmental budgets often conceal more than they show. Let's take a look at the purposes the money is spent for, not the departments that spend it.

Welfare. First, social-welfare spending accounts for an even higher proportion of the total than the HHS budget would appear to suggest: In 1981, about half of the federal government's expenditures provided income supplements, health and education benefits, job training, direct employment, and so on to the poor, the sick, the disabled, and the aged. In the late 1950s, social-welfare spending accounted for only 25 percent of the budget, defense for 50 percent. What some call the *welfare shift* had by 1975 reversed those proportions. This reversal was the main theme of the budgetary—and, therefore, the political—history of the 1960s and 1970s.

Economic and Social Regulation. The other part of that history was the growth of spending for social and economic regulation. Economic regulation affects specific industries. Social regulation covers broad areas of public policy—environmental and consumer protection and job safety, for instance. From 1970 to 1980, government spending for social and economic regulation soared from less than $900 million to $6.5 billion—about 90 percent of it for social regulation. During those 10 years, the number of regulatory agencies increased by more than 60 percent; the number of their employees increased from fewer than 28,000 to more than 88,000 positions; and Congress passed about as many major new regulatory laws as it had in all the years from the New Deal to 1970.

Summing Up. If the number of federal bureaucrats was no greater in 1980 than it had been in 1952, why do politicians get elected and reelected by making claims to the contrary? Why are our perceptions of the bureaucracy's size so much at odds with reality? Why do we suppose that an occupying army of federal time-servers has steadily and noisily proliferated throughout all these years?

There is a reason. Although the number of federal bureaucrats has not grown steadily in the years since 1952, the functions of the bureaucracy have changed. As a result, it is now a much more obvious and, some would say, intrusive force in our lives. Before 1932, the only bureaucrat most Americans met regularly was a postal employee. We expected little from government, and we got little. We now get vastly more; but as a result, the government orders us about vastly more, sometimes in very controversial ways—like

---

[9] The first was during the Depression.

school busing. At few, if any, times in all our national history have the powers and policies of the federal bureaucracy been as controversial as they are right now.

CONTROLLING BUREAUCRACY

Take a look at the chart that shows the organization of the Defense Department. On its face, it looks quite clear. At the top, though not shown, is the President of the United States, the commander-in-chief of our armed forces on land, sea, and in the air. Below the President is the head of the department itself, the secretary of defense, and the secretary's chief assistant, the deputy secretary. Below them are the officials who head the department's staff (or advisory) units and its line units, which operate programs. At this level, we have the assistant secretaries for legislative affairs and public affairs, and below them the under secretaries for defense policy and for research and engineering.

From the secretary on down, these officials preside over the department as a whole. However, the armed forces comprise three separate fighting services—the army, the navy (including the marines), and the air force—so there must be secretaries, under secretaries, and assistant secretaries for each.

Now, the officials mentioned so far are civilians, people who make policy and administer programs but who do not command military units. That is a job for uniformed personnel. Each fighting unit is ultimately responsible to the chiefs of staff of the army or the air force, the chief of naval operations, or the marine corps commandant. These four make up the Joint Chiefs of Staff, which reports directly to the secretary of defense.

Below all these high-ranking officials and military officers are 2 million uniformed men and women and 893,000 civilians who actually defend the United States.

The details of this organization are not what is important. Except at the very top—the secretary, the deputy secretary, the assistant secretaries, and the under secretaries—such details vary from department to department. What does not vary, first, is the fact that official posts and titles tend to proliferate, especially at the top. Once, for example, our ambassador to Chile

"reported directly to the Secretary of State. But soon a Chile desk officer was interposed in the hierarchy, followed by an Assistant Secretary for Latin America (with deputy), and then a regional director for the West Coast of Latin America, with his deputy. So now there are at least six layers of titled officials between the Secretary and the ambassador." The embassy's staff, too, has become more complicated.[10]

Second, every department comprises very diverse and sometimes conflicting parts—in this case, the three services and the multitude of individual units they include. Third, the official organization of every department often conflicts with its real organization. The President stands at the head of the chart, but a department that attempted to satisfy the President and only the President would soon be voted out of existence.

What is the *real* organization of the executive departments? Let's take another look at the Department of Defense.

---

[10] Charles Peters, *How Washington Really Works* (Reading, Mass.: Addison, 1980), p. 63.

Figure 12-3 Department of Defense

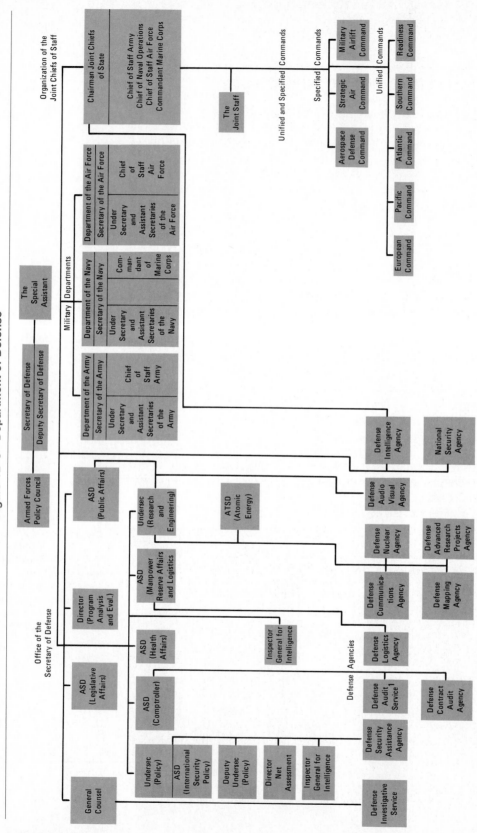

¹Effective April 20, 1981, the Defense Audit Service will report to the Assistant Secretary of Defense (Review and Oversight), a new position.

The "Iron Triangle"

The President nominates the secretary of defense and is supposed to be the secretary's boss. But the secretary cannot buy even a typewriter or a pencil sharpener if Congress does not approve the relevant program and appropriate funds for it. And without the consent of Congress, the secretary cannot set up or spend money for a weapons program. Moreover, the Department of Defense, like other departments, does not confront Congress as a monolith. Defense comprises three separate services, and the secretary must attempt to satisfy each of them because each has its own ties to Congress, independent of the department's.

Congress, too, is complicated. The responsibility for considering the department's requests belongs first to the House and Senate Armed Services Committees and to their subcommittees on defense appropriations. Many of their members have served for years and regard themselves, rightly or wrongly, as experts. They have their own pet ideas and programs and do not blindly follow the President's or the secretary's pet ideas and programs. In Congress, moreover, military considerations are not the only ones. Defense contracts run to billions of dollars, and powerful congressmen and senators want some of that money for companies in their own districts. In short, the funding battles that are first fought within the department are fought again in Congress. Should the army, the navy, or the air force fail to persuade the department to adopt a particular program, it can always try again in Congress.

Finally, many pressure groups have an interest in the activities of the Defense Department: veterans' groups, manufacturers of military equipment, labor unions that organize defense-industry workers, and people who live in districts with big defense plants or military bases. Then, too, there are many people who simply follow defense problems out of curiosity or patriotism. All these groups make up the "interested public," and the secretary of defense must try to please them, too.

Over the decades, our government bureaucracies, the committees of Congress that oversee them, and the interest groups affected by their activities

AP/Wide World Photos

General John Vessey, chairman of the Joint Chiefs of Staff, and Defense Secretary Caspar Weinberger appear before the Senate Armed Services Committee to discuss defense funding reductions.

constantly bargain with one another. The need to defend these bargains, gains, common interests, and opinions fuse the three into what some would call an iron triangle, which can and does defy the President, the commander-in-chief and head of the executive branch.

It is important to note that although iron triangles can directly involve the heads of departments, they can also comprise *bureau chiefs*, congressional subcommittees, and interest groups. In this case, career bureaucrats may be critical actors in public policy making—and they may be considerably resistant to direction by department heads or other politically appointed federal executives. Since the tenure of such bureau chiefs and membership on congressional subcommittees are generally longer than the term of a political executive, iron triangles of this kind are sometimes referred to as the "permanent government." It is this aspect of the federal bureaucracy against which presidential candidates often complain most.

A Textbook Case. The year was 1944, and the United States was fighting the most devastating war in modern history. President Franklin D. Roosevelt had sent to Congress a proposal to have the Interior Department's Bureau of Reclamation build an agricultural irrigation dam on the Kings river in California. Another part of the executive branch, the Army Corps of Engineers, also wanted to build the project and had submitted a rival plan. The bureau would have limited the amount of land that any one owner could irrigate with water from the project, imposed controls on local land speculation, and required the project's beneficiaries to repay much of its cost. The corps' plan imposed no limits or controls, and it was much more attractive to local property owners.

The Army Corps of Engineers has general responsibility for river and harbor development throughout the United States, so it is very powerful and has very good connections in Congress. Usually, they are better than the President's connections. Spokesmen for the Corps went up to Capitol Hill and persuaded the House Interior Committee to recommend making the Corps responsible for the project, in defiance of its commander-in-chief, the President. Mr. Roosevelt then fired off letters to the secretary of war and the chairman of the House Interior Committee, repeating his support for the Bureau of Reclamation. No matter; the committee and the full House awarded the project to the Army Corps of Engineers.

When the measure went up to the Senate, the President again wrote to the secretary of war to remind him that the administration, of which he was himself an important member, supported the bureau's plan, not the Corps.' The secretary of war reported the President's views to the Senate but did nothing to muzzle the Corps, which took its case to the Senate Commerce Committee. The committee, and later the full Senate, supported the Corps. With the help of its friends in Congress and powerful local interests, the Army Corps of Engineers had defied the President of the United States and prevailed. The Kings River Dam was duly built—by the Army Corps of Engineers.[11]

Let us consider these truly astonishing events. President Roosevelt was commander-in-chief of the U.S. Armed Forces, and a global war was under way. By tradition (and also by provision of the Uniform Code of Military

---

[11] This account is drawn from David B. Truman, *The Governmental Process*, 2nd ed. (New York: Knopf, 1971), pp. 410–15.

Justice), soldiers who disobey a direct order of their commanders in wartime can be sentenced to death. Yet here is a case where the general who commanded the Corps defied direct orders from *his* commander-in-chief, the President of the United States—not once, but several times. There was no punishment, nor even thought of any, and in the end it was the general, not the President, who got his way.

The Rules of the Game. Chains of command, with the President at the top, are not always quite so irrelevant as they were in the Kings River project. Yet the unwritten rules of the game require all heads of departments and agencies to engage in continuous and intense struggles for power. When a bureau can fuse its own interests with those of Congress and of the interested public, it is hard for a President to break the iron triangle. Besides, Presidents come and go, but the permanent government of the bureaucracy and Congress abides, generating its own code of behavior and way of life.

"Agency Culture"

Ernest Fitzgerald, a civilian employee of the Defense Department, went before a committee of Congress in 1968. He claimed that the Lockheed C-5A transport plane, then being built for the air force, had cost vastly more than the sum Congress had appropriated for it and was a bad plane to boot. Fitzgerald's accusations were accurate. Was he promoted and given a large raise? No. He was fired. And when a court ordered the department to give him back his job, the department gave him the title and an office—and no work. Read this story carefully and think about it. Should you ever work for a bureaucracy, public *or* private, and do what Ernest Fitzgerald did, you may well suffer the same fate. Bureaucracies have their own interests to protect.

Each department, each agency, each office is a little world unto itself, with its own agency culture. If you work in an office where men wear pinstripe suits and sober ties, you too should wear pinstripe suits and sober ties. In all likelihood, you will not even be hired unless you do, because agencies want to recruit people who fit in. There are several ways to attempt this. In the first place, a boss can usually manipulate job descriptions to make them fit only the desired person. Quite often, this person emerges not through competitive exams but through the buddy system, the friends and relations of the bureau's staff. Finally, would-be employees of an agency tend to select themselves: Most people want to work for agencies whose programs they support and whose agency culture is compatible with their own.

Should nonconformists like Ernest Fitzgerald manage to slip through, they can be "encouraged" to leave, despite tenure. True, most federal bureaucrats can be fired only on conviction for some act of malfeasance—just about impossible to prove—or in the event of a "reduction-in-force" (RIF) dismissal of excess employees. Short of these catastrophes, nonconformists can be made miserable in a number of ways: Their positions can be stripped of functions and power, they can be transferred to northern Alaska, or their colleagues can be persistently nasty to them.

Like the iron triangle, agency culture isolates each department from the rest of the world—and from democratic control. We cannot vote bureaucrats out of office. Are those we elect to run the bureaucracy—the President and the members of Congress—better able to control it? Let us see.

Presidential Controls

Our President is the sole head of the executive branch—a "monarch" of sorts (see Chapter 10). Not every monarch is a strong one, nor equally strong in all areas of responsibility. The present queen of Great Britain is said to reign but not rule. At some times, and in some ways, our Presidents find it hard to rule, too.

For one thing, Presidents are not necessarily managers. Unlike prime ministers, they often come into office lacking executive experience in the federal government or in any large organization. Presidents Carter and Reagan had been governors but had never held federal office. Presidents Truman, Kennedy, Johnson, Nixon, and Ford had served mostly in Congress, not in the executive branch. President Eisenhower had been the highest-ranking general in the army, but had never served in Congress. This division of experience is one result of the separation of powers (see Chapter 2), which keeps the Congress apart from the executive branch and thus prevents members of Congress from getting executive experience unless they resign their seats.

As a necessary and unfortunate result, the President and the President's chief assistants often come into office largely ignorant of the federal government and its workings. They may know little or nothing of the character of agency cultures and other aspects of the ways federal agencies function. This lack of experience and knowledge can sap the President's power to run the government and the bureaucracy.

Appointment and Removal. The President *does* appoint the heads of all executive departments and all executive agencies. The presidential choice must then be confirmed by two-thirds of those senators present and voting. Outright rejections, though rare, do happen, and the very possibility imposes certain constraints on the President.

Department heads, once appointed, do not form a "team," since most are strangers to the President and to one another. Some appointments—especially to the Departments of Labor, Agriculture, and Commerce—usually buy off important interest groups. Others may reward political loyalty to the President. Still others may actually have relevant experience or expertise.

When the members of the cabinet show up for work at their departments, they find that their bureaucratic subordinates regard them as mere temporary interlopers—just what they are. Listen to the words of President Carter's first treasury secretary, W. Michael Blumenthal (1977–1979):

> Out of 120,000 people in the Treasury [Department], I was able to select 25, maybe. The other 119,975 are outside my control. . . . So it's hard to talk about running something. If you wish to make substantive changes, policy changes, and the department employees don't like what you're doing, they have ways of frustrating you, or stopping you, that do not exist in private industry.[12]

What is more, department chiefs are surrounded almost the whole day long by people who work within their departments. From these people, they get most of their advice. They absorb the agency culture and come to look at the department as it looks at itself; the problems of the department become their problems, the importance of the department, their importance. Usually, they

---

[12] Quoted in Thomas E. Cronin, *The State of the Presidency*, 2nd ed. (Boston: Little, Brown, 1980), p. 242.

see that departmental policies, right or wrong, have remained fairly constant from administration to administration, party to party. They realize, too, that members of Congress who have a stake in departmental policies cannot be ignored, and neither can the interested public. Pretty soon, the department heads have become both captives and advocates of the bureaucracy.

Back at the White House, the President and the President's staff resent this state of affairs. After all, the department heads were chosen to represent the President to the bureaucracy, not the bureaucracy to the President. The President comes to rely on the White House staff, the inner core of loyalists, who snipe at those department heads with responsibilities that overlap their own. The conflict between the President's national security adviser and the secretary of state, so frequently in the news in recent years, is usually the most open symbol of the disaffection between the President and the department heads.

After simmering below the surface for a few weeks or months, the conflict comes into public view, where journalists eagerly seize on it. The President may now decide that certain department heads have been intolerably disloyal and demand their resignations. President Carter, for example, fired three of his cabinet members in 1979 and accepted the resignations of two others, amid charges that they had been poor "team players." The contrived air of drama surrounding these events was unusual, but not the turnover itself or the tensions that produced it. Secretary of State Alexander Haig was dismissed in 1982 for similar reasons. Presidents pay dearly for these dismissals, which give their administrations an appearance of derangement. Moreover, the dismissed cabinet officers not infrequently make embarrassing disclosures about the Presidents who no longer needed their services.

Regulatory Agencies and Career Officials. Whatever good it may do, the President can dismiss cabinet and subcabinet officials at will. But members of independent regulatory commissions can be dismissed only for neglect of duty or malfeasance in office, not for sabotaging the President's policies. And the civil-service system so protects workers within its domain that, according to some critics, it is just about impossible to fire them.

As mentioned earlier, the federal Civil Service Reform Act of 1978 created a Senior Executive Service to give cabinet members and other political executives more flexibility in dealing with top-level civil servants. Members of the SES can be moved out of programs where they seem unresponsive to the policy directions being pursued by the presidential administration, and replaced by other SES members more in tune with these directions. If such flexibility is employed on a widespread basis, the transferring of SESers among programs and agencies may weaken the iron triangle, because congressional committees and interest groups would constantly be dealing with new bureau chiefs presumably having different perspectives on the programs under their jurisdiction. There are currently about 8,000 members of the SES.

Reorganization. President Nixon, who knew that the power of appointment would not make him master of the bureaucracy, thought he had a better idea: to break up existing departments and, therefore, the iron triangles that upheld them. In 1971, Mr. Nixon sent to Congress a proposal to consolidate the Departments of Agriculture, Commerce, HEW, HUD, Interior, Labor, and Transportation. Out of these seven would have come four new units: Human Resources, Natural Resources, Economic Development, and Community Development.

Interest groups and congressional committees that worked with the existing departments fought and blocked Mr. Nixon's plan, but hard upon his triumphant reelection in 1972, he again proposed to consolidate the seven departments into four. Mr. Nixon was never very popular in Congress, whose members did not wish to break up the iron triangles of which they themselves were an important part. Once again, his plan never got anywhere, but this time because it was derailed by the Senate Watergate investigation.

In any case, then and now the power to create and abolish departments belongs to Congress and to it alone, along with the power to prescribe their duties and structure. Since 1939, however, Congress has delegated a part—though only a part—of that authority to the President, most recently in a 1977 act that permits the President to propose changes in the internal organization of each department and agency, although not to abolish, merge, or create them. The act gives either house sixty days to veto such proposals. Most earlier reorganization acts also provided for a "legislative veto." Today, however, it appears that such legislative vetoes are unconstitutional. (We will discuss this later.)

Congress has actually accepted many more reorganization proposals than it has rejected—from 1939 to 1977 it accepted 92 out of 115. These presidential victories have probably made little difference, if only because they concern relatively unimportant matters. President Nixon could not get Congress even to consider the idea of reorganizing the departments as a whole; neither could President Carter, although he did persuade it to set up two new departments.

Suppose that Mr. Nixon or Mr. Carter had gotten his way, or that both had. In either case, a President can stay in office for 8 years at most, unless he succeeds to the presidency from being Vice-President and finishes out two years or less of the former President's term, in which case he is eligible to be elected for two additional terms. Bureaucracies are able to persist indefinitely. Even if Mr. Nixon had controlled the four new departments more fully than he controlled the seven old ones, would his successors have done the same? Eventually, new departments would have built up new ties with Congress, new ties with interest groups. There would still have been iron trangles, a permanent government, and resistance to presidential domination.

Budgeting. No department or agency can function without money, so they are all preoccupied with their budgets, the staff of bureaucratic life. The federal budget is drawn up deep in the bosom of the White House, in the Office of Management and Budget (OMB). Why can't Presidents bring a department or an agency to heel merely by turning off the spigot? They can't because they lack the authority to make such threats credible. First, the President merely proposes the budget; Congress can cut or add as it pleases. The President and the OMB do not even have anything like complete control over the proposals themselves. For every agency, in its

> annual struggle to protect or enlarge its budget, has a decisive advantage over its natural enemy, the Office of Management and Budget, which appraises budget requests. The OMB might assign 6 or 7 employees to size up a cabinet-level department's budget, but the department will have 450 or 500 budget people whose job is to keep the OMB from finding out the truth. The agency may ask for four or five times what it needs for a program, confident that the OMB can't possibly track down all the overestimates, thus assuring that a more than satisfactory final figure will emerge.[13]

_____
[13] Charles Peters, *How Washington Really Works* (Reading, Mass.: Addison, 1980), pp. 39–40.

Office of Management and Budget Director David Stockman testifies before the House Appropriations Committee in 1985 on President Reagan's budget proposals.

Even this state of affairs, despite its encouragement of departmental free enterprise, is better than the mess it replaced. Before 1921, the President did not make budget proposals; the budget was simply what the two houses of Congress decided to spend, appropriation by appropriation. World War I budgeting was the decisive proof that something less primitive was needed. Under the Budget and Accounting Act of 1921, the President got the authority to prepare an executive budget each year, assisted by the Bureau of the Budget, OMB's direct ancestor. In 1970, Richard Nixon tinkered with some of the bureau's duties and changed its name to the present one.

Each year, budget making starts when OMB, acting directly under the President, works out the administration's overall spending target and its relative generosity to each department and agency. Then OMB gives all of them their own spending targets and asks each to keep its budget proposal within those limits. When the departments and agencies return their budget proposals to OMB, it must reconcile them with the President's spending targets—which may, by now, have changed. After both houses of Congress pass the budget—not necessarily as the President submitted it—OMB monitors the departments and agencies so that they do not overspend.

Because the budget is so enormously important, the OMB director is at times one of the great figures of Washington. But not always. Jimmy Carter's OMB director James McIntyre, was not so regarded by most Washington observers—perhaps a reflection on Mr. Carter's lack of clear priorities? The budget director who came in with President Reagan in 1981, David Stockman, acted in that year as a virtual economic vice-president, perhaps because the President who appointed *him* had very clear priorities. But Stockman's preeminence was also in part due to his way with numbers and words. It was Stockman who carried out Mr. Reagan's instructions to cut departmental spending, Stockman who persuaded the President to accept OMB's decisions, and Stockman who forced those decisions down the throats of unwilling departments. It was he who went before congressional committees to defend the budget and other aspects of "Reaganomics." When "Reaganomics" failed

How to Win at Wordsmanship

After years of backing through etymological thickets at the U.S. Public Health Service, a 63-year-old official named Philip Broughton hit upon a sure-fire method for converting frustrations into fulfillment (jargonwise). Euphemistically called the Systematic Buzz Phrase Projector, Broughton's system employs a lexicon of 30 carefully chosen "buzzwords":

Column 1	Column 2	Column 3
0. integrated	0. management	0. options
1. total	1. organizational	1. flexibility
2. systematized	2. monitored	2. capability
3. parallel	3. reciprocal	3. mobility
4. functional	4. digital	4. programming
5. responsive	5. logistical	5. concept
6. optional	6. transitional	6. time-phrase
7. synchronized	7. incremental	7. projection
8. compatible	8. third-generation	8. hardware
9. balanced	9. policy	9. contingency

The procedure is simple. Think of any three-digit number, then select the corresponding buzzword from each column. For instance, number 257 produced "systematized logistical projection," a phrase that can be dropped into virtually any report with that ring of decisive, knowledgeable authority. "No one will have the remotest idea of what you're talking about," says Broughton, "but the important thing is that they're not about to admit it."

Reproduced from *Newsweek* (May 6, 1968), pp. 104, 104B, 104D, May 1968, Newsweek, Inc.

to work as promised, thus endangering many Republican members of Congress, these earlier heroics earned Stockman many enemies on Capitol Hill.

Impoundment. About three-quarters of federal spending is described by the government itself as "relatively uncontrollable under federal law." Unemployment benefits, for example, must be paid out to anyone who meets certain criteria, however high total expenditures may climb. Congress hates to cut these programs, for "it is an axiom of politics that it is easier to give things away than to take things away."[14] So even the President's power to make budget *proposals* is more or less restricted to the remaining quarter, and Congress can do as it pleases with this quarter, too. Suppose that Congress appropriates more money to fund a department or agency than the President wishes to spend. Must it be spent anyway? In general, yes. Until President Nixon's time, 1969–1974, there was no real need for a clear or absolute answer; Presidents would occasionally *impound*, or refuse to spend, sums appropriated by Congress—but never very large sums or for very long. Mr. Nixon, however, sent up to Capitol Hill more than 100 proposals to reduce domestic spending; and when Congress refused to go along, he simply impounded the money—tens of billions of dollars, in fact.

---

[14] Elizabeth Drew, "A Reporter in Washington, D.C.: Sketchbook," *The New Yorker*, May 31, 1982, p. 94.

In 1974, Congress—still redolent with unpleasant memories of Mr. Nixon's presidency—decided to put a statutory limit on the power of impoundment.[15] It gave the President a right not to spend funds it had appropriated, but only a temporary right. If Congress did not agree within 45 days to pass a new act, a **rescission bill** to cancel the spending, the money would indeed have to be spent. When Mr. Reagan first came into office, he proposed to drop or change these controls. Congress ignored him.

Morale. A President can attempt to control the departments and agencies by manipulating their morale. Presidents, after all, must favor some programs over others. Programs that bask in the sunshine of the President's approval get money, jobs, and power; the men and women who work for them feel important. Programs that the President dislikes can defend themselves, of course; the President alone cannot trim or drop them. But such agencies enter into a state of siege. Vacant positions may not be filled. Threats of impending budget and personnel cutbacks lower morale. Employees find new jobs and leave the government; the agency is seized by a kind of paralysis.

President Reagan came into office full of plans to change the direction of federal spending. At the outset, he got his own way to a remarkable extent. The Defense Department flourished; domestic programs and agencies went into retreat. The President cut the work force in many of these domestic agencies by so demoralizing them that many employees looked for new jobs. Consider this, however: It is usually the brightest and therefore the most employable people who leave first; the rest stick it out.

Congressional Controls

In 1975, President Ford cut the budget of Amtrak, the government corporation that runs most of this country's intercity railroads. Amtrak then announced that if Congress approved the cuts, four routes would be dropped: San Francisco to Bakersfield, California; St. Louis, Missouri, to Laredo, Texas; Chicago, Illinois, to Seattle, Washington; and Norfolk, Virginia, to Chicago.

Why these four routes? Perhaps because the first one passed through the district represented by the chairman of the transportation subcommittee of the House Appropriations Committee; the second, through the state represented by the chairman of the Senate Appropriations Committee; the third, through the states of the Senate majority leader and the chairman of the Senate Commerce Committee; and the fourth, through the states of the chairmen of the Senate Commerce Committee and of its surface-transportation subcommittee, the state of the Senate majority whip, and the district of the House Commerce Committee's chairman. The seven members of Congress were duly enlisted in the cause of saving Amtrak's budget.[16]

This story has two morals. First, when bureaucrats lose a fight within the executive branch, they appeal to Congress. Second, Congress itself does not control the bureaucracy, because its members are concerned with their own reelection.

---

[15] In the Congressional Budget and Impoundment Control Act (1974).

[16] Charles Peters, *How Washington Really Works* (Reading, Mass.: Addison, 1980), p. 40.

The Birth of an Agency. The two houses of Congress are present at the creation: They pass the act that gives birth to each department and agency and sets forth its duties and organization. Congress can later add new functions or take away old ones or even kill off departments and agencies altogether. It rarely does so, but the mere possibility that it might gives it some degree of power. Congress usually refuses to *create* new departments requested by Presidents.

Funding. Journalists used to call it "the power of the purse strings"; political science professors called it the "appropriations check." By whatever name, Congress must approve the budget and therefore, in theory at least, congress control federal spending. Bureaucracies do know where the money comes from, so they are responsive to Congress—though more to the committees that must approve their budgets than to individual congressmen. Good relations with important committees and congressmen can also help an agency survive the dark night of presidential hostility. Presidents come and go, after all, but Congress and the bureaucracy are the permanent government.

But Congress has the power of the purse strings only as far as it uses that power, and often it does not. By the early 1970s, for example, many members of Congress were convinced that the Vietnam War (see Chapter 17) was a disaster, but because few of them would vote to cut off funding for it, the disaster went on and on.

Advice and Consent. Both houses of Congress must agree to set up a department or an agency and to fund it. But only the Senate confirms the President's nominee to head it. Senators use confirmation hearings to dispute the President's policies, but in the end, most of them think it wrong to block a nomination purely out of political disagreement with the nominee. Sometimes, however, the confirmation hearings become so hostile that the President decides to withdraw the nomination. A President last suffered the extreme embarrassment of actually losing a confirmation vote in 1959. The nominee who was voted down on that occasion, Lewis Strauss, was defeated not for reasons of policy but because, as one senator put it, he "was a very arrogant fellow. He's the only guy I know that could strut sitting down."[17]

Restrictive Legislation. Not only can Congress cut whole areas out of a department's or agency's jurisdiction, but it can also force a department to drop specific policies. Since 1976, for example, Congress has imposed more and more restrictions on the use of Medicaid funds for abortions. In the late 1970s it forbade the Justice Department to take part in suits that involved school busing. Similar restrictions and outright prohibitions have been included in certain foreign-aid bills.

Legislative Veto. On some issues, Congress feels sufficiently confident of public support to demand that certain kinds of administrative actions be submitted to it for approval or disapproval, usually for a sixty- to ninety-day period, before going into effect. (See Chapter 6 for a discussion of one such

---

[17] Merle Miller, *Lyndon* (New York: Putnam, 1980), p. 221.

Rita Lavelle, of the Environmental Protection Agency, testifies before a congressional committee investigating the agency.

case, the AWACS affair.) This *legislative veto* is in some cases exercised by certain committees in both houses, in others by either house (*one-house veto*), and in still others by both (*concurrent resolution*). The President cannot veto a legislative veto. The Supreme Court's decision in *Immigration and Naturalization Service* v. *Chadha* (1983) held that the *one house* legislative veto was unconstitutional because it violated the separation of powers and the process for legislating created by the Constitution. Based on the Court's reasoning and language, the two-house legislative veto may also be unconstitutional, but that has not been specifically decided upon as of this writing.

Congressional Investigations. Bureaucrats hate investigations, especially congressional investigations. The mere possibility that Congress might be stirred to look into dark corners sometimes weighs heavily on bureaucrats and keeps them on good behavior. Actually, the typical investigation is not terribly revealing, because the bureaucratic witnesses tend to "stonewall," and the congressmen do not know enough to ask good questions. Sometimes much interesting information comes out nonetheless—in the probes of the CIA carried out in the mid-1970s, for example. These hearings were so fruitful because relatively little had been known about the CIA before then.

Aid to Constituents. Suppose that your application for a federal student loan is held up. You decide against appealing to a higher level of bureaucracy, where the officials may be even less sympathetic to your case. Instead, you write to your representative and senators and ask for help. It would be unwise to expect very much; they can do little but have their aides call the department. But its employees, knowing that higher powers have an interest in you, might deal with your problems more carefully—if not more sympathetically.

Much of the work in congressional offices involves dispensing this kind of help. Congressmen rather like it because it gets them votes, without commit-

Governmental Free Enterprise

The Economic Opportunity Act provided support for new programs to train and employ the hard-core poor. But the new programs depended upon old institutions—the State Employment Services—for their implementation. Set up during the New Deal as an exchange between the business community and the unemployed, the offices of the Employment Service were primarily located in the business districts of the central cities, not easily accessible to the residents of the slums. For thirty years, the employees at each local office had filled out the same report, documenting the number of people serviced that week. Now there suddenly appeared a new clientele, more difficult to place in jobs. The forms to be filled out at the end of the week, however, remained the same, pressuring the employees to "cream the crop," servicing the least needy and least difficult to place first.

In an effort to reverse the situation, the executives in the Labor Department prescribed a new weekly form; local Employment Service employees were now called upon to report only the hard core's placement, those who'd been out of work for eighteen months and made under $3,000 a year. The shift in the pattern of incentives finally focused attention on the hard core, but now a different problem emerged. Evaluated only on the basis of how many of the most difficult people were placed in their training programs, the local employees began waving advance payments to drag in off the streets drug addicts, prison convicts, and anyone they could find. Evaluators of the training program in the Cardozo section in Washington, D.C., discovered that heroin addicts made up more than half the trainees. The word had spread in the heroin community that one had only to enter the program, stay long enough to collect the advance, and then return to the streets, providing a successful placement for the Civil Service employees and $50 to the addict for another day's fix.

The director of the Cardozo program knew what was going on, but could not admit it publicly. His program, he said to me, had to compete for money and staff with the program in Anacostia, the other slum area in the District of Columbia, and such a revelation would hurt his chances for funding in the following year. Better to keep it quiet and work from within to change the situation.

Doris Kearns, *Lyndon Johnson and the American Dream* (New York: Signet, 1977), pp. 303–4.

ting them to controversial positions that might also cost them votes. In fact, some critics intimate that Congress actually creates this sort of work for itself:

> Legislation is drafted in very general terms, so some agency, existing or newly established, must translate a vague policy mandate into a functioning program, a process that necessitates the promulgation of numerous rules and regulations and, incidentally, the trampling of numerous toes. At the next stage, aggrieved and/or hopeful constituents petition their congressmen to intervene in the complex (or at least obscure) decision processes of the bureaucracy. The cycle closes when the congressman lends a sympathetic ear, piously denounces the evils of bureaucracy, intervenes in the latter's decisions, and rides a grateful electorate to even more impressive electoral showings. Congressmen take credit coming and going. [18]

Practical Limits. In fact, most congressmen want to be reelected far more urgently than they want to control the bureaucracy. Congress has enough power to limit the President's control over the executive branch but is too decentralized and fragmented to exert much control itself. Oversight of policy tends to be sporadic and careless—when it occurs at all. Congress did make more of an effort in the 1970s—especially in budget making and foreign policy. By the early 1980s, however, it had become much less vigilant.

---

[18] Morris P. Fiorina, *Congress: Keystone of the Washington Establishment* (New Haven: Yale Univ., 1977), p. 49.

Judicial Control

Historically, the federal judiciary has played only a minimal role in controlling public bureaucracies. Aside from opposing the delegation of legislative powers to federal agencies during the 1930s, the federal courts have only infrequently interpreted the Constitution as a barrier to the exercise of authority by public bureaucrats. Beginning in the 1950s, however, this began to change. Since that time the courts have declared broad protections for people as they come into contact with administrative agencies. Nowadays, for instance, recipients of welfare benefits may have some rights to due process before their payments can be terminated. Public employees have extensive due process, First Amendment, and other substantive constitutional rights. The Eighth Amendment's proscription of cruel and unusual punishment has been the vehicle for court-ordered extensive reforms of prisons. A right to treatment has been declared for those confined to public mental health facilities. Moreover, the constitutional right to equal protection under the law has been interpreted to compel widespread reforms of public school systems, prisons, and other public institutions. Of course, the nature of judicial power is such that simply articulating such rights does not automatically lead to their enforcement. The courts have taken steps to deal with this limitation. In civil suits, courts generally hold public administrators personally liable for monetary damages if they have violated constitutional rights they could reasonably have been expected to know during the performance of their functions.[19]

SUMMARY

All modern governments—and most modern private enterprises—are run by bureaucracies. But our system of government, with its fragmentation of power among different groups of elected officials, liberates the bureaucracy and permits it to forge ties with all of them. "Free enterprise" rages within the executive branch: Agencies and departments compete against each other and for the good will of the President and Congress. Congress and the President compete for control over the bureaucracy. "Iron triangles" of executive departments and agencies, the interest groups they affect, and the congressional committees they report to often make the President relatively powerless. The President does not appoint the heads of departments and agencies and proposes a budget, but the Senate must consent to these appointments, and Congress as a whole must pass the budget. Congress can frustrate the President's efforts to control the bureaucracy but cannot itself exert control, for it is too decentralized, and its members are too often preoccupied with improving their chances of reelection.

Like all other mortals, bureaucrats have their own personal and organizational interests to protect and promote. Yet, the federal bureaucracy manages to do quite a good job of serving the public interest as Congress has defined it. No large organization is without its time-servers, its incompetents, its hacks. But most of the people who work for the federal government work hard and

---

[19] See David H. Rosenbloom, *Public Administration and Law* (New York: Marcel Dekker, 1983) for a comprehensive analysis of judicial involvement in public administration.

honorably. The great issue of public administration at present is not the quality or inner worth of our civil servants but the impact of divided government on administration. However hard department heads and senior civil servants may work to implement the President's policies, the fragmented nature of our political system encourages bureaucrats, like other policy makers in Washington, to go into business for themselves.

SUGGESTED READINGS

LAWRENCE DODD and RICHARD SCHOTT, *Congress and the Administrative State*. New York: Wiley, 1979. Knowledgeable and up-to-date analysis of the complex network of relationships between Congress and the bureaucracy.

ANTHONY DOWNS, *Inside Bureaucracy*. Boston: Little, Brown, 1967. Fine, theoretically focused analysis of the subject, concentrating on bureaucratic politics.

JAMES W. FESLER, *Public Administration: Theory and Practice*. Englewood Cliffs, N.J.: Prentice-Hall, 1980. Comprehensive text on public administration and bureaucracy by one of the leading students of the subject.

HUGH HECLO, *A Government of Strangers*. Washington, D.C.: Brookings Institution, 1977. In Britain, Japan, and many other countries the top administrative elite is drawn from a very narrow circle of people, most of whom know each other and have gone to the same elite universities. The situation is wholly different in the United States, and Heclo's analysis attempts to clarify the consequences of the difference.

C. NORTHCOTE PARKINSON, *Parkinson's Law*. Boston: Houghton Mifflin, 1957. A humorous but also very serious classic on the subject of bureaucratic growth and appetites. Useful not only for students of government but of big corporate bureaucracies. One famous aspect of Parkinson's Law is the proposition that work expands to fill the space available to it. A corollary of this (often not explicitly seen as such) is the Bureaucrat's First Duty: to leave no unexpended balance on hand at the end of the fiscal year.

B. GUY PETERS, *The Politics of Bureaucracy: A Comparative Perspective*. New York: Longmans, 1978. There are many puzzles about American government that can be cleared up with the help of comparative analysis. This book provides very important insights about American public administration and civil servants from this perspective.

DAVID H. ROSENBLOOM, *Public Administration and Law*. New York: Marcel Dekker, 1983. An in-depth discussion of the involvement of the federal judiciary in controlling public administrative activities. The book explains why administrative values often lead to action that infringes upon the constitutional rights of individual citizens.

HAROLD SEIDMAN, *Politics, Position and Power*. New York: Oxford Univ. Press, 1975. Very illuminating account of relations between Presidents and bureaucrats by an insider.

For the historically minded, who may be interested in the development of American public administration from 1789 to the beginning of the twentieth century, there stands the classic administrative history by LEONARD D. WHITE: Vol. I, *The Federalists* (1948); Vol. II, *The Jeffersonians* (1951); Vol. III, *The Jacksonians* (1954), and Vol. IV, *The Republican Era, 1869–1901* (1958), all published in New York by Macmillan. This may seem like ancient history, but as is so often the case with American political institutions and practices, this series is full of insights as to how American bureaucracy became *American* bureaucracy, with patterns of behavior that are still very important today.

The National Journal should also be mentioned here. This periodical appears monthly. It is extremely informative about current developments in Washington and excels in reporting about federal bureaucracies, their political contexts, and the programs they administer.

chapter thirteen

CONGRESS

Delbert Kalhoun's Minnesota farm has been in his family six generations, since 1864. His great grandfather and grandfather cleared the 600 acres of land where Delbert's own grandchildren now live. But the Kalhoun farm, like many other American farms, is seeing hard times. Delbert and his son Philip share a debt of $250,000 that they are unable to pay back, and the value of the farm has dropped in recent years. Philip now drives a milk delivery route to bring in extra money, and the family is considering food stamps.

In Kansas, C. David Jensen and his family lost all their farm equipment and personal property in an involuntary auction held under orders from the sheriff to repay the Citizens Bank of Grainfield. The auctioned property included Jensen family heirlooms such as a set of oak bedroom furniture and a rocking chair. Another involuntary auction was held recently to sell their 1,210 acres of farmland to repay a $400,000 mortgage. The Jensens had raised wheat on their land for 27 years.

In Georgia, forty of Ray Parks's friends joined together to sing—loudly—to prevent an auctioneer from hearing bids on his foreclosed farm.

Hope for these farmers rested in the Congress. Farmers wanted their representatives in Washington to ease their burden of heavy debts and decreasing returns by passing a bill that would guarantee loans and reduced interest rates. Many farms are so heavily steeped in debt today because during a period of prosperity in the 1970s, they borrowed to expand their farms and operations. Many blame the government for getting them in over their heads. The recession of the early 1980s and lowered costs of imported farm products are two causes of the 1985 farm crisis.

In Washington, representatives in Congress have recently been faced with cries for help from farm constituents. The entire South Dakota legislature, made up of 105 members, flew to Washington to lobby for a day. In Ames, Iowa, 15,000 people packed a coliseum protest rally. The ribbons they wore read FARM CRISIS, and they carried signs, saying, "FARMS, NOT ARMS," and "NO BILL, NO TILL."

Senate Majority Leader Robert Dole had been trying to postpone the congressional vote on a farm relief bill. The bill was a setback for the President's budget plan. Dole argued that the way to help the farmers was with smaller deficits and lower interest rates. Iowa Senator Tom Harkin led his fellow senators from farm states in voicing their constituents' views. In Lafayette Park, opposite the White House, Harkin had 250 white crosses put into the ground to represent the number of farms estimated to be going out of business daily.

Finally, eight Republican senators, all of them from farm states, joined Democrats in approving the bill. In doing so, they granted $1.85 billion to farmers in guaranteed loans, and $100 million for banks as an aid in reducing interest rates. The senate also passed a bill to give farmers half of the price-support loans they normally get in the fall. Meanwhile in the House, Democrats recognized farmers' needs with similar legislation.

Senator Dole was deeply disappointed with these measures because he believed that they undermined plans to reduce the national deficit. However, as Iowa Senator Charles Grassley, who incidentally was up for reelection in 1986, pointed out that if he had voted not to help the farmers, he would have been turning his back on the seven out of ten people in his state whose jobs depend directly on farming.[1]

WHAT IS CONGRESS?

Most tourists on Capitol Hill see little but the miles of marble hallways, the chandeliers, heroic statuary, the House and Senate chambers, and if they wish, their own congressman's outer office. The longer they stay, the more confusing Congress becomes to them. Floor debate usually plays to very small audiences of obviously bored people. Committees and subcommittees investigate obscure topics at interminable length, pausing occasionally to let their members rush to the floor for votes. These votes sometimes mean just the opposite of what they seem to mean: "Nay" on some key questions—for example, "motion to recommit" a bill to committee—is actually a vote in favor of the bill in question.

Meanwhile, much of the real business of legislating goes on in the halls, in the Senate gym, in the members' elevator, in hideaway offices the public never sees, and over the telephone. Members converse in a unique legislative dialect that is hardly intelligible to outsiders—an elliptical code studded with terms such as *mark, teller,* and *whip check.*

Congress and Parliament

Most of the world's legislatures are parliaments, but not Congress. Parliaments, in general, are controlled by strong parties. By manipulating an array

[1] George J. Church, "Playing Hardball in February," *Time*, March 4, 1985, pp. 19–20; Jacob V. Lamar, "When Push Comes to Shove," *Time*, March 11, 1985, p. 26; Ed Magnuson, "Clinging to the Land," *Time*, February 18, 1985, pp. 32–39

The U.S. Capitol Building, on Capitol Hill, contains both houses of the legislature. The Senate meets in one wing and the House of Representatives in the other.

of rewards and punishments that our own congressional leaders envy, the leadership of a parliamentary party enforces a high degree of voting loyalty among its followers. At certain times in the past, American parties may have been almost as cohesive as parliamentary parties now are, but if so, those days are long since gone. Members of Congress can now defy their party leaderships with near-impunity.

Parliamentary parties are strong because a parliamentary government can hold office only with the support of a majority of the legislature's membership. The government, in fact, is the executive committee of the legislature itself. Without strong parties, a stable parliamentary government would not be possible, for such a government must resign if it is defeated on any important issue. Such defeats occur only at moments of grave political crisis; ordinarily, a government places its policies before parliament expecting them to be adopted, and parliament duly adopts them. Because parliaments usually accept government policy, they do not examine it in detail, and therefore they usually lack developed committee systems. Nor do members, in general, specialize in particular areas of policy.

Our system is utterly different. Congress, which does not elect the President and cannot simply vote the President out of office,[2] is constitutionally independent of the executive. It has the right and, more important, the ability to modify or reject anything the President may put to it. It can and does

---

[2] Except in cases of impeachment, which is for criminal, not political, offenses.

initiate new legislation—sometimes against the President's will. Unlike most parliaments, it is *bicameral* (two-chambered) in fact as well as in form: The Senate, representing states as states, is quite as powerful as the House of Representatives and has rather more public prestige.[3] For any measure to become law, the Senate and the House must come into full agreement on it. Sometimes, the two houses are controlled by different parties, as they were in the Congress of 1981–1983. Always, their leaderships are entirely separate from, and independent of, each other. Even in earlier times, when the influence of party was stronger than it is now (see Chapter 9) this coequality left much less scope for party responsibility—party control over government policy—than is characteristic of parliamentary regimes. There is still less scope for it now.

Congress and the President

Congress is more powerful and independent than a parliament. Yet it must compete for power with the courts, the bureaucracy, and above all, with the President. Throughout most of the nineteenth century, and well into the twentieth, our federal government was usually "congressional government," to use President Woodrow Wilson's (1913–1921) unadmiring phrase. But from 1941 onward, wars and rumors of wars basically transformed this country's role in international affairs, which had been quite modest (see Chapter 17). The President, not Congress, directed this new role and the interventionist bureaucratic state that had emerged during the economic crisis of the 1930s (see Chapter 15). From the end of World War II, in 1945, to the beginning of Richard Nixon's engulfment in the Watergate affair, in 1973, the position of Congress in Washington's permanent power struggle declined steadily.

Congress then responded on a number of fronts. The 1973 War Powers Act limited the President's power to commit American troops to action abroad, without explicit congressional approval (see Chapters 11 and 17). The creation of the Congressional Budget Office (CBO) and a comprehensive congressional budget process liberated Congress from its dependence on information supplied by the executive branch. The 1974 Impoundment and Budget Control Act attempted to prevent any repetitions of Mr. Nixon's refusal to spend billions of dollars appropriated by Congress (see Chapter 11).

Congress and the Interest Groups

Oddly enough, the years when Congress attempted to save itself from the clutches of the executive branch were the very years when it fell ever more deeply into the web of organized interest groups surrounding it (see Chapter 6), most of which defend some sort of economic turf. The halls of Congress are redolent with their influence, and sometimes it is the public that loses out. For instance, during the 1981 "tax auction," traders in commodity "futures" (the right to purchase a certain amount of a commodity in the future) won tax exemptions worth $400 million a year. Why? Most of these traders work at the Chicago Board of Trade, located in the home district of the chairman of the House Ways and Means Committee, which is very influential, especially in tax matters.

_____

[3] Many parliaments have "upper houses"—Britain's House of Lords, for instance—but most of them have little or no power.

GETTING ELECTED

As Lyndon Johnson used to say, "You have to get the election certificate before you can be a statesman."[4] Senators and members of the House are elected in 50 and 435 separate electoral districts, respectively. All of these elections are local elections, and local issues often predominate in them—if there are any issues at all.

In the past, candidates for both houses of Congress received financial help and campaign workers from their state and local parties. Today, those parties do not have much help to give; neither do the Democratic and Republican National Committees (see Chapter 11). Major-party candidates can no longer rely on a rock-solid regional base, as Democrats once could in the South and Republicans in much of New England and the Midwest. Largely on their own, candidates have turned for salvation to a personal, almost nonpartisan, political style inspired mainly by consumer advertising (see Chapter 10).

Campaign Spending

New-style campaigns are expensive—colossally, when they are campaigns for the Senate. In 1984, total campaign spending on all Senate races rose above $172 million, and the 33 victorious candidates spent more than $97 million— an average of $3 million per victor. Campaigns for the House do not reach quite these heights, but they, too, are expensive: In 1984, each of 17 successful candidates spent more than $700,000 per campaign; Rep. James Jones (D-Okla.) spent $1.1 million. Only a handful of candidates for the House managed to keep campaign expenses below $50,000; the winners, on average, spent $291,000.[5]

Members of the House run for office every two years, senators every six, so the average spending of congressmen should be multiplied by three to make a fair comparison of campaign costs. By that standard, the average congressman spends about 40 percent as much as the average senator to stay in office for six years. Senators spend more because their constituencies comprise whole states, most of which have more voters than a mere congressional district. Vote for vote, however, Senate seats are usually cheaper. In Illinois, for example, Democrat Alan J. Dixon was elected to the Senate in 1980 for $2,346,897. Republican John E. Porter was elected to the House at a cost of $667,662. Dixon won the general election with 2,565,302 votes, slightly less than $1 a vote. Porter won his seat with only 137,707 votes, nearly $5 a vote.

Representative Porter outspent most of his colleagues but even so, congressmen, senators, and challengers to both have to spend more and more money to get elected—or even defeated. High campaign costs make them more dependent on political action committees (PACs; see Chapters 6, 10).

Getting Elected to the House

Candidates for the House are the unknown soldiers of American politics: Most voters know little more than their names. Give the voters a choice between a name they know vaguely and a name they do not know at all, and they choose

Owen Franken, Stock, Boston

Fund raising is an important part of the campaign, especially these days, when candidates do not receive financial help from their state and local parties.

---

[4] *Newsweek* October 25, 1971.

[5] *The Almanac of American Politics*, 1986 (Washington, D.C.: Barone, 1985).

the incumbent about nine times out of ten. When no incumbent is to be had, they usually vote for the candidate of the party they identify with.

Political wise men used to harp on the importance of presidential "coat-tails," the ability of strong presidential candidates to pull in votes for their parties' congressional nominees. This could happen when party-line voting was the rule, but because it no longer is, presidential coattails have been largely, sometimes completely, tailored out of politics. For example, in 1972, President Nixon (R) won reelection in a landslide over Senator George S. McGovern (D–S.D.). Mr Nixon carried 382 congressional districts to McGovern's 53, while in the same election, Democratic House candidates won 243 districts and Republicans only 192.

No wonder congressional incumbents often minimize their connection with political parties and run completely independent campaigns. Even this independence does not always insulate them from any disaster that may befall the top of the ticket: In 1980, more than two dozen incumbent Democratic congressmen, about 11 percent of all Democractic incumbents seeking reelection, were defeated, and 26 of 126 Republican incumbents, 15.5 percent, were defeated in 1982.

The Incumbent's Advantage. Members of the House have done everything they can to protect and expand the **incumbent's advantage.** Congress gives senators and congressmen several ways of keeping in touch with constituents at taxpayers' expense: radio and television studios to tape statements for home-town stations; a computer system to store names and addresses of voters; and free postage, the "franking privilege," for sending newsletters back home. (These mailings are supposed to be "nonpolitical," but incumbents always contrive to find "nonpolitical" ways of tooting their own horns.) Congress also provides each of its members with a large staff, in part to answer mail and do casework—efforts to help solve constituents' problems (See Chapter 12 for a description of congressional efforts to influence bureaucracies on behalf of constituents).

JAMES R. MILFORD —
ENJOYING ALL THE
ADVANTAGES OF INCUMBENCY

The Gerrymander. House incumbents enjoy a high rate of survival for another reason, too: Many congressional districts are designed to protect them. Seats in the House are reapportioned every ten years, just after the federal census. States that gain population usually gain seats in the House, and vice versa. After the 1980 census, New York lost five congressional seats and Florida gained four. Both states, along with many others, had to rearrange the boundaries of their congressional districts. New boundaries are drawn by state legislatures, in part by the lights of party advantage.

Assume, for example, that two House districts are to be drawn within the imaginary city of Gerryburgh. One-third of its residents are Republicans, all of whom live in north Gerryburgh; two-thirds are Democrats, all living in south Gerryburgh. When the legislature draws the city's two districts, it must follow only one basic rule, handed down by the U.S. Supreme Court: They must be almost exactly equal in population.[6] The Gerryburgh district line could therefore be drawn from north to south, creating two equal districts containing Democrats and Republicans. Or it could be drawn from east to west, creating one district with only Democrats and a second with a mixture of Democrats and Republicans. If the legislature is controlled by the Democrats, the choice is clear: One "safe" district and one marginal district beats two marginal districts.

The Tide of Incumbency. Gerrymanders are hardly new; they were invented in 1812. But the tremendous advantage that House incumbents usually enjoy is new, indeed. Few signs of an "incumbent insulation" effect appear in the electoral data before 1960 or so, almost none at all before 1952. Without doubt, the professionalization of the House as a career goes back much earlier than this, to about the turn of the twentieth century, in fact. At that point, the average tenure of congressmen began to increase and the proportion of seats without incumbents in any given election—a proportion that had been slowly falling for about fifty years—plummeted rather suddenly to present-day levels (as a rule, between 10 percent and 15 percent of all House seats). Nonetheless, partisan electoral tides rolled back and forth in House elections and in extreme cases (like 1920, 1932, 1946, and 1948) swept many incumbents out of office.

Such tides have not altogether ceased, but in recent years they have lost much of their force, as a result of the tendency of incumbents of both major parties to get a much higher share of the total vote than their party's presidential candidates get. There is plenty of evidence that incumbents who are attuned to this new electoral game play their Washington roles to full advantage. Moreover, PACs and other givers of cash contribute most of it to incumbents, regardless of party; "to him that hath shall be given."

Senate incumbents get more PAC money than Senate challengers get yet still they do not benefit from an incumbent-insulation effect comparable to the one that protects most congressmen. House incumbents are much less visible than Senate incumbents. Once, party identification and party voting gave the electorate most of the "cues" it relied on at the ballot box. Today, party loyalties have been weakened. If the voters know anything about congressional candidates, it is the name of the incumbent, and they vote for the name they know.

Like senators, House incumbents who rise sufficiently high above the crowd to attract unfavorable attention can be exceptionally vulnerable to

---

[6] *Wesberry* v. *Sanders*, 376 U.S. 1 (1964).

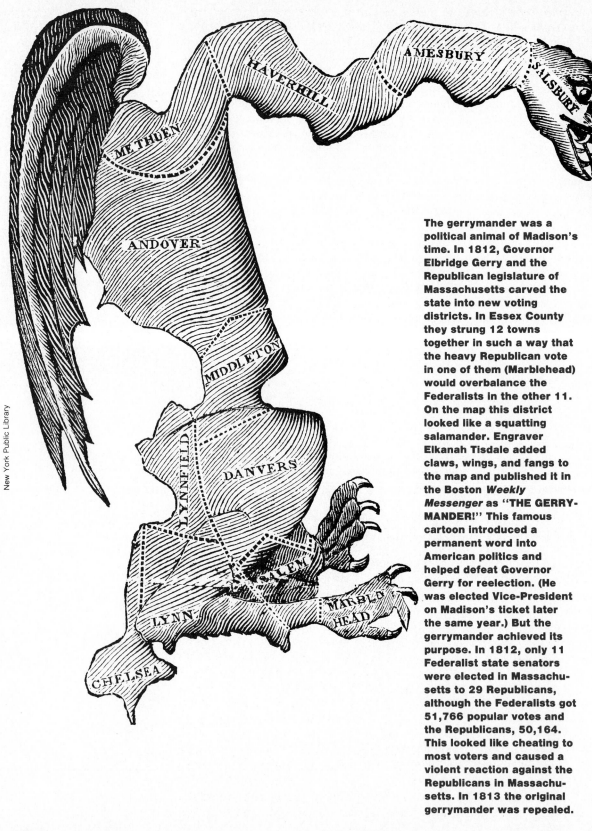

The gerrymander was a political animal of Madison's time. In 1812, Governor Elbridge Gerry and the Republican legislature of Massachusetts carved the state into new voting districts. In Essex County they strung 12 towns together in such a way that the heavy Republican vote in one of them (Marblehead) would overbalance the Federalists in the other 11. On the map this district looked like a squatting salamander. Engraver Elkanah Tisdale added claws, wings, and fangs to the map and published it in the Boston *Weekly Messenger* as "THE GERRY-MANDER!" This famous cartoon introduced a permanent word into American politics and helped defeat Governor Gerry for reelection. (He was elected Vice-President on Madison's ticket later the same year.) But the gerrymander achieved its purpose. In 1812, only 11 Federalist state senators were elected in Massachusetts to 29 Republicans, although the Federalists got 51,766 popular votes and the Republicans, 50,164. This looked like cheating to most voters and caused a violent reaction against the Republicans in Massachusetts. In 1813 the original gerrymander was repealed.

Table 13-1 The Competitiveness of Congressional Elections: 1984 Outcomes

	SUPERCLOSE	MARGINAL	SAFE	SUPERSAFE	UNCONTESTED
House	5%	7%	28%	44%	15%
Senate	9	9	36	45	0

SOURCE: The data are for the 1984 election. The classifications are drawn from the *Congressional Quarterly Weekly Report,* November 6, 1976, pp. 3147–54. Elections are defined as follows: superclose, won by less than 52 percent of the vote; marginal, won by 52–54.9 percent of the vote; safe, won by 55–64.9 percent of the vote; supersafe, won by 65 percent of the vote.

challengers. Even congressmen elevated to leadership positions may be hurt by the anti-Washington feeling that has built up in recent years. Congressmen without really safe seats are well advised to keep their heads down.

The Democratic Advantage. Since 1931, the Democrats have controlled the House almost continuously. The Democrats benefit most from the incumbent-insulation effect because a clear majority of incumbents are Democrats. Indeed, this alone gave them a 71-seat majority in the 1984 House elections, although 15 Democratic incumbents were dragged down in the Republican tide. We cannot be absolutely sure, but it seems likely that straight party voting—from the top of the Republican ticket, Ronald Reagan, on down—would have produced a House majority of 100 seats or more.

Strategies. Suppose you decided to run for a seat in the House. Your strategy would depend on whether you were running as an incumbent, against an incumbent, or for a seat without an incumbent.

The first stage is the nomination, and with it, you may have to stand in a party primary. If the primary is contested—and if there is an incumbent, that is less likely—you will certainly have to build up a personal campaign organization, but this would be necessary in any case. Incumbents have a head start because they already have such organizations.

Organizations cost money, and here too the incumbent has the advantage. If you are running for the first time, especially against an incumbent, you will need political connections and connections to wealth. Without them, you might as well spend your time turning lead into gold.

Let us say that you have money and connections and that you win the primary. You are now the party's candidate, the proud bearer of a tradition stretching far back—in the one case, to Lincoln and Teddy Roosevelt; in the other, to Jefferson, Jackson, and Franklin D. Roosevelt. Parties may be weak, but you can still count on the votes of a good number of people who regard themselves as Democrats or Republicans and vote accordingly. (In Texas, for example, some people still call themselves "Wooden-Nickel Democrats"; they would vote for the party's candidate if it were a wooden nickel.) Your party may also give you a certain amount of money. But unless your district is stoutly loyal to one party and you belong to it, the party's voters and the party's money are not at all likely to get you elected. To win over the extra money and votes you will need, you must use the personal organization you built up during the primaries. Getting campaign contributions will take up a lot of your time because candidates for the House and Senate, unlike presidential candidates, receive no federal subsidies (see Chapter 10).

"Bread and Butter." Incumbents usually campaign on their records of personal service to constituents, not on political issues. They tell their

Neither, Nor?

There are two ways of looking at this week's Democratic primary results in Washington's Fifth Congressional District: Either Representative Thomas S. Foley was so popular that he was renominated with 95 percent of the vote, or 5 percent of his constituents were so violently opposed to him that they backed Kerry D. Pinard, an inmate in the Washington State Penitentiary serving time for auto theft and escape.

The New York Times, September 17, 1982, p. A18, © 1982. Reprinted by permission.

Cooling It

There is a tradition that Thomas Jefferson, upon his return from France, was protesting to George Washington against the establishment of two houses in the legislature. The incident occurred at the breakfast table, and Washington asked: "Why did you pour that coffee into your saucer?" "To cool it," replied Jefferson." "Even so," said Washington, "we pour legislation into the senatorial saucer to cool it."

From Max Farrand, *The Framing of the Constitution of the United States* (New Haven: Yale Univ., 1978).

constituents how they defended them against the Washington Establishment, as though they themselves did not belong to it. Many of the unusually large number of Democratic incumbents defeated in 1980 in fact belonged to the House leadership. In 1984, on the other hand, congressmen in general and the House leadership in particular fared well. Of course, the challenger brands the incumbent as a man or woman filled with the evils commonly thought to be raging in the capital.

Getting Elected to the Senate

The Constitution's Framers conceived of the Senate as an "aristocratic" council of state, insulated from "the excesses of a wild democracy." The Senate, as they designed it, was elected by state legislatures, and it continued to be so elected until 1913. Even now, Senate elections are staggered—all are not held at once like elections to the House—and each state has two senators, whatever its population.

Staggered elections mean that only one-third of the Senate's seats are contested in any federal election, a schedule designed to protect the Senate from sudden shifts in popular opinion. The equal number of senators allotted to each state was chiefly meant to protect the small states from the larger ones and further to dilute the impact of popular democracy, since some senators represent many more people than others do. For example, in 1980, California's Senator Alan Cranston, a Democrat, was reelected with 4,705,399 votes—more than 10 times the whole population of Alaska; whereas Alaska's Frank H. Murkowski, a Republican, needed only 84,159 votes to win his Senate seat. So one vote for a U.S. senator in Alaska is worth 56 votes in California.

It is very hard to generalize about the electoral problems of all 100 senators. California's Senate races are almost like presidential elections, complete with sophisticated media drives and intricate coalitions of organized interest

Running for the Senate is usually tougher than running for the House—in general, only about half of Senate incumbents are reelected if they choose to run. Senator Bill Bradley is shown here celebrating his reelection to a second term.

UPI/Bettmann Newsphotos

groups. A Senate campaign in a small state is no more complex than a bid for a seat in the House. In 1980, more Alaskans voted for the state's only seat in the House than voted for U.S. senator.

Nonetheless, running for the Senate is usually tougher than running for the House. Senators are better known to the voters than congressmen are, and in an age of media politics, that ought to be an advantage. Most of the time, it is. But when, as now, the voters seem to fear and reject the federal government, they sometimes reject those politicians they know best. Even 20 years ago, senators running for third terms had a very high electoral mortality rate, apparently because 12 years in Washington put a lot of distance between them and their constituents. There is at least one other reason for the high electoral mortality of senators: Despite the growing weakness of parties in general, Senate elections have grown more partisan in recent years. In 1960, the election of a Republican senator from any of the 11 states of the old Confederacy was hardly conceivable; in 1982, those states were represented by 11 Democratic senators, 10 Republicans, and an independent. A Democratic senator from the South no longer has a guaranteed lifetime job.

The result? For the last 25 or so years, Senate incumbents have been more at risk of defeat than House incumbents—quite a paradox, since the Constitution was designed to produce exactly the opposite result. About 9 out of 10 House incumbents are reelected if they choose to run; in general, only about half of Senate incumbents are. But this is not always so. In 1984, for example, only 3 Senate incumbents out of 29 incumbents seeking reelection lost their seats—2 Republicans and one Democrat. As we have pointed out (see Chapter 10), 1984 was a very good year for incumbents of both parties.

Disaster in 1980. The election of 1980 was a disaster for Democratic incumbents in both houses. About 11 percent of Democratic incumbents in the House went down to defeat, either in the primaries or in the November election—enough to permit a conservative coalition of Republicans and boll weevil Democrats to pass President Reagan's program. But the Democratic rout was much worse in the Senate, where 22 Democrats sought reelection. Twelve—55 percent—were defeated, either by other Democrats in the primaries or by Republicans in the general election and Republicans took control of the Senate for the first time since 1954. Such tidal waves are very unusual in the Senate. Before 1980, the most recent surge had been in 1958, when Republicans were the victims and Democrats took the large majority they held for a generation.

The 1982 Election

For many months after the 1980 election, Republicans hoped and Democrats feared that Ronald Reagan's success and the Republican takeover of the U.S. Senate had launched a conservative realignment (see Chapter 10). In at least one respect, the election did resemble a true realignment: It produced drastic changes in policy, especially economic policy (see Chapter 16). But soon after Congress, at President Reagan's behest, drastically cut federal taxes and expenditure, the economy went into a recession that lingered throughout 1982. By October 1982, the last full month before the election of that year, the national unemployment rate had reached 10.4 percent, the highest since the end of World War II, in 1945. At some point in 1982, about one American worker in five had been unemployed, and many Americans who did have jobs were worried about them. In fact, Americans feared unemployment more than they feared inflation—a significant change from 1980. And the social issues so important in 1978 and 1980—abortion, school prayers, and the like—could not withstand the blast of a near-depression economy.

The Republicans' 1982 slogan was no longer, "Join the realignment," as in 1980, but the more modest, "Save the Senate." Democrats attacked the fairness and adequacy of "Reaganomics"; Republicans urged the voters to "Stay the course." The election was widely billed as a referendum on the President's policies. Some pundits and forecasters were predicting Democratic gains of 40 to 60 seats in the House.

The Republican party did save the Senate, where the Democrats made no gains at all in 1982. In the House, Democrats won 26 additional seats, giving them a majority of 103 seats, up from 51 in the House elected in 1980. Yet even though they snatched many governorships and state legislatures from the Republicans, the results fell far short of a landslide against Reaganomics. Indeed, their gains in the House fell short of the average number of seats, 30, won over the last 30 years by the "out party" in midterm elections.

But the 26 seats they did pick up were won in the teeth of an important force that usually works to the President's advantage: the "patience factor." Although the President's party has on average lost 30 House seats in midterm elections, not all midterm elections are alike. Two years after one party or the other has won control of the White House, the President's party has, on average, lost only 10 seats. But 2 years after the President's reelection, the average loss has been 48 seats. Until 1982, the actual figures varied little from election to election. Two years after a new President takes office, many voters are still angry at the opposition party. (In 1982, for example, many voters could still remember how much they had disliked Jimmy Carter.) By the sixth year of a President's tenure in office, they blame the President and the President's party for the country's problems. In the past generation, the sixth-year judgment has been uniformly and crushingly negative.

In fact, the 1982 Democratic gain of 26 House seats was the best showing in 60 years for an out party in a second-year midterm election. That, in a sense, makes it all the more odd that the Democrats did not do even better. Why didn't they? In the first place, despite the electorate's unhappiness with an unemployment rate of 10.4 percent, political parties have so declined in importance that voters who disliked the economic policies of a Republican President did not necessarily vote for the Democrats. (This is one reason for thinking that the 1982 results may not have prefigured those of 1984.) As parties have become less important as a "cue" for voters, "name identification" has become more important. Voters remember the names of very few politicians, and they tend to vote for those few. This tendency helps reelect incumbents, including Republican incumbents who might otherwise have been defeated in 1982 (see Chapters 10 and 13).

The weaknesses of party and the incumbent's advantage manifest themselves in almost all congressional districts. Marginal (closely contested) districts were, in addition, swayed by the power of big money. True, the 1982 election was filled with the political corpses of wealthy candidates who spent millions for the privilege of losing. The Republican governor of Texas, Bill Clements, vainly spent $14 million, and Mark Dayton, the Democratic senatorial candidate in Minnesota, wasted at least $5 million. But in closely contested districts, money can tell; and the big money is skewed to the right, to the Republicans. Just after the election, *The New York Times* published a

Table 13–2 1982 House Election: *The New York Times* Postelection Poll

| | DEMOGRAPHIC GROUPS: MAXIMUM TO MINIMUM PERCENTAGE DEMOCRATIC, 1982 | | | | | |
| | 1982 | | 1978 | | SHIFT | |
	D	R	D	R	D	R
Blacks	82	18	83	17	−1	+1
Jews	78	22	79	21	−1	+1
Unemployed	73	27				
Hispanics	68	32				
Labor union household	68	32	67	33	+1	−1
Eastern region	65	35	61	39	+4	−4
Blue-collar workers	64	36				
Catholics	62	38	66	34	−4	+4
Aged 18–29	61	39	62	38	−1	+1
Southern region	59	41	58	42	+1	−1
Farmers	59	41				
Retirees	59	41				
Females	58	42	57	43	+1	−1
Aged 45–59	57	43	56	44	+1	−1
Aged 60 and over	57	43	53	47	+4	−4
National sample	56.3	43.7	56.5	43.5	−0.2	+0.2
Males	55	45	57	43	−2	+2
Whites	54	46	54	46	0	0
Midwestern region	53	47	55	45	−2	+2
Aged 30–44	53	37	57	43	−4	+4
No labor union member in household	52	48	52	48	0	0
Western region	49	51	51	49	−2	+2
White-collar workers	49	51				
Protestants	46	54	48	52	−2	+2
	PARTY IDENTIFICATION AND ATTITUDE					
Liberal Democrats	91	9	90	10	+1	−1
Moderate Democrats	89	11	87	13	+2	−2
Conservative Democrats	87	13	81	19	+6	−6
Liberal Independents	77	23	70	30	+7	−7
Moderate Independents	55	45	57	43	−2	+2
Conservative Independents	34	66	41	59	−7	+7
Liberal Republicans	20	80	24	76	−4	+4
Moderate Republicans	15	85	17	83	−2	+2
Conservative Republicans	8	92	10	90	−2	+2
Attitude: Those to blame for economic problems—						
Reagan and Republicans	91	9				
Previous Democratic policies	27	73				

SOURCE: *The New York Times*, November 8, 1982. Data reworked on a two-party basis (excluding "others" and "don't know/no response").

most illuminating article on this point. It appears that no fewer than 35 House candidates won by less than 55 percent of the vote and also raised at least $50,000 more than their opponents did. Six of these candidates were Democrats, and 29 were Republicans. At least two-thirds of them, in both parties, were conservatives. There is little doubt that campaign money saved a few Republican Senate seats, too.

U.S. Rep. William M. Brodhead (D–Mich.) was a "Watergate baby"—one of the many young Democrats elected to the House in 1974, in the aftermath of the Watergate scandal and President Nixon's resignation. When Brodhead moved his family to Washington, in January 1975, he radiated enthusiasm for his new job as congressman from Michigan's 17th district, a cross section of suburban Detroit.

"I kept saying I couldn't believe I got paid for this, it was so much fun," he recalled in 1982. "I wanted to do everything. I didn't want there to be one unemployed person in my district; I didn't want there to be one handicapped child without an opportunity to get a full education. I was thinking that, someday, I'd like to be Speaker of the House."

Over the next eight years, Brodhead achieved a great deal. He was reelected three times, by heavy majorities. The Democratic leadership appointed him to a seat on the powerful Ways and Means Committee, and he was elected chairman of the Democratic Study Group, a coalition of liberals and moderates. As a member of Ways and Means, Brodhead advised Presidents, helped write the federal budget, and proposed multibillion dollar amendments to tax bills.

By the spring of 1982, Bill Brodhead—forty years old and facing his fifth term in the House—was fed up. "This job is a killer—it eats up your life," he complained. "How can you work seventy, eighty, ninety hours a week and still keep your health, your perspective, and your integrity? When I get home at night, I'm really too tired to talk. I eat my dinner and get into bed with my reading. My personal life has disappeared—I have no friends, no outside interests, no energy—nothing except my job."

Brodhead was deeply troubled, as well, by "the constant, growing pressure from lobbyists" and beginning to feel that Congress was being "sold off piece by piece" to special-interest groups whose campaign contributions, he said, have "almost become bribes." And he was upset by polls showing that most people regard members of Congress as political used-car salesmen. He was unhappy, too, about press coverage that seemed to focus on the blunders of Congress, not its achievements. All in all, Brodhead concluded, "Congress is a nuthouse," and he decided not to run for reelection. Yet he was "terrified" that he would later regret leaving Congress. For despite all the pain and disillusionment, "I love the institution, my colleagues, and my job."

The Hill

Congress is the hothouse of Washington's political community, an intensely human assemblage of politicians, lawyers, lobbyists, and bureaucrats. Along with the president and the cabinet, members of Congress are the stars of Washington's ongoing political show—celebrities, rather like movie stars in Hollywood. The waiters in Washington's expensive restaurants memorize the names and positions of important senators and congressmen, and woe unto him that seats a member of the Merchant Marine Committee when the chairman of Ways and Means is waiting for a table!

Constituent Mail

Congressmen of either party mostly flatter their constituents, whatever they may really feel. Occasionally, the truth will out, as it did in this letter from a California congressman to a constituent, way back in 1934:

One of the countless drawbacks of being in Congress is that I am compelled to receive impertinent letters from a jackass like you in which you say I promised to have the Sierra Madre mountains reforested and I have been in Congress two months and haven't done it. Will you please take two running jumps and go to hell.

Art Stein, Photo Researchers, Inc.

The Congressional Staff

Like the stars of Hollywood and the recording studio, our political stars need backup. The workload of Congress simply crushes those members who take it seriously. By any measure—the number of days spent in session, the number of bills filed, the number of pieces of mail from constituents—Congress is now a full-time legislature, and legislating is now a full-time occupation for its members. They must therefore rely on battalions of lawyers, policy specialists, researchers, secretaries, go-fers—in short, the congressional staff. Many of these people regard themselves as "the real congressman" or "the real senator," much as the wives and husbands of congressmen and senators do.

Over the past twenty years, the congressional staff has just about doubled. Congress even has its own bureaucracy, its staff agencies—for example, the General Accounting Office (GAO) and the Congressional Budget Office (CBO). In 1983 these agencies had 10,116 employees; members' staffs, 11,165 people; and the committees, an additional 3,045. The office suite of a senator from a large state looks like the headquarters of a small business firm, which in a sense it is.

Members of Congress depend on their staffs to answer the flow of mail from constituents, to apprise them about bills and issues, and to keep the boss's name in print, especially in hometown newspapers. Committee staffs try to keep an eye on the federal bureaucracy and its programs. Some staffers draft bills and negotiate for votes and concessions, and even pursue their own political careers.

Without question, the increase in staff makes Congress more effective but also increases its workload by searching out new problems that need attention. The ubiquity and importance of the congressional staff also helps make Capital Hill less intimate than it was not very long ago.

Fred Asbill, administrative assistant to Congressman Clay Shaw, leads a morning staff meeting in the congressman's office.

Figure 13–1   Staff of Members and of Committees in Congress, 1891–1983

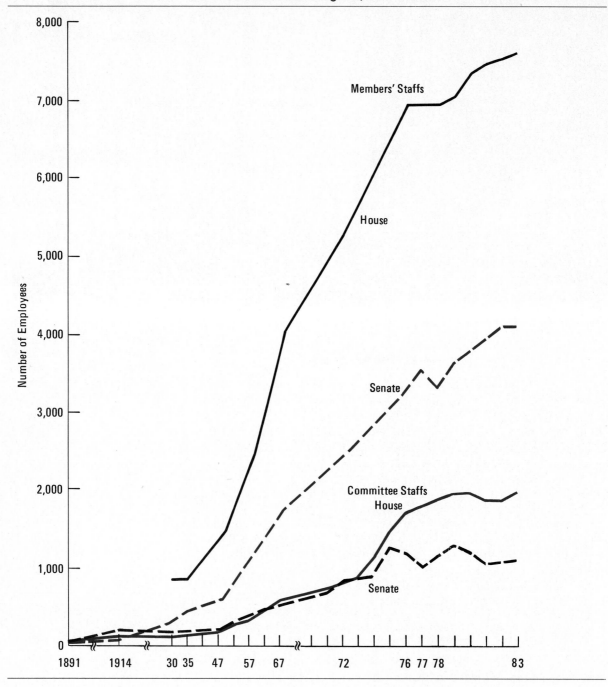

Length of Service

When Congress is in session, senators and congressmen struggle to follow debate on the floor of their respective houses, to attend committee and subcommittee hearings, to study bills, and to see that their staffs respond promptly to constituents. On weekends and when Congress is not in session, wise members go home to humor and study their constituents.

It is a demanding life. In recent years, more and more incumbents have decided that it is too demanding and have retired voluntarily. For one thing, Congress no longer rewards long years of service in the old style. Throughout most of this century, House veterans could expect that the seniority system would eventually raise them to chair committees, positions that assured them of undisputed and tyrannical authority. In 1974–1975, however, the House Democratic caucus overrode the seniority rule, and since then, the power of chairperson over a committee has been limited by revised rules. When you consider that Congress has greatly improved its members' retirement benefits, it is easy to explain so many new faces.

In 1972, for example, 19 percent of all members of the House belonged to the "20-year club," and 38 percent had served 6 years or fewer. In 1984 those proportions were 13 percent and 49 percent, respectively. Turnover in the Senate was almost as high: The number of voluntary retirements had gone up; so, too, had the number of less experienced members. In 1971, only 27 senators were serving their first terms; by 1984, there were 43.

Group Portrait: The Demographics

Congress had not been revolutionized by these changes; the new members were pretty much like the old ones. In fact, the social composition of Congress today is remarkably similar to that of the Constitutional Convention of 1787, when neither women nor blacks could vote and the white population of the United States was almost exclusively British stock. There are many more Roman Catholics in Congress now, and the number of women has been rising—but slowly. In 1984, 22 women were serving in the House and 2 in the Senate. The number of blacks in the House is rising too and stood at 20 in 1984. Congress also has a bare sprinkling of Hispanics and Asian-Americans. But the vast majority of the members are white, middle-aged, middle class, and especially, Protestant—74 percent in the Senate, 63 percent in the House (1984).

First and foremost, members typify the economic and social elites in their states and districts, including the poor ones. One reason for this is the enduring "rule of locality," the custom that all congressmen must live in their own districts.[7] Most members of Congress describe themselves either as lawyers, businessmen, bankers, farmers, or teachers. Congress is so dominated by the upper and upper-middle classes because American politics has not, as a rule, turned on class conflict. In Europe, leftist parties make great efforts to recruit working- and lower-middle-class men and women to serve in parliament, but the United States has no serious left-wing party. The differences between Republican and Democratic members of Congress are con-

---

[7] The Constitution merely requires congressmen to live in the states in which their districts are located.

fined largely to ethnic and racial background. Democrats, especially in the House, are often Catholic or Jewish, and Republicans are white Anglo-Saxon Protestants; every black in the 1985–1986 Congress was a Democrat. But these Catholics, Jews, and blacks are mostly upper-middle-class Catholics, Jews, and blacks, for Americans apparently prefer to be represented by persons of higher social standing than themselves.[8]

The Lawyers. One particular *occupational* group dominates Congress and has dominated it since the very beginning: lawyers. They were as prominent in the 98th Congress as they had been in the 78th, the 58th, the 38th, and the 8th, and as prominent as they will probably be in the 108th. The domination of Congress by lawyers was first pointed out by Alexis de Tocqueville in the 1830s. Tocqueville, himself an aristocrat, regarded lawyers as our substitute for an aristocracy. That, perhaps, is not their image today, why many of us object to them. Jimmy Carter, you may recall, claimed that not being a lawyer was among his qualifications for the presidency. In 1985, 250 out of 535 Senators and House members were lawyers.

But many Americans seem to find a certain rough-and-ready common sense in the idea that lawyers should dominate the writing of laws. Lawyers themselves find the idea supremely sensible; they run for office in much greater numbers than other people do, perhaps because it is relatively easy for them to leave their jobs and then go back when they lose or retire.

Professional Legislator-Politicians. One more thing remains to be said about the lawyers, businessmen, bankers, teachers, and farmers in Congress. Most of them are no longer lawyers, businessmen, bankers, teachers, or farmers. Time and circumstances have made them professional legislator-politicians. Legislating is at least a full-time job, and most members now regard congressional service as a career. This was not always so: Until around 1900, Congress met

---

[8] This may in part reflect a folk theory to the effect that rich legislators might be more resistant to corruption. The slogan, "He's too rich to steal," is sometimes heard in today's campaigns.

Table 13–3   98th Congress: Members' Occupations (1983–1984)

	SENATE			HOUSE		
	D	R	Total	D	R	Total
Agriculture	2	7	9	13	13	26
Business/Banking	14	15	29	73	65	138
Education	5	7	12	29	14	43
Engineering	0	0	0	2	3	5
Journalism	5	2	7	13	9	22
Labor leaders	0	0	0	2	0	2
Law	32	29	61	132	68	200
Law enforcement	0	0	0	2	3	5
Medicine	1	0	1	2	4	6
Clergymen	0	1	1	2	0	2
Military	0	1	1	0	1	1
Pro sports	1	0	1	2	1	3
Aeronautics	1	1	2	0	3	3

SOURCE: VSC 84–85.

for legislative business during about half the year. In those days, too, most members of the House held their seats for only one or two terms.

About the turn of the present century, sessions of Congress began to lengthen, and more and more congressmen ran for reelection. Most congressmen and senators now enter public life at the state or local level, then run for federal office. In 1982, the Senate had 71 members with some form of state or local government experience; 29 had served in the House. More than 300 (out of 435) members of the House had experience in state or local government, many of them in state legislatures. Most members of Congress spend much of their adult lives running for office, holding office, and running for other offices.

Congressional Ethics

The great majority of congressmen and senators are decent, hard-working men and women who conscientiously serve the public interest as they see it. Many are deeply troubled by the public's long-standing doubts about the average member's moral character. Still, ever so often, Washington's political air reeks of scandal and appears to confirm the public's worst suspicions. There have been quite a few such scandals in the recent past.

The worst of them burst into public view in early 1980, when the Federal Bureau of Investigation made public its ABSCAM ("Arab scam") investigation. Agents of the bureau, posing as Arab sheiks and businessmen, had dangled bribes before members of Congress of doubtful political virtue. Six congressmen and one senator, Harrison Williams (D–N.J.), were videotaped while conversing with a "sheik" and his accomplices. One congressman, Richard Kelly (R–Fla.), was shown happily stuffing his pocket full of FBI cash.

A CBS News drawing of FBI technicians videotaping an attempt by a so-called Arab sheik (actually an FBI agent) to bribe a member of Congress during the ABSCAM investigation.

Representative Michael ("Ozzie") Myers (D–Pa.) complained that his share of a bribe was too small. A third ABSCAM congressman, Representative John W. Jenrette (D–S.C.), observed, "I've got larceny in my blood." These and similar conversations were shown on national television. The others involved were Representatives John Murphy (D–N.Y.), Frank Thompson (D–N.J.), and Raymond Lederer (D–Pa.).

Senator Williams and all six congressmen were convicted on charges stemming from the investigation. A reluctant Congress then had to discipline them. In 1980, Myers became the first congressman since the Civil War to be expelled from the House. Kelly, Murphy, and Thompson were defeated for reelection, and Lederer, who ran and won, resigned to avoid expulsion. Jenrette and Williams resigned, too—Williams, literally on the eve of a Senate disciplinary vote to expel him.

The ABSCAM scandal was only the latest in a long line of congressional peccadilloes. In 1980, for example, Senator Herman Talmadge (D–Ga.) was defeated after disclosures that he had used political funds—discovered (according to him) in the pocket of his "magic overcoat"—for personal gain. In the mid-1970s, many congressmen were tainted by the so-called Koreagate scandal, concerning a mysterious Korean businessman named Tongsun Park, who had attempted to make friends and influence people on his government's behalf. In 1976, Representative Wayne Hays (D–Ohio), one of the most powerful and least-liked members of the House, retired from office when his secretary, Elizabeth Ray, revealed that she could neither type nor file, although she does seem to have performed certain other services for him. In the same year, Representative Wilbur Mills (D–Ark.), then chairman of the Ways and Means Committee, was driven from office after a fling with an "exotic dancer."

Is it true, someone asked the famous humorist Will Rogers years ago, that Congress is filled with thieves and rascals? "Of course," Rogers replied, "but it's a good cross section of its constituency." The sins of the present generation of congressmen are as old as sin itself. What does seem to have changed, at least temporarily, is the atmosphere of genial cynicism that once prevailed on the Hill. (In the 1930s and 1940s, for instance, two members of the House were reelected while serving prison terms for political corruption, and the House did nothing about either one.) Above all, the Capitol Hill press corps is no longer willing to overlook the personal failings of members. Both the House and Senate have adopted fairly tough ethics codes that restrict the outside income members can earn, limit the value of gifts they can accept from lobbyists, require detailed financial disclosures, and prohibit slush funds that can be spent at a congressman's discretion. Some parts of the ethics codes—particularly the limitations on outside income—are bitterly resented by the members, who argue that they have trouble getting by on their salaries.

They have some reason for complaint. As of 1985, the base salary of each senator and representative (except the Speaker of the House) was $75,100 a year. On average, the American *family* (in 1981) made a little less than $24,500 a year, but members of Congress must maintain two places of residence, and they have other substantial expenses, like travel, only some of which are paid for by congressional allowances. Some members feel, as Senator James Abourezk (D–S.D.) felt in 1978, that they must retire because they cannot afford to stay. The ethics codes, whatever their benefits, place very great financial pressures on those senators and congressmen who lack private wealth.

THE STRUCTURE OF CONGRESS

In the spring of 1982, more than 10 million Americans were out of work, partly because interest rates were so high that many companies could borrow neither to invest (and thus add new employment) nor to maintain current levels of employment. The Reagan administration's 1982 record budget deficits (see Chapter 16) were an albatross on Capitol Hill, where political soothsayers regarded them as a major cause of high interest rates and, therefore, of high unemployment.

So Mr. Reagan's first proposed budget for 1983 was unanimously rejected by the Senate budget committee, which proceeded to write a new one, calling for a substantially lower deficit. But the committee's version, too, met with strong resistance, and it, too, was greatly modified before passage by the full Senate. The House, meanwhile, was considering six proposals, none quite like the President's or the Senate's. In late May, well beyond its deadline under the law, the House finally took up all the proposed budgets, as well as a grab bag of 68 amendments to them. One by one, it voted each of them down. Then, without passing any budget resolution at all, it coolly adjourned for a long weekend.

When Mr. Reagan discovered what the House had done, he was understandably and publicly annoyed. "We worked for four months . . . to present the President's budget to the Congress, and [the House] spent six days going at—not our budget, but a half a dozen or more budgets and sixty-eight amendments. And they finally came up with nothing," he said. "It's called the President's budget, but there is nothing binding about it. It is submitted to the Congress, and they don't even have to consider it."

"The United States government's program for arriving at a budget," concluded the President, "is about the most irresponsible, Mickey-Mouse arrangement that any governmental body has ever practiced."

In the second year of his presidency, Ronald Reagan was learning about Congress the hard way—discovering, as had other Presidents before him, that its long corridors often lead nowhere. "Being fed up," as one veteran House member has observed, "is part of the legislative process."

Congress makes laws through a maze of internal circuitry. Some of the circuits are formalized and long-lasting, like the rules of debate, the powers of the leadership, the committee system, and the procedures that govern a bill's progress. Other circuits, no less real and no less important, change continually: patterns of party loyalty, voting coalitions, the force field of ideology, and the pull of constituencies. The power that makes the system move is pure politics—invisible, mercurial, and like electricity itself, capable of jumping out of its customary circuits at any time, often with startling results.

The Committee System

Let us begin with a simple and useful statistic: On average, only about one bill in twenty becomes law. The other nineteen are sucked up by the committee system, which screens, evaluates, and modifies almost every bill introduced in Congress. Committees come in four kinds. *Select committees* are usually created for specific, limited purposes—investigating drug abuse, for example—and rarely have the power to draft bills. *Joint committees,* are formed to

Table 13-4 Select and Special Committees: Senate, 1983-1984

COMMITTEE	CHAIRMAN
Select Committee on Ethics	Ted Stevens (R–Alaska)
Select, Indian Affairs	Mark Andrews (R–N.D.)
Select, Intelligence	Barry M. Goldwater (R–Ariz.)
Special, Aging	John Heinz (R–Pa.)

Subtotal:
Number of select and special committees = 0
Number of subcommittees of special committees = 4
Grand total:
All Senate committees = 20
All Senate subcommittees = 107

Table 13-5 Joint Committees of Congress, 1983-1984

COMMITTEE	CHAIRMAN
Joint Committee on the Library	Sen. Charles McC. Mathias, Jr. (R–Md.)
Joint Committee on Printing	Rep. Augustus J. Hawkins (D–Cal.)
Joint Committee on Taxation	Rep. Dan Rostenkowski (D–Ill.)
Joint Economic Committee	Sen. Roger W. Jepsen (R–Iowa)

Total number of joint committees of Congress, 1983–1984: 4 (6 subcommittees)

study specific kinds of problems and do not ordinarily draft bills; they coordinate policy between the two houses of Congress, and their members are drawn from both.

Standing Committees—15 in the Senate, 22 in the House—are the basic units of Congress, its chief mechanism for sharing the burdens of legislation. Each standing committee covers a broad area of policy, and most comprise an elaborate system of subcommittees. Often the subcommittees, not the committees, hold hearings on bills and draft them. Standing committees are not equal in power. Under the Constitution, the House must originate all "money bills"—bills on spending and taxation—so its most important committees are the "money committees." Ways and Means (taxes) and Appropri-

Table 13-6 Standing Committees: Senate, 1983-1984

COMMITTEE	CHAIRMAN	NUMBER OF SUBCOMMITTEES
*Agriculture, Nutrition and Forestry	Jesse Helms (R–N.C.)	7
*Appropriations	Mark O. Hatfield (R–Ore.)	13
*Armed Services	John Tower (R–Texas)	6
*Banking, Housing and Urban Affairs	Jake Garn (R–Utah)	9
*Budget	Pete V. Dominici (R–N.M.)	0
*Commerce, Science and Transportation	Bob Packwood (R–Ore.)	8
*Energy and Natural Resources	James A. McClure (R–Idaho)	6
*Environment and Public Works	Robert T. Stafford (R–Vt.)	6
*Finance	Robert Dole (R–Kans.)	9
*Foreign Relations	Charles H. Percy (R–Ill.)	7
*Governmental Affairs	William V. Roth, Jr. (R–Del.)	7
*Judiciary	Strom Thurmond (R–S.C.)	9
*Labor and Human Resources	Orrin G. Hatch (R–Utah)	7
Rules and Administration	Charles McC. Mathias, Jr. (R–Md.)	0
Small Business	Lowell P. Weicker, Jr. (R–Conn.)	9
Veterans' Affairs	Alan K. Simpson (R–Wyo.)	0

Number of standing committees: 16   *Total subcommittees:* 103

*Major committee: No senator can serve on more than two. On minor committees, no senator can serve on more than one.

Table 13-7 Standing Committees of the House, 1983–1984

Agriculture (8 subcommittees)	Interior and Insular Affairs (6 subcommittees)
Appropriations (13 subcommittees)	Judiciary (7 subcommittees)
Armed Services (7 subcommittees)	Merchant Marine and Fisheries (5 subcommittees)
Banking, Finance and Urban Affairs (8 subcommittees)	Post Office and Civil Service (7 subcommittees)
Budget (9 "task forces")	Public Works and Transportation (6 subcommittees)
District of Columbia (3 subcommittees)	Rules (2 subcommittees)
Education and Labor (8 subcommittees)	Science and Technology (7 subcommittees)
Energy and Commerce (6 subcommittees)	Small Business (6 subcommittees)
Foreign Affairs (8 subcommittees)	Standards of Official Conduct
Government Operations (7 subcommittees)	Veterans Affairs (5 subcommittees)
House Administration (5 subcommittees)	Ways and Means (6 subcommittees)

Select and special committees of the House:
Federal Government Service Task Force
House Recording Studio
Permanent Select Committee on Intelligence (3 subcommittees)
Select Committee on Aging (4 subcommittees)
Select Committee on Children, Youth, and Families
Select Committee on Narcotics Abuse and Control

ations (spending).[9] The Constitution gives the Senate the duty of ratifying foreign treaties, so ambitious senators hope to sit on the Foreign Relations Committee.

Finally, *conference committees* are in many respects the most interesting of the lot. Like joint committees, their members are drawn from both chambers, and they are usually created for specific, limited purposes. But they often have great influence on the course of legislation. A conference committee's work begins when all the other committees, and both houses of Congress, have finished theirs. Its job is to reconcile any differences between House and Senate versions of a bill. In theory, the members of conference committees are supposed merely to juggle elements in the existing bills and to avoid introducing new ideas. But that is just the theory. In practice, the conferees, usually the most experienced and powerful members of the Senate and the House, have great freedom to rewrite the bills.

In fact, conference committees often have an overwhelmingly powerful position—in part because amendments cannot be added to their proposals, which must be voted up or down. And these committees seem to be growing more powerful over time. An old joke goes, "The bill shall be read twice and, without further debate, sent to conference committee." In August 1982, life very nearly imitated humor, when President Reagan's tax-increase package was passed and signed into law. Critics of that performance would only add that the House did not read the tax bill even once, much less twice!

The Coming of Reform

For most of this century, the committee system often resembled a collection of autonomous tribes wandering about Capitol Hill under close supervision by

---

[9] This does not prevent the Senate from drafting money bills first, if the House is willing to go along. This is exactly what happened with the 1982 package of tax increases, drafted very largely by the Senate Finance Committee under the chairmanship of Senator Robert J. Dole (R–Kans.). House conservatives who opposed the tax increase repeatedly raised the "constitutional question." Although the conservatives had a point, it mattered little in the end: The final package passed both houses and was signed into law by President Reagan.

elderly chiefs. The committee chairpersons were selected automatically by seniority, from the ranks of the majority party—since 1933, usually the Democrats. With good reason, critics charged that many of these committees were too isolated from the country's changing political needs, too independent of congressional party leaders and the President, and too intimate with the federal bureaucracy and the interest groups served by it (see the section on "Iron Triangles," Chapter 12).

In the session of 1974–1975, the old order was overthrown, especially in the House, where the Democratic caucus decided to elect committee chairpersons itself, by majority vote. (The caucus is notably partial to the claims of seniority, but they are no longer absolute.) Committees were also forced to adopt written rules of procedure and to follow them; Committee heads were stripped of many powers and forced to respond to the views of individual members, including the Republican minority, and a number of committees were consolidated into others. Standing committees began to delegate much of the workload to subcommittees, and committee staffs were expanded and made less partisan and more professional. Except for hearings on sensitive national security matters, the committees were largely prohibited from meeting in secret.

These changes, together with the very rapid turnover of membership in both houses, made Congress much less autocratic and much more open. But every change has unintended consequences, every reform its price. The bad news is that Congress has now compounded the problems of "committee government" with those of "subcommittee government." Congressional decision making was always cumbersome and slow—in a word, indecisive. Now it is even more cumbersome and even slower. Congress is more open, but its openness mainly benefits special interest groups. The publicity that now attends all its workings actually makes congressmen less free to vote their consciences and to support the national interest over the interests of their particular constituencies.

By the late 1970s, Congress was often too rudderless and too buffeted by outside influences to act at all. Party loyalties were low; each bill seemed to require a new coalition. Deadlock replaced compromise as the basic state of the congressional mind. As one of President Carter's aides, Stuart Eizenstat, complained, "Moses would have difficulty getting the Ten Commandments through Congress today." In any case, the reforms of the mid-1970s raised the political costs of passing legislation and therefore made legislation harder to pass.

The Leadership

It would be reasonable to suppose that the leaders of the House and the Senate have gained the powers that the committees and, especially, the committee chairmen were forced to surrender. Reasonable, but incorrect, perhaps because these leaders are first and foremost party leaders, and our parties are only somewhat stronger in Congress than outside it. They have other, nonparty, sources of power as well. Ordinarily, the leaders control the formal devices that help Congress set its agenda: the House and Senate calendars, the rules of floor debate, and the referral of bills to committees. Usually, too, they convey the wishes of the President to Capitol Hill.

(Left) Mirrored elegance marks the formal office of the Speaker of the House.

(Right) Crystal chandeliers embellish the offices of the majority and minority leaders of the House.

The House of Representatives. The **Speaker of the House** is both its presiding officer and the real leader of the majority party. Speakers are elected by the House on a straight party vote (see below), usually one of the few such votes in any session. The House **majority leader** (who is in fact subordinate to the Speaker) and the *assistant majority leaders*, the *whips*, help manage floor debate and voting and keep the Speaker informed about the state of feeling among the troops. The Speaker, although formally elected by the House as a whole, is in fact chosen by the majority caucus, as are the majority leader and the assistant majority leaders. The minority causus chooses the minority leader and assistant leaders. (See the section "The Two Houses" for an account of the Speaker's role and power.)

The Senate. The presiding officer of the Senate is the Vice-President of the United States. Acting as the president of the Senate—as its presiding officer, that is—the Vice-President gets an occasional chance to break a tie by casting a vote, but on the whole, there is little to do, so most Vice-Presidents rarely come to the Senate. In their absence, the presiding officer is the president pro tem, usually the majority-party senator with the greatest seniority. This too is largely an honorific post. Ordinarily, the Senate is presided over by a junior senator filling in, as a chore, for the president pro tem. The most powerful senator is the majority leader, elected by the majority caucus. As in the House, there are assistant majority leaders, as well as leaders and assistant leaders of the minority, elected by the minority caucus.

Voting Cues

Compared with typical business corporations, Congress is loosely organized. Its leaders rely chiefly on compromise and accommodation. "To get along, go along" is a congressional aphorism. With few weapons at hand, today's leaders often fail not only to deliver the vote but even to predict it.

Now that leaders no longer command and followers no longer obey, members of Congress must look for cues, signals about the most correct or prudent way to vote. The President's position is one such cue, especially for members of the President's party. Another is the stand taken by the parties in their national platforms (see Chapter 9). For almost all congressmen, a vital cue is the vote within the committee that sends a bill to the floor, especially the vote of like-minded members of that committee. Often, too, congressmen are influenced by the views of their constituents, especially their better organized constituents.

Party Voting

Since all of the members of the 1985–1986 Congress called themselves Republicans or Democrats, it may seem odd that party positions are only one among a number of cues. The reason is that the decline of party loyalties in the electorate has been paced by a corresponding decline in Congress.

Nonetheless, the disintegration of parties has not progressed as far within Congress as it has outside it. Congress still chooses the Speaker in a straight party vote. All in all, party is even now the single best indicator of any congressman's or senator's actions. Yet for a century, the proportion of votes solidly pitting the two parties against each other has declined steadily. If we define a **party vote** as one in which a majority of Democrats oppose a majority of Republicans, such votes account for only about one-third of the House

Table 13–8	Party Voting, House of Representatives, 1861–1982	
CONGRESSES	YEARS	ROLL CALL VOTES WITH MAJORITY OF DEMOCRATS AGAINST MAJORITY OF REPUBLICANS
37th–41st	(1861–1871)	74%
42nd–46th	(1871–1881)	73
47th–51st	(1881–1891)	67
52nd–56th	(1891–1901)	63
57th–61st	(1901–1911)	74
62nd–66th	(1911–1921)	54
67th–71st	(1921–1931)	55
72nd–76th	(1931–1941)	65
77th–81st	(1941–1951)	47
82nd–86th	(1951–1961)	50
87th–91st	(1961–1971)	43
92nd–96th	(1971–1981)	38
97th	(1981–1982)	36

SOURCE: Jerome M. Clubb and Santa A. Traugott, "Partisan Cleavage and Cohesion in the House of Representatives, 1861–1974," *Journal of Interdisciplinary History*, 7, No. 3 (Winter 1977), 382–83 (as adapted).

The percentages shown are the averages for the five Congresses of each decade. This study should also be consulted for other tests of party voting.

total—a standard so loose that even in a party vote, the majority party does not necessarily triumph. In 1981, for instance, 83 percent of House Democrats voted with their party and against President Reagan's proposed budget cuts. But a group of 43 conservative southern Democrats—the "boll weevils"—voted with the President and gave him an important victory.

In the Republican party, senators and congressmen from the Northeast are less disposed than Republicans from the rest of the country to vote the party line, generally because the Northeasterners are more liberal and represent constituencies with important liberal—labor interests. Within the Democratic party, the conservative congressmen and senators from the Deep South tend to vote against the party's majority.

The Conservative Coalition

Much of the time, the real majority in Congress is neither the Democrats nor the Republicans but the so-called **conservative coalition,** a remarkably stable grouping of conservatives from both parties. Every so often, the coalition is overwhelmed by a liberal Democratic majority, as it was after the 1964 and 1974 elections. Since the 1930s, however, the coalition has blocked a great many social-welfare proposals and slowed down others.

The conservative coalition's durability and effectiveness spawned a variety of ideological, regional, and issue-oriented groups, especially in the House. Today's typical congressman might belong to half a dozen of them.

THE TWO HOUSES

The Framers created a Congress of two houses, and that is still the most important thing about it. All bills must survive two completely separate committee systems, move through two completely separate floor debates, and then get a majority of votes in each house. To control Congress, it is necessary to control both of its coequal parts.

The House of Representatives

Let us begin with the House of Representatives, for the Framers meant it to be the living heart of American government, comparable to the British House of Commons (see Chapter 2). Not until the 1830s did the presidency and the Senate assert themselves.

The Speaker of the House. The Senate is often compared to a sort of gentleman's club but the House is a three-ring circus—with the Speaker of the House its ringmaster. With its 435 members, the House of Representatives is unwieldy, and that fact has shaped its rules. The Speaker, the chief parliamentarian and leader of the majority party in the House, has much more control over it than any senator wields in the upper chamber.

When, for example, there is any ambiguity about which committee should examine a bill—and there often is—the Speaker can send it to a committee that shares his own view. A decision of this sort can more or less seal the bill's fate. The Speaker, too, decides which amendments from the floor are **germane** (or relevant) to a bill under discussion and, therefore, permissible. (In the Senate, bills can be amended without restriction.) When the Speaker decrees that an amendment is not germane, it is killed, packed off to the burial ground of legislative impossibilities.

Since 1975, the Speaker has also in effect controlled the House Rules Committee, its "traffic cop," which determines when and if bills will be sent from committee to the floor, and in what order. The Rules Committee regulates debate by issuing "rules" that decide how a bill may be dealt with on the House floor. If, for example, the committee issues a **closed rule,** and it is approved by the House, the members cannot amend the bill on the floor. And the House, unlike the Senate, routinely limits the time allotted to debate, so filibusters are out of the question.

The Speaker controls the Rules Committee by appointing those of its members who belong to the majority party and by setting the ratio between the majority and minority parties. On most other standing committees, the party ratio, by tradition, reflects the partisan balance of the House as a whole: In the 1985–1986 Congress, there were about three Democrats for every two Republicans. The Rules Committee was an exception. Since 1983, Speaker O'Neill had ignored the protests of House and Senate Republicans and decreed a committee of nine Democrats and four Republicans. The Democrats remained solidly in control of the mechanics of legislation in the House.

These changes in part repealed the famous St. Patrick's Day revolt against the Speaker and his powers, in 1910. Before then, a strong partisan Speaker appointed the majority members of the Rules Committee and thus controlled the flow of business through the House. Speaker Joseph G. Cannon (R–Ill., Speaker: 1903–1911) was a conservative "standpatter" who met with increasing resistance from a group of about fifty progressive–liberal House Republicans. In March 1910, they joined with Democrats to strip the Speaker of many powers, including the right to appoint the majority members and chairman of the Rules Committee.

During the generation after 1938—years when the Democrats controlled the House—the Rules Committee and its chairman were selected by seniority, as were all others. Under its long-time chairman, Howard W. Smith (D–Va.), the Rules Committee became a key power point for the conservative coalition. Finally, in 1961, Speaker of the House Sam Rayburn (D–Tex., Speaker: 1940–1947, 1949–1953, 1955–1962) joined forces with incoming President John F. Kennedy (1961–1963) to bypass the conservative bottleneck. The size of the Rules Committee was expanded and packed with liberal Democrats. By a close vote, 217 to 212, the House went along with this change.

Even after this struggle, the Speaker still could not appoint the majority members of the committee and therefore could not fully control the agenda of the House. Like so many reforms in American political history, the reforms of 1910 (which remained in force) had been meant to promote democracy, but in fact they had merely fragmented power and weakened the ability of government to govern. In 1974, awareness of that reality restored the Speaker's influence over the Rules Committee to something like its pre-1910 state.

Committees. Yet the 1974 reforms also *undercut* the Speaker by requiring that each member of the House be assigned to at least one major committee. They also barred any member from serving as chairman of more than one major committee or subcommittee. Democrats receive their committee assignments from the Steering and Policy Committee, Republicans, from the Committee on Committees.

Competition for seats on the most prestigious committees is even more intense in the House than it is in the Senate, where it is quite intense. The budget committees are the most important ones, followed by Ways and Means (taxes) and Appropriations (spending).

Voting. The reforms of the mid-1970s promoted the House's drift toward deadlock, but with an added, technological aspect. In the past, it was hard to demand a **record vote**—in which all congressmen cast their votes openly, by name—because it took a long time for the Clerk of the House to read out the names of 435 members. Now the House has an electronic voting system, and record votes are common—about 600 of them a year, up from fewer than 100 in the early 1960s. In the old days, the members would simply rise at their seats to signify "yea" or "nay" and the Speaker would decide which side had won—a **standing vote.** Or the members would form two lines, one for "yea," one for "nay," and file past the teller—a **teller vote.**

Now that votes are on record, each congressman can be observed by such people as lobbyists, political opponents, journalists, and voters. As a result, congressmen are less free to use their judgment, and they must often pretend to support positions they do not really share. Often, too, it is a lot easier to vote against a bill than for it. In early 1982, for example, the House defeated all six budget resolutions because, in the words of one congressman, "enough members figure they can't get hurt by voting against all of them."[10]

"How someone votes gets down to whether he has an opponent in a primary and whether he has a serious opponent in the general election. For a moderate Republican, it's whether he has a primary opponent on the right; it's what the victory margin was last time. The decision on the final vote is very personal. It's: Can I survive with this?"

Representative Brian Donnelly,

(D–Mass.)

The Senate

The Framers created the U.S. Senate on the model of the British House of Lords plus the Senate of ancient Rome. It was meant to institutionalize the power of the well-to-do. It was also meant to represent states as political bodies. The coming of democracy killed off many "second chambers" and turned the rest into tourist traps without political importance, like the House of Lords. But the U.S. Senate had a very different fate—almost the opposite, in fact. Elected, after 1913, by the same voters who elected the House, it acquired democratic legitimacy and survived as a coequal branch of the legislature—one of the very few coequal second chambers in the world.

Senatorial Courtesy. The Senate is small. All 100 members of the Senate can get to know each other quite well, and all can march to their own drummers without getting in one another's way. Senators used to treat one another to displays of Oriental courtesy. One senator will rarely campaign against another senator—of either party. Senate Democrats usually cooperate with Republicans on procedural matters like setting the agenda. Yet the Senate's majority and minority leaders and their assistants are, above all, party leaders, elected by the party caucuses, working through party policy committees, and setting party priorities.

---

[10] "A Reporter in Washington, D.C.," *The New Yorker*, June 21, 1982, p. 102.

Committees. The nerve center of the Senate's partisan machinery consists of the two committees that assign senators to their standing committees: for the Democrats, the Steering Committee; for the Republicans, the Committee on Committees. Tradition assigns a clear pecking order to the Senate's sixteen standing committees, thirteen of which are called "major." Every senator gets assigned to at least one major committee, and no senator may serve as chairman of more than one major committee at a time. These rules were meant to distribute choice committee assignments fairly—especially to Appropriations and Foreign Affairs. Senators must still compete for those assignments, though, and it can take years to get them.

Even the most junior senators have great, perhaps unreasonable, freedom of maneuver when bills reach the floor. Unlike congressmen, they can amend bills in almost any way they please—hence, many so-called amendments are in fact substitute bills. And the Senate does little to restrict the amount of time its members can spend (or waste) debating bills.

Senator Strom Thurmond leaving the Senate after a 24-hour filibuster against the Civil Rights Bill in 1957.

UPI/Bettmann Newsphotos

Filibusters. Unrestricted debate created that most colorful of American political traditions, the **filibuster,** in which a group of senators attempts to defeat a bill by prolonged debate. The filibusterers, who can replace one another, drone on (sometimes for weeks) until they so wear out their colleagues that the Senate does not have a **quorum,** the minimum number of senators required to carry on business. They then demand a "quorum call." The senators on the opposing side must quickly appear in the Senate chamber to register their presence. If they do not muster sufficient numbers, the bill dies for want of a quorum.

Until quite recently, most filibusters were organized by conservatives, particularly southerners seeking to obstruct civil-rights bills. The solo record in these matters is held by the redoubtable Senator Strom Thurmond (R–S.C.), who spoke without a break for 24 hours and 18 minutes in a failed effort to kill the 1957 Civil Rights Act. His speech included readings from the Washington, D.C., telephone book. Another senator once described, at remarkable length, his celebrated recipe for shrimp stew—a delicious one, by all accounts. And the accounts are available in the *Congressional Record.* In recent years, liberals, too, have increasingly resorted to filibusters to obstruct legislation desired by conservatives. In mid-1982, for instance, they were able to talk to death a proposed antiabortion amendment offered by Senator Jesse Helms (R–N.C.) and supported by President Reagan.

And in early 1985, farm-state senators held a filibuster on the confirmation of Edwin Meese as Attorney General. These senators weren't concerned with the Meese confirmation; rather, they were demanding loan money for farmers who might go bankrupt before the spring planting. Although President Reagan opposed any additional aid, and Senate majority leader Bob Dole (R–Kans.) called the tactics "blackmail," a farm loan agreement was reached within a week. Before 1975, **cloture** motions, cutting off debate, required a two-thirds vote of senators present and voting. Only about one such motion in four succeeded. In 1975, the rule was changed; cloture now requires a three-fifths vote of the entire Senate (sixty members), and that slight difference made such motions easier to pass.

"The Old Southern Home." The New Deal realignment of the 1930s gave the Democrats control over the Senate. For a generation thereafter it was widely

known as "the old southern home." Southern Senators—many quite conservative—chaired most of the Senate's important committees. Its "folkways" tended to reflect the manners of the South: It was generally expected, for example, that freshmen senators would deliver a major speech when a leading "insider" determined that one was wanted.

Today's Senate is very different. The pressures of congressional business, the reality of perpetual electioneering, and the new kinds of people who have gotten into the Senate have made it a rather nasty, snarling place. Senators who worry about the new trend also place part of the blame on the 1974 rules changes, which "opened up" committee meetings to public view; for this, in their view, encouraged "grandstanding" and personal abrasiveness.

Connected to the "grandstanding" is what some observers call "the new obstructionism," an outgrowth of the individualism that is running riot as parties decay. One critic of the Senate, Senator Joseph R. Biden (D–Del.), says, "We've spawned a very negative thing. We've abandoned any discipline. We end up with 100 Proxmires in the Senate.[11] One Proxmire makes a real contribution. All you need is thirty of them to guarantee that the place doesn't work."[12] For whatever reason, the Senate's effectiveness has declined, which rightly bothers thoughtful senators of both parties.

Congress in Action: The Budget

Each kind of legislature tends to produce certain kinds of legislation and, quite as important, fails to produce other kinds. Were Congress a parliament, with a parliamentary organization, we could expect laws of a very different sort, passed in a very different way.

The peculiarities of Congress—its structure, rules, and folkways—mark every bill and resolution. But nothing so reveals the bond between the legislative process and the legislative product as the way Congress attempts to scrutinize, change, debate, and pass the federal budget. That process is among the great continuing battles of American political life—so important and so complex that absolutely nothing is left out of it.

The Old Budget System. Congress has no overall system for reviewing the federal budget until 1974–1975.[13] Before then, it normally approved the annual budgets of each federal department, program by program. To understand the budget procedure created in 1974–1975, you must understand the old one, for it was incorporated into the new.

Congress has always regulated government spending through a two-step process: Each department's budget must be *authorized* in one bill, then the money must be *appropriated* in a second bill. Authorization bills are handled by those House and Senate committees that oversee the various departments and programs: Defense Department authorizations, for example, are ap-

---

[11] Senator William Proxmire (D–Wis.) has played the role of individualist and critic during his quarter-century in the senate.

[12] Congressional Quarterly Weekly Report, September 4, 1982, p. 2181.

[13] It had attempted to produce one in 1949–1950, but the effort fell apart under the pressure of interest-group demands.

proved by House and Senate armed-services committees. These committees consider both the department's overall spending requests and its specific programs.

Once Congress has approved a department's authorization bill, it must then pass a second bill to appropriate actual funds for spending—the appropriations bill. This bill must be reviewed by the appropriations committees of the House and Senate. In many cases, less money is appropriated than was formerly, which usually means that the department must tighten its belt. Congress might, for example, authorize new fighter planes, but appropriate less money than the Pentagon requested. The Pentagon must then buy fewer planes than it had wanted, or it must "stretch out" its purchases over a longer period.

The budgets and programs of every department and agency were, and still are, reviewed at least four times—twice (once in each house) for authorization and twice for appropriations. Congress can modify these programs, kill them, or start wholly new ones; it can also try to ensure that they are well run. Yet the defects of the old system were many and great. For one thing, getting a budget through was so complex that Congress often failed to approve it on time. The federal government's **fiscal year** runs from October 1 to September 30 of the following calendar year. When the new fiscal year begins, the budget should be ready. If the appropriations bill for a particular department has not been approved by September 30, Congress can pass a **continuing resolution** to operate the department at the previous level of funding. Under the old system, this often happened and was often criticized. (Unfortunately, it seems to be happening even more frequently these days, under the new system.)

The traditional budget system gave Congress no means of examining the federal budget as a whole. Both houses approved each department's spending, program by program, dollar by dollar, but never did Congress decide what the government's total spending could be or how that total should be divided among the departments and agencies. Congress could not even be sure just how much spending it had approved until the fiscal year was out. Conservatives complained that this lack of overall control encouraged Congress to spend more money than it raised in taxes—that it led, in other words, to constantly higher spending and to federal deficits (see Chapter 16). Government spending had increased during the 1970s, partly from inflation and partly from the cost of the social programs Congress approved during the 1960s. The bottom line? Between 1970 and 1980, total federal spending rose from $196 billion to $580 billion a year, and the federal deficit, from $2.8 billion to $59.6 billion. This increase, often called an "explosion," was nothing of the sort—though inflation made it seem like one. The rise in federal expenditures over the past thirty years is best described as an "upward creep," at least if these expenditures are computed as a percentage of gross national product (GNP, see Chapter 16). Among the governments of a dozen and a half leading industrial countries, only Japan's spent a smaller percentage of the GNP than the government of the United States did (at all levels). And over the decade from 1966 to 1976, the *growth* in the share of GNP spent by governments at all levels (federal, state, and local) was less in the United States than in *any* other country.

The real political problem was not an explosion in the amount of money spent by the federal government but a radical change in the *composition* of the federal spending. For after 1970, "traditional" expenditures (such as defense) took second place to spending on domestic welfare, which was quite controversial. The sheer multiplication of dollar amounts and programs forced the weaknesses of the old budgetary system into the public eye. As Senator Everett M. Dirksen (R–Ill.) once said, "A billion dollars here, and a billion dollars there, and pretty soon it adds up to real money."

Even liberals had a reason to want a more efficient way of passing budgets. In the early 1970s, they were upset by the evils of the "imperial presidency," since the old budget procedure put Congress at the mercy of the President for almost all information regarding the budget. In fact, Congress sometimes voted appropriations without even knowing how much money the executive branch expected to raise through taxation. To the extent that Congress was managing the budget at all, it was doing a poor job. Worse still, its lapses had become notorious.

The 1974 Impoundment and Budget Control Act. At about this time, Congress made many attempts to cut the President's power and revive its own. One of them was the 1974 Impoundment and Budget Control Act, which created a new congressional budget system, grafted on to the old authorization-appropriations procedure. The new system was more complicated, not less so. Both the House and the Senate created budget committees to recommend spending totals for each standing committee's programs and for the federal budget as a whole. The act also created an important new agency, the Congressional Budget Office (CBO), which gave Congress its own source of information about economic matters.

Under the new system, both houses' budget committees, together with the other standing committees and the CBO, are supposed to approve two budget resolutions each year. Ideally, the procedure follows this course:

— JANUARY: The President submits budget proposals to Congress.
— MAY 15: The first major deadline. By this date, standing committees have finished work on the authorization bills, and Congress has passed its first budget resolution, setting tentative spending targets for every part of the federal budget.
— SEPTEMBER 15: The next deadline. It is two weeks before the start of the new federal fiscal year. Both houses have now approved all appropriations bills, and Congress passes a second, binding budget resolution. Throughout, the budget committees tell the standing committees when their spending proposals have risen above the overall budget targets.
— LATE SEPTEMBER: The final step, reconciliation. The House and Senate match their spending totals for every part of the federal budget.

Sometimes the new budget process works, and sometimes it does not. As always, politicians still find it much easier to give than to take away. Ronald Reagan became President in 1981 intending to cut the total size of the federal budget and, at the same time, to raise defense spending. He won a major victory in the summer of 1981, when his supporters in Congress used the reconciliation bill to cut about $35 billion from the 1982 federal budget. In so doing, however, the President seized control of the reconciliation process and used it to get his own way—the opposite of what Congress had in mind when it passed the 1974 budget act. But in 1982, President Reagan's first budget proposals were flatly rejected on Capitol Hill because of disputes over defense spending. So were the budget resolutions drawn up by both houses' budget committees. The first budget resolution finally passed Congress about a month

President Reagan presents his fiscal 1986 budget to congressional leaders at the White House. From left to right: Vice-President George Bush; Senate Majority Leader Robert Dole; Senate Minority Leader Robert Byrd; Senator Strom Thurmond; and House Minority Leader Robert Michel.

after its deadline. And in 1984, Congress did not pass a budget resolution until late September—over four months past the deadline.

By creating two new budget committees, moreover, the 1974 law has undermined the authority of the four traditional money committees; in the Houses: (1) Ways and Means, (2) Appropriations; in the Senate: (1) Finance, (2) Appropriations. Worst of all, according to some critics, the new system makes it very hard for the standing committees to scrutinize particular federal programs carefully, and it has forced both houses to adopt the budget in a hurried and often confused manner. Critics say that even the quality of congressional deliberation has declined.

Still, the budget reforms of 1974 represent a historic attempt by Congress to cope. Perhaps, in the long run, they will help undo the trend toward political deadlock and allow Congress to assert itself against the executive. For the time being, at least, the reformed budget system is its best and only hope. Indeed, Senator Mark Hatfield (R–Ore.) argues that additional reforms would not help: "Difficult decisions are always left until the end. In the Senate, legislation only gets done by unanimous consent or exhaustion."

Mr. Reagan's reconciliation package of 1981 did cut federal budget spending significantly below the levels that had been expected before its passage. But his supply-side, three-year tax cut slashed federal revenues far more severely than the budget cuts reduced spending. Those revenues declined even further as a result of a recession that was more serious and

Table 13–9 Number of Legislative Activities in the House of Representatives, 80th–98th Congresses

CONGRESS	TIME IN SESSION Days	Hours	BILLS Introduced	Reported	Passed	RESOLUTIONS Introduced	Reported	Passed	COMMITTEE MEETINGS	QUORUM CALLS	YEA AND NAY VOTES	RECORDED VOTES
80th	254	1,221	7,611	1,840	1,739	950	340	481	na	122	159	0
81st	315	1,501	10,502	2,523	2,482	1,193	401	586	na	268	275	0
82nd	271	1,163	9,065	2,018	2,008	990	279	432	na	183	181	0
83rd	240	1,033	10,875	2,093	2,129	989	349	519	na	124	147	0
84th	230	937	13,169	2,334	2,360	935	364	473	3,210	132	147	0
85th	276	1,147	14,580	2,094	2,064	1,080	356	482	3,750	222	193	0
86th	265	1,039	14,112	1,676	1,636	1,394	318	481	3,059	202	180	0
87th	304	1,227	14,328	1,941	1,927	1,381	368	497	3,402	284	240	0
88th	334	1,251	14,022	1,375	1,267	1,277	367	467	3,596	296	232	0
89th	336	1,547	19,874	1,613	1,565	2,125	436	583	4,367	388	394	0
90th	328	1,595	22,060	1,369	1,213	2,167	376	446	4,386	397	478	0
91st	350	1,613	21,436	1,137	1,130	2,139	405	512	5,066	369	443	0
92nd	298	1,429	18,561	1,010	970	1,897	391	499	5,114	285	456	193
93rd	318	1,487	18,872	906	923	2,223	457	601	5,888	375	632	446
94th	311	1,789	16,982	985	968	2,389	510	656	6,975	419	810	463
95th	323	1,897	14,414	1,001	955	3,386	489	660	6,771	184	1,035	505
96th	326	1,876	9,103	na	929	na	na	na	7,022	na	1,276	
97th	303	1,420	7,458	575	572	1,717	229	486	6,179	47	519	293
98th	266	1,705	6,442	711	755	1,662	272	620	na	90	524	382

SOURCE: Commission on Administrative Review, U.S. House of Representatives, *Scheduling the Work of the House*, 94th Cong., 2nd sess., 1976, p. 24, Congressional Record for 95th–98th Congresses.

protracted than anything the administration (and most economists) had expected. The result: federal deficits greater than $150 billion, even with economic recovery in 1983 and 1984—the highest ever as a percentage of GNP, except for those of the two world wars. Senators and congressmen loudly complained that in the first half of the 1980s, Congress was overwhelmed by budget and tax measures almost the whole session long. Under these conditions, missed deadlines and government-by-continuing-resolution have become fixtures of the legislative process. Will all this eventually swamp the new budgetary system even more seriously than it did in 1984? It may.

SUMMARY

Since World War II, and especially since the early 1970s, Congress has attempted to adapt to the modern American superstate. It has a very long way to go. Both the House and Senate delegate much authority to their committees and subcommittees, and the extreme fragmentation of Congress creates many opportunities for special-interest groups. The general decay of party politics had eroded the strongest force for maintaining stable voting coalitions in the Congress and the bond of common interest between it and the presidency.

Today's congressional candidates often campaign as outsiders who owe nothing to the party organizations. They try to depoliticize themselves, relying heavily on service to constituents and name-recognition, and on portraying themselves as defenders of their districts against big government in Washington. On important votes, most members of the House and Senate are increasingly vulnerable to the pressures of their constituencies and of special interests.

Today, as always, Congress competes with the presidency and the bureaucracy, a rivalry created by the constitutional separation of powers. Congress tried to take the initiative from the President in the mid-1970s, after Watergate, with laws such as the 1973 War Powers Act and the 1974 Impoundment and Budget Control Act. Congressional prerogatives were tested and, to some extent, found wanting in the budget fights of 1981 and 1982. The first time around, President Reagan scored great tax and budget victories, since he was able to control the new budget process himself—which was not its creators' intention. So it is hardly clear that Congress will be able to hold its own.

Congress today is younger, probably richer, probably less corrupt, and decidely more vigorous than it has been in a very long time. In recent years, it has made heroic efforts to come to grips with its political environment, and it remains—as the Framers of the Constitution intended—a branch of government fully equal to the executive branch. But these efforts have been undercut by other developments, especially the decay of party bonds and serious economic and budgetary problems. Congress is in trouble, like our other institutions. But despite its obvious, sometimes tragicomic flaws, it deserves more support and encouragement than it seems to be getting.

SUGGESTED READINGS

LAWRENCE C. DODD and BRUCE I. OPPENHEIMER eds., *Congress Reconsidered*, 2nd ed. Washington, D.C.: Congressional Quarterly Press, 1981. A collection of very timely essays by leading analysts of our national legislature.

RICHARD F. FENNO, JR., *Home Style: House Members in their Districts*. Boston: Little, Brown, 1978. Vivid, illuminating description of the links between congressmen and their constituencies, and how they cultivate them.

MORRIS FIORINA, *Congress: Keystone of the Washington Establishment*. New Haven: Yale Univ., 1977. A worried view of Congress's performance by one of the leading American political scientists.

MICHAEL MALBIN, *Unelected Representatives: Congressional Staff and the Future of Representation*. New York: Basic Books, 1980. Detailed and penetrating analysis of the growth of staff support in the "new" Congress and some of the implications of this bureaucratization process.

WALTER J. OLESZEK, *Congressional Procedures and the Policy Process*. Washington, D.C.: Congressional Quarterly Press, 1978. Straightforward, factual account of procedures in the contemporary Congress, helping the student to sort out what often seems to outsiders to be an impenetrable maze.

GARY ORFIELD, *Congressional Power: Congress and Social Change*. New York: Harcourt, 1975. Analyzes the shift in power and policy making following the adoption of the reform cluster in the mid-1970s.

ROBERT L. PEABODY, *Leadership in Congress: Stability, Succession and Change*. Boston: Little, Brown, 1976. Detailed analysis of change and continuity in congressional leadership patterns over two decades, giving important insights into the qualities that leaders have the limitations on their capacity to lead.

DAVID B. TRUMAN, ed., *The Congress and America's Future*, 2nd ed. Englewood Cliffs, N.J.: Prentice-Hall, 1973. Collection of first-rate essays on leading aspects of Congress and its relationships to other parts of the American political process—notably the presidency. Very much influenced by the "imperial presidency" phase of the power cycle.

chapter fourteen

THE COURTS

Sitting with his law clerks one day, Mr. Justice Powell felt uneasy in his mind. About half a year earlier, in the spring of 1972, the U.S. Supreme Court had listened to oral arguments in a suit that challenged the constitutionality of laws prohibiting abortion. Powell was quite sure that the U.S. Constitution, which says nothing about abortion, also implies nothing about it. And yet, as he told the clerks, he found these laws "atrocious"—so much so that he had made up his mind to vote against them. There had been no sudden flash of constitutional insight. Against what he viewed as his better judgment, Powell had decided to vote his "gut."

By fall 1972, six justices—a majority—had committed themselves to a decision that would strike down most of this country's laws against abortion. Mr. Justice Blackmun then started to write the majority opinion, setting forth the Court's decision and the reasons for it. His first draft argued that until the fetus (or unborn child) was viable—able to live outside the mother's womb—the state had no legitimate interest in abortion and therefore no right to ban it.

Mr. Justice Brennan, another of the six justices, disliked the viability standard. He believed that the Court should consider the state's interest in the mother's life, not just the child's. Blackmun then rewrote his opinion to incorporate Brennan's views. At this point, Blackmun distinguished among the three trimesters (twelve-week periods) of pregnancy. During the first trimester, the state had no interest in the matter at all; during the second, it could regulate abortion to save the mother's life; during the third, it could intervene to save the fetus, now assumed to be viable.

Another of the six justices, Mr. Justice Marshall, read the opinion at this point and discovered a new set of problems. Marshall was and is the only black member of the Court. He felt that many poor women would get no medical help until the second trimester, in which case the Court's decision might change little or nothing. Blackmun then decided to incorporate Marshall's objections, too, by stipulating that states could ban (as opposed to regulate) abortions in the third trimester only.

Chief Justice Burger had by now decided to support the opinion of his good friend Justice Blackmun. Burger's main interest was not the reasoning behind the opinion but the date of its release. The decision was sure to offend conservatives, so he wanted it to come out after the second inauguration of President Richard Nixon, who had appointed both him and Blackmun.

The justices were now "openly brokering their decision like a group of legislators." Even many of the Court's law clerks thought the opinion was less a constitutional thesis than a medical textbook.

Mr. Justice Stewart agreed with them. He, too, had decided to vote with the majority, but he wanted a firmer constitutional basis for doing so. Eventually, he rested his case on a doctrine called "substantive due process," a line of reasoning once much used by the Court but now in disfavor. Under it, from 1890 to 1937, the Court had struck down just about any economic-regulation law its majority disliked. Stewart himself did not really think much of substantive due process, but he considered it more honest than the argument worked out by Blackmun, Brennan, and Marshall. So he wrote a concurring opinion, one that supported the majority's decision but for different reasons.

Many years earlier, another of the justices, William O. Douglas, had been among the leading opponents of substantive due process. He found Stewart's views "laughable" but, like Stewart, wrote a concurring opinion—not because he disagreed with the majority opinion, but because he wanted to stress one of its points: the right to privacy.

Only two justices now dissented: Mr. Justice Rehnquist and Mr. Justice White. In January 1973, the Court announced its decision, striking down almost all antiabortion laws and permitting states to ban abortion only in the third trimester.[1] But the Court's decision did not settle the abortion issue.

Charles Evans Hughes, Chief Justice of the United States from 1930 to 1941, once said "we live under a Constitution, but the Constitution is what the judges say it is." Hughes was right. Because Americans expect the justices to enforce the commands of the Constitution and because the Constitution's meaning is always not clear, the Court's decisions have provoked bitter controversy since the earliest days of the Republic. Today, there is no shortage of people willing to argue that some law violates a right guaranteed by the Constitution. As long as the Court sits, its decisions will continue to spark debate. The American system of constitutional government invites rule by judges.

THE ROOTS OF AMERICAN LAW

The United States has 51 separate legal systems: those of the 50 states and that of the federal court system. Most of the laws of this country are passed, executed, and interpreted by the states. Most suits are tried and appealed in state courts.

---

[1] This account is derived from Bob Woodward and Scott Armstrong, *The Brethren* (New York: Simon & Schuster, 1979).

Actually, the courts of the original thirteen states are older than the federal courts, and they passed on to them the legal traditions that repose at the bottom of all American law. Those traditions came largely from England.

Roman Law and English Law

The English legal system was different from the legal systems of continental Europe, which were and are based on the law code of the Roman Empire. These European codes are systematic, precise, and detailed; the German code, for example, goes into such detail that, among many other things, it defines the ownership of swarms of wild bees.

Limits on Judges. The Roman law code, and those based on it, provide rule comprehensive enough to settle all disputes. In principle, judges merely monitor and direct the application of the code, which gives them little room for discretion and flexibility. The English legal tradition gave much more scope to judicial creativity, although judicial review of legislation did not survive there, as it has here.

The Common Law. The English tradition was created case by case, through real disputes between people. Judges settled these cases by applying **precedents,** past judicial decisions, but because they did not always have a clear precedent to apply, they often had to make up their own minds. "Case law," comprising thousands of decisions, was built up over centuries, rather like a coral reef.

Eventually, English judges built up a set of common standards: customary practices that were applied throughout the entire kingdom of England. These **common laws,** worked over by legal scholars, evolved into a body of legal rules but never into a systematic legal code. Even English **statutes**—laws enacted by Parliament—did not have this degree of detail. Judges acquired the power to develop the law, a power that would not be thinkable under the Roman system.

Stare Decisis. One Roman heritage that the English picked up and never lost was a fascination with Latin phrases. The most important principle of the common law is what lawyers call **stare decisis,** meaning "let the decision stand." In practice, it means that the principles spelled out in earlier decisions should be followed unless there is an extremely strong reason not to. Even when judges apply *stare decisis*, they still have a lot of leeway. Rarely does a case present every feature of a previous case and only those features.

The Adversary System. Another aspect of English law (not, however, peculiar to it) is the so-called **adversary system.** In England, and also in the United States, people who are accused of crimes have a right to be represented by lawyers of their own choosing. These lawyers may not tell lies on their clients' behalf or suppress evidence, but they can and do shape the truth in their clients' favor and try to get the best possible outcomes for their clients, even if guilty. Defense and prosecution do not work together in a common pursuit of truth; they clash as adversaries, and the court elicits the truth for itself. The adversary system makes the law very complicated, cumbersome, and expensive, but it is an inevitable corollary of another basic legal principle: the presumption of innocence.

Writs

Writs of *mandamus* and *certiorari* are discussed in the text. Others include the following:

Writ of *quo warranto* (literally, "By what warrant?"). A writ filed when there is reason to believe that officials have acted outside their legal jurisdiction. If a court in a *quo warranto* proceeding finds that they have done so, their actions are declared null and void.

Writ of *habeas corpus* (literally, "You will have the body"). Originally authorized and defined in British law by the Habeas Corpus Act of 1678. A writ requiring police officials to bring a prisoner before a properly authorized court within a (very short) specified time. A fundamental aspect of civil liberties, this writ is designed to make arbitrary imprisonment for indefinite periods of time unlawful and, since 1787, unconstitutional. It may not be suspended constitutionally except by Congress, and then only "when in Cases of Rebellion or Invasion the public Safety may require it" (Article 1, Section 9, Clause 2).

Ultra vires (literally, "Beyond the powers"). Used by the Supreme Court in some cases to strike down the constitutionality of statutes or other official actions by federal or state authorities. The concept means that the body or official in question has acted beyond the constitutional scope of authority. For example, in *Schechter Bros. Corp.* v. *United States* 295 U.S. 495 (1935), the Supreme Court declared the National Industrial Recovery Act of 1933 to be *ultra vires,* hence unconstitutional. The act set up the National Recovery Administration (NRA) and delegated to it very sweeping powers to regulate prices, working conditions, and other aspects of the private economy. The Court in striking it down invoked yet another latinism: *delegata protestas non potest delegari* (literally: delegated power cannot [itself] be delegated). By this, it meant that the legislative powers of Congress were delegated to it by the people through the Constitution, and it could not then delegate these legislative powers to other bodies. After 1937, Congress was given almost complete latitude to do just that (see Chapter 12).

Stare decisis (approximately, "Let the decision stand") A long-time rule in English and American jurisprudence, stressing that precedents (earlier judicial decisions) should normally be regarded as applicable to current cases with similar legal and factual circumstances. *Stare decisis* is meant to promote order, predictability, and continuity in the development of case law. So strong is the need for these virtues that Justice Brandeis once went so far as to say in an opinion, "It is normally better that the law be settled than that it be settled right." However, his long-time ally on the Court, Justice Oliver Wendell Holmes, once observed in a lecture, "It is revolting to have no better justification for a legal rule than that it was laid down in the reign of Henry IV." The more that courts rely on *stare decisis*, the more rigid and unchanging the law will be. Yet some argue that *stare decisis* keeps courts from being unelected legislatures, if anything does. Today, for better or worse, *stare decisis* is very often more honored in the breach than in the observance; and the more important the constitutional issues are, the less this self-restraint rule seems to matter.

In the United States, defense lawyers, whatever they actually believe, must act on the assumption that their clients are innocent. So, too, must our courts, which cannot find defendants guilty just because no evidence has been presented to prove their innocence. Positive proof of guilt is required for conviction, and the burden of providing it rests with the prosecution.

Criminal Law and Civil Law

Every society is full of rules: baseball's infield fly rule, for example, and etiquette's rule that bids us to place a fork to the left of a dish. Neither of these rules is enforced by the government; they are rules of private society. Even those rules, or laws, that are enforced by the government vary in kind.

THE RULES OF THE GAME

Drawing by Mischa Richter © 1981 The New Yorker Magazine, Inc.

Violations of certain rules amount to an attack on society itself. Others essentially involve disputes among private persons, with the government stepping in as referee. The boundaries among these different kinds of rules are set by public opinion, not by logic. They therefore change. Translating the Bible into English was a heinous crime punished by burning—500 years ago.

Criminal Law. The range covered by the criminal law is immense: from throwing garbage on the sidewalk to homicide. What do these acts have in common? In themselves, nothing. The common thread is our attitude toward them—our belief that they injure society itself, not just the immediate victim. That is why the government, not the victim, acts as prosecutor and punishes the guilty. In legal jargon, serious crimes are called **felonies,** and punishments for them can be severe. Lesser crimes, with correspondingly lesser punishments, are **misdemeanors.**

Civil Law. Consider the case of an automobile accident in which a drunk driver kills a pedestrian. That driver could well be accused, under the criminal law, of committing vehicular homicide, for the state has a public interest to maintain—society is threatened by such drivers. In addition, the relatives of the person killed in the accident may bring a suit against the driver for damages, demanding compensation both for the victim and for the property destroyed in the wreck. Such suits involve private interests rather than directly public ones. They form part of the **civil law,** tried and decided in a different forum: the civil courts.

The crucial distinction is that the state is not a party to civil cases. People who feel they have been injured by the actions of another person—for example, through slander, willful negligence, libel, or breach of contract—must themselves bring suit if any civil-court action is to occur. If the civil court finds for this **plaintiff** and against the **defendant,** the latter usually has to pay damages, a money fine. Prison sentences are never directly involved in such cases, unless the defendant defies the court's ruling and refuses to pay, committing **contempt of court.** In that event, the state itself has been injured and becomes a party to this aspect of the case.

Irene Springer

An automobile accident could end up as a criminal case against a drunken driver or a civil case in which the injured party brings suit against the driver for damages. The major distinction between criminal law and civil law is that the state is not a party to civil cases.

Birth of the Judiciary

The early colonists brought the common law and the adversary system over from England. Each colony then developed its own judicial system and body of precedents, the ancestors of today's legal systems in 49 of the 50 states. The exception is Louisiana, originally settled by French rather than English colonists. Its legal system includes large parts of the French *code civil* (or the *Code Napoleon)*, based on Roman rather than common law.

The Colonial Period

During the early period, the governor and his council, usually members of the upper house of the colonial legislature, acted as judges. The executive, judiciary, and legislature were fused, as in England. When the colonies became more populous, they set up local courts, county by county, but the governor and council continued to hear appeals.

Because few early settlers had legal training, most judges were laymen. Both in England and the United States, lay judges are still commonplace at the very primary level of justice of the peace.[2] Some states still authorize lay judges even for higher levels of their judicial systems. Nevertheless, the legal systems of both countries became increasingly elaborate and professional, complete with professional lawyers to argue cases before courts, a stage reached in many colonies by the time of American independence. As a group, lawyers were well represented at the Constitutional Convention of 1787.

The Constitutional Convention. The Framers of the U.S. Constitution therefore did not start out from a judicial blank slate, though when they met in 1787, there had never been a national court system.

---

[2] The author's father, who was no lawyer, served for some years not so very long ago as justice of the peace in a small Pennsylvania borough.

Library of Congress

During the early colonial period, members of the upper house of the legislature acted as judges—the executive, judiciary, and legislature were fused, as in England. Here is shown the first Legislative Assembly in America—at Jamestown, Virginia, August 1619.

The Framers aimed to create a stronger national government, yet they feared such a government. The delegates limited the powers of the federal such a government by dividing them among three coequal branches: the legislature, the executive, and the judiciary. Each is independent of the others, yet entwined with them as well.

The Framers lavished much detail on the form and powers of the federal executive and legislature. As for the judiciary, they contended themselves by stating that "the judicial Power of the United States shall be vested in one supreme Court, and in such inferior Courts as the Congress may from time to time ordain and establish." There are few details, and those mostly establish the independence of the judiciary, not its structure or powers.

"Good Behavior." One of these details provided that federal judges should serve during "good behavior"—not, that is, for a specified term or at the pleasure of Congress or the President. Federal judges can only be removed through the rare and difficult process of impeachment by the House and conviction by the Senate. As a practical matter, once appointed, they stay in office as long as they wish. They do not have to do the bidding of Congress or the President and cannot be removed for handing down unpopular decisions.

Shared Appointments. To prevent either the President or Congress from dominating the federal courts, the delegates divided the appointment of federal judges between the two. The President starts the process by nominating candidates, but the Senate must confirm them by a simple majority.

Guaranteed Annual Wage. The Constitution prohibits Congress from cutting the salaries of federal judges, again to insulate them from congressional pressures. This protection was undermined in recent years by inflation, for the Constitution does not require Congress to increase judicial salaries when the dollar's value declines. Judicial raises have for years been tardy, slow, and inadequate. Exactly as the Framers must have feared, proposals in Congress to raise judges' salaries often bog down in highly political debates about the correctness of judicial decisions, especially those of the Supreme Court.

A FEDERAL CASE

The Constitution added this very complicated system of national government to an already quite complicated system of state and local governments. The states were still to pass, enforce, and interpret all laws within their own sphere of power. In fact, as we have said, they conduct most of the legal business of this country.

What then is a "federal case?" The answer is twofold. First, the case must in some way involve a **federal question**—the interests of the federal government. Second, the parties to the case, even if it does involve those interests, must also meet certain criteria: They must have what lawyers call **standing to sue.**

Federal Questions

Cases can involve federal questions either because they arise under federal law or because they involve certain kinds of parties, notably the federal government.

Federal Law. Anyone accused of breaking a federal law will be tried in a federal court, before a federal judge and a federal jury, and prosecuted by a federal prosecutor. Federal law in this sense includes the U.S. Constitution, all statutes passed by Congress, all regulations issued under those statutes, and all federal treaties.

The Parties. The second kind of federal question is more complex. Say that a state accuses the federal government of violating a state law. Who tries the case? The federal courts. Federal courts, in fact, try any and all cases involving the federal government as a party, to protect it from the possible rivalry of state courts.

As ratified in 1788, the Constitution also gave the federal courts jurisdiction over cases involving state governments as parties. But the Eleventh Amendment (1798) took away some of these cases: those in which individuals or foreign countries bring suit against states.[3] States, though, must still sue one another in federal court.

Federal courts also hear cases (called **diversity cases)** in which citizens of different states sue each other, as long as those cases involve claims of $10,000 or more.

Finally, the U.S. Supreme Court hears all cases involving foreign diplomats, a power that complements the federal government's power over foreign policy.

---

[3] This amendment was adopted in a fervid states' rights atmosphere following the Supreme Court's decision in *Chisholm* v. *Georgia*, 2 Dall. 419 (1793), in which the Court had accepted jurisdiction of a suit by a citizen of one state against another state.

Cases that do not fit any of these categories do not involve federal questions and are left to state courts.

Most cases that involve both state and federal questions can be heard either by state or federal courts, depending on the preference of the party filing the suit. This overlapping jurisdiction means that state judges apply and interpret federal law and that federal judges do the same for state law.

Standing to Sue

In 1974, a civil-rights group petitioned the U.S. Supreme Court to review a zoning law that required all houses in a suburb of Rochester, New York, to be single-family units on large lots. In effect, the law kept poor people out of the suburb. The case, however, was hypothetical; none of the petitioners had attempted to build any house forbidden by the law, and therefore none could claim any personal injury from it. Two lower federal courts had already refused to hear the case on just those grounds.

Chief Justice Burger and Justices Stewart, Blackmun, Rehnquist, and Powell agreed with the two lower courts. As Justice Stewart put it, the petitioners were not challenging a law; "what they are really asking us to do is to overrule the capitalist system," which makes it possible for rich people to build houses that poor people cannot afford.

Justice Brennan, together with Justice Marshall, took a different view and argued that the need to show a real injury from a real attempt to build a house was a mere legal technicality, one that the court should overlook. The petitioners did not have the money to commission and file a plan and thereby give the zoning board a chance to reject it.[4]

The Court's majority did not base its ruling on the rights and wrongs of the zoning law but on what lawyers call standing to sue. The petitioners did not have that standing because they had suffered no personal injury from the law they wanted to challenge. We shall look into this matter of "standing" in a moment. But before we even begin, bear in mind that it means what the courts say it means. If for any reason, four justices had wanted to hear the case, it would have been heard—personal injury or not. The court makes its own rules and also bends, stretches, and ignores them.

"Standing to sue" has four elements. In principle, any case heard in federal court should embody all four:

1. "*Adverse Parties.*" First, federal courts can hear only cases between truly hostile parties. Parties that merely wish to test the constitutionality of a law cannot agree to contrive a dispute and take it to the federal courts.

2. "*Substantial Legal Interest.*" The two parties must also stand to gain or lose by the outcome of the case. They must show that real pain or punishment may result from the dispute—that they stand to lose life, liberty, or assets.

Hence, the doctrine of **mootness.** When a legal action is overtaken by events—in other words, if it should be made irrelevant before it is decided—it is *moot,* and the court can drop the case. Suppose that a convicted murderer appeals a death sentence but before the appeal is decided, the legislature of that state rescinds the death penalty. Because the convict can no longer be executed, no one any longer has a "substantial legal interest" in the suit.

3. "*A Real Set of Facts.*" Federal courts will hear only controversies that have really occurred, not those that might occur in the future. Congress

---

[4] This account is drawn from Woodward and Armstrong, *The Brethren.*

The U.S. Supreme Court was petitioned to review a zoning law that required all houses in a suburb of Rochester, New York, to be single-family units on large lots. It challenged a law that kept poor people out of the suburb.

cannot, for instance, ask the U.S. Supreme Court to review the constitutionality of a bill, nor can the President ask the Court if a certain line of policy does or does not "faithfully execute the law." To find out if they have acted constitutionally, Congress and the President must wait for real disputes to arise. Many state courts do issue **advisory opinions** of the sort that the federal courts refuse to give.

4. *"A Legal Question."* Federal courts are restricted to cases that can be settled through what legal jargon insists on calling "an enforceable determination of rights." In other words, they will attempt to resolve disputes based on **legal questions** only. Suppose, for example, that a losing candidate for public office brings suit to have an election thrown out. If the candidate's legal rights were violated, there may very well be a federal case. But no federal court would hear a case brought on the ground that the defeated candidate would make a better officeholder.

Political Questions. The Court has also long insisted that certain kinds of questions are **political questions** and therefore outside the scope of judicial review. Back in 1849, it was asked to decide which of two rival Rhode Island governments had been the lawful one in the so-called Dorr War (1842). The Court refused to do so on the grounds that this was a political question.[5] Much later, a Northwestern University professor of political science, Kenneth W. Colegrove, brought suit against the state of Illinois, charging that its legislature had failed to reapportion the state's congressional districts for more than forty years. As a result of population changes in the meantime, his vote was worth only one-ninth, or less, of a vote cast by someone living in a nearby Chicago district. The Court again refused to intervene because, in the majority's view, this was a "political question," too, and "would cut very deep into the very being of Congress. Courts ought not to enter this political thicket."[6]

"Silent gerrymanders" were an unsolved and growing problem of American representative institutions. In Connecticut, for example, the 1818 state constitution gave each town two members in the state House of Representatives, producing inequalities as high as 680 to 1 in the weighting of votes. Vermont had not reapportioned its lower house since 1793! In 1962, the U.S. Supreme Court changed its mind and decided that federal courts could set constitutional standards for state legislative apportionment.[7] By 1964, the justices had ruled that all legislative districts (congressional as well as state) had to be equal in population. This was the famous one-person/one-vote rule.[8]

Access to the Federal Courts

"The law, in its majestic impartiality, forbids the rich as well as the poor from sleeping beneath bridges," as the nineteenth-century novelist Anatole France put it. So, too, the rich and poor alike can take their grievances to federal court. American justice, though, is colossally expensive. A trial is bad enough; the costs of an appeal can be absolutely ruinous, for our courts—unlike those of Europe—usually insist that both parties pay their own way. Learned Hand, a famous federal judge of the first half of this century, said he would fear a lawsuit more than anything but a long illness or death.

Help for Defendants. The problem of financing lawsuits is especially bad in civil cases, since both parties must always pay their own costs. Criminal matters can be easier for poor people—financially, at any rate. A series of decisions, mostly handed down by the U.S. Supreme Court under Chief Justice Earl Warren (1953–1969), required governments at all levels to provide a lawyer for any criminal defendant too poor to pay for one. Appellate courts also absolve poor people from many procedural requirements.

Collective Access. Poverty is only one of the obstacles to justice. Some people are neither poor enough to be classified as indigent nor rich enough to afford a lawsuit. The claims of others are not sufficiently large to justify that expense.

---

[5] *Luther* v. *Borden*, 7 Howard 1 (1849).

[6] *Colegrove* v. *Green*, 328 U.S. 549 (1946).

[7] *Baker* v. *Carr*, 369 U.S. 186 (1962).

[8] *Wesberry* v. *Sanders*, 376 U.S. 1 (1964); *Reynolds* v. *Sims*, 377 U.S. 533 (1964).

One example of a class-action suit was a suit brought by Vietnam veterans against the makers of the herbicide Agent Orange. Some of the groups involved felt that the $180 million settlement was not fair; they are shown here protesting the settlement outside the federal courthouse in Brooklyn.

Still others simply may not wish to make their way alone through the innumerable hazards and annoyances of the court system. Such people can join with others or with groups and take their cases to court collectively, either through **class-action suits** or cooperation with interest groups.

Class Actions. Suppose a utility company illegally overcharges each of its customers a dollar or two a month. No one files suit for a dollar a month; the costs would far outweigh the potential gains. The utility, however, would be making huge sums of money when all the overcharges were added together. So a consumer might file a class-action suit on behalf of all the utility's customers—a suit that might bring a judgment for millions of dollars, not the few dollars that any one individual might hope to win.

During the Warren era, a liberal Court made it much easier for class-action suits to be filed, which then became an important weapon in the hands of consumer, environmental, and civil-rights groups—liberals, in short. Later on, a conservative Court made it much harder to file such suits and drastically cut their number. This no doubt reduced the workload of the federal courts. Some people argue that it also reduced the rights of many people.

Interest Groups. People who cannot or will not finance their own lawsuits sometimes get massive aid from interest groups. The National Association for the Advancement of Colored People (NAACP) prepared the long trail of litigation and preparation behind the U.S. Supreme Court's school desegregation decision, *Brown* v. *Board of Education.*[9] The NAACP had substantial financial resources, an expert legal staff, and, of course, a vital interest in the

---

[9] 347 U.S. 423 (1954).

outcome of the suit. Many other such cases abound. In fact, it is commonly understood that constitutional litigation is an important aspect of interest-group activity. Most, if not almost all, major constitutional cases now involve substantial efforts by interest groups.

Moreover—and perhaps more centrally—when interest groups are concerned about a case before the U.S. Supreme Court, they often apply for leave (permission) to file briefs **amicus curiae** ("friend of the court"). Leave is very often granted, although less often under Chief Justice Burger than under his predecessor, Chief Justice Warren. Such briefs tell the Court what the group's position is and often provide important information that the lawyers for the contending parties may not have raised at all, or not to the interest group's satisfaction. This information sometimes plays an important part in the processes of decision. Otherwise, the justices would have to rely solely on the arguments submitted by the opposing parties in the case. And one or both sides may not have been argued well.

THE STRUCTURE OF THE FEDERAL COURT SYSTEM

A federal criminal case begins with an arrest. Federal attorneys, who work for the Justice Department then bring the suspect before a **grand jury** of twenty "good men and true"—today, of course, women are jurors too. Should the grand jury find merit in the government's case, it returns an **indictment**, declaring that a crime has been committed and accusing some person or persons of committing it. "The suspect" is now "the accused" and must stand trial. Federal civil cases are simpler to bring to trial. One party, the **plaintiff**, files a suit accusing the other party, the **defendant**, of damaging his or her interests. The defendant then stands trial.

District Courts

Federal trials, and the events leading up to them, take place in one of 94 **U.S. District Courts.** U.S. District Courts are the only federal courts in which juries rule on the facts of each case and find defendants guilty or innocent of the offenses "whereof they are charged." These courts do not hear appeals.

Created by Congress. The number of U.S. District Courts and the number of judges sitting on each are fixed by Congress. In the Judiciary Act of 1789, Congress set up 13 district courts, one for each state. Over the years, Congress has increased the number of judicial districts to 94—with 89 in the states, and one each in the District of Columbia (Washington, D.C.) and the U.S. territories of Northern Mariana Islands, Guam, Puerto Rico, and Virgin Islands. Each state has at least one district; states with heavy caseloads—New York, Texas, and California, for instance—have several. No district crosses a state line.

Distributed throughout these districts are 578 district judges. New York's southern district has the largest number: 27 judges; Guam and the Northern Mariana Islands have only one judge each. Among the states, the least populated district court benches are those for Wyoming, Vermont, North

A federal judge presided over the breakup of the American Telephone and Telegraph Company. Here AT&T employees are shown delivering to the court documents connected with the breakup of the Bell System.

Dakota, New Hampshire, Maine, and Idaho, with 2 each. Each court is equipped with clerks for administrative chores, U.S. marshals to serve papers and stand guard, probation officers, and court reporters. Certain districts also have lower-ranking judges: bankruptcy judges, for example, to deal with creditors, and U.S. magistrates to handle minor cases and pretrial matters.

Responsibilities: Trials and Oversight. U.S. District Courts chiefly conduct trials. In 1982, they handled about 230,000 cases—398 for each judge, on the average. All but 14 percent of these cases were civil rather than criminal, and most were based on federal law. Like courts at all levels, U.S. District Courts conduct trials by receiving evidence, hearing testimony, and handling down decisions, sometimes with the help of juries. Most of these decisions are not appealed.

Oversight. From the early 1970s to the early 1980s, a judge of the U.S. District Court more or less ran Boston's school system. A few years later, another such judge halted construction of a highway project in New York City. Still another presided over the breakup of the American Telephone and Telegraph Company (the Bell System). Some litigation can run on for years.

The U.S. Courts of Appeals

For every 100,000 of us, we seem to need 143 lawyers. The Japanese somehow make do with 9 per 100,000. We Americans are a litigious people, and we often carry our litigations beyond the trial stage, by appealing them to a higher level of the court system. To meet the demand for such appeals, Congress had to create the intermediate level of the federal judicial hierarchy, now called the **U.S. Courts of Appeals.** These courts hear appeals not only from the district courts but also from executive agencies such as the Interstate Commerce Commission (ICC), the Federal Trade Commission (FTC), the Environmental Protection Agency (EPA)—in short, from the whole alphabet soup of federal regulation.

An Unsettled History. The Judiciary Act of 1789 created four courts of appeals, then called "circuit courts." During the next fifteen years, the Federalists and the Jeffersonians (see Chapter 9) battled to control them; they were created, abolished, then created anew in modified form.

During most of the nineteenth century, the circuit courts lacked a separate staff of judges. Instead, U.S. District Court judges and U.S. Supreme Court justices doubled, whenever they could, as circuit court judges. This *riding circuit*, was especially burdensome to the Supreme Court. In 1869, Congress finally created a separate panel of circuit court judge—but too few of them; the Supreme Court was still overburdened.

Not until 1891 did Congress create enough appellate judgeships to reduce the justices' workload. This time, it set up the whole new level of appeals courts that eventually replaced the circuit courts. Since 1948, the courts on this level have been called the U.S. Courts of Appeals.

Current Structure. Today there are thirteen U.S. Courts of Appeals.[10] Each covers a geographical area still called a circuit. One circuit comprises the District of Columbia; others comprise states. The thirteenth, and newest, is the Court of Appeals for the Federal Circuit, which accepts cases involving patents, copyrights, and trademarks from any district court, as well as all appeals from the U.S. Claims Court and the U.S. Court of International Trade.

The 13 circuits divide among them 168 judges, in proportion to their caseloads. U.S. Courts of Appeals hear most cases by dividing into panels of 3 judges each. Very important cases may be heard and decided en banc, meaning that all of the circuit's judges sit on the case.

More than 27,000 cases were filed in the U.S. Courts of Appeals in 1982, an 11 percent increase over 1981.

How They Work. The U.S. Courts of Appeals are not trial courts. They hear no witnesses, receive no evidence, have no juries. Lawyers simply present arguments, both written and oral, before the judges. The U.S. Courts of Appeals do not make decisions about the guilt or innocence of any defendant, and they receive no new evidence. Their job is to examine the record of the original trial and determine if it was held according to the rules.

Suppose, for example, that during a trial, a federal district court admitted evidence that had been seized illegally. The U.S. Supreme Court first barred such evidence in 1914 (see Chapter 4).[11] If the district judge had somehow overlooked this "Weeks rule," the Court of Appeals would issue a reminder by overturning the conviction. Such gross mistakes are not at all common, in part because they would be detected by appeals courts.

---

[10] In 1976, Congress added another circuit, the Temporary Emergency Court of Appeals, to deal with the overflow of work from other courts. Because it is temporary, it is not assured of continuing institutional life and is therefore not included in the total of thirteen circuits.
[11] *Weeks* v. *U.S.*, 232 U.S. 383 (1914).

A Time of Transition for No. 2 Court

"It's sort of the last bastion of liberalism, and the question is whether it will hold," said Joseph L. Rauh Jr., a leading public interest lawyer here, who fervently hopes that it will.

"It's giving one damned good last hurrah for the maintenance of a powerful regulatory system run out of Washington," complained a Reagan Administration official who sometimes would like to see it disappear in a puff of smoke.

Both were talking about the United States Court of Appeals for the District of Columbia Circuit.

Sitting in tranquil dignity in the Federal Courthouse just down the street from the Capitol, the D.C. Circuit, as lawyers call it, is the nation's principal judicial reviewer of Federal regulations, and is widely regarded as its most powerful tribunal after the Supreme Court.

It is also a target of efforts by conservatives and business lobbyists in Congress who want to take away some of its powers by shifting part of its caseload to other Federal courts, and of efforts by President Reagan to use his power of appointment to make the Federal judiciary more conservative.

Ruling on Auto Safety

Known for more than three decades as a hotbed of liberal judicial activism, the D.C. Circuit remains a favorite of environmentalists, consumer activists, labor unions and civil rights groups and a bete noir of conservatives and business interests.

Just last month, for example, a three-judge panel of the appeals court delighted consumer activists and enraged Administration officials by ruling that all new automobiles sold after September 1983 must be equipped with air bags or automatic seat belts.

The panel's action, together with a related decision in June, overruled a centerpiece of the Administration's program of regulatory relief for business and reinstated a regulation that the Administration had rescinded because it would cost consumers and the auto industry $1 billion annually.

The Justice Department plans to appeal to the Supreme Court on Wednesday. It has already appealed several other recent D.C. Circuit decisions, including a ruling written by Judge J. Skelly Wright this spring that barred operation of the second, undamaged nuclear reactor at Three Mile Island until the Nuclear Regulatory Commission assessed the "psychological stress" on people in the neighborhood.

Reversals by Supreme Court

In still another case being appealed by the Justice Department, a three-judge panel of the D.C. Circuit awarded more than $90,000 in attorney's fees and costs to two environmental groups for bringing a lawsuit against the Government, even though the Government prevailed against them on every issue in the suit.

The D.C. Circuit's vast, although not exclusive, power to review the legality of regulatory actions stems from its jurisdiction over appeals from decisions of the Federal District Court here, where many suits against the Government are filed, and from dozens of statutes that make actions by various agencies directly appealable to it.

The more conservative Supreme Court has reversed a considerable number of D.C. Circuit decisions on politically charged issues in recent years.

But the appeals court has the final say on the legality of many regulations and other issues that involve billions of dollars and have a national impact because the Supreme Court has time to review only a small fraction of its decisions.

Conservatives and business interests seeking to cut the D.C. Circuit's powers have waged innumerable tugs of war in Congress over the years against liberal public interest types who like to take their cases to the D.C. Circuit.

Currently, Congress is considering a complex "venue" bill, favored by the Administration and such conservative Senators as Alan K. Simpson, Republican of Wyoming, and Paul Laxalt, Republican of Nevada, to cut the D.C. Circuit's powers by shifting much of its regulatory caseload to Federal courts in the parts of the country where the regulatory actions in question would have the greatest impact.

The proposal has little chance of passing this year, but it will be back after this fall's elections.

Meanwhile, the D.C. Circuit's future as a bastion of liberalism is very much in doubt.

In the past year, Mr. Reagan has appointed to the court two politically conservative academics with impeccable scholarly credentials: Robert H. Bork, formerly of Yale Law School, and Antonin Scalia, formerly of the University of Chicago Law School.

These appointments cut the D.C. Circuit's liberal majority, long led by Judge Wright and Judge David L. Bazelon, to six of the court's 11 fulltime judges.

One more vacancy would give the President an opportunity to tip the balance against the liberal wing, which includes Chief Judge Spottswoods W. Robinson 2d and the four judges appointed by President Carter. Judge Bazelon, 73 years old, who joined in the recent decision on air bags, took part-time, senior status two years ago and thus has no vote in cases before the full court.

Judges Wright and Bork represent the philosophical antipodes of the court, although the shorthand labels "liberal" and "conservative" tend to obscure the fact that they agree with each other and their colleagues on many of the legal issues that come before them.

Appointed to the court by President Kennedy in 1962 after a pioneering role in desegregating schools as a Federal District Judge in New Orleans, Judge Wright, 71, has been a champion of minorities, the poor and the powerless, rarely hesitating to strike down actions by other branches of Government that offend his sense of justice.

A Household Name

He has also voted for aggressive implementation a vaguely worded Federal regulatory laws designed to protect the health and safety of workers, consumers and the environment, as in the Three Mile Island opinion.

Judge Bork, who became a household name by carrying out President Nixon's order to dismiss Archibald Cox as Watergate special prosecutor in 1973, has long been an apostle of judicial restraint and deference to legislative and executive branches in setting national policies.

Before his appointment, he was a cogent critic of many of the Supreme Court's constitutional innovations of recent decades, such as those reapportioning state legislatures, requiring large-scale busing to desegregate schools and legalizing abortion.

What Judges Wright, Bork, Bazelon, Scalia and others on the D.C. Circuit have in common is a reputation for exceptional intellectual ability and for a scholarly approach that has produced some of the longest, most elaborately reasoned, most heavily footnoted judicial opinions ever written. Many of those decisions are excerpted in law school textbooks.

Explaining why he was not overly concerned about the political conservatism of the two Reagan appointees, Alan B. Morrison, a public interest lawyer and consumer activist who heads the Public Citizen Litigation Group, remarked recently, "As a litigator, I'll take a smart judge any time."

Stuart Taylor Jr., September 7, 1982, © 1982 by the New York Times Company. Reprinted by permission.

Special Courts

There is a saying that "military justice is to justice as military music is to music." Whatever the merits of military music, military justice has greatly improved in recent years. But the United States continues to maintain separate courts to try violations of military law and of certain other specialized branches of law.

Congress sets up special courts under two distinct grants of constitutional power: Article III, which permits Congress to create lower courts, and Article I, which gives it the power to regulate matters such as taxation and the local government of Washington, D.C. They are called **Article III courts** and **Article I courts.**

Article III Courts. The special courts created under Article III are courts in the true sense: They render justice, not administrative decisions, and they are armed with the protections of judicial independence set forth in Article III. The judges of these courts serve during good behavior, and Congress cannot cut their salaries. The President nominates them, and the Senate must confirm them by a simple majority.

The first special court created under Article III, the Court of Claims, was set up in 1855. It hears suits for damages that private individuals and companies bring against the federal government. The Court of International Trade hears disputes involving customs duties (taxes on imports).

Article I Courts. Certain federal courts are courts only in appearance. Article I of the U.S. Constitution (see Chapter 2) bestows on Congress a long shopping list of powers: taxation, for instance, and governing the U.S. territories and the District of Columbia. These powers generate disputes that do not fall under ordinary federal statutes. Courts set up under Article I are courts in the sense that they hear testimony, receive evidence, and hand down decisions. But they are not true courts, because they do not carry out the judicial power of the United States. As mere administrative arms of Congress, these Article I courts do not enjoy the protections of judicial independence set forth in Article III. Their judges are appointed by Congress for specific terms, not for life.

The three main Article I courts are the U.S. Court of Military Appeals, created in 1950 to hear appeals from military tribunals (courts-martial); local courts in the District of Columbia and other places under the direct control of Congress; and the U.S. Tax Court, which chiefly decides appeals from rulings of the Internal Revenue Service (see Chapter 16).

Article I courts are outside the basic federal hierarchy of district courts, circuit courts, and the U.S. Supreme Court. Article III courts are parallel to the lower and middle parts of that hierarchy: Some try cases, others hear appeals, and their decisions can be appealed to the U.S. Supreme Court.

THE U.S. SUPREME COURT

The Constitution created the U.S. Supreme Court, made it the highest court of appeal, and defined its jurisdiction—the kinds of cases it can handle. But never did the Constitution really define the Court's power. In continental Europe, judges merely applied the law; in England, they also interpreted it, but they judged only *cases*. The U.S. Supreme Court took for itself the power to judge *the law*.

Because it judges the law, not just the merits of particular cases, the Court's power is unique. It was the Court that ordained the desegregation of the public schools and made busing a means of achieving integration. It was the Court that legalized the right to abortion. And it was the Court that forced state legislatures to distribute their seats according to population. No other court system, no other court, would presume to do such things on its own authority.

The Court is asked to consider appeals from about 4,000 cases a year—not, in itself, a particularly large number, especially since all but a few are dismissed. But cases of such importance cannot be decided casually. Indeed, the Court cannot casually refuse to hear a case. Everything it does and does not do takes time. Chief Justice Warren Burger has repeatedly complained that the Court, groaning under the burden of a constantly rising volume of appeals, is grossly overworked.

Jurisdiction

The U.S. Supreme Court confronts the great legal issues as the ultimate court of appeals, and we are mainly aware of it in that role. But the Framers of the Constitution also thought of it as a court of *original jurisdiction*, a trial court. Although the former role has crowded out the latter, the Court still holds trials.

Justices of the Supreme Court, 1985

	Appointed	President
William J. Brennan, Jr.	1956	Dwight D. Eisenhower
Byron R. White	1962	John F. Kennedy
Thurgood Marshall	1967	Lyndon B. Johnson
Warren E. Burger, *chief*	1969	Richard M. Nixon
Harry A. Blackmun	1970	Richard M. Nixon
Lewis F. Powell, Jr.	1972	Richard M. Nixon
William H. Rehnquist	1972	Richard M. Nixon
John Paul Stevens	1975	Gerald R. Ford
Sandra Day O'Connor	1981	Ronald W. Reagan

U.S. Supreme Court

The U.S. Supreme Court, 1985. *Bottom row* **(left to right): Thurgood Marshall, William J. Brennan, Jr., Warren E. Burger, Byron R. White, Harry A. Blackmun. Top row (left to right): John Paul Stevens, Lewis F. Powell, Jr., William H. Rehnquist, Sandra Day O'Connor.**

Original Jurisdiction. Under Article III, the Court had original jurisdiction in all suits that involved the states or foreign diplomats as parties. The Court, however, regards its jurisdiction over foreign diplomat as concurrent, not exclusive, so Congress has been able to assign such cases to other courts. The Eleventh Amendment removed from federal jurisdiction all cases involving states sued by private citizens or by foreign governments. In recent decades, therefore, just about all the cases tried by the U.S. Supreme Court have been suits between states themselves, usually over boundaries or water rights. There are few of these cases, and even fewer are important; rarely does the Court's original-jurisdiction docket (list of cases) account for more than 2 percent of the total number of cases before it.

Special Masters. The appellate demands on the Court are so great that it cannot conduct a full trial even for these few cases. So it has devised a way of speeding them up: appointing a *special master,* usually a lawyer with expertise

Precedent is important in American courts of law.

University of Kansas

in the issues presented by the case. The special master collects evidence and testimony from the parties, listens to their arguments, and gives the Court a report of findings and recommendations, which it then uses to issue a decision.

Appellate Jurisdiction. All other cases that reach the U.S. Supreme Court have been appealed from state courts or from lower federal courts. In each of these cases, the losing party hopes to persuade the Court to reverse a lower court's decision. Some appeals challenge the procedures leading up to that decision; others dispute a lower court's interpretation of the law. Still others challenge a law's constitutionality.

The Constitution says that "the supreme Court shall have appellate Jurisdiction, both as to Law and Fact, with such Exceptions, and under such Regulations as the Congress shall make." Members of Congress who dislike the Court's rulings often respond by proposing to strip the Court of jurisdiction over various kinds of appeals. In one case, Congress did just that. (See "The Supreme Court's Jurisdiction" on p. 458.) Some constitutional lawyers today claim that any such act would be unconstitutional. Even so, we should perhaps amend Chief Justice Charles Evans Hughes's famous remark to read: We live under a Constitution, but the Constitution is what the judges say it is, *provided that Congress allows them jurisdiction to say anything.*

Obligatory Jurisdiction. Articles III gave Congress the power to regulate the U.S. Supreme Court's appellate jurisdiction. Under that grant of power, Congress requires the Court to accept certain kinds of appeals, which are thus said to make up its **obligatory jurisdiction.** Most of these suits involve parties claiming that an action by officials at some level of government violated the U.S. Constitution. Some such cases are trivial, however, and the Court often deals with them by listening only to preliminary arguments, without calling for full briefs and arguments. Such cases are said to be decided "summarily."

Despite these procedures, and even though many obligatory appeals are dismissed on grounds that they do not involve federal questions, the Court is being crushed under the load of obligatory jurisdiction. Chief Justice Burger has petitioned Congress to abolish it altogether, but Congress has so far not agreed.

Discretionary Jurisdiction. Until 1925, just about all of the U.S. Supreme Court's appeals fell under its obligatory jurisdiction. By then, however, the Court was so swamped with business that it petitioned Congress to give it greater control over its caseload, a request that was granted in the 1925 Judges Bill.

Since then, almost all parties wishing to bring cases before the Court have requested what lawyers call a **writ of certiorari** (an order from a higher to a lower court, requesting the record of a case for review). If the Court grants the writ, the case is accepted for full review. If the justices feel that the case does not merit their further attention, they deny the application for a writ, and the lower court's ruling is allowed to stand. Those cases accepted by the Court for full review make up its **discretionary jurisdiction.**

Many of these certiorari petitions are frivolous. The term " *discretionary jurisdiction*" means just what it says: In recent years, about 95 percent of all petitions for certiorari have been denied. Nonetheless, each must receive scrutiny. As the number of petitions continues to rise, so does the justices' workload.

Judicial Review

The 5 percent of certiorari petitions granted by the Court make up almost all its important cases. In some appeals, it decides whether or not lower courts used proper procedures; in others, it interprets the law by divining the intentions of Congress. Such appeals do not involve the greatest of the Court's powers, judicial review. This involves nothing less than the power to judge the constitutionality of any act by any level of government and, therefore, the power to nullify any act by any level of government. This power was given to the Supreme Court not by the Constitution but by the Court itself.

Marbury v. *Madison.* In 1801 a man named William Marbury asked the U.S. Supreme Court to issue a writ of **mandamus**,[12] compelling Secretary of State James Madison to deliver a commission making Marbury a justice of the peace for the District of Columbia. *Marbury* v. *Madison* was already a complicated case. Marbury was a Federalist, a member of the party defeated by Thomas Jefferson in the presidential election of 1800 (see Chapter 9). After the Federalists' defeat, but before Jefferson took office, the lame-duck Federalist Congress passed the 1801 Judiciary Act. The act created a sort of Federalist government-in-exile of 16 new circuit judgeships and, in a second statute, established an unspecified number of justices of the peace for the District of Columbia. Just before leaving office, President Adams made 42 "midnight appointments" under the latter act, including the appointment of William Marbury, whose commission was signed and sealed by President Adams's secretary of state, John Marshall. (Marshall was also President-elect Jefferson's cousin.) Marbury's commission and those of at least three others were not delivered, however, before the change in administrations occurred.

When the Jeffersonians took office, they repealed the 1801 Judiciary Act, thus abolishing all the new circuit judgeships. At about the same time, Marbury and three other would-be justices of the peace asked the new Secretary of State Madison for their commissions. President Jefferson instructed Madison to refuse. At this point, Marbury came before the Court to ask it, as a court of original jurisdiction, to issue a writ of mandamus against Madison. Oddly enough, the chief justice was the same John Marshall who had been President Adams's secretary of state.

Chief Justice Marshall disliked his cousin, President Jefferson, who warmly returned the feeling. Marshall would no doubt have liked to grant Marbury's plea for a writ. Had he done so, however, Secretary of State Madison would surely have ignored it, for the Jeffersonians were popular and the U.S. Supreme Court's powers largely untested. If, however, the Court ruled against Marbury, Marshall would be surrendering to Jefferson.

Marshall cut through this dilemma with the skill of a supreme political and legal strategist. Speaking for a unanimous Court, Marshall declared that Jefferson and Madison had indeed acted unjustly in refusing to deliver Marbury's commission.

More important, the Court declared that the "judicial power" of Article III extended even to issuing orders to a cabinet official who was acting at the

---

[12] *Mandamus* (Latin, "We command"). When an executive official who by law has a certain duty fails to perform it, those injured by this nonaction can file for a writ of mandamus in federal court. If the court grants the petition, the official becomes judicially compelled to perform the duty that has been ignored.

President's direction. But Marbury and the others still lost their case because, Marshall declared, the Court's original jurisdiction did not include the authority to issue a writ of mandamus.

The ruling was no tactical retreat; in fact, it involved a vast claim to power. The chief justice, who wrote the court's decision, argued that Congress had no right to expand the Court's jurisdiction—as it had in the Judiciary Act of 1789, which authorized the Court to issue writs of mandamus. This section of the act was therefore unconstitutional, null, and void. Marshall thus claimed for the U.S. Supreme Court the power to override acts of Congress by subjecting them to judicial review. The fact that this particular act of Congress had given the Court a power of much lesser importance was trivial by comparison.

The decision did not require anyone to do anything. Jefferson, Madison, and their party could not prevent it from being implemented, for there was simply nothing to implement.

Besides, they were far more offended by Marshall's invasion of executive authority than by any judicial usurpation in sitting in judgment over acts of Congress. On constitutional grounds, the Court refrained from doing what, on political grounds, it could not have done in any case. There was no practical point to challenge, so the legal point was allowed to stand. *Marbury* v. *Madison* was one of the great political masterpieces in the history of American jurisprudence.

The Silent Constitution. Until John Marshall asserted the U.S. Supreme Court's power of judicial review, in *Marbury* v. *Madison*, it did not clearly exist.[13] The Constitution says nothing about it. There is indeed some evidence that some delegates to the Constitutional Convention may have wanted the federal courts to exercise judicial review over the states, but much less evidence that they wanted the federal courts to ride herd over Congress and the President.

Why then has judicial review endured since 1803? First, because 54 years elapsed before the Court declared void another *congressional* statute. Although the Court declared many state laws unconstitutional during this period, the justices were plainly hesitant to use this power against Congress. Second, simply because judicial review was needed. Our Constitution set each branch of the federal government against the others, and the states against one another and against the federal government. It did not create any mechanism for resolving these struggles. Insofar as we have such a mechanism, it was created by Chief Justice Marshall. In the words of Justice Felix Frankfurter (1939-1962), John Marshall "gave institutional direction to the inert ideas of a paper scheme of government."

The Supreme Court's Work Routine

Justice Lewis Powell has remarked that the U.S. Supreme Court is much less efficient than his old law firm. Despite all the improvements of the last century, today's Court is still overworked. Even discretionary jurisdiction has not solved the problem, because the number of certiorari petitions continues

---

[13] In any event, *Marbury* v. *Madison* was not the first case in which the Court considered the constitutionality of an act of Congress. Earlier, the Court (in *Hylton* v. *U.S.*) had ruled that Congress did have the power, under the Constitution, to levy a tax on carriages. Since the law was ruled constitutional, rather than unconstitutional, the Court's exercise of judicial review attracted little attention.

to increase. The justices must spend more and more time considering them and, therefore, less and less time hearing cases.

The "Rule of Four." Certiorari petitions are examined by the law clerks, who write reports on them. Should four justices wish to hear a case, it is accepted for review—the so-called **rule of four.**

The Dockets. Cases accepted for a full hearing are placed on one of three dockets. The **original docket** consists of those few cases that come to the U.S. Supreme Court in its role as a trial court. The misleadingly named **appellate docket** comprises those appeals in which both parties pay their own court costs.

Also for appeals—but for those of indigents, very often prison inmates—is the **miscellaneous docket.** Petitions from indigents, called *in forma pauperis* petitions, are spared some of the Court's rigid (and expensive) administrative procedures. Through such a petition, Clarence Earl Gideon persuaded the Court to review the landmark case of *Gideon* v. *Wainwright* (1963), which forced the states to provide lawyers for all defendants too poor to do so themselves (see Chapter 4). The vast majority of these petitions do *not* win hearings, of course. Justice William O. Douglas (1939–1975) once summed them up as "fantastic" and "for the most part frivolous."

Submission of Briefs. After the Court accepts an appeal, the lawyers submit briefs (written arguments). Often running for hundreds of pages, briefs refer to precedents, laws, and legal history and may also be peppered with the findings of sociology, psychology, history, economics, and other academic specialties. All the justices must read all the briefs and all transcripts from lower courts, because the U.S. Supreme Court, unlike Congress, does not divide itself into committees.

Oral Argument. When the justices feel they have digested the briefs and transcripts, a case is scheduled for oral argument, the only point at which the lawyers confront the Court face-to-face. On such days, the Court convenes at 10 A.M. Each side argues its case for a half hour—an hour in cases of exceptional importance. The lawyers ordinarily spend most of that time answering questions thrown out by the justices, for oral argument is a free-for-all. Lawyers who participate in it must think well, quickly, and on their feet.

Oral arguments do not often win cases by themselves, but a blunder may help lose one. More than anything else, they simply show the public that the Court is actually hearing a case, and the arguments provide the public with information about it. Oral arguments also give justices a chance to ask questions inspired by briefs and transcripts.

Conference. Cases are decided (and writs of certiorari granted or denied) not in open court but in conference, held on Wednesday afternoons and Fridays in complete secrecy. Only the justices are present, and no transcripts or official notes are made. Justices of the U.S. Supreme Court are human. They can be willful and even unreasonable. Conferences do not always ring with lofty philosophical discussions. Sometimes they are redolent with personal likes and dislikes, sometimes with power plays.

Fred Ward, Black Star

Oral argument on a case takes place in the Court, and is the only point at which the lawyers on the case confront the Court face to face.

A Power Play. Chief Justice Warren E. Burger joined the Court in the fall of 1969. At that time, a case reached Justice Hugo L. Black (1937–1971), who was acting as supervisory justice for the 5th Circuit, not as a justice of the U.S. Supreme Court. It was a petition to prevent the delay of desegregation in 33 Mississippi school districts.

Mr. Justice Black was especially sensitive about cases like this one. When President Franklin D. Roosevelt first appointed him to the Court, in 1937, it came out that Black had once belonged to the notorious and racist Ku Klux Klan. Many people came to believe—quite incorrectly, in fact—that Black was a racist and a segregationist. Perhaps as a result, he usually took a hard line in desegregation cases, insisting on integration immediately, not with "all deliberate speed."

This particular case soon reached the full Court. After oral argument, the justices met in conference. First, they had to decide whether or not to issue a desegregation order and second, whether to issue a simple and short order or a longer and more detailed one.

Black was adamant on both points. He insisted that there had already been too much delay and that no more should be tolerated. He insisted as well on a short, direct, blunt order. On this last point, he was opposed by Chief Justice Burger and by Justices Harlan, Stewart, and White.

Black then issued an ultimatum: "If anyone writes, I dissent." In other words, if he did not get his way, he would vote against the majority. The Court does not like split decisions in desegregation cases, so the other justices capitulated to Mr. Justice Black.[14]

---

[14] This account comes from Woodward and Armstrong, *The Brethren.*

The Three Terms

The Court assembles in the fall (usually the first Monday in October) and sits, with a few short holiday breaks, until the end of June or the first days of July, when it recesses for the summer. When legal journals and scholars refer to the 1985 Term of the Supreme Court, they mean the period extending from October 1985 to July 1986.

Normally, the overall flow of work falls into three phases:

Summer Recess: Review of certiorari petitions, though this also goes on, at a reduced rate, all year.

Early Term: Hearing oral arguments in all cases that have been placed on the docket, followed by conferences, votes, and assignment of majority opinions.

Late Term: Decisions and filing of opinions, espe-cially in the more important and controversial cases. In particular, the last few weeks of the term usually see a hugh spate of decisions and opinions.

In cases of the utmost urgency and national impor-tance, the Court will occasionally reconvene during the summer. Years, or even decades, can pass be-tween one such exceptional session and the next.

The three phases are not divided by Chinese walls. Some decisions are handed down early in a term (usually when they have been argued in an earlier term). Some are not made when expected but are set aside for reargument in a subsequent term. (This happened with the epochal school desegregation case, *Brown* v. *Board of Education* (1954).) Similarly, oral arguments can be and are scheduled in the later part of the term.

The Opinion. In a real sense, handing down decisions is not the most important part of the Court's job. The rest of us had no overwhelming reason to care whether Allen Bakke, as an individual, was admitted to medical school in California, or Louise Brown was enrolled in an elementary school in Kansas (see Chapter 4). What *was* important were the *grounds* for those decisions, for those grounds would be extended to anyone in a similar situation. Justices who agree about how to decide particular cases very often do not agree about why they should be so decided.

A chief justice voting with the majority selects the justice who writes an opinion, the legal document explaining the majority's decision and the reasons for it. (In all other respects, the chief justice is no more than the "first among equals.") If the chief justice dissents, the most senior justice in the majority assigns the **majority opinion.** Some cases—particularly those involving desegregation—seem to cry out for unanimity and to get it. Most issues are less sensitive. Justices will try to accept the majority decision and the majority opinion if they can, if they cannot, they may write a **concurring opinion,** which accepts the decision but not the reasons for it, or a **dissenting opinion,** which rejects the majority decision.

The Majority Opinion. Because the justices in the majority may have different reasons for supporting the same decision, not all of them necessarily support the majority opinion. The question is a vitally important one because the reasons for a decision are usually more important than the decision itself. At one extreme, when the justices decide a case unanimously and they all agree to support the majority opinion, they create a strong precedent, one that is likely to be followed by lower court judges handling similar cases. At the other extreme, a bare majority—five members of the full Court—that cannot agree on a majority opinion creates a confusing precedent or none at all. If three out of five justices who vote for the majority decision sign one opinion, and two justices issue another opinion, what line of legal reasoning are the justices in the lower courts supposed to follow? Sometimes it is difficult to know.

So the justice who writes the majority opinion will try to win support for it from the rest of the majority. Like Mr. Justice Blackmun's opinion in the abortion case, the majority opinion is more often cooked up by all the members of the majority, rather than by the justice whose name appears on the opinion.

The Legal Public. Lawyers, law professors, and judges scrutinize the Court's opinions, especially majority opinions. The legal public is a demanding and, at times, a harsh audience. Some justices, for example, are thought to be better than others at writing opinions that are clear and that identify the real issues in dispute. Some are thought to have more sophisticated views and to express them in a more sophisticated way.

And the justices take note of what members of the legal public say. A not closely guarded secret around the Court is that the first fall issue of the *Harvard Law Review* is quickly examined by each justice. This is the issue that reviews and critiques the Court's opinions issued during the most recent term.

Influential members of the legal profession do not always think highly of the Court's legal and intellectual abilities. And sometimes the Court takes positions that many influential lawyers reject. After World War I, for example, and especially after 1929, many lawyers and law professors began to doubt the wisdom of laissez-faire economics (see Chapters 15 and 16). The Supreme Court, however, stood by those principles until 1937, in the face of growing criticism from many law school professors. Two of these outspoken professors, William O. Douglas and Felix Frankfurter, were soon added to the Court.

In recent years, this professional public has become even more critical of the Court's performance. Before 1969, some commentators accused the liberal majority led by Chief Justice Warren of being too result-oriented, of being more interested in coming up with the "right answer" than in justifying their decisions. Recent critics of the present, more conservative Court see a lack of intellectual distinction. Others claim that, liberal or conservative, the justices often think and act like legislators, not judges. Walter Berns, for one, has argued that "the cause of constitutional government, and with it liberty, is not advanced by proposing that the Supreme Court follow the election returns."[15] Even more serious are the loud and frequent complaints about the quality of the Court's opinions and their usefulness for the legal community; for when many justices issue their own opinions, lawyers and lower courts do not know whom to follow.

Importance of Dissent. U.S. Supreme Court justices who write dissenting opinions are not just bearing witness before God. They are also taking their views from the Court to the wider legal public, hoping to see those views eventually upheld by the Court's majority. That has indeed happened. Justices Oliver Wendell Holmes (1902–1932) and Louis Brandeis (1916–1939) opposed the Court's predilection for laissez faire, and in time, the Court embraced their views and rejected those of the former majority. Likewise, the dissents of Justices Black and Douglas, especially on civil liberties (see Chapter 5) were more influential in the long run than the majority opinions the two men rejected.

Importance of the Law Clerks. Some justices write their own decisions and use their law clerks mainly as researchers and critics. Other justices more or

---

[15] Walter Berns, "Has the Burger Court Gone Too Far?" *Commentary* (Oct. 1984), 33.

Justice William Rehnquist meets with his law clerks to discuss cases.

less let their law clerks write early drafts of their decisions. Even justices who do their own writing may fall under the influence of their law clerks.

Who are these law clerks? Each year, all the justices choose three or four graduates of top law schools. These appointments, which last only a year, carry great prestige and set their holders on the high and straight road to legal eminence. Of the present Court, Justice Rehnquist clerked for Justice Robert H. Jackson (1941–1954), Justice White for Chief Justice Fred Vinson (1946–1953), and Justice Stevens for Justice Wiley Rutledge (1943–1949).

POLITICS OF THE FEDERAL COURT SYSTEM

To become a federal judge, it is not necessary to be the smartest lawyer in the state. Strictly speaking, you don't even need a law degree. The Constitution merely empowers the President to nominate a person—any person—to fill a judicial vacancy, and the nominee must then be confirmed by a majority vote of the Senate.

Selecting the Federal Bench

The President, however, does *not* nominate just any person. Political reality imposes a great many informal requirements on would-be federal judges.

Partisan Considerations. For one thing, ever since George Washington's day, Presidents have looked to their own parties for judicial candidates. Lawyers, a vital force in party politics, become involved in it because politicians control so many of the legal loaves and fishes—judgeships, for example. Political parties in turn rely on lawyers, whose loyalty they secure by distributing judgeships and other rewards at their disposal. That is why Republican Presidents nominate Republican judges and Democratic Presidents nominate Democratic judges, especially at lower levels of the system—the district and circuit courts. Nominations to the U.S. Supreme Court are different because some Presidents do not want to be criticized for making very unsuitable or very partisan appointments to it. But not every President gets a chance to nominate, since vacancies on the highest Court occur infrequently, on the average of one every two or three years. President Carter, for example, made no Supreme Court appointments during his term in office.

Ideological Factors. So important and visible is the U.S. Supreme Court that Presidents look less for Democrats or Republicans than for lawyers who share their own legal and political outlook—their "ideology." Many of our Presidents were lawyers themselves, and all knew that the people they appointed to the Court might well hold office for a generation or so after they themselves had left it. (John Adams, for instance, had been dead 9 years, and the Federalists out of power for 34, when John Marshall died in office. Franklin D. Roosevelt had been dead 30 years when one of his appointees, William O. Douglas, retired from the Court.) This longevity in office gives them all the more reason to nominate justices who share their own views.

Unfortunately for them, a law of politics is that "appointees disappoint the appointer," sometimes, at any rate. Teddy Roosevelt cried in anger that the justice he had appointed, Oliver Wendell Holmes, had "the backbone of a chocolate eclair" because of his position in an important antitrust case. Dwight Eisenhower described his appointment of the staunchly liberal Chief Justice Earl Warren as "the biggest damn fool mistake I ever made." And Harry Blackmun has not turned out to be the strict constructionist Richard Nixon thought he was.

On the other hand, over the long run the direction of the Supreme Court's constitutional doctrine has been vitally shaped by the political views and ideologies of Presidents. This is one reason why critical realignments, producing a pretty stable majority and policy leadership, have involved fundamental changes in constitutional doctrine. One classic case was the Court's abandonment of economic supervision after its "switch in time that saved nine" in 1937. The New Deal had come to stay; Franklin D. Roosevelt was eventually to appoint seven of the Court's nine justices; and constitutional law was adapted to the new political dispensation. By the same token, Ronald Reagan—the most ideological President of modern times—used his appointing power to shift the federal judiciary in a conservative direction. As of late 1985, he had been able to make only one Supreme Court appointment (Justice O'Connor). But his appointments to the district courts and courts of appeals have been far more numerous, and the conservatizing process is now clear enough to stimulate considerable comment from the press. By the end of Reagan's term in 1989, the change in judicial direction should be still more obvious.

Justices often try to resign when their successor can be chosen by a President of similar legal and political views. In the 1970s, for example, Justice Douglas hung on long after he had become desperately ill, hoping to survive until the next liberal Democratic President came along. He did not make it.

"I don't know what got into me. He was no damn good as attorney general, and on the Supreme Court . . . it doesn't seem possible, but he's been even worse. He hasn't made one right decision that I can think of."

President Harry Truman,
on one of his Supreme Court appointments, Tom Clark

"Balance." Another consideration in choosing justices is "balance." Our country has six major regions, three major religious groups, and at least a dozen important ethnic and racial groups. The U.S. Supreme Court, however, has only nine seats. Most Presidents would like to see all of our major regions and religious groups represented on the Court, but that ideal, as you can see, must be honored more in the breach than in the observance. Many people, for instance, speak of a "Jewish seat." There was one from 1916 to 1969, but there has been no Jewish justice since 1969. In 1982, only one Catholic was on the Court—William Brennan—and the only black ever—Thurgood Marshall. In 1981, President Reagan set a precedent by appointing the first woman, Justice Sandra Day O'Connor. It is likely that, from now on, we shall hear about "a woman's seat," though on past showing, it may not always be filled by a woman. Likewise, many people think that one seat should be filled by a justice promoted from the ranks of law professors. Yet since 1962 when Felix Frankfurter retired, no one has gone directly from a law school faculty to the U.S. Supreme Court.

The Appointment Process

The stratagems, maneuvers, and compromises that produce federal judges begin long before vacancies occur. Lawyers and judges are constantly parading themselves before politicians, and Presidents know which judges are old or sick and who is likely to resign. When a vacancy occurs at last, the President puts together a list of possibilities. They must then be checked out in several ways.

Senatorial Courtesy. One hallowed tradition requires the President to consult senators from the state involved (if they belong to the President's party) before making any appointment to a U.S. District Court. Senatorial courtesy, as it is called, in effect means that no one can get such an appointment without senatorial approval. Often senators will have recommended the nominee to the President. Someone has described district judges as lawyers who know U.S. senators. Senators have less influence in selecting judges of the twelve circuit courts and the U.S. Supreme Court, which do not serve individual states.

Investigation. When only a few candidates remain on the list, the FBI investigates them. So too does a special committee of the American Bar Association, which looks into their legal qualifications and sends the Senate and the President an evaluation ranging from "exceptionally well qualified" to "not qualified." Republican Presidents tend to give these ratings more weight than Democratic Presidents do.

Senate Confirmation. The President finally makes the nomination and sends it to the Senate, where it is first examined in committee. The Judiciary Committee's staff conducts yet another investigation of the nominee's background and talents. Then the committee itself, usually after public hearings, makes its recommendation to the full Senate. At last the Senate itself votes on the nominee, whose confirmation requires the support of a majority of those senators voting.

Curbing the Court

The Senate's confirming power has its limits. It is the power to reject nominees, not to choose them, and senators rarely exercise their power to reject. Few senators think it wise or proper to reject a nominee they regard as competent, but whose legal views differ from their own.

At one point, members of Congress were much less inhibited in these matters than they are now. In 1804, the Jeffersonians attempted to impeach all the Federalist Supreme Court justices and actually did impeach Justice Samuel Chase (1796–1811)—the only one to bear that dubious distinction. But Chase was acquitted in the Senate. The failure to remove Chase helped to establish a tradition of judicial independence.

A number of efforts to impeach the entire Warren Court were made in the 1960s, when "Impeach Earl Warren" billboards sprouted along highways in the South and West. No member of that Court provoked more fury in conservative hearts than Mr. Justice Douglas. At one point, Gerald Ford, then House Republican leader, actually asked the House to impeach Douglas on the grounds that "an impeachable offense is anything Congress says it is." That is true, in a sense, but Congress has never made unpopular Court decisions a ground for impeachment. No wonder Justice Douglas was reluctant to retire in 1975 while Gerald Ford was President!

Conventions of propriety therefore prevent Congress from having any great impact on the Court's makeup. Propriety, however, does not prevent Congress from trying to reverse the Court's decisions.

Constitutional Amendments. Occasionally Congress has met the Court on its own ground by proposing constitutional amendments intended to reverse its decisions. Four of these amendments were later ratified, the most recent being the Twenty-sixth (1971), which undid a ruling that Congress could not give eighteen-year-olds the right to vote in *state* elections.[16] By and large, however, it is much easier for the unelected Court to rule on controversial issues than it is for Congress to reverse those rulings. Despite the anger generated by the Court's decisions on school prayer, reapportionment, and abortion, Congress has refused to propose amendments against them, despite the strong efforts of individual representatives and senators.

Funding. At times, however, Congress will strike at a ruling indirectly—not by trying to reverse it but by cutting the federal funds appropriated to carry it out. For instance, Congress has voted to ban the use of Medicaid to pay for most abortions.

The Court's Size. Congress does not have to reverse the Court rulings directly or indirectly. It can also add to the number of justices on the Court and thus

---

[16] The other three were the Eleventh Amendment (1798), reversing a decision in which the Court ruled that the citizen of a state could sue another state in the federal courts; the Fourteenth Amendment (1868), which reversed the Court's decision (in the Dred Scott case) that slaves had no rights, and the Sixteenth Amendment (1912), which reversed a ruling that made income taxes unconstitutional.

The justices' robes await their day in Court.

create a new and different majority, that might be prepared to issue new and different rulings. Remember, the number of justices on the U.S. Supreme Court is fixed by Congress, not by the Constitution. Congress has already tinkered with that number. In one 6-year period, Congress did so no fewer than 3 times: from 9 to 10 in 1863, from 10 to 7 in 1866, and from 7 to 9 in 1869. Since then, the number has stood at 9—the chief justice and 8 associate justices.

The most serious of later efforts to change the Court's size came in 1937, at the start of Franklin D. Roosevelt's second presidential term. Mr. Roosevelt first took office in 1933, at the height of the Great Depression. His predecessor, Herbert Hoover, had insisted that the depression would "burn itself out" with little or no government interference. It did not, so under Roosevelt the government tried to stimulate and regulate the economy and provide work for the jobless. Legal challenges to New Deal policies found their way to the U.S. Supreme Court. For two generations, the Court had been protecting the private economy from government interference at all levels, and it continued to do just that, striking down policy after New Deal policy.

In 1936, Mr. Roosevelt and a Democratic Congress were reelected by a landslide. The next year, the vengeful President struck back at the Court by proposing to expand it to fifteen members. The six new justices that Mr. Roosevelt wanted to nominate under the "court-packing" plan would have given him a majority. He had a particularly long way to go, for up to then, he had not nominated one.

Despite Mr. Roosevelt's popularity, the U.S. Supreme Court was and is a kind of sacred institution. Most people disliked the idea of naked political interference with its makeup; the public outcry against the plan was so strong that a Democratic Congress defeated it. In any case, Mr. Roosevelt's plan turned out to be unnecessary, since in the "switch in time that saved nine," the Court reconciled itself to economic regulation. Then, age began to take its toll among the older justices, and Mr. Roosevelt was able to nominate his own candidates; from 1937 to 1945, he filled nine vacancies. No more has been heard of court packing.

The Supreme Court's Jurisdiction. We have already seen that the Constitution gave Congress an apparently unlimited power to define the Court's appellate jurisdiction. What Congress has given (or tolerated through inaction), Congress can take away. Many serious efforts have been made to strip the Supreme Court of jurisdiction in certain especially controversial areas. One, but only one, succeeded. Fearing that the Court might invalidate the Reconstruction Acts (see Chapter 5), in 1868, Congress passed a law that withdrew the Court's jurisdiction over a case that had already been argued and was ready for decision.[17] Some legal scholars think such laws are unconstitutional.

This is not merely a point of quaint historical interest. In 1963, the Warren Court ruled against school prayers (see Chapter 4),[18] a decision that has been controversial ever since. The controversy shows no signs of abating. In 1982, certain Senate conservatives offered a bill to reverse the decision by denying to all federal courts, including the Supreme Court, jurisdiction in school-prayer cases. A combination of liberal filibustering and the overwork of an election year derailed this particular bill. But the jurisdictional gun is still loaded, should Congress see fit to use it again.

Activism and Self-Restraint

Our acceptance of the Supreme Court's extraordinary power runs very deep, but it is not absolute, and neither is the Court's power: It is revocable and has in fact been revoked from time to time. Chief Justice Hughes, who said that the Constitution is what the justices say it is, understood this fact very well. He understood, too, that every time the scope of judicial power was reduced, the justices had paved the way by overreaching themselves. In Holmes's day, the most important example of judicial overreaching, and its consequences, was the Dred Scott decision,[19] in which the Court ruled that "the black man has no rights that the white man is bound to respect." Northern antislavery opinion was enraged by the ruling; and in the 1860s, the Court's power went temporarily into eclipse. Hughes called such cases the Court's "self-inflicted wounds." They are most likely to occur when the justices attempt to solve some important nationwide problem by fiat. Constitutional politics is politics at the very highest and most intellectual level. But it is politics nevertheless, and the justices forget this at their, and the Court's peril.

What is the Court's proper role in our political system? From nearly the outset of the Court's existence, two broad schools of thought have disputed the question, each with its own phalanx of justices, lawyers, scholars, and interested citizens. The supporters of **judicial activism** have argued that the Court should use its powers to frustrate Congress, state legislatures, and other

---

[17] *Ex Parte McCardle,* 7 Wall. 506 (1869).
[18] *Abington School Dist.* v. *Schempp,* 374 U.S. 203 (1963).
[19] *Dred Scott* v. *Sandford,* 19 How. 393 (1857).

authorities whenever they attempt to violate the constitutional rights of individuals and corporations. The supporters of **judicial self-restraint** have argued that the Court should use its powers of judicial review sparingly and respect the popular will as expressed through elected officials, especially legislatures, even when the Court does not applaud their policies.

The political implications of each position changed dramatically in the late 1930s. Before then, the Court's activism was very largely used to obstruct economic regulation (see Chapter 3). A kind of intellectual sleight-of-hand permitted the justices to disclaim all merely political power while using the Court's veto to the utmost. For instance, in 1936, when the Court struck down a New Deal agricultural-relief law,[20] Justice Owen Roberts claimed that the Court's sole power was the power of decision; its task was merely to lay a statute alongside the Constitution and determine whether the former was compatible with the latter.

Justices Holmes and Louis Brandeis—and later Benjamin N. Cardozo (1932–1938) and Harlan F. Stone (1925–1946)—cast "cynical acid" on this line of reasoning. (Some law school critics called it the "slot-machine" theory of jurisprudence.) Holmes, Brandeis, Cardozo, and Stone repeatedly called on the Court's majority to face up to its conservative political motives. They also demanded that the Court abandon its claim to act as an economic superlegis-lature. As Justice Holmes wrote in a classic dissent, "This case[21] is decided on an economic theory which a large part of the country does not entertain. The Fourteenth Amendment does not enact Mr. Herbert Spencer's *Social Statics.*"[22]

In those days, it was the *liberals* who embraced judicial self-restraint and the power of elected officials. Many conservatives, no doubt sincerely, believed that the Fourteenth Amendment *did* enact Herbert Spencer's *Social Statics* and therefore did support the Court's judicial activism in striking down both national and state economic legislation.

After 1937, the Court reconciled itself to economic regulation and turned its constitutional sights toward new issues, particularly civil liberties and civil rights. The debate between the judicial activists and those who favored self-restraint continued with full intensity. As a professor of the Harvard Law School, Felix Frankfurter had been one of the leaders of the attack on the old Court's activism, its attempt to read laissez faire into the Constitution. On the Supreme Court from 1939 to 1962, Frankfurter became its leading spokesman for judicial self-restraint, even in cases that involved civil liberties.

Justices Black and Douglas—like Frankfurter, appointed to the Court by Franklin Roosevelt—believed, on the contrary, that judicial activism was required by the spirit and very often by the letter of the Constitution, particularly when laws infringed on basic political and religious rights. For Black, when the First Amendment said, "Congress shall make no law . . . abridging the freedom of speech, or of the press," it meant that and nothing less, and the Court had the bounden duty of striking down any law that dared to stray into forbidden territory.[23]

Frankfurter found Black's rigidity "fundamentalist" and simple-minded. He tried to balance civil liberties against the right of Congress to deal with

[20] *U.S.* v. *Butler,* 297 U.S. 1 (1936).
[21] *Lochner* v. *New York,* 198 U.S. 45 (1905).
[22] A classic Social Darwinist presentation of the case for total laissez faire.
[23] See especially Black's dissent in *Dennis* v. *U.S.,* 341 U.S. 494 (1951).

evils that might, in fact, exist. For a very long time Frankfurter rather than Black was in the majority, especially in the "cold war cases" (see Chapter 4). In 1953, Governor Earl Warren (R) of California was appointed chief justice by President Dwight D. Eisenhower (1953–1961). From about the mid-1950s until his retirement in 1969, he gave his name to an era of the Supreme Court's history: the Warren Court. The Court's majority defected to activism and pursued it across an enormously wide front, including desegregation, civil liberties, and reapportionment. (Many of the details are developed in Chapters 4 and 5, which deal with civil liberties and civil rights, respectively.) Only the similarly creative judicial activism on behalf of laissez faire, between 1890 and 1937, equalled it.

By the late 1960s, the Court had been transformed into the universal bogeyman of the American right. One of the innumerable politicians who traded on hostility to the Court was Richard Nixon. In the 1968 presidential campaign he promised that, if elected, he would nominate conservative justices. In 1969 he nominated Warren Earl Burger to succeed Earl Warren as chief justice. Thereafter, the Supreme Court's decisions in many areas of civil-liberties law became somewhat more conservative. But judicial activism continued to flourish, most notably in the Court's 1973 abortion decision, *Roe* v. *Wade*.[24] At some point in the 1960s, the Court tacitly abandoned many of the judicial norms on which "self-restraint" rests. It looked more to results, less to precedents, and lost any sense of bashfulness in asserting its own policy preferences. The old judicial activists were usually careful to make judicial, rather than legislative arguments; they based their decisions on law, or on the appearance of law, not on claims that their views would produce beneficial consequences if implemented. Their successors have borne that self-limiting yoke much less willingly, and the legal credibility of the Court's decisions has suffered as a result. It is inevitable that the Constitution should today mean many things that could never have occurred to the Founders. But it also seems to mean a great many things it did not mean thirty years ago.

The exercise of judicial power in a democracy is among the highest and most difficult of political arts. Even those who think that the Court would benefit from a wholesome dose of judicial self-restraint might not carry it far enough to let state authorities persecute Jehovah's Witnesses who refuse to salute the flag (see Chapter 4). Any Court bent on achieving results is asking for serious political trouble, sooner or later; professional critics and much of public opinion are bound to ask quo warranto? By what warrant? Why should nine unelected men and women, given lifetime tenure, presume to act as a superlegislature? This question always arises in the wake of the Court's "self-inflicted wounds." If the doubts persist and grow, they could at some point be fatal to the tradition of judicial review in a democratic political system.

SUMMARY

American courts and American law inherited the English "common law" tradition. Legal decisions tend to follow the pattern of previous decisions—what the lawyers call "precedents"—far more than in European legal systems,

---

[24] 410 U.S. 113 (1973).

based on rigid and comprehensive legal codes. Judges have much power in the English legal system and still more in ours, for they do not mechanically apply an all-embracing code to particular cases. Often, they actually make law.

The delegates to the Constitutional Convention set up the federal courts as a coequal branch of the government, together with the executive and the legislative branches. Alongside the federal courts, they maintained separate state court systems. Both in the federal system and in those of the states, criminal law punishes offenses against society as a whole, while the civil law regulates disputes, usually over property, between private citizens.

At the bottom of the federal court structure are the U.S. District Courts. These are trials courts, where judges and juries rule on the facts of cases. Losing parties can appeal to the next level of the system, the thirteen U.S. Courts of Appeals. At the highest level is the U.S. Supreme Court. Judges of all these courts are nominated by the President and confirmed by a majority vote of the Senate. They serve during "good behavior," and their salaries cannot be cut.

To be heard in federal court, a case must involve a violation of federal law, including the Constitution, or certain kinds of parties—two states, for example. The parties must also have "standing to sue."

Getting a case heard by the U.S. Supreme Court is even harder. Most parties must ask the court for a writ of certiorari, a judgment by at least four of the nine justices that a case is worth hearing. If they do grant the writ, lawyers for both sides submit briefs and then appear in open court for oral argument. The Court's decision and the reasons for it often require elaborate negotiations among the justices. Majority opinions, as well as dissenting and concurring opinions, if any, are closely scrutinized by lawyers, law professors, and politicians. In the long run, dissents are sometimes more influential than majority opinions.

Most of the Court's cases come to it on appeal from lower federal courts or from state courts. Its most important power is judicial review of the constitutionality of all actions by all other branches and levels of government. That power was set forth by Chief Justice John Marshall in *Marbury* v. *Madison* (1803) and has endured to the present day, even though it is not specifically mentioned in the Constitution.

Judicial review has been with us for so long that most of us accept it as a part of the "living Constitution." It is hard to imagine how the Constitution could survive without it. Yet it creates controversy over the Supreme Court's role in the American political system—debate about the proper balance between judicial activism and judicial self-restraint. This debate is not likely to disappear soon. Nor, so long as judicial review survives, is political controversy over the Supreme Court and its decisions. For the Court is up to its neck in politics, and the essence of politics is controversy.

SUGGESTED READINGS

Lawrence Baum, *The Supreme Court*, 2nd ed. Washington, D.C.: Congressional Quarterly Press, 1984. Up-to-date, highly competent review of the Court, giving ample weight to the "political aspects of its activities but with a matter-of-fact style."

RAOUL BERGER, *Congress versus the Supreme Court*, Cambridge: Harvard Univ., 1969. Careful review by a leading scholar of congressional efforts to curb the Court. Generally hostile to such efforts, as are almost all leading studies on this subject.

ALEXANDER M. BICKEL, *The Least Dangerous Branch: The Supreme Court at the Bar of Politics*. Indianapolis: Bobs-Merrill, 1962. Adopts a modified Frankfurterian (self-restraint) position, but is particularly concerned to defend the institution of judicial review against the many congressional (and other) critics of the Warren Court's decisions.

CHARLES L. BLACK, *The People and the Court*. Englewood Cliffs, N.J.: Prentice-Hall, 1960. Strongly supportive of a judicial-activist role for the Supreme Court, by a leading law school professor.

ALFRED KELLEY and WINIFRED HARBISON, *The American Constitution*, 5th ed. New York: Norton, 1970. An excellent historical review of the growth of judicial doctrine. Much more detailed than McCloskey's *The American Supreme Court*.

PHILIP B. KURLAND and GERHARD CASPER, eds. *Landmark Briefs and Arguments of the Supreme Court of the United States: Constitutional Law*. Washington, D.C.: University Publications of America, 1975– . A collection of more than 100 volumes containing briefs and summaries or transcripts of oral arguments in major constitutional cases decided by the Supreme Court. These are documents not otherwise easily available. Student wishing to see the raw material for a Supreme Court decision in the form of written briefs and oral argument have a fine resource in this set.

ROBERT G. MCCLOSKEY, *The American Supreme Court*. Chicago: Univ. of Chicago, 1960; also *The Modern Supreme Court*. Cambridge: Harvard Univ., 1972. Perhaps the finest short historical surveys of the Court. Elegantly written, they repay close and attentive reading.

ALPHEUS THOMAS MASON, *Harlan Fiske Stone: Pillar of the Law*. New York: Viking, 1956. Pioneering judicial biography that broke new ground by making use of Chief Justice Stone's letters, personal notes, and intracourt memoranda. Stone was a key figure on the twentieth century Court. His years of service (1925–1946) spanned the Court's attention before 1937 to protection of property and after 1937 to protection of civil liberties and other civil rights.

BERNARD SCHWARTZ, *Super Chief: Earl Warren and His Supreme Court—A Judicial Biography*. New York: New York Univ., 1983. Detailed account of decision making by the Warren Court, relying mainly on the private notes and memoranda of some justices. Because Schwartz's account is documented for the most part (and therefore verifiable), the emergent picture of the Court is probably more reliable than the one found in *The Brethren*, noted below.

D. GRIER STEPHENSON, Jr., *The Supreme Court and the American Republic: An Annotated Bibliography*. New York: Garland, 1981. Listing of some 1,300 books and articles about the Court and its justices, including a guide to available personal papers of the justices, published and unpublished.

BOB WOODWARD and SCOTT ARMSTRONG, *The Brethren*. New York: Simon & Schuster, 1979. Anecdotal and entertaining, if sometimes flawed "inside story," mostly of the early Burger years, based mainly on interviews with unidentified law clerks.

Primary source materials and references: Opinions of the Supreme Court. The official publication is *United States Reports* (before about 1880, these appear in the name of the court reporter). Privately published sources are *U.S. Reports, Lawyers' Edition,* and *Supreme Court Reporter* (purists cite all three, and the two last-named come out much more promptly than the first). A loose-leaf service is the privately published *U.S. Law Week*.

Congressional Quarterly, *Guide to the Supreme Court*. Washington, D.C.: Congressional Quarterly, 1979. The last word down through the date of publication.

Casebooks. These reprint leading constitutional decisions (and dissents) from the beginning. Most of them also contain useful interpretive material. One of the very best is Alpheus Thomas Mason, William M. Beaney, and Donald Grier Stephenson, Jr., *American Constitutional Law*, 7th ed. Englewood Cliffs, N.J.: Prentice-Hall, 1983. Another excellent casebook is Martin Shapiro and Rocco J. Tresolini, *American Constitutional Law*, 6th ed. New York: Macmillan, 1983.

chapter fifteen

PUBLIC POLICY AND THE FREE MARKET

A cold wind blew through Washington, D.C., on March 4, 1933, as Franklin D. Roosevelt took the oath of office as 32nd President of the United States. The mood of the country matched the weather. Thirteen million people were out of work. Banks everywhere were closing. Families were being evicted from their homes, their businesses, their farms. "We are at the end of our string," cried the outgoing President, Herbert Hoover.[1]

Huge numbers of people gathered in front of the Capitol to hear Mr. Roosevelt's inauguration address. "Our primary task is to put people to work," he said, and he proposed to do this through "direct recruiting by the government itself," if necessary. He demanded that homes and farms be protected against foreclosure and that "speculation with other people's money" cease. And if his current proposals did not end the Depression, he vowed to ask Congress for as much power as "would be given to me if we were in fact invaded by a foreign foe."

Mr. Roosevelt did not request wartime powers until 1941, when we actually went to war (see Chapter 17). But during his first three months in office, he pushed through Congress a series of bills that changed the United States forever. An agriculture act gave farmers more time to repay their mortgages and increased the amount they could borrow from banks. A Civilian Conservation Corps (CCC) put 250,000 young men to work building dams, draining marshlands, fighting forest fires, and planting trees. Federal grants (see Chapter 3) helped the states pay out unemployment relief. The federal government got the power to supervise trading in stocks and bonds. The Tennessee Valley Authority (TVA) harnessed the Tennessee river's power and provided cheap electricity. Homes were protected from foreclosure. And the National

---
[1] James MacGregor Burns, *Roosevelt: The Lion and the Fox* (New York: Harcourt, 1956).

Industrial Recovery Act—perhaps, as Mr. Roosevelt described it, the most far-reaching law ever passed by Congress—cut the workweek, raised wages, and set up a $3.3 billion publicworks program that created jobs for the unemployed.[2]

These measures did not end the Depression—World War II did. But they did change, and change forever, our attitudes toward the federal government and its role. Nothing like these programs had ever been seriously proposed, let alone carried out. The New Deal did not take them out of the realm of controversy, but it established them as realities. Each program created its own constituency and new expectations about the role and powers of government. These constituencies and expectations had not existed in 1880.

———— LOOKING BACKWARD, 1980s TO 1880s ————

A hundred years ago, the domestic programs that today make up the core of federal public policy did not exist. Most people accepted the theory and practice of **laissez faire:** the idea that government should not regulate business, industry, or commerce, and that each individual should have an unlimited opportunity to amass wealth and to lose it. When regulation was needed to protect the public health and safety, Americans overwhelmingly preferred state and local regulation. For promoting the public health and safety was an aspect of the "police powers" of government, and police powers were almost entirely a state and local responsibility. (See Chapter 16 for a longer account of laissez-faire theory.)

The Long Death of Laissez Faire

Before the 1930s, health and safety were construed quite narrowly. Until 1863, for example, when the bank notes of "wildcat" banks were outlawed, banks could do as they pleased (see Chapter 16). So, until 1934, could stock speculators. Congress did not attempt to regulate any other area of the economy until 1887, when—partly at the behest of the railroad industry—it set up the Interstate Commerce Commission (ICC, see Chapter 12). In 1890, Congress responded to intense public fear of monopolies by passing the Sherman Antitrust Act to fight "combinations in restraint of trade." But the act was not very effective. As for consumers, they had no federal protection against dangerous foods and drugs until 1906, when Congress passed the Pure Food and Drug Act, largely as a result of Upton Sinclair's descriptions of the Chicago stockyards in *The Jungle* (1905).[3]

The old, the poor, the sick, and the weak had no protection, no safety nets. There was no Social Security in the nineteenth century, no unemployment benefits, no worker's compensation. Job-related injuries were common because working conditions were not regulated. Men and women who suffered injuries on the job were laid off, without pay, and they had to rely on public or private charity—if it was available. Even employed people worked many more hours for less pay and died much sooner than average Americans

---

[2] James MacGregor Burns, *Roosevelt: The Lion and the Fox.*

[3] Sinclair's main purpose in writing *The Jungle* was to popularize socialism, and he was somewhat disappointed by the reaction to his book. "I aimed at the public's heart, and by accident I hit it in the stomach," he wrote.

do today. A hundred years ago, *average* life expectancy was 42 years; today it is 72.

Measured by 1981 dollars, in the early 1880s the average annual disposable income of the people of the United States was $1,500, compared with more than $10,000 in the early 1980s. For manufacturing workers, the typical 1880s workweek was 60 hours—10 hours a day, 6 days a week. The average pay was 20 cents an hour, about $2 in today's money. (Today's average workweek is 40 hours, and average pay is $8 an hour.) Even middle-class people worked 6 days a week. In banks and on the New York Stock Exchange, the 6-day week survived until the end of World War II.

Hours were even longer in some industries. Steelworkers had to work 12 hours a day, 6 days a week, until 1921; in addition, they periodically worked 24 hours straight to permit the day and the night shifts to change places without interrupting production. No federal laws limited the hours that men, women, or children could work.[4]

Because the federal government was so little involved in the lives of the people, it made few demands on them. Consider taxes. In the 1880s, federal taxes amounted to about 2 percent of the gross national product (GNP) and consisted chiefly of excise (luxury) taxes and customs receipts from the tariff on imported goods. To help pay for the Civil War, a temporary income tax had been levied in the 1860s; a second income tax, enacted in 1894, was struck down the following year by the U.S. Supreme Court.[5] Not until 1913, when the Sixteenth Amendment was ratified, was the income tax put on a firm constitutional footing. Yet even then it was a pittance, ranging from a flat rate of 1 percent on incomes up to $20,000 ($200,000 in today's values) to a maximum of 7 percent on incomes of $50,000 and over. Because average incomes were low, the tax was levied on only one-sixth of the adult population—single persons earning at least $3,000 a year (the equivalent of $30,000 today) and families earning at least $4,000 (the equivalent of $40,000). In fact, a majority of Americans did not pay income taxes until 1943, when the government introduced withholding. Massive federal taxation was an outgrowth of World War II and the resulting revolution in this country's position as a world power. (See Chapter 16 for a further account of federal taxation.) "Macroeconomic" policy—the manipulation of the budget, interest rates, and the money supply to influence levels of employment and inflation—developed even later (see Chapter 16). The federal government's first permanent efforts to stimulate employment came in 1946, when Congress passed the Employment Act, and the full range of macroeconomic policies was not applied until the 1960s.

Working conditions were much worse around the turn of the century—children had to work long shifts and there were many job-related injuries due to lack of regulation of factories.

Back to Eden?

Even now, this country's economy and society are still founded on free enterprise, so we often dispute the proper boundaries between private business and government. A substantial minority still believes that government should stick to traditional duties, like national defense. A substantial minority, but not a majority, is for dismantling the activist state, which would mean the end of Medicare, Social Security, and unemployment benefits; of

---

[4] An exception: Congress had set an eight-hour day as standard for employees of the federal government.

[5] *Pollock* v. *Farmers' Loan & Trust Co.*, 158 U.S. 601 (1895).

Black people found it almost impossible to register and vote in the South after 1877, but it was not until the civil-rights movement made the problem harder to ignore that Congress passed the Voting Rights Act of 1965.

farm-price supports, tobacco subsidies, bank-deposit insurance; of controls on toxic poisoning of the environment. It would put an end to the Federal Reserve Board and "sound money" (see Chapter 16) and would dry up federal aid for research and development, and for local highways, bridges, and sewage treatment. These programs have constituencies too large to be ignored. Debate over the costs and benefits of public policy will continue, but the real debate will concern the *limits* of public policy, not its existence.

STAGES OF POLICY MAKING

Before public policy can be implemented, it must be conceived and planned. Let's examine the natural history of public policy.

Identifying the Problem

The first step is simply to identify a problem. Many problems festered away for years before the government acknowledged their existence and decided to do something about them. Consider the problem of black voting rights in the South. In 1877, they were sharply curtailed and, from 1890 to 1908, were virtually abolished (see Chapter 5). Although such machinations obviously nullified the Fifteenth Amendment, national policy makers ignored them for more than half a century. Not until the rise of the civil-rights movement did Congress pass the Voting Rights Act of 1965. The official consciousness was raised only when the cost of ignoring the problem rose above the cost of confronting it.

Many problems less politically explosive than civil rights received prompter attention from public officials. For example, in 1976, the federal government feared that an epidemic of swine flu might sweep the country. Federal health officials were particularly troubled by the similarity between the swine flu virus and the one believed to have caused the great influenza epidemic of 1918–1920, which may have killed about 20 million people throughout the world. President Ford asked for, and Congress quickly authorized, an immunization program with $135 million in federal funds. Public health forces all over the country were mobilized, and more than 40 million Americans were inoculated. In this case, it turned out that delay might well have had its uses: Hundreds of people who had received the shots suffered adverse reactions, of which the most serious was Guillain-Barre Syndrome, a rare and serious neurological disorder. What is more, to get the program started as quickly as possible, the government had agreed to assume sole responsibility for legal damages. More than $9 million has been paid out thus far to settle claims. Ironically, the immunization program may not have been necessary in the first place. The winter of 1976 turned out to be one of the mildest flu seasons on record.

What Is to Be Done?

The next step is deciding what to do and who should do it—the government or the private sector. The policy makers must now weigh the costs and benefits of the alternatives, and their effects on different groups of people. Sometimes, some evidence may argue for inaction. Democratic Presidents and congressional leaders delayed restoring the constitutional rights of black people as a result of fears, which proved to be correct, that civil rights would split the Democratic party. Eventually, the federal government had to act anyway.

Adopting a Policy

At this point, policy makers must decide how to implement the policy they want. Is new legislation needed? If so, Congress must be persuaded to act. In matters touching on constitutional rights, the government may need a favorable court decision.

At times, the government's policy is just to do nothing and hope that the problem will go away of its own accord, and on occasion it actually does. Some problems are found to be quite unreal. During the 1960 presidential campaign, John F. Kennedy warned of a "missile gap" between the Soviet Union and the United States. When he took office, in 1961, he discovered that the United States had a comfortable lead in missiles.

Implementing a Policy

Government officials do not always take their own policies seriously; at times, they simply want the people to believe that something is being done about a problem that they themselves find unreal or hopeless. Even serious policies do not always succeed. Most successful policies have broad public support. Look at our tax system, for example. In many foreign countries, tax cheating is a popular national sport. We Americans, however, pay most of what we owe, most of the time. One reason: The Internal Revenue Service (IRS) has a comprehensive and up-to-date auditing and enforcement operation. People who avoid paying taxes run a high risk of exposure, fine, or imprisonment. Another: Most Americans believed that our tax system was fair and served the public interest—a belief that has been eroded recently.

When public policies lack broad support, the results are often unhappy and sometimes calamitous. In the mid-1960s, for example, the federal government attempted to provide jobs and reduce racial tension in Oakland, California, by giving the city's agencies $23 million to construct a ship terminal and an airport maintenance hangar. Four years after the program started in 1966, little had been done, mainly because local politicians and local public opinion were indifferent to the project. (See Chapter 3 for a longer description of the Oakland project and the reasons for its failure.)

Evaluating the Programs

Once a policy has been adopted and implemented, many players in the policy game must try to evaluate it. First, there are the staffs of the government agencies that operate the policies. Often these evaluations submitted to the Office of Management and Budget (OMB) or to Congress are strongly self-interested. Even if the agency report is not hopelessly biased, OMB and Congress may have trouble deciding whether a program operates effectively, because devising accurate and meaningful ways of judging a program's impact is very difficult. The federal government has stuck its nose into many more complex policy problems than it knows how to solve, and it has many more "solutions" than ways of evaluating them.

In any case, formulating and evaluating public policy are political acts. Information—even when available—often takes second place to the political will of the electorate and its representatives.

THEORIES OF POLICY MAKING

Politicians, bureaucrats, interest groups, journalists, and the general public work upon, and dance around, problems and policies as they move through the tube of policy making. Each group has its own game to play, its own interests. Real-world pressures are a part of the game, too, for we would not have the technical means to solve all of our problems even if we had the political will—and the solutions to some may make others worse.

How do the players, their interests, the rules of the game, and the pressures of the real world combine to produce public policy? There is much disagreement, and several distinct theories contend for support.

Technocratic Theories

In one group of theories the heart of policy making is the adjustment of means (policies) to ends (goals). These theories take the ends of the players at face value and concentrate on the means by which they seek to attain those ends.

The "Rational-Man" Theory. One technocratic theory is the so-called rational-man view of policy analysis, which assumes that all the players in the game of public policy attempt to maximize their own self-interest. To that end, each player attempts to clarify goals, ranks them in order of preference, and devises means of attaining them.

Let us say that the Defense Department wants to buy a weapons system, and several companies compete for the contract. The department analyzes all the companies and selects the one that will build the best system at the lowest possible cost. Often it will be necessary to balance costs against benefits, **cost-benefit analysis,** since the company that can build the best system will not always be willing to charge the lowest price. The results of these analyses at times leave much to be desired—consider the billions of dollars spent for sophisticated weapons, like the M-1 tank, that are plagued by breakdowns and cost overruns. But if cost-benefit analysis did not exist, the government would have no way, even in theory, of assessing any policy.

The Policy-Systems Approach. Another technocratic theory is the **policy-systems approach,** which originated in computer programming and corporate flow analysis. Its heart is the *input–output* model of policy. *Input*—in the form, let us say, of pressure from interest groups—triggers a response from political institutions. That response is policy *outputs,* such as new laws or judicial decisions. These in turn have measurable consequences, some unintended—both for good and ill. In any case, those whom the policy affects give the policy makers *feedback*—reactions that provide them with various kinds of information.

As an example of feedback, let's take a look at the controversy that followed the Clean Air Act of 1970. The law significantly reduced air pollution,

Pogo

but many industries complained about the high cost of complying with it. Beginning in 1980, they mounted a campaign (feedback) to get the standards relaxed, and the Reagan administration, which regarded government overregulation of industry as a cause of low economic growth, did relax them. The problem appeared to be, "How much clean air can we Americans afford?"—a cost-benefit issue. But the real problem was political: "Who should pay for clean air?"

The policy-systems approach permits the making of detailed, comprehensive analyses of policy making. Unlike the rational-man approach, it takes political influences into account. But it works best when applied to case studies of specific policies, rather than to basic questions of social, economic, and political power.

Incrementalist Models

The various technocratic theories assume that the heart of policy making is the desire and ability of human beings to devise solutions to narrowly defined problems. By contrast, the incrementalist theories assume that no problem can be solved by a single solution or set of solutions; as E. E. Schattschneider put it, "nobody knows enough to run the government."[6] Or as one group of incrementalists, the pluralists, would say, "For every policy problem there is a solution which is simple, straightforward—and wrong."

Better, say the incrementalists, to devise policies that accommodate most of the groups interested in a problem than to impose "rationalistic" policies that may satisfy no one and promise more than policy makers can possibly deliver. For if an incremental policy change spawns unintended and undesirable effects, they can be limited and overcome. Besides, our political system, with its separations and divisions of power (see Chapters 2 and 3, respectively), makes broad public support absolutely essential to adopt and carry out any policy.

Bureaucratic Politics. Related to incrementalism are theories that point to the importance of bureaucratic politics. The federal government is not a monolith but a fusion of many separate agencies that compete for power and influence. One thing these individual agencies do have in common is a strong preference for policies that permit them to expand their own authority and budgets.

Elitist Models

Yet another group of theories starts with the fact that not all players in the game of public policy are equal, for wealth and power are not distributed equally. These theories stress that some of us have far more influence on public policy than others do.

Conservative proponents of the elitist model think that this inequality is prudent, if not just. But many "power elite" theorists are radical, though not necessarily Marxist. Still others are Marxists or persons influenced by them. What all elitists share is the idea that economic power decisively shapes political power and public policy. The state's basic function, they claim, is to preserve and promote the national wealth at home and abroad. Since the modern capitalist system is dominated by large corporations and banks, these institutions bulk large in policy making. The more important any area of public policy may be, the more they will dominate it.

Critics of the elitist theory argue that if it is true, we should find specific cases where elites have united behind specific policies and imposed them. But concrete local studies do not seem to reveal such elite conspiracies.[7] In reality, this country has several overlapping elites, and even corporate businesspeople do not agree on many issues. Some groups that have great influence on policy making—labor leaders, for example—do not belong to the corporate elite.

Sophisticated proponents of the elite theory have an answer to these criticisms. They point out that powerful groups want to get their own way on some issues more than on others. The chairman of International Business Machines (IBM) can afford to take a broad view of the company's interests in matters such as Social Security and even the minimum wage, since IBM pays well above it. But he cannot be equally broad-minded in dealing with international trade policy, since foreign sales are IBM's lifeblood. Businesspeople in many other sectors of American industry—those who are *not* dependent on foreign sales—would like the United States to adopt trade

---

[6] E. E. Schattschneider, *The Semisovereign People: A Realist's View of Democracy in America* (New York: Holt, 1960), p. 136.

[7] See Robert A. Dahl, *Who Governs?* (New Haven: Yale Univ., 1961).

policies that would not be to IBM's liking. Sophisticated proponents of the elitist theory admit that our elite is not at all monolithic, and certainly not on all possible issues, even important ones. Foreign-policy issues (including foreign economic policy) tend to mobilize the elite, yet the elite is no longer united behind the Cold War consensus (see Chapter 17).

PROMOTION: THE SERVICE STATE

Some public policies are meant to promote the general welfare, especially the welfare of business; some to regulate business; and some to provide welfare benefits to people who need help in coping with the rigors of the private economy, and to those who cannot cope at all. Regulation, promotion, and welfare do have this much in common: They all reflect a widespread belief that private enterprise must be protected from its own excesses. All three—though in differing proportions—enter into both our liberal and conservative public policies, if only because both liberals and conservatives must sell their respective public policies in the same pluralist democratic system.

Even when laissez faire was most in vogue, during the second half of the nineteenth century, it applied only to government regulation, not promotion, of business. Promotion, in fact, is older than laissez faire: It goes back to the earliest days of the Republic, and even to colonial times. President George Washington's first proposal dealt with the need for a **tariff** (a tax on imports) to protect our industry from foreign competition. And in 1791, Treasury Secretary Alexander Hamilton issued a *Report on Manufactures* full of schemes for promoting business at the taxpayers' expense.

At the high-water mark of laissez faire, the federal government went on promoting the interests of American business—for example, by setting up the "service" departments: Interior (1849), Agriculture (1889), and Commerce (1903). In fact, the whole laissez-faire era, especially 1897 to 1933, was the acme of one very important promotional policy: the protective tariff, warmly supported by most business conservatives.

Promotion involves subsidies paid directly or indirectly to private businesses to help them achieve their private economic goals—which are assumed to be national goals as well. Let us first consider the more obvious kind of subsidy, that paid directly to individual business.

Direct Subsidies

When the government buys dairy products at fixed prices (see Chapter 6), or pays airlines for carrying the U.S. mail, it pays in cash. Like all other aspects of promotion, direct subsidies are of very long standing. In the 1860s, for instance, the federal government owned vast land tracts in unpopulated areas (as it does today). Policy makers believed, correctly, that the construction of a transcontinental railroad linking the West Coast with the rest of the country was a great national objective. But the railroad companies, which were privately owned, could not profitably build the railroad across vast tracts of uninhabited land. The solution: give very large areas of government-owned land to these companies, which could then sell the land, thus raising capital and encouraging farmers to emigrate into the West—where they became customers for the railroad companies' freight-haulage services. The railroad was built—profitably.

The transcontinental railway might not have been built if government hadn't subsidized its cost by huge grants of land to the railroad companies.

Indirect Subsidies

Most subsidies, however, are indirect. Some are paid not by the government but by consumers and taxpayers. Others do not go directly to business but tend nonetheless to promote its interests.

Protection. From the beginnings of our national government until the 1930s, the federal government attempted to protect American industries from foreign competition. Protection, chiefly in the form of tariffs (a tax) on foreign goods, made it possible for domestic producers to raise their own prices; the subsidy thus came from the pockets of consumers. From 1897 to 1933, tariffs were steadily increased—most dramatically in 1930, with the enactment of the Smoot–Hawley tariff. Many economists believe that Smoot–Hawley made the Great Depression more severe by fragmenting world trade.

When Franklin D. Roosevelt took office as President, in 1933, our tariff policy started to change. In 1934, without explicitly repealing Smoot–Hawley, Congress passed the Reciprocal Trade Agreement Act, which authorized the President to negotiate mutual tariff reductions. By the end of World War II (1945) the economies of Europe and Japan were in shambles, and the United States had incomparably the most powerful economy in the world. Our economy was then so strong that **free trade** (the abolition of tariffs and other barriers to trade) became the linchpin of our international economic policy, for other countries were having trouble competing with us. Besides, many of our new-found allies were highly dependent on trade, and our international responsibilities forced us to take their interests into account.

Free trade remained the basis of our policy for a generation. But in the 1970s, the international balance of economic power shifted. Japan and Europe began to compete with us vigorously—and often successfully. OPEC (Organization of Petroleum Exporting Countries) became a power in the world. Our share of world production and trade declined. Foreign imports—including automobiles, electronic equipment, and textiles—flooded the American market and provided such stiff competition that, by the early 1980s, television sets (among many other things) were no longer manufactured in the United States, even by American companies. Many industries and labor unions demanded protection.

There had been another change. In the old days, few American industries were at all dependent on foreign sales. By the 1970s, two sectors of our economy—agriculture and high technology—had become very dependent indeed. These industries, vulnerable to foreign retaliation, pressured the government to maintain free trade. Meanwhile, our government failed to provide American business with the kinds of export subsidies that were routine in Europe and Japan. (So close is the relationship between the Japanese government and leading sectors of its industry that it is sometimes very hard to distinguish between the two.) By the early 1980s, a worldwide recession had in part undermined the international political consensus behind free trade. Each country's political leadership was subjected to intense pressures for and against free trade. Unless economic conditions drastically change, the debate will continue, and protectionist action may well follow.

U.S. Postal Service

The postal system is an example of a service to business that is subsidized by the government. We all get advantages from it, of course, but the benefits go chiefly to business.

Subsidized Services. Consider the census. In some ways, no doubt, we all derive advantages from it. But the benefits go chiefly to business, although the costs are borne by the general taxpayer. The census is one example of a second category of indirect subsidies to business: services wholly or partly subsidized by the government. Many of these services benefit society in general yet they benefit business most. The postal system is one such service. So, too, are the National Oceanic and Atmosphere Administration, which follows and predicts the weather, the National Bureau of Standards, and the United States Patent & Trademark Office.

Public Works. Many subsidized services are provided, not by the federal government, but by the states and localities, sometimes with federal help. Roads, bridges, and other public works are built and maintained chiefly at state and local expense; in fact, the federal government did not begin to allocate large sums for interstate highways until 1957. Still later, it helped pay for local sewage treatment facilities and other public works projects. These funds were cut under the Reagan administration, at a time when existing public works throughout the country were deteriorating quite rapidly.

Loan Guarantees. Corporations threatened with bankruptcy must find new sources of funding; however, the very fact that they are likely to fail makes lenders unwilling to lend. Until recently, companies in this position simply went under. In the 1970s, a number of them sought and won federal **loan guarantees,** promises by the federal government to repay their loans if they could not do so. This permitted some very large companies—notably Chrysler and Lockheed—to get loans that would not otherwise have been available to them, often at interest rates lower than the prevailing commercial rate.

Loan guarantees are as much a question of politics as of economics. When a large corporation is threatened with bankruptcy, the local politicians—liberal and conservative alike—want the federal government to bail it out.

Liberals elsewhere tend to attack such guarantees as "socialism for the rich," and conservatives, as "lemon socialism," government assistance to inefficient companies in declining industries. President Reagan has not been sympathetic to requests for loan guarantees and similar kinds of assistance.

Tax Subsidies. The federal government permits homeowners to deduct from their taxable incomes (the base on which taxes are computed) the money they pay in interest on their mortgages. As a result, their taxes are lower than the taxes of renters with identical pretax incomes. (Renters cannot make such deductions, although they pay their landlords' interest charges in their rents.) The lower taxes paid by homeowners benefit the homebuilding industry, whose product become less expensive through the courtesy of the general taxpayer. And all industries can deduct "depreciation" (lost value as a result of age and use) from their taxable incomes. The lower taxes that homeowners and businesses pay as a result of these (and other) subsidies must be made good by other, usually poorer, taxpayers.

Even so, proponents of these subsidies argue that they benefit the country as a whole by benefiting the economy as a whole, helping business generate jobs, goods, and services. Such arguments were the basis of President Reagan's three-year tax cut, which slashed corporate income taxes far more than taxes paid by individuals. Such arguments were also the basis of business's objections to the tax reform package proposed by the Treasury Department in early 1985. Business leaders argued that by reducing tax incentives for investment, innovation, and growth, "tax simplification" threatened economic recovery and long-term economic growth.

REGULATION

Before and for a little while after the United States was founded, extensive government regulation of business was commonplace—a policy called **mercantilism.** Governments regulated the prices of goods and services, the kinds and quality of products, and the right of entry into markets. British mercantilism, for example, attempted to thwart industrial development in the American colonies, a policy that was among the causes of the American Revolution.

In 1776, the year of American independence, Adam Smith argued in *Wealth of Nations* that government regulation of business was inefficient and contradictory. Whatever regulation might be needed, Smith taught, should be left mostly to consumers. *Wealth of Nations* was a sensation; it molded the minds of statesmen for generations and dominated our economic policy making throughout the nineteenth century and into the twentieth (see Chapter 16).

Even so, business was still regulated in some ways and promoted in others. Never has our economy functioned without any regulation, although for a long time it was much more common at the state than at the federal level.[8] State regulation concentrated on two major problems: monopoly—the breakdown of the market—and working conditions and hours. For example, Illinois, with the consent of the U.S. Supreme Court,[9] regulated the rates

---

[8] In part because from 1890 through 1937, the U.S. Supreme Court did all it could to limit the federal government's power over private business (see Chapter 3).

[9] *Munn* v. *Illinois*, 94 U.S. 113 (1877).

Some Leading Independent Regulatory Commissions and Agencies

Organization	Year Created	Mission
Interstate Commerce Commission	1887	Regulates rates, routes, and activities of major land transport (railroads, trucking, bus lines, etc.).
Federal Reserve System	1914	Central banking functions, including regulations (when congressionally authorized) of credit.
Federal Trade Commission	1914	Pursuant to Clayton Antitrust Act, issues regulations to protect consumers from "unfair and deceptive" business practices, especially in marketing.
Federal Maritime Commission	1916	(Originally set up as U.S. Shipping Board.) Regulates the American merchant marine.
Securities and Exchange Commission	1934	Regulates the security industry through full disclosure rules and through actions against malpractices in securities markets.
National Labor Relations Board	1935	Administers provisions of Wagner (1935) and Taft–Hartley (1947) Acts; vested with power to safeguard workers rights to organize, to prevent unfair labor practices, etc.
Federal Communications Commission	1934	Regulates interstate and foreign communications by radio, television, wire, and cable.
Occupational Safety and Health Review Commission	1970	Adjudicates disputes arising from OSHA findings, making final decisions.
Consumer Product Safety Commission	1972	Issues uniform safety standards for consumer products; bans sales of products that do not comply.
Commodity Futures Trading Commission	1974	Prevents malpractices in commodity markets and the dissemination of misleading information affecting market-price levels. Regulatory functions set up as early as 1922 in the Department of Agriculture; made independent commission 1974.
Nuclear Regulatory Commission	1975	Licenses and regulates the nuclear-energy industry to protect environment, public health, and safety. Regulatory functions are part of the work of the old Atomic Energy Commission (1946–1974).

It should be noted that nearly 100 federal organizations (including administrations, agencies, bureaus, etc.) have some significant national regulatory function. Among the most important of these are the Food and Drug Administration (created in its present form in 1931, now in the Department of Health and Human Services, but with ancestor organizations going back to 1907); the Environmental Protection Agency (created in 1970 as an executive-branch, rather than a fully independent regulatory agency); and the Occupational Safety and Health Administration (created in 1971 within the Department of Labor). All are discussed in the text of this chapter.

The "good old days": child
workers in 1910.

charged by grain-elevator operators and railroads, on the ground that they
were monopolies; and Utah's eight-hour day for miners was sustained by the
Court in 1898.[10] But when (in 1905) the justices decided that the work of
bakers was not unhealthful, they struck down a New York ten-hour law.[11] The
New York decision provoked a classic dissent from Justice Oliver Wendell
Holmes:

> This case is decided upon an economic theory which a large part of the
> country does not entertain. . . . The Fourteenth Amendment does not enact
> Mr. Herbert Spencer's *Social Statics.* . . . A constitution is not intended to
> embody a particular economic theory, whether of paternalism and the
> organic relation of the citizen to the state or of laissez faire. It is made for
> people of fundamentally differing views, and the accident of our finding
> certain opinions natural and familiar, or novel and even shocking, ought not
> to conclude our judgment upon the question whether statutes embodying
> them conflict with the Constitution of the United States.

Nonetheless, the Court went on striking down state efforts to regulate
business, although it also struck down federal regulatory laws that, in its view,
violated the "reserved rights of the states" under the Tenth Amendment.

One such law, overturned in 1918, prohibited child labor,[12] whose employment remained a protected right until, many years later, the Court ruled in
favor of the 1938 Fair Labor Standards Act.[13] By then, such regulations had
been commonplace for decades in other industrial countries.

---

[10] *Holden* v. *Hardy,* 169 U.S. 366 (1898).

[11] *Lochner* v. *New York,* 198 U.S. 45 (1905).

[12] *Hammer* v. *Dagenhart,* 247 U.S. 251 (1918).

[13] *U.S.* v. *Darby,* 312 U.S. 100 (1941).

Monopolies

Even in the heyday of constitutional conservatism, however, the Court did accept the idea that "natural monopolies," like the telephone company, could be regulated if they were given a "fair rate of return" on their investment. In principle, the Court thus admitted that, in some instances, competition was lacking and regulation therefore acceptable. On these grounds, privately owned transit systems, telephone companies, and public utilities in general were regulated.

Like the states, the federal government attempted to curb the power of monopolies, for by the late 1880s, powerful cartels, pools, and trusts had begun to alarm public opinion. Congress first responded to that fear, in 1890, by passing the Sherman Antitrust Act, which outlawed "combinations in restraint of trade." In 1890, as today, Republicans generally opposed government regulation, but the outcry against monopolies was so strong that the Sherman Act was sponsored by a Republican (Senator John Sherman of Ohio), enacted by the Republican-controlled Congress, and signed by a Republican President (Benjamin Harrison).

The act was not very effective and was further limited by the U.S. Supreme Court's 1895 ruling in the so-called Sugar Trust Case, which made "production" a local activity, exempt from the Sherman Act (see Chapter 3).[14] A wave of mergers then swept the country. In 1914, partly as a result, Congress passed the Clayton Antitrust Act, which is still the core of modern antitrust law. But the mergers have continued—first in the 1920s and, again, from the 1960s to the present. After 1981, the Reagan administration actually encouraged corporate mergers, on the ground that they encouraged efficiency. Despite antitrust legislation, the concentration of economic power has continued throughout the century.

Food and Drugs

Monopolies were fair targets for regulation because they had themselves undermined the ideal: the market. The prevailing rule of the marketplace was still *caveat emptor*, "let the buyer beware."

Most of the country's produce was grown by the people who consumed it, or was sold and consumed locally. Not until large cities emerged did food processing become a big and, literally, dirty business. Upton Sinclair's novel *The Jungle* generated such fear and anger that Congress had to pass the 1906 Pure Food and Drug Act, which created an agency in the Agriculture Department to force standards on the industry. The government had now admitted that buyers could no longer be held personally responsible for investigating the products they bought. This was a momentous admission.

Types of Regulation: "Old" and "New"

Up to and including the New Deal, most kinds of regulation were meant to resolve specific problems in specific industries. This so-called **old regulation** has often been contrasted with a **new regulation**—for instance, environmental regulation—which aims to protect society in general. The truth is that much of

Ken Karp

The Pure Food and Drug Act was passed in 1906 to force standards on the industry—such as ingredient and instruction labeling.

---

[14] *U.S. v. E. C. Knight Co.,* 156 U.S. 1 (1895).

the new regulation is not so new. The Pure Food and Drug Act was an early example of it, since almost everyone eats processed foods. So too were the setting of minimum wages, the prohibition of child labor (in 1938), and occupational health and safety standards (which, on the state level, sometimes date back to the late nineteenth century).

Social regulation—even more than regulation of specific industries—was opposed by big business, conservatives, and the political institutions they dominated. Private business must operate at a profit, and profits depend in large part on costs. If the government forces industry to pay for reducing pollution, that adds to its costs of production. If industry must permit its employees to join unions and bargain for wages and working conditions, that, too, adds to its costs.

If business does not bear these costs, the public does. In fact, the public pays many of the costs of business directly, for example, when local governments build roads to factories, install traffic lights near hotels, issue bonds for industrial parks, or grant tax breaks to industries.[15]

Labor–Management Relations

Few manifestations of the new regulation were resisted as long or as stoutly as the right to unionize. The struggle is still going on.

Skilled workers organized the first successful unions in the nineteenth century. More easily replaceable workers in heavy industry had much greater difficulty organizing. In 1935, the National Labor Relations Act (also called the Wagner Act) gave workers the right to organize unions and legal protection against "unfair labor practices." It also legalized the so-called **union shop,** which requires every worker hired by a company to join the union within a certain period,[16] and even permitted the **closed shop,** which requires employers to hire no one but workers who already belong to a union.

The Wagner Act abruptly tipped the social balance of power toward labor, and business fought it bitterly. In 1937, however, a conservative U.S. Supreme Court upheld the law's constitutionality by a five-to-four vote.[17] Nine years later, the tide turned in favor of business: The Republicans, who had won control of Congress in 1946, passed the Labor–Management Relations Act (called the Taft–Hartley Act) the following year and overrode the veto of President Harry S Truman, a Democrat. Taft–Hartley permits states to pass "right-to-work" laws that outlaw both the closed and the union shops. Although organized labor is adamantly opposed to the law, efforts to make significant changes in it have failed, even when the Democrats occupied the White House and had overwhelming majorities in both houses.

Right-to-work laws have been passed mostly in the Sunbelt. (Business and conservative groups attempted to enact similar laws through referenda in other, industrial states,[18] but these efforts were overwhelmingly defeated by the voters.) Where right-to-work laws exist, they have undoubtedly inhibited unions and cut local labor costs, one reason for the remarkable economic growth—and low wages—of the Sunbelt.

---

[15] Consumers indirectly bear *all* of the costs of business when they purchase its products.
[16] The union shop was not established under the law; it must still be won by individual unions in collective bargaining.
[17] *N.L.R.B.* v. *Jones-Laughlin*, 301 U.S. 1 (1937).
[18] Such as Massachusetts in 1948, Ohio in 1958, and Kansas in 1968.

HEALTH AND SAFETY

We have already seen that public opinion drew the federal government into the health and safety business as long ago as 1906. Yet the Occupational Health and Safety Act of 1970 was quite controversial—perhaps because the injury and mortality rates of many American industries are high, so the cost of cutting those rates must be high as well.

The act created the Occupational Safety and Health Administration (OSHA) and gives it a broad mandate to regulate the working conditions of more than 70 million workers (over two-thirds of this country's work force). OSHA has promulgated more than 4,000 rules, covering several hundred pages in the Code of Federal Regulations and enforced by 1,200 health and safety inspectors. They visit plants and inspect them, often without previous warning.

General Motors claimed in 1974 that compliance with OSHA's rules would cost it some $80 million. Small businesses complain even more bitterly about the cost of OSHA's regulations and paperwork. Unluckily for OSHA, it emerged at a time of high inflation, and business was able to persuade many members of Congress that its regulations were partly to blame. Since the mid-1970s, OSHA has concentrated on a few especially hazardous industries, such as transportation, construction, and petrochemicals.

Some argue that companies might more willingly comply with health and safety standards if they were given economic incentives to do so. That might be done, for example, by giving tax breaks to companies with good safety records. Such policies might not work better than the present ones, but business and the general public usually prefer self-regulation to government regulation.

ENVIRONMENTAL PROTECTION

On September 28, 1982, a freight train was wrecked near the small town of Livingston, Louisiana. Toxic chemicals on the train caught fire, and the police had to evacuate the entire town. Not for two weeks could Livingston's residents return to their homes.

So many toxic chemicals and wastes have been dumped into Lake Erie that its marine life and vegetation have been killed off and the entire lake pronounced dead.

In Love Canal, near Buffalo, New York, a newspaper reporter discovered, in the late 1970s, that a number of homes had been built on a site where more than 15,000 tons of toxic wastes had been dumped years earlier. Residents of the community suffered higher-than-normal rates of cancer, and in 1978 part of the area had to be evacuated.

Most frightening of all, in 1979, the core reactor of a nuclear generating plant at Three Mile Island, near Harrisburg, Pennsylvania, came perilously close to melting down. Had it done so, radiation would have been released into the atmosphere, requiring a large and densely populated area to be evacuated.

Collective Goods. Among other things, these incidents show that the wonders of industry are dangerous. Protection against environmental hazards is a

Michael Hayman, Photo Researchers, Inc.

Protection against environmental hazards is a collective good, something that is to everyone's interest to have and to no one's interest to provide, at least through private means.

collective good, something that is to everyone's interest to have and to no one's interest to provide, least of all privately. Collective goods of this kind often go unprovided unless government, with its powers of coercion, steps in and compels business and industry to clean up after the mess. The higher the antipollution standards, the more expensive it is to comply with them— especially those that prevent the mess to begin with. When making decisions about pollution, we must consider not only what is technically possible but what it costs.

A Success Story. Business and industry sometimes clean up after themselves quite voluntarily. For more than a century, air pollution was a problem in Pittsburgh, the center of the American steel industry. (Charles Dickens, the English novelist, who visited the city in 1842, described it as "Hell with the lid off.") By 1945, the city was intolerably polluted; the sky over it turned black by noon. Many major corporations warned that they would move if conditions failed to improve. Pittsburgh's political, banking, business, and industrial leaders worked out a successful plan that committed the steel companies to pay for and install emission-control devices and to cut the pollution in other ways as well.

Why was Pittsburgh different? In this case, the steel industry was pressured by the business community itself to provide for the collective good. There and then, the cost of the antipollution devices was lower than the cost of inaction. Today's costs are much higher.

Love Canal. Voluntary cleanup is the exception, not the rule. Much more typical was the course of events at Love Canal, where Hooker Chemical Company, which had dumped the toxic wastes, refused to pay the costs of evacuating the neighborhood or compensating its residents. To complicate matters, the ownership of the company had changed between the dumping and the discovery of its consequences. The federal government paid to move

ENVIRONMENTAL LEGISLATION

The federal government first took a really active role in environmental matters in the late 1960s, that fabled time of social activism.

The Clean Air Act. In 1967, Congress passed the Clean Air Act, substantially amended in 1970, to establish strict emission-control standards for automobiles. Those standards have been repeatedly modified and, in some cases, set aside—largely as a result of the energy crisis and lobbying by the automobile industry.

The National Environmental Policy Act. In 1969, Congress passed the National Environmental Policy Act, which requires that *environmental impact statements* be filed with the Environmental Protection Agency (created in 1970) before any project that uses federal funds can proceed. Preparing these statements is often a lengthy, complex task, which critics have attacked on the ground that it creates unnecessary red tape. Environmentalists reply that the statements publicize the possible dangers of such projects and thus permit reasoned decisions about them.

The Water Quality Improvement Act. Not until 1970 and the passing of the Water Quality Improvement Act were companies made responsible for accidental oil spills or deliberate dumping of toxic wastes and pollutants into rivers, lakes, and harbors. The act required the offending companies to pay clean-up costs and made them liable to fines. It also promoted state and local investment in improved waste-treatment facilities.

The Toxic Substances Control Act. In 1976, Congress tried to deal with the problem of poisonous chemicals by passing the Toxic Substances Control Act, which requires that many chemicals used to manufacture everything from fertilizers to plastics be tested and controlled.

only the people living in the unhealthiest part of the Love Canal area, and New York State did not provide funds to move the others.

Conflict. During the 1980s, we might have to spend as much as $300 billion to clean up the environment, unless standards are lower then costs might be lower, too, at least in the short run. Billions will be spent in any case, at the expense of business and, ultimately, the consumer. Expect serious and protracted conflict, especially if the overall economic climate makes it more difficult for business to pass on its costs by raising prices.

Energy

Keeping our industries in production is quite as important as cleaning up after them—some might say more so. Industries need energy, and so do our homes and our cars. Not long ago, energy was hardly a problem, for we had (and still have) vast reserves of coal, which until recently was our single most important source of energy. After World War II, many homes and electric-power plants converted from coal to oil or natural gas, fuels that then were cheaper than coal and generated no solid wastes. We were ourselves a major oil and gas producer, but huge increases in consumption and the discovery of cheap oil supplies abroad, especially in the Middle East, made us dependent on foreigners. In 1973, our Arab oil suppliers put an embargo on their oil; and when they started shipping it again, they and other oil producers that united in the Organization of Petroleum Exporting Countries (OPEC) raised oil prices drastically.

These events prompted us to look for other sources of energy. The United States has vast reserves of coal, but coal is a dirty fuel. Nuclear energy was another obvious, expensive alternative—in some European countries, the most important one. But as the events at Three Mile Island showed, the dangers of nuclear power are very great. Even if no such problem strikes again, we must still close down old nuclear plants and dispose of nuclear wastes, which can remain radioactive, and thus lethally toxic, for hundreds of thousands of years. They are usually stored deep underground in stable geological settings, but who knows how long they will remain stable?

After Three Mile Island, the building of nuclear plants ceased in this country, at least for a time. The Reagan administration wanted to start building them again; the 1980 Democratic platform called for the shutting down of existing nuclear plants whenever possible, and for a freeze on licensing new plants until a safe way of dumping nuclear wastes has been developed. During the first half of the 1980s, the controversy was overtaken by events. Massive cost overruns, court challenges by opponents of nuclear energy, diminished energy use, and lowered prices for competing energy sources made nuclear energy much less profitable and therefore much less appealing to the power industry.

The Deregulation Movement

Conservatives and business leaders have long opposed government regulation. By the late 1970s, deregulation had become fashionable even in certain liberal circles. Some kinds of regulation, it was felt, had outlived their usefulness. Yet by the 1980s, after several years of deregulation had weakened a number of industries, notably airlines, the whole idea became much less fashionable, even among businesspeople.

First, majorities form around support for one kind of regulation or another. But these majorities are often grassy and dissipate when the actual costs of regulation have to be paid. But deregulation does not satisfy public opinion for long. Our attitudes on such issues are notoriously unstable. Why? Remember that the United States does not have an age-old tradition of a strong state—quite the contrary. We reconciled ourselves to such a state rather quickly in the 1930s, not because it seemed theoretically desirable but because laissez faire did not seem to be working. Even then, we never really acquired statist attitudes, and we continued to oppose big government in principle, although in practice we took it for granted and came to desire the specific benefits it provided. (See Chapter 7 for a longer account of this dualism in public opinion.)

A Test Case. One of the first targets of the liberal deregulators, under President Carter, was the airline industry, which since 1938 had been closely regulated by the Civil Aeronautics Board (CAB), an independent regulatory commission. In 1938, the airlines industry was young, and the government decided that protecting and promoting it would serve the national interest. To that end, the CAB controlled the routes the airlines flew and the prices they charged. It even determined who could get into the airlines business.

By the late 1970s, the airlines industry was no longer an infant and, as President Carter saw it, had long outgrown the need for such regulation. Airlines were big businesses with tens of thousands of employees and assets worth hundreds of millions of dollars. Government regulation was now widely thought to protect the airlines from the need to compete, not to protect the public from the airlines. In 1978, Congress passed the Airline Deregulation Act,

Anita Duncan

Surface mining, called strip mining. In an effort to prevent soil erosion, one of the nation's greatest problems, federal law requires that land on any strip mine be restored after mining ceases. The law is often evaded.

which phased out the CAB's authority over routes and prices and provided for its complete elimination by January 1, 1985. The law established competitive market conditions in the airlines industry—to the dismay of many airlines, which are in deep financial trouble. The recession that began in the summer of 1981 cost the airlines many passengers, and the airlines tried to lure them back with lowered fares. Between the recession and increased competition, many airlines found that they could not charge enough for their services to stay in business, and two major carriers, Braniff and Continental, went bankrupt for a short period of time. Other major carriers have followed two cost-cutting strategies. First, a number of major carriers entered into concessionary bargaining, demanding large "givebacks" from their workers and changes in work rules. Second, many major carriers abandoned their less profitable routes—those servicing small, out-of-the-way cities and towns—since the CAB no longer insisted on them.

President Reagan. When President Reagan took office in 1981, he too, had committed himself to deregulate industry, but he did so more by administrative action, and inaction, than by law. For example, former EPA chief Anne Gorsuch refused to enforce many of the regulations issued under the environmental laws of the 1960s and 1970s. The Justice Department dismissed an antitrust case against IBM and settled another suit against the American Telephone and Telegraph Company (AT&T) on what many regarded as the

Deregulation

Without consulting brewers, distillers or vintners last fall, the Reagan Administration offered the alcoholic beverage industry what might be considered the ultimate White House gift—almost total deregulation.

The Federal Bureau of Alcohol, Tobacco and Firearms, the regulatory agency that monitors the industry, was to be dissolved. Enforcement of Federal laws governing licensing, unfair trade practices, labeling and advertising would be "discontinued to the extent legally possible." Government would get off the industry's back, industry would police its own affairs and, presumably, consumers and taxpayers would notice some savings.

As might be expected, consumer groups were appalled by the Administration's attitude toward the only product once banned by the United States Constitution. More regulation of the industry's advertising and ingredient labeling was needed, not less, asserted the Center for Science in the Public Interest, a group concerned with health issues.

But, as things have turned out, the industry is appalled, too, although for different reasons. "We were dumbfounded," said Douglas Metz, executive vice president of the Wine and Spirits Wholesalers of America, a trade group.

The nation's distillers, brewers and vintners, the Administration has discovered, learned long ago to live with the entangling vines of Federal regulation and do not wish to be freed. Almost with a single voice, the many segments of the alcoholic beverage industry, which has retail sales of about $40 billion a year, have thanked the Administration for its good intentions. But they have quickly added that the gift of deregulation could create such chaos in the marketplace that it might even prompt another Prohibition era.

Speaking frankly, they have told the Administration that they would rather deal with a single set of Federal regulations than with 50 sets of state regulations.

Richard B. Thornburg, spokesman for the National Beer Wholesalers Association, said that "the industry has grown up with the act and feels very comfortable with it."

"If the Administration does away with the Bureau of Alcohol, Tobacco and Firearms and stops enforcing the act," he continued, "we could see a return of the abuses that caused Prohibition."

Before the 13-year "noble experiment," as Prohibition is sometimes called, began on Jan. 16, 1920, Mr. Thornburg said the industry was rife with monopolies, criminals and unethical promotions used to encourage the consumption of alcohol. "We're dealing with a controlled substance, a drug, if you will," he said. "It is in the best interests of industry and consumers to have a Federal involvement."

The regulated industry also views its Federal regulators with great respect. The bureau, said Mr. Meister, "is a very lean, highly efficient organization staffed with very professional, highly competent people." "The public is getting a very high return for its tax dollar in the functions performed by the bureau," he added.

From "Deregulation Plan Has an Industry 'Dumfounded,'" by Michael de Courcy Hinds, *The New York Times*, August 27, 1982. By permission.

company's terms. In the Interior Department, Secretary James G. Watt not only changed his department's policy direction but also proposed to modify existing policies.[19] President Reagan also set up a special committee, headed by Vice-President Bush, to weed out "unnecessary" regulation. This committee finished its work in 1984, claiming that it had met all its goals. Skeptics, however, argued that the political will to push for deregulation had eroded and that ending the committee simply reflected political realities.

The FTC. Another attack on the principle and practice of regulation was chiefly the doing of Congress, not the Reagan administration. Since 1914, the

---

[19] Among other things, he wanted to replace the 1977 Control and Reclamation Act, which requires strip-mining companies to pay for restoring the land they mine, with an act that would transfer authority over strip mining to the states. Another Watt objective: permitting speeded-up economic development of lands owned by the federal government and of offshore areas where the federal government can grant leases for oil exploration and drilling.

Federal Trade Commission (FTC) has policed unfair and deceptive business practices. After nearly a decade of hearings, investigations, and study, in 1981 the FTC issued a regulation that would have required used-car dealers to disclose the major defects of their cars. Its supporters claimed that honest car dealers would not be hurt, but critics[20] insisted it would add to dealers' costs, which would then be passed on to consumers. Congress, increasingly irate about the growth of the FTC's activities, voted overwhelmingly in 1982 against the used-car (or "lemon") rule, thus killing it.

WELFARE: REGULATING THE POOR?

Twenty-five percent of the country's wage earners were out of work in 1933, and another 25 percent could find only part-time jobs. Our economic system had collapsed. Not only from sheer pity but also to prevent social and political unrest, the federal government started to underwrite the national standard of living.

Relief

Some of the government's attempts to do so could be described as welfare because they provided support for indigent people who would not or could not work. But many programs gave "relief," low-paying jobs administered through new agencies like the Federal Emergency Relief Administration (FERA), the Public Works Administration (PWA), the National Youth Administration (NYA), the Works Progress Administration (WPA), and the Civilian Conservation Corps (CCC).

During World War II, unemployment almost vanished, and the relief programs came to an end—the last in 1943. But the government's commitment to full employment was written into law in the 1946 Employment Act. The idea that government should be the "employer of last resort," was by no means accepted by all Americans. Liberals supported it, but conservatives did not.

Hard-Core Poverty

Likewise, not all Americans regarded poverty as a problem amenable to state action. "The poor," the Bible tells us, "ye shall always have with you," and many Americans agreed. Oddly enough, persistent poverty (as opposed to poverty induced by major economic disasters like the Depression) stayed off the national agenda until the early 1960s, a time of economic prosperity. Why then? For one thing, the economic boom not only made poverty a glaring national embarrassment but also provided the government with large financial resources. The riots and disorders that broke out among blacks in many central cities during the mid-1960s were a second reason.

In a sense, the whole problem of persistent poverty—and the welfare problem, which grew out of it—became more entrenched during these fat years and then during the lean years that followed them. Many people were

---

[20] Including the National Automobile Dealers Association, which contributed more than $1 million to congressional campaigns in 1979 and 1980.

pushed into "structural unemployment" that resulted from a long-term shift away from unskilled labor. More and more, our economy is a service economy that can use only skilled workers, professionals, and the like. Many people who come to the labor market with nothing but strong arms and backs cannot find work—ever. Once started, structural unemployment, poverty, and welfare dependency become entrenched. Welfare dependents develop their own language, style, and cultural outlook, one at war with the middle-class culture that dominates this country and pays the bill.

Solutions? Is poverty a problem that can be solved? If so, how? Some liberals and radicals urge the poor to organize politically, so they will be better placed to demand job training, jobs, better education, or even direct-income supplements—a guaranteed annual income.

Such proposals, whatever their merits, strike at a basic American value: the idea that normal, competent adults provide for themselves. Indeed, that principle is already somewhat compromised by the most controversial of all existing welfare schemes: the Aid to Families with Dependent Children (AFDC) program. Any fatherless family (mothers and children) whose income falls below a certain point is eligible, so that the program includes many recipients who are clearly "normal." For better or for worse, AFDC breaks down the distinction between the "deserving" poor—people whose disabilities prevent them from earning a living—and those who used to be called "sturdy beggars."[21]

Political conservatives complain that AFDC's rapidly increasing cost burdens the taxpayers. Liberals reply that the Defense Department's cost overruns are just as high. But both liberals and conservatives agree that programs like AFDC raise disturbing questions. Do these programs contribute to a welfare dependency that is being handed down from generation to generation? Do they weaken the structure of poor families by encouraging men to desert their wives, since AFDC funds are supposed to go only to women without men to support them? Why should anyone work if everyone doesn't?

Some conservatives argue that the cycle of dependency could be broken by requiring able-bodied welfare recipients to work for their own benefits— "workfare," as it is called. Some states have done just that; and so, in fact, did the old New Deal relief programs. Workfare cannot make its recipients really independent, however, unless they do work that teaches them real skills. Most workfare jobs are menial—seen as a form of punishment, not a source of pride.

Disorganization. Swedish sociologist Gunnar Myrdal once noted that although Sweden is the classic welfare state, it has no minimum-wage law, whereas the United States has had such a law since 1938. Sweden did not need to legislate a national minimum wage; its people were so effectively organized, in labor unions and other associations, that they won a minimum wage through collective bargaining. The United States had no effective industrial

---

[21] An evocative term from the time of Queen Elizabeth I of England (1558–1603). In those days, "sturdy beggars" who were found soliciting rather than working could be imprisoned, branded, mutilated, or—the supreme punishment, for repeated offenses—transported "for life" to the colonies, which eventually became the eastern seaboard of the United States.

unions before 1935, and even today the very poor still lack organization. If the thing was to be done, the government had to do it.

Despite the exceptional wealth in our country, many of our people have problems that seem to be more intractable than those confronting similar groups in the other industrial democracies. There are no Harlems in, say, Switzerland or Sweden, but the reason is not that those countries are richer than the United States or better, in general, at solving their problems. Our poor people are at a disadvantage because they are unorganized, both socially and politically. Generally, they do not turn out to vote in large numbers, and relatively few belong to labor unions. As a result, the poor depend on the government, but the government itself has relatively little incentive (other than sheer good will) to satisfy their demands.

Social Security

One income-maintenance program is not at all like the other income-maintenance programs: It is politically popular. Of course, that program is Social Security. Politicians propose to change the retirement benefits at their political peril, and they know this. In 1981, for example, the Reagan administration asked Congress for a very limited curtailment of benefits. At the time, Congress gave him the tax and spending policies he had demanded (see Chapter 16), but his Social Security proposal was defeated in the Senate by a vote of 96 to 0. President Reagan apparently learned a lesson from this debacle, because during the 1984 campaign he promised he would "never" reduce benefits to Social Security recipients. In early 1985 he said he would consider cuts only if an "overwhelming bipartisan majority" demanded them. The elderly, unlike the poor, are a potent force, well-organized and ever more numerous.

What accounts for the magic of Social Security? Mainly this: It is not, strictly speaking, a welfare program, for it is based on a specific tax—the Federal Insurance Contributions Act (FICA) payroll tax—paid by all workers. FICA has been much criticized. Some economists call it inflationary because the part paid by employers gets passed on to the public, through higher prices. Liberals contend that the tax is not progressive (does not tax the wealthy at higher rates) and thus falls hardest on those who earn least. But there is a political logic, a political beauty, to FICA: Those who pay it—about 90 percent of the American labor force—establish a legitimate claim on society. President Franklin D. Roosevelt realized that this claim was a key to Social Security's political invulnerability. When a visitor complained one day about the economic impact of the payroll tax, Roosevelt replied,

> I guess you're right on the economics, but those taxes were never a problem of economics. They are politics all the way through. We put those payroll contributions there so as to give the contributors a legal, moral, and political right to collect their pensions. . . . With those taxes in there, no damn politician can ever scrap my social security program.[22]

He was right. No damn politician can.

---

[22] Arthur M. Schlesinger, Jr., *The Age of Roosevelt: The Coming of the New Deal* (Boston: Houghton Mifflin, 1958), II, 308–9.

The Social-Security Scandals

Hester McLean is 56 years old, poor and sick. Her pancreas is shot. Her bowels work erratically. Her duodenal ulcer acts up. Her left knee continues to deteriorate from arthritis. Four years ago she stopped working as a maid, and began collecting $297 a month under a social-security program for the disabled. In April 1982, however, the federal aid was cut off: her health, a bureaucrat ruled, had improved. This year McLean's case reached a federal judge, who reviewed her medical history and promptly lost his judicial detachment. "This case presents an appalling example of sheer bureaucratic dishonesty," federal district court Judge Joseph S. Lord III wrote last May. "If the purpose of the U.S. Department of Health and Human Services is to crush defenseless human beings, as it seems to be, it would succeed unless . . . courts interposed a protective arm." But when Social Security is involved, even the long arm of the law is without muscle. Lord ordered the agency to pay her benefits immediately. Four months later, McLean has yet to receive a dime.

The McLean case is just one of hundreds of thousands that constitute the Great Disability Disaster of 1981–84. According to official reports, at least 215,000 ailing Americans were sent tumbling through a porous "safety net" only to be told later that a dreadful mistake had been made. The blunderbuss clearing of the disability rolls has been attacked by Senate and House committees, state officials and even Social Security's in-house administrative law judges. The critics charge that the agency, spurred by Reagan administration budget cutters, has reversed the American notion of social justice so that it now reads: better that one crippled person go begging, than one deadbeat get an extra check.

Even Social Security recognizes the crisis—and the potential fodder for Democrats eager to attack Reagan on the "fairness issue." Last week the agency released an internal memo that described the department's credibility as at "an all time low" and recommended a cease-fire in the battle against "sympathetic" claimants. And at the weekend, congressional conferees reached an agreement between the Senate and the House on long-awaited legislation that will cure some of the program's ills. The bill will bar terminations except where the agency can show a disabled person has improved enough to hold a "substantial gainful" job. And it will allow people who have lost benefits to appeal under the new law—a big loss for the administration, which advocated leaving the current appealers stuck in the pipeline.

Haven: The current mess grew out of good intentions. Four years ago, a General Accounting Office report estimated that up to 584,000 people on the disability rolls were capable of working. The program—begun in 1956 as a lifeline for workers forced to quit because of severe physical or mental illness—seemed just another haven for welfare cheats—at an annual cost of about $19 billion. Congress responded by directing Social Security to review the eligibility of recipients every three years. When the Reagan administration took office, it ordered the reviews to begin in March 1981 and toughened the eligibility standards. Headquarters sent out 30,000 cases a month to state offices unprepared to review them.

Two years later the GAO found that disabled people who had been on the rolls for several years—and had not improved medically—were being tossed off. Nevertheless, the Reagan administration did not back down. Since 1981, 1.2 million cases have been reviewed: 491,000 lost their benefits. Those decisions have been reversed in 215,000 cases and others remain on appeal.

Fear: But even a reversal takes its toll. Vera Heiser of Darien, Ill., lost her disability support in 1982, shortly after her third open-heart operation. Along with her check, the Feds also lifted her Medicare card; for eight months she couldn't afford to see her doctor and, with her husband, borrowed money for her medicine. After she was reinstated, she said, "Now I live with fear 24 hours a day. I'm so afraid that it's going to happen again." In the wake of such horror stories, 26 states—voluntarily or under court order—stopped cooperating with the reviews. And even friendly legislators such as Sen. John Heinz, Republican of Pennsylvania, began calling the policy a "holocaust of the nation's disabled."

Recently, federal judges have denounced new disability regulations adopted by the Reagan administration. In June, Judge Morris E. Lasker overruled the agency's policy of judging a claimant's diseases separately without looking at their combined "severity." He compared the policy's logic to that of "a mathematician [who] might prove that because two does not equal four, two plus two never equals four either." A fortnight ago, an appeals panel in New York rejected the agency's practice of honoring only mental disabilities that appeared on its approved list—without judging whether the person was capable of working.

Tension: Even when the feds win in court, the judges take them to task. Last week Judge Joyce

Hens Green ruled against a group of administrative-law judges who claimed that Social Security singled them out for review if they reversed aid cutoffs in more than 70 percent of their cases. Green said the agency had that power, but concluded that exercising it had "created an untenable atmosphere of tension and unfairness."

The tension is systemwide. Health and Human Services Secretary Margaret Heckler tried to ease it by declaring a moratorium on cutoffs and ordered the resumption of payment to those pursuing administrative appeals. Spokesman Jim Brown says the agency is sorry for the mistakes and hopes to be more "humane" in the future. But for the moment, the agency is unable to keep pace with its tasks. L. C. Rentie went without payments for three years until a judge in San Francisco ordered him back onto the rolls last December. Five months later his lawyer moved to hold Heckler in contempt of court for not paying Rentie; within a few weeks, his check arrived. Social Security apologized: his form was lost in the computer.

In Philadelphia, Hester McLean is still waiting for her payment ordered by Judge Lord last May. Three weeks ago an assistant U.S. attorney asked Social Security's counsel where McLean's money was. He's still waiting for an answer.

Hester McLean at home: an improvement in health, according to bureaucratic diagnosis.

Brad Bower, Picture Group

As a matter of fact, the Social Security tax has given rise to a number of illusions about the program—mainly the idea that it is a true insurance program and that the payroll tax is a premium that can be collected, with interest, upon retirement.[23] In fact, Social Security is only a transfer program;

---

[23] In an insurance program, the premiums are invested and earn dividends and yields, all of which are paid out to beneficiaries.

Table 15–1 Income Security as Percentage of GNP and of Total Federal Outlays, 1948–1983

YEAR	RAW TOTALS IN $ BILLIONS				AS PERCENTAGES			
	GNP	Total Outlays	Income Security	Payroll Taxes (receipts)	Of GNP Total Outlays	Of Federal Outlays	Of GNP Income Security	Of GNP Payroll Taxes
1948	$243.5	$33.0	$2.8	$2.4	13.5%	8.4%	1.1%	1.0%
1953	358.9	74.1	6.1	4.7	20.7	8.3	1.7	1.3
1958	440.3	82.6	15.0	8.6	18.8	18.2	3.4	1.9
1963	573.4	111.3	24.1	14.9	19.4	21.6	4.2	2.6
1968	826.0	178.8	33.7	29.2	21.7	18.8	4.1	3.5
1973	1,252.0	245.6	73.0	54.9	19.6	29.7	5.8	4.4
1978	2,083.8	448.4	146.2	103.9	21.5	32.6	7.0	5.0
1983	3,221.4	808.3	307.6	204.6	25.1	38.1	9.5	6.4
1986*	4,198.5	973.7	333.1	284.6	23.2	34.2	7.9	6.8

* Estimated in Administration's Fiscal Year 1986 budget.

the taxes we contribute today are not invested but simply transferred to people who have already retired. From today's payroll to today's retirees. The benefits have been raised many times since the program was begun, in 1935, so people in the first generation covered by Social Security are now receiving benefits far larger than the amount of their total payments into the system. Later generations of workers are not likely to be so fortunate.

Why is the Social Security system in financial trouble? One reason is that Congress has increased the benefits rather generously over the past twenty years. It added Medicare for the elderly in 1965. In 1972, it tacked on a provision that automatically tied benefits to the inflation rate. But the legislation was so hastily and carelessly drawn that it authorized raising benefits at twice the level of inflation. Social Security is a politician's dream come true: Congress can increase benefits in election years, while carefully increasing FICA in nonelection years.

Even major increases in payroll taxes have not kept pace with benefits, in part because high unemployment has reduced the amount of revenues generated by the payroll tax. Better medical care has kept more people alive longer, so more people survive to receive benefits. At the same time, the birthrate—especially among whites—has dropped sharply. Fewer and fewer workers contribute; more and more retirees collect. Unless something is done to correct the problems created by this imbalance, they will threaten the system by the year 2010 or so.

Even now, the costs of Social Security are skyrocketing. In 1984, the system's price tag was $178.2 billion, expected to rise to $202.2 billion in 1983 and to $259.9 billion in 1990. What is to be done?

In late 1982, President Reagan established a bipartisan National Commission on Social Security Reform in order to find solutions for the social security funding crisis. In March 1983, Congress approved a "rescue plan" designed to stave off immediate financial collapse and provide solvency into the twenty-first century. The major provisions approved by Congress were based largely on the commission's recommendations. Congress voted to increase the retirement age to 67 by the year 2027, to delay cost-of-living adjustments for six months, to increase payroll taxes for both employers and employees, to tax benefits of high-income recipients for the first time; and to bring new federal employees, Congress itself, the President, Vice-President, and federal judges into the social security system for the first time. Along with a number of minor provisions, these changes aimed to spread the pain of social security reform to numerous segments of the population. Representative Barber Conable, Jr. (R–NY) noted that the plan "may not be a work of art, but it is artful work." Many rescue plans in the past promised long-term solvency for the social security system, promises that turned out to be impossible to fulfill. Whether the recent reforms will fare any better is still an open question.

SUMMARY

Before the Great Depression of the 1930s, there was in many fields little need and less demand for a federal domestic policy. Alexander Hamilton did not propose a farm price-support program in the 1790s, when American farmers raised crops chiefly for their own consumption and sold their surpluses, if any, in local markets. As the scale of production and the extent of the market grew, the public came to accept certain kinds of regulation—the 1906 Pure Food and Drug Act, for instance. Moreover, the ideal of laissez faire did not prevent the government from providing business with a wide variety of subsidies and grants-in-aid. Even federal regulation of business started no later than 1887, with the Interstate Commerce Act, and 1890, when Congress passed the Sherman Antitrust Act.

As for welfare, the federal government's involvement began in 1933, with the coming of the New Deal. In a society and political culture saturated by the values of free enterprise, welfare policy occupies an ambiguous position. Policies that are, in effect, "welfare for business" are rarely so regarded by the public, much less subjected to large-scale political controversy. Welfare for the poor has always occupied a very different position. For many years, public opinion on the subject has distinguished between the "deserving" and the "undeserving" poor. Most Americans do support government aid to those who are physically or mentally incapable of working. But some welfare programs help people who are more or less "normal" and, as a result these programs are much more controversial, because public opinion feels that they dissolve the connection between the fruits of labor and labor itself. After all, *someone* has to pay the bill!

Two kinds of welfare programs, and only two, are popular: unemployment insurance and Social Security. When unemployment rises over 7 percent or so, it becomes rather obvious that millions of people would work if they could, but can't, because they can't find jobs. Social Security, however, is not even perceived as a welfare program, because wage earners pay taxes, FICA, to finance it. These taxes were built into the system at the very beginning because its drafters knew that they would make it politically invulnerable. They succeeded brilliantly, and the system now has a chronic solvency problem. Its solvency eroded more seriously than expected and sooner than expected—partly as a result of the economic slump of the early 1980s, which diminished FICA collections. By the turn of the century, the changing balance between active workers and retirees will generate a much greater crisis.

We may well be pardoned for looking nostalgically at the simpler and vastly less expensive world of a century ago. Yet nostalgia is not likely to help us deal with our domestic policy needs. Chemical and nuclear waste hazards, environmental pollution, and safety and health issues will not go away. Neither, it seems, will our welfare underclass of men and women who lack the skills needed for today's service economy. Slumps and high unemployment still plague us.

Changes in our economy and society can also make some kinds of government activity irrelevant. Beginning in the late 1970s and continuing into the 1980s, the deregulation movement sought to create true market conditions in some parts of the economy, such as the airlines industry, on which the government had imposed a shared monopoly. President Reagan sought to go beyond this by deregulating to cut the costs of industry. One kind of government subsidy, the protective tariff, was effectively eliminated decades ago, very largely because American industry no longer needed protection and wanted to expand international trade. But in the 1970s, as the competitive position of our economy declined, protectionist sentiments mounted.

Action and reaction, debate and change are the only unchanging features of American public policy. The basic limitations on government action—public acceptance of free enterprise and fear of centralized power—will probably survive, though perhaps in new forms. But they will survive only if they can deliver the goods: jobs and income. If they cannot, there may be some surprises ahead.

_____ SUGGESTED READINGS _____

AMERICAN ENTERPRISE INSTITUTE FOR PUBLIC POLICY RESEARCH, *Regulation*. Washington, D.C. A bimonthly journal produced by the country's leading conservative think tank. Generally, there is a point of view, but this journal—like most of AEI's other publications—is of very high quality, containing valuable articles by experts.

J. CLARENCE DAVIES III and BARBARA S. DAVIES, *The Politics of Pollution*, 2nd ed. Indianapolis: Bobbs-Merrill, 1975. Survey of the development of environmental-protection laws and regulations, written from a favorable perspective. Explains why the demand for these laws and regulations grew so intense.

HARRISON W. FOX, JR., and MARTIN SCHNITZER, *Doing Business in Washington: How to Win Friends and Influence Government*. New York: Free Press, 1981. As the title implies, this is a kind of how-to-do-it manual for corporate executives and thus has a good deal on lobbying. In addition, it contains a useful and vivid profile of the political and administrative environment affecting businesspeople and business regulation.

PAUL W. MACAVOY, *The Regulated Industries and the Economy*. New York: Norton, 1979. A valuable part of the contemporary literature on regulation and its costs by a leading economist.

MARTIN C. SCHNITZER, *Contemporary Government and Business Relations*. Chicago: Rand McNally, 1978. One of many textbooks on the subject; quite thorough and comprehensive.

ALAN STONE, *Economic Regulation and the Public Interest: The Federal Trade Commission in Theory and in Practice*. Ithaca, N.Y.: Cornell Univ., 1977.

Excellent case study of the regulatory process in the FTC by a political scientist who once worked for it.

JAMES Q. WILSON, ed., *The Politics of Regulation*. New York: Basic Books, 1980. A series of sometimes excellent case studies in the regulatory process, reflecting the increased sensitivity in recent years to the economic and other costs of such government regulation of business.

chapter sixteen

MANAGING THE
ECONOMY

Some people called the Bank of United States the "pantspressers' bank," because so many of its 440,000 depositors worked in New York's garment district. Quite a few of them thought it was a government bank, but it was, in fact, a wholly private enterprise quite unconnected with the first and second Banks of the United States, central banks owned and operated by the federal government in the late eighteenth and early nineteenth centuries (see Chapters 3 and 8). Private though it might be, the Bank of United States was huge: 57 branches strong, with total resources of $314.7 million and deposits of $220 million. The men who controlled it also controlled many affiliates, including an insurance company, 3 financial companies, and more than 20 real estate companies.

These men were swindlers. In the summer of 1929, they bought 118,000 shares of their own bank's stock in hopes of driving up the price and selling at a profit. But the stock market crashed in late October, so they could not unload their shares on the public. Instead, they negotiated a loan to the bank from the government Federal Reserve System; in turn, the bank loaned $11 million to the swindlers' affiliates, which used the money to buy the stock.

For years, the swindlers had been speculating wildly, especially in real estate, and the bank was in trouble—bad trouble. Why then could they waste an additional $11 million? For one thing, the members of the bank's board of directors had asked no awkward questions, because they had received from it loans of more than $2.5 million. For another, the New York State Banking Department, which routinely investigated the bank twice a year, largely ignored its responsibility. After the stock sale, for instance, the state's investigators reported quite critically on the bank and its methods, and the state banking superintendent even suggested certain changes. He

497

dropped them, however, when the bank came up with its own proposal: a merger with other banks.

Although the merger deal collapsed, the bank persisted in its wild stock and real estate binge and went on lending money to its affiliates. To make the Banking Department think they had paid off their loans, the swindlers fiddled with the books. They needed more money, too, and tried to get it by luring new depositors. All to no effect. In September, state inspectors reported that the bank owed $2.9 million more than it held in assets; in other words, it was broke. These charges were not publicized, and the swindlers, who were again trying to arrange a merger, told their stockholders that the bank had a surplus of $10 million. All the proposed mergers again fell through.

In November 1930 while these machinations were in progress, banks failed in Tennessee, Missouri, Indiana, Illinois, Iowa, Arkansas, and North Carolina. On December 10, 1930, the troubles of the Bank of United States at last hit the streets of New York. On that one day, rumors of its impending collapse raced from door to door, tenement to tenement, block to block, and neighborhood to neighborhood; crossed the East River and the Harlem River and passed into Brooklyn and the Bronx; and generated massive lines of angry and confused depositors who waited in the rain to withdraw their money. On December 11, the state banking commissioner closed the bank.

The swindlers later went to jail, but the 440,000 depositors—75 percent with deposits of less than $400—recovered only 50 cents on the dollar. They were lucky to get even that, because in those days bank deposit insurance did not exist. A bank account was an investment; investments sometimes go bust; and by the lights of that era, the government had no right to diminish that risk. The economy, like nature itself, was then thought to be governed by immutable laws, and woe unto any nation that meddled with them.

ECONOMICS AS A SOCIAL SCIENCE

Like all other social sciences, economics studies human behavior. It is not a pure science, like mathematics or physics, where clearly definable causes produce clearly definable effects that can be investigated in laboratories and relied on always to operate in the same way. Economics is bound up with the passions and material interests of humanity, so it is saturated with politics and political preferences. That is why we have radical, liberal, moderate, and conservative economics (and several schools of each), but not moderate physics, liberal chemistry, or conservative calculus.

Even so, economics has great mathematical rigor, and economists have accumulated a large body of real knowledge. In this field as in others, one person's opinion is not as good as another's. Why then does economics fail to achieve the predictive accuracy and practical effectiveness of physics? Because, once again, economics is a social science, based on the study of human behavior, which is bafflingly complex and not always very rational.

The Two Levels

Economists generally specialize in one of two broad categories of economic behavior: **microeconomics** or **macroeconomics.** Microeconomics deals with

Van Bucher, Photo Researchers, Inc.

Supply and demand, or demand and supply?

economic behavior at the level of individual firms and people and attempts to explain how the decisions of individual consumers, households, and companies jointly change the price of goods and services relative to one another, the quantity of goods and services produced and purchased, and the amount of labor and capital used to produce them.

Macroeconomics studies the economy at a higher level. In a sense, macroeconomists add up all the individual and corporate responses observed by microeconomists and try to make sense of their impact on the national economy. For example, if the government is considering a tax cut, macroeconomists would try to predict how much of it the consumers would be likely to spend and how much they might save. This level of economic behavior is far more complex than individual behavior. Take the example of a tax cut. The proportion of the cut that consumers (as a whole) might save will be influenced, among other things, by its level (10 percent, say, or 12 percent); by the number of Americans who are out of work at that time; by the past and present level of consumer income; by the past and present value of financial assets such as stock holdings and tangible assets such as homes and cars; by the level of consumer debt; and by popular expectations about the future course of employment, income, assets, and debt.

Once the macroeconomists have guessed how much of a tax cut its recipients will spend or save, they try to assess the impact of that national spending or saving. How will it affect business investment in plant and equipment? How much will it change the total amount of goods and services produced in the United States in the immediate future? The monetary value of all goods and services produced in a country is what economists call its

Table 16–1 United States: Per Capita Disposable Income and Unemployment, 1911–1984, and Rate of Inflation, 1939–1984

YEAR	INCOME ($ 1972)	RATE OF UNEMPLOYMENT	RATE OF INFLA-TION	YEAR	INCOME ($ 1972)	RATE OF UNEMPLOYMENT	RATE OF INFLA-TION
1911	$1,445	6.7%		1951	$2,415	3.3%	6.6%
1912	1,498	4.6		1952	2,441	3.0	1.4
1913	1,511	4.3		1953	2,501	2.9	1.6
1914	1,458	7.9		1954	2,483	5.5	1.2
1915	1,514	8.5		1955	2,582	4.4	2.2
1916	1,632	5.1		1956	2,653	4.1	3.2
1917	1,650	4.6		1957	2,660	4.3	3.4
1918	1,569	1.4		1958	2,645	6.8	1.7
1919	1,535	1.4		1959	2,709	5.5	2.4
1920	1,367	5.2		1960	2,709	5.5	1.6
1921	1,187	11.7		1961	2,742	6.7	0.9
1922	1,353	6.7		1962	2,813	5.5	1.8
1923	1,510	2.4		1963	2,865	5.7	1.5
1924	1,493	5.0		1964	3,026	5.2	1.5
1925	1,518	3.2		1965	3,171	4.5	2.2
1926	1,539	1.8		1966	3,290	3.8	3.2
1927	1,552	3.3		1967	3,389	3.8	3.0
1928	1,595	4.2		1968	3,493	3.6	4.4
1929	1,788	3.2		1969	3,564	3.5	5.1
1930	1,635	8.7		1970	3,665	4.9	5.4
1931	1,559	15.9		1971	3,752	5.9	5.0
1932	1,336	23.6		1972	3,860	5.6	4.2
1933	1,288	24.9		1973	4,080	4.9	5.8
1934	1,375	21.7		1974	4,009	5.6	8.8
1935	1,495	20.1		1975	4,051	8.5	9.3
1936	1,676	16.9		1976	4,158	7.7	5.2
1937	1,719	14.3		1977	4,280	7.1	5.8
1938	1,600	19.0		1978	4,441	6.1	7.4
1939	1,754	17.2	−.8	1979	4,512	5.8	8.6
1940	1,847	14.6	2.2	1980	4,487	7.1	9.2
1941	2,083	9.9	7.5	1981	4,561	7.6	9.6
1942	2,354	4.7	9.9	1982	4,555	9.7	6.0
1943	2,429	1.9	5.3	1983	4,670	9.6	3.8
1944	2,483	1.2	2.4	1984 (est.)	4,941	7.5	3.7
1945	2,416	1.9	2.4				
1946	2,353	3.9	15.7				
1947	2,212	3.9	12.9				
1948	2,290	3.8	6.9				
1949	2,257	5.9	−.9				
1950	2,392	5.3	2.1				

* Inflation: Measured from year-on-year change in implicit price deflator used by the government to compute "real" GNP.
SOURCE: ERP 85.

national output or **gross national product,** better known as **GNP.** The rate at which GNP rises in any one year is an economist's measure of a national economy's health. It is also a key element in the unemployment rate, in the level of personal incomes and corporate profits, and in the inflation rate. All these are political dynamite.

So many variables (factors) affect the course of the U.S. economy that its vicissitudes are hard to predict, even with computer-run econometric models. No economist can identify all the variables or know in advance how they will interact. Economists cannot predict when the people will behave unpredictably or when important variables (for instance, the price of oil) will change. Few if any economists predicted the extent or persistence of the recession that began in the summer of 1981.

The Policy Options: Monetary Policy and Fiscal Policy

Two broad types of policies can directly influence the national economy. The first one to be implemented in the United States was **monetary policy,** control over the money supply, granted to Congress by the Constitution. Since 1914, that power has been delegated to the Federal Reserve Board. In some ways, little has changed since the days when James Madison first commented on the decisive political importance of the conflict between "creditors and debtors."[1] Even now, the federal government must steer between groups that want "easy money" (relatively low interest rates, making it cheap to borrow) and those that want "sound money"—price stability—which often requires high interest rates.

The federal government's second macroeconomic policy choice, **fiscal policy,** is carried out by manipulating the federal budget and federal taxes. In the United States, fiscal policy did not even emerge until the Great Depression of the 1930s was well under way. One aspect of fiscal policy, **budgetary policy,** deals with matters such as the total level of federal spending each year, its distribution among particular departments and programs, and the circumstances—if any—in which spending should exceed revenues (deficit spending). These are all political questions of the most basic and explosive kind. The other part of fiscal policy, **tax policy,** provides the revenue for the government's activities. Each year, policy makers have to decide how much federal revenue should be raised from personal income taxes, how much from

---

[1] See Appendix for *The Federalist*, Paper 10.

Monetary policy, control over the money supply, was granted to Congress by the Constitution. Since 1914, that power has been delegated to the Federal Reserve Board.

Marc Loonan

corporate taxes, how much from excise (luxury) taxes. What level of taxes should each income group be made to bear? And what *aggregate* (or total) amount of taxation should the President and Congress accept? If aggregate taxes are to be raised or lowered, by how much, when, and under what circumstances? These are all bottom-line questions. They determine how much money each of us will have left in our pockets.

HOW U.S. ECONOMIC POLICY EVOLVED

Before the 1930s and the onset of the Great Depression, the people and government of the United States believed that an economy works best when left more or less alone. This policy of economic noninterference, or **laissez faire,** was set forth in the works of the so-called **classical economists,** who dominated economic thinking for more than a century. The classical doctrine interpreted human behavior by the lights of the cash register. Each individual, in this view, takes part in economic exchanges solely because of hope of personal gain. That hope—when it is not regulated by the government— inspires us to work as hard as we can and therefore to produce as much as we can. Since production is as high as it can possibly be, so too is consumption. Whatever regulation may be needed is supplied directly by the market.

Suppose, for example, that there is a sudden rage for alligator shoes. The price of alligator shoes then goes up, for demand exceeds supply. Selfish men and women notice this. Some go out into the jungles and massacre the beasts; others learn to make their skins into footwear. Soon, alligator shoes flood the market. The supply overtakes the demand; then the price falls. Selfish men and women now look for other employment. In short, economies regulate themselves, or so the classical economists taught. "It is not from the benevolence of the butcher that we can expect our dinner," Adam Smith observed in Wealth of Nations, "but from his regard to his own interest."[2]

The classical economists believed that cycles of boom and bust were inevitable, and that depressions could end only when they had burned themselves out—when excess supplies and financial speculation had been cleared away. This was supposed to happen quickly. The more a nation produced, the higher the demand for its goods and services—and for labor to meet that demand. A depression, in this scheme of things, could never last very long. (See the section on Say's "Law of Markets.")

The Magic of Gold

Because the classical economists viewed the market as "self-correcting," they conceded very few economic responsibilities to government: to maintain stable currencies, balance the budgets, enforce contracts, hang thieves, and maintain the international gold standard. Before 1914, the currencies of all industrial nations were fully backed by gold; in other words, each government would exchange its own paper currency for gold coin. The value of each currency in terms of gold was fixed for long periods of time, and this meant that the relative values of these currencies also remained stable.

The beauty of the **gold standard** was that it functioned automatically. Money backed by gold, it was thought, could not grow at the whim of

---

[2] Adam Smith, *Wealth of Nations* (1776).

Gold being weighed in the Federal Reserve Bank in New York. The metal shoes shown are protection against dropping gold bars on one's feet.

politicians. If any government suddenly increased the supply of paper money without a parallel increase in that country's stock of gold, the cost of all its goods would rise. Under a system of free trade (see Chapter 15), the higher price of goods in that country would make its citizens import goods at the cheaper prices prevailing abroad. At the same time, because its goods were now more costly than foreign goods, it would sell fewer of them in foreign markets.

Net result: Its **balance of trade** would turn negative as its trading partners abroad purchased fewer of its goods and acquired more of its currency and gold in exchange for their own goods. To halt this outward flow of gold and the increasingly negative trade balance, officials in the first country would have to accept the so-called discipline of gold, by curbing the growth in the money supply—usually through increased taxation. The contraction of the money supply would then force prices down and make goods competitive abroad. In the end, the balance of trade would again be in surplus.

Another virtue of the gold standard—to its past and present admirers, at any rate—was that it kept prices, including the price of labor, more or less stable. If one country started paying its workers significantly more than any other nation did, and it could not absorb those costs through higher **productivity** (increased output of goods per laborer), its domestic prices would rise and create a negative trade balance, with all the undesirable consequences.

Finally, the international gold standard kept government finance "pure" by prohibiting budget deficits, which might flood an economy with money not backed by gold. For these reasons, the gold standard seems as desirable to this country's conservatives today as it did to conservatives of the past, and many would like to reintroduce it. Others seek to achieve the same end through a constitutional amendment prohibiting unbalanced budgets.

Where Gold Fell Short. It seems so simple, so logical, so automatic. Why then did the gold standard collapse? The problem was that it always collapsed during serious wars. We discovered this in 1861, when the federal government had to issue currency well above its gold holdings to pay the cost of the Civil War. After the war, officials restored the gold standard by imposing a stringent policy of **deflation,** contracting the money supply. Federal spending was cut so rapidly that the country went through a severe depression. Many economists believe that the Great Depression of the 1930s was deepened, if not caused, by attempts to restore the worldwide gold standard after its collapse during World War I. In any case, those attempts failed and had to be abandoned almost everywhere by 1933.

First Priority: A Balanced Budget

Before the Great Depression, most people assumed that the **public sector** (government) should balance its income versus expenditures, rather like the budgets of private firms and households. Fiscal—that is, budgetary—policy was simply a matter of running a budget surplus, often for decades or years.

The 1929 Depression, like those before it, cut tax receipts more rapidly than the government could cut expenditures. Result: a budget deficit. Classical economic theory declared that a deficit should be eliminated, pronto, by drastic cuts in public spending, but in 1929, such cuts merely worsened the Depression. Unemployment was high and rose still higher, demand plummeted, and prices fell so low that companies could not make a profit. Survival of the gold standard, however, made budget cuts more or less inevitable. Understandably, almost the first major step of the incoming President Franklin D. Roosevelt was to end the free convertibility between gold and the paper dollar. So, far from cutting the budget (as he had promised to do in the 1932 campaign), Mr. Roosevelt set up many economic-relief programs that created a large federal budget deficit. He had little choice. With 25 percent of the labor force out of work, the fiscal policies of the 1920s were dead.

But Mr. Roosevelt did not abandon the ideal of a balanced budget. He almost achieved one in 1937—only to encounter the 1937–1938 recession,[3] which many economists blame on his effort to cut spending. Then and only then was the goal of a balanced budget abandoned.

Upsetting the Classical Apple Cart

Even before the Great Depression, a small but vocal group of economists—including John Maynard Keynes (1887–1946), an Englishman—had begun to challenge classical theory's assumption that a free market economy is self-regulating.

---

[3] President Roosevelt invented the term *recession* at this time so that he would not have to call the 1937–1938 slump a "depression." Presidents ever since have found the term invaluable.

UPI/Bettmann Newsphotos

During the Depression, President Roosevelt set up many economic-relief programs, such as this W.P.A. water conservation project in South Dakota; programs like this created a large federal budget deficit.

Say's "Law of Markets." One of the most important classical theorists, Jean Baptiste Say (1767–1832), had argued in his so-called Law of Markets that "supply creates its own demand." This law presupposes that economies run in repetitive cycles. At the onset of the cycle, the supply of goods is plentiful and interest rates are low. (You must read to the end of the cycle to see why.) Consumers have little incentive to save their money, so they spend it. With spending high, business invests in new facilities to satisfy demand. Since businesses now apply for loans, the interest rate goes up. As it rises, consumers have more incentive to save their money, less to spend it. Banks have more money to lend to business; businesses have more money to invest. They do invest it, and the supply of goods and services goes up. Meanwhile, however, the consumers are saving their money, not spending it. Business finds itself with goods it cannot sell, so it begins slowing down production and cutting back on investment. Bankers then receive fewer requests for loans, so they lower interest rates. Consumers again have less incentive to save their money and start to spend it on the now-plentiful goods. Thus the cycle begins anew.

The Trouble with Thrift. Like most classical theories, the Law of Markets is simple, logical, beautiful. But it does not always work. In 1924, Dennis H. Robertson showed that high savings did not always produce new investment and that excess savings did not invariably raise consumer spending. Keynes took the next step. During depressions, he observed, consumers tended to save, not because interest rates were high but because they feared for their jobs. Savings exceeded the amounts that business wanted to invest and, worse, kept consumer spending low, so they only intensified the economy's downward spiral. In this event, savings "simply represented potential production" that went unproduced.[4]

Keynes reasoned that if economic relief could come from neither the thrift of individuals nor the profit seeking of business, it could come only from increased government spending, particularly on public-works projects. By hiring extra workers to construct public works, he argued, governments would end up generating additional jobs because their new employees would make the purchases that would, in turn, permit business to hire workers to produce those goods. These workers would spend their earnings on further goods, generating even more jobs in the private sector.

This so-called **multiplier effect** would not go on indefinitely, because there would be a certain leakage of money along the way as each newly employed worker put a certain amount of cash aside as savings. How large would the multiplier actually be? According to Keynes, that would depend on the volume of unused resources in the economy. If it is small, then extra government spending might raise prices, thereby generating domestic inflation. When the volume of unused resources is large—and in the 1930s it was—Keynes put the multiplier at about 1.5 or 2: For every two workers the government employed directly on public-works projects, a third worker would be reemployed by private business. Keynes claimed as well that public-works spending would cost about a third less than it seemed to, since the government would get some of its money back through taxes and would be able to cut spending on welfare and unemployment assistance.

The Revolution in Economic Policy

Keynes's *General Theory of Employment, Interest and Money* (1936) was an intellectual milestone of the twentieth century. It moved away from the lovely but largely theoretical constructions of classical economics and attempted to explain the actual workings of the private economy. Even more important, the *General Theory* proposed to manage free-enterprise economies to abolish the cycle of boom and bust, but not private property. He made full employment into a major and apparently realistic aim of public policy and invented modern macroeconomic management.

Demand-side Economics. Keynes, the father of **demand-side economics,** interpreted the Great Depression as a "demand crisis," an inability of consumers to buy the economy's full productive capacity. **Effective demand,** demand backed by money, was too low, so there was little incentive to produce more, little incentive to invest, and little incentive to hire. Keynes argued that at this stage of the business cycle, government should "prime the pump" by stimulating effective demand in a number of ways, including planned budget deficits. During economic booms, or upturns, however, the economy's problems were inflation and unsound speculation. At such times, Keynes thought, government should impose **countercyclical policy,** restraining the nation's "excesses" by running budget surpluses, curtailing credit, and

---

[4] Robert Lekachman, The Age of Keynes (New York: Random House, 1966), pp. 67-71.

even, if necessary, raising taxes. During booms, governments were to deflate, retrench, and restrain; during busts, to reflate, spend, and hire.

Economists now realize that it is much easier, politically, to stimulate demand by spending the government's money and cutting taxes than it is to curb demand by placing restraints upon borrowing and spending. Nowhere, perhaps, is this more true than in the United States, where a relatively weak and fragmented central government contends with powerful and effective interest groups (see Chapter 6).

Keynes in Action. President Roosevelt's advisers were not strongly influenced by Keynes until 1938, nor does it seem that Mr. Roosevelt himself ever fully accepted the idea of unbalanced budgets, deficit spending, and a larger national debt. "From a Keynesian standpoint," one sympathetic economist contends, Mr. Roosevelt's policies were "too timid, too wavering, and too often contradicted by other measures with quite different tendencies."[5] Huge government spending to build armaments and armed forces in World War II—not the New Deal—put an end to the Great Depression.

By the end of the war, there was little public support for the kinds of deflationary policies that had been usual in these circumstances. In 1946, Congress passed an employment act that called upon the federal government to create and maintain "useful employment opportunities." It also created the President's Council of Economic Advisers (see Chapter 11), which later played a key role in directing macroeconomic policy. Finally, it laid the groundwork for the use of Keynesian-style economic management. Modern fiscal policy had been born.

_____ MONETARY POLICY AND MONETARISM _____

Our economy, of course, is a money economy greatly dependent on credit, or borrowing. it is also therefore a debt economy. In the best of all possible worlds, the government would keep interest rates low enough to permit most would-be borrowers to borrow, so that enough money entered the economy to fund it and permit it to grow. But the real world often falls short of the best of all possible worlds.

In the days of the gold standard, the government defined the dollar's value in terms of gold—from 1837 to 1933, at $20.67 the troy ounce—and that valuation limited the amount of money the government could mint and print. Since the early 1970s, when the United States formally abandoned the gold standard, gold has been a commodity like any other; in the third quarter of 1982, for example, it traded at from $400 to $450 an ounce. For all practical purposes, the dollar has value merely because the government says it does, and because we accept that claim, not because it is backed by the gleaming power of gold. This kind of money is called **fiat money,** its value defined by government decree rather than by intrinsic worth.

In the past, fiat money (which has a very long history) aroused great skepticism because it was easily inflated to suit the interests and whims of government. Revolutionary America knew some of this skepticism, for an entirely fiat Continental currency financed that war. (The saying, "Not worth a

---

[5] Lekachman *The Age of Keynes*, p. 113.

Continental," persisted for at least a century afterward.) When James Madison, in *The Federalist*, Paper 10, describes the "rage for paper money" as one of the "wicked and improper projects" the Constitution had been designed to thwart, he was saying that the Framers hoped to eliminate fiat money from the American economy.

A Chaotic Banking Tradition

The Constitution gave Congress essentially unlimited powers to create money and regulate its value—and explicitly denied such powers to the states. Money is dispensed to the people chiefly through banks. At the prodding of Treasury Secretary Alexander Hamilton (1789–1795) one of the federal government's earliest acts was to charter the first Bank of the United States as the central banker for our capital-short republic. In those days, each state and private bank printed its own currency. A second Bank of the United States was chartered in 1816, five years after the first one lapsed. The second bank died in 1836, after President Andrew Jackson (1829–1837) vetoed an attempt to recharter it.

For about three decades, from the 1830s to the 1860s, an era of free enterprise in the most literal sense permitted every state-chartered bank to issue currency when and as it pleased. The United States came to be known as "the promised land of paper money." During the Civil War, Congress tried once again to establish a national banking system by permitting private banks to receive federal charters and by suppressing state bank notes.[6] But the federal banks could issue their own notes and were not subjected to any central coordination. When business was bad, they tended to reduce lending and cut down the amount and value of the notes they issued, which only made matters worse.

---

[6] Upheld by the Supreme Court in *Veazie Bank* v. *Fenno*, 8 Wall. 533 (1869).

Teri Leigh Stratford

The Federal Reserve System

The need for coordination, if not regulation, was clear, and by the turn of the century, bankers themselves recognized it. Congress came to the rescue in 1913. The Federal Reserve Act was a typical compromise between those who wanted a strong central bank and those who did not want any. It divided the United States into 12 Federal Reserve districts, each with a regional Federal Reserve Bank, but concentrated the system's national policy-making powers in a Board of Governors in Washington, D.C. As of 1985, about 5,806 (out of 15,023) commercial banks belonged to the system.[7] They control 71 percent of all American bank deposits.

Each of the 12 Federal Reserve banks[8] is headed by a board of 9 directors, 6 elected by the local member banks, 3 by the Fed Board in Washington. The regional directors choose the president of their local Federal Reserve Bank. The Federal Reserve Board in Washington consists of 7 members appointed by the President of the United States and confirmed by the Senate for 14-year terms. From among those 7, the President selects the board's chairman, who serves as its principal spokesman. The terms of the members are staggered, so that no President can appoint more than 2 of the 7 during any one term, except in the event of deaths or resignations. Fed Chairman Paul Volcker, who was appointed in 1979 by President Carter, continued in office under President Reagan.

The Federal Reserve Board meets in Washington, D.C.

What Is Money, Anyway? The Federal Reserve Board's main job is to adjust the flow of money in the United States. Yet experts do not agree among themselves just what money is. Purists would have the Fed track the amount of cash in circulation and in demand deposits (checking accounts) at commercial banks. Some economists think it should add checking accounts at savings banks and some or all savings accounts. Other economists would also include the deposits in money-market mutual funds,[9] because they are so easily convertible into cash, and some or all of the many other financial instruments invented in the 1970s.

The Fed has partly bypassed debate by offering an array of so-called **monetary aggregates,** or measures, each of which includes a different mix of financial instruments: M_1, M_2, M_3, and so on. To confuse matters further, new Ms are constantly added, and the old ones are sometimes redefined to keep up with the public's desperate appetite for new high-interest-earning financial vehicles that can easily be converted into cash.

The Fed's Monetary Tools. Whatever the definition of money, the Fed's basic long-term aim is to supply us with enough of it to buy all the goods and services the economy can produce. If we spend less money than that,

---

[7] In recent years, many state-chartered member banks have considered withdrawing from the Federal Reserve System, partly because they would then no longer have to comply with its requirement that they keep a cash reserve on deposit with the Federal Reserve, instead of investing it. Some banks have actually gone through the motions of withdrawal, which is quite legal under the compromise statute of 1913.

[8] The seal on the left front of every piece of paper currency tells you which of the twelve regional banks issued it.

[9] Money-market mutual funds are more or less like banks, in that investors deposit their money, earn interest, and can withdraw their money as they please. Money-market funds are regulated by laws that are much less restrictive than those that govern banks, and they can therefore offer higher interest.

production will decline and unemployment will rise. If we spend more, we pay higher prices for fewer goods and services. The general idea is to keep everyone who wants to work employed but to avoid stirring up inflation. The ideal state of affairs is called a "full employment equilibrium." To achieve it, the Fed has four major policy tools.

Reserve Requirements. Within certain statutory limits, the Federal Reserve Board can raise or lower the amount of cash reserves that member banks must keep on deposit with the Fed. If the Fed raises these reserve requirements, banks can lend less money, thus tightening credit and the supply of new money. If the Fed lowers reserves, banks can lend more, thereby making credit easier and putting more money into circulation.

The Discount Rate. A bank is a store that sells money. Like every other commodity, money and credit have a price, which we call the *interest rate.* The interest rate that member banks must pay to borrow from the Federal Reserve System is called the *discount rate.* Lowering it makes the cost of money cheaper for member banks and permits them to offer it to their customers more cheaply, too. Corporations and individuals then have more incentive to borrow, and economic activity—and, perhaps, inflation—heats up. Raising the discount rate has the opposite effect.

There is also a second, less well-publicized, side to the Fed's discount policy: The Federal Reserve has the power to limit the actual amount that member banks borrow. Both policies have a similar effect: When banks can borrow from the Fed, they can afford to lend that money to their own customers; when they cannot borrow, some of their own loan applicants must be turned down, and less money enters the economy.

Open-Market Operations. The Fed's most important policy tool is its ability to undertake so-called **open-market operations** by buying or selling government securities on a daily basis.

By early 1985, many billions of dollars in securities had been issued by the U.S. Treasury to finance federal budget deficits. These securities were held as investments by individuals, banks, insurance companies, and other corporations. When the Federal Reserve sells these securities to investors on the open market, it gets from them a check that is drawn on a commercial bank. The Fed collects on this check by reducing that bank's reserves. For the time being, that money is withdrawn from the economy. When the Fed buys back government securities, it pays for the purchase by a check drawn on its own accounts. The buyer then deposits that check at a commercial bank. Result: The bank in question can now make new loans and boost the money supply.

Margin Requirements. Since the 1930s, the Federal Reserve has also had the power to regulate margin requirements (the minimum down payment) for buying stocks and bonds. If the margin rate is 50 percent, for instance (as it is for stocks), you must pay at least half the purchase price of any stock you wish to buy; and in essence, you must borrow the rest from the broker. Lowering margin requirements has the effect of making credit easier; raising them has the opposite impact. For the Fed, however, this policy tool has been used not so much to control the money supply as to prevent the kind of speculative fever that helped produce the 1929 stock market crash.[10]

---

[10] Before the creation of the Securities and Exchange Commission (SEC) in 1934, investors could buy stocks on a 10 percent margin rate, buying often and driving stock prices up quickly on very little cash investment but taking profits in full. The market thus functioned till it went bankrupt, so it crashed.

Credit Controls. In early 1980, the U.S. inflation rate (calculated on an annual basis) was pushing 20 percent, and the Fed imposed a new range of credit controls: a stiff reserve requirement (15 percent) on the popular money-market mutual funds rules that made it harder to get and use credit cards, other efforts to hold down borrowing, and a requirement that American companies report any borrowing they intended to do overseas.

These credit controls had an immediate and momentous impact on consumer borrowing. Many banks, credit-card companies, and department stores increased the minimum monthly payments that consumers had to make on their accounts and shortened repayment times for major purchases. Unfortunately, all this coincided with (and probably provoked) the 1980 recession, so that many debt-ridden customers were pushed into personal bankruptcy.

The Fed soon lifted its credit controls, but memory of the credit crunch persisted. On the one hand, it may have cut the use of credit back to much healthier levels. On the other, credit-shy consumers may have slowed our recovery from the recession that began in the summer of 1981. A huge increase in debt-fueled consumer spending has produced every economic recovery since World War II. No such increase took place in 1982.

A Potent Political Force. The Federal Reserve was originally almost a service agency (see Chapter 12) designed to smooth out the bumps in the banking system, in part by providing banks and credit markets with ready money in

Stock certificates are issued to buyers of shares in a company. Since the 1930s, the Federal Reserve has had the power to regulate margin requirements for securities bought that way.

times of stress.. Eventually, the Fed evolved into an important policy maker, able and willing to stimulate and contract the economy. As it grew more powerful, so did its Board of Governors in Washington. But the system was and still is almost totally insulated from any kind of public accountability. Even its policy meetings are usually held behind closed doors, away from public scrutiny, and minutes are published months after major policy changes. Finally, and most importantly, many economists and politicians believe that the Fed promotes the interests of big business and big banking. It has certainly feared inflation much more than unemployment and has consistently bemoaned unbalanced budgets.

Volcker's Tight Rein. Just before the appointment of Paul Volcker as chairman of the Federal Reserve Board, in 1979, the Fed had been regulating interest rates directly and trying to keep them low enough to avoid much higher unemployment and lower consumer spending. That policy had the undesirable, though perhaps inevitable, side effect of fueling inflation. In October 1979, Chairman Volcker announced that the Fed would try to control the actual growth of the money supply instead of imposing an interest rate. The new policy influenced interest rates too, though indirectly, since the more money that may enter the economy, the lower interest rates will tend to be, and vice versa. In fact, the new policy raised interest rates and was meant to do so, and by 1982 the inflation rate was down to single digits. But high interest rates also deepened (and perhaps caused) a simultaneous, and quite severe recession. There was much debate about the causes of that recession, but no doubt at all that unemployment rates and business failures then rose to their highest levels since the late 1930s and that real, inflation-adjusted interest rates—the interest rate minus the inflation rate—reached their highest point since that same era.

The Fed's Independence. Like other independent regulatory agencies, the Fed is insulated not only from public opinion but also from the President and from Congress.[11] When possible, however, the Board of Governors clearly tries to accommodate the political branches of government, for the philosophy of "getting along by going along" runs deep in Washington. Then, too, what Congress gives it can always take away."[12] During 1984, some politicians—both liberal and conservative—were demanding that Congress require the Federal Reserve to target desired interest rates rather than growth in the money supply. These individuals believed that high interest rates posed more of a threat to economic growth than did fluctuations in the money supply.

Protecting Banks and Depositors

As the example of the Bank of United States shows, bank depositors were once expected to take risks, like everyone else. When banks failed, their

---

[11] In one respect, however, the Fed takes its orders from officials appointed by the President: when it buys and sells the dollar in foreign-exchange markets to affect the price of our currency relative to that of other nations (see Chapter 12).

[12] That statute has already been amended once, in 1934. The basic reason for the 1934 change was the desire to concentrate general decision-making power in the Board of Governors. During the 1920s, the governors of the New York Federal Reserve Bank had greater influence over policy making than the Board in Washington. The links between the New York governors and Wall Street, on the one hand, and the Bank of England, on the other, were notoriously close. The basic point of the 1934 reforms was to move the financial policy making center from Wall Street to Washington—for the first time—some would argue, by drastically reducing the autonomy of the regional Fed governors.

deposits could be wholly wiped out, and the bank's customers could do nothing. The result was that if a bank's solvency came into doubt, its depositors would rush to take their money out.

Banks never had enough cash on hand to pay off all their depositors. (They do not today, either.) So "runs" could, and did, bring down institutions that were perfectly sound and well managed. Financial panics could and did capsize the financial system. The last of these panics struck during the winter of 1932–1933. On March 6, 1933, President Roosevelt shut down the *entire* national banking system.

Insuring against Runs.   Congress had to respond. In 1934, it created the Federal Deposit Insurance Corporation (FDIC), which guaranteed deposits up to a limit ($100,000 per account, as of 1985). Depositors were given peace of mind, and so were banks, which were now less threatened by runs. The price for this peace of mind was more federal regulation, of course. Banks with federal charters were required to participate in the FDIC program, and state banks were permitted to participate if they met certain standards. Even most banks that do not belong to the Federal Reserve System accept examiners from the FDIC to qualify for the insurance. A parallel agency, the Federal Savings & Loan Insurance Corporation (FSLIC), guarantees deposits in savings and loan associations.

There is, however, a little-noted catch. Much as banks cannot simultaneously meet claims by all depositors, the FDIC and FSLIC would not have enough funds to reimburse all depositors in the event of a major bank collapse. Congress would have to appropriate additional funds—and would probably do so. These funds, of course, would have to come from either of two sources: additional taxes, which would mean that many people would in practice be reimbursing themselves for their own losses, or by printing whatever additional funds might be needed.

The latter course, which would generate inflation of very large proportions, is by no means inconceivable. The specter appeared to many people as they read of foreign countries' inability to meet payments on large loans from U.S. banks. By early 1985, the U.S. banks' troubles seemed somewhat alleviated by a series of bilateral agreements between banks and specific debtor nations. But these agreements still rest on the assumption that economies of the debtor nations will grow in the coming years. It is by no means obvious that such growth will occur or that anything less than severe austerity programs demanded by the International Monetary Fund will produce growth. Such austerity programs are intensely unpopular in debtor countries, where public opinion could be expressed in political and social uprisings. If that happens, the debtor governments may be the ones who are tempted to stop the rot by starting the presses.[13]

SETTING FISCAL POLICY

From the end of World War II to the early 1970s, John Maynard Keynes replaced the classical economists as the policy oracle of the U.S. government. Many **neo-Keynesians,** the followers of Keynes, had experienced the Depres-

---

[13] Martin Mayer, *The Fate of the Dollar* (New York: Signet, 1981).

sion at first hand. For them, the chief aim of national economic policy was to ensure that jobs would be available to anyone who wanted to work. More fundamentally, they urged the federal government to use its budget and tax policies to level the ups and downs of the business cycle, stimulate economic growth, and correct unbalanced international trade.

The years from 1945 to the early 1970s were a time of unprecedented prosperity and growth, both in the United States and abroad. To everyone but the most obdurate conservatives, the neo-Keynesians were largely responsible for this economic miracle. But the political priority of the neo-Keynesians—their insistence on holding down unemployment at almost any cost—helped fuel the inflation of the 1970s.[14] By 1981, when Ronald Reagan took office as President, Keynesian economics confronted a major challenge.

How Fiscal Policy Works

The federal budget affects the economy chiefly through *aggregate expenditure:* total spending by consumers, business, and the various levels of government. The simple truth is that "increased federal spending results in added income for someone."[15] For instance, when the federal government buys goods from a particular company, that company's income rises, and it can afford to hire additional workers to fill the government contract. Businesses and consumers can also choose to spend on themselves the extra income generated by government orders.

Tax policy, too, can affect private expenditure, since changes in the amount of taxes levied on individuals or business can raise or lower their disposable (after-tax) income. Lower levels of government spending tend to lower output and employment; higher government spending does the opposite.

By fiddling with the mix of spending and tax policies, the government can change the economy's direction. Say that effective demand for goods and services is higher than the economy's output, even under full employment. More and more dollars then chase an unchanging quantity of goods: inflation. The reverse, too, may happen: Private spending may not keep up with the volume of goods that enter the economy. Federal officials might propose five combinations of tax and spending changes to produce a better match between demand and output at full employment: (1) reduce government purchases of goods and services, without changing tax rates; (2) increase tax rates, without changing the level of government purchases; (3) simultaneously reduce spending and raise tax rates; (4) reduce both spending and taxes; and (5) raise spending, while increasing taxes.[16] Making and implementing such decisions is called **fine-tuning** the economy.

The Politics of Spending

From the 1870s to 1929 and, again, from 1947 to about 1960, about 75 percent of all federal spending was concentrated in a few traditional areas that generated little controversy: national defense, foreign affairs, general ex-

---

[14] In part, because the deflationary side of neo-Keynesianism was not applied in times of economic expansion.

[15] David J. and Attiat F. Ott, *Federal Budget Policy* (Washington, D.C.: The Brookings Institution, 1977), p. 80.

[16] Ott, *Federal Budget Policy*, pp. 85–86.

Table 16-2 The Changing Composition of the Federal Budget: Selected Categories as a Percentage of All Federal Outlays, 1940–1987

YEAR	DEFENSE, INTERNATIONAL RELATIONS, AND SPACE	HEALTH	EDUCATION	INCOME SECURITY	ALL OTHER
1940	15.7%	0.5%	0.7%	14.7%	68.4%
1941	43.1	0.4	1.0	11.3	44.2
1942	71.7	0.2	0.5	4.0	23.6
1943	82.9	0.1	2.5	1.4	13.1
1944	84.0	0.2	0.2	1.1	14.5
1945	86.4	0.2	0.2	1.2	12.0
1946	77.3	0.3	0.2	4.1	18.1
1947	48.4	0.4	0.3	7.6	43.3
1948	48.8	0.4	0.5	7.7	42.6
1949	46.2	0.4	0.4	8.6	44.4
1950	40.1	0.6	0.5	10.5	48.3
1951	55.2	0.6	0.5	9.3	34.4
1952	66.8	0.5	0.5	7.4	24.8
1953	67.0	0.4	0.5	7.8	24.3
1954	65.7	0.4	0.6	10.6	22.7
1955	60.7	0.4	0.8	13.1	25.0
1956	59.2	0.5	0.9	13.6	25.8
1957	58.4	0.6	0.9	14.7	25.4
1958	56.2	0.6	1.0	17.8	24.4
1959	52.9	0.7	0.9	18.3	27.2
1960	52.2	0.8	1.1	19.3	26.6
1961	51.3	0.9	1.2	21.2	25.4
1962	51.9	1.0	1.3	20.6	25.2
1963	51.0	1.2	1.3	20.8	25.7
1964	50.8	1.4	1.4	20.6	25.8
1965	48.6	1.4	1.9	21.1	27.0
1966	48.7	1.8	3.1	21.0	25.4
1967	49.3	4.1	3.6	19.2	23.8
1968	49.0	5.2	3.7	18.6	23.5
1969	47.0	6.1	3.4	19.9	23.6
1970	43.2	6.4	3.6	21.6	25.2
1971	38.2	6.7	4.1	25.2	25.8
1972	35.5	7.3	4.9	26.6	25.7
1973	31.9	7.3	4.6	28.1	28.1
1974	30.5	7.7	4.1	29.5	28.2
1975	29.4	8.1	4.5	31.9	26.1
1976	26.0	8.8	4.8	33.4	27.0
1977	25.7	9.1	5.1	32.7	27.4
1978	24.8	9.4	5.7	31.3	28.8
1979	24.8	9.6	6.0	31.0	28.6
1980	25.4	9.7	5.5	32.5	26.9
1981	25.2	9.9	6.3	33.2	25.4
1982	27.2	9.9	3.6	37.2	22.1
1983	28.2	10.0	3.3	38.1	20.4
1984	29.3	10.3	3.2	35.8	21.4
1985*	29.2	10.3	3.2	34.7	22.6
1986*	32.0	10.5	3.0	34.2	20.3
1987*	33.6	10.5	2.7	34.1	19.1

* Estimated

penses (including salaries), interest payments on the public debt, and veterans' benefits.

By 1939, during the New Deal, emergency relief programs made it necessary to cut traditional expenditures to 30 percent of the budget. These emergency relief items were always reported, in italics, as temporary. And they were; the last of them ended in 1943.

By that time, the budget patterns of the 1930s had been reversed by World War II. After the war, the United States, the new leader of a world wide military and diplomatic alliance, continued to spend heavily on defense, foreign aid, and related programs (see Chapter 17). From the late 1940s through the late 1960s, national-security expenditures (defense, international relations, and the space program) made up about one-half to three-fifths of the entire federal budget, and they accounted for nearly 10 percent, and sometimes a bit more, of the country's GNP.

Shifting Priorities. Government spending embodies a political system's priorities. The priorities of our political system changed radically in recent decades. With the coming of the Reagan administration, in 1981, they changed once again.

Until the 1960s, the federal government had almost no programs to aid health and education. Income security, mostly Social Security (see Chapter 15), accounted in 1960 for less than half its 1980 share of the budget and of GNP. The shift from the warfare–welfare state to the welfare–warfare state began in the late 1960s. President Lyndon Johnson's Great Society expanded the budget share spent on welfare and on **entitlements,** the whole range of benefits—including Social Security, Medicare, Aid to Families with Dependent Children, and unemployment and disability insurance—that qualified citizens are "entitled" to by law (see Chapters 3 and 15).

A few years later the Vietnam War finally came to an end, and detente with the Soviet Union and China (see Chapter 17) produced quite drastic reductions in defense spending, relative to all other items of expenditure as a share of GNP. In 1972, for the first time in postwar history, spending on income security, health, and education surpassed national defense outlays, and by 1977, the traditional expenditures accounted for only 39 percent of the total budget.

Guns or Butter? Bear in mind that this **welfare shift** did not hugely increase the share of GNP absorbed by the federal budget; from 1976 to 1981, that share was a bit higher than 22 percent, compared with 19 percent in the period from 1958 to 1967. To be sure, it was only 3 percent of GNP in 1929. But the real—and explosive—political question is not the size of the federal budget but rather its composition. The federal budget's share of GNP did not rise dramatically after 1970, mainly because relatively higher domestic spending was mostly offset by relatively lower defense spending. If we allocated about 10 percent of our GNP for defense, as we did from 1955 to 1975, and did not trim domestic spending, the federal government's "take" of the GNP would be 27 percent, not 22 percent. The share of the total public sector (including state and local spending) would be pushing 40 percent.

Even at that level, the total share of our GNP absorbed by the public sector would remain significantly below the levels in almost all other industrial democracies but Japan. Many Americans would find those levels hard to accept. In addition, many people—not only conservatives—think that defense outlays must rise above their late-1970s troughs.

Table 16–3 Federal Government Receipts: Selected Years, 1795–1984

RECEIPTS AS PERCENTAGE OF TOTAL RECEIPTS

YEAR	CUSTOMS	PUBLIC LAND SALE	INTERNAL REVENUE					ALL OTHER RECEIPTS	TOTAL RECEIPTS ($ THOU-SANDS)
			Individual	Corporate	Employ-ment Tax	Others (mostly excise)	Total I.R.		
1795	91.4%	0%	0%	0%	0%	5.5%	5.5%	3.1%	6,115
1816	76.2	3.6	0	0	0	10.7	10.7	9.5	47,678
1836	46.1	48.9	0	0	0	0	0	5.0	50,827
1860	94.9	3.2	0	0	0	0	0	2.0	56,065
1866	32.1	0.2	20.0	0	0	35.4	55.4	12.4	558,033
1885	56.1	1.8	0	0	0	34.8	34.8	7.4	323,691
1905	48.1	0.9	0	0	0	43.0	43.0	8.0	544,275
1916	27.2	0.2	8.7	7.3	0	49.6	65.5	7.0	782,535
1925	14.5	0.0	22.4	24.2	0	21.9	68.5	17.0	3,780,149
1939	5.6	0.0	18.2	20.4	13.1	39.4	91.1	3.3	5,667,823
									($ millions)
1945	0.7	0	36.7	32.6	6.9	13.0	89.2	10.2	50,162
1960	1.2	0	44.0	23.2	15.9	14.4	97.5	1.3	92,492
1970	1.3	0	46.7	6.9	23.4	10.0	97.0	1.8	193,743
1980	1.4	0	46.9	12.4	30.9	5.9	96.2	2.5	520,051
1984	1.7	0	44.4	8.5	36.3	6.5	95.7	2.6	666,457

Finally, GNP was growing slowly, very slowly. Even before Ronald Reagan's election it was clear that a bitter budget struggle, turning on guns versus butter, was imminent.[17] The policy choices of the Reagan administration have only—though very considerably—speeded up and embittered that struggle.

Taxation

Like other good things, government has a price, and the money comes out of our pockets. One source of income is the money the government collects for some of its services—for example, the fee you pay when issued a passport. Another source is the levying of tariffs on goods imported from foreign countries. From about 1840 to 1930, the tariff generated most of the government's income. It was also a way of protecting American industry from foreign competition and therefore a source of bitter political controversy (see Chapter 15).

Individuals Foot the Bill. At present, by far the biggest source of government revenue is the individual American wage earner, for the more the government spends, the more taxes it must levy and the broader its base of taxation must be. Federal spending has skyrocketed since 1929, making the revenue from tariffs inadequate. Only income taxes—income taxes on individuals—could sustain the new level of spending. Such taxes now raise almost half of all federal revenues. The United States had no individual income taxes until 1863,

[17] Walter Dean Burnham, "American Politics in the 1980s," *Dissent*, Spring 1980.

It is not income, but taxable income, that gets taxed. At present, the biggest source of government revenues comes from the individual wage earner.

during the Civil War. The taxes lapsed in the 1870s and were declared unconstitutional by the U.S. Supreme Court in 1895.[18] In 1913, just in time for World War I, the Sixteenth Amendment to the Constitution gave Congress the clear right to levy such taxes, and it has levied them ever since. Most of our working population did not pay income taxes until 1942–1943, however, at the height of World War II, when the government started the practice of withholding taxes from salary checks—"pay-as-you-go" collection.

The first income tax was levied at a rate ranging from a flat 1 percent on incomes up to $200,000 (in today's values) to a maximum of 7 percent on incomes of $500,000 and over. At present our system is progressive, that is, tax rates rise with individual incomes. In fact, however, it is not income, but taxable income, that is taxed; and the well-to-do are well supplied with loopholes for reducing their taxable income. Liberal economists think that these loopholes should be closed so that the tax burden falls most heavily on those best able to bear it, and so that the rest of our people have enough after-tax income to buy the goods and services that business and industry produce. Conservatives argue that lower taxation for the well-to-do promotes investment and, therefore, employment and output.

Corporate Income Taxes. Until the end of World War II, the corporate income tax often raised as much revenue as the personal income tax did. Ever since, the corporate bite has relaxed, falling from 7 percent of GNP (30 percent of federal revenues) in 1945 to only 1.6 percent (8.5 percent) in 1984 and 1.7 percent (9.0 percent) estimated in 1985.

Many economists—by no means all of them conservative—think that corporate taxes cannot be made "progressive," since corporations always pass expenses on to consumers, in the form of higher prices. In effect, the corporate income tax is a kind of sales tax.

---

[18] *Pollock* v. *Farmers' Loan Trust Co.,* 158 U.S. 601 (1895).

Social Security and Excise Taxes. Many poorer Americans pay more money in FICA, or Social Security taxes, than in personal income taxes. Constantly increasing benefits have required constantly higher taxes. Yet the Social Security system is still in trouble; around the year 2010, recipients will come rather close to equaling the number of active workers who pay into the fund, (see Chapter 15).

Excise Taxes. Some of the most spectacular early political battles in American history were provoked by the levying of excise (luxury) taxes, derisively called "nuisance" and even "sin" taxes. They are more difficult and expensive to collect than income taxes, and proposals to raise them or extend them to additional products regularly bring out floods of hostile lobbyists. Federal excise taxes are today levied on liquor, tobacco, telephones, air travel, gasoline, and other so-called luxury items.

Deficit Financing

The federal budget last ran a surplus in fiscal 1969. Since then, the government has run a deficit every year. In fact, there have been 19 budget deficits in the past 20 years, 32 since 1945 and 45 since 1932. All these budget shortfalls taken together have produced a national debt now in excess of $1 trillion.

Do these deficits betoken a national crisis of fiscal morality? Public opinion seems to think so (see Chapter 7). Some economists argue that the national debt is owed to ourselves rather than to foreigners, since it has been financed chiefly by selling U.S. Treasury notes and bonds to Americans. As a share of GNP, the national debt has steadily declined. During the first term of President Reagan, however, this direction was reversed. Debt was 44 percent of GNP in 1984 and projected to reach 52 percent by 1988.

Conversely, the budgets of state and local governments run at a considerable surplus. Federal, state, and local governments as a whole ran budget surpluses during several years in the 1970s, including 1979. Even the federal budget has been in surplus, or very slightly in deficit, when the economy flourished, but it ran a clear deficit when it was in recession. Because this pattern approximates the Keynesian model of budgetary policy, it cannot unarguably be said that the deficit is out of control—at least it seems that it was not until 1981.

A Lot of Interest. The early 1980s were years of very high interest rates. By mid-1982, the federal funds rate—the interest rate paid out to people who bought federal bonds—had risen to almost 15 percent, compared with a high of about 8 percent in 1978. Although the federal funds rate dropped back to 11.6 percent in mid-1984 and 8.4 percent by year's end, real interest rates (the rate over and above the inflation rate) was still high. Financing the national debt had become a burden, though not so much of a burden that the federal government could not borrow whatever money it needed. Unlike the revenue-earning power of a private company, the taxing power of the federal government is unlimited. When the pool of lendable funds is not expanding very fast and the demand for credit is high, the federal government can bid up the interest rate to entice enough capital to meet its needs.

Private industry can be crowded out of credit markets. In the early 1980s, projections of future federal budget deficits rose dramatically, and many economists and businesspeople feared that such a crowding out was imminent. Their fears vanished by mid-1982, when industry's borrowing fell as business declined in a recession. Two years later, by mid-1984 when business investment picked up during the recovery, crowding out once again became a concern. The economy itself is vulnerable. Huge federal deficits now loom ahead as far as anyone can see; and if federal and industrial borrowing both drive up interest rates, economic growth could be stunted.

CONTEMPORARY PROBLEMS AND ISSUES: THE REAGAN YEARS

By Election Day 1980, it was clear that the U.S. economy was sick. Corporate profits were down, and the savings rate (a key to capital formation and investment) was much lower here than in most other countries. Inflation had climbed into the double-digit range and at one point earlier in the year had bumped dangerously close to 20 percent. Growth in U.S. labor's output per hour, a key measure of productivity, fell from 2.9 percent a year (1960–1969) to 0.7 percent (1974–1979) and then rose to only 1.6 percent (1980–1984). That is a drop of more than 75 percent, one that prefigured stagnation even before the slump began in 1981. For every extra dollar that business paid its workers, it was getting a much smaller increase than it had in the past, and our goods were becoming less competitive in world markets.

Just as troubling was the growth of real interest rates (interest rates minus the rate of inflation) to historically unprecedented levels. These levels were so high that corporations were finding it more and more difficult to cover them and still make a profit. Long-term investment in new plant and machinery was now hard to justify, so corporate resources were diverted into short-term projects for which returns were more easily calculated. Billions upon billions of dollars were spent by companies in unproductive bids to acquire one another.

The Monetarist Challenge

What had gone awry? Neo-Keynesianism received what was perhaps undue credit for the economic expansion that took place immediately after World War II. Now it was asked to take much of the blame for the marked slowdown that had set in since the mid-1970s.

The Phillips Curve. The economy resisted all efforts at fine-tuning. The neo-Keynesian fine-tuners thought they had found an inverse, or opposite, relationship between unemployment and inflation—lower levels of unemployment lead to higher but stable levels of inflation, and higher levels of unemployment lead to lower but stable levels of inflation. Government officials could literally trade off a certain level of inflation for the level of unemployment they wished to achieve, and vice versa. This idea is based on the Phillips curve.

The stability of that trade-off has long been challenged by the monetarists, who argue that once started, both inflation and deflation tend to progress uncontrollably. As a result, they are more fearful of inflation than the neo-Keynesians tend to be, and monetarists tend to support policies that limit economic growth by restricting the money supply. **Monetarism,** like neo-

Keynesianism, is a theory of demand management. But where neo-Keynesians emphasize expanding and contracting demand by manipulating the size of the federal deficit, the monetarists emphasize expanding or contracting the money supply. When the money supply contracts, interest rates rise; business find it harder to borrow and, therefore, to invest and to hire additional workers. Companies that are losing money cannot borrow in order to keep those workers they already have. Unemployment rises, and unemployed workers spend less money than employed ones do. As demand falls, so do prices. Workers who keep their jobs are scared. They demand smaller wage increases—if they demand any at all—and this, too, cuts any increase in the costs that business must pass along to consumers. During the Nixon and Ford administrations (1969–1974 and 1974–1977, respectively), monetarism was embraced by the "establishment" faction of the Republican party (see Chapter 9). President Carter, a Democrat who often acted like a Republican, applied monetarism, also, as he approached the end of his presidency.

Supply-Side Economics

The monetarists, although associated with restrictive economic policies, would propose to increase the money supply in suitable circumstances. For them, however, suitable circumstances must include cuts in government expenditure or higher taxes. Unlike the neo-Keynesians, they do not believe in deficit financing. As for the neo-Keynesians, we associate them chiefly with expansionary policies, yet their theory requires the government to cut expenditures or raise taxes during a boom. The expansionary side of Keynes's medicine proved much easier to take than the restrictive side, for it is much easier to propose, appropriate, and spend than to cut back.

From the point of view of almost all politicians, both neo-Keynesianism and monetarism were defective, since both, in certain circumstances, required spending cuts or higher taxes or both. Monetarism had the additional defect, even for many conservatives, of producing high interest rates, and although these interest rates could cut inflation, they could also increase unemployment and cause recessions. It is not at all surprising that many conservatives wanted a new and less painful alternative to neo-Keynesianism. "Seek and ye shall find." The result was supply-side economics.

According to the adherents of this view—who are more numerous among politicians than among economists—the problems of the 1970s resulted from the federal government's attempt to control only the demand side of the economy. The key to restoring corporate profits, they said, was to cut taxes in order to spur business investment and consumer savings, and to eliminate as much government regulation of business as possible. Arthur Laffer (of the University of Southern California), a leader of the pure supply-siders, believed that lower tax levels would stimulate investment and raise the GNP, thereby generating as much tax revenue as higher levels did.[19] Spending cuts would not be needed; neither would high interest rates. As an extra benefit, the higher volume of production would tip the balance of supply and demand toward supply, so inflation would be cut or even halted.

It was this theory, more than any other, that formed the intellectual backdrop for the massive three-year tax cut that President Reagan proposed and Congress adopted in 1981.

---

[19] This had actually happened, unintentionally, under President John F. Kennedy (1961–1963).

A Look at the Fairness Issue

What we have today is government of the rich, by the rich and for the rich.

Walter F. Mondale

No matter how the U.S. economy performs between now and Election Day, the Democrats will challenge Ronald Reagan's economic policies on the fundamental ground of fairness—and the polls suggest that candidate Reagan is somewhat vulnerable to this favorite Democratic theme. Since his election in 1980, the percentage of Americans who believe that Ronald Reagan cares about people like *them* has steadily declined, and even some Republicans think their president is biased toward the rich. As a result, the "fairness issue" offers Mondale and the Democrats a target on Reagan's flank.

Last week the Urban Institute, a respected nonpartisan research organization based in Washington, D.C., gave them some new ammunition. "The Reagan Record," a new study based on three years of cross-disciplinary analysis, is a judicious and systematic examination of the administration's accomplishments in all areas of domestic policy. Quite properly, it praises Reagan for reversing the precipitous decline in consumer confidence during the Carter adminis-

tration, and it gives him partial credit (the Federal Reserve Board gets the lion's share) for reducing inflation. But the book's 13 authors and editors are critical of Reaganomics, and their research suggests that the fairness issue is more than partisan rhetoric. For one thing, they argue that Reagan's policies needlessly exacerbated the impact of the 1981–1982 recession. And they conclude that Reaganomics—combined with the recession—has widened the gap between rich and poor.

Inequality: The crux of their argument is an analysis of changes in family income between 1980 and 1984—and the bottom line, after taxes and inflation are taken into account, is a small but significant trend toward inequality. Over all, the average family income, adjusted for inflation, rose from $20,333 to $21,038, or 3.5 percent, during the past four years. But the trend is less positive when the family-income data is broken down by quintiles—into five statistically equal groups from the richest fifth to the poorest fifth.

By that measure, the richest fifth got richer: its relative share of total family income rose from 37 percent to 38.9 percent, and its average income climbed from $37,618 to $40,880. The next richest

Reaganomics

In the space of a century, economics appears to have come full circle. A good part of what the supply-side economists propose is a return to laissez faire, including the gold standard. One of their earliest converts was Ronald Reagan. As President, Mr. Reagan propounded his own version of supply-side economics, one that was rapidly dubbed "Reaganomics."

From the supply-siders, Mr. Reagan took the idea of massive tax cuts, primarily for corporations and wealthy individuals, carrying a price tag of $750 billion or so. Cutting the taxes of the rich was not an end in itself but a means of giving them extra capital to invest. If they actually did so, the result would be new factories, new machinery—and new jobs.

Unlike the supply-siders, however, Mr. Reagan proposed to cut funding for entitlement programs. His administration argued that those programs were responsible for much of the federal budget deficit, and that the deficit, in turn, was responsible for inflation. You will remember that the supply-siders had argued that the tax cuts would generate extra revenue and therefore make budget cuts unnecessary. It was the monetarists who emphasized the need for budget cuts. In fact, many important members of Mr. Reagan's economic team were monetarists, not supply-siders. These administration monetarists also supported the efforts of the Federal Reserve Board—strongly criticized by the supply-siders—to hold down the growth of the money supply. Many

fifth—the "upper middle class"—stayed dead even in income share. The other three-fifths lost ground: the middle fifth's share declined from 18.5 percent to 18.1 percent, the second lowest fifth dropped from 13.2 percent to 12.5 percent and the poorest fifth fell from a 6.8 percent share to 6.1 percent. Moreover, the two bottom fifths also lost ground in absolute terms: family income for the second-lowest quintile dropped from $13,391 to $13,163, and from $6,913 to $6,391 for the bottom fifth.

The income shift "may not at first glance seem very large," the study's authors write, "but it represents a very large transfer of disposable income to the top quintile group . . . of $25 billion overall and translates into an extra $2,000 per family" for the most affluent fifth. Furthermore, as the authors note, this is the first such shift since the mid-1960s.

The causes of that shift are complex, and Reagan's spending policies are far from the only factor affecting family income. Indeed, the authors conclude that "the social safety net remains largely intact," although cutbacks in food stamps, welfare and other safety-net programs contributed to reducing the family income of the poor. Over all, the study argues, the double-digit unemployment of the 1981–82 recession is probably the biggest single reason why the poor have lost ground. And though the well-to-do have gained the most from Reagan's 1981 tax cuts,

the study concludes that the overall tax burden on Americans has actually risen, not dropped, since 1980. The reason: for most, Reagan's cuts in income-tax rates have been canceled out by rising local, state and social-security taxes.

Like any study of a complex reality, the Urban Institute report is based on methodological strategies that affect its findings. One such choice is the authors' reliance on data from census surveys. Those statistics do not include a variety of transfer payments, such as Medicare and company fringe benefits, that tend to brighten the picture. Government surveys that include such benefits show a 10.3 percent jump in per capita income during the same four years—almost three times the rise in average family income. Still, the overall pattern is troubling to many Americans—and at the weekend, Reagan himself criticized such studies as the work of "pessimists" who have been consistently "wrong" about his policies. He also complained that news stories on the Urban Institute study had ignored the fact that the elderly, at least, enjoyed healthy income gains over the past four years—and if nothing else, his reaction suggested that the fairness issue is still alive in campaign '84.

Tom Morganthau, "A Look at the Fairness Issue," *Newsweek*, August 27, 1984, p. 33. © 1984 by Newsweek, Inc. All rights reserved. Reprinted by permission.

economists believed that the Reagan administration was following a monetarist policy and supporting it with supply-side rhetoric.

The spending side of the Reagan program was not consistently monetarist, however. Entitlement programs were only one cause of the federal deficit. Another was the very high increase in defense spending the administration proposed. How then to cut the deficit? The Reagan administration supported the movement for a constitutional amendment requiring the federal budget to be kept in balance except during declared wars or when 60 percent majorities in both houses voted for a deficit. This proposal nicely closes the circle of conservative macroeconomic policy; if adopted, it would prevent the use of neo-Keynesian economic techniques by national policy makers.

A Deficit to Beat All Deficits. Oddly enough, the same Ronald Reagan who supported such an amendment ended up presiding over the highest peacetime budget deficit in U.S. history—one that rose well above $120 billion in 1982 and was estimated at $178.50 billion for 1985. Even when adjusted downward for inflation, that sum was twice as large as all federal spending in 1940, including the cost of the New Deal's relief programs.

What had gone wrong? To begin with, the Reaganomics tax cuts, which had gone into effect in mid-1981, *cut* the federal government's revenue instead of adding to it, as planned. On the spending side, the cost of Social Security had risen from $64 billion in 1975 to $155 billion in 1982, but the Senate refused to limit benefits for fear of the voting power of the elderly. (See

**Table 16–4 Size of the Budget and Its Composition,
Fiscal Years 1979 and 1981–1986**

BUDGET COMPONENT	1979	1981	1982	1983	1984	PROJECTED 1985	1986
Share of GNP:							
National defense	4.9%	5.5%	6.1%	6.5%	6.4%	6.6%	6.8%
Payments for individuals	9.9	11.2	11.7	12.3	11.2	11.0	10.5
Net interest	1.8	2.4	2.8	2.8	3.1	3.4	4.0
Other nondefense outlays	5.6	5.4	4.8	4.6	4.1	4.6	3.3
Offsetting undistributed receipts	−0.7	−1.0	−0.9	−1.1	−0.9	−0.8	−0.9
Total outlays	21.3	23.5	24.5	25.1	23.8	24.8	23.2
Total receipts	19.7	20.8	20.3	18.6	18.6	19.0	18.9
Deficit	−1.2	−2.0	−3.6	−6.1	−4.9	−5.4	−4.3
Share of Total Outlays:							
National defense	23.1	23.2	24.8	26.0	26.7	26.5	29.3
Payments for individuals	46.2	47.7	47.8	48.9	46.9	44.6	45.5
New interest	8.5	10.1	11.4	11.1	13.0	13.6	17.4
Other nondefense outlays	26.4	23.1	19.4	18.2	17.1	18.7	14.3
Offsetting undistributed receipts*	−3.5	−4.1	−3.5	−4.2	−3.8	−3.4	−3.9
Total outlays	100.0	100.0	100.0	100.0	100.0	100.0	100.0

*Includes the following receipts which are not distributed by function in the budget: the federal contribution to the employee retirement fund, rents and royalties on the outer continental shelf lands, and receipts from disposition of federal surplus property.

Source: Budget of the United States Government, Fiscal Year 1986, pp. 9–58, 9–59. Figures are rounded.

Chapter 15 for a longer account of the Social Security problem and Mr. Reagan's efforts to deal with it.) Meanwhile, Mr. Reagan proposed a 17 percent increase in expenditures from 1981 to 1982, with similarly high increases in the following years (see Table 17–2 in Chapter 17).

The Reagan administration suddenly found itself blamed for the deepest recession in postwar history. Inflation went down dramatically, falling to an annual rate of between 6 percent and 7 percent by late summer 1982. That decline, however, was partly the result of very high real interest rates, which deprived many companies of cash and helped raise business bankruptcies to the highest levels since the Depression. By the fall, unemployment pushed past 10 percent, and most economists were forecasting that it would stay at that level for at least another year, even if the recession ended.

The Debate. By changing the direction of the government's economic policy, Ronald Reagan provoked a national debate about the causes of this country's economic malaise. Not everyone was convinced that Keynesian policies and government spending were at fault. This country's tax burden is quite low compared with that of almost all other advanced capitalist countries. Total U.S. tax revenues—local, state, and federal—were 26.9 percent of GNP in 1966—admittedly much higher than the 10 percent of GNP that Americans paid to all levels of government in 1929. Yet in 1966, the United States ranked no higher than 15th among 23 advanced capitalist nations. By 1976, the United States had fallen to 18th place. Even more remarkably, the percentage by which our levels of taxation had changed during those 10 years—the Great Society years of growth in domestic entitlement programs—was actually the

"Reindustrialization"

Ours is not the only country that has suffered from inflation and underinvestment over the past decade. Many economists now contend that the stagnation of the late 1970s and 1980s resulted from a worldwide revolution. The Western countries, in this view, could no longer compete with Japan and certain Third World countries, notably Korea, in manufacturing industries—steel, automobiles, and textiles. To survive, they would have to move their economies into such services as finance, medicine, and computer software. This massive shift upset the structure of the Western economies—jobs, investment capital, and support systems—much as the industrial revolution did. But how shall we deal with these changes?

Some, including President Reagan, say that the market will do the job. Others, including economists and businesspeople, call for a national policy of reindustrialization to raise the national productivity by encouraging automation, job-retraining programs, increased cooperation between labor and management, and the movement of businesses into high-growth industries. Still other economists argue that a radical reconstruction of the economic order is called for, a reconstruction going far beyond Keynesian prescriptions. They are only a minority, but they are more numerous and influential than they have been for decades—a fact that reflects the gravity of the economic situation today.

lowest among all 23 nations. Among the advanced industrial countries, only Japan had a lower overall tax burden in 1976. Despite the widespread belief that government spending is out of control, the fundamental conflict between liberals and conservatives has turned much more on the *composition* of federal spending than on its *size*. For *whom* and for *what* should money be spent? These are the basic questions of politics today.

If high taxes and government spending are not the cause of our present economic discontents, what is? Let's go back to 1939, when federal budget outlays accounted for only 9.7 percent of GNP. Interest rates were in the neighborhood of 1 percent. Yet 1939 was not a good year for the economy. Business did not stampede to the credit markets to borrow money at these nominal rates. Why not? Because there was something missing: the opportunity for profitable investment. Without such opportunities, investment will not occur. And why were there no such opportunities? The neo-Keynesians argue that business was not eager to borrow and invest because demand was feeble. No demand, no sales. The recession that began in 1981 seemed to show that tax cuts, like low interest rates, have no magic power to stimulate investment—not, at least, as quickly as the Reagan administration had hoped.

Economists of the left stress that underconsumption seems to plague private-enterprise economies. The capacity to produce goods and services tends to outstrip the capacity of most consumers to buy them at prevailing price levels. Much of modern big government has been created to overcome underconsumption. But some kinds of government spending tend to do so less than others. For instance, military spending does generate demand, cash flows, and profits. But this spending, as it enriches particular parts of the private economy, does not produce goods and services that can be purchased by consumers, and its beneficiaries tend to be relatively few in number. Welfare and income-maintenance programs derive in part from altruism and "politics," but they also generate income for millions of people who would otherwise not be able to push the wheels of industry by consuming its products. By stimulating demand, they give business an incentive to invest, and thus to hire.

The last general crisis of consumption was the Great Depression, in the 1930s. Already, the 1980s resemble that earlier decade in two basic ways. First, both decades began with severe and protracted economic crises. Second, they began with large and comprehensive attempts to change the basis of public policy. Such periods differ fundamentally from quieter times. Conflict becomes more common and bitter. Ideological politics goes on the march. Nothing can any longer be taken for granted; "politics as usual" goes up in smoke; almost everyone, ends up taking sides. Politicians propose and carry out comprehensive policy changes. Reaganomics—whatever you may think about it—is surely and by a wide margin the most comprehensive and controversial change in American public policy in the past fifty years.

SUMMARY

Whatever may have caused our current economic problems, the solutions to them clearly will involve economic and political trade offs. As Lester Thurow, an economist at the Massachusetts Institute of Technology points out, today's economic policy making, like chess, is a "zero-sum" game, where the gains of winners can come only at the expense of losers. Only at a time of economic growth can economic policy making be a "positive-sum game," a game in which most players can win. It might well be possible to cut inflation to the vanishing point. But there would be a price: a sharp contraction of economic activity, higher unemployment, and human misery on a grand scale. *Cui bono:* Who gains? And who loses? The people who worry most about inflation are clearly the well-to-do. The poor worry about unemployment. Keynesian policies therefore fit more easily into a liberal political framework than do monetarist or supply-side theories, which are politically conservative in their assumptions and effects.

Before the twentieth century, laissez-faire theories and the self-adjusting mechanism of the gold standard permitted governments to ignore such trade offs or, rather, to make them without realizing that they had been made. Economics was then thought to be part of the natural order of things. Government officials had responsibility only for maintaining law and order, national defense, and balancing the budget. The self-regulating mechanisms of the market and the gold standard did the rest.

John Maynard Keynes tried to undermine the theoretical basis of laissez faire, and he worked out the practical mechanisms by which governments could control the bumps in the business cycle. In fact, however, it was the Depression and the massive unemployment it produced that undermined laissez faire in practice. Most people now expect government actively to promote prosperity, and they punish political leaders who fail to deliver the goods.

Now that economic policy in the active sense has been brought into being, we must decide what kind of policy we shall have. No policy can benefit all groups equally, and many policies benefit some groups at the expense of others. Economic management is more a question of deciding which group to favor than of choosing the correct technical means of achieving any goal. The future of economic policy making in the next few years will hang on the balance of political forces.

SUGGESTED READINGS

BRUCE BARTLETT, *Reaganomics: Supply-Side Economics in Action*. Westport, Conn.: Arlington House, 1981. An advocacy treatment of Reaganomics by someone who has worked with Representative Jack Kemp (R-N.Y.), a leading proponent of supply-side economics.

JAMES M. BUCHANAN, *Democracy in Deficit*. Charlottesville: Univ. of Virginia, 1977. Neo-Keynesianism's inflationary implications.

MARTIN CARNOY and DEREK SHEARER, *Economic Democracy: The Challenge of the 1980s*. New York: Basic Books, 1980. Two very able younger economists on the left present alternatives.

ROBERT LEKACHMAN, *The Age of Keynes*. New York: Random House, 1966. The best nontechnical discussion of Keynes and his economics theories.

————, *Greed Is Not Enough: Reaganomics*. New York: Pantheon, 1982. A harshly critical treatment of President Reagan's macroeconomic policies from this prominent left-liberal economist.

MARTIN MAYER, *The Fate of the Dollar*. New York: Times Books, 1980. A very knowledgeable, conservative, and readable account of the management and mismanagement of our currency, from Eisenhower to Carter. Sheds useful light on the international central-banking community, its operations, and the relationships among the Federal Reserve Board, its chairmen, and the President.

JAMES D. O'CONNOR, *The Fiscal Crisis of the State*. New York: St. Martin's, 1973. An intelligent Marxist analysis of the macroeconomic functions and politics of American government. It casts powerful light upon important structural problems of economic management.

JOSEPH A. PECHMAN, *Federal Tax Policy*, 3rd ed. Washington, D.C.: Brookings, 1977. Detailed description and analysis of pre-Reagan tax policy, with proposals for reform, by a leading expert.

JOSEPH A. PECHMAN, ed., *Setting National Priorities: The 1983 Budget*. Washington, D.C.: Brookings, 1982. Belonging to an annual series extending back over the past decade, this is essential reading for anyone who seeks expert guidance in the changing priorities of federal budgets during the early Reagan years. This Brookings volume (and the series) may be written dryly, but it presents a wealth of information on a subject of overwhelming and dramatic political importance, in a fairly neutral way.

MICHAEL L. WACHTER and SUSAN M. WACHTER, eds., *Toward a New U.S. Industrial Policy?* Philadelphia: Univ. of Pennsylvania, 1981. Up-to-date collection of articles and essays, from all points of the ideological spectrum, on many aspects of government macroeconomic management.

chapter seventeen

FOREIGN AND DEFENSE POLICY

On October 23, 1983, a suicide terrorist blew up the barracks of the U.S. Marines in Lebanon, killing 241 soldiers. Although the next logical step might have been a strong counterattack by the U.S., that step was never taken. First of all, the identity of the group responsible for the terrorist act was uncertain. Second, policy makers reasoned that retaliation might bring on additional attacks by terrorist factions.

Terrorism had characterized the fighting for some time, in this area of heated, often bloody conflict. Confusion in U.S. foreign policy on the terrorism and chaotic political scene was another characteristic of the crisis in Lebanon. In 1982, a terrorist murder of Lebanon's president-elect, Bashir Gemayel, led to fighting between Israeli and Lebanese Christian factions on one side and Syrian and Lebanese Muslim factions on the other. One result of the fighting was the surprise slaughter of over 700 Palestinians, including men, women, and children, in a refugee camp.

President Reagan responded to this brutal attack by sending in the U.S. Marines to establish some kind of peace while the slain Gemayel's brother, Amin, attempted to form a new government. But U.S. policy seemed contradictory even from the beginning. On the one hand, foreign policy makers stated a commitment to the establishment of a democratic Lebanese government; on the other, they pledged support for a government whose control was in the hands of Gamayel and the Christians, clearly a minority in Lebanon.

When Secretary of State George Shultz negotiated with Israelis to sign an Israeli–Syrian peace agreement, he assumed that the Syrians would also sign. Unfortunately, he was wrong. Fortified by Soviet arms, Syrian forces gained military strength. Syrian President Hafez Assad also strengthened his relations with Lebanese Muslim factions, the Shiite and Druze militiamen, as well as with Iranian terrorist groups. To quell Druze–Christian fighting that followed an Israeli retreat, U.S. Marines entered into the fighting with gunfire of their own, casting a dark shadow of doubt on the belief in the U.S.'s role as peacemaker. Then came the terrorist attack on the Marine barracks.

There are a number of morals to this tale. The actual or potential military element in American foreign policy is quite large where responses to revolutions and civil wars in developing countries are concerned. But the uses of military power are often very poorly defined and the risks to American servicemen can be excessive. They certainly were in Lebanon. Another problem is that it is tremendously difficult to work out a good response to terrorism, particularly when the terrorism is well organized and internationally supported. Still another issue arises. Can American foreign-policy makers intervene in other people's civil wars with any chance of success when the people fighting the war are determined and prepared to pay a heavy price to win? Perhaps we should remind ourselves that every one of these problems plagued American intervention in Vietnam from beginning to end. We assert global responsibilities, but parts of the globe very stubbornly insist on doing things their own way. American foreign policy has achieved much in the forty years since World War II ended. Can the people who make it also learn from their mistakes?

——— THE UNITED STATES AND THE WORLD———

The Lebanese crisis reminds us of two things. First, the United States is inescapably part of a larger world, and much of that world is not friendly to us. Second, what happens in that world has an impact on politics at home. President John F. Kennedy (1961–1963), with his usual intelligent wit, said, "Domestic policy can hurt you, but foreign policy can kill you." That remark embodies one of the few really great revolutions in American history: our shift from isolation to world power and, parallel to it, our shift from invulnerability to the constant threat of nuclear annihilation.

Even before foreigners influenced our domestic politics, our domestic politics strongly influenced the way we did business with foreigners, for we have always framed our foreign-policy goals in the language of domestic politics. President Woodrow Wilson (1913–1921) wanted to "make the world safe for democracy." Yet no aspect of U.S. government policy is made with less democratic participation than foreign policy, always the happy hunting ground of a small elite in the White House, the bureaucracy, Congress, and a few law firms and universities. Many people argue that this must be so, because international politics demands expertise that few of us have and because diplomacy, to succeed, must be carried on more or less secretly.

These arguments cannot be dismissed out of hand, yet they do not answer obvious questions: If foreign policy has more and more impact on our domestic politics, prosperity, and perhaps even survival, does the way we make foreign policy undermine democracy itself? Is a democratic foreign policy desirable? If it is desirable, is it feasible?

In one sense, we already have a democratic foreign policy. The elite that charts its course does not live in seclusion from the rest of us. The values of that elite are to a great extent our own values, so that the oddities of our political, social, and cultural development have shaped a distinctly American foreign-policy style.

THE AMERICAN FOREIGN–POLICY STYLE

The foundation of American foreign policy is an attitude toward world politics and our role in it. We Americans have always imputed a special virtue to ourselves and doubted the politics, morals, and hygiene of foreigners. (Foreigners wishing to travel to the United States, for example, must fill out an immigration form that asks them, among other things, if they are coming to this country for immoral or subversive purposes!)

Our world role, as we see and act on it, is to help good triumph over evil. We like to think of foreign policy as a moral battleground, not as a contest for limited and selfish objectives. Our statesmen, of course, do not neglect American national interests in conducting our foreign policy. But they, like the rest of us, prefer to think that our foreign policy works for democracy, prosperity, and justice among nations, not that it serves our own selfish interests. (There are exceptions, however. Franklin D. Roosevelt (1933–1945) once said of a Caribbean dictator friendly to the United States, "He is a son of a bitch, but he is *our* son of a bitch." He was.) We like to feel that our policy is inspired by a few grand, simple, and self-evident principles, which have changed little, while our position in world politics has changed considerably.

Isolationism. At the outset of our national history, we had little need of foreign policy. We kept ourselves in a state of principled isolation, maintainable by our geographical isolation from Europe, by the great differences between its political systems and ours, and by our opportunities for westward expansion. Some of the founding fathers, especially Alexander Hamilton, thought the United States should involve itself in the wars and diplomacy of Europe and become a great power. Most Americans agreed with Thomas Jefferson that our society should remain inward-looking and agricultural. Even President Washington (1789–1797), Hamilton's boss, argued (in his Farewell Address) that "in extending our commercial relations, the United States should have as little political connection as possible" with foreign states. Americans believed that liberty and commerce made us peaceful and virtuous and that oligarchy and monarchy made the peoples of Europe warlike and corrupt. These simple assumptions continually reappear in the history of our foreign relations.

Manifest Destiny. Our isolation was both possible and necessary. It was possible because our nearest plausible enemies lived more than 3,000 miles across the Atlantic Ocean. It was necessary because the United States was developing its resources and melding many different groups of immigrants into a new nationality—*e pluribus unum,* "out of many, one," the Latin phrase that is our national motto. A sense of separateness from Europe was needed to turn our energies both inward and westward, to form our new nationality. We sustained our sense of separateness by creating a national myth: that the United States was a uniquely principled nation in world politics; that our moral superiority justified isolationism; that we had a Manifest Destiny, given to us by God, to expand to the Pacific Ocean.

These myths flourished as long as the United States did not have to deal regularly with the great powers. They were, nonetheless, myths. It was not our moral superiority that separated us from European power politics but our preoccupation with our own continent and the fact that Africa and Asia made much easier targets for European imperialism than we did.

President McKinley's Prayer

In this passage of William McKinley's diary, the President recalls how he decided in the spring of 1898, during the Spanish-American War, what to do with the Philippines, after learning that Manila harbor had fallen to the American naval commander, Commodore George Dewey:

I walked the floor of the White House night after night until midnight; and I am not ashamed to tell you, gentlemen, that I went down on my knees and prayed Almighty God for light and guidance more than one night. And one night late it came to me this way—I don't know how it was, but it came. (1) That we could not give them [the Philippines] back to Spain—that would be cowardly and dishonorable; (2) that we could not turn them over to France or Germany—our commercial rivals in the Orient—that would be bad business and discreditable; (3) that we could not leave them to themselves—they were unfit for self-government—and they would soon have anarchy and misrule over there worse than Spain's was; and (4) that there was nothing left for us to do but to take them all and to educate the Filipinos, and uplift and Christianize them, and by God's grace do the very best we could by them, as our fellow-men for whom Christ also died.

McKinley goes on to say that he slept sounder, confident that the Philippines came to the United States "in the province of God," by virtue of "His plans for human progress."

THE GREAT REVERSAL

The conditions that had made our isolation possible were overthrown temporarily by World War I and permanently by World War II. For the first time, the "entangling alliances" President Washington had warned us against became (or seemed to become) vital to our national security. Yet the old tradition endures. So far, at least, this great reversal has had remarkably little effect either on our national myth or on our foreign-policy style.

World War I and Its Aftermath

When the war began in Europe in 1914, we did not join it; in fact, President Wilson was reelected in 1916 with the slogan, "He kept us out of war." By 1917, it had become clear that an Allied defeat, especially the defeat of Britain, to which we had loaned a great deal of money, would be a disaster for the United States. We then entered the war on the side of the Allies. World War I became our first major involvement in European politics.

At the war's end, in 1918, Mr. Wilson went to the peace conference at Versailles with a plan for promoting universal peace, his famous Fourteen Points. "Even God," French Premier Clemenceau joked, "needed only ten." Wilson's two key principles were "open covenants, openly arrived at"—no more secret diplomacy—and national self-determination, especially for the peoples of the former Austrian and Russian empires.

Although Mr. Wilson rejected isolationism, his premises were, in most respects, traditional. He assumed that wars were promoted by oligarchies secretly plotting with, and against, one another. Everyone else shared a common interest in peace, so democracy and open diplomacy would create the conditions for universal peace. These were doubtful ideas, unfortunately. To cite two episodes from our own history: It was the United States, not Mexico, that provoked the Mexican War (1846–1848); and it was the United States, not Spain, that provoked the Spanish-American War (1898) and then

Teri Leigh Stratford

fought a nasty three-year war against Filipino guerrillas to keep the Philippines, a territory won from Spain.[1]

The Treaty of Versailles (1919), which ended the war, provided for an international organization called the League of Nations. Since the U.S. Senate refused to ratify the treaty, the United States did not join the league. At the urging of our next president, Warren G. Harding (1921–1923), we went "back to normalcy." *Normalcy* meant that the United States was for all intents and purposes beyond the reach of any powerful enemy; therefore, we did not need large military forces. Except during the Civil War and World War I, defense spending had rarely gone above 1 percent of our gross national product.

In the "normal" world before 1941, the United States was merely one power among many in the game of nations. Of all the great powers, it was the least involved in international power politics. Many nations, especially Germany and Japan, made the mistake of underestimating us.

Normalcy means that the United States is at peace, prosperous, and beyond the reach of any powerful enemy.

The Day That Lives in Infamy

On December 7, 1941—"a day that will live in infamy," said Franklin D. Roosevelt, our President at the time—the U.S. Naval Base at Pearl Harbor,

---

[1] It is only fair to note that the United States never really took to territorial imperialism. While the U.S. Army finally suppressed the Filipino guerrillas in 1902, it moved immediately to set up a colonial government that was remarkably progressive and humane. The United States granted the Philippines independence on July 4, 1946 (though retaining important naval and air bases there to the present day).

On December 7, 1941, a U.S. naval base was attacked and destroyed— and so was a state of mind. For the first time since 1812, we were no longer unreachable.

Hawaii, was attacked and destroyed by Japanese warplanes. What was destroyed on that day was not just a naval base but also a state of mind. Hawaii, though not then a state, was a U.S. territory. For the first time since 1812 (when the British burned Washington), a foreign enemy had attacked us on what was more or less home soil. We were no longer unreachable. From that day forward, we have lived with the knowledge that a foreign enemy might launch a devastating surprise attack against us. This possibility has been central to our strategic-defense planning ever since. We entered World War II on December 8, 1941.

The war changed our government beyond recognition. In 1939, the federal government had only about 80,000 civilian employees working in matters connected with national security. At the war's end, in 1945, it had *3 million* such employees. In 1939, the defense budget was about 1.4 percent of our gross national product (GNP); during the war, defense spending rose to 38.5 percent of GNP by 1945; and after the war, it never fell below 4.6 percent. In 1939, we had naval bases only in Hawaii, Guam, and the Philippines; by 1945, there were 434 U.S. bases around the world.

This transformation was not just a change in numbers. During most of American history, national security was a backwater of the federal government. By 1945, it dominated the executive branch. The government as a whole had a new sense of priorities: It had become "militarized."

At the war's end, the other great powers—Britian, France, Germany, Italy, Japan, and the Soviet Union—were exhausted and devasted. We became the mightiest of nations, with a network of alliances and military commitments that reached around the globe.

Cold War

As Germany was about to surrender, the troops of the United States and the Soviet Union met in the German town of Torgau, on the Elbe river. It was April 25, 1945, and they met as allies, yet the wartime alliance between them had already begun to crumble. Soon, the United States and the Soviet Union were lining up allies against each other. Each group of states quickly formed a bloc. By 1946, Winston Churchill, Britain's World War II prime minister, was pointing to the "Iron Curtain" that the Soviets had put up in the middle of Europe to cut off their bloc from the West.

In the beginning, the struggle between the United States and the Soviet Union was grossly unequal. The Soviet Union had been exhausted by the war. The United States had not. The United States had nuclear weapons. The Soviet Union did not. The United States was the richest nation in history. The

Table 17-1 Defense Expenditures as Percentage of Gross National Product, 1940–1984

YEAR	DEFENSE EXPENDITURES*	TOTAL "IMPERIAL" EXPENDITURES**	YEAR	DEFENSE EXPENDITURES	TOTAL "IMPERIAL" EXPENDITURES
1940	1.5%	1.6%	1965	7.2%	8.5%
1941	4.9	5.0	1966	7.6	9.0
1942	15.2	16.4	1967	8.8	10.1
1943	33.2	34.9	1968	9.3	10.3
1944	36.6	38.3	1969	8.7	9.6
1945	38.5	40.1	1970	8.2	9.0
1946	21.4	22.7	1971	7.2	7.9
1947	5.6	7.6	1972	6.6	7.3
1948	5.1	6.9	1973	5.7	6.3
1949	5.1	7.5	1974	5.6	6.2
1950	4.6	6.3	1975	5.7	6.4
1951	6.9	8.1	1976	5.3	5.9
1952	12.7	13.6	1977	5.3	5.9
1953	13.8	14.4	1978	5.3	5.9
1954	12.8	13.2	1979	5.0	5.5
1955	10.1	10.6	1980	5.2	5.7
1956	9.6	10.1	1981	5.5	5.7
1957	9.7	10.4	1982	6.0	6.7
1958	9.9	10.6	1983	6.4	7.0
1959	9.6	10.3	1984	6.2	6.9
1960	9.1	9.7			
1961	9.1	9.7			
1962	9.1	10.1			
1963	8.8	9.9			
1964	8.5	9.9			

* Excluding all other externally oriented expenditures.

**Including defense, international relations, and space-program spending.

Note: 1941–1946: World War II and reconversion; 1947–1950: Low military spending, considerable foreign-aid spending (Marshall Plan). Also Veterans' benefits, G. I. Bill, etc., equaled 3 percent of GNP in 1947, 31 percent in 1950; 1951–1954: Korean War mobilization; 1955–1964: Cold War arms race; 1966–1969: Vietnam War period (note how much less of an increase in GNP for defense than for the Korean War); 1971–1976: "Détente," drastic cut in *relative* defense spending, and as percent of GNP and of budget totals.

Soviet Union was a poor country that also happened to be the second most powerful country in the world.

Because these two countries were so much more powerful than all the others, they were called the "superpowers." This was new, for in the past there had always been more than two great powers. Until the 1970s, the United States was the stronger of the two. In 1949, however, the Soviets jiggled the balance a bit by exploding their first nuclear device. The Soviet bomb made the cost of a shooting war between the superpowers incredibly high. But this did not deter each superpower from spreading its own network of alliances and sociopolitical institutions. The rivalry, the **Cold War,** was not confined to any one part of the world or to any one kind of competition. It became a confrontation of ideologies, or political principles—Soviet-style Marxism–Leninism, versus Western capitalistic democracy as well as a struggle over tangible military and economic interests. Finally, it was an armed struggle, though only between client states of the superpowers. Occasionally the United States intervened in these struggles directly, as in Korea and Vietnam, but we always avoided armed conflict with the Soviet Union. Both sides feared a conflict that might escalate into a nuclear war. Some argue that nuclear weapons have actually reduced the likelihood of a hot war between the superpowers. Had there been no such weapons, they argue, the superpowers would already have come to blows.

The standoff between the superpowers has also, perversely, created greater freedom for violence among their client states. While Moscow and Washington carefully restrict their own involvement in limited wars, such wars stay limited; and the client states who fear them less get involved in them more. Small indecisive wars have been frustrating to Americans, who are accustomed to demanding, if not getting, unconditional surrender.

Responsibility. Was the Cold War inevitable? Who caused it, if anyone? Remember that the Soviet Union was our country's wartime ally. Why did we not remain allies? There are two broad explanations of why the Cold War happened, and each points a finger in a different direction.

The Orthodox Version. The orthodox anti-Communist version points to long-term hostility between Soviet communism and the West. As seen through the eyes of orthodoxy, the Soviet Union was a militant Communist dictatorship bent on promoting worldwide revolution. In pursuit of the international "dictatorship of the proletariat," the Soviets subverted every government in Eastern Europe and set up Communist satellite states. Communism was seen as an aggressive international conspiracy with headquarters in Moscow. The West, in responding to the Soviets, was acting defensively, to preserve national sovereignty, liberty, democracy, and free enterprise.

By the 1970s, even those who blamed the Cold War solely on the Communists admitted that the Soviets no longer controlled all the other Communist states, that the Communist bloc was no longer a monolith. But although they conceded the emergence of rivalries within the Communist world—notably the split between the Soviet Union and the People's Republic of China (mainland China)—they claimed that all these independent and not-so-independent Communist states still had aggressive designs against the West.

The Revisionist Version. Without necessarily denying the often hostile intentions of Communist states, **revisionists** argue that the West was at least as much responsible for the Cold War as the Soviet Union was, perhaps more so. More than twenty *million* Soviet citizens died in World War II. This great loss of life, they claim, gave the Soviets a profound fear of encirclement and invasion—a fear that, according to the revisionists, is essentially defensive. Communism, they say, is something of a conventional religion, and the Soviets are no more eager to spread it than Britain, let us say, is eager to convert the world to Episcopalianism. When the Soviets have imposed Communist governments on their neighbors, they have done so to promote their own national interests, not ideological interest. According to the revisionists, it was the United States that developed a militant ideology, anticommunism, and a ring of alliances and military bases around the Soviet Union and its allies.

As part of this argument, revisionists also claim that we have imposed our struggle with the Soviet Union on the **Third World** developing countries of Asia, Africa, and Latin America. That is, *we* have been the aggressors in such countries, opposing social and political change while attempting to build a transnational capitalist empire with the help of client governments, multinational corporations, and where necessary, military intervention.

Still other revisionist point to the size of the so-called **military-industrial complex**—the foreign policy, defense, intelligence communities, and industries that serve them—and to the militarization of American foreign policy resulting from this complex. These government agencies and the industries associated with them have to justify their existence and size; therefore (say the revisionists) they go fishing for trouble.

Who Is Right? The Soviet leadership's hostility to the West is real, not illusory; and it is rooted not just in Russian national goals but also in Communist beliefs. One thing is clear: At the end of World War II, the Soviet Union meant to dominate Eastern Europe and ensure a divided Germany. It is not quite clear how the Soviets, at first, thought they would achieve their aims. In the end, the Soviets occupied Eastern Europe and established and inspired Communist dictatorships everywhere in it. Was this inevitable? Might the Soviets have been satisfied with some less total form of control? Perhaps not.

For all we know, the Soviets might never have felt truly secure until they had installed satellite governments throughout Eastern Europe. If so, their motive was not zeal for communism alone, but fear of renewed invasion from the West, especially from Germany. That fear must be seen in the light of their World War II losses: remember, more than twenty million deaths at the hands of the Germans. The physical damage was correspondingly heavy. By contrast, the total number of American servicemen who died during World War II was 407,316. We suffered an extremely small number of civilian casualties, almost all in Hawaii on December 7, 1941; property damage on American home soil was limited to the naval base at Pearl Harbor and the army air base at adjacent Hickam Field.

In any event, the Western powers agreed at the Yalta conference (1945) to give the Soviets a preponderant influence in most of postwar Eastern Europe. In addition, however, President Roosevelt called for free elections to be held there. Perhaps the Soviets interpreted this call as an ideological campaign against them, of the sort that they are wont to undertake against us. In all likelihood, the President took such appeals for granted; they were commonplace Wilsonian rhetoric. The Soviets underestimated the force behind Mr. Roosevelt's idealism; the West underestimated Soviet insecurity. Each side prepared to resist what it interpreted as the other's aggressiveness; such preparations further worsened the general wartime climate of insecurity.

Perhaps this climate was less the fault of either side than of the conditions that created their rivalry and sharpened it. At the core of international politics lie insecurity and fear. No collective authority checks the pride and folly of nations. International society is and always has been a war of all against all, tempered, at best, by prudent realism. No nation is obliged to consider the rights or common humanity of its neighbors; each nation must ultimately defend its rights and interests by itself. So it was after World War II, when the Cold War began, and so it is today. Such insecurity also in part explains our maintenance of a large national security establishment and the strident role that we have often played in the developing world.

The Cold War Develops. Before World War II, Europe was the center of the world's stage. After it, there were two centers—the United States and the Soviet Union—each on the fringes of Europe, not quite in it, not quite out of it. Although their rivalry soon outgrew the European theater, the earliest disagreements centered on it.

A number of specific events and concerns marked the beginnings of a more contentious relationship between the American and Soviet superpowers.

Germany. Understandably enough, the Soviets demanded economic reparations from Germany and wanted to see the Germans permanently divided and disarmed. The United States, however, wanted to restore Germany as a trading partner, not to wreck its economy. In addition, as the Cold War developed, Washington began to see an independent West Germany as a potentially important military asset for the Western alliance.

Greece. With Soviet support, Greek Communists in 1944 launched a revolution against the royal government, which was supported militarily and financially by Britain. By 1947, the British, who had held the line against the insurgents, informed Washington that they could no longer afford the financial burden of assisting the Greek government. The United States, in response, not only helped the Greek Royalists but informally offered to assist any government threatened by communism. This policy was called the **Truman Doctrine** after President Harry S Truman (1945–1953).

Czechoslovakia. A Soviet-backed coup in 1948 toppled the noncommunist government of Czechoslovakia in Eastern Europe and replaced it with a Soviet puppet regime. This action seriously disabused those in the West who thought that Soviet intentions in Eastern Europe might still be benign.

Berlin. From June 1948 to June 1949 the Soviets shut off land access to West Berlin, a city occupied by all four wartime allies—the U.S., Britain, France, and the Soviet Union—but surrounded by Soviet-controlled East Germany. In the end the Soviets were foiled by a Western airlift of supplies to West Berlin, and the confrontation they generated was one of the major factors behind U.S. congressional support for the creation of the North Atlantic Treaty Organization (NATO). Germany (and Berlin) remained divided between East and West.

China. In 1949 Mao Tse-tung's Chinese Communists routed the Nationalists, who had received massive American support. By the end of 1949, the Communists controlled all of China's mainland, and the Nationalists were eventually forced to pull back to the island of Taiwan. Everywhere, communism seemed to be on the rise.

Containment. In July 1947, George Kennan, the State Department's leading Kremlinologist (expert on the Soviet Union), published a very important article in *Foreign Affairs*, which is more or less the organ of the American foreign-policy establishment (see the final section in this chapter, "the Establishment"). Kennan argued that the Soviet leaders were inspired by unrelenting hostility to Western capitalism and that Soviet expansionism was

In 1948 the Soviets shut off land access to West Berlin. For a year Western allies kept the city supplied by airlift, until in June 1949 the roads were opened again by the Soviets.

in many respects merely a variant of the tradition of Russian expansionism. If the West did not create "unassailable barriers" to the growth of Soviet power and influence, that power would indeed grow, especially in the politically and economically weak states along the thousands of miles of Soviet border. The United States, Kennan noted, had a new responsibility of maintaining world peace through a "long-term, patient, but firm and vigilant **containment**" of Soviet power. (In his memoirs, Kennan criticizes himself for not having made it clear that he meant political, not military containment.)

The Marshall Plan and NATO. In 1947 the United States created the first such barrier, a plan to restore Western Europe to economic and political health. It was called the **Marshall Plan,** after George C. Marshall, President Truman's second secretary of state. Under its auspices, billions of dollars eventually flowed to the war-shattered economies of Western Europe. By 1949, the logic of the Cold War also prompted Mr. Truman and Congress to enter into a commitment that made the United States permanently responsible for Western Europe's security. This commitment was institutionalized in the North Atlantic Treaty Organization (NATO), which in subsequent decades became a principal instrument of the policy of containment.

The Korean War. Despite the civil war in China and a "dirty little war" between the Communists and the French in a part of French Indochina called Vietnam, the Cold War was not truly globalized until June 1950, when the Soviet Union's North Korean ally crossed the 38th parallel and invaded South Korea, an ally of the United States.

Korea had been a divided nation since 1945, when Soviet forces had moved into the northern part of the country and set up a Communist government. North Korea's attack on South Korea took us and our allies by surprise, but the Truman administration quickly decided it was a threat. Because the Soviet representative on the U.N.[2] Security Council had walked out of it (in protest) earlier in the year, the Soviets were not in a position to use their veto when the United States proposed, successfully, that the U.N. authorize a "police action" to aid the South Korean side.

Eventually the struggle stabilized around the 38th parallel, the border between North and South Korea. In line with the strategy of containment, the objective became the restoration of South Korea's sovereignty. In July 1953, the Eisenhower administration (1953–1961) signed an armistice agreement with North Korea. Containment had been globalized.

Massive Retaliation. But the Eisenhower administration, guided in its foreign policy by Secretary of State John Foster Dulles (1953–1959), regarded containment as a passive and perhaps immoral strategy for coexisting with godless communism. As the Korean War showed, it was an expensive policy as well. President Eisenhower and Secretary Dulles therefore looked for a cheaper means to support containment and, if possible, a way to roll back Communist power and influence.

The policy they devised to facilitate containment was known as **massive retaliation.** In the mid-1950s, American nuclear weapons were vastly superior in number and quality to those of the Soviet Union. More important still, we could get those weapons to Soviet cities; the Soviets could not yet launch a credible nuclear attack against us. Massive retaliation was the Eisenhower administration's threat to respond to Soviet aggression by using the bomb. This was a convenient strategy. We would not have to spend a lot of money to build up large conventional forces, while our allies, particularly those in Europe, could feel secure under our nuclear umbrella. From this point on, nuclear deterrence became an important facet of America's effort to contain Soviet power.

Massive retaliation and Mr. Eisenhower's foreign policy in general were based on a transient phenomenon: the invulnerability of U.S. air space. Things were bound to change as soon as the Soviets developed a way to drop their own bombs on American cities. Many people still look back on these times as "normal" and do not understand why, later on, we did not always get our way.

Kennedy and Flexible Response

On October 4, 1957, the Soviet Union successfully launched into space the world's first mechanical satellite, *Sputnik*. The same rocket booster that carried the 184-pound spheroid into outer space could easily have dropped a nuclear warhead on the United States; moreover, there was no known defense against such weapons. Again we faced a Pearl Harbor, this time a nuclear one. The intercontinental-missile age had dawned.

Sputnik undermined our strategy of massive retaliation. We could still threaten the Soviets with nuclear destruction, but they could now make the same threat against us. Did it make sense for the President to risk New York, Chicago, and Los Angeles for the sake of Frankfurt, Brussels, or Paris? Would the Soviets believe our willingness to do so? If not, the United States had no

---

[2] The United Nations (U.N.), now with headquarters in New York City, was formed in San Francisco, California, in 1945, as an international organization of nations pledged to promote world peace and security, maintain treaty organizations, observe international law, and cooperate in furthering social progress.

defense strategy that would serve to protect its NATO allies. When John F. Kennedy (1961–1963) took office as President, he and his senior officials cast about for alternatives to massive retaliation. Nuclear strategy had to be rethought.

The Kennedy administration was also looking for an effective way to mount **counterinsurgency operations** against leftist guerrillas who were operating in developing countries with the support and tolerance of local populations. With good reason, the Kennedy administration feared that many Third World countries were vulnerable to guerrilla conquest and that our global interests might be outflanked by the Communists, without a single Soviet casualty. This was the era of the Green Berets, a time when high officials of the U.S. government were said to be reading Mao's book on guerrilla warfare.

The Cuban Missile Crisis. The sort of thing that worried President Kennedy had already come to pass on the island of Cuba, ninety miles south of Florida. Fidel Castro's guerrilla forces had overthrown a U.S.-supported dictatorship at the start of 1959; and by 1960, Cuba had in effect joined the Communist bloc. In April 1961, shortly after Mr. Kennedy took office, the United States sponsored an invasion of Cuba by anti-Castro exiles, who were totally routed at the Bay of Pigs.

A year later, in the summer of 1962, the Soviet premier, Nikita Khrushchev, decided to place in Cuba about ninety medium-range missiles and bombers, both capable of reaching the United States. On October 14, U.S. spy planes photographed the Soviet missile sites. Kennedy wanted the missiles out of Cuba, but he also wanted to avoid a war, especially a nuclear war. Finally, he decided on a naval quarantine of Cuba—really a blockade, a word he did not wish to use since a blockade is an act of war—to prevent new Soviet arms or technicians from reaching the island.

Soviet missiles aboard a Soviet ship being withdrawn from Cuba while a U.S. Navy patrol plane and destroyer keep close watch over the operation.

AP/Wide World Photos

On October 22, the President, in a broadcast to the American people, called upon Khrushchev to withdraw the missiles as soon as possible, and he announced the "quarantine." Soviet ships carrying offensive weapons continued to sail ominously toward the U.S. Navy's quarantine line. Then, on October 28, Khrushchev agreed to withdraw the missiles in exchange for an American pledge not to invade Cuba or to overthrow Castro's government. Sixteen Soviet ships sailing toward the quarantine line turned around in midocean and returned to their home ports; soon after, the missile sites were dismantled. The crisis was over.

But only this particular crisis. More, perhaps, than anything before or since, these events, so close to home, made us aware that nuclear weapons and nuclear war are a real and present danger.

The War in Vietnam

The French had lost their "dirty little war" in Vietnam.[3] In 1954,[4] the Geneva Accords divided the former colony into the sovereign states of Cambodia, Laos, and Vietnam. Vietnam itself was divided at the 17th parallel, with the Communists in control north of that line, anti-Communists south of it. A government of a reunified Vietnam was to be elected in 1956.

The Beginnings (1954–1963). President Eisenhower and Secretary of State Dulles disdained to accept these agreements. Instead of working toward a unified (and very probably Communist) Vietnam, the Eisenhower administration encouraged South Vietnam's anti-Communist government in Saigon (now Ho Chi Minh City), led by one Ngo Dinh Diem. In 1956, it supported Diem when he refused to permit elections for a unified government. Diem had some success at first. But a Communist-led insurgent movement, the National Liberation Front (NLF), or Vietcong, began a guerrilla war in South Vietnam's countryside in 1960. Supported and probably controlled by North Vietnam, the NLF sought to overthrow Diem and reunite the country.

These events were still not a great threat. President Kennedy, however, was committed to fighting Communist mischief wherever it might turn up. He sent 16,000 U.S. military "advisers" to help South Vietnam fight the NLF. (They were called advisers because, in theory, they could not fire weapons unless fired upon.) The war, however, did not go well for South Vietnam, and it is not clear what Kennedy meant to do about it. In any case, by the time of his death in November 1963, we had 16,500 advisers in South Vietnam.

Escalation (1963–1969). The war in the Vietnamese countryside went from bad to worse. In Saigon, Diem, who had been assassinated just a few weeks before Kennedy, was followed by one ambitious general after another. The last of these generals was a man named Nguyen Cao Ky, who said that his "only hero" was Adolf Hitler. The government was corrupt, unstable, and unpopular, and we supported it.

President Lyndon B. Johnson (1963–1969) and his advisers believed that the

---

[3] President Eisenhower announced in 1953 that the United States had given France aid for their Indochina War, and in 1954 it was reported that 75 percent of that war's costs were met by the United States.

[4] Also in 1954, the Southeast Asia Treaty Organization (SEATO) was formed as a collective defense pact by the United States, Britain, France, Australia, New Zealand, Philippines, Pakistan, and Thailand.

real problem was North Vietnam, the NLF's patron, not the South's internal disunity, however serious that might be. In 1964, Mr. Johnson was elected President by a landslide, largely with the slogan, "American boys should not be doing the job of Asian boys" in Vietnam. While he was saying this, the President had already concluded that Asian boys could *not* do the job and that American boys would have to do it for them. Later on, many Americans felt that he had simply lied to them. This feeling accounted for much of the later bitterness against the war.

Mr. Johnson needed an excuse to escalate our involvement. In August 1964, North Vietnam obliged him by attacking two U.S. torpedo boats in the Gulf of Tonkin, in what may or may not have been North Vietnamese waters. In retaliation, the President then ordered air strikes against North Vietnam, and he prevailed on the Senate (by a vote of 88 to 2) to pass the so-called Gulf of Tonkin Resolution supporting his actions. He did not ask for a declaration of war, perhaps in fear that it might increase public pressure for an all-out war— a war that might bring the Soviets directly into the conflict. Direct Soviet or Chinese participation was the last thing Mr. Johnson and his staff wanted. For the rest of the war, the Gulf of Tonkin Resolution had to serve as the legal justification of our involvement.

Regular bombing of North Vietnam began in February 1965. In March, Mr. Johnson sent the first U.S. combat troops—no longer just as advisers—to Vietnam. Very soon we found ourselves with a major war on our hands: 148,000 American troops were stationed in Vietnam by October 1965. Three and a half years later there were 541,000. After 1966, regular units of the North Vietnamese Army took over much of the fighting from the NLF.

As for the bombings, from 1965 to the end of 1971 the United States dropped 3.6 million tons of bombs on South Vietnam alone. (Compare this with the mere 2 million tons dropped by *all* the combatants in World War II.) The total tonnage of bombs dropped on Vietnam, Cambodia, and Laos by mid-1973 was over 7 million—300 pounds of bombs for every man, woman, and child; 22 *tons* of bombs for every square mile.

The human toll of the war is horrifying to contemplate. Perhaps 2 million or so Vietnamese were killed from 1960 to 1975, and an additional 4 million were made homeless. At the height of the war, under President Richard M. Nixon (1969-1974), in 1971, 130,000 South Vietnamese *civilians* were killed each month. The United States, too, paid with its blood: the blood of more than 55,000 dead and 220,000 wounded American service men.

Yet our will did not prevail in Vietnam. How many times were we told, in the 1960s and 1970s, that victory was around the corner? At first, public opinion wanted to believe. The period of believing came to an end with the so-called Tet Offensive of January–February 1968, when NLF and North Vietnamese forces attacked several large cities in South Vietnam and held them briefly. The attacks were repelled, but they showed that North Vietnam was able and willing to continue the war.

Many people now began to think that what we were calling "the war in Vietnam" was in fact a Vietnamese civil war, a fight between different factions of one country, not between international communism and the West. In any case, there seemed to be little prospect of achieving the administration's announced objective of forcing North Vietnam to leave South Vietnam alone. Many Americans, including Americans who did not oppose the war in principle, saw no point in having their sons drafted "to die of foreign fevers and foreign shot and shell" in a war that seemed to lack a clear or feasible objective.

Deescalation and Defeat (1969–1975). President Nixon, who was aware of the strength of domestic opposition to the war, attempted gradually to unload the actual fighting on South Vietnam's army. At the same time, in 1971, in hopes of cutting off the supply lines of the NLF and the North Vietnamese, Mr. Nixon extended the war to Cambodia and Laos. Still the war went on; the prospect that South Vietnam might ever be able to defend itself seemed as distant as always. Confronted by the prospect of a congressional cutoff of funding for the war, in early 1973 the administration signed a cease-fire agreement with North Vietnam, which returned our prisoners of war in return for a U.S. military withdrawal.

President Nixon's opponents argue that he was merely attempting to buy a "decent interval" between our withdrawal and the victory of North Vietnam. Mr. Nixon claimed that he meant to continue support of South Vietnam with anything it might take to repel the enemy—anything, that is, except U.S. troops. No matter. In the spring of 1975, North Vietnam launched a major offensive, but Congress refused President Gerald Ford's (1974–1977) request to appropriate funds to help South Vietnam.

On May 1, 1975, units of the North Vietnamese army entered Saigon. Just a few hours before, the last Americans had left the country by boarding a helicopter on the roof of the U.S. embassy. The United States had lost a war for the first time.

Why? First, the French failed in Vietnam. President Eisenhower succeeded in propping up Diem, but President Kennedy failed to prevent Diem's over-throw. President Johnson failed to keep the North Vietmanese out of South Vietnam and, indeed, brought them directly into the war. President Nixon failed to get South Vietnam to accept the burden of responsibility for its own defense and failed to deter North Vietnam from continuing the war effort. He failed as well to buy a "decent interval" between our withdrawal and North Vietnam's victory, and President Ford failed to prevent that victory.

We like to think of ourselves as a pragmatic people, a people who judge any course of action by its results. The results of our policy in Vietnam were twenty years of failure, costly to ourselves, and far more costly to the Vietnamese. How on earth did we get into this mess? Why did it take us so long to get out?

The Munich Analogy. Generals, according to an old witticism, prepare to fight the last war, not the next one. Diplomats and politicians, too, often make policy with their eyes on the past, not the present or future.

The men who made our foreign policy during the Vietnam years had mostly come to adulthood in the 1930s, the "devil's decade." They were obsessed with what is called the Munich analogy. In the years before World War II, Britain and France had appeased Nazi Germany by submitting to its demands, a policy that came to a climax in the Munich Agreement of 1938, when they agreed to cut up Czechoslovakia and give part of it to Germany. Yet in little more than a year they were forced into the very war they had done everything in their power to avoid. Perhaps if Britain and France had resisted the Nazis from the start, Germany might have concluded that aggression does not pay. At any rate, this experience and its apparent lessons profoundly affected the Americans who lived through it. *They* did not want to have to explain to *their* children why *they* had not resisted evil. When the National Liberation Front and North Vietnam started to wage war against South Vietnam, our policy makers looked on the two as the Nazis of the present era. They quoted George Santayana (1863–1952), an American philosopher:

"Those who do not remember the past are condemned to relive it," and they acted accordingly.

It would be convenient, in a sense, if history repeated itself exactly. But it rarely does. From the viewpoint of many people in Vietnam—North and South—North Vietnam was not a foreign aggressor but one side in a civil war. To such people, *we*, the Americans, were the foreign aggressors. This in itself diluted the force of the Munich analogy. Our policy makers, besides, never really considered the limits of one nation's ability to help another. Czechoslovakia in 1938 was a powerful, heavily armed state that might well have been able to resist the Germans had it gotten support from Britain and France. South Vietnam was a paper country with little will to defend itself, and our presence in it compounded its lack of will.

The Domino Theory. Closely linked with the Munich analogy was the view that Southeast Asia was like a set of dominoes in a row: Push the first over, and all the others would fall. We had a deep-seated fear that insurgencies, rather like a plague virus, would spread without control throughout the Third World. By adhering to the domino theory we demonstrated once again a long-standing American cultural tendency to think of foreign policy in terms of grand principles rather than in terms of the more limited political and economic facts of the particular circumstances at hand.

Some Lessons. We cannot undo the disaster of Vietnam, but we can learn from it. History is not likely to repeat itself, but certain patterns of thought, particularly among our political leaders, may well do so.

Stereotypes. In the first place, our political leaders are prone to interpret the outside world, especially the Third World, through stereotypes. American and French critics pointed out that Vietnam was special, that its conditions did not necessarily apply to all of Southeast Asia. Vietnamese communism was fused tightly with a fervent nationalism, and the Communist leader, Ho Chi Minh, was in effect the country's George Washington. Perhaps there were no dominoes to fall, except Laos and Cambodia, which we created ourselves.

Mental Isolation. Henry Ford said, "History is bunk." Many American policy makers seem to agree with him; they ignore the histories, languages, and cultures of foreign countries. Americans expect foreigners to behave and think as we do, and when they do not, we are often surprised, annoyed, and confused.

Inattention. A third point is that managing a global network of alliances is enormously difficult, complicated, and time consuming. High policy makers, from the President on down, have only so much time, too little to pay attention to every problem, crisis, and flash point. Lack of time for thought and reflection is one of the most striking aspects of life in Washington, most of all at the highest levels. When policy makers are forced to make decisions about problems they have done their best to ignore, they tend to respond as leaders of a fire brigade: They want to go in and douse the problem.

Détente

We were sucked into the Vietnam War because we regarded North Vietnam and the NLF Vietcong as the cutting edge of world communism. Yet we did not come to blows with the leading power of world communism, the Soviet Union. In fact, from the mid-1960s, we worked at better relations with the Soviets.

Our will did not prevail in Vietnam. In fact, the war is now recognized by many to have been a civil war between different factions of one country. Today, the former National Assembly Building in Saigon is used as offices for the Communist Saigon authorities.

The Cold War began to wind down a bit under President Kennedy. In June 1963, in the aftermath of the Cuban missile crisis, the superpowers signed the Hot Line Agreement, which gave Washington and Moscow a quick way of communicating in a crisis. Later that year, they both assented to the Partial Nuclear-Test Ban Treaty, which stopped the testing of nuclear weapons in the atmosphere. More important than either of these agreements was the growing awareness on both sides of the need for a stable relationship.

Mutual Assured Destruction (MAD). Large disparities between Soviet and American nuclear forces created instability and, perforce, a growing threat of nuclear war. The weaker side would always fear a disarming first strike by the stronger and thus in a crisis, might, be tempted to launch a **preemptive strike,** one that anticipates a first strike from the other side. Strategic stability, it was now thought, required both the United States and the Soviet Union to have an assured second-strike capability. Both, in other words, should be able to absorb a first strike by the other side and still have enough weapons and delivery systems to destroy the enemy. Neither should become so strong that it would start a nuclear war, believing it could limit damage to itself and win. Nor should either be so weak that it would start a war to preempt a first strike by the other side. These ideas were the kernel of the so-called theory of **Mutual Assured Destruction,** MAD for short.

The basic prerequisite of MAD was and is that the United States and the Soviet Union must have large and reasonably invulnerable nuclear forces and that neither country be able to protect its population against the consequences of nuclear war. Because the United States was far ahead of the Soviet Union in such matters in the 1960s, we had to slow down our deployment of nuclear weapons to allow the Soviets to catch up and therefore create a roughly equal—and stable—strategic relationship. Because of this and the resources being expended on the Vietnam War, the United States added no strategic nuclear delivery vehicles (missiles or bombers) to its arsenal between 1967 and 1983, although we did qualitatively improve those we already had.

Salt I. These qualitative improvements were themselves a problem, however, for they, too, could upset the stability of the balance of terror. The superpowers therefore tried to limit their impact. One development was especially ominous, for a number of reasons. In the late 1960s, both the Soviet Union and the United States for the first time developed interceptor missiles, called **antiballistic missiles** (ABMs), which could shoot down incoming intercontinental missiles from the other side, although many specialists doubted their effectiveness. In response, the United States began to outfit its offensive missiles with **multiple independently targetable warheads** (MIRVs), as many as eight or nine warheads on a single missile booster. These made it possible to swamp any ABM defensive system. An action–reaction arms technology race started. Both sides were set, at enormous cost, to deploy ABMs that would not really make them more secure, since both sides also meant to deploy MIRVs. This made little sense, and the two governments knew it.

Because neither really wanted the ABM, it proved relatively simple to control. By May 1972, the leaders of the two superpowers were able to sign the first Strategic Arms Limitation Treaty **(SALT I),** which permanently limited the development and deployment of the ABM. SALT I also limited for five years the number of offensive missiles each side was permitted to deploy. The U.S. Senate approved this first SALT treaty in September 1972.

Trade. President Nixon was now officially committed to **détente**, the policy of better relations with the Soviet Union. From the mid-1960s to the early 1980s, the level of trade between East and West rose steadily. The Soviet bloc, whose economies were largely stagnant, benefited not only from Western goods but also from Western money and Western technology. In the West, many people thought that the United States and its allies did not reap comparable benefits. The Soviets, for example, continued to supply aid and weapons to North Vietnam.

The China Strategy. Mr. Nixon, however, also had a plan for encouraging the Soviets to halt their aid to North Vietnam. The plan was daring. Since the foundation of the People's Republic of China—Communist China—in 1949, the United States had proudly refused to have any dealings with it. Yet after 1960, Communist China not only broke with the Soviets but became their bitterest enemy. We continued to keep our distance from Communist China, whose complaint against the Soviets was that they were no longer sufficiently militant against the West. That aspect of the dispute was superficial and short-lived, for the hostility between the world's leading Communist powers, in the long run, rested on major differences of national interest and cultural outlook. China was too large to be brought to heel as a Soviet satellite. A decade after the rupture surfaced, even our policy makers realized that it was genuine, that it would be long-lived, and that American foreign policy should be changed accordingly.

President Nixon, who in the matter of anticommunism had always been among the purest of the pure, went on television in 1971 with a piece of shocking news. His national security adviser, Henry Kissinger, had visited Peking, held discussions with the Chinese, and even set up a visit to the mainland for Mr. Nixon. The President calculated that the prospect of a reconciliation between the Soviet Union's two greatest opponents, the United States and Communist China, would so terrify Soviet leaders that they would force North Vietnam to call off its designs on the South. Like a great many clever ideas, this one did not quite work. Nonetheless, it created a triangular relationship among the three nations, a relationship that was sometimes relatively friendly, sometimes hostile, and always distrustful.

At first glance, it may seem odd that the era of détente coincided with Richard Nixon's conservative Republican administration. But the oddity is deceptive. Nixon and Kissinger, although conservatives dedicated to maintaining American world power, were also realists. (Wilsonian idealism is characteristic more of Democratic than Republican administrations.) There were important *domestic* reasons why détente and the opening to China had to occur under a Republican administration if they were to have any long-term chances of success. In the early 1950s, Republican and Democratic conservatives accused the Democratic leadership of having lost China and promoting the spread of world communism in general. Ever since, Democratic administrations had leaned over backwards to prove they were not soft on communism. In this line, Republican conservatives had nothing to prove.

The United States and the Third World

In the opening days of the Cold War, world politics appeared to be simpler and more straightforward than it does today. World communism seemed to be the root of all great threats to American national interests. The American economy, then much more self-sufficient than it is now, was supreme in the world. We were even a net *exporter* of oil.

Decolonization in Africa and Asia produced scores of new nations, mainly Third World countries, rapidly swelling the size of the United Nations and greatly changing its political tone. Some of these new nations had won their independence through guerrilla warfare, and most of them were led by left-wing governments. In those days, however, the United States could and did overthrow threatening Third World regimes, as it did in Iran in 1953 and in Guatemala in 1954. Since then, direct intervention has become much more costly. American policy toward the Third World now tends to combine force (or threats of force) with support for pro-American (or at least anti-Communist) politicians and military men, the judicious use of foreign aid, and assistance to multinational corporations, most of which have American home bases. In addition, American liberals have pressured our Third World allies to hold free elections and respect human rights. American conservatives usually ask little of them but the crushing of local leftist movements.

What Is the Third World? The countries of the so-called Third World, also known as the **less developed countries** (LDCs), comprise a majority of the world's population and a very large majority of the United Nations' membership (161 countries in all as of 1985). Some of these countries (chiefly those in Latin America) have been politically independent for at least 150 years; some are primitive and underdeveloped; some have considerable industry. A cluster of them (mostly, but not entirely, in the Arab Middle East) produces most of the world's oil for export. Other LDCs—like Zaire, Zambia, and Zimbabwe, all in Africa—have vital strategic mineral resources. But a great many of them have few such assets or none. They differ in economics, culture, religion, and politics. No one policy is likely to cover them all.

What most LDCs do have in common, in one way or another, is deep and massive poverty and a recent history of economic or political colonization by the West, including the United States. That history, and its continuing

Along with many economists, most Third World countries believe that the development of a unified world economy distorted and impoverished their own economies. The Organization of Petroleum Exporting Countries (OPEC) was formed to assert its own interests against those of the developed world.

UPI

aftermath, have bred great resentments. The Mexicans, for example, have not forgotten that the "colossus of the North" took half of their former national territory in 1848, and they believe that the United States continues to promote American corporate interests in Mexico at the expense of Mexican interests. Even more dramatic was the passionate anti-Americanism that accompanied the Iranian revolution of 1979.

North-South Dialogue. In fact, all the LDCs wish to assert their own interests against those of the developed world. One expression of that desire was the emergence during the early 1970s of the Organization of Petroleum Exporting Countries (OPEC). Along with many economists, most Third World countries believe that the development of a unified world economy distorted and impoverished their own economies, and they are demanding a global redistribution of wealth from the rich North to the poor South. OPEC actually forced such a redistribution, although it benefited only countries with exportable oil. But it occurred on a huge scale that did sap American industrial and financial power and brought the international banking system to the verge of collapse.

The Limits of Power

Very much in the way that American policy from 1945 to the late 1960s was dominated by the Munich analogy, after 1972 the prevailing wisdom called for "No more Vietnams." American power went into retreat. As a substitute for the direct use of American forces, the Nixon administration devised what it called the **Nixon Doctrine:** helping our Third World allies—for example, Iran—to help themselves by selling them modern arms. But U.S. military forces were not to be made automatically available to such allies.

The administration of President Jimmy Carter (1977–1981) attempted to meet these new realities by supporting a much more circumscribed role for the United States in world affairs. In constant dollars (after adjusting for inflation), the U.S. defense budget was reduced. The administration attempted to substitute America's moral suasion for more tangible instruments of power, in part by waging a global human rights campaign. And when domestic unrest occured in Nicaragua and Iran, Carter refused to intervene militarily or covertly in a way that previous administrations might have done. (Perhaps as a result, the revolutionary Sandinista government took power in Nicaragua, and the theocratic Khomeini regime, as we have seen, seized power in Iran.) Only toward the end of his term in office, following the Soviet Union's invasion of Afghanistan in December 1979, did President Carter begin to understand the price of not pursuing a more aggressive foreign policy based on *Realpolitik* and traditional instruments of power.

Soviet Pipeline. As far as events have permitted—and in the Falkland Islands war[5] and the Middle East they did not—the Reagan administration

---

[5] In 1982 Argentina seized control of the Falkland Islands, in the South Atlantic, from Britain. Most of the people living on the islands wanted to remain a British dependency. British Prime Minister Margaret Thatcher dispatched a naval force to the South Atlantic which, after several sea and air battles with Argentine forces, landed marines on the Falklands and took back control of them for Britain. The Reagan administration was put in a difficult position by the war because it wanted to support its NATO ally, Britain, but did not want to alienate Argentina and the rest of Latin America. Opinion was divided concerning the degree to which Argentina had violated international law by seizing military control of the islands in the first place.

Table 17–2 National Defense Budget, 1973–1988 ($ millions)*

YEAR	DEFENSE OUTLAYS	PERCENTAGE OF GNP	PERCENTAGE OF BUDGET OUTLAYS
1973	$ 74,541	5.7%	30.3%
1974	77,781	5.6	29.0
1975	85,552	5.7	26.3
1976	89,430	5.3	24.5
1977	97,501	5.3	24.3
1978	105,186	5.3	23.5
1979	117,681	5.0	24.0
1980	135,856	5.2	23.6
1981	159,765	5.5	24.3
1982	185,309	6.0	24.9
1983	209,903	6.4	26.0
1984	227,413	6.2	26.7
1985**	253,830	6.4	26.5
1986**	285,669	6.7	29.3
1987**	321,160	6.9	31.3
1988**	358,378	7.1	32.7

*Absolute dollar volume of all defense outlays.

**Estimated.

Note: The GNP figures for 1985–1988 are projections and long-range economic forecasts, which may or may not be justified by events. Projected total budget and defense outlays for 1985 and beyond are based on administration objectives, which Congress will modify.

SOURCE: Budget of the United States Government, Fiscal Year 1986, pp. 5–6, 9–48.

tried to unite the West in common resistance to the Soviets. Wilsonian idealism crept back into American foreign policy. In 1982, the administration imposed a ban on the use of American technology for equipment used to construct a pipeline from Siberia to Western Europe. Europeans wanted the pipeline because they needed a stable and relatively cheap source of energy for their vulnerable economies. Besides, they were to produce most of the equipment used to build it. The Soviets, with vast natural gas reserves, wanted to sell them to Western Europe to earn hard currency. In December 1981, however, Poland's Communist government proclaimed martial law and suppressed the country's independent labor movement, called Solidarity. The Soviets were not directly involved, but the Reagan administration and many others blamed them for the repression in Poland. By this time, contracts for the pipeline had long been signed. Nonetheless, the administration issued its ban. Mr. Reagan argued that in the wake of martial law in Poland, it would be wrong to help the Soviets acquire hard-currency reserves and resources for a further military buildup. (The Soviets have been spending as much as 15 percent of their GNP on arms, compared with our 5 or 6 percent.) He also claimed that the pipeline would "Finlandize" Western Europe, that is, drive it toward neutralism.

Our European allies pointed out that on the one hand, they would be left without a cheap and abundant source of energy, and on the other large numbers of Europeans would be thrown out of work at a time of already high unemployment. Meanwhile, they noted, President Reagan had ended the grain embargo that President Carter imposed on the Soviets after they invaded Afghanistan in 1979. And the pipeline would be built in any case, they claimed, because the economic interests of Western Europe and the Soviet Union required it. Our allies defied the administration's ban.

Antinuclear Protest. When the Carter administration ended, a follow-on **SALT II** treaty still had not been ratified by the Senate. **SALT I,** ratified in 1972, had been expected to begin the very long process of capping the nuclear arms race. These expectations were dashed, in part because many well-informed people concluded, not without some reason, that the Soviets had used our weakness in the period after Vietnam to expand their global influence and their conventional and strategic military forces. Mr. Reagan, who shared this opinion, came into office intending to avoid further arms negotiations with the Soviets, except of the most cosmetic type, until the United States had built many new weapons, including nuclear ones.

One striking result, both internationally and domestically, was an explosion of antinuclear sentiment and activity. In the spring of 1982, proposals for a freeze on the proliferation of nuclear weapons were adopted in hundreds of New England town meetings. In the November 1982 elections, nuclear-freeze referenda were on the ballots of nine states. They won in all but Arizona. The long-term effect of the nuclear-freeze movement was hardly clear, but in the short run, at least, it forced the Reagan administration to accept ongoing negotiations with the Soviets much earlier than it had meant to accept them. One thing was certain: The whole area of nuclear weapons, formerly the preserve of our political and military elite, had been thrown open to a much wider public.

The Soviet pipeline designed to carry natural gas from the USSR to Western Europe caused an international uproar.

Reagan and the Third World. Just as the Reagan administration reverted to a traditional Cold War stance with respect to nuclear weapons and U.S. dealings with the Soviet Union, it reverted to a pre-Vietnam view of developing countries as principally battlegrounds in the global conflict between East and West. This was especially evident in Central America and the Caribbean. Large amounts of military and economic assistance were provided to the government of El Salvador, which in the early 1980s faced a challenge from both left-wing revolutionaries and right-wing extremists. U.S. troops participated in military exercises in Honduras, the purpose of which was in part to intimidate the new, revolutionary Sandinista government in Nicaragua (Honduras's neighbor to the south). In Nicaragua itself, the CIA, with the Reagan White House's support, provided covert assistance to Contra guerrillas who sought to overthrow the Sandinistas. In October 1983, United States military forces landed on the island of Grenada in the Caribbean, to oust a Marxist regime that had come to power there and appeared ready to permit the construction of Cuban and Soviet military facilities. The United States was once more projecting its military power abroad and pursuing a "forward" policy in the Third World.

To be fair, we must observe that the Reagan administration did not initiate all of its involvement in Third World turmoil. American troops were sent to Lebanon, which had been undergoing civil war since 1975, as part of Washington's enduring security commitment to Israel and as a result of an activist role that the U.S. had played in the Middle East since the early 1970s. When more than two hundred American soldiers were killed in the fall of 1983, when their barracks were blown up by Islamic extremists driving a truck loaded with explosives, Reagan's policies in the Middle East and elsewhere came under serious criticism. Congressional opponents of the administration accused it of lacking any clear-cut view of its objectives in the Middle East.

Members of Sandinista Popular Militia mark fifth anniversary of their founding.

They argued that America's new militance in the Third World would eventually bring about a repetition of Vietnam. Either such arguments were not convincing to the bulk of the American people, or the issues to which they pointed were not considered critical, because in November 1984 Ronald Reagan was elected to a second term by a landslide victory over Walter Mondale.

THE CONSTITUTIONAL SETTING

Foreign policy does not fit easily into our political system. The Constitution divided the powers of government among the President, Congress, and the federal courts, and between the entire federal government and the states. No one person or institution is sovereign, no one person or institution has the ultimate power to make basic decisions (see Chapters 2 and 3).

We manage to get along without a sovereign domestic power; sometimes just barely. Foreign policy is different. The lack of any world government *requires* the government of each nation to act as a sovereign power against all other nations. So we have always conceded to the federal government as a whole (though not to any one branch of it) full *external* sovereignty, the power to protect and promote the interests of this country against those of all others.

Another constitutional oddity of foreign policy is the extent of the President's control over it; not, of course, that the President has anything like complete control. Foreign policy, in Alexander Hamilton's words, calls for "unity, secrecy and dispatch," but the Constitution divides authority between Congress and the President, and as usual the Constitution is not always clear. The result, also as usual, is that Congress and the President continually bicker.

Treaties

The President, for example, negotiates treaties, but the Senate must ratify them by a two-thirds vote. At times, this shared power over treaties leads to very serious problems. Jimmy Carter had to struggle to secure the ratification of a treaty that by the year 2000 will transfer control over the Panama Canal from the United States to Panama, and in the end he won his two-thirds vote with a margin of only one vote to spare. Opposition to another treaty of Carter's, the SALT II agreement with the Soviet Union, was so strong that he did not even dare to bring the question to a vote.

Such difficulties and delays make foreign governments wonder if anyone is really in charge of our country. Sometimes, too, they wonder if it is worth the trouble negotiating an agreement that the Senate may decline to ratify.

Executive Agreements. Precisely to avoid these infuriating difficulties, Presidents often try to bypass the Senate altogether by signing **executive agreements,** rather than treaties, with foreign powers. Such agreements have a long history; one of the first, the Rush–Bagot agreement (1817), demilitarized the Great Lakes and is still in force. Another famous executive agreement with Britain, the "destroyer deal" of 1940, sent forty old American destroyers to Britain in return for long-term leases on U.S. naval bases in the Western Hemisphere.

Presidents argue that executive agreements are not treaties but mere attempts to "take care that the laws be faithfully executed." In the destroyer deal, for example, the Attorney General of the day suggested that the President's power to "dispose [that is, position] the armed forces of the United States" included a power to "dispose of the armed forces of the United States."

The President as Commander-in-Chief

The President, *is* commander-in-chief of the armed forces, but this rank does not—and was not meant to—confer the constitutional power to declare war, a power explicitly reserved for Congress. As commander-in-chief, the President does have the power to repel sudden attacks and can in certain circumstances *get us into* war. In other words, the ability to *make* war is distinct from the constitutional power to *declare* it, and these two coexist uneasily.

Nonetheless, the President does not in the strictest sense have a constitutional power even to make war. At the start of the nineteenth century, the U.S. Supreme Court ruled that it is for Congress to initiate all hostile acts against foreign powers, and that the President must stay within the limits set by Congress. The Court did concede (in 1863) that the President has the right to resist sudden attacks, including acts of insurrection. But the Court would give the President only the right to command the armed forces in the manner prescribed by Congress.

Congress, too, and only Congress, has the constitutional power to raise and support armies, to provide and maintain the navy, and to make rules for U.S. forces on land and sea. From the beginning, the President's powers in this and in all other respects were limited by the exclusive right of Congress to appropriate money.

Congress does not always use its exclusive rights effectively, however. Dozens of times, Presidents have sent American forces into large-scale combat without bothering to get (or even ask for) a declaration of war. Such cases go right back to the beginning. In 1798, for example, after long provocations from the French revolutionary government, President John Adams launched what official sources described as a "quasi war" with France. The last declaration of war was made on December 8, 1941, against Japan, Germany, and Italy. Yet the United States subsequently fought major wars in Korea and Vietnam, neither of which was declared by Congress. "Presidential wars" have become the norm rather than the exception, and it is quite possible that there may never again be a congressional declaration of war.

In the event of a nuclear war, a formal declaration would be utterly impossible. If the Soviets were to launch a first strike against us, we would have perhaps twenty minutes of advance warning—less if they used their missile-carrying submarines off our coast. If we were to launch a first strike against them—something we have explicitly threatened to do in certain circumstances—we would not wish to advertise the fact beforehand.

The Imperial Presidency

Why has Congress failed to assert its rights? The main reason is that even when the superpowers fight each other indirectly, through client states, they want to limit their involvement. Declarations of war lock countries into postures of violence and hostility that make nuclear catastrophe much more possible. After 1968 or so, there was a new reason. The Vietnam War was by then bitterly controversial. Had President Johnson or President Nixon asked for a formal war vote, he might have lost it. In fact, all foreign-policy questions have become more controversial in the last twenty years. No President is likely to ask for a declaration of war while this state of mind persists.

Because the President does have the ability to make war, if not the right to make or declare it, there is a strong urge to avoid these problems by simply presenting Congress with a *fait accompli*, the accomplished fact of American involvement. You will remember, for example, that in 1964 Lyndon Johnson sought congressional approval for the air strikes he launched against North Vietnam in retaliation for its attack on two U.S. ships. But he went to Congress *after* launching those attacks.

Mr. Johnson could do so because the Congress and the Supreme Court almost always accept whatever the President sees fit to order on grounds of "military necessity." Among other things, the Court has permitted the President to declare martial law, suspend *habeas corpus*, and seize control of economic assets in the United States, and it has not effectively prevented the President from waging war abroad.

No President would attempt to suspend *habeas corpus* in peacetime, and no Congress can let the President do so. The presidency and its powers feed upon crises, especially foreign crises. At such times, the fragmentation usually characteristic of American political institutions suddenly succumbs to a kind of temporary presidential authoritarianism. Since December 7, 1941, the United States has continually been thrust into foreign crises. Yet even now, short of a really major crisis, the division of powers still sometimes limits the President's power to commit the United States to any policy or action. So we find one group of writers bemoaning the evils of the imperial presidency, while another claims that the President does not have enough power and should be granted more.

Checking the President

Vietnam intensified the fear of an imperial presidency. Congress was unwilling to halt the war, but it did try to prevent future wars like it. Congress, in short, attempted to cut the President down to size.

The 1973 War Powers Act. The first step in doing so was to limit the President's ability to make war. The 1973 War Powers Act (passed over Richard Nixon's veto) requires the President to consult with Congress before sending troops abroad. Within 48 hours of sending troops into a combat zone, the President must report to Congress. If Congress does not approve the President's actions within sixty days, the President has a further thirty days to withdraw our forces. The act also permits Congress to end an undeclared war at any time by passing a **concurrent resolution,** one approved by a majority in both houses.

Some people viewed the War Powers Act as a symptom of the very problem it meant to cure. Before the act, the President had never had any explicit permission from Congress to wage undeclared wars. The act just gave him that and in this sense expanded the President's powers instead of limiting them.

The Congressional Veto. The War Powers Act permitted Congress to end undeclared wars by using a device of doubtful constitutionality: the congressional veto (see Chapters 6 and 12). Acts that incorporate congressional vetoes permit the President to do certain things for the time being but give Congress the right to veto those acts in the future. In some cases, a committee of one or both houses can stymie the President; in others, one house; and in still others,

"The blue countries are our staunch allies, the green are less staunch, and the yellow are not staunch at all."

both houses. These resolutions, even if passed by both houses, are not acts of Congress and therefore cannot be vetoed by the President.

Whatever the constitutionality of the congressional veto (and in 1983 the Supreme Court found some uses of it to be *un*constitutional), a good many acts of Congress embody it. Besides the War Powers Act, for example, there is also the Nelson–Bingham Act (1974), which permits Congress to veto arms sales by concurrent resolution. (See Chapter 6 for an account of a recent attempt to veto such a sale.)

Intelligence Oversight. The year after forcing the War Powers Act on Richard Nixon, in 1974, Congress passed the Hughes–Ryan Act, which required the President to approve secret intelligence operations and to report them to six, later eight, committees of Congress. The discovery, shortly thereafter, that the Central Intelligence Agency (CIA) had mounted intelligence operations against domestic antiwar activists inspired Congress to create two special oversight committees: the Senate and House select committees on intelligence. Executive Order 12036, issued by President Carter in 1978, still further restricted our intelligence agencies.

By then, however, the climate of opinion had shifted. Many people were now more worried about the Soviets than about the imperial presidency, and they felt that our intelligence agencies were overregulated. Some of the regulations were then relaxed or abolished; in the early 1980s, for instance, the CIA reported to only two committees of Congress, the House and Senate select committees on intelligence.

INSTITUTIONS

The Constitution gives the President an unusual degree of control over diplomatic and military matters because they commonly were and are thought to require "unity, secrecy, and dispatch." In fact, however, the executive branch is immense, so the goals of one of its policies often conflict with the goals of another. In 1979, when the Soviets invaded Afghanistan, President Carter responded by placing a partial embargo on sales of grain to the Soviet Union. That embargo frustrated the same administration's efforts to improve the U.S. balance of trade.

Often, executive departments and agencies lack information about the problems they are dealing with or about the possible consequences of various policies. The Soviet grain embargo, for instance, simply forced the Soviets to buy grain from Argentina instead of the United States. Argentina's former customers then turned to us. The embargo changed the patterns of the world grain trade, but it did not get the Soviets out of Afghanistan.

Various agencies often see the same problems from very different points of view; therefore, they propose very different solutions. In the grain embargo, the Department of Agriculture, with its constituency of farmers, did not wish to cut off a major source of farm income. The State Department, however, wanted to retaliate against the Soviet invasion by some means short of direct American involvement in the conflict. Like all other large organizations, the executive departments and agencies that make our foreign policy have an institutional view of the world and of their role in it. In a real sense, the struggle between the United States and the Soviet Union often takes a back seat to the struggle between the differing agencies in our own government.

The White House

The most important of all players in the game of foreign policy is the President of the United States. Until quite recently, the secretary of state was the President's chief foreign-policy adviser, but most secretaries get absorbed by the institutional interests and outlook of the State Department. Recent Presidents wanted to have foreign-policy advisers within the White House advisers beholden only to them. To that end, the post of the President's national security adviser (NSA) was created.

Competition between the secretary of state and the national security adviser is by now fixed in our system of government, although it ebbs and flows, depending on the personalities involved. It is for the President to decide whose advice to accept. During Richard Nixon's first term, Henry Kissinger, his NSA, had far more influence than William Rogers, the secretary of state. Hostility between the White House staff and the State Department was open and strong. During Nixon's second term, Kissinger wore two hats: He was both the NSA and secretary of state. President Carter's NSA, Zbigniew Brzezinski, competed with the secretary of state, Cyrus Vance. And Ronald Reagan's first NSA, Richard Allen, was driven out of office in part by the efforts of Mr. Reagan's first secretary of state, Alexander Haig—who was himself dismissed with a push from William Clark, Allen's successor and a former aide to Haig. In 1985, Robert C. McFarlane was President Reagan's national security adviser.

In Washington, a large staff and budget is the mark of a heavy hitter. The NSA has a large staff: about sixty foreign-policy specialists who, in some ways, duplicate the functions of the State Department.

The Intelligence Agencies

The humorist Art Buchwald once suggested that the United States could place its secret documents beyond the reach of foreign spies simply by putting them all on open file in the Library of Congress. We would then no longer be identifying the important ones by labeling them "top secret," and a good spy would be as hard to find as a good researcher.

As a matter of fact, however, most good spies really are good researchers, because the work done by intelligence agencies mostly involves compiling and evaluating information, chiefly from published and broadcast sources.

The Central Intelligence Agency (CIA). Since 1947, when it was formed, the Central Intelligence Agency has been the most important single part of U.S. intelligence. Its chief, the director of central intelligence (DCI), is among the President's most important advisers. The CIA's budget is a classified secret, divided (to confuse enemies) among the budgets of other departments and agencies. Best guesses are that the CIA spends more than $1 billion each year and that it employs about 15,000 people. Under President Reagan, William J. Casey has been DCI.

The CIA is not the only U.S. intelligence agency. Others include the Defense Intelligence Agency (DIA), the Office of Strategic Reconnaissance, and the intelligence branches of the army, navy, air force, and marines.

The "Dark Side." In 1931, when Secretary of State Henry L. Stimson was asked to permit intelligence gathering that involved interception and reading of mail, he refused on the ground that "gentlemen do not read each other's mail." Today's policy makers have long since lost such charming scruples; our efforts to gather intelligence involve every known tactic and device.

The CIA has always had two sides: *overt* intelligence gathering and evaluation, and *covert* (or secret) operations, often to support regimes friendly to the United States or to overthrow unfriendly regimes. From 1951 onward, covert operations were planned and carried out under the agency's deputy director for plans (after March 1973, the deputy director for operations). Some of these deputy directors—such as Allen W. Dulles, Richard Helms, and William Colby—later became directors of Central Intelligence.

Quite a few of these covert actions were truly spectacular. In 1953 and 1954, the CIA overthrew leftist governments in Iran and Guatemala, respectively. For years, it fought a "secret war" in Laos and attempted to "destabilize" the Sukarno government in Indonesia. It organized the Bay of Pigs invasion of Cuba in 1961 and, when that failed, tried to assassinate Castro with "hit men" from the American mafia. After Salvadore Allende had won Chile's 1970 presidential election, it attempted (unsuccessfully) to prevent him from taking office. Later on, in 1973, the CIA may have organized or aided the coup that overthrew Allende.

Very disturbing questions continue to surround the use of the CIA for covert operations known only to the President and a few aides, for there is no doubt that the President relied on the CIA as time went on. Some light was finally shed on the "dark side," in the mid-1970s, when the Senate investigated it. These investigations, most notably by the Senate Select Committee on Intelligence, chaired by Senator Frank Church (D–Idaho), discovered most of what we know about the CIA, including the fact that it had routinely spied on American citizens within the United States—a strictly illegal activity expressly prohibited by the National Security Act of 1947, which established the CIA in the first place. (Domestic surveillance is supposed to be carried out by *domestic* agencies, chiefly the Federal Bureau of Investigation.)

Even the overseas operations of the CIA came into disrepute. This no doubt has its dangers. The United States must deal with hostile powers that have no scruples about their own clandestine intelligence activities. The overseas commitments of our government probably require a CIA, including at least some secret operations. But if our standards, even of espionage, are not better than those of the Soviets, can we be so much better than they are? And if we do not ensure that the CIA obeys the law, can we claim to live under a constitutional government?

The State Department

The Department of State is supposed to be the chief foreign-policy arm of the U.S. government; its head, the secretary of state (in 1985, George P. Schultz), is supposed to be the President's chief foreign-policy adviser. Yet during the Johnson administration, the Defense Department had more impact on U.S. foreign policy than the State Department; and during the Nixon administration, the national security adviser overshadowed the secretary of state.

State is still responsible for the day-to-day conduct of foreign relations. It negotiates most agreements with foreign powers and international organizations. It protects our citizens and interests, particularly our commercial interests, abroad. And it coordinates, as far as possible, the doings of the forty federal agencies involved in foreign policy.

The department's operating units are organized in two ways: by region and by function. Regional bureaus, subregional offices, and country desks deal with specific areas and countries; among other things, they oversee the work of U.S. embassies and consulates. Functional bureaus—for example, the Bureau of Educational and Cultural Affairs and the Bureau of Politico-Military Affairs (P-M)—deal with different kinds of policy problems. Also connected to State are certain independent supporting agencies: the Agency for International Development (AID); the Arms Control and Disarmament Agency (ACDA), whose director often negotiates arms-control agreements; the U.S. Information Agency (USIA); and the Peace Corps.

State has changed a good deal since World War II, and not only because it has lost its automatic domination of U.S. foreign policy. In days gone by, ambassadors had a great deal of independence because communications with Washington were slow, expensive, and (by modern standards) infrequent. Ambassadors had to make up their own minds much of the time. Sometimes their independence had world-historical consequences. In 1803, for example, our ambassadors in Paris accepted the French government's offer to sell all of the Louisiana Territory. President Jefferson was horrified when he learned that they spent $15 million on it, but he and Congress went along with a decision that doubled the size of the United States.

Today, executives in Washington can monitor our ambassadors very closely. The President or the secretary can easily send out roving ambassadors to replace the men and women on the scene. Secretaries of state themselves are often tempted to engage in "shuttle diplomacy." As a result, the power and independence of our ambassadors are reduced. Negotiations are often conducted or directed by people from Washington, people who do not know local conditions or host governments.

Moreover, although the State Department enjoys a certain prestige, it is comparatively small. State has the lowest budget of any government depart-

The Department of State is responsible for the day-to-day conduct of foreign relations. Here, Secretary of State George Schultz meets with Soviet counterpart Andrei Gromyko.

Bill Fitz-Patrick, The White House

ment—less than 2 percent of the Defense Department's—and it has a staff of only 27,000. (Three million people work for Defense.) State also has a reputation—sometimes deserved, unfortunately—as a tradition-bound, indecisive, inefficient "fudge factory."

These very real problems notwithstanding, the State Department gets more than its fair share of criticism, in part because of its socially elite tone. (One congressman, who was perhaps not aware of all the dimensions of the struggle against communism, used to introduce bills to force the department to serve lemonade, rather than wine, at its social functions.) Our attitudes toward the rest of the world have changed much less since December 7, 1941, than might be supposed. By and large we are still suspicious of foreigners. State thus suffers from its association with them.

The Defense Department

The founding fathers and their generation inherited from the English a strong dislike of large standing (or permanent) armies. A standing army, as they saw it, was a standing threat to liberty. Until the Civil War, the United States neither had nor needed a large army of any kind. At the end of that war, the large army created to fight it was dismantled. World War I brought into being another large army, and this one, too, was dismantled at the war's end.

But the large army created to fight World War II never really went away. Since that war we have not only maintained a large standing army, but have forgotten that we had ever, on principle, refused to do so. An enormous amount of money has been poured into our armed forces and the weapons they use. This money gives them and our allies political clout, the kind of clout that in turn creates pressure for large and growing armed forces.

Originally, the army and navy were run by separate departments, and the air force was a part of the army. In 1947, the War and the Navy departments were fused into the new Department of Defense. At first the DoD was a "holding company" for the four military services—the army, navy, air force, and marines—which pretty much controlled it. In the 1960s, under Secretary of Defense Robert S. McNamara, civilians took effective control of the DoD and used its departmental structure (as distinct from the military structure of the four services) to impose a greater degree of control on the military's sometimes wasteful spending. Of course, the civilians in DoD have not *always* sought to limit the expenditure of resources on defense. Under President Reagan, the political appointees who run the Defense Department demand more ambitious defense programs and higher defense budgets. Caspar Weinberger, secretary of defense since 1981, has been in the forefront of the drive for military buildup. Such appointees play a major role in formulating and implementing Mr. Reagan's militantly anti-Communist foreign policy.

Interservice Rivalries. The DoD arose from the ashes of the old War and Navy departments because, among other reasons, the government wanted to restrain the rivalry for money, programs, and support among the four services. That rivalry, however, is still a political fact of life in Washington. Consider a classic case: the bickering, in the 1950s, between the navy and the air force over the power (and money) to build the Polaris submarine-launched ballistic missile.

The air force argued that Polaris should belong to the air force because the missile, if used, would be launched at "air force targets" in the Soviet Union—

that is, cities and other strategic targets—whereas the navy's proper task was keeping sea lanes open. The navy countered by claiming that Polaris should belong to the navy because the missile would be based on submarines, and submarines were the navy's sole preserve, whereas the air force had no proper business in the ocean at all.

The navy won but then turned around and argued that Polaris funding should *not* be taken out of the navy's share of the DoD budget because "Polaris is a *national* program, not a navy program." That, as two defense experts later commented, "was a rather disappointing thought for those who liked to think of the whole navy as a national program."[6]

The Defense Budget. During the 1950s and 1960s, the defense budget accounted for about half of the U.S. government's total spending and about 9 or 10 percent of the U.S. gross national product (see Chapter 16). Although the dollar totals for military spending continued to rise, by 1980, inflation and the so-called welfare shift (see Chapter 12) had reduced the defense budget to only a quarter of all government spending and to 5 percent of our GNP.

Rightly or wrongly, conservatives argued that this shift in the federal government's priorities had allowed the Soviets to create a more powerful military machine than ours, both in nuclear and conventional forces. Many experts deny that the Soviets are any stronger than we are, but no one denies that this widespread fear of Soviet strength affected our political behavior in the late 1970s and early 1980s. Its most dramatic effect was the election of President Reagan, who on taking office called for very large real increases (that is, over inflation) in the defense budget.

What would such higher defense budgets permit us to do? Some argue that with the extra money we could build weapons to neutralize weapons the Soviets have or are now building. Others reply that these weapons would increase our arsenal in an essentially meaningless way, since both sides can already destroy each other many times over.

Spending on military personnel gets more public support than spending on equipment, and everyone agrees that personnel costs have gone up more rapidly than almost any other part of the defense budget—one result of the ending of the military draft in the early 1970s. The draft is a tax on the bodies and time of the young men subject to it, and it is justified by the call to patriotism. That justification was accepted as a matter of course in both world wars and in Korea. It wore out its welcome in Vietnam—partly because the war itself did not command universal support, and partly because, during the Vietnam era, the draft was grossly unfair. Relatively few working-class men could claim the deferments (especially the educational deferment for college students) that were widely available to the middle and upper classes.

The demise of the draft required the United States to develop an all volunteer army. There were obvious costs involved. This army had to be paid wages high enough to attract volunteers, so a large share of the defense budget had to be diverted from weapons to paychecks. Ending the draft also meant that the lower ranks of the armed forces came to be staffed chiefly by blacks, Chicanos, and poor, rural whites. This fact gave rise to serious debate, which is still going on. Should the United States hire a mercenary army recruited from the poor, so that middle-class young men do not have to help

---

[6] Alain L. Enthoven and K. Wayne Smith, *How Much Is Enough? Shaping the Defense Program, 1961-1969* (New York: Harper, 1971), p. 17.

defend their country? Can we rely on an army that is less educated than the population it defends?

The high unemployment rate of the early 1980s increased the pool of young men and women who volunteered for military service. That in itself raised the standard of recruits. Assuming that such high unemployment does not become a long-standing feature of the economy, this improvement will be only temporary. What is not temporary is the federal defense budget crisis of recent years. How can the government liberate enough funds to spend more on weapons? An obvious way is to return to the military draft, which would eliminate the need to pay competitive wages to lower-ranked enlisted personnel. But short of major war, that would be politically controversial, to say the least.

Civilian Contractors. Another reason for the yearly rise in the defense budget is the truly gigantic cost of developing and buying weapons. Let's take just one example. The 1981 cost of one Trident submarine was $960.8 million, just for the vessel and its contents, not for the multibillion-dollar research, development, and start-up costs that made it possible. For $353 million or so you could buy *all* the activities of the Food and Drug Administration (in 1982); for $374.6 million, the entire Community Health Center Program.

Trident's development costs are even more impressive. Weapons and weapons systems cost a lot to develop, in part because new weapons push the frontiers of high technology, and their cost cannot be fully anticipated; but also because expenses are not tightly controlled (though Trident was one of the few programs to be developed *within* cost projections). The Defense Department's efforts to control cost overruns, currently running at billions of dollars per project, have mostly been anything but vigorous.

Systems of Payment. Cost-plus-fixed-fee (CPFF) contracts guarantee contractors a fixed fee over and above a project's cost. The CPFF system gave many contractors in the 1950s little reason to save taxpayers' money, and certain contractors were not above padding their costs. When Robert McNamara took over as defense secretary, in 1961, he imposed a new system: firm-fixed-price (FFP) contracts. Contractors competing for projects had to stipulate a firm fixed price that included a profit. Large cost overruns had to be paid out of the contractor's pocket. This system, too, had serious flaws, for at a time of high inflation few contractors could predict the cost of a high-technology project lasting five or six years. Companies would either pad their estimates or demand new infusions of cash when their original payments had run out. In the post-McNamara years, the Defense Department generally returned to the old cost-plus system.

The Joint Chiefs. The civilian hierarchy of the Defense Department was imposed on an elaborate military hierarchy, which culminates in the Joint Chiefs of Staff (JCS). The JCS comprises the chiefs of staff of the army and air force, the chief of naval operations, and the marine corps commandant. (See Chapter 12 for a description of the civilian and military commands.) Although it is supposed to report to the secretary of defense, it in fact has direct access to the President. Most of the time, if need be, it will take its case to Congress.

Despite appearances, the JCS does not really operate as a unified military command. Mainly, it works to perpetuate the rights, identities, and rivalries of the four services, which are sometimes neither simple nor straightforward. For example, President Reagan and the civilians he appointed to run the DoD rejected the SALT II treaty with the Soviets; the joint chiefs supported it.

Bill Fitz-Patrick, The White House

The President is commander-in-chief of the armed forces and appoints the secretary of defense.

The Outlook for Defense. When Ronald Reagan took office as President in 1981, defense experts—not only conservatives—generally agreed that the United States would have to rearm. But there was much dispute as to how much new weaponry would be needed, what kinds, and how fast we would need them. In fact, many experts would describe President Reagan's approach to arms spending rather as he would describe the liberal approach to social spending: an attempt to "throw money" at problems.

There was widespread distrust of Ronald Reagan on the war–peace issue. That distrust created the nuclear-freeze movement, which is essentially without precedent in the United States. It also reversed the post-Afghanistan drift to greater hawkishness on foreign policy issues (see Chapter 7). Certainly, "big defense" did not, in the early 1980s, have the kind of support it enjoyed in the Cold War to Vietnam era. Today, no Establishment enjoys the kind of undisputed, unruffled control over the discussion of foreign and military policy that it had before Vietnam. It's a new ballgame, with many more players, and no team can count on winning.

The Establishment

In the past, foreign policy was very much an elite undertaking, if only because relatively few people knew or cared about it. That, however, is not the only reason. Foreign affairs are conducted much more secretively and undemocratically than domestic politics. The people who participate in foreign affairs come almost exclusively from the most exalted and atypical ranks of American society.

Besides high-ranking government officials, the foreign-policy establishment includes three elements. First are the top executives of major business corporations. Some of these people merely influence the government; others actually enter it. Defense secretaries of the Eisenhower, Kennedy, Johnson, and Reagan administrations came into office directly from business. Most of the companies they had left, by the way, had extensive foreign interests and fat defense contracts.

The second segment of the Establishment consists of the "action" intellectuals, mostly linked to major universities such as Harvard (Henry Kissinger), Columbia (Zbigniew Brzezinski), and MIT (Walt W. Rostow) or to think tanks (private foundations) such as the Rand Corporation (James R. Schlesinger, secretary of defense for Nixon and Ford; secretary of energy for Carter). People like Kissinger enter the Establishment not only because they are smart but also because they know how to make contacts.

The Establishment's third components consists of the national law firms concentrated in New York City, firms with major ties to American domestic and multinational corporations. Many recent secretaries of state—for example, Truman's (Dean Acheson), Eisenhower's (John Foster Dulles), one of Nixon's (William P. Rogers), and one of Carter's (Cyrus R. Vance)—were partners in such law firms.

The voice of the Establishment, as far as it still has one, is the Council on Foreign Relations and its quarterly review, *Foreign Affairs*. But this Establishment is no longer really united. Until Vietnam, most of its members agreed on the wisdom of containing communism. Vietnam shattered this consensus, especially after 1968. Since then, the Establishment has become divided. Its more liberal wing advocates arms control and reduced American involvement overseas, and the conservatives (in groups such as the Committee on the Present Danger) look back fondly to the Cold War consensus. These divisions within the Establishment have given Congress and public opinion increased influence in shaping our foreign policy.

SUMMARY

Foreign policy is tied in with the day-to-day economic welfare of all Americans. It and its consequences now influence and sometimes dominate our domestic politics. Our moralizing, isolationist, and at times unrealistic national foreign policy has led us to see international politics as an arena for peaceful and profitable trade and as a field for fighting the battle between good and evil. With the Cold War, the United States slowly and painfully came of age as a great power, only to realize by the mid-1970s that its power and influence had declined. Our use of that power and influence must, in the aftermath of Vietnam, be measured, and disagreement about the most appropriate way to do this has generated dissension within the traditional foreign-policy elite.

The President and Congress share power over foreign policy. Even in the most strictly constitutional sense, however, the president has more authority in this area than in any other. The President's ability to make both overt and clandestine war created the "imperial presidency"; but after Vietnam, Congress took steps to limit the President's war-making power. Some people now think that the powers of the office are not sufficient to the demands of foreign affairs. Others wonder if any executive power, however broadly and imperially defined, can possibly be enough to meet what they regard as the excessive demands of our foreign policy.

As with other areas of policy, foreign and defense policies are very much affected by organizational interests and the struggle for influence in Washington. By and large, the State Department has been on the losing end of that struggle. What State has given up, the President's national security adviser and the Defense Department have won. The role of Defense, in particular, reflects the militarization of our foreign policy since December 7, 1941, the day when the United States ceased to be invulnerable to foreign attack.

This militarization continues, and it continues to raise disturbing questions on two levels: international and domestic. American foreign policy is conservative in its aims. Significant political and economic change in any part of the world, no matter how it is produced, seems almost always to be against the interests of the United States. But is it, really? The Soviet Union is not and cannot be responsible for all the discontent in the world. And at times, we appear to be saying that the future must be prevented from happening.

The domestic consequences of a military foreign policy could be serious. They boil down to two questions. Abraham Lincoln asked one of them: How we can hope to preserve liberty for ourselves if we deny it to others? The other question is: How long can we have a military foreign policy before it fatally corrupts our domestic political institutions?

Fears of this sort, in the mid-1970s, produced the hue and cry about the imperial presidency; the trigger was Watergate. The problem endures. Does liberty at home conflict with our interests abroad? Do we dare admit that it does?

SUGGESTED READINGS

STEPHEN E. AMBROSE, *Rise to Globalism: American Foreign Policy, 1938–1980*, 2nd ed. New York: Penguin, 1980. A useful history of American foreign policy from Pearl Harbor to the present.

THOMAS A. BAILEY, *The Pugnacious President*. New York: Free Press, 1980. A distinguished historian's hostile critique of militarized foreign policy and the imperial presidency.

RICHARD BARNET, *The Roots of War*. New York: Penguin, 1972. Written very much under the influence of the Vietnam War, a passionately anti-Establishment analysis of American foreign policy.

FRED L. BLOCK, *The Origins of International Economic Disorder*. Berkeley: Univ. of Calif., 1977. A revealing analysis of how the United States came to dominate the international economy in the 1940s and of how our economic leadership decayed in the 1970s.

JOHN F. CAMPBELL, *The Foreign Affairs Fudge Factory*. New York: Basic Books, 1971. A useful analysis of the State Department and its reputed lack of effectiveness.

CECIL V. CRABB, JR., *Policy-Makers and Critics: Conflicting Theories of American Foreign Policy*. New York: Praeger, 1976. A sensible and thorough discussion of Vietnam and post-Vietnam foreign-policy debates.

ROBERT O. KEOHANE and JOSEPH NYE, *Power and Interdependence: World Politics in Transition*. Boston: Little, Brown, 1977. Very useful for analyzing important aspects of global politics after 1945.

LAWRENCE J. KORB, *The Fall and Rise of the Pentagon: American Defense Policies in the 1980s*. Westport, Conn.: Greenwood Press, 1979. An analysis of the fiscal and moral impact of Vietnam on the Pentagon. Korb believed that the Pentagon's semieclipse during the 1970s was temporary, and he was right.

MARTIN MAYER, *The Fate of the Dollar*. New York: Signet (paperback), 1981. An extremely revealing, startling, and conservative account of the role played by central banks and bankers in international economic relations. Among other things, it reminds us that the governors of the Federal Reserve Board, like the leaders of the State and Defense Departments, play an important role in world politics.

THOMAS POWERS, *The Man Who Kept the Secrets: Richard Helms and the CIA.* New York: Knopf, 1979; Pocket Books (paperback), 1981. An extraordinarily illuminating study of the Central Intelligence Agency. The notes and bibliography are also extremely useful.

SENATE SELECT COMMITTEE ON GOVERNMENT OPERATIONS WITH RESPECT TO INTELLIGENCE ACTIVITIES (also called the Church Committee), *Alleged Assassination Plots Involving Foreign Leaders* (1975); *Covert Action Report* (1975); and *Hearings and Final Report* (1976). All published in Washington, D.C., by the U.S. Government Printing Office. Reports issued by the most important of the congressional committees that, in the mid-1970s, investigated U.S. intelligence activities abroad.

W. SCOTT THOMPSON, ed., *National Security in the 1980s: From Weakness to Strength.* San Francisco: Institute of Contemporary Studies, 1980. A collection of essays, some quite penetrating, that make the argument for much larger defense spending.

DANIEL YERGIN, *Shattered Peace: The Origins of the Cold War and the National Security State.* Boston: Houghton Mifflin, 1978. A more or less traditional and first-rate American view of origins of the Cold War and Soviet–American confrontation.

EPILOGUE

_____ **"A REPUBLIC, IF YOU CAN KEEP IT"** _____

On September 18, 1787, the day after the U.S. Constitution was signed,[1] Benjamin Franklin was asked by a Mrs. Powel, "Well, Doctor, what have we got, a republic or a monarchy?" "A republic," replied Franklin—"if you can keep it."[2] Ben Franklin knew that creating a free republic in a world of aristocracy and despotism was an immense achievement. But he also knew that our republic would not, and will not, necessarily survive. In fact, it must be created anew by each generation of Americans, a responsibility that now rests with us.

We Americans have now lived under the same republican constitution for some 200 years, and we have always more or less abided by it. When Ronald Reagan defeated President Carter's bid for reelection, everyone expected Mr. Carter to retire peaceably, and of course he did. Consider the reaction to the death (in 1982) of President Leonid Brezhnev, of the Soviet Union. Mr. Brezhnev's chief office was not the largely ceremonial presidency but the chairmanship of the Soviet Communist party. The Soviet system could not automatically replace him, nor could any of the contenders appeal to the legitimacy of a free election. Mr. Brezhnev was soon followed by Yuri Andropov, a former head of the Soviet secret police—and then, in quick

---

[1] By the delegates to the Constitutional Convention.
[2] Recorded by James McHenry in his diary.

sucession, by Konstantin Chernenko (1983) and Mikhail Gorbachev (1984). The 1982 transition was the first "legal" transfer of power in Soviet history.

We *can* be reasonably sure that whoever wins the next presidential election in the United States will take office on the appointed day. By the standards of most of the world, our system of government is almost inconceivably strong, because it is legitimate in the eyes of the people. Yet our system has real weaknesses, too. Of course, you don't have to read a textbook to discover them: They fill our newspapers and television shows, not to mention everyday life. Since John F. Kennedy's assassination in 1963, we have repudiated each of our Presidents. For the first time, we have been defeated in war—an unpopular war that divided us deeply. In the name of "national security," both Democratic and Republican administrations have committed misdeeds that cannot possibly be squared with our democratic values. In the fullness of time, the mentality of the national-security state penetrated our domestic politics and gave birth to the Watergate affair.

President Richard M. Nixon (1969–1974) was forced out of office by a national consensus against these threats to democracy. Yet many aspects of our national consensus were unraveling, and still are. During and after the late 1960s, the weight of federal spending shifted from "traditional" categories, such as defense and foreign relations, toward domestic social programs, which were and are controversial. Congress created and funded such programs believing that economic growth, rapid in the 1960s, would roll on forever—an assumption that was cruelly falsified by inflation, stagnation, and eventually, near-depression. During the same two decades, the coming of the civil rights revolution forced the country to pay more attention to the needs and demands of its black citizens, and these demands, and the policies they generated, were controversial too.

Of course, if the pie of society's wealth had grown, relative to the number of Americans who came to sit at the table, we might have bought off poor and black people simply by giving them their portion of the increase. To use the language of theory, society would then have resembled a **positive-sum game,** in which everyone wins by becoming absolutely (though not always relatively) better off. But the economy did not cooperate. The amount of wealth available for distribution to each individual grew more slowly in the 1970s than it had in the 1960s. At times it did not grow at all, and in the 1980s, it actually began to contract. If poor and black people were to gain absolutely, they would gave to gain relatively. In other words, their gains would come at the expense of others, who would then be absolutely and relatively worse off—a **zero-sum game.** In fact, however, no such gains occurred, because those who stood to lose were more powerful than their opponents. But the demand for such a redistribution persisted. Economic conflict became a standing feature of our society.

The Role of Politics

One school of thought argues that a political system can perform two basic functions. One is promoting the health of the economy and the interests of those who control it. The other (according to this view) is maintaining social harmony, or "legitimacy"—in part by manipulating the climate of political attitudes and expectations, in part by maintaining living standards. At times, of course, these two functions conflict. The government may then decide to cut social spending to free resources for the private sector, whose interests are paramount.

This line of reasoning, with its frank admission that different social interests cannot necessarily be reconciled, seems new and threatening to many of us. For three decades after the Great Depression and World War II, the dominating idea in American politics and government was what one political scientist called "interest-group liberalism."[3] By these lights, the federal government's proper function was to broker among organized interest groups, whose goals were thought to be compatible, and to underwrite the national standard of living. This conception of government required high levels of economic growth.

During the heyday of "interest-group liberalism," in the 1950s and early 1960s, our political and economic order did appear to satisfy the rival claims of competing interest groups. Without any need for large-scale economic management by the state, the cut-and-thrust of political competition seemed itself to ensure the greatest good of the greatest number.[4] This competition was the political equivalent of Adam Smith's "hidden hand"—the market forces that, so we are told, balance supply and demand (see Chapter 16). Our political scientists regarded the state as a barometer acted on by conflicting interests, not as a force in its own right, so they thought that we did not have to answer (or even ask!) the most basic of political questions: How can political leaders amass enough power to defend the common good?

The Crisis of Governability

These ideas won over our political scientists' hearts and minds in an age of prosperity at home and supremacy abroad. As that prosperity and supremacy wanted, "interest-group liberalism" waned along with them. At the same time, the number and composition of organized interest groups changed. With more groups competing for a share of the pie, and the pie itself growing little or not at all, "interest-group liberalism" lost credibility. Many scholars and writers concluded that the country was suffering from a "crisis of governability" produced (among other causes) by an excess of democracy. What most political scientists of the 1950s and early 1960s had regarded as the virtues of our political system—its lack of central coordination and its free-wheeling interest groups competing to shape public policy—now seemed to be pushing our national steering mechanism in too many directions.[5]

Other critics pointed to the "cultural contradictions of capitalism." Accord-

---

[3] Theodore Lowi, *The End of Liberalism*, 2nd ed. (New York: Norton, 1979).

[4] The classic expression of this view was undoubtedly David B. Truman, *The Governmental Process* (New York: Knopf, 1951), which is still well worth reading. For a more theoretical study in the same school, by one of the greatest living political scientists, see Robert A. Dahl, *A Preface to Democratic Theory* (Chicago: University of Chicago Press, 1956).

[5] These attacks were particularly associated with the journal *The Public Interest*. See Nathan Glazer and Irving Kristol, eds., *The American Commonwealth 1976* (New York: Basic Books, 1976), a collection of essays by authors on various aspects of the "governability crisis." See also the report to the Trilateral Commission: Samuel P. Huntington, Michael Crozier, and Joji Watanuki, *The Crisis of Democracy* (New York: New York University Press, 1975). Huntington's essay on the American political situation is particularly relevant. He extended this line of analysis further in *American Politics: The Promise of Disharmony* (Cambridge: Harvard University Press, 1982).

ing to them,[6] the years of prosperity had produced a generation of hedonists who cared only for the proverbial "sex, drugs, and rock and roll" and were undermining the ethic of hard work and self-denial that had built our society. The contradiction: If it were somehow possible to restore Victorian levels of saving and investment, our levels of consumption would be too low to sustain mass production (see Chapter 10). These dangers were embodied in three concrete developments: "stagflation" in our economy; the foreign-policy "drift" that followed the Vietnam War; and the proliferation of demands from such newly organized groups as blacks, women, environmentalists, and critics of our foreign and defense policies. The conservative critics were looking for a way back to the 1950s, at home and abroad: the Cold-War consensus, and lower levels of social spending. With some success, these critics waged an intellectual guerilla war against the interest-group liberalism that had so long dominated public policy.

Now, the United States, unlike almost all other industrial democracies, has no mass left-wing political party. When the center and its gospel of social harmony went into eclipse, conservatism was the only game in town. So these attacks on the theory and practice of "interest-group liberalism" paved the way for Ronald Reagan's election as President in 1980, and his reelection in 1984. Of course, Reagan sought to explain his own policies by appealing to social harmony, not by summoning the American people to a class war. Yet these policies were classic examples of zero-sum politics in action.

President Reagan had three main objectives. The first was more or less straightforwardly to transfer wealth from the poor and a large part of the middle class, on the one hand, to the wealthy, on the other—a transfer defended as the only means of providing capital for investment (and thus job-creation) in the private sector. The second objective was to reduce federal domestic spending fast enough and far enough to make room for a vast and rapid defense buildup. The third, and probably most basic, objective was to reduce permanently the federal government's power to manage the economy.

Except in times of crisis, our political system does not encourage large-scale policy changes inspired by a coherent point of view. The enactment in 1981 of much of the President's program was a symptom of crisis, and these symptoms have not been limited to changes in policy. In recent years, our political institutions have been challenged too. For example, certain very important people, in both parties, would like to limit the President to a single 6-year term, with no opportunity for reelection. Why? Because, as Cyrus Vance, President Carter's first secretary of state, put it, "In the last 18 months of a 4-year term" presidential decision-making is distorted by political considerations that "may change at the time of any given primary."[7]

Political Action: "Which Side Are You On?"

Around 1800, Thomas Jefferson expressed a hope that our people would not reach the Pacific Ocean for a thousand years. Mr. Jefferson believed that the

---

[6] The classic contemporary expression of this is Daniel Bell, *The Cultural Contradictions of Capitalism* (New York: Basic Books, 1976). Much of Bell's argument was first made long ago by the eminent economist Joseph Schumpeter, in *Capitalism, Socialism and Democracy*, 3rd ed. (New York: Harper & Row, 1950). Schumpeter argued that although the Marxist economic analysis of capitalism and its prospects was largely false and misleading, capitalism would probably pass away. Neither Schumpeter nor Bell could be called a radical, either in politics or economics.

[7] *Boston Globe*, November 25, 1982, p. 6.

passing of the frontier would also mean the passing of the social and economic bases of democracy: the family farm and, along with it, truly broad-based property ownership. By the time of Abraham Lincoln's presidency, in the early 1860s, the family farm was already ceasing to be the foundation of our country. American society had become more complex and therefore more open to the possibility of conflict among interests and interest groups. Labor (the working people) now confronted capital (the employers) as a distinct and potentially hostile force. President Lincoln commented on the competition between them in his first annual message to Congress, in 1861. "Labor [he wrote] is prior to and independent of capital. Capital is only the fruit of labor, and could never have existed if labor had not first existed. Labor is the superior of capital, and deserves much the higher consideration."[8] He added that "the effort to place capital on an equal footing with, if not above, labor" seemed to undermine "popular institutions."[9]

Nonetheless, until the Great Depression, the federal government stood shoulder-to-shoulder with employers, not with working people. But the Depression so shook our social harmony that for almost half a century thereafter, the federal government tried to keep economic and social conflict out of sight and out of mind. Inequality persisted, of course, but its effects were contained by rapid economic growth. By controlling the possibility of conflict between economic inequality and political democracy, our politicians hoped to legitimate both.

These politicians were not, as individuals, more generous than those of the present. But the disasters of the 1930s and 1940s—disasters that not only reversed the progress of centuries but eclipsed the very hope of progress—made them wise. They had seen with their own eyes that a democracy must satisfy at least some of the people's expectations if it is also to protect the privileges of the well-to-do. And they had also seen that the real alternative to democracy is dictatorship. In this sense, even the most liberal among them practiced a sort of conservatism—a conservatism that we ignore at our peril.

As every thoughtful student of this country has observed for generations, beneath our fabled national consensus lies a vast amount of explosive tinder: racial, ethnic, and religious conflicts in greater profusion than anywhere else. One conservative writer, Kevin Phillips, even suggests that should Reaganomics (see Chapter 16) fail, it may be followed by a right-wing populism similar to fascism.[10] Such fears probably do not give enough weight to our liberal and democratic values, yet the fact that these fears seriously bother serious people shows that something, somewhere, may be seriously wrong.

"More Equal." All systems of power have a characteristic "mobilization of bias."[11] To put the same thought another way, certain people in every system have more and better opportunities for political action than most others do.

---

[8] Abraham Lincoln, Message to Congress, Dec. 3, 1861: Reprinted in *Appleton's Annual Cyclopedia for 1861* (New York: D. Appleton, 1862), p. 612.

[9] Ibid. Thaddeus Stevens, a canny businessman who was chairman of the House Ways and Means Committee, was asked by a colleague what Congress should do about this part of the President's message. He replied that he didn't know, since the House had no Committee on Metaphysics.

[10] Kevin P. Phillips, *Post-Conservative America: People, Politics and Ideology in a Time of Crisis* (New York: Random House, 1982).

[11] E. E. Schattschneider, *The Semisovereign People: A Realist's View of Democracy in America* (New York: Holt, Rinehart & Winston, 1960), esp. pp. 30ff. This little book is a genuine classic, whose profound insights into American politics make it worth reading carefully, and more than once.

Even when all individuals and organized interests are equal before the law, as they are in this country, some (to use George Orwell's phrase[12]) are "more equal than others." Every citizen has one and only vote but the members of our corporate and banking elite not only vote but also give large sums of money to candidates and PACs, and support lobbying before Congress and the executive agencies. Indeed, some are important enough to be personally involved in executive decision-making—as "wise men," especially in foreign-policy matters.

The Possibilities for Political Action. For better or worse, our political system (like all others) divides society into the rulers and the ruled. In this country (as in all others), some individuals and interest groups are "more equal than others." Yet—as so many critics complain—the privileges and power of our elite are anything but unassailable, and all but the most apathetic of our people can and, in certain circumstances, do play a part in our political life.

Of course, those who benefit from our system tend to work within it—through electoral politics and interest-group activity. Those who reject our system and its basic premises will—if they dare—work against it. There is also a third way, the way of those who do not reject the fundamentals of our political culture but cannot accept specific policies. These people may work "around" the system.

For example, the civil-rights movement broke state and local laws that it (and the federal government) held to be unjust. So too did those who opposed the Vietnam War. "Civil disobedience" of this sort raises the most serious questions of law and political morality. No government worthy of the name can be expected to play dead when authority is challenged, nor can a society based on equality under law exempt citizens from the duty to obey it. Yet our country itself was created in a revolution, the supreme act of illegality, so it would not, perhaps, be wise to "damn a rebel out of hand." When, if ever, should citizens break the law to achieve political goals? If we cannot resolve that vexed a question here, perhaps we can at least clarify the issue.

Certainly, those who would violate the law on grounds of conscience must care intensely about the issues that force them to such extremes. They must be convinced that it would be immoral not to act. They must be prepared to accept the consequences of their illegal acts—imprisonment or fines—otherwise, their cause is mere anarchy. Last, they must recognize that such tactics are not likely to succeed unless substantial parts of public and official opinion sympathize with their cause and their methods.

The Importance of Electoral Politics. Protest politics sometimes does succeed. But if any theme unites the writings of our characteristic political thinkers, it is the idea that electoral politics must in the long run be the most important means of expressing the popular will. Electoral politics can only play that role to the extent that our people choose to participate. And they cannot participate effectively if political parties are too weak to involve them in the business of electing candidates with common aims. Like it or not, political parties have been the only means of balancing the concentrated power of the Few and the dispersed power of the Many. Parties and only parties allow politicians to accumulate enough power to achieve their goals.

So the acute decay of American political parties worries people who love and understand our political ideals. Whatever else you might say about the

---

[12] In *Animal Farm* (1945).

Reagan Revolution, it could revive our political parties and sharpen the differences between them. For if we again start to debate issues of basic importance, we must again turn to the only institutions capable of bringing about basic change.

The American Dream

"America," the poet sang, "was promises."[13] Or as a philosopher (invoking the words of Lincoln's Gettysburg Address) put it, the United States is the only country "dedicated to a proposition."[14] Our nation is based not on common blood but on common ideas: the fourfold American creed of political and civil liberty, private property, political democracy, and religious freedom. Many people believe that these four make up a seamless web, that there can be no serious tensions or contradictions among them. The fact that we Americans agree on so many basic political questions that elsewhere have generated controversy, hatred, and genocide appears to support this idea. Yet we Americans have argued about the meaning of the American Dream, sometimes in debating chambers, sometimes on the battlefield. As President Lincoln said, we have never had a common definition of liberty:

> We all declare for liberty; but in using the same word we do not mean the same thing. With some, the word liberty may mean for each man to do as he pleases with himself and the product of his labor; while with others the same word may mean for some men to do as they please with other men and the product of other men's labor. Here are two not only different, but incompatible things, called by the same name, liberty. And it follows that each of the things is by the respective parties called by two different and incompatible names, liberty and tyranny.[15]

How much individual liberty should each of us enjoy? Should it be limited by the general interest and to what extent? How can we control the tensions between capital and labor, between an unequal economic system and a political democracy? Since the coming of independence, such basic questions have divided patriotic, sincere Americans. They divide us now.

Conflict over fundamentals is painful, but it is also necessary. For ideas, and visions of the good society based upon them, are the ultimate source of all that happens in politics. As John Maynard Keynes (see Chapter 16) put it:

> The ideas of economists and political philosophers, both when they are right and when they are wrong, are more powerful than is commonly understood. Indeed the world is ruled by little else. Practical men, who believe themselves to be quite exempt from any intellectual influences, are usually the slaves of some defunct economist. Madmen in authority, who hear voices in the air, are distilling their frenzy from some academic scribbler of a few years back . . . Soon or late, it is ideas, not vested interests, which are dangerous for good or evil.[16]

---

[13] Archibald MacLeish, *America Was Promises* (1939).

[14] i.e., "that all men are created equal." Lincoln here refers to legal and political equality, not to equality of property. The philosopher was Bertrand Russell.

[15] Address at the Sanitary Fair, Baltimore, April 18, 1864. Lincoln's comment is echoed in the folk saying, "Freedom to the shark is death to the minnows."

[16] John Maynard Keynes, *The General Theory of Employment, Interest and Money* (New York: Harcourt, Brace, 1936), pp. 383–84. Consider also a comment by Percy Bysshe Shelly, in *A Defense of Poetry* (1821): "Poets are the unacknowledged legislators of the world."

Disagreement about ideas is the bone and muscle of a free society, proclaiming the vigor of the American dream, not its decay. Our political tradition speaks with many voices, not just one, and within that tradition we might easily find room for libertarian conservatism, on the right, or social democracy, on the left. Remember: What separates human beings from beasts of the field is the ability to reflect on our condition and change it if we want to. No doubt, we cannot change it all at once—and in some ways, not at all. But in the long run, the philosophers, the poets, and the dreamers often get their way. President Reagan won the election because he and his supporters had ideas, and a vision based upon them, and the losers did not. "Greater than the tread of mighty armies is an idea whose time has come."[17]

Consider the Alternatives

We cannot deal with any problem unless we agree that it exists and that it can and should be resolved. That is why no aspect of politics is so important as its "agenda": our belief that the time has come to address certain issues, and that certain kinds of solutions are (or are not) possible. For "political conflict is not like an intercollegiate debate in which the opponents agree in advance on a definition of the issues."

> As a matter of fact, the definition of the alternatives is the supreme instrument of power; the antagonists can rarely agree on what the issues are because power is involved in the definition. He who determines what politics is about runs the country, because the definition of the alternatives is the choice of conflicts, and the choice of conflicts allocates power.[18]

There are two main players in the effort to shape our national agenda. The first is the President of the United States, our chief source of official information and inspiration. Unofficial opinion comes to us mainly from the second, the mass media. Even at their most powerful, the mass media do not tell us what to think, but they tell many of us what to think about, and that is the "supreme instrument of power." You, too, will be subject to that power if you do not free yourself from the "images of the tribe" and the "images of the cave" that make up TV's stock-in-trade.

What can you do? Careful reading of our best newspapers, like *The New York Times*, and specialist publications like *Congressional Quarterly Weekly Report* and the *National Journal*, can be quite eye-opening. So too can the C-SPAN cable-TV channel, which covers the House of Representatives and much else besides. Finally, you might investigate the writings of those who have studied our government and history. They are anything but infallible, yet the best of them often raise important issues that elude the mass media.

This book itself is a beginning, not an end. The more you know about our institutions, processes, and history, the more you can do to change—or preserve—them. If you do not set your own agenda and work to promote it, someone else's agenda must prevail.

The Years Ahead

Last but not least, remember the words of Sherlock Holmes, "Assume nothing, Watson."[19] Times of crisis awaken sleeping dogs; they raise anew

---

[17] Victor Hugo, *History of a Crime* (1852).

[18] Schattschneider, *The Semisovereign People*, p. 68.

[19] Dr. John Watson, the sidekick of Sir Arthur Conan Doyle's famous detective.

questions we thought we had settled long ago. We can now take very little for granted. Whatever you may think of President Reagan's policies, he and his supporters have asked many basic questions. Rightly or not, they believe that the needs of private enterprise—from which we all, ultimately, derive our incomes—require us to accept higher levels of unemployment and pollution, and lower levels of government services, especially social services. These ideas cannot be dismissed out of hand. But the effort to carry them out affects different groups of Americans quite differently. Will you benefit from such policies or pay the price for them? You ought to know.

Some opponents of President Reagan claim that the problems of our economy are so deeply entrenched that only the government can break the necessary logjams and mobilize the necessary resources. But how can a government that lacks internal sovereignty (see Chapters 2 and 3) amass the power to plan our economy? And if it did, can we be sure that its plans would work? If the United States does have a crisis of governability, can it be overcome by any means compatible with political democracy? Or by any means at all?

APPENDIX

In Congress, July 4, 1776.

A Declaration by the Representatives of the United States of America, in General Congress assembled. When in the Course of human Events, it becomes necessary for one People to dissolve the Political Bands which have connected them with another, and to assume among the Powers of the Earth, the separate and equal Station to which the Laws of Nature and Nature's God entitle them, a decent Respect to the Opinions of Mankind requires that they should declare the causes which impel them to the Separation.

We hold these Truths to be self-evident, that all Men are created equal, that they are endowed by their Creator with certain unalienable Rights, that among these are Life, Liberty, and the Pursuit of Happiness—That to secure these Rights, Governments are instituted among Men, deriving their just Powers from the Consent of the Governed, that whenever any Form of Government becomes destructive of these Ends, it is the Right of the People to alter or to abolish it, and to institute new Government, laying its Foundation on such Principles, and organizing its Powers in such Forms, as to them shall seem most likely to effect their Safety and Happiness. Prudence, indeed, will dictate that Governments long established should not be changed for light and transient Causes; and accordingly all Experience hath shewn, that Mankind are more disposed to suffer, while Evils are sufferable, than to right themselves by abolishing the Forms to which they are accustomed. But when a long Train of Abuses and Usurpations, pursuing invariably the same Object, evinces a Design to reduce them under absolute Despotism, it is their Right, it is their Duty, to throw off such Government, and to provide new Guards for their future Security. Such has been the patient Sufferance of these Colonies; and such is now the Necessity which constrains them to alter their former

Systems of Government. The History of the present King of Great-Britain is a History of repeated Injuries and Usurpations, all having in direct Object the Establishment of an absolute Tyranny over these States. To prove this, let Facts be submitted to a candid World.

He has refused his Assent to Laws, the most wholesome and necessary for the public Good.

He has forbidden his Governors to pass Laws of immediate and pressing Importance, unless suspended in their Operation till his Assent should be obtained; and when so suspended, he has utterly neglected to attend to them.

He has refused to pass other Laws for the Accommodation of large Districts of People, unless those People would relinquish the Right of Representation in the Legislature, a Right inestimable to them, and formidable to Tyrants only.

He has called together Legislative Bodies at Places unusual, uncomfortable, and distant from the Depository of their Public Records, for the sole Purpose of fatiguing them into Compliance with his Measures.

He has dissolved Representative Houses repeatedly, for opposing with manly Firmness his Invasions on the Rights of the People.

He has refused for a long Time, after such Dissolutions, to cause others to be elected; whereby the Legislative Powers, incapable of Annihilation, have returned to the People at large for their exercise; the State remaining in the mean time exposed to all the Dangers of Invasion from without, and Convulsions within.

He has endeavoured to prevent the Population of these States; for that Purpose obstructing the Laws for Naturalization of Foreigners; refusing to pass others to encourage their Migrations hither, and raising the Conditions of new Appropriations of Lands.

He has obstructed the Administration of Justice, by refusing his Assent to Laws for establishing Judiciary Powers.

He has made Judges dependent on his Will alone, for the Tenure of their offices, and the Amount and payment of their Salaries.

He has erected a Multitude of new Offices, and sent higher Swarms of Officers to harrass our People, and eat out their Substance.

He has kept among us, in Times of Peace, Standing Armies, without the consent of our Legislatures.

He has affected to render the Military independent of, and superior to the Civil Power.

He has combined with others to subject us to a Jurisdiction foreign to our Constitution, and unacknowledged by our Laws; giving his Assent to their Acts of pretended Legislation:

For quartering large Bodies of Armed Troops among us:

For protecting them, by a mock Trial, from Punishment for any Murders which they should commit on the Inhabitants of these States:

For cutting off our Trade with all Parts of the World:

For imposing Taxes on us without our Consent:

For depriving us, in many cases, of the Benefits of Trial by Jury:

For transporting us beyond Seas to be tried for pretended Offences:

For abolishing the free System of English Laws in a neighbouring Province, establishing therein an arbitrary Government, and enlarging its Boundaries, so as to render it at once an Example and fit Instrument for introducing the same absolute Rule into these Colonies:

For taking away our Charters, abolishing our most valuable Laws, and altering fundamentally the Forms of our Governments:

For suspending our own Legislatures, and declaring themselves invested with Power to legislate for us in all Cases whatsoever.

He has abdicated Government here, by declaring us out of his Protection and waging War against us.

He has plundered our Seas, ravaged our Coasts, burnt our towns, and destroyed the Lives of our People.

He is, at this Time, transporting large Armies of foreign Mercenaries to compleat the works of Death, Desolation, and Tyranny, already begun with circumstances of Cruelty and Perfidy, scarcely paralleled in the most barbarous Ages, and totally unworthy the Head of a civilized Nation.

He has constrained our fellow Citizens taken Captive on the high Seas to bear Arms against their Country, to become the Executioners of their Friends and Brethren, or to fall themselves by their Hands.

He has excited domestic Insurrections amongst us, and has endeavoured to bring on the Inhabitants of our Frontiers, the merciless Indian Savages, whose known Rule of Warfare, is an undistinguished Destruction, of all Ages, Sexes and Conditions.

In every stage of these Oppressions we have Petitioned for Redress in the most humble Terms: Our repeated Petitions have been answered only by repeated Injury. A Prince, whose Character is thus marked by every act which may define a Tyrant, is unfit to be the Ruler of a free People.

Nor have we been wanting in Attentions to our British Brethren. We have warned them from Time to Time of Attempts by their Legislature to extend an unwarrantable Jurisdiction over us. We have reminded them of the Circumstances of our Emigration and Settlement here. We have appealed to their native Justice and Magnanimity, and we have conjured them by the Ties of our common Kindred to disavow these Usurpations, which, would inevitably interrupt our Connections and Correspondence. They too have been deaf to the Voice of Justice and of Consanguinity. We must, therefore, acquiesce in the Necessity, which denounces our Separation, and hold them, as we hold the rest of Mankind, Enemies in War, in Peace, Friends.

We, therefore, the Representatives of the UNITED STATES OF AMERICA, in General Congress Assembled, appealing to the Supreme Judge of the World for the Rectitude of our Intentions, do, in the Name, and by Authority of the good People of these Colonies, solemnly Publish and Declare, That these United Colonies are, and of Right ought to be, Free and Independent States; that they are absolved from all Allegiance to the British Crown, and that all political Connection between them and the State of Great-Britain, is and ought to be totally dissolved; and that as Free and Independent States, they have full Power to levy War, conclude Peace, contract Alliances, establish Commerce, and to do all other Acts and Things which Independent States may of right do. And for the support of this declaration, with a firm Reliance on the Protection of divine Providence, we mutually pledge to each other our lives, our Fortunes, and our sacred Honor.

THE CONSTITUTION OF THE UNITED STATES OF AMERICA

We the people of the United States, in Order to form a more perfect Union, establish Justice, insure domestic Tranquility, provide for the common defence, promote the general Welfare, and secure the Blessings of Liberty to ourselves and our Posterity, do ordain and establish this Constitution for the United States of America.

Article 1

Section 1. All legislative Powers herein granted shall be vested in a Congress of the United States, which shall consist of a Senate and House of Representatives.

Section 2. The House of Representatives shall be composed of Members chosen every second Year by the People of the several States, and the Electors in each State shall have the Qualifications requisite for Electors of the most numerous Branch of the State Legislature.

No person shall be Representative who shall not have attained to the Age of twenty-five Years, and been seven Years a Citizen of the United States, and who shall not, when elected, be an Inhabitant of that state in which he shall be chosen.

Representatives and *direct Taxes* shall be apportioned among the several States which may be included within this Union, according to their respective Numbers, *which shall be determined by adding to the whole Number of free Persons, including those bound to Service for a Term of Years, and excluding Indians not taxed, three fifths of all other Persons.*[1] The actual Enumeration shall be made within three Years after the first Meeting of the Congress of the United States, and within every subsequent Term of ten Years, in such Manner as they shall by Law direct. The Number of Representatives shall not exceed one for every thirty Thousand, but each State shall have at Least one Representative; and until such enumeration shall be made, the State of New Hampshire shall be entitled to chuse three, Massachusetts eight, Rhode-Island and Providence Plantations one, Connecticut five, New-York six, New Jersey four, Pennsylvania eight, Delaware one, Maryland six, Virginia ten, North Carolina five, South Carolina five, and Georgia three.

When vacancies happen in the Representation from any State, the Executive Authority thereof shall issue Writs of Election to fill such Vacancies.

The House of Representatives shall chuse their Speaker and other officers; and shall have the sole Power of Impeachment.

Section 3. The Senate of the United States shall be composed of two Senators from each State, *chosen by the Legislature thereof,*[2] for six Years; and each Senator shall have one Vote.

Immediately after they shall be assembled in Consequence of the first Election, they shall be divided as equally as may be into three Classes. The Seats of the Senators of the first Class shall be vacated at the Expiration of the second Year, of the second Class at the Expiration of the fourth Year, and of the third Class at the Expiration of the sixth Year, so that one-third may be chosen every second Year; *and if Vacancies happen by Resignation, or otherwise, during the Recess of the Legislature of any State, the Executive*

---

[1] Those parts of the Constitution later changed by amendment have been set in italics. Changed by the Fourteenth and Sixteenth Amendments.

[2] Repealed by the Seventeenth Amendment.

thereof may make temporary Appointments until the next Meeting of the Legislature, which shall then fill such Vacancies.[3]

No Person shall be a senator who shall not have attained to the Age of Thirty Years, and been nine Years a Citizen of the United States, and who shall not, when elected, be an Inhabitant of that State in which he shall be chosen.

The Vice-President of the United States shall be President of the Senate, but shall have no vote, unless they be equally divided.

The Senate shall chuse their other Officers, and also a President pro tempore, in the absence of the Vice-President, or when he shall exercise the Office of the President of the United States.

The Senate shall have the sole Power to try all Impeachments. When sitting for that purpose, they shall be on Oath or Affirmation. When the President of the United States is tried, the Chief Justice shall preside: And no person shall be convicted without the Concurrence of two thirds of the Members present.

Judgment in Cases of Impeachment shall not extend further than to removal from Office, and disqualification to hold and enjoy any Office of honor, Trust, or Profit under the United States: but the Party convicted shall nevertheless be liable and subject to Indictment, Trial, Judgment, and Punishment, according to Law.

Section 4. The Times, Places and Manner of holding Elections for Senators and Representatives, shall be prescribed in each state by the Legislature thereof; but the Congress may at any time by Law make or alter such Regulations, except as to the Places of Chusing Senators.

The Congress shall assemble at least once in every Year, and such Meeting shall be on the first Monday in December, unless they shall by Law appoint a different Day.[4]

Section 5. Each House shall be the Judge of the Elections, Returns and Qualifications of its own Members, and a Majority of each shall constitute a Quorum to do Business; but a smaller number may adjourn from day to day, and may be authorized to compel the Attendance of absent Members, in such Manner, and under such Penalties, as each House may provide.

Each House may determine the Rules of its proceedings, punish its members for disorderly Behavior, and, with the Concurrence of two thirds, expel a Member.

Each House shall keep a Journal of its Proceedings, and from time to time publish the same, excepting such Parts as may in their Judgment require Secrecy; and the Yeas and Nays of the Members of either House on any question shall, at the Desire of one fifth of those Present, be entered on the Journal.

Neither House, during the Session of Congress, shall, without the Consent of the other, adjourn for more than three days, nor to any other Place than that in which the two Houses shall be sitting.

Section 6. The Senators and Representatives shall receive a Compensation for their Services, to be ascertained by Law, and paid out of the Treasury of the

---

[3] Changed by the Seventeenth Amendment.
[4] Changed by the Twentieth Amendment.

United States. They shall in all Cases, except Treason, Felony, and Breach of the Peace, be privileged from Arrest during their Attendance at the Session of their respective Houses, and in going to and returning from the same; and for any Speech or Debate in either House, they shall not be questioned in any other Place.

No Senator or Representative shall, during the Time for which he was elected, be appointed to any civil Office under the Authority of the United States, which shall have been created, or the Emoluments whereof shall have been increased, during such time; and no Person holding any Office under the United States shall be a Member of either House during his continuance in Office.

Section 7. All Bills for raising Revenue shall originate in the House of Representatives; but the Senate may propose or concur with Amendments as on other bills.

Every Bill which shall have passed the House of Representatives and the Senate, shall, before it become a Law, be presented to the President of the United States; If he approve he shall sign it, but if not he shall return it, with his Objections, to that House in which it shall have originated, who shall enter the Objections at large on their Journal, and proceed to reconsider it. If after such Reconsideration two thirds of that House, it shall agree to pass the bill, it shall be sent, together with the objections, to the other House, by which it shall likewise to reconsidered, and if approved by two thirds of that House, it shall become a Law. But in all such Cases the Votes of both Houses shall be determined by Yeas and Nays, and the Names of the Persons voting for and against the Bill shall be entered on the Journal of each House respectively. If any Bill shall not be returned by the President within ten Days (Sundays excepted) after it shall have been presented to him, the Same shall be a Law, in like Manner as if he had signed it, unless the Congress by their Adjournment prevent its Return, in which Case it shall not be a Law.

Every Order, Resolution, or Vote to which the Concurrence of the Senate and House of Representatives may be necessary (except on a question of Adjournment) shall be presented to the President of the United States; and before the Same shall take Effect, shall be approved by him, or being disapproved by him, shall be repassed by two thirds of the Senate and House of Representatives, according to the Rules and Limitations prescribed in the Case of a Bill.

Section 8. The Congress shall have Power To lay and collect Taxes, Duties, Imposts and Excises, to pay the Debts and provide for the common Defence and general Welfare of the United States; but all Duties, Imposts and Excises shall be uniform throughout the United States;

To borrow Money on the credit of the United States;

To regulate Commerce with foreign Nations, and among the several States, and with the Indian Tribes;

To establish an uniform Rule of Naturalization, and uniform Laws on the subject of Bankruptcies throughout the United States;

To coin Money, regulate the Value thereof, and of foreign Coin, and fix the Standard of Weights and Measures;

To provide for the Punishment of counterfeiting the Securities and current Coin of the United States;

To establish Post Offices and post Roads;

To promote the Progress of Science and useful Arts, by securing for limited Times to Authors and Inventors the exclusive Right to their respective Writings and Discoveries;

To constitute Tribunals inferior to the supreme Court;

To define and punish Piracies and Felonies committed on the high Seas, and Offenses against the Law of Nations;

To declare War, grant Letters of Marque and Reprisal, and make Rules concerning Captures on Land and Water;

To raise and support Armies, but no Appropriation of Money to that Use shall be for a longer Term than two Years;

To provide and maintain a Navy;

To make Rules for the Government and Regulation of the land and naval forces;

To provide for calling forth the Militia to execute the Laws of the Union, suppress Insurrections and repel Invasions;

To provide for organizing, arming, and disciplining the Militia, and for governing such Part of them as may be employed in the Service of the United States, reserving to the States respectively, the Appointment of the Officers, and the Authority of training the Militia according to the discipline prescribed by Congress;

To exercise exclusive Legislation in all Cases whatsoever, over such District (not exceeding ten Miles square) as may, by Cession of particular States, and the acceptance of Congress, become the Seat of the Government of the United States, and to exercise like Authority over all Places purchased by the Consent of the Legislature of the State in which the Same shall be, for the Erection of Forts, Magazines, Arsenals, dock-Yards, and other needful Buildings; —And

To make all Laws which shall be necessary and proper for carrying into Execution the foregoing Powers, and all other Powers vested by this Constitution in the Government of the United States, or in any Department or Officer thereof.

Section 9. The Migration or Importation of such Persons as any of the States now existing shall think proper to admit shall not be prohibited by the Congress prior to the Year one thousand eight hundred and eight, but a Tax or duty may be imposed on such Importation, not exceeding ten dollars for each Person.

The privilege of the Writ of Habeas Corpus shall not be suspended, unless when in Cases of Rebellion or Invasion the public Safety may require it.

No Bill of Attainder or ex post facto Law shall be passed.

No capitation, or other direct, Tax shall be laid unless in Proportion to the Census or Enumeration herein before directed to be taken.[5]

No Tax or Duty shall be laid on Articles exported from any State.

No Preference shall be given by any Regulation of Revenue to the Ports of one State over those of another: nor shall Vessels bound to, or from, one State, be obliged to enter, clear, or pay Duties in another.

No Money shall be drawn from the Treasury, but in Consequence of Appropriations made by Law; and a regular Statement and Account of the Receipts and Expenditures of all public Money shall be published from time to time.

No Title of Nobility shall be granted by the United States: And no Person holding any Office of Profit or Trust under them, shall, without the Consent of

---

[5] Changed by the Sixteenth Amendment.

the Congress, accept of any present, Emolument, Office, or Title, of any kind whatever, from any King, Prince, or foreign State.

Section 10. No State shall enter into any Treaty, Alliance, or Confederation; grant Letters of Marque and Reprisal; coin Money; emit Bills of Credit; make any Thing but gold and silver Coin a Tender in Payment of Debts; pass any Bill of Attainder, ex post facto Law, or Law impairing the Obligation of Contracts, or grant any Title of Nobility.

No State shall, without the Consent of the Congress, lay any Imposts or Duties on Imports or Exports, except what may be absolutely necessary for executing its inspection Laws: and the net Produce of all Duties and Imposts, laid by any State on Imports or Exports, shall be for the Use of the Treasury of the United States; and all such Laws shall be subject to the Revision and Control of the Congress.

No State shall, without the Consent of Congress, lay any duty of Tonnage, keep Troops, or Ships of War in time of Peace, enter into any Agreement or Compact with another State, or with a foreign Power, or engage in War, unless actually invaded, or in such imminent Danger as will not admit of delay.

Article II

Section 1. The executive Power shall be vested in a President of the United States of America. He shall hold his Office during the Term of four years, and, together with the Vice-President, chosen for the same Term, be elected, as follows:

Each State shall appoint, in such Manner as the Legislature thereof may direct, a Number of Electors, equal to the whole Number of Senators and Representatives to which the State may be entitled in the Congress: but no Senator or Representative, or Person holding an Office of Trust or Profit under the United States, shall be appointed an Elector.

The Electors shall meet in their respective States, and vote by Ballot for two persons, of whom one at least shall not be an Inhabitant of the same State with themselves. And they shall make a List of all the Persons voted for, and of the Number of Votes for each; which List they shall sign and certify, and transmit sealed to the Seat of the Government of the United States, directed to the President of the Senate. The President of the Senate shall, in the Presence of the Senate and House of Representatives, open all the Certificates, and the Votes shall then be counted. The Person having the greatest Number of Votes shall be the President, if such Number be a Majority of the whole Number of Electors appointed; and if there be more than one who have such Majority, and have an equal Number of Votes, then the House of Representatives shall immediately chuse by Ballot one of them for President; and if no Person have a Majority, then from the five highest on the List the said House shall in like Manner chuse the President. But in chusing the President, the Votes shall be taken by States, the Representation from each State having one Vote; a quorum for this Purpose shall consist of a Member or Members from two-thirds of the States, and a Majority of all the States shall be necessary to a Choice. In every Case, after the Choice of the President, the Person having the greatest Number of Votes of the Electors shall be the Vice-President. But if there should remain two or more who have equal votes, the Senate shall chuse from them by Ballot the Vice-President.[6]

---

[6] Changed by the Twelfth and Twentieth Amendments.

The Congress may determine the Time of chusing the Electors, and the Day on which they shall give their Votes; which Day shall be the same throughout the United States.

No person except a natural-born Citizen, or a Citizen of the United States, at the time of the Adoption of this Constitution, shall be eligible to the Office of President; neither shall any Person be eligible to that Office who shall not have attained to the Age of thirty-five years, and been fourteen Years a Resident within the United States.

In Case of the Removal of the President from Office, or of his Death, Resignation, or Inability to discharge the Powers and Duties of the said Office, the same shall devolve on the Vice-President, and the Congress may by Law provide for the Case of Removal, Death, Resignation, or Inability, both of the President and Vice-President, declaring what Officer shall then act as President, and such Officer shall act accordingly, until the disability be removed, or a President shall be elected.[7]

The President shall, at stated Times, receive for his Services a Compensation, which shall neither be increased nor diminished during the Period for which he shall have been elected, and he shall not receive within that Period any other Emolument from the United States, or any of them.

Before he enter on the execution of his Office, he shall take the following Oath or Affirmation: —"I do solemnly swear (or affirm) that I will faithfully execute the Office of President of the United States, and will, to the best of my Ability, preserve, protect, and defend the Constitution of the United States."

Section 2. The President shall be Commander in Chief of the Army and Navy of the United States, and of the Militia of the several States, when called into the actual Service of the United States; he may require the Opinion, in writing, of the principal Officer in each of the executive Departments, upon any subject relating to the Duties of their respective Offices, and he shall have Power to Grant Reprieves and Pardons for Offenses against the United States, except in Cases of Impeachment.

He shall have Power, by and with the Advice and Consent of the Senate, to make Treaties, provided two thirds of the Senators present concur; and he shall nominate, and by and with the Advice and Consent of the Senate, shall appoint Ambassadors, other public Ministers and Consuls, Judges of the supreme Court, and all other Officers of the United States, whose Appointments are not herein otherwise provided for, and which shall be established by Law: but the Congress may by Law vest the Appointment of such inferior Officers, as they think proper, in the President alone, in the Courts of Law, or in the Heads of Departments.

The President shall have Power to fill up all Vacancies that may happen during the Recess of the Senate, by granting Commissions which shall expire at the End of their next Session.

Section 3. He shall from time to time give to the Congress Information of the State of the Union, and recommend to their Consideration such Measures as he shall judge necessary and expedient; he may, on extraordinary occasions, convene both Houses, or either of them, and in Case of Disagreement between them, with respect to the Time of Adjoinment, he may adjoin them to such Time as he shall think proper; he shall receive Ambassadors and other public

---

[7] Changed by the Twenty-fifth Amendment.

Ministers; he shall take Care that the Laws be faithfully executed, and shall Commission all the Officers of the United States.

Section 4. The President, Vice-President and all civil Officers of the United States, shall be removed from Office on Impeachment for, and Conviction of, Treason, Bribery, or other high Crimes and Misdemeanors.

Article III

Section 1. The judicial Power of the United States, shall be vested in one supreme Court, and in such inferior Courts as the Congress may from time to time ordain and establish. The Judges, both of the supreme and inferior Courts, shall hold their Offices during good Behaviour, and shall, at stated Times, receive for their Services, a Compensation, which shall not be diminished during their Continuance in Office.

Section 2. The judicial Power shall extend to all Cases, in Law and Equity, arising under this Constitution, the Laws of the United States, and Treaties made, or which shall be made, under their Authority;—to all Cases affecting Ambassadors, other Public Ministers and consuls;—to all Cases of admiralty and maritime Jurisdiction;—to Controversies to which the United States shall be a Party;—to Controversies between two or more States;—*between a State and Citizens of another State;*[8]—between Citizens of different States,— between Citizens of the same State claiming Lands under Grants of different States, *and between a State, or the Citizens thereof, and foreign States, Citizens or Subjects.*

In all Cases affecting Ambassadors, other public Ministers and Consuls, and those in which a State shall be Party, the supreme Court shall have original Jurisdiction. In all the other Cases before mentioned, the supreme Court shall have appellate Jurisdiction, both as to Law and Fact, with such Exceptions, and under such Regulations as the Congress shall make.

The trial of all Crimes, except in Cases of Impeachment, shall be by Jury; and such Trial shall be held in the State where the said Crimes shall have been committed; but when not committed within any State, the Trial shall be at such Place or Places as the Congress may by Law have directed.

Section 3. Treason against the United States, shall consist only in levying War against them, or in adhering to their Enemies, giving them Aid and Comfort. No Person shall be convicted of Treason unless on the Testimony of two Witnesses to the same overt Act, or on Confession in open Court.

The Congress shall have power to declare the Punishment of Treason, but no Attainder of Treason shall work Corruption of Blood, or Forfeiture except during the Life of the Person attained.

Article IV

Section 1. Full Faith and Credit shall be given in each State to the public Acts, Records, and judicial Proceedings of every other State. And the Congress may

---

[8] Changed by the Eleventh Amendment

by general Laws prescribe the Manner in which such Acts, Records and Proceedings shall be proved, and the Effect thereof.

Section 2. The Citizens of each State shall be entitled to all Privileges and Immunities of Citizens in the several States.

A Person charged in any State with Treason, Felony, or other Crime, who shall flee from Justice, and be found in another State, shall on demand of the executive Authority of the State from which he fled, be delivered up, to be removed to the State having Jurisdiction of the crime.

No Person held to Service or Labour in one State, under the Laws thereof, escaping into another, shall, in Consequence of any Law or Regulation therein, be discharged from such Service or Labour, but shall be delivered up on Claim of the Party to whom such Service or Labour may be due.[9]

Section 3. New States may be admitted by the Congress into this Union; but no new State shall be formed or erected within the Jurisdiction of any other State; nor any State be formed by the Junction of two or more States, or parts of States, without the Consent of the Legislatures of the States concerned as well as of the Congress.

The Congress shall have Power to dispose of and make all needful Rules and Regulations respecting the Territory or other Property belonging to the United States; and nothing in this Constitution shall be so construed as to Prejudice any Claims of the United States, or of any particular State.

Section 4. The United States shall guarantee to every State in this Union a Republican Form of Government, and shall protect each of them against Invasion; and on Application of the Legislature, or of the Executive (when the Legislature cannot be convened) against domestic Violence.

Article V

The Congress, whenever two-thirds of both Houses shall deem it necessary, shall propose Amendments to this Constitution, or, on the Application of the Legislatures of two-thirds of the several States, shall call a Convention for proposing Amendments, which, in either Case, shall be valid to all Intents and Purposes, as part of this Constitution, when ratified by the Legislatures of three-fourths of the several States, or by Conventions in three-fourths thereof, as the one or the other Mode of Ratification may be proposed by the Congress; Provided that no Amendment which may be made prior to the Year One thousand eight hundred and eight shall in any Manner affect the first and fourth Clauses in the Ninth Section of the first Article; and that no State, without its Consent, shall be deprived of its equal Suffrage in the Senate.

Article VI

All Debts contracted and Engagements entered into, before the Adoption of this Constitution, shall be as valid against the United States under this Constitution, as under the Confederation.

This Constitution, and the Laws of the United States which shall be made in Pursuance thereof; and all Treaties made, or which shall be made, under

---

[9] Repealed by the Thirteenth Amendment.

the Authority of the United States, shall be the supreme Law of the Land; and the Judges in every State shall be bound thereby, any Thing in the Constitution or Laws of any State to the Contrary notwithstanding.

The Senators and Representatives before mentioned, and the Members of the several State Legislatures, and all executive and judicial Officers, both of the United States and of the several States, shall be bound by Oath or Affirmation to support this Constitution; but no religious Test shall ever be required as a Qualification to any Office or public Trust under the United States.

Article VII

The Ratification of the Conventions of nine states shall be sufficient for the Establishment of this Constitution between the States so ratifying the same.

Done in Convention by the Unanimous Consent of the States present the Seventeenth Day of September in the Year of our Lord one thousand seven hundred and Eighty seven, and of the Independence of the United States of America the Twelfth. In Witness whereof We have hereunto subscribed our Names.

AMENDMENTS TO THE CONSTITUTION

Amendment 1[10]
Congress shall make no law respecting an establishment of religion, or prohibiting the free exercise thereof; or abridging the freedom of speech, or of the press; or the right of the people peaceably to assemble, and to petition the Government for a redress of grievances.

Amendment II

A well-regulated Militia, being necessary to the security of a free State, the right of the people to keep and bear Arms shall not be infringed.

Amendment III

No Soldier shall, in time of peace, be quartered in any house, without the consent of the Owner, nor in time of war, but in a manner to be prescribed by law.

Amendment IV

The right of the people to be secure in their persons, houses, papers, and effects, against unreasonable searches and seizures, shall not be violated, and no Warrants shall issue, but upon probable cause, supported by Oath or affirmation, and particularly describing the place to be searched, and the persons or things to be seized.

---

[10] The first ten amendments, ratified by 1791, are commonly called the U.S. Bill of Rights (see Chapter 4).

Amendment V

No person shall be held to answer for a capital or otherwise infamous crime, unless on a presentment or indictment of a Grand Jury, except in cases arising in the land or naval forces, or in the Militia, when in actual service in time of War or public danger; nor shall any person be subject for the same offence to be twice put in jeopardy of life or limb; nor shall be compelled in any criminal case to be a witness against himself, nor be deprived of life, liberty, or property, without due process of law; nor shall private property be taken for public use, without just compensation.

Amendment VI

In all criminal prosecutions, the accused shall enjoy the right to a speedy and public trial, by an impartial jury of the State and district wherein the crime shall have been committed, which district shall have been previously ascertained by law, and to be informed of the nature and cause of the accusation; to be confronted with the witnesses against him; to have compulsory process for obtaining witnesses in his favor, and to have the Assistance of Counsel for his defence.

Amendment VII

In Suits at common law, where the value in controversy shall exceed twenty dollars, the right of trial by jury shall be preserved, and no fact tried by a jury, shall be otherwise reexamined in any Court of the United States, than according to the rules of the common law.

Amendment VIII

Excessive bail shall not be required, nor excessive fines imposed, nor cruel and unusual punishments inflicted.

Amendment IX

The enumeration in the Constitution, of certain rights, shall not be construed to deny or disparage others retained by the people.

Amendment X

The powers not delegated to the United States by the Constitution, nor prohibited by it to the States, are reserved to the States respectively, or to the people.

Amendment XI (1795)[11]

The Judicial power of the United States shall not be construed to extend to any suit in law or equity, commenced or prosecuted against one of the United States by Citizens of another State, or by Citizens or Subjects of any Foreign State.

------

[11] Ratification date.

Amendment XII (1804)

The Electors shall meet in their respective States and vote by ballot for President and Vice-President, one of whom, at least, shall not be an inhabitant of the same State with themselves; they shall name in their ballots the person voted for as President, and in distinct ballots the person voted for as Vice-President, and they shall make distinct lists of all persons voted for as President, and of all persons voted for as Vice-President, and of the number of votes for each, which lists they shall sign and certify, and transmit sealed to the seat of the government of the United States, directed to the President of the Senate;—The President of the Senate shall, in the presence of the Senate and House of Representatives, open all the certificates and the votes shall then be counted;—The person having the greatest number of votes for President, shall be the President, if such number be a majority of the whole number of Electors appointed; and if no person have such majority, then from the persons having the highest numbers not exceeding three on the list of those voted for as President, the House of Representatives shall choose immediately, by ballot, the President. But in choosing the President, the votes shall be taken by states, the representation from each state having one vote; a quorum for this purpose shall consist of a member or members from two-thirds of the states, and a majority of all the states shall be necessary to a choice. *And if the House of Representatives shall not choose a President whenever the right of choice shall devolve upon them, before the fourth day of March next following, then the Vice-President shall act as President, as in the case of the death or other constitutional disability of the President.*[12]—The person having the greatest number of votes as Vice-President, shall be the Vice-President, if such number be a majority of the whole number of Electors appointed, and if no person have a majority, then from the two highest numbers on the list, the Senate shall choose the Vice-President; a quorum for the purpose shall consist of two-thirds of the whole number of Senators, and a majority of the whole number shall be necessary to a choice. But no person constitutionally ineligible to the office of President shall be eligible to that of Vice-President of the United States.

Amendment XIII (1865)

Section 1. Neither slavery nor involuntary servitude, except as a punishment for crime whereof the party shall have been duly convicted, shall exist within the United States, or any place subject to their jurisdiction.

Section 2. Congress shall have power to enforce this article by appropriate legislation.

Amendment XIV (1868)

Section 1. All persons born or naturalized in the United States, and subject to the jurisdiction thereof, are citizens of the United States and of the State wherein they reside. No State shall make or enforce any law which shall abridge the privileges or immunities of citizens of the United States; nor shall

---

[12] Changed by the Twentieth Amendment.

any State deprive any person of life, liberty, or property, without due process of law; nor deny to any person within its jurisdiction the equal protection of the laws.

Section 2. Representatives shall be apportioned among the several States according to their respective numbers, counting the whole number of persons in each State, excluding Indians not taxed. But when the right to vote at any election for the choice of electors for President and Vice-President of the United States, Representatives in Congress, the Executive and Judicial officers of a State, or the members of the Legislature thereof, is denied to any of the male inhabitants of such State, being twenty-one years of age, and citizens of the United States, or in any way abridged, except for participation in rebellion, or other crime, the basis of representation therein shall be reduced in the proportion which the number of such male citizens shall bear to the whole number of male citizens twenty-one years of age in such State.

Section 3. No person shall be a Senator or Representative in Congress, or elector of President and Vice-President, or hold any office, civil or military, under the United States, or under any State, who, having previously taken an oath, as a member of Congress, or as an officer of the United States, or as a member of any State legislature, or as an executive or judicial officer of any State, to support the Constitution of the United States, shall have engaged in insurrection or rebellion against the same, or given aid or comfort to the enemies thereof. But Congress may by a vote of two-thirds of each House, remove such disability.

Section 4. The validity of the public debt of the United States, authorized by law, including debts incurred for payment of pensions and bounties for services in suppressing insurrection or rebellion, shall not be questioned. But neither the United States nor any State shall assume or pay any debt or obligation incurred in aid of insurrection or rebellion against the United States, or any claim for the loss or emancipation of any slave; but all such debts, obligations, and claims shall be held illegal and void.

Section 5. The Congress shall have the power to enforce, by appropriate legislation, the provisions of this article.

Amendment XV (1870)

Section 1. The right of citizens of the United States to vote shall not be denied or abridged by the United States or by any State on account of race, color, or previous condition of servitude.

Section 2. The Congress shall have power to enforce this article by appropriate legislation.

Amendment XVI (1913)

The Congress shall have power to lay and collect taxes on incomes, from whatever source derived, without apportionment among the several States, and without regard to any census or enumeration.

Amendment XVII (1913)

The Senate of the United States shall be composed of two Senators from each State, elected by the people thereof, for six years; and each Senator shall have one vote. The electors in each State shall have the qualifications requisite for electors of the most numerous branch of the State legislatures.

When vacancies happen in the representation of any State in the Senate, the executive authority of such State shall issue writs of election to fill such vacancies: *Provided,* That the legislature of any State may empower the executive thereof to make temporary appointments until the people fill the vacancies by election as the legislature may direct.

This amendment shall not be so construed as to affect the election or term of any Senator chosen before it becomes valid as part of the Constitution.

Amendment XVIII (1919)[13]

Section 1. After one year from the ratification of this article the manufacture, sale, or transportation of intoxicating liquors within, the importation thereof into, or the exportation thereof from the United States and all territory subject to the jurisdiction thereof for beverage purposes is hereby prohibited.

Section 2. The Congress and the several States shall have concurrent power to enforce this article by appropriate legislation.

Section 3. This article shall be inoperative unless it shall have been ratified as an amendment to the Constitution by the legislatures of the several States, as provided in the Constitution, within seven years from the date of the submission hereof to the States by the Congress.

Amendment XIX (1920)

The right of citizens of the United States to vote shall not be denied or abridged by the United States or by any State on account of sex.

Congress shall have power to enforce this article by appropriate legislation.

Amendment XX (1933)

Section 1. The terms of the President and Vice-President shall end at noon on the 20th day of January, and the terms of Senators and Representatives at noon on the 3d day of January, of the years in which such terms would have ended if this article had not been ratified; and the terms of their successors shall then begin.

Section 2. The Congress shall assemble at least once in every year, and such meeting shall begin at noon on the 3d day of January, unless they shall by law appoint a different day.

Section 3. If, at the time fixed for the beginning of the term of the President, the President elect shall have died, the Vice-President elect shall become

---

[13] Repealed by the Twenty-first Amendment.

President. If a President shall not have been chosen before the time fixed for the beginning of his term, or if the President elect shall have failed to qualify, then the Vice-President elect shall act as President until a President shall have qualified; and the Congress may by law provide for the case wherein neither a President elect nor a Vice-President elect shall have qualified, declaring who shall then act as President, or the manner in which one who is to act shall be selected, and such person shall act accordingly until a President or Vice-President shall have qualified.

Section 4. The Congress may by law provide for the case of the death of any of the persons from whom the House of Representatives may choose a President whenever the right of choice shall have devolved upon them, and for the case of the death of any of the persons from whom the Senate may choose a Vice-President whenever the right of choice shall have devolved upon them.

Section 5. Sections 1 and 2 shall take effect on the 15th day of October following the ratification of this article.

Section 6. This article shall be inoperative unless it shall have been ratified as an amendment to the Constitution by the legislatures of three-fourths of the several States within seven years from the date of its submission.

Amendment XXI (1933)

Section 1. The eighteenth article of amendment to the Constitution of the United States is hereby repealed.

Section 2. The transportation or importation into any State, Territory, or possession of the United States for delivery or use therein of intoxicating liquors, in violation of the laws thereof, is hereby prohibited.

Section 3. This article shall be inoperative unless it shall have been ratified as an amendment to the Constitution by conventions in the several States, as provided in the Constitution, within seven years from the date of the submission hereof to the States by the Congress.

Amendment XXII (1951)

No person shall be elected to the office of the President more than twice, and no person who has held the office of President, or acted as President, for more than two years of a term to which some other person was elected President shall be elected to the office of the President more than once.

But this Article shall not apply to any person holding the office of President when this Article was proposed by the Congress, and shall not prevent any person who may be holding the office of President, or acting as President, during the term within which this Article becomes operative from holding the office of President or acting as President during the remainder of such term.

Amendment XXIII (1961)

Section 1. The District constituting the seat of Government of the United States shall appoint in such manner as the Congress may direct:

A number of electors of President and Vice-President equal to the whole number of Senators and Representatives in Congress to which the District would be entitled if it were a State, but in no event more than the least populous State; they shall be in addition to those appointed by the States, but they shall be considered, for the purposes of the election of President and Vice-President, to be electors appointed by the State; and they shall meet in the District and perform such duties as provided by the twelfth article of amendment.

Section 2. The Congress shall have power to enforce this article by appropriate legislation.

Amendment XXIV (1964)

Section 1. The right of citizens of the United States to vote in any primary or other election for President or Vice-President, for electors for President or Vice-President, or for Senator or Representative in Congress, shall not be denied or abridged by the United States or any State by reason of failure to pay any poll tax or other tax.

Section 2. The Congress shall have power to enforce this article by appropriate legislation.

Amendment XXV (1967)

Section 1. In case of the removal of the President from office or of his death or resignation, the Vice-President shall become President.

Section 2. Whenever there is a vacancy in the office of the Vice-President, the President shall nominate a Vice-President who shall take office upon confirmation by a majority vote of both Houses of Congress.

Section 3. Whenever the President transmits to the President pro tempore of the Senate and the Speaker of the House of Representatives his written declaration that he is unable to discharge the powers and duties of his office, and until he transmits to them a written declaration to the contrary, such powers and duties shall be discharged by the Vice-President as Acting President.

Section 4. Whenever the Vice-President and a majority of either the principal officers of the executive department or of such other body as Congress may by law provide, transmit to the President pro tempore of the Senate and the Speaker of the House of Representatives their written declaration that the President is unable to discharge the powers and duties of his office, the Vice-President shall immediately assume the powers and duties of the office as Acting President.

Thereafter, when the President transmits to the President pro tempore of the Senate and the Speaker of the House of Representatives his written declaration that no inability exists, he shall resume the powers and duties of his office unless the Vice-President and a majority of either the principal officers of the executive department or of such other body as Congress may by law provide, transmit within four days to the President pro tempore of the

Senate and the Speaker of the House of Representatives their written declaration that the President is unable to discharge the powers and duties of his office. Thereupon Congress shall decide the issue, assembling within forty-eight hours for that purpose if not in session. If the Congress, within twenty-one days after receipt of the latter written declaration, or, if Congress is not in session, within twenty-one days after Congress is required to assemble, determines by two-thirds vote of both Houses that the President is unable to discharge the powers and duties of his office, the Vice-President shall continue to discharge the same as Acting President; otherwise, the President shall resume the powers and duties of his office.

Amendment XXVI (1971)

Section 1. The right of citizens of the United States, who are eighteen years of age or older, to vote shall not be denied or abridged by the United States or by any State on account of age.

Section 2. The Congress shall have power to enforce this article by appropriate legislation.

THE FEDERALIST, PAPER 10
BY JAMES MADISON

Although all the state delegations to the Constitutional Convention voted in 1787 to accept the Constitution, it still had to be ratified by nine of the thirteen states. In New York State (among others), public opinion was divided more or less evenly between the Constitution's supporters (the Federalists) and its opponents (the Anti-Federalists). To influence the hard-fought and sometimes bitter contest, Alexander Hamilton, James Madison, and John Jay wrote The Federalist, *a series of essays about the Constitution, political theory, and American politics. Published in a local newspaper,* The New York Packet, *these essays helped ratify the Constitution in New York.*

The most famous selection of The Federalist *is Paper 10, by James Madison, "father of the Constitution" and fourth President of the United States (1809–1817). It has been quoted many times in this and all other texts on American government.*

Paper 10: James Madison

To the People of the State of New York:
   Among the numerous advantages promised by a well-constructed Union, none deserves to be more accurately developed than its tendency to break and control the violence of faction. The friend of popular governments never finds himself so much alarmed for their character and fate as when he contemplates their propensity to this dangerous vice. He will not fail, therefore, to set a due value on any plan which, without violating the principles to which he is attached, provides a proper cure for it. The instability, injustice, and confusion introduced into the public councils have, in truth, been the mortal diseases under which popular governments have everywhere perished, as they continue to be the favorite and fruitful topics from which the adversaries to liberty derive their most specious declamations. The valuable improvements

594   APPENDIX

made by the American constitutions on the popular models, both ancient and modern, cannot certainly be too much admired; but it would be an unwarrantable partiality to contend that they have as effectually obviated the danger on this side, as was wished and expected. Complaints are everywhere heard from our most considerate and virtuous citizens, equally the friends of public and private faith and of public and personal liberty, that our governments are too unstable, that the public good is disregarded in the conflicts of rival parties, and that measures are too often decided, not according to the rules of justice and the rights of the minor party, but by the superior force of an interested and overbearing majority. However anxiously we may wish that these complaints had no foundation, the evidence of known facts will not permit us to deny that they are in some degree true. It will be found, indeed, on a candid review of our situation, that some of the distresses under which we labor have been erroneously charged on the operation of our governments; but it will be found, at the same time, that other causes will not alone account for many of our heaviest misfortunes; and, particularly, for that prevailing and increasing distrust of public engagements and alarm for private rights which are echoed from one end of the continent to the other. These must be chiefly, if not wholly, effects of the unsteadiness and injustice with which a factious spirit has tainted our public administrations.

By a faction I understand a number of citizens, whether amounting to a majority or minority of the whole, who are united and actuated by some common impulse of passion, or of interest, adverse to the rights of other citizens, or to the permanent and aggregate interests of the community.

There are two methods of curing the mischiefs of faction: the one, by removing its causes; the other, by controlling its effects.

There are again two methods of removing the causes of faction: the one, by destroying the liberty which is essential to its existence; the other, by giving to every citizen the same opinions, the same passions, and the same interests.

It could never be more truly said than of the first remedy that it was worse than the disease. Liberty is to faction what air is to fire, an aliment without which it instantly expires. But it could not be a less folly to abolish liberty, which is essential to political life, because it nourishes faction than it would be to wish the annihilation of air, which is essential to animal life, because it imparts to fire its destructive agency.

The second expedient is as impracticable as the first would be unwise. As long as the reason of man continues fallible, and he is at liberty to exercise it, different opinions will be formed. As long as the connection subsists between his reason and his self-love, his opinions and his passions will have a reciprocal influence on each other; and the former will be objects to which the latter will attach themselves. The diversity in the faculties of men, from which the rights of property originate, is not less an insuperable obstacle to a uniformity of interests. The protection of these faculties is the first object of government. From the protection of different and unequal faculties of acquiring property, the possession of different degrees and kinds of property immediately results; and from the influence of these on the sentiments and views of the respective proprietors ensues a division of the society into different interests and parties.

The latent causes of faction are thus sown in the nature of man; and we see them everywhere brought into different degrees of activity, according to the different circumstances of civil society. A zeal for different opinions concerning religion, concerning government, and many other points, as well of speculation as of practice; an attachment to different leaders ambitiously contending for pre-eminence and power; or to persons of other descriptions whose fortunes have been interesting to the human passions, have, in turn, divided mankind into parties, inflamed them with mutual animosity, and rendered them much more disposed to vex and oppress each other than to co-operate for their common good. So strong is this propensity of manking to fall into mutual animosities that where no substantial occasion presents itself the most frivolous and fanciful distinctions have been sufficient to kindle their unfriendly passions and excite their most violent conflicts. But the most common and durable source of factions has been the various and unequal distribution of property. Those who hold and those who are without property have ever formed distinct interests in society. Those who are creditors, and those who are debtors, fall under a like discrimination. A landed interest, a manufacturing interest, a mercantile interest, a moneyed interest, with many lesser interests, grow up of necessity in civilized nations, and divide them into different classes, actuated by different sentiments and views. The regulation of these various and interfering interests forms the principal task of modern legislation and involves the spirit of party and faction in the necessary and ordinary operations of government.

No man is allowed to be a judge in his own cause, because his interest would certainly bias his judgment, and, not improbably, corrupt his integrity. With equal, nay with greater reason, a body of men are unfit to be both judges and parties at the same time; yet what are many of the most important acts of legislation but so many judicial determinations, not indeed concerning the rights of single persons, but concerning the rights of large bodies of citizens? And what are the different classes of legislators but advocates and parties to the causes which they determine? Is a law proposed concerning private debts? It is a question to which the creditors are parties on one side and the debtors on the other. Justice ought to hold the balance between them. Yet the parties are, and must be, themselves the judges; and the most numerous party, or in other words, the most powerful faction must be expected to prevail. Shall domestic manufacturers be encouraged, and in what degree, by restrictions on foreign manufacturers? are questions which would be differently decided by the landed and the manufacturing classes, and probably by neither with a sole regard to justice and the public good. The apportionment of taxes on the various descriptions of property is an act which seems to require the most exact impartiality; yet there is, perhaps, no legislative act in which greater opportunity and temptation are given to a predominant party to trample on the rules of justice. Every shilling with which they overburden the inferior number is a shilling saved to their own pockets.

It is in vain to say that enlightened statesmen will be able to adjust these clashing interests and render them all subservient to the public good. Enlightened statesmen will not always be at the helm. Nor, in many cases, can such an adjustment be made at all without taking into view indirect and remote considerations, which will rarely prevail over the immediate interest which one party may find in disregarding the rights of another or the good of the whole.

The inference to which we are brought is that the *causes* of faction cannot be removed and that relief is only to be sought in the means of controlling its *effects*.

If a faction consists of less than a majority, relief is supplied by the republican principle, which enables the majority to defeat its sinister views by regular vote. It may clog the administration, it may convulse the society; but it will be unable to execute and mask its violence under the forms of the

Constitution. When a majority is included in a faction, the form of popular government, on the other hand, enables it to sacrifice to its ruling passion or interest both the public good and the rights of other citizens. To secure the public good and private rights against the danger of such a faction, and at the same time to preserve the spirit and the form of popular government, is then the great object to which our inquiries are directed. Let me add that it is the great desideratum by which alone this form of government can be rescued from the opprobrium under which it has so long labored and be recommended to the esteem and adoption of mankind.

By what means is this object attainable? Evidently by one of two only. Either the existence of the same passion or interest in a majority at the same time must be prevented, or the majority, having such coexistent passion or interest, must be rendered, by their number and local situation, unable to concert and carry into effect schemes of oppression. If the impulse and the opportunity be suffered to coincide, we well know that neither moral nor religious motives can be relied on as an adequate control. They are not found to be such on the injustice and violence of individuals, and lose their efficacy in proportion to the number combined together, that is, in proportion as their efficacy becomes needful.

From this view of the subject it may be concluded that a pure democracy, by which I mean a society consisting of a small number of citizens, who assemble and administer the government in person, can admit of no cure for the mischiefs of faction. A common passion or interest will, in almost every case, be felt by a majority of the whole; a communication and concert results from the form of government itself; and there is nothing to check the inducements to sacrifice the weaker party or an obnoxious individual. Hence it is that such democracies have ever been spectacles of turbulence and contention; have ever been found incompatible with personal security or the rights of property; and have in general been as short in their lives as they have been violent in their deaths. Theoretic politicians, who have patronized this species of government, have erroneously supposed that by reducing mankind to a perfect equality in their political rights, they would at the same time be perfectly equalized and assimilated in their possessions, their opinions, and their passions.

A republic, by which I mean a government in which the scheme of representation takes place, opens a different prospect and promises the cure for which we are seeking. Let us examine the points in which it varies from pure democracy, and we shall comprehend both the nature of the cure and the efficacy which it must derive from the Union.

The two great points of difference between a democracy and a republic are: first, the delegation of the government, in the latter, to a small number of citizens elected by the rest; secondly, the greater number of citizens and greater sphere of country over which the latter may be extended.

The effect of the first difference is, on the one hand, to refine and enlarge the public views by passing them through the medium of a chosen body of citizens, whose wisdom may best discern the true interest of their country and whose patriotism and love of justice will be least likely to sacrifice it to temporary or partial considerations. Under such a regulation it may well happen that the public voice, pronounced by the representatives of the people, will be more consonant to the public good than if pronounced by the people themselves, convened for the purpose. On the other hand, the effect may be inverted. Men of factious tempers, of local prejudices, or of sinister designs, may, by intrigue, by corruption, or by other means, first obtain the suffrages, and then betray the interests of the people. The question resulting is, whether small or extensive republics are most favorable to the election of proper guardians of the public weal; and it is clearly decided in favor of the latter by two obvious considerations.

In the first place it is to be remarked that however small the republic may be the representatives must be raised to a certain number in order to guard against the cabals of a few; and that however large it may be they must be limited to a certain number in order to guard against the confusion of a multitude. Hence, the number of representatives in the two cases not being in proportion to that of the constituents, and being proportionally greatest in the small republic, it follows that if the proportion of fit characters be not less in the large than in the small republic, the former will present a greater opinion, and consequently a greater probability of a fit choice.

In the next place, as each representative will be chosen by a greater number of citizens in the large than in the small republic, it will be more difficult for unworthy candidates to practise with success the vicious arts by which elections are too often carried; and the suffrages of the people being more free, will be more likely to center on men who possess the most attractive merit and the most diffusive and established characters.

It must be confessed that in this, as in most other cases, there is a mean, on both sides of which inconveniencies will be found to lie. By enlarging too much the number of electors, you render the representative too little acquainted with all their local circumstances and lesser interests; as by reducing it too much, you render him unduly attached to these, and too little fit to comprehend and pursue great and national objects. The federal Constitution forms a happy combination in this respect; the great and aggregate interests being referred to the national, the local and particular to the State legislatures.

The other point of difference is the greater number of citizens and extent of territory which may be brought within the compass of republican than of democratic government; and it is this circumstance principally which renders factious combinations less to be dreaded in the former than in the latter. The smaller the society, the fewer probably will be the distinct parties and interests composing it; the fewer the distinct parties and interests, the more frequently will a majority be found of the same party; and the smaller the number of individuals composing a majority, and the smaller the compass within which they are placed, the more easily will they concert and execute their plans of oppression. Extend the sphere and you take in a greater variety of parties and interests; you make it less probable that a majority of the whole will have a common motive to invade the rights of other citizens; or if such a common motive exists, it will be more difficult for all who feel it to discover their own strength and to act in unison with each other. Besides other impediments, it may be remarked that, where there is a consciousness of unjust or dishonorable purposes, communication is always checked by distrust in proportion to the number whose concurrence is necessary.

Hence, it clearly appears that the same advantage which a republic has over a democracy in controlling the effects of faction is enjoyed by a large over a small republic—is enjoyed by the Union over the States composing it. Does this advantage consist in the substitution of representatives whose enlightened views and virtuous sentiments render them superior to local prejudices and to schemes of injustice? It will not be denied that the representation of the Union will be most likely to possess these requisite endowments. Does it consist in the greater security afforded by a greater variety of parties, against the event of any one party being able to outnumber and oppress the rest? In an equal degree does the increased variety of parties comprised within the Union increase this security. Does it, in fine, consist in the greater obstacles opposed to the concert and accomplishment of the secret wishes of an unjust and interested majority? Here again the extent of the Union gives it the most palpable advantage.

The influence of factious leaders may kindle a flame within their particular States but will be unable to spread a general conflagration through the other States. A religious sect may degenerate into a political faction in a part of the Confederacy but the variety of sects dispersed over the entire face of it must secure the national councils against any danger from that source. A rage for paper money, for an abolition of debts, for an equal division of property, or for any other improper or wicked project, will be less apt to pervade the whole body of the Union than a particular member of it, in the same proportion as such a malady is more likely to taint a particular county or district than an entire State.

In the extent and proper structure of the Union, therefore, we behold a republican remedy for the diseases most incident to republican government. And according to the degree of pleasure and pride we feel in being republicans ought to be our zeal in cherishing the spirit and supporting the character of federalists.

PRESIDENTS, VICE-PRESIDENTS, AND CONGRESSES

	PRESIDENT	SERVICE		VICE-PRESIDENT	CON-GRESS
1	George Washington	Apr. 30, 1789–Mar. 3, 1797	1	John Adams	1, 2, 3, 4
2	John Adams	Mar. 4, 1797–Mar. 3, 1801	2	Thomas Jefferson	5, 6
3	Thomas Jefferson	Mar. 4, 1801–Mar. 3, 1805	3	Aaron Burr	7, 8
	"	Mar. 4, 1805–Mar. 3, 1809	4	George Clinton	9, 10
4	James Madison	Mar. 4, 1809–Mar. 3, 1813		"[1]	11, 12
	"	Mar. 4, 1813–Mar. 3, 1817	5	Elbridge Gerry[2]	13, 14
5	James Monroe	Mar. 4, 1817–Mar. 3, 1825	6	Daniel D. Tompkins	15, 16, 17, 18
6	John Quincy Adams	Mar. 4, 1825–Mar. 3, 1829	7	John C. Calhoun	19, 20
7	Andrew Jackson	Mar. 4, 1829–Mar. 3, 1833		"[3]	21, 22
	"	Mar. 4, 1833–Mar. 3, 1837	8	Martin Van Buren	23, 24
8	Martin Van Buren	Mar. 4, 1837–Mar. 3, 1841	9	Richard M. Johnson	25, 26
9	William Henry Harrison[4]	Mar. 4, 1841–Apr. 4, 1841	10	John Tyler	27
10	John Tyler	Apr. 6, 1841–Mar. 3, 1845			27, 28
11	James K. Polk	Mar. 4, 1845–Mar. 3, 1849	11	George M. Dallas	29, 30
12	Zachary Taylor[4]	Mar. 5, 1849–July 9, 1850	12	Millard Fillmore	31
13	Millard Fillmore	July 10, 1850–Mar. 3, 1853			31, 32
14	Franklin Pierce	Mar. 4, 1853–Mar. 3, 1857	13	William R. King[5]	33, 34
15	James Buchanan	Mar. 4, 1857–Mar. 3, 1861	14	John C. Breckinridge	35, 36
16	Abraham Lincoln	Mar. 4, 1861–Mar. 3, 1865	15	Hannibal Hamlin	37, 38
	"[4]	Mar. 4, 1865–Apr. 15, 1865	16	Andrew Johnson	39
17	Andrew Johnson	Apr. 15, 1865–Mar. 3, 1869			39, 40
18	Ulysses S. Grant	Mar. 4, 1869–Mar. 3, 1873	17	Schuyler Colfax	41, 42
	"	Mar. 4, 1873–Mar. 3, 1877	18	Henry Wilson[6]	43, 44

PRESIDENT	SERVICE	VICE-PRESIDENT	CON-GRESS
19 Rutherford B. Hayes	Mar. 4, 1877–Mar. 3, 1881	19 William A. Wheeler	45, 46
20 James A. Garfield[4]	Mar. 4, 1881–Sept. 19, 1881	20 Chester A. Arthur	47
21 Chester A. Arthur	Sept. 20, 1881–Mar. 3, 1885		47, 48
22 Grover Cleveland[7]	Mar. 4, 1885–Mar. 3, 1889	21 Thomas A. Hendricks[8]	49, 50
23 Benjamin Harrison	Mar. 4, 1889–Mar. 3, 1893	22 Levi P. Morton	51, 52
24 Grover Cleveland	Mar. 4, 1893–Mar. 3, 1897	23 Adlai E. Stevenson	53, 54
25 William McKinley	Mar. 4, 1897–Mar. 3, 1901	24 Garret A. Hobard[9]	55, 56
"	Mar. 4, 1901–Sept. 14, 1901	25 Theodore Roosevelt	57
26 Theodore Roosevelt	Sept. 14, 1901–Mar. 3, 1905		57, 58
"	Mar. 4, 1905–Mar. 3, 1909	26 Charles W. Fairbanks	59, 60
27 William H. Taft	Mar. 4, 1909–Mar. 3, 1919	27 James S. Sherman[10]	61, 62
28 Woodrow Wilson	Mar. 4, 1913–Mar. 3, 1921	28 Thomas R. Marshall	63, 64, 65, 66
29 Warren G. Harding[4]	Mar. 4, 1921–Aug. 2, 1923	29 Calvin Coolidge	67
30 Calvin Coolidge	Aug. 3, 1923–Mar. 3, 1925		68
"	Mar. 4, 1925–Mar. 3, 1929	30 Charles G. Dawes	69, 70
31 Herbert C. Hoover	Mar. 4, 1929–Mar. 3, 1933	31 Charles Curtis	71, 72
32 Franklin D. Roosevelt[16]	Mar. 4, 1933–Jan. 20, 1941	32 John N. Garner	73, 74, 75, 76
"	Jan. 20, 1941–Jan. 20, 1945	33 Henry A. Wallace	77, 78
"[4]	Jan. 20, 1945–Apr. 12, 1945	34 Harry S Truman	79
33 Harry S Truman	Apr. 12, 1945–Jan. 20 1949		79, 80
"	Jan. 20, 1949–Jan. 20, 1953	35 Alben W. Barkley	81, 82
34 Dwight D. Eisenhower	Jan. 20, 1953–Jan. 20, 1961	36 Richard M. Nixon	83, 84, 85, 86
35 John F. Kennedy[4]	Jan. 20, 1961–Nov. 22, 1963	37 Lyndon B. Johnson	87, 88
36 Lyndon B. Johnson	Nov. 22, 1963–Jan. 20, 1965		88
"	Jan. 20, 1965–Jan. 20, 1969	38 Hubert H. Humphrey	89, 90
37 Richard M. Nixon	Jan. 20, 1969–Jan. 20, 1973	39 Spiro T. Agnew[11]	91, 92, 93
"[12]	Jan. 20, 1973–Aug. 9, 1974	40 Gerald R. Ford[13]	93
38 Gerald R. Ford[14]	Aug. 9, 1974–Jan. 20, 1977	41 Nelson A. Rockefeller[15]	93, 94
39 Jimmy (James Earl) Carter	Jan. 20, 1977–Jan. 20, 1981	42 Walter F. Mondale	95, 96
40 Ronald Reagan	Jan. 20, 1981–Jan. 20, 1985	43 George Bush	97, 98
"	Jan. 20, 1985–	"	99

[1]Died Apr. 20, 1812. [2]Died Nov. 23, 1814. [3]Resigned Dec. 28, 1832, to become U.S. Senator. [4]Died in office. [5]Died Apr. 18, 1853. [6]Died Nov. 22, 1875. [7]Terms not consecutive. [8]Died Nov. 25, 1885. [9]Died Nov. 21, 1899. [10]Died Oct. 30, 1912. [11]Resigned Oct. 10, 1973. [12]Resigned Aug. 9, 1974. [13]First nonelected Vice-President, chosen under Twenty-fifth Amendment procedure. [14]First nonelected President. [15]Second nonelected Vice-President. [16]First President to be inaugurated under Twentieth Amendment. Jan. 20, 1937.

GLOSSARY

active-negative presidents James D. Barber's term for compulsive, aggressive executives who seek to gain and keep power; for example, Woodrow Wilson and Richard M. Nixon.

active-positive presidents James D. Barber's term for Presidents of flexible outlook and high self-esteem who emphasize results; for example, Franklin D. Roosevelt and John F. Kennedy.

activist state An approach to government that emerged in the 1930s and 1940s; it opposed the power of business and advocated the creation of social welfare and management of the business cycle.

adversary system A system of law in which the defense and prosecution do not work together in a common pursuit of truth, but clash as adversaries, each arguing its case as strongly as possible and leaving the court to elicit the truth for itself.

advisory opinion An opinion given by a state court about the legality or constitutionality of an action or bill that has yet to provoke a court case.

affirmative action The policy of schools and employees to admit and recruit more minority and female students and workers in order to overcome the effects of previous discrimination.

agency culture The tendency of government agencies and departments to be composed of people with similar points of view and interests; they thus tend to create and follow their own policies and become immune to democratic controls and presidential directives.

aggregate expenditure The total spending by consumers, businesses, and government.

amendment A change or addition to the Constitution, usually to expand civil liberties and civil rights.

amicus curiae briefs Latin for "friend of the court"; briefs filed in Supreme Court cases that inform the Court of an interested party's position and provide information that the contending parties may not have supplied.

antiballistic missiles (ABMs) Defensive interceptor missiles that can shoot down incoming intercontinental missiles (ICBMs).

Anti-Federalists A political party in the early years of the United States that opposed ratifying the Constitution and favored protection of political liberties.

appellate docket Appeals to the Supreme Court in which both parties pay their own court costs.

aristocracy A form of government in which power is vested in a small privileged class felt to be best qualified to rule.

Articles of Confederation The first constitution of the United States, ratified on March 1, 1781, which created the original thirteen states and Congress, but granted Congress few powers to tax, regulate commerce, make foreign policy, or wage war.

Article I courts Federal courts that settle disputes not falling under ordinary federal statutes such as those involving appeals from military tribunals, local courts in the District of Columbia, and tax courts.

Article III courts The regular federal court system (Supreme Court, courts of appeals, district courts) plus special federal courts such as the Court of Claims that hear suits brought against the federal government by private individuals and companies.

assimilation The process by which a minority group becomes integrated into a society by adopting the lifestyle of the majority.

balance of trade The difference in value over a period of time between a country's exports and imports.

Bill of Rights The first ten amendments to the Constitution restricting the federal government's power to threaten life, liberty, and property.

Black Codes Laws passed by Southern state legislatures in 1865 and 1866 nullifying the Thirteenth Amendment, which banned slavery.

blockbusting The practice by real estate agents of settling one black family in an all-white neighborhood in the hope that white homeowners will panic and sell their houses to the realtors at bargain prices.

block (broad-based) grants Federal grants to states that can be spent at the states' discretion on any program within broad limits; for example, grants for employment training, public health, and community development.

bolts (party) A type of third political party that results when factions within a major party lose power struggles and leave to run their own candidates; for example, the Progressive party of 1912.

budgetary policy An aspect of fiscal policy that deals with total federal spending, its distribution among departments and programs, and the circumstances in which deficit spending should occur. *See also* tax policy.

bureaucracy Any large administrative organization that is arranged hierarchically with specialized functions at each level and that operates according to rules instead of personal relations.

busing The transportation of public school students from areas where they live to schools in other areas in order to overcome de facto residential segregation in cities.

cabinet A council of heads of government departments that advises a prime minister or other head of government.

canvass A camping technique in which a candidate's supporters deliver by car to polling places those registered voters who support the candidate but have not yet voted.

capital punishment The death penalty; considered by many to be a "cruel and unusual punishment." Its application was very severely restricted in 1972 by the Supreme Court; today thirty-five states have restored it, but only for the most heinous crimes, usually murder.

categorical grants Money given by the federal government to states for specific purposes with uniform rules.

caucus A closed meeting of a group of people belonging to the same political party, usually to select candidates or decide on policy.

caucus system The system by which political leaders meeting locally choose delegates to state conventions, which in turn elect delegates to national conventions.

certiorari, writ of Latin for "to be informed"; an order from an appeals court to a lower court to send up the records of a case so that it can be studied on appeal.

charismatic leaders Leaders with magnetic appeal who often emerge during revolutions and other times of crisis; for example, Moses, Jesus, Mohammed, Abraham Lincoln.

checks and balances The system among the branches of the federal government by which each branch has powers separate from the others and by which no one branch can act without the cooperation of the others. *See also* separation of powers.

city manager A nonpartisan urban executive who is elected by a city council.

civil law Law governing private as opposed to public, or state, interests; applies to people who feel they have been injured by the actions of another person.

civil liberties The right of every citizen to a fair trial and to speak, meet, read, and worship freely without state interference.

civil religion A shared belief in God, in the divinely inspired destiny of the United States, and in the divine origin of property, liberty, and democracy.

Civil War amendments The Thirteenth, Fourteenth, and Fifteenth Amendments to the Constitution freeing the slaves, giving blacks legal citizenship, and protecting their rights as citizens.

class-action suits The joining of many individuals or groups in taking a case to court.

class consciousness Personal awareness of membership in a social class; the belief that class membership should influence political action.

classical economics The doctrine that individuals take part in economic exchanges solely for personal gain, and therefore produce and consume as much as they can; the law of market supply and demand is thus the only regulation necessary.

clear and present danger A standard of constitutional law in which a citizen's First Amendment rights to free speech are not protected if his or her remarks present a "clear and present danger" to the peace.

closed rule A decision on a bill by the House Rules Committee that prevents the bill from being amended on the House floor.

closed shop A hiring policy that requires employers to hire no one but workers who already belong to a certain union.

cloture A provision in the Senate to cut off debate if three-fifths of the total number of senators (today 100) vote to do so.

Cold War The unarmed conflict between Communist and Western countries after World War II involving an ideological clash between Marxism-Leninism and capitalist democracy and a struggle over tangible military and economic interest.

comity The practice among states of recognizing each other's laws and treating each other's citizens as they do their own.

common law Legal principles and applications under common law are derived from custom, precedent, and previous judicial decisions. This is the basis of the Anglo-American legal system and is distinguished from Roman law codes, which prevail on the European continent and are important in the legal system of Louisiana.

compulsory process A rule that allows defendants in trials to compel witnesses to testify.

concurrent powers Powers such as taxation that are granted to both the federal government and the states.

concurrent resolution A measure passed by both Houses of Congress that does not have the force of law and does not require the President's signature; frequently used for expressions of congressional opinion on an issue or for internal housekeeping rules. But *see also* legislative veto.

confederation A league of governments, with each of these governments having essentially sovereign powers, and the powers of the central government limited by and derived from the governments that have joined to create the confederation. Somewhat analogous to the United Nations today, though some confederation governments have had more effective power than the UN does.

conference committees Congressional committees, the members of which are drawn from both houses, that reconcile any differences between House and Senate versions of a bill.

congressional committees See conference committees; joint committees; select committees; standing committees.

congressional veto *See* legislative veto; *see also* concurrent resolution.

Connecticut Plan (Great Compromise) A plan introduced at the Constitutional Convention in which Congress would be composed of two houses; each state would send two members to the upper house (Senate), while membership in the lower (House of Representatives) would be determined by the size of each state's population.

consensus A general agreement on a wide variety of economic, political, social, and religious issues.

conservative coalition A stable group of conservatives from both parties that often forms a majority in Congress.

containment policy The post–World War II foreign policy of the United States toward the USSR; in it, the United States felt it necessary to create barriers to the growth of Soviet power in weak states along the Soviet border.

contempt of court The act of defying a court ruling.

continuing resolution A resolution passed by Congress to operate a government department at its current level of funding when its appropriations bill has not been approved by the end of the fiscal year.

contract theory of government A compact between a government and its people in which the people accept the authority of the government in return for protection of their lives, liberty, and property.

cost-benefit analysis A method of policy assessment that tries to balance costs against benefits; for example, the best system or product may not be available at the lowest possible price.

countercyclical policy Keynes's doctrine of economic management calling for governments to engage in deficit spending and to stimulate demand in depression periods; and to run a budget surplus and restrain demand in boom periods.

courts of original jurisdiction *See* trial courts.

cross-cutters People whose political opinions embrace contradictory theories; for example, an ideological conservative who favors a diminishing role for government but supports large-scale government activities in health and education.

culture The network of beliefs, behavior, and social communications which is specific to large-scale human communities at specific points in historical time; closely associated with language, religion, and the arts (both high and low), each of which reflects one aspect of "culture" in a given society.

dark-horse candidates Obscure or apparently unimportant nominees at national political conventions who sometimes win because the major nominees are in deadlock.

defendant A person required to make answer in a lawsuit.

deflation A contraction in the money supply, accompanied by falling wages and prices.

demand-side economics Keynes's identification of mass underconsumption of goods and services as a key causal factor in economic depressions, coupled with two remedies: (a) management by the state of the business cycle through macroeconomic policy; (b) transfer-payment programs funneling money to individuals who would otherwise not be able to consume. Called "demand-side" because it identifies the structure and volume of aggregate demand as the crucial problem for state policy to deal with.

de novo trial The right to begin a new case if either side does not accept a minor court's decision.

détente The relaxation of strained relations between nations.

deviating elections Elections in which public opinion shifts in one direction or another but without permanent effect.

direct primary A preliminary election in which voters nominate a party's candidate to run in a general election.

discount rate The interest rate that member banks must pay to borrow money from the Federal Reserve System.

discretionary jurisdiction Those cases accepted by the Supreme Court for full review after granting a writ of *certiorari*.

discretionary powers Broad general powers granted by Congress to government agencies that enable them to make their own policy.

discretionary spending Federal spending over which the government has a measure of control; for example, aid to state and local governments.

diversity cases Federal court cases in which citizens of different states sue each other; must involve claims of $10,000 or more.

division of powers The separation of powers between the national and state governments in the federal system.

double jeopardy Being tried a second time for the same crime if previously acquitted.

dual federalism The doctrine that goods and services remain under state regulation until they cross state lines, at which point they become subject to federal regulation.

due process The course of legal proceedings that protects citizens against unreasonable searches and seizures, double jeopardy, compulsory self-incrimination in trials, cruel and unusual punishments, and excessive bails; ensures that trials are open, public, and speedy; gives defendants a right to counsel; and guarantees just compensation to people whose property has been seized by the government.

due process clause A clause of the Fourteenth Amendment that prohibits state governments from violating the civil rights of citizens, i.e., from depriving "any person of life, liberty, or property, without due process of law."

effective demand The public's ability, backed by money, to buy the economy's full productive capacity.

elastic clause The clause in the Constitution that gives Congress power "to make all laws which shall be necessary and proper for carrying into execution" the enumerated powers; also called the "necessary and proper" clause.

elections *See* deviating elections; maintaining elections; realigning elections.

Electoral College A group of presidential electors that meets state by state after a presidential election to cast the official votes for President.

electronic media Mass media such as radio and television.

elites Groups who dominate political, business, labor, or professional institutions.

eminent domain Government seizure of private property for public purposes.

entitlements Federal government benefits—such as Social Security, Medicare, unemployment and disability insurance—that qualified citizens are "entitled" to by law.

entrepreneurship The ability to organize resources and make them produce wealth.

enumerated powers Powers specifically granted to a branch of government by the Constitution.

equal protection clause A clause in the first section of the Fourteenth Amendment prohibiting states from denying "any person . . . equal protection of the laws"; intended to permit blacks to challenge acts of group discrimination committed against them.

Equal Rights Amendment (ERA) The recently defeated Twenty-seventh Amendment to the Constitution that would have read, "Equality of rights under the law shall not be denied or abridged by the United States or by any state on account of sex."

equal-time rule A Federal Communications Commission (FCC) regulation that requires broadcasters to give all candidates for public office equal opportunity to present their cases.

excise taxes Federal taxes on so-called luxury goods such as liquor, tobacco, telephones, air travel, and gasoline.

exclusionary rule A Supreme Court ruling that evidence obtained by illegal search and seizure cannot be used against someone accused of a crime.

executive agency A government agency under the direct control of the President.

executive agreements Agreements signed by the President with foreign powers in order to bypass the need for Senate ratification of treaties.

ex post facto laws Laws that make actions illegal only after they have been committed.

extradition The practice of surrendering an accused criminal who has fled from one state to another to the jurisdiction of the accusing state.

fairness doctrine An FCC regulation that requires broadcasters to present a variety of viewpoints on issues of public importance.

faithful-delegate rule A rule in national presidential conventions that requires all delegates to vote on the first ballot for the candidates to whom they are pledged.

favorite-son candidates Politicians favored by their state delegation at national presidential conventions in order to bargain with front-running contenders.

federalism A system of government in which power is divided and shared between the national government and state governments.

Federalist Papers A series of essays written in 1787–1788 by Alexander Hamilton, James Madison, and John Jay advocating ratification of the Constitution and stressing the need for a strong national government.

Federalists An early U.S. political party that supported the Constitution and advocated a strong central government.

federal question The interests of the federal government in federal court cases.

felony A serious crime with a correspondingly severe punishment.

fiat money Money whose value is defined by government decree rather than by intrinsic worth.

filibuster A procedure in which a group of senators attempts to defeat a bill by prolonged debate.

fine tuning An economic policy in which the federal government manipulates taxation and government purchasing in order to change the direction of the economy.

fiscal policy A policy that calls for manipulating the rate and incidence of federal taxes to influence the national economy. *See also* monetary policy; budgetary policy; tax policy; fine tuning.

fiscal year The federal government's accounting period, which runs from October 1 to September 30 of the following year.

free trade The abolition of tariffs and other barriers to trade.

full faith and credit A section of the Constitution that requires states to recognize one another's laws and court decisions.

gerrymandering Dividing a territorial unit into election districts to give one political party an electoral majority in a larger number of districts while concentrating the voting strength of the opposition in as few districts as possible.

gold standard The monetary system by which all currency is fully backed by gold and freely convertible into gold coin.

grandfather clause A post–Civil War ruling by some state governments that allowed the voting franchise to anyone who could prove that his or her grandfather had voted before a certain date; enacted to keep blacks from voting. Outlawed by the Supreme Court in 1915.

grand jury A group of citizens convened to decide whether or not there is enough evidence in a given case to merit a trial. *See also* indictment.

grants-in-aid Money and resources given by the federal government to states for roads, schools, and social programs.

gross national product (GNP) The monetary value of all goods and services produced in a country in a given year.

habeas corpus, **writ of** Latin for "you should have the body"; a legal order requiring legal authorities to charge a person they arrested with a specific violation of the law within a few days.

home rule The power of a local government to govern itself under its own charter.

implied powers Congressional powers that are assumed to be constitutional because they are implied rather than being specifically enumerated by the Constitution. *See also* elastic clause.

incorporation theory An interpretation of the due process clause of the Fourteenth Amendment that extends the federal Bill of Rights to the states.

incumbents' advantages Privileges enjoyed by sitting congressmen and senators—such as the use of radio and television studios and free postage—that give them an advantage over their opponents in elections.

indentured servants Laborers who came to the United States from Europe at the behest of large American landholders; in return for the cost of the voyage, they agreed to spend several years working for the landholder.

indictment A declaration by a grand jury that a crime has been committed and that a certain person (or persons) has committed it.

indirect lobbying Influencing members of Congress through public opinion, or the appearance of public opinion, as in protests, demonstrations, media campaigns, and "grassroots" letter-sending campaigns.

individualist subculture A political subculture which assumes that political systems exist only to help individuals get what they want; such subcultures tolerate Boss rule and corruption.

in forma pauperis **petitions** Petitions to the Supreme Court from people who cannot pay a lawyer or court costs.

infrastructure Permanent public works installations such as roads, sewers, bridges, subways, and water systems.

inherent powers Powers mostly dealing with foreign relations that belong to any national government by virtue of its being a state or nation.

interest groups Organizations of people who share common material concerns or points of view. *See also* public interest groups; single-issue groups; lobbying.

intergovernmental immunities The doctrine that prohibits federal and state governments from taxing each other's "instrumentalities," such as bonds.

interstate commerce Commerce among states.

intrastate commerce Commerce within a state.

iron triangle The bargains, compromises, and common interests of government bureaucracies, congressional committees, and special-interest groups that combine to work against executive policy and often defy it.

island communities Communities of like-minded people with similar social, ethnic, or cultural backgrounds that keep to themselves and attempt to run their own affairs.

item veto The power of a state governor to veto specific items in appropriations bills. The President does not have such a power.

Jim Crow laws State laws enforcing racial segregation in public accommodations and conveyances.

joint committees Committees formed to coordinate policy between the two houses of Congress, with members drawn from both; they study specific problems and do not usually draft bills.

judicial activism The belief that the Supreme Court should oppose Congress, state legislatures, and other authorities whenever they attempt to violate the constitutional rights of individuals and corporations.

judicial review The Supreme Court's right to judge the actions of other branches and levels of government and to declare them unconstitutional.

judicial self-restraint The belief that the Supreme Court should use its powers of judicial review sparingly and respect the popular will as expressed through elected officials and legislatures.

justice-of-the-peace courts *See* minor courts.

Keynesian economics *See* countercyclical policy; demand-side economics; multiplier effect.

Know Nothing movement A political movement in the 1850s that opposed further Irish immigration.

laissez-faire capitalism The policy of economic noninterference; that is, the government should not regulate business, industry, or commerce, and each individual should have an unlimited opportunity to amass wealth and to lose it.

legal questions One of the criteria for standing to sue in federal courts; that is, a dispute must involve a clearcut violation of legal rights. *See also* political questions.

legislative veto The power claimed by Congress or a congressional committee to veto by majority vote an executive act; when exercised by either the House or the Senate, it is called a *one-house veto;* when exercised by both houses, a *concurrent veto. See also* concurrent resolution.

less developed countries (LDCs) Countries of Asia, Africa, and Latin America marked by deep poverty and a history of economic or political colonization by the West.

libel Publishing untruthful statements that attack the character or reputation of a person or group.

libertarian Democrats Democrats who are economic conservatives and social liberals.

limited presidency (Whig theory) A view of the presidency in which the office retains only those powers specifically granted to it by the Constitution.

lobbying The efforts by special-interest groups to influence the legislating and policymaking of members of Congress. *See also* indirect lobbying.

Machines Highly organized political groups in cities, under the leadership of a boss or small clique, that sell influence in return for cash or votes.

macroeconomics The study of the impact of individual, corporate, and government decisions on the national economy; for example, the study of how manipulation of the federal budget, interest rates, and money supply affects levels of employment and inflation.

maintaining elections Elections in which the balance of forces between the major parties is not changed; for example the elections of 1940, 1944, and 1948.

majority leader The head of the majority political party in the House of Representatives.

majority of votes The number of votes equal to 50 percent plus one vote. *See also* plurality of votes.

mandamus, **writ of** Latin for "we command"; a writ from a superior court that orders a government official or lower court to perform duties required of it by law.

margin requirement The minimum down payment necessary to purchase stocks and bonds.

Marshall Plan A program of U.S. foreign aid to help rebuild the economies of Europe after World War II.

massive retaliation The Eisenhower Administration's policy to force a rollback of Communist power and influence by threatening the use of nuclear weapons.

mass media Mass audience communications—such as magazines, radio and TV programs, and newspapers—that transmit standardized messages and that are owned and controlled by relatively few persons.

matching funds Federal subsidies to the primary campaigns of presidential candidates; candidates must have raised a minimum of $100,000 and have met certain other conditions.

media events Public events that take place mostly for the sake of being reported in the mass media.

mercantilism Government regulation of the prices of goods and services, the kinds and quality of products, and the right of entry into markets.

merit system The appointment and promotion of government officials on the basis of competitive examination.

microeconomics A theory of the economic behavior of individual firms and people; analyzes how individual decisions change the price of goods and services, the quantity of goods produced and purchased, and the amount of labor and capital used to produce them.

midterm conferences National conferences of political parties that are called at the midpoint of each presidential term in order to give the party a chance to decide on policies and ideas for the forthcoming presidential campaign.

military-industrial complex President Eisenhower's term for an alliance between the foreign policy, military, and intelligence communities and the defense industries, who combine to influence defense spending for mutual gain.

minor courts Local courts that handle routine civil and criminal cases.

miscellaneous docket Appeals to the Supreme Court in which the parties are too poor to pay a lawyer or court costs.

misdemeanor A lesser crime than a felony with a correspondingly lesser punishment.

mobocracy A term used by delegates to the Constitutional Convention for those with little or no property.

monetarism An economic theory that demand can be controlled by expanding or contracting the money supply.

monetary aggregates The Federal Reserve System's definition of money that includes, in addition to cash in circulation, various financial instruments such as demand deposits, savings accounts, and money-market mutual fund deposits.

mootness, doctrine of A rule that a court can drop a case when any legal action or appeal would be overtaken by events and made irrelevant before it is decided.

moralist subculture A political subculture originating with early New England Puritans, which holds that a good society can be created by effective political action and improved by reform movements.

multiple independently targetable warheads (MIRVs) An intercontinental missile with eight or nine warheads that can evade antiballistic missiles.

multiplier effect Keynes's theory that the government's creation of jobs in public works projects generates additional jobs in the private sector.

Mutual Assured Destruction (MAD) A nuclear war policy in which both sides are able to absorb a first strike by the other side and have enough weapons and delivery systems left to destroy each other.

national output *See* gross national product.

natural law The asserted law of human nature by which all human beings seek to protect their lives, liberty, and property.

natural rights Each individual's asserted right to life, liberty, and property.

necessary and proper clause *See* elastic clause.

neo-Keynesians Followers of John Maynard Keynes, who believe that the government has a responsibility to create full employment, stimulate economic growth, and correct trade imbalances.

"New Class" Democrats Persons from Republican families or newly prosperous professionals and managers from Democratic families who have taken liberal positions on foreign policy, women's rights, abortion, and the environment.

New Deal coalition A coalition formed in the 1930s among white Southerners, labor unionists, Northern ethnics, blacks, and middle-class liberals; some had been traditional Democrats, others traditional Republicans.

New Federalism President Reagan's plan to limit the national government's power to regulate and to restore power to state governments; it emphasizes self-reliance and voter accountability.

new immigration Roman Catholic, Jewish, and Eastern Orthodox immigrants arriving in the United States between 1880 and 1923 from Southern and Eastern Europe.

New Jersey Plan A plan introduced at the Constitutional Convention that made acts of Congress enforceable in every state and gave each state only one representative in Congress. *See also* Virginia Plan; Connecticut Plan.

new regulation Government regulation aimed at protecting society in general; for example, minimum wage laws, environmental laws, the Pure Food and Drug Act. *See also* old regulation.

Nixon Doctrine A policy devised by the Nixon Administration to help Third World allies resist communism by selling them modern arms but withholding military forces.

nondiscretionary spending Spending, over which the federal government has little control (e.g., direct aid to individuals).

obligatory jurisdiction Appeals that the Supreme Court is obligated to accept, most of them involving the constitutionality of acts by government officials.

obscenity According to the most recent Supreme Court ruling, works are obscene if they meet the following criteria: "appeal to the prurient interest in sex," "portray sexual conduct in a patently offensive way," and "do not have serious literary, artistic, political, or scientific value."

old regulation Until the 1960s, government regulation directed at solving specific problems in specific industries.

one-house veto *See* legislative veto.

one-party politics Intense identification by voters of a particular locality with one political party or another.

open-market operations The Federal Reserve's practice of buying and selling government securities on a daily basis and thereby maintaining control over the money supply.

original docket Trial cases that the Supreme Court accepts for a full hearing.

original jurisdiction The trial jurisdiction of the Supreme Court over disputes involving foreign diplomats or interstate affairs.

parliamentary party The members of a political party who sit in parliament.

parliamentary system A political system in which an elected assembly of legislators chooses the executive and enacts laws.

party identification A tendency, often acquired early in life, to support one political party or another.

party-line voting Voting for only the candidates of a given party.

party vote Congressional voting in which a majority of Democrats opposes a majority of Republicans.

passive-negative presidents James D. Barber's term for Presidents who are dutiful, vague, and bent on avoiding conflict; for example, Calvin Coolidge and Dwight Eisenhower.

passive-positive presidents James D. Barber's term for Presidents who are compliant and want the affection of others; for example, William H. Taft and Warren G. Harding.

passive segregation Racial segregation that comes about as a result of local residential patterns.

peonage A relationship between employer and worker in which the worker is held in compulsory servitude to the employer in order to work off indebtedness. *See also* indentured servants.

Phillips Curve The economic theory that low levels of unemployment lead to high, stable levels of inflation, and vice versa.

plaintiff A person who brings a lawsuit to obtain a remedy for an injury to his or her rights.

plural executives The practice in state government of making several state offices independently elective.

pluralist society A society in which members of diverse ethnic, racial, religious, or social groups independently participate in and maintain their traditional culture.

plurality of votes The largest number of votes, not necessarily the majority of votes; with a plurality, a candidate could win an election with less than 50 percent of the votes. The basic rule in American general elections.

political action committee (PAC) A committee set up by an interest group solely for the purpose of electing or defeating a candidate for public office.

political culture The part of human culture that deals with power and the institutions that channel power.

political questions A criterion used by the Supreme Court in deciding that a case does not lie within the scope of judicial review; for example, cases involving state reapportionment. *See also* legal questions.

political socialization The process of acquiring political opinions.

polygamy The marriage of one man to several women or vice versa.

population (universe) The large group of people whose opinions a pollster wants to assess.

populist Democrats Democrats who are economic liberals and social conservatives.

position issue A social or political issue on which people can hold opposing views. *See also* valence issue.

precedents Past judicial decisions that establish a new approach and set examples for the future. See also *stare decisis.*

preemptive strike In nuclear war, a strike launched in anticipation of a first strike from the other side.

prerogative powers Presidential powers claimed to be inherent in the executive office, requiring neither constitutional nor legislative approval.

President pro tem The presiding officer of the Senate in the absence of the Vice-President; usually the majority-party senator with the greatest seniority.

price supports The setting of minimum prices for crops by the federal government.

primary elections Elections in which voters choose each major party's candidates for state and national offices. *See also* direct primaries; faithful delegate rule; preference primaries; unit rule; white primaries; winner-take-all primaries.

prime minister The head of government under the parliamentary system; is not the sole head of the executive branch but rather the head of a cabinet, which has collective responsibility for running the government.

prior restraint A form of censorship in which publications are suppressed not for the malicious attacks and defamatory articles they have already published but for those they might publish in the future.

privacy, right to A civil liberty created by judicial interpretation that guarantees citizens freedom from government interference in such matters as the use of birth control devices and termination of pregnancies; also protects citizens from undue exposure of their private lives in the public media.

privileges and immunities clause A section of the Fourteenth Amendment to the Constitution, requiring states not to discriminate against each other's citizens.

productivity The output of goods per laborer.

proportional representation The system of giving political parties seats in a legislature in proportion to the total number of votes those parties win.

protection, protectionism The practice of setting high taxes on imported goods in order to protect domestic industry from foreign competition.

protest movements A type of third party formed in order to draw attention to national issues that are being ignored by the major parties; for example, the Progressive party of 1924 and the American Independent party of 1968.

public interest groups (PIGs) Groups such as consumer protection organizations and the American Civil Liberties Union (ACLU) who represent what they view as the public interest against special interest groups.

public sector That part of the political economy controlled or directly funded by government (federal, state, or local).

quo warranto, **writ of** Latin for "by what warrant?"; a writ filed when there is reason to believe that officials have acted outside their legal jurisdiction.

"rational man" theory A theory of policymaking which assumes that all persons involved in making public policy attempt to maximize their own self-interest.

realigning elections Elections in which the political balance between the parties and the shape of public policy both change in a fundamental way; for example the elections of 1828, 1860, 1896, and 1932.

realpolitik "Realistic" politics based on practical and material rather than on ethical or theoretical factors.

record vote A procedure in the House of Representatives in which all congressmen cast their votes openly, by name.

redlining A bank's refusal to grant mortgages in an area that blacks are moving into, thus speeding up "white flight" from the neighborhood.

representative sample A sample of people who possess the same mixture of traits and qualities that characterizes all members of the sampling universe.

rescission bill A congressional act canceling or rescinding the spending authority of a government agency or department.

restrictive covenants Real-estate contracts that bind buyers not to sell their houses to members of certain minority groups.

revenue-sharing President Nixon's policy of allowing state and local officials the unrestricted use of federal grant money.

right-to-work laws Laws that prohibit labor contracts that require union membership as a condition of employment.

rubber-stamp conventions National presidential conventions in which the delegates have already decided who will be the major candidates.

rule of four The Supreme Court's practice of accepting a case if four justices wish to hear it.

rule of locality The custom that all congressmen must live in their own districts.

SALT I (Strategic Arms Limitations Treaty) An agreement reached in 1972 between the United States and the USSR to limit permanently the development and deployment of the ABM, and limit the deployment of offensive missiles for five years.

SALT II An agreement begun in 1974 between the United States and the USSR to end the nuclear arms race; it has yet to be ratified by the U.S. Senate.

sample The people actually questioned in a poll, whose opinions are representative of those of the larger population.

sampling error The degree to which the actual opinion of a large population differs from that of a sample taken from it.

scientific polls Polls that try to ensure that the respondents are representative of the population under study.

select committees Congressional committees created for specific, limited purposes; they rarely have the power to draft bills.

senatorial courtesy The unwritten rule that the President should consult with senators of a state before appointing a federal judge in that state, and should allow a senator of the President's own party an absolute veto over the nomination.

separate-but-equal doctrine A doctrine holding that racial segregation in schools and public accommodations does not imply the superiority of one race to another, rather that each race is entitled to equal but separate facilities.

separation of powers The division of power between branches of the federal government so that one branch makes laws (legislative), one enforces them (executive), and one interprets them (judicial); also the division of power between the federal government and the states.

severance taxes Taxes levied by states on natural resources that are exported to other states.

single-issue groups Special-interest groups that are united around one serious, non-negotiable issue, such as abortion.

slander Spoken defamation of character. *See also* libel.

small-claims courts *See* minor courts

Snowbelt The states of the North and Midwest.

social contract The contract between a government and its people in which the people accept the government's authority and obey its laws in return for protection of their lives, liberty, and property.

Social Darwinism A turn of the century idea that individuals who rise to the top of society are innately superior, or the most fit.

socialism A system of government in which all the people own the means of production and control the distribution of goods.

social issues Controversial topics such as abortion, school prayer, and the death penalty that sharply divide public opinion.

socialization Learning to participate actively in a social group.

sovereignty Absolute, unlimited power of a person or institution over a group of people or a state.

Speaker of the House The powerful presiding officer of the House of Representatives; elected by the majority party on a straight-party vote.

special district A unit of local government that serves a special function such as a school, sanitation, fire protection, or water district; may overlap with counties, cities, or towns.

special master A lawyer appointed by the Supreme Court to collect evidence and testimony in original jurisdiction suits.

split ticket voting Voting for candidates of more than one party.

spoils system The system by which the winner of an election awards political offices to supporters.

standing committees Permanent congressional committees that hold hearings on bills and draft them.

standing to sue Criteria that must be met before persons can bring a lawsuit in federal courts. The parties to the lawsuit must be truly hostile; they must stand to gain or lose by the outcome of the case; the controversy involved must really have occurred; and it must be based on a legal question.

standing vote A procedure in the House of Representatives in which congressmen rise from their seats to signify their vote and the Speaker decides which side wins.

stare decisis Latin for "let the decision stand"; a legal custom in which principles spelled out in earlier decisions should be followed unless there is a strong reason not to do so.

statutes Laws enacted by Parliament.

stewardship theory A view of the presidency in which the President is the custodian of the national interest and has the right and duty to take any action to protect it.

straw polls (straw votes) Surveys taken of self-selected groups of people who may or may not be typical or the population under study.

strict construction The practice of judges of taking the text of the Constitution literally.

subsidy A grant by a government to an individual or a company to help an enterprise or stimulate an activity deemed advantageous to the public.

suburbanization A population trend in which people move out of the central cities to nearby communities.

sumptuary laws Laws that regulate and restrict the wearing of extravagant or luxurious clothing in public.

Sunbelt The states of the South and Southwest.

supply-side economics Economic policy favoring lower marginal tax rates to stimulate investment, productivity, and savings; sharp cuts in federal spending; and as little government regulation of business as possible.

tariff A tax on imports to protect domestic industry from foreign competition.

tax policy An aspect of fiscal policy that deals with how much revenue should be raised from taxes on personal income, corporations, and luxury goods, what level of taxation each income group should be made to bear, and the aggregate amount of taxation the government should accept.

teller vote A procedure in the House of Representatives in which congressmen form two lines, one for "yea," one for "nay," and file past the teller.

third parties Minor political parties; they remain weak in the United States because the electoral system lacks proportional representation and awards elections only on the basis of a plurality of votes. *See also* bolts; protest movements.

Third World The developing countries of the world.

township A unit of local government, usually a subdivision of a county.

traditional subculture A political subculture that values family life, community ties, and tradition.

transfer payments Money payments made by the federal government directly to individuals; for example, Social Security checks.

trial courts (courts of original jurisdiction) State courts that receive evidence, bear witnesses, rule on the facts, and deliver verdicts.

Truman Doctrine A post–World War II policy in which the United States formally offered to assist any government threatened by communism.

two-thirds rule A rule in the Democratic national conventions, in effect through the year 1936, that a presidential nominee had to receive two-thirds of the delegate vote.

two-tiered electoral system An electoral system in which a second election is held in districts where no candidate has won a majority of votes.

***ultra vires,* writ of** Latin for "beyond the powers"; used by the Supreme Court to strike down statutes or other official acts when the body or official in question has acted beyond the constitutional scope of its authority.

union shops Hiring policies that require every worker to join the union within a certain period.

unitary states States in which the national government has absolute power over regional governments.

unit rule A rule in national presidential conventions by which a state's entire delegate vote is cast unanimously for one candidate on the basis of a simple majority agreement.

universe *See* population.

urbanization A population trend in which most of a country's people live in cities and towns.

U.S. Court of Appeals An intermediate federal court that examines the record of an original trial and determines if it was held according to the rules.

U.S. District Court A federal court that conducts mostly civil trials by receiving evidence, hearing testimony, and handing down decisions, sometimes with the help of a jury; it does not hear appeals.

valence issue A social or political issue on which there is only one side. *See also* position issue.

veto The President's power to refuse to sign a bill passed by Congress; it then becomes law only if two-thirds of each house votes in favor of overriding the veto. *See also* congressional veto; legislative veto; item veto.

Virginia Plan A plan introduced at the Constitutional Convention under which Congress would be given many powers, and the states would be represented according to population. *See also* New Jersey Plan; Connecticut Plan.

voluntarism A belief in self-regulation and the least possible government interference.

welfare shift The reversal in government spending patterns on defense and social welfare programs between 1950 and 1975; in 1950, 25 percent of government spending went for welfare programs and 50 percent for defense; by 1975 these proportions had been reversed.

Whig party The major opposition party to the (Jacksonian) Democrats, 1834–1854, advocating "positive liberalism" (protective tariffs, a central bank, aid to business, etc.). Shattered by the North–South critical realignment of the 1850s, with the Northern Whigs forming the core of the new Republican party.

Whig theory *See* limited presidency.

white primary State primary elections that restrict voting only to whites. Outlawed by the Supreme Court in 1944.

winner-take-all primaries The practice in national conventions of giving all of a state's delegate vote to whichever candidate receives a mere plurality of the popular vote.

writs *See certiorari; habeas corpus; mandamus; stare decisis; ultra vires.*

yellow journalism Politically neutral news writing marked by sensationalism on such topics as sports, social events, and crime that appeals to readers with a broad range of interests.

INDEX

Italicized page numbers preceded by *f*, *m*, and *p* refer to *figures*, *maps*, and *photographs*.